AACRAO®
1910

2010 FERPA Guide

edited by LeRoy Rooker

with TINA M. FALKNER, DENNIS J. HICKS,
BRAD A. MYERS & SHARON SHIRLEY

American Association of Collegiate
Registrars and Admissions Officers
One Dupont Circle, NW, Suite 520
Washington, DC 20036–1135

Tel: (202) 293–9161 | Fax: (202) 872–8857 | www.aacrao.org

For a complete listing of AACRAO publications, visit www.aacrao.org/publications.

The American Association of Collegiate Registrars and Admissions Officers, founded in 1910, is a
nonprofit, voluntary, professional association of more than 10,000 higher education administrators
who represent more than 2,600 institutions and agencies in the United States and in twenty-eight
countries around the world. The mission of the Association is to provide leadership in policy
initiation, interpretation, and implementation in the global educational community. This is
accomplished through the identification and promotion of standards and best practices in
enrollment management, information technology, instructional management, and student services.

LIBRARY OF CONGRESS CATALOGING-IN-PUBLICATION DATA

The AACRAO 2010 FERPA guide / Leroy S. Rooker, managing editor ; Brad A. Myers ... [et al.].
    — 2010 update.

    p. cm.
    ISBN 978-1-57858-092-7

  1. United States. Family Educational Rights and Privacy Act.
  2. Student records—Law and legislation—United States.
  3. Privacy, Right of—United States.
  4. College registrars—United States.—Handbooks, manuals, etc.
  5. College admission officers—United States.—Handbooks, manuals, etc.
  I. Rooker, Leroy S.
  II. Myers, Brad A.

KF4156.5.A318A5 2010
344.73'0793—dc22
2010010758

Table of Contents

Preface..i

Acknowledgements..v

FERPA at-a-Glance..vii

Chapter One
Introduction..1

Historical Background...1

Essence of the Act...4

To Whose Records Does the Act Apply?................5

To What Records Does the Act Apply?.................5

To Which Institutions Does the Act Apply?..............5

Enforcement and Penalties.....................................5

Conflict With State Law..5

The "Musts" and "Mays" in FERPA...........................6

Chapter Two
Definition of Terms......................................7

Chapter Three
Compliance: Requirements, Procedures, and Strategies......................13

Notice to Students of Their Privacy Rights (§99.7)..13

Notification to Students of the Institution's
Directory Information; Student's Right to Non-
Disclosure (§99.37)...14

Students' Access to Their
Education Records (§99.10)....................................14

Limitations on the Students' Rights to Inspect
Their Education Records (§99.12)............................15

Student's Waiver of Right to Review Confidential
Letters of Recommendation (§99.12)........................15

Retention & Destruction of Education Records
(§99.10, §99.20 and §99.32).....................................15

Disclosure of Education Record
Information (§99.30)...16

Exceptions to Written Consent
Requirement (§99.31)..16

*Release of Personally
Identifiable Information*......................................17

Release of Directory Information (§99.37)..........17

*Release of Non-Directory
Information (§99.30, 99.31)*.................................17

Disclosure to Parents..17

Challenging the Contents of
Education Records (§99.20 – §99.22)........................18

A FERPA Hearing Request:
Policy and Procedures.......................................18

Right to Challenge Information in Records........19

Hearings to Challenge Records.........................19

Records of Requests and
Disclosures (§99.32, §99.33)..................................19

Chapter Four
FERPA Issues: Analysis & Application.......21

Academic Standing..21

Access to Education Records.................................21

Admissions Files...21

Admitted vs. Enrolled/In Attendance Students......22

Agents/Contractors...22

Alumni Records...22

Annual Notification and FERPA Policy...................22

Athletes (Student-Athletes)....................................23

Campus Security/Police Records...........................23

Challenging Student Records.................................23

Charging a Fee for Copying/Search/Retrieval.........23

Computer Access to Records..................................23

Conducting Studies..24

Contractors/Agents...24

Deceased Students..24

Destruction and Retention of Records...................24

Directory Information...24

Disciplinary Records..25

Releasing Disciplinary Records..........................25

Disciplinary Information on a Transcript.............26

Distance Education; Using Technology in the Classroom Setting.................................26

   Sharing Email Addresses, Grades and Other Personally Identifiable Information Among Students in the Same Class 26

Dual-Enrolled Students..27

Electronic Signatures 27

   Implementing Institutional Electronic Signatures—Helpful Hints & Resources 27

Electronic Transmission of Student Data.................28

Emailing Grades...28

Email Transcript Requests.......................................28

Emergency Situations 28

Enforcement Procedures and Penalties (§99.60–99.67) 28

Facsimile Records (Fax) 29

   Receiving Requests..29

   Sending Information...29

Financial Aid 29

Former Students' Rights...30

Health or Safety Emergency.....................................30

   Contacting a Student for an Emergency..............30

HIPAA and FERPA..30

IRS Summons...31

Law Enforcement Records 31

Legitimate Educational Interest/ School Officials 31

   "School Officials"..32

   Articulating Legitimate Educational Interest 33

   Computer Access and Legitimate Educational Interest 33

Letters of Recommendation.....................................34

The Media 35

Medical Treatment Records 35

Non-Disclosure of Directory Information (Opt Out; FERPA Block) 35

Outsourcing...36

Parental Access to a Student's Education Records 36

   Biological, Custodial, and Non-Custodial Parents.......................................36

   Student Permission to Share Grades with Parents..36

Penalties Under FERPA 37

PINs/Passwords...37

Posting of Grades (§99.3)...38

   Other Acceptable Methods for Notifying Students of their Grades......................38

Postsecondary Feedback to High Schools 39

Records Retention..39

Record Keeping of Disclosures.................................40

Redisclosure 40

Releasing Non-Directory Information Over the Phone 40

   To the Student 40

   To Third Parties 40

Religion as Directory Information 40

Safeguarding 41

School Officials 41

SEVIS..41

Use of the Social Security Number...........................41

   Using SSN to Verify Student Information 41

"Sole Possession" (Anecdotal) Notes on a Student...42

The Solomon Amendment and FERPA...................42

State or Federal Program Data Releases....................43

States' Open Records/ Disclosure Laws and FERPA...................................44

   State Law Conflict with FERPA (§99.61)...........44

Student Access to Education Records—Electronic 44

Student Directories..44

Student Right-To-Know Act and FERPA................44

Students' Right to Review Records 45

Students as Members of Institutional Committees 46

Subpoenas 46

   What FERPA Says About Subpoenas 46

   Ex Parte Court Orders..47

   Jurisdiction 47

   What to Do When Presented with a Subpoena...47

   Rights of a Person When Served with a Subpoena...48

   Notifying the Student...49

   Complying with the Subpoena 49

Chapter Five

Training Materials 51

Frequently Asked Questions 51

Key Terms/Concepts in FERPA 52

How Do You Determine What is an
Education Record? 52

What Does FERPA Say About Parents? 52

Written Authorization by Student to
Share Grades with Parents 52

The Student's Rights of Non-Disclosure
Under FERPA 53

FERPA-Related College/Registrar Web Sites 53

A FERPA Brochure 54

FERPA Basics for Faculty/Instructional Staff 57

FERPA Basics for Staff 59

A FERPA Workshop/Presentation 61

FERPA Case Studies with Answers 72

True/False Quiz 82

A FERPA Final Exam 83

A FERPA Audit 93

True/False Quiz Answer Key 97

FERPA Final Exam Answer Key 98

Chapter Six

Sample Forms 101

Sample Form 1:
Permission to Release
Education Record Information—Version A 103

Sample Form 2:
Permission to Release
Education Record Information—Version B 104

Sample Form 3:
Permission to Release
Education Record Information—Version C 105

Sample Form 4:
Authorization of
Grade Disclosure 106

Sample Form 5:
Consent to
Send Grades to Parents 107

Sample Form 6:
Authorization to
Disclose Education Records to Parents/
Opt Out of Directory Information 108

Sample Form 7:
Consent to Return Graded Assignments in a Public
Manner 109

Sample Form 8:
Request to Opt Out of
Directory Information—Version A 110

Sample Form 9:
Request to Opt Out of
Directory Information—Version B 111

Sample Form 10:
Request to Opt Out of
Directory Information—Version C 112

Sample Form 11:
Request for Revocation of
Non-Disclosure of Directory Information 113

Sample Form 12:
Request to Review
Education Records 114

Sample Form 13:
Request to Inspect and
Review Education Records 115

Sample Form 14:
Request to Amend or
Remove Education Records 116

Sample Form 15:
Request for Formal
Hearing to Amend or Remove Education
Records—Version A 117

Sample Form 16:
Request for Formal
Hearing to Amend or Remove Education
Records—Version B 118

Sample Form 17:
Code of Responsibility for
Security and Confidentiality of Data 119

Sample Form 18:
Student Worker—
Statement of FERPA Understanding 120

Sample Form 19:
Request for Computer
Access to Student Records in the Student
Information System (SIS) 121

Sample Form 20:
Agreement for Accessing
Private Electronic Student Data by Staff 122

Sample Form 21:
Staff Login Notice for
Accessing Private Electronic Student Data 123

Sample Form 22:
Request to Change SSN to
Another Personal Identifier 124

Sample Form 23:
Notice of Intent to
Comply with a Subpoena 125

Sample Form 24:
Agent/Contractor Agreement 126

Sample Form 25:
Authorization to
Release Grades/Transcripts for
Dual-Enrolled Students 127

Sample Form 26:
Notification of Student
Privacy Rights under FERPA (Email Version) 128

Sample Form 27:
Transcript Notice of
FERPA Redisclosure Limitation 129

Sample Form 28:
Student Dependent Status/
Consent to Disclosure to Parents 130

Sample Form 29:
Student Dependent Status 131

Sample Form 30:
Student-Athlete's
Authorization to Disclose Information in
Education Records Pursuant to FERPA 132

Sample Form 31:
NCAA Student-Athlete
Statement 133

Appendices

Appendix A
The Family Educational Rights and
Privacy Act of 1974 as Amended 137

Appendix B
Family Educational Rights and
Privacy Act Regulations 147

Appendix C
FERPA Section-by-Section Analysis 165

Appendix D
Model Notification of Rights under FERPA for
Postsecondary Institutions 177

Appendix E
FPCO Letters 179

Appendix F
FPCO Guidance Brochures 301

Appendix G
Definition of Dependent 305

Appendix H
HIPAA/FERPA Guidance 309

Appendix I
Electronic Signature Regulations 321

Appendix J
Solomon Amendment Regulations 327

Appendix K
Anti-Terrorism Related Amendments &
SEVIS Guidance 333

FPCO Letter to AACRAO on SEVIS 337

ICE Sample Information Request Form
for Foreign Students 340

Appendix L
State Laws Relating to FERPA 341

Bibliography 345
Index 347

Preface

The primary purpose of this AACRAO publication is to provide guidance and suggested implementation procedures for complying with the Family Educational Rights and Privacy Act of 1974, as Amended (subsequently referred to as "The Act" or FERPA). The publication has been updated to include the new changes to the FERPA Regulations which became effective in January 2009. These changes were the first extensive modification of the regulations since 1988 and incorporate changes reflecting a new world for postsecondary institutions following the Virginia Tech tragedy. The publication is intended to 1) assist institutional record-keepers and other school officials to understand their roles and responsibilities for implementing The Act, and 2) provide many practical training tips that can be used on a daily basis in training other institutional employees on FERPA.

A Preliminary Caution

As with most publications dealing with legal issues, federal legislation, interpretations, and new regulations can amplify and change what is included in this publication. For example, the tragedy at Virginia Tech brought to light the need for clarification of FERPA's "health and safety" exception, as well as the need to provide guidance on the interplay between FERPA and HIPAA. Similarly, the increased use of technology, including for creating fraudulent documents, has led to changes in the FERPA definition of a "disclosure." Such issues have impacted and will continue to affect the need for clarification and/or modification of the law. As such, these guidelines are, by definition, interpretive. They are not to be construed as law and are intended for use along with The Act and its published regulations. While consulting this document, the reader should be aware of any applicable privacy or public information laws of your state, which may be at variance with FERPA (*see* "Conflict with State Law" on page 5).

FERPA applies to all levels of education in the United States, but there are significant differences in how the law applies to postsecondary institutions as compared to K–12 schools. This publication applies to postsecondary education only. A companion volume covering FERPA at the K–12 levels, *FERPA and Secondary Education* (1997), sponsored by the National Association for College Admission Counseling and AACRAO, is available from AACRAO.

History and Contents of This Publication

The *Family Educational Rights and Privacy Act* (FERPA) was enacted by the United States Congress in 1974. In response, the AACRAO *Guide to Postsecondary Institutions for Implementation of the Family Educational Rights and Privacy Act of 1974* was first printed in 1976.

In this original edition, AACRAO was assisted by representatives of the following associations in developing a comprehensive and concise set of recommended institutional guidelines and procedures for postsecondary institutions implementing this law: the American Council on Education, the National Association of College and University Attorneys, The College Board, and Educational Testing Service.

In 1984, the *1984 AACRAO FERPA Guide* was published, and it contained, for the first time, the format and content that is found in subsequent editions.

In 1988, new FERPA regulations brought about significant changes, of which the most prominent was the identification of two types of parental statuses: custodial and non-custodial. These new regulations outlined the role and rights of both types of parents under FERPA. The AACRAO Board of Director responded to this change by appointing a committee to revise the *1984 FERPA Guide*. This committee surveyed a randomly selected group of 500 AACRAO member institutions to assess current knowledge, procedures, and attitudes regarding FERPA. Their responses enabled the committee to identify key areas and topics that needed to be discussed and included in the next FERPA publication. This publication eventually became the 1995 edition of *The Guide to Postsecondary Institutions for Implementation of the Family Educational Rights and Privacy Act of 1974 as Amended*. The *1995 FERPA Guide* followed the outline of the 1984 publication, and expanded the appendices and added a bibliography.

The 1998 edition followed the same format. It also provided updated information on events, policies, rulings, and legislation that affected FERPA since the 1995 publication of the *Guide*. Following this publication, significant changes occurred with the issuance of the 2000 FERPA regulations, including: disclosure of records information when the student has been found in violation of substance abuse policies; disclosure of results from disciplinary hearings; and clarifying conditions under which an institution may disclose records in defending itself. In response, the AACRAO Executive Board appointed a committee of records administrators who had direct responsibility for administering FERPA on their campuses, and who also had extensive experience with FERPA, to develop the *2001 FERPA Guide*. It addressed the 2000 FERPA regulations and followed the same general format of previous *Guides*, while adding a new Chapter 6 which included training materials that practitioners could use on their campuses for training others about their responsibilities under FERPA.

By 2006, numerous social, political, and technological factors were influencing the implementation of The Act. The 2006 *Guide* discussed these and incorporated the changes made to the FERPA regulations since 2001. In addition, a few of the topics and issues contained in the 2006 edition included: e-signatures as they apply to FERPA; dual-enrolled students; U.S. Supreme Court cases: *Falvo* and *Gonzaga*; *Miami/OSU* federal court case; the

Solomon Amendment; the *Patriot Act*; SEVIS; Graham-Leach-Bliley; and the *Digital Millennium Copyright Act*. A new enhancement in the 2006 Guide was the inclusion of a CD-ROM containing a digital version of FERPA training materials and forms.

What's New in this Publication?

This most recent revision of the *Guide* (2010) provides updates based on the recently revised FERPA regulations that were published in December 2008 and became effective in January 2009. While the scope of each chapter remains the same as the 2006 version, they have been updated to reflect all the changes in the 2009 regulations. Where applicable, section citations to the regulations preceded by the section symbol "§" (*e.g.*, §99.32) have been added to the relevant text to aide readers in locating the source of the provision. In addition, a revised format and index make it easier to find topics being researched.

Chapter 1 contains a summary of the changes to FERPA that are discussed throughout this edition of the *Guide*.

Some noteworthy items in the 2010 edition include:

- A copy of the FERPA regulations in Appendix B, with the 2009 amendments highlighted.
- A section-by-section analysis of the 2009 amendments in Appendix C.
- Updated training materials and forms for you to use at your institution.

  Note: All the training materials and forms in the 2010 *Guide* are available on the AACRAO Web site at www.aacrao.org/compliance/ferpa/.

- Appendix H was newly added and focuses on the intersection between FERPA and HIPAA. In the wake of the shootings at Virginia Tech, the U.S. Department of Education and U.S. Department of Health and Human Services published *Joint Guidance on the Application of FERPA and HIPAA to Student Health Records*, to address confusion of school administrators, health care professionals and others on the application of these laws to records maintained on students. This appendix includes the *Joint Guidance*, along with an article on FERPA and HIPAA myths, penned by the former heads of the offices at the Departments of Education and Health and Human Services, which are responsible for FERPA and HIPAA compliance respectively.

- Additional appendices, including background materials (*e.g.*, FPCO opinion letters in Appendix E) related to various 2009 regulatory changes and other

FERPA issues of interest to the postsecondary education community.

The 2010 Guide Team

Recognized and respected for their expertise in implementation, compliance, and training in FERPA, the editorial team for the 2010 *Guide* includes:

- Tina Falkner, Associate Registrar, University of Minnesota, Twin Cities
- Dennis Hicks, Registrar, Indiana University–East
- Brad Myers, University Registrar, Ohio State University
- LeRoy Rooker, Senior Fellow, AACRAO; former Director, Family Policy Compliance Office, U.S. Department of Education (chair)
- Sharon Shirley, Consultant; former staff member, Family Policy Compliance Office, U.S. Department of Education
- Rick Campanelli, Esq., Baker and Daniels, LLP, and former Director of the Office for Civil Rights at the U.S. Department of Health & Human Services

This publication is the culmination of their combined efforts.

Acknowledgements

One of my greatest pleasures, during my 21 years as director of the Family Policy Compliance Office (FPCO) at the U.S. Department of Education, was partnering with so many wonderful people in the postsecondary community. You—the admissions officers, registrars, and other college and university officials of this country—hold my highest regard as a truly distinguished group of professionals. Thus, I naturally feel privileged to continue working with you in my current capacity as a Senior Fellow at AACRAO.

You played a large part in contributing to what we at FPCO attempted to accomplish in the 2009 amendments to FERPA regulations and the publication of the *FERPA-HIPPA Guidance*. Through discussions with you about how to address issues ranging from fraudulent documents to campus safety, I came to understand FERPA's impact on your daily efforts to serve your students and profession with integrity and fairness. From working with officials such as those of you at Virginia Tech, I learned how significant the consequences can be when the nuances of the law are misunderstood, especially with regard to the intersection between FERPA, HIPPA, health and safety, and campus security issues. Thus, your input helped clarify for FPCO the directions the new regulations needed to take; true to the statute, but meaningfully updated to assist you in performing your jobs effectively.

This 2010 *Guide* is a continuation of the process the FPCO staff and I began at the Department. Grounded in the law, and especially the 2009 amendments, this document is the most up-to-date and reliable reference on FERPA for postsecondary institutions. And, just as the 2009 amendments were accomplished by the collaborative efforts of dedicated staff at FPCO, so has this *Guide* come to successful publication by the collaborative efforts of several AACRAO associates. We feel certain that the 2010 *Guide* will aid you in responding to the many challenges you face in your efforts to protect student privacy and records on your campuses.

This *Guide* could not have successfully reached publication apart from the expertise and tireless effort of the volunteer AACRAO editorial team, which consisted of AACRAO members: Tina Falkner, Associate Registrar,

University of Minnesota-Twin Cities; Dennis Hicks, Registrar, Indiana University-East; and Brad Myers, University Registrar, Ohio State University. The four of us met late last summer to determine the content and carve out assignments. Thereafter, Brad, Tina, and Dennis worked countless hours on their own time to write initial drafts of various sections, then revise and edit them in concert. Brad pulled everyone's edits together to supply me with the material to make a final product. He made a few trips to the AACRAO office in D.C. to collaborate with me on content, initial drafts, and polishing the final draft of the document, working late nights and early mornings to meet our deadlines. I also want to thank Sharon Shirley, former member of my FPCO staff, who took time off from her teaching duties in Connecticut to add her FERPA insights and her writing and editing skills to the mix, trekking through the infamous D.C. blizzard to do so.

Additionally, I want to acknowledge the ever-astute contributions of AACRAO's Associate Executive Director, Barmak Nassirian; the Director of Membership and Publications, Martha Henebry, who attempted to keep us on schedule; and, in particular, Paula McArdle, who interpreted my edits and compiled the many pieces to produce a publication of which we can all be proud.

Finally, I would like to recognize my former staff at FPCO, dedicated public servants all, without whose extraordinary efforts the new 2009 regulations discussed in this *Guide* might not have been published.

As then Committee Chair Dennis Hicks said in his acknowledgements for the 2006 *Guide*, AACRAO is "an organization of volunteers. Volunteers accept a challenge, not for self, but for the good of the whole." In completing this project, I've witnessed first-hand the unselfishness with which AACRAO members serve their colleagues in the post-secondary community. This *AACRAO 2010 FERPA Guide* is a product of that unselfish dedication and sacrifice and a reminder to me of how privileged I am to be associated with professionals of such caliber.

Leroy Rooker, Managing Editor
March 8, 2010

FERPA at-a-Glance

If you are looking for a summary of what FERPA is all about, the following statements capture its essence:

★ Students at postsecondary institutions must be permitted to inspect and review their education records.

★ School officials may not disclose personally identifiable information from a student's education record, without written permission, unless such a disclosure is permitted by one of the FERPA signed-consent exceptions.

★ Institutions are responsible for ensuring that all of its school officials comply with FERPA.

If you are looking for a more detailed summary of FERPA, the following will be helpful.

What is FERPA?

The *Family Educational Rights and Privacy Act of 1974*, as amended, sets forth requirements regarding the privacy of student records. This law applies to postsecondary institutions as well as K–12 schools.

FERPA governs:
- ✕ The disclosure of education records maintained by an educational institution; and
- ✕ Access to these records.

Who *must* comply with FERPA?

Any educational institution (school or other entity that provides educational services and is attended by students) or educational agency (entity that administers schools directly linked to it) that receive funds under any program administered by the U.S. Secretary of Education.

What does FERPA require for colleges to be in compliance?

- ✕ Institutions must notify students annually of their FERPA rights (*see* Appendix D, "Model Notification of Rights," on page 177).

There is no specific method that schools must use to notify students—it is up to the institution. Notice must take a form that is "reasonably likely" to notify students. Recommended and most frequently used ways include: student bulletin, handbook or catalog; school or local newspaper; student registration packet; email notice of basic issues with a link to additional information.

- ✕ Ensure students' rights to inspect and review their education records.
- ✕ Ensure students' rights to request to amend their education records.
- ✕ Ensure students' rights to limit disclosure of personally identifiable information contained in education records.
- ✕ Notify third parties of the redisclosure prohibition of personally identifiable information (except under a few circumstances).
- ✕ Keep records of requests for and disclosures of student education records.

Who has FERPA rights at the postsecondary level?

- ◘ FERPA rights belong to the student at a postsecondary institution regardless of age.
- ◘ *Student* applies to all students—including continuing education students, students auditing a class, distance education students, and former students.
- ◘ *In attendance* can be defined by the institution, but it cannot be later than the day that the student first attends a class at the institution.

What FERPA rights are given to students?

- ◘ Right to inspect and review their education records.
- ◘ Right to request to amend their education records.
- ◘ Right to limit disclosure of "personally identifiable information" (information that would directly identify the student or make the student's identity easily traceable) known as *directory information*.
- ◘ Right to file a complaint with the Department of Education concerning an alleged failure by the institution to comply with FERPA.

What are education records under FERPA?

- ◘ Education records are defined as records that are:
  - ▶ Directly related to a student, and
  - ▶ Maintained by an educational agency or institution or by a party acting for the agency or institution, if certain conditions are met.
- ◘ Education records are not: sole possession records, law enforcement unit records, employment records, medical records, or post-attendance records.

To whom, and under what conditions, can colleges disclose personally identifiable information?

- ◘ Anyone, if the college has obtained the prior written consent of the student
- ◘ Anyone, in response to requests for directory information (Information that is generally not considered harmful or an invasion of privacy if disclosed)
  - ▶ Institutions must identify those items it considers directory information and notify students.
  - ▶ Institutions must inform students that they can withhold release of this information.
- ◘ Authorized representatives of the following government entities, if the disclosure is in connection with an audit or evaluation of federal or state supported education programs, or for the enforcement of or compliance with federal legal requirements that relate to those programs:
  - ▶ Comptroller General of the U.S.
  - ▶ Secretary of Education
  - ▶ U.S. Attorney General (for law enforcement purposes only)
  - ▶ State and local educational authorities
- ◘ School officials determined by the institution to have a legitimate educational interest
- ◘ Agents acting on behalf of the institution (*e.g.* contractors, consultants)
- ◘ Schools in which the student seeks or intends to enroll (additional conditions exist)
- ◘ A party, such as the Department of Veteran's Affairs or an employer, providing financial aid to the student ("financial aid" does not include any payments made by parents); (additional conditions exist)
- ◘ Organizations conducting studies for or on behalf of educational institutions (additional conditions exist)
- ◘ Accrediting organizations for accreditation purposes
- ◘ Parents of a dependent student (as defined by the IRS code)
- ◘ Parents when their student (under 21) is found to have violated the alcohol or drug policy of the institution
- ◘ To comply with a judicial order or subpoena, including *ex parte* orders under the USA Patriot Act
- ◘ Appropriate parties if a health or safety emergency exists and the information will assist in resolving the emergency (additional conditions exist)
- ◘ The student
- ◘ An alleged victim of a crime of violence when the disclosure is the results of a disciplinary hearing regarding the alleged perpetrator of that crime with respect to that crime
- ◘ Anyone requesting the final results of a disciplinary hearing against an alleged perpetrator who has been found in violation of the campus code relating to a crime of violence or non-forcible sex offense
- ◘ The Department of Homeland Security (DHS), Immigration and Customs Enforcement (ICE) for purpose of complying with Request Form ICE relative to the institution's participation in SEVIS
- ◘ Military recruiters who request "Student Recruiting Information" for recruiting purposes only (Solomon Amendment). Student recruiting information is name, address, telephone listing, age (or year of birth), class level, major, degrees received and most recent educational institution of enrollment. (conditions exist)
- ◘ The Internal Revenue Service (IRS), for purposes of complying with the *Taxpayer Relief Act of 1997*

✦ Anyone, when the disclosure concerns information provided by sex offenders required to register under state or federal law

How does technology impact FERPA guidelines?

As we move toward an environment with less paper, it is important to note that the same principles of access and confidentiality must be applied to all media, including but not limited to, electronic data, email, and video or audio tapes.

What happens if a college does *not* comply with FERPA?

The Department of Education may issue a notice to cease the non-compliance and could ultimately withhold funds administered by the Secretary of Education.

Where can I get more information regarding FERPA?

Family Policy Compliance Office
U.S. Department of Education
400 Maryland Avenue, SW
Washington, DC 20202–5901
Phone (202) 260–3887
Fax (202) 260–9001
Email: ferpa@ed.gov
Web: www.ed.gov/policy/gen/guid/fpco/index.html

Assistance is also available from AACRAO at ferpa@aacrao.org.

Chapter One

Introduction

Under the *Family Educational Rights and Privacy Act* (hereafter referred to as The Act or FERPA), students are given three primary rights. They have the right to:

- Inspect and review their education records.
- Have some control over the disclosure of information from their education records.
- Seek to amend incorrect education records.

Educational institutions and agencies should conform to fair information practices. This means that persons who are subjects of data systems (*i.e.*, students at an institution) must:

- Be informed of the existence of such systems.
- Be apprised of what data about them is on record.
- Be given assurances that such data is used only for intended purposes.
- Be given the opportunity to request an amendment or correction to their records.
- Be certain that those responsible for data systems take reasonable precautions to prevent misuse of the data.
- Know that the institution will reasonably respond when an alleged misuse of, or access to, data is brought to the attention of those responsible for data systems.

Although The Act does not require it, those responsible for data systems are obliged to consider properly disposing of, or destroying, information when 1) the conditions under which that information was collected no longer exist and 2) there are no legal restrictions preventing such disposal.

Historical Background

On March 2, 1976, the Department of Health, Education, and Welfare issued the initial implementation regulations in the *Federal Register* for the *Family Educational Rights and Privacy Act of 1976* (P.L. 93–568, Sec. 2), as amended

(P.L. 93–568, Sec. 2; 20 U.S.C. 1232g), known as the "Buckley Amendment," after its congressional author. Final regulations appeared in the June 17, 1976 issue of the *Federal Register*.

When the Department of Education (DOE) was established, the responsibility for implementing the regulations was transferred to the Department of Education and codified in Part 99 of Title 34 of the Code of Federal Regulations (34 C.F.R. 99). Slightly modified final regulations were issued in the *Federal Register* on May 9, 1980, Vol. 45, No. 92. In 1988 revised final regulations to the *Family Educational Rights and Privacy Act* were promulgated (34 C.F.R. 99). The stated purpose of that revision was to simplify and clarify the previous provisions and to reduce, where possible, the regulatory burden on colleges and universities. In 1988, the Department rewrote the regulations for clarity and eliminated some of the regulatory requirements placed on schools. The final regulations were published April 11, 1988 in the *Federal Register*. In 1990 the *Crime Awareness and Campus Security Act* modified the disclosure rules in FERPA. These changes to FERPA were published in the *Federal Register* on January 7, 1993.

FERPA was amended by the *Higher Education Amendments of 1992* which excluded, under certain conditions, law enforcement records of an institution of higher education from the provisions of FERPA (*see Federal Register*, Department of Education, 34 C.F.R. 99, Notice of Proposed Rule Making, December 14, 1993, pp. 65298–65300). The final regulations regarding law enforcement records were published in the *Federal Register* on January 17, 1995. The 1996 changes to FERPA affecting higher education included:

- Eliminating the requirement that each institution have a FERPA institutional policy statement and substituting an expanded annual notification requirement to satisfy the requirements of the law.

◪ Requiring State Educational Agencies (SEAs) to afford eligible students access to education records maintained by the SEA. This right of access is the only right parents and eligible students are afforded at the SEA level. SEA also includes state governing bodies of higher education.

◪ Clarifying that, if an educational agency or institution initiates legal action against an eligible student, it must make a reasonable effort to notify the student in advance of its intent to disclose the information from education records to a court of law.

◪ Amending FERPA so that a school is not required to notify an eligible student before complying with certain subpoenas. A college does not have to notify the student of the existence of a subpoena if it receives a federal grand jury subpoena and the court has ordered that the college not disclose to any person the existence or contents of the subpoena. Additionally, if a court or other issuing agency issues a subpoena for a law enforcement purpose and orders the school not to disclose the existence or contents of the subpoena to the student, FERPA does not require notification before compliance with the subpoena.

◪ Clarifying that a college may include information in a student's education records concerning disciplinary action taken against the student for conduct that posed a significant risk to the safety or well being of that student, other students, or other members of the college community.

◪ Clarifying that a college may disclose, without prior consent, information contained in a student's education records concerning disciplinary action taken against the student, described in the previous bullet, to teachers and school officials who have legitimate educational interests in the behavior of the student. FERPA was amended to allow this type of disclosure to teachers and school officials in other schools who have legitimate educational interests in the behavior of the student.

◪ Adding a provision that, if a third party re-discloses personally identifiable student information in violation of FERPA, the college which disclosed the information to the third party shall be prohibited from permitting access to education records to that third party for a period of not less than five years.

◪ Clarifying that persons filing complaints with the Department of Education under FERPA must have legal standing. That is, a complainant must be an eligible student affected by an alleged violation. This is consistent with other laws affording specific rights to persons.

The changes and additions to FERPA in 2000 included:

◪ Permitting disclosure of education records to authorized representatives of the U.S. Attorney General in connection with an investigation or enforcement of federal legal requirements of federally supported education programs.

◪ Permitting non-consensual disclosure of the final results of a disciplinary proceeding against a postsecondary student in specified circumstances.

◪ Permitting non-consensual disclosure to parents and legal guardians of students under the age of 21, regardless of their dependency status, of information regarding a student's violation of laws or policies governing the use or possession of alcohol or a controlled substance.

◪ Clarifying the conditions under which the institution may disclose records in defending itself.

◪ A clarification of "directory information" and revision of the examples illustrative of "directory information."

◪ Clarifying what information can be disclosed from an institutional disciplinary proceeding and under what conditions.

◪ New definitions of dates of attendance, non-forcible sex offenses, crimes of violence (including a more specific list of examples), alleged perpetrator of a crime of violence, sole possession records, alleged perpetrator of a non-forcible sex offense, and final results of a disciplinary hearing.

In 2004, §99.30 of the FERPA regulations was amended to permit a school to accept an electronic signature as consent to disclose education records to a third party under specified conditions. The process used must both identify and authenticate a particular person as the source of the electronic consent; and the transaction must indicate the person's approval of the information contained in the electronic consent. (*See Federal Register*, Vol. 69, No. 77, April 21, 2004.)

In December of 2008 the Department of Education published significant regulatory changes to FERPA. However, those changes did not become effective until January 2009. Although they have sometimes been referred to as the 2008 amendments, they will hereinafter be referred to in this *Guide* as the "2009 amendments" or "2009 regulations." The following statutory revisions and court rulings are reflected in the 2009 regulations, as are several clarifications based on Department case history. These include:

- In response to the September 11, 2001 terrorist attacks on the United States, Congress passed the *USA Patriot Act* which amended FERPA to permit educational agencies and institutions to disclose—without the consent or knowledge of the student or parent—personally identifiable information from the student's education records to the Attorney General of the United States or to his designee in response to an *ex parte* order in connection with the investigation or prosecution of terrorism crimes specified in sections 2331 and 2332b(g)(5)(B) of Title 18, U.S. Code.

- *The Campus Sex Crimes Prevention Act* amended FERPA in 2000 to permit educational institutions to disclose information concerning registered sex offenders that they receive under community notification programs and pursuant to the Wetterling Act.

- In *Owasso Independent School District* v. *Falvo* (2002), the Court held that peer grading does not violate FERPA as long as an education record has not yet been created. This elementary school case may not have reasonable applicability in a higher education setting.

- In *Gonzaga University* v. *John Doe* (2002), the Court confirmed earlier case law that precluded a student or former student from using FERPA as the foundation for a legal cause of action in a civil court because, under The Act, "the Secretary is expressly authorized to deal with violations.'" Of course, this would not preclude an individual from suing an institution under common law privacy rights (*e.g.*, libel, slander) if an individual felt the institution had violated his rights regarding release of student record information.

- In *United States v. Miami Univ. and Ohio State Univ.* (2002), the United States Court of Appeals for the Sixth Circuit unanimously affirmed a lower court's ruling that university disciplinary records are "education records" under the *Family Educational Rights and Privacy Act* (FERPA) and that disclosing such records without students' consent, or meeting one of the exceptions to signed consent in §99.31, constitutes a violation of FERPA.

The following points summarize the major revisions from the 2009 amendments:

- Clarifying that the phrase "in attendance" applies to students who may not be physically present in class, such as through online courses.

- Clarifying that "biometric records" can be "personally identifiable" and what constitutes "biometric records."

- Clarifying that social security numbers, or any part thereof, cannot be designated as directory information.

- Clarifying that student identification numbers cannot be designated as directory information, except when they are used as student identifiers to gain access to information from education records, and then, only if in combination with other authentication factors.

- Allowing the return of information included in an education record to the originator or purported originator of the information by excluding such transfer of information from the definition of "disclosure."

- Clarifying that records pertaining to an individual's previous attendance as a student are "education records" under FERPA, regardless of when they were created or received by the institution.

- Summarizing the exceptions that permit postsecondary institutions to disclose information from education records to parents of eligible students.

- Clarifying that "personally identifiable information" includes information that alone or in combination, is linked to or linkable to a specific student with reasonable certainty. This replaces the "easily traceable" standard that previously existed within FERPA.

- Expanding the "school officials" exception to include contractors, consultants, volunteers, and other outside service providers used by an institution to perform institutional services and functions that it would otherwise perform for itself.

- Requiring postsecondary institutions to use "reasonable methods" to ensure that teachers and other school officials (including outside service providers) obtain access to only those education records—paper or electronic—in which they have legitimate educational interests.

- Requiring institutions to establish with contractors and other outside service providers expectations about direct control and appropriate use of student data to which they have access.

- Allowing a student's previous school to supplement, update, or correct any records it sent during the student's application or transfer period, including disciplinary records.

◘ Requiring a postsecondary institution to enter into a written agreement with an organization that is conducting a study "for or on behalf of" the institution and clarifying that the institution does not have to initiate the study. The agreement should include expectations about appropriate use of student data to which they have access.

◘ Allowing the disclosure of information de-identified through the removal of all "personally identifiable information."

◘ Requiring the use of reasonable methods to identify and authenticate the identity of the student, school officials, parents, and any other parties to whom information from education records is disclosed.

◘ Allowing federal and state officials who receive education records for audit, evaluation, or compliance and enforcement purposes to re-disclose such records in certain circumstances.

◘ Clarifying that, by removing the limitation on redisclosure in §99.33, that releasing the outcome of a disciplinary proceeding to a victim of an alleged crime of violence or a non-forcible sex offense, mandated under the Clery Act, is appropriate under FERPA, and that an institution cannot require such a victim to sign a confidentiality agreement prior to disclosing the outcome of the disciplinary hearing to the victim.

◘ Requiring state or federal officials to whom an institution has disclosed education records to keep a record of redisclosures and provide it to the postsecondary institution upon request.

◘ Revising the conditions under which information from education records may be disclosed in a health or safety emergency, to allow disclosures, including to parents of eligible students, when an institution determines that there is "an articulable and significant threat to the health and safety of the student or other individuals." If such disclosures are made, institutions must record the disclosure and its basis.

◘ Clarifying that directory information may not be disclosed on former students who opted out at their last opportunity to do so while still a student.

◘ Clarifying that opting out of directory information does not provide a student anonymity within a class.

◘ Clarifying that using social security numbers to disclose or confirm directory information is prohibited.

◘ Clarifying that information from education records that has been de-identified can be disclosed by the institution, so long as the information could not reasonably be linked to a specific student.

◘ Clarifying that student identifiable information released to a federal or state educational authority by an institution can be re-disclosed, on behalf of the institution, to another party which could have initially received the information directly from the institution under any of the exceptions in §99.31.

◘ Clarifying and enhancing enforcement provisions of FERPA, pursuant to *Gonzaga University* v. *Doe* 536 U.S. 273 (2002), including that alleged violations brought by someone other than the affected student may be investigated and that a complaint does not have to allege a policy or practice of violating FERPA in order to investigate or find a violation in a specific alleged incident.

◘ Providing additional safeguarding recommendations to help ensure compliance with FERPA.

Copies of the original 1974 law, as amended, as well as the final regulations, are included in Appendices A and B of this publication. The reader should always check to see if the Department of Education has issued any regulations since publication of this Guide through the Web page of the Family Policy Compliance Office (FPCO), the office in the Department of Education that has responsibility for administering FERPA, at: www.ed.gov/policy/gen/guid/fpco/index.html *or* www.aacrao.org.

Essence of the Act

FERPA deals specifically with the education records of students, affording them certain rights with respect to those records. For purposes of definition, education records are those records which are 1) directly related to a student and 2) maintained by an institution or a party acting for the institution.

FERPA gives students who reach the age of 18, or who attend a postsecondary institution, the right to inspect and review their own education records. Furthermore, students have other rights including the right to request amendment of records and to have some control over the disclosure of personally identifiable information from these records.

FERPA applies to all educational agencies and institutions that receive funding under most programs administered by the Secretary of Education (34 C.F.R. 99.1). Almost all postsecondary institutions, both public and private, generally receive such funding and must, therefore, comply with FERPA.

Institutions must annually notify students currently in attendance of their rights by any means that are likely to be read by students. The most common examples are found in the student handbook, catalog, or student newspaper. This notice also applies to any students pursuing education via distance education or any other non-traditional educational delivery processes. (*See* Appendix D, on page 177, for a sample of a model annual notification statement provided by the Family Policy Compliance Office.)

The regulations do not specify the means to be used for annually notifying students regarding their FERPA rights. Schools are not required by FERPA to notify former students of their FERPA rights. Although it is highly recommended that each institution publish its annual notification on its Web site, this method is only acceptable for fulfilling the annual notification requirement if all students are required to have personal computers or free and convenient access to computers that can access the institution's Web site.

If every enrolled student is given an institutional email address, schools may send their annual notification via email to their students.

Institutions may not disclose information contained in education records without the student's written consent except under conditions specified in The Act. An institution is not required to disclose information from a student's education records to the parents of dependent students but may exercise its discretion to do so. It is the responsibility of an institution to ensure that information is not improperly disclosed to the parents of students.

To Whose Records Does the Act Apply?

FERPA applies to the education records of persons who are, or have been, in attendance in postsecondary institutions, including students in cooperative and correspondence study programs and in any non-traditional educational delivery processes, such as distance learning.

FERPA does not apply to records of applicants for admission who are denied acceptance or, if accepted, do not attend an institution. Furthermore, rights are not given by FERPA to students enrolled in one component of an institution who seek to be admitted in another component of a school (*e.g.*, a student, admitted to one college within a university, but denied admission in another college, does not have any FERPA rights in the college which denied him/her admission).

To What Records Does the Act Apply?

The Act applies to all education records maintained by a postsecondary institution, or by a party acting for the institution, which are directly related to a student. Records containing a student's name, social security number or other personally identifiable information, in whatever medium, are covered by FERPA unless identified in one of The Act's excluded categories (*see* "Education Records," on page 9, for excluded categories).

To Which Institutions Does the Act Apply?

The Act applies to all institutions that receive funds administered by the Secretary of Education. This funding can either be in direct grants to the institution or to students attending the institution (financial aid). The Act applies to the entire institution even though only one component, *e.g.*, department or college, of the institution receives such funding.

Enforcement and Penalties

Responsibility for administering The Act has been assigned to the Family Policy Compliance Office within the Department of Education. This office reviews and investigates complaints, whether brought by the affected eligible student or otherwise brought to the attention of that office. When a violation has been found, FPCO attempts to bring about compliance through voluntary means, including any changes to the policies or practices of the institution. The penalty for noncompliance with FERPA can be withholding payments of Department of Education funds from the institution, issuing a cease and desist order, or terminating eligibility to receive funds; such actions generally will be taken only if compliance cannot be secured by voluntary means. See "Enforcement Procedures," on page 28, for more information.

Conflict With State Law

FERPA may be more permissive than the privacy laws of some states. If a conflict exists between FERPA and a state or local law, and if an institution determines that it cannot comply with the requirements of The Act, it should advise the Family Policy Compliance Office, U.S. Department of Education, 400 Maryland Avenue, SW, Washington, D.C. 20202–5901; phone: (202) 260–3887; fax: (202) 260–9001, within 45 days of that determination, giving the text and legal citation of the conflicting law. These guidelines, therefore, should not be interpreted to reduce the stringency of such state laws. They counsel common sense, good judgment, perspective, and integrity for compliance by postsecondary institutions in the implementation of The Act.

Several challenges to FERPA were made during the 1990s based on various states' open records/meetings laws. In general, sunshine/open records laws do not supersede FERPA; thus, schools must continue to comply with FERPA. Any perceived conflict between a state open records law and FERPA should be brought to the attention of the Family Policy Compliance Office. See discussion on "States' Open Records/Disclosure Laws and FERPA," on page 44 for more information on this issue.

The "Musts" and "Mays" in FERPA

Throughout The Act, the words "may" and "must" are used. These words are usually used in connection with sections of The Act that either permit or require an institution to perform an action to comply with FERPA. In the former case, the institution has control over a decision; in other words, it *may* do something. In the latter case, the institution has no choice; in other words, it *must* do something.

There are many "mays" and a few "musts" in FERPA. The reader should be aware of these words and not consider an institution legally obliged to release education record information when FERPA actually states that the institution *may* release education record information. For example, FERPA states that each institution may identify certain items as directory information; however, this is an institutional decision. By deciding not to identify any items as directory information, the institution would be making a decision that could have a major administrative impact on all offices. For example, consider the challenges of producing a commencement program if the names of all the graduates and their degrees were not identified as directory information.

Note that the "may" under FERPA could become a "must" for public institutions in a state where the Open Records Law requires release of information that FERPA permits to be released, or under other legislation that might require all institutions in that state to release information releasable under FERPA.

Chapter Two

Definition of Terms

[7]

Understanding key terms is essential to the interpretation of The Act and the final regulations for its implementation. Some definitions and explanations which carry substantive meaning for understanding The Act are listed here for the convenience of the reader. The regulations, as contained in Appendix B to this guide, provide all legal definitions.

ACT: Refers to the *Family Educational Rights and Privacy Act of 1974*, as amended, enacted as Section 444 of the *General Education Provisions Act* (20 U.S.C. 1232g).

AGENCY: An organization, company, or bureau that provides some service for another; a company having a franchise to represent another.

AGENT: A person or business formally authorized to act on another's behalf, *e.g.* within the scope of a contract between the two parties.

ALLEGED PERPETRATOR OF A CRIME OF VIOLENCE: A student who is alleged to have committed a crime of violence or a non-forcible sex offense.

ALUMNI RECORD: A record created by an educational institution that may contain personally identifiable information about a former student; is related solely to that student's activities as an alumnus; and is not related to attendance as a student.

ALUMNUS: A graduate or former student of a specific school, college, or university

ATTENDANCE: Includes but is not limited to:
- Attendance in person or by paper correspondence, videoconference, satellite, Internet, or other electronic information and telecommunications technologies for students who are not physically present in the classroom; and
- The period during which a person is working in a work-study program.

BIOMETRIC RECORD: As used in the definition of "personally identifiable information," a record of one or more mea-

surable biological or behavioral characteristics that can be used for automated recognition of an individual. Examples include fingerprints; retina and iris patterns; voiceprints; DNA sequence; facial characteristics; and handwriting.

C.F.R.: See "Code of Federal Regulations."

CLERY ACT: The *Jeanne Clery Disclosure of Campus Security Policy and Campus Crime Statistics Act,* codified at 20 U.S.C. 1092 (f) as a part of the *Higher Education Act of 1965,* is a federal law that requires colleges and universities to disclose certain timely and annual information about campus crime and security policies. All public and private postsecondary educational institutions participating in federal student aid programs are subject to it. The Clery Act was originally enacted by Congress in 1990 as the Campus Security Act. It requires colleges and universities to publish an annual report every year by October 1st containing three years worth of crime statistics and certain security policy statements, including sexual assault policies, which assure basic victims' rights, the law enforcement authority of campus police and where the students should go to report crimes.

CODE OF FEDERAL REGULATIONS: The annual accumulation of executive agency regulations published in the daily Federal Register, combined with regulations issued previously and still in effect. The C.F.R. contains the general body of regulatory laws governing practice and procedure before federal administrative agencies. The regulations pertaining to FERPA are found in 34 C.F.R. Part 99 (*see* Appendix B, on page 147).

CONTRACTOR: Outside parties who, for the purposes of The Act, qualify as school officials in that they are acting for the agency or institution and are subject to the same conditions governing the access and use of records that apply to other school officials.

COURT ORDER: A directive issued by a Court of Law, requiring an entity to take some specified action.

CRIME OF VIOLENCE: Refers to acts that would, if proven, constitute any of the following offenses or attempts to commit the following offenses: arson, assault offenses, burglary, negligent homicide, criminal homicide, destruction/damage/vandalism of property, kidnapping/abduction, robbery, forcible sex offenses.

DATES OF ATTENDANCE: The period of time during which a student attends or attended an institution. Examples of dates of attendance include an academic year, a spring semester, or a first quarter. The term does not include specific daily records or a student's attendance at the institution.

DE-IDENTIFIED RECORDS AND INFORMATION: An educational record that has had all personally identifiable information, as defined in §99.31(b), removed.

> **FERPA TIPS**
>
> Items that can never be designated and disclosed as directory information include a student's social security number, gender, race, ethnicity, citizenship, country of origin, religious preference, grades, GPA.

DIGITAL MILLENNIUM COPYRIGHT ACT, THE: The Recording Industry Association of America continues to issue hundreds of subpoenas for names and addresses of students whose internet service provider address or internet names correlate to evidence of music sharing. In response to campus inquiries about whether or not to disclose an education record pursuant to a subpoena, the FPCO advises that institutions may do so *as long as* a reasonable attempt is made to give the student prior notice.

DIRECTORY INFORMATION: Information contained in an education record of a student that would not generally be considered harmful or an invasion of privacy if disclosed. It includes, but is not limited to, the student's name; address; telephone listing; electronic mail address; photograph; date and place of birth; major field of study; grade level; enrollment status (*e.g.*, undergraduate or graduate, full-time or part-time); dates of attendance; participation in officially recog-

nized activities and sports; weight and height of members of athletic teams; degrees, honors and awards received; and the most recent educational agency or institution attended. (a) Directory information does *not* include a student's—(1) Social security number; or (2) Student identification (ID) number, except as provided in paragraph (b) of this section. (b) Directory information includes a student ID number, user ID, or other unique personal identifier used by the student for purposes of accessing or communicating in electronic systems, but only if the identifier cannot be used to gain access to education records except when used in conjunction with one or more factors that authenticate the user's identity, such as a personal identification number (PIN), password, or other factor known or possessed only by the authorized user.

NON-DISCLOSURE / OPT OUT / NO RELEASE OF DIRECTORY INFORMATION: The requirement that an educational institution must provide the opportunity for a student to refuse to let the institution release information designated as Directory Information, as outlined in §99.37.

DISCIPLINARY ACTION OR PROCEEDING: The investigation, adjudication, or imposition of sanctions by an educational agency or institution with respect to an infraction or violation of the internal rules of conduct applicable to students of the agency or institution.

"FINAL RESULTS" OF A DISCIPLINARY PROCEEDING: A decision or determination, made by an honor court or council, committee, commission, or other entity authorized to resolve disciplinary matters within the institution. The disclosure of final results must include only the name of the student, the violation committed, and any sanction imposed by the institution against the student.

DISCLOSURE: To permit access to, or the release, transfer, or other communication of, personally identifiable information contained in education records by any means, including oral, written, or electronic means, to any party except the party identified as the party that provided or created the record.

EASILY TRACEABLE: This term was removed from the new regulations and replaced with the language in §99.3, "personally identifiable information," (f) and (g).

ELECTRONIC SIGNATURE: An electronic sound, symbol, or process, attached to or logically associated with a contract or other record and executed or adopted by a person with the intent to sign the record that identifies and authenticates that person as the source of the electronic consent, and indicates such person's approval of the information contained in the electronic consent.

EDI: *See* "Electronic Data Interchange."

EDUCATIONAL INSTITUTION (OR AGENCY): Generally means any public or private agency, institution (including governing boards which provide administrative control or direction of a university system) of postsecondary education, which receives funds from any federal program under the administrative responsibility of the Secretary of Education. The term refers to the institution as a whole, including all of its components (*e.g.*, schools or departments in a university).

EDUCATION RECORDS: Those records directly related to a student and maintained by the institution or by a party acting for the institution.

The term "education records" does not include the following:

(1) Records that are kept in the sole possession of the maker, are used only as a personal memory aid, and are not accessible or revealed to any other person except a temporary substitute for the maker of the record.

(2) Records of the law enforcement unit of an educational agency or institution, subject to the provisions of § 99.8.

(3)(i) Records relating to an individual who is employed by an educational agency or institution, that:

(A) Are made and maintained in the normal course of business;

(B) Relate exclusively to the individual in that individual's capacity as an employee; and

(C) Are not available for use for any other purpose.

(ii) Records relating to an individual in attendance at the agency or institution who is employed as a result of his or her status as a student are education records and not excepted under paragraph(3)(i) of this definition.

(4) Records on a student who is 18 years of age or older, or is attending an institution of postsecondary education, that are:

(i) Made or maintained by a physician, psychiatrist, psychologist, or other recognized professional or paraprofessional acting in his or her professional capacity or assisting in a paraprofessional capacity;

(ii) Made, maintained, or used only in connection with treatment of the student; and

(iii) Disclosed only to individuals providing the treatment. For the purpose of this definition, "treatment" does not include remedial educational activities or activities that are part of the program of instruction at the agency or institution;

(5) Records created or received by an educational agency or institution after an individual is no longer a student in attendance and that are not directly related to the individual's attendance as a student.

(6) Grades on peer-graded papers before they are collected and recorded by a teacher.

ELECTRONIC DATA INTERCHANGE: Utilizes standard data formats for transmitting data from one computer to another.

ELIGIBLE STUDENT: Refers to a student who has reached the age of 18 *or* is attending an institution of postsecondary education. Since these guidelines are specifically for postsecondary institutions, "student" as used in this document is presumed always to refer to an eligible student. In non-postsecondary institutions, parents of students have additional rights not covered in this guide.

ENROLLED STUDENT: For the purposes of this publication, this term refers to a student who has satisfied all of the institutional requirements for attendance at the institution. The Family Policy Compliance Office has stated that each institution may determine when a student is "*in attendance*" in accordance with its own enrollment procedures. (*Federal Register*, July 6, 2000, p. 41856).

EX PARTE ORDER: An order issued by a court of competent jurisdiction without notice to an adverse party in connection with the investigation or prosecution of terrorism crimes specified in sections 2331 and 2332b(g)(5)(B) of Title 18, U.S. Code.

> **FERPA TIPS**
>
> If the institution does not make a determination of what "in attendance" means, the student is considered "in attendance" when they begin attending classes. Although FERPA is silent on whether a student is "in attendance" during vacations and summer breaks, FERPA applies to all students past and present. Therefore, "in attendance" establishes the time when student's FERPA rights begin initially as a college or "eligible" student.

FAMILY POLICY COMPLIANCE OFFICE: The office within the U.S. Department of Education that is responsible for enforcing/administering the *Family Educational Rights and Privacy Act of 1974* as amended. This office has responsibility for FERPA at all levels of education (K–12, postsecondary).

FINANCIAL AID: A payment of funds to an individual (or a payment in kind of tangible or intangible property to the individual), which is conditioned on the individual's attendance at an educational agency or institution. Financial aid does not include payments made by parents.

GRAMM-LEACH-BLILEY: The *Gramm-Leach-Bliley Act of 1999* prohibits an institution that provides financial products or services from sharing a customer's "nonpublic personal information" with non-affiliated third parties unless the institution first discloses its privacy policy to consumers and allows them to "opt out" of that disclosure. The Act restricts the ability to sell, give or otherwise disclose personal information to third parties without permission.

HEALTH AND SAFETY EMERGENCY: An educational agency or institution may disclose personally identifiable information from an educational record to appropriate parties including parents of an eligible student, in connection with an emergency if knowledge of the information is necessary to protect the health or safety of the student or other individuals.

HIPAA: The *Health Insurance Portability and Accountability Act of 1996* requires the establishment of national standards for electronic health care transactions and national identifiers for providers, health insurance plans, and employers with the intention of keeping patient information private.

"IN ATTENDANCE" (OR WHEN IS A STUDENT "IN ATTENDANCE"?): *See* "Enrolled Student" on page 9.

INSTITUTION OF POSTSECONDARY EDUCATION: An institution that provides education to students beyond the secondary school level. "Secondary school level" means the educational level (not beyond grade 12) at which secondary education is provided.

LAW ENFORCEMENT UNIT: Any individual or other component of an institution, including commissioned police officers and noncommissioned security guards, officially authorized by the institution to enforce any local, state, or federal law and maintain the physical security and safety of the institution. (Although the unit may perform other non-law enforcement functions, it retains its status as a law enforcement unit.)

LAW ENFORCEMENT UNIT RECORDS: These records are not education records as defined by The Act, so long as the records are files, documents, and other materials that are: 1) created by a law enforcement unit, 2) created for a law enforcement purpose, and 3) maintained by the law enforcement unit. Law enforcement records *do not* include: 1) records created by a law enforcement unit for law enforcement purposes other than those of the law enforcement unit; 2) records created and maintained by a law enforcement unit exclusively for non–law enforcement purposes, such as a disciplinary action or proceeding conducted by the institution.

LEGITIMATE EDUCATIONAL INTEREST: The demonstrated "need to know" by those officials of an institution who act in the student's educational interest, including faculty, administration, clerical and professional employees, and other persons who manage student record information including student employees or agents. (Although The Act does not define "legitimate educational interest," it states that institutions must establish their own criteria, according to their own procedures and requirements, for determining when their school officials have a legitimate educational interest in a student's education records.) *See* the "FERPA Model Notification of Rights" in Appendix D, on page 177, which contains sample language.

MEGAN'S LAW: Established the minimum national standards for sex offender registration and community notification programs. States must establish programs that require a sexually violent predator (and anyone convicted of specified criminal offenses against minors) to register their name and address with the appropriate authority where the offender lives, works, or is enrolled as a student. States are also required to release relevant information necessary to protect the public concerning persons required to register, excluding the identity of any victim. Under FERPA, prior consent is not required if the disclosure concerns sex offenders under Section 170101 of the *Violent Crime Control and Law Enforcement Act of 1994*, 42 U.S.C. 14071, and the information was provided to the educational agency or institution under 42 U.S.C. 14071 and applicable federal guidelines.

NON-DISCLOSURE / OPT OUT / NO RELEASE OF DIRECTORY INFORMATION: *See* "Directory Information" on page 8.

NON-FORCIBLE SEX OFFENSE: Statutory rape or incest.

OUTSOURCING: The circumstances under which a business contracts with another business to conduct a service or function that it would otherwise provide itself. In many cases the contracted business will be acting as an "agent" (*see also* "Agent" on page 7) of the contracting business.

PARENT: Includes a natural parent (custodial and/or non-custodial), a guardian, or an individual acting as a parent in the absence of a parent or a guardian.

PARTY: Refers to an individual, agency, institution, or organization.

PERSONALLY IDENTIFIABLE: Data or information which includes, but is not limited to—(a) The student's name; (b) The name of the student's parent or other family members; (c) The address of the student or student's family; (d) A personal identifier, such as the student's social security number, student number, or biometric record; (e) Other indirect identifiers, such as the student's date of birth, place of birth, and mother's maiden name; (f) Other information that, alone or in combination, is linked or linkable to a specific student that would allow a reasonable person in the school community, who does not have personal knowledge of the relevant circumstances, to identify the student with reasonable certainty; or (g) Information requested by a person who the educational agency or institution reasonably believes knows the identity of the student to whom the education record relates.

RECORD: Any information or data recorded in any medium (*e.g.*, handwriting, print, tapes, film, microfilm, microfiche, any form of electronic data storage including emails).

RECORDKEEPING: Recordation of releases of personally identifiable information from a student's education records to a party outside of the institution. Includes health or safety emergency releases. *See* §99.32 of the FERPA regulations (on page 158) for more details, including exceptions.

REDISCLOSURE: Notification requirement for institutions of higher education and state educational authorities acting on behalf of the institution, concerning the disclosure of personally identifiable information from education records to parties outside the institution. See §99.33 (on page 159) for details, including exceptions.

REGULATIONS, THE: Federal regulations implementing the statutory requirements of FERPA and found in Appendix B (on page 147). Also cited in this publication as 34 C.F.R. Part 99. Throughout this Guide, we have eliminated the "C.F.R." symbol where possible and have substituted the section symbol (§) before the specific regulation discussed.

SEVIS: The Student and Exchange Visitor Information System (SEVIS) is an Internet-based system that establishes a process for electronic reporting by designated school officials of information required to be reported to the Department of Homeland Security's Immigration and Customs Enforcement (ICE), previously known as the Immigration and Naturalization Service (INS). SEVIS maintains accurate and current information on non-immigrant students (F and M visa), exchange visitors (J visa), and their dependents (F-2, M-2, and J-2). SEVIS enables schools and program sponsors to transmit mandatory information and event notifications via the Internet, to the Department of Homeland Security, Immigration and Customs Enforcement (ICE) throughout a student's or exchange visitor's stay in the United States, in order to certify an institution as eligible to participate in SEVIS.

SCHOOL OFFICIALS: Those members of an institution who act in the student's educational interest within the limitations of their "need to know." These may include faculty, administration, clerical and professional employees and other persons who manage student education record information including student employees or agents. It may also include contractors, volunteers, and others performing institutional functions. (Although The Act does not define "school officials," it states that institutions must establish their own criteria, according to their own procedures and requirements for determining them. This is a recommended definition.)

SOLE POSSESSION RECORDS: Records that are kept in the sole possession of the maker, are used only as a personal memory aid, and are not accessible or revealed to any other person except a temporary substitute for the maker of the record. Any record that is made in conjunction with a student or other school official, such as an evaluation of a student or the student's performance, is *not* a sole possession record.

SOLOMON AMENDMENT: Sometimes referred to in this publication simply as "Solomon." This 1996 amendment requires postsecondary institutions to provide Department of Defense representatives, among other things, access to student recruiting information (defined below).

STUDENT: Any individual for whom an educational institution maintains education records. The term does not include an individual who has not been in attendance at the institution. An individual who is or has been enrolled in one component unit of an institution and applies for admission to a second unit has no right to inspect the records accumulated by the second unit until enrolled therein.

STUDENT RECRUITING INFORMATION: Information identified in the Solomon Amendment that institutions are required to provide military recruiters upon request. Those items are: student name, addresses, telephone listings, age or year of birth, class level, academic major, degrees received and the most recent previous educational institution in which the student was enrolled.

STUDENT RIGHT-TO-KNOW ACT OF 1990: Referred to in this publication as SRTK. SRTK requires colleges and universities to report graduation rates to current and prospective students.

SUBPOENA: A command from a court to require the person named in the subpoena to appear at a stated time and place to provide testimony or evidence. There are two main types of subpoenas: *duces tecum* (requires the production of documents, papers or other tangibles) and *ad testificandum* (requires person to testify in a particular court case).

USA PATRIOT ACT: The *Uniting and Strengthening America by Providing Appropriate Tools Required to Intercept and Obstruct Terrorism (USA PATRIOT) Act of 2001* permits a postsecondary institution to disclose personally identifiable information from a student's education records—without notification of the student—to the U.S. Attorney General or his designee in order to comply with an *ex parte* order in connection with the investigation or prosecution of an offense listed in 18 U.S.C. 2332(g)(5)(B).

U.S.C.: United States Code. A compilation of all federal legislation organized into 50 titles. Revised every six years with supplementary volumes issued in intervening years. The legislation related to FERPA is found in 20 U.S.C. 1232g (*see* Appendix A, on page 137).

Chapter Three

Compliance:
Requirements, Procedures, and Strategies

To fulfill the basic requirements for compliance with The Act, each educational institution must:

★ Provide students access to their education records.

★ Prevent improper disclosure of personally identifiable information from education records.

★ Provide opportunity for challenge of the contents of education records as required by FERPA and the regulations.

★ Maintain adequate records of requests and disclosures as detailed in this chapter.

Students have three primary rights under FERPA. They have the right to:

■ Inspect and review their education records.
■ Have some control over the disclosure of information from their education records.
■ Seek to amend incorrect education records.

In addition, students have a right to file a complaint with the Department if they believe one of their primary rights have been violated.

To comply with these rights and all of the provisions of The Act, its regulations, and disclosure provisions, each educational institution must annually notify students of their FERPA rights including the right to file a complaint with the U.S. Department of Education and provide students access to their education records.

Notice to Students of Their Privacy Rights (§99.7)

Each institution is required to annually notify students in attendance of their FERPA rights. To assist institutions in complying with the annual notification we have provided

in Appendix D (on page 177) a model annual notification of FERPA rights, developed by the Family Policy Compliance Office.

The annual notification *must* specify student rights covered by The Act, including the right to:

■ Inspect and review information contained in education records (*see* "Students' Access to Their Education Records," on page 14).
■ Request the amendment of the student's education records to ensure that they are not inaccurate, misleading, or otherwise in violation of the student's privacy or other rights (*see* "Challenging the Contents of Education Records," on page 18).
■ Consent to disclosure, with certain exceptions specified in The Act, of personally identifiable information from education records (*see* "Disclosure of Education Record Information," on page 16).
■ File complaints with the Department of Education concerning alleged failures by institutions to comply with The Act. Written complaints should be directed to:

The Family Policy Compliance Office, U.S. Department of Education, 400 Maryland Avenue, SW, Washington, DC 20202; phone: (202) 260–3887, fax: (202) 260–9001; email: ferpa@ed.gov.

In addition, the annual notice must include:

- The procedure to inspect and review education records.
- The procedure for requesting an amendment to education records.
- How the institution defines "school officials" and what constitutes a "legitimate educational interest."

Former students do not have to be notified. The method of annually notifying students is left to the discretion of the institution, as long as the means employed are reasonably effective to communicate those rights. For example, it may be met by individual student notification or by publication in college catalogs (printed or electronic), schedules, or student newspapers. A 2005 survey of AACRAO member institutions found that the most common methods of annual notification were the printed college catalog, student Web site, and schedule of classes.

As mentioned in Chapter 1, although it is highly recommended that each institution publish its annual notification on its Web site, this method is only acceptable for fulfilling the annual notification requirement if all students have ready access to computers at the institution. In addition, if the institution provides each student with an email address, notification can be provided via email.

FERPA TIPS

Students have the right to access their education records. A copy may be refused, but only if in doing so the institution does not limit the student's right to inspect and review that record and does not violate your state's open records law.

Notification to Students of the Institution's Directory Information; Student's Right to Non-Disclosure (§99.37)

FERPA requires institutions to give public notice to students in attendance of the categories of personally identifiable information which the institution has designated as directory information (*see* Appendix D for a "Model Notification of Directory Information," on page 177).

This notification should include:

- Types of information which *may* be designated as directory information. See "Definition of Terms" (Chapter 2) of these guidelines.

  These items of directory information may be "grouped" into categories for release to the public for specific purposes. In such cases, institutions may restrict the dissemination of an entire category if the student requests exclusion of any items of directory information.

- Specific procedures to inform students how to withhold categories of public or directory information. Generally, an institution would give students a specific period of time (as determined by the institution) within which they must inform institutions, in writing, that such categories of information are to be withheld (*see* "Disclosure of Education Record Information," on page 16). Although not a FERPA requirement, institutions should alert students to the possible undesirable consequences of withholding directory information. Institutions are advised to formulate procedures that will permit students to make informed decisions when they exercise their right to exclude directory information.

Institutions *may* disclose directory information about former students without meeting the notification requirements. However, if a student—at his/her last opportunity as a student—requested that directory information not be disclosed, the institution *must* continue to honor that request until informed to the contrary by the former student.

If requested to withhold directory information by a student after he or she has left the university, institutions *may*, but are not required to, comply with the request.

Students' Access to Their Education Records (§99.10)

Students and former students have rights to inspect and review their education records.

Procedures must be developed to permit students to inspect and review education records (with some limitations as noted in the next section) within a reasonable period of time, but not more than 45 days after the institution has received the request. The right to inspect and review includes the:

- Right to access, with an explanation and interpretation of the record. While FERPA does not state that students have a right to receive a copy of their records (except as follows), your state's open records law may.

- Right to a copy of the education record when failure to provide a copy of the record would effectively prevent the student from inspecting and reviewing the record, such as when the student no longer lives within commuting distance. The institution may, however, make other arrangements for the student to inspect and review the requested records, such as at a school located closer to the student. A copy may be refused, but only if, in doing so, the institution does not limit the student's right to inspect and review that record.

- While many student information systems now provide students the "self-service" option of viewing a great deal of their education record, none provides them with online access to "all" of their education record. This must be taken into consideration when students request to exercise their right to review their education record.

Limitations on the Students' Rights to Inspect Their Education Records (§99.12)

Limitations exist on students' rights to inspect and review their education records. The institution is not required to, but could, permit students to inspect and review the following:

- Financial information submitted by parents.

- Confidential letters and recommendations placed in their files prior to January 1, 1975, provided these letters were collected under established policies of confidentiality and were used only for the purposes for which they were specifically collected.

- Confidential letters and statements of recommendation, placed in the records after January 1, 1975, regarding which the student has waived his or her right to inspect and review and that are related to the student's admission, application for employment or job placement, or receipt of honors (*see* the next section, "Student's Waiver of Right to Review...").

- Students *must* not be permitted to view their education records if they contain information about another student; however, in such cases the institution must permit access to that part of the record which pertains only to the inquiring student.

Student's Waiver of Right to Review Confidential Letters of Recommendation (§99.12)

Students may waive any or all of their rights to review confidential letters and statements of recommendation

under The Act. The right of waiver is subject to the following conditions:

- That institutions do not require waivers as a condition for admission to or receipt of a service or benefit from the institution (although institutions are free to request waivers).

- That the documents to which students have waived the right to access are used only for the purposes for which they were collected. If used for other purposes, the waivers are void and the documents may be inspected by students. Institutions would be well advised to assure all parties concerned that the instruments used for soliciting recommendations and evaluations contain the specific purposes for which they will be used and the timeframe in which such forms will be destroyed.

- That the waiver is in writing and signed by the student, regardless of age. Students may waive their rights to inspect and review either individual documents or classes of documents (*e.g.*, part or all of an admission or job placement file). They may revoke the waiver in writing; however, by revoking it, they do not have the right to inspect and review documents collected while the waiver was in force.

Note: When "applicants" who waive their rights to access documents become students, they may specifically request and be given the names of all individuals who submitted letters and statements of recommendation for them.

Retention & Destruction of Education Records (§99.10, §99.20 and §99.32)

FERPA does not contain a Records Retention Plan. The regulations do not specify what records must be kept or how long they are to be maintained. In fact, the regulations contain only one condition pertaining to the destruction of education records. This is that once students have requested access to their education records, such students' records cannot be destroyed until inspection and review have been provided.

Two additional items *must not* be destroyed unless the records to which they pertain are destroyed: 1) "explanations" placed in the records by students as a result of a request for amendment that has been denied, and 2) records of disclosures and requests for disclosures.

Reference is made throughout these guidelines to various documents. Among them are forms documenting waiver of rights and consent for disclosure, subpoenas, requests for and notices of hearings, and summary proceedings of the hearings. Neither The Act nor the regulations stipulate procedures for retention of such written documents. Most questions about the accuracy of education records have been and will continue to be settled informally.

Nevertheless, it is clear that if a complaint alleging violations of the student's rights under FERPA should be filed against an institution, the institution's defense will depend largely upon documentation of its procedures and practices in any individual case. Therefore, these guidelines advise institutions to take necessary precautions to retain all documentation pertaining to compliance with The Act. The manner in which these records are kept is at the discretion of the institution. It is recommended that the institution establish a record's retention/management policy according to the guidelines found in the most recent *Retention of Records: Guide for Retention and Disposal of Student Records* published by AACRAO. In addition, the institution may need to meet other federal or state records retention requirements (*e.g.* public institutions will typically have record retention requirements issued by a state agency and/or legislature).

> **FERPA TIPS**
>
> Although there is no records retention policy in FERPA, each institution *should have* a records retention policy that follows the guidelines in AACRAO's most recent Retention of Records: Guide for Retention and Disposal of Student Records.

> **FERPA TIPS**
>
> The words "may" and "must" have different meanings. The FERPA practitioner should pay close attention to these words throughout this publication. They have a significant impact on how each institution develops its annual notification and policies in complying with FERPA.

Disclosure of Education Record Information (§99.30)

With Written Consent (§99.30)

A student *must* provide written consent before an institution may disclose personally identifiable information from their education records (note the "Exceptions" in the next section). Such written consent *must*:

- Specify the records to be released.
- State the purpose of the disclosure.
- Identify the party or class of parties to whom disclosure may be made.

- Be signed and dated by the student.

Institutions *must* disclose education records, or components thereof, without written consent to students who request information from their own records. An institution, at its discretion, could accept an electronic signature from a student as long as the conditions in §99.30 (d) are met.

Exceptions to Written Consent Requirement (§99.31)

An institution may release personally identifiable information from a student's education record without the student's written consent as required in §99.30 if the disclosure meets one or more of the following conditions:

- The disclosure is to other school officials, including teachers, whom the institution has determined to have legitimate educational interests. A contractor or other party to whom an agency or institution has outsourced institutional services or functions may be considered a school official. An educational agency or institution must use reasonable methods to ensure that school officials obtain access to only those education records in which they have legitimate educational interests.
- The disclosure is to officials of another institution of postsecondary education where the student seeks or intends to enroll.
- The disclosure is to authorized representatives of federal, state or local educational authorities.
- The disclosure is in connection with financial aid for which the student has applied or the student has received.
- The disclosure is to organizations conducting studies for, or on behalf of, the institution.
- The disclosure is to accrediting organizations.
- The disclosure is to parents of a dependent student.
- The disclosure is to comply with a judicial order or lawfully issued subpoena, including *ex parte* orders under the *USA Patriot Act*.
- The disclosure is in connection with a health or safety emergency.
- The disclosure is information the educational agency or institution has designated as "directory information."
- The disclosure is to the student.
- The disclosure is to a victim of an alleged perpetrator of a crime of violence or a non-forcible sex offense.

- The disclosure, subject to the requirements in §99.39, is in connection with a disciplinary proceeding at an institution of postsecondary education.
- The disclosure is to a parent of a student under the age of 21 concerning the student's violation of any law or policy regarding the use or possession of alcohol or a controlled substance.
- The disclosure concerns sex offenders and other individuals required to register under state or federal law.

There are specific conditions attached to these exceptions to the signed consent requirement, which are found in §99.31.

In addition, specific state laws may require or prohibit disclosure under certain of these exceptions.

RELEASE OF PERSONALLY IDENTIFIABLE INFORMATION

All information that is directly related to a student is considered "personally identifiable." This information includes both "directory information" and "non-directory information."

RELEASE OF DIRECTORY INFORMATION (§99.37)

Institutions *may* release, without written consent, those items specified as directory information:
- For students who are currently enrolled, provided the following conditions are met prior to disclosure:
  - ▶ That the institution inform the students of information or categories designated as public or directory information (*see* Appendix D, on page 177).
  - ▶ That students be given the opportunity to opt out or suppress disclosures of information for any or all categories of directory information.
  - ▶ That the students be given a reasonable period of time in which to state such refusals in writing.
- Institutions *may* release without written consent, those items designated as directory information on any student not currently enrolled unless that student, at his/her last opportunity as a student, requested otherwise.

RELEASE OF NON-DIRECTORY INFORMATION (§99.30, 99.31)

- Institutions *may* disclose personally identifiable information from a student's education records to a third party if the eligible student has signed and dated a written consent form which is presented to a school official by the third party.
- Institutions are responsible for informing parties to whom personally identifiable information is released that recipients, as a general rule, are not permitted to disclose the information to others without the written consent of the student. An example of such wording follows:

"The attached information has been forwarded to you at the request of the student with the understanding that it will not be released to other parties. The Family Educational Rights and Privacy Act of 1974, as amended, prohibits release of this information without the student's written consent. Please return this material to us if you are unable to comply with this condition of release."

Or

"This document contains personal information from a student's education records. It is protected by the Family Educational Rights and Privacy Act (20 U.S.C. 1232g) and may not be re-released without consent of the parent or eligible student."

In certain circumstances, found in 34 C.F.R. 99.33, the recipient of the information *may* legally redisclose that information. However, the 1996 final regulations added a provision that, if a third party rediscloses personally identifiable student information in violation of FERPA, the college which discloses the information to the third party shall be prohibited from permitting access to education records to that third party for a period of not less than five years.

Disclosure to Parents

Parents have a unique role with students and the institution with regard to FERPA.

Terms under which institutions may disclose information to parents of students are:
- By obtaining the student's written consent, which institutions do if the student is not a dependent.
- By establishing the student's dependency as defined by Internal Revenue Code of 1986, Section 152. An explicit institutional policy, covering "dependency" determination, should be available if release is to be made to parents under this provision (*see* "Parental Access to a Student's Education Records," on page 36). That policy, for example, might include:

▶ Advising each student, during the registration process, that their records may be disclosed to their parents upon request if their parents claim them as dependents for income tax purposes and the institution has verified that fact. Students should be asked to indicate if they are claimed as a dependent by their parents, or by one of their parents in cases of divorce, and to sign an acknowledgment that they were provided the opportunity to notify the school that they are not dependents for income tax purposes. Thereafter, if a parent of a student, who has indicated that one or both of the parents claims the student as a dependent, requests access, the school may give access to either parent (custodial or non-custodial) unless there is a court order, state statute, or other legally binding document prohibiting such. (See page 130 for sample forms.)

▶ Requiring a certified copy of the parents' most recent Federal Income Tax Form.

Challenging the Contents of Education Records (§99.20–§99.22)

The Act and regulations do not provide details about required grievance and hearing mechanisms to be employed, but institutions should have clear channels of appeal which a) are stated in the annual FERPA notification, b) involve an impartial individual, and c) take the following provisions of the regulations into account:

▪ Institutions *must* provide students with an opportunity to challenge and amend the contents of their education records which the students consider to be inaccurate, misleading, or otherwise in violation of their privacy or other rights (see 34 C.F.R. 99.20, 99.21, 99.22 for additional information).

▪ Officials who receive challenge requests *must* decide within a reasonable period of time whether corrective action consistent with the student's request will be taken. The student *must* be notified of the decision. If the decision is in agreement with the student's request, the appropriate record(s) *must* be amended.

▪ A student who is not provided full relief sought by his/her challenge *must* be informed by the appropriate official of the decision and his/her right to a formal hearing on the matter.

▪ A student's request for a formal hearing should be in writing. Within a reasonable period of time after receiving the requests, the appropriate official *must*

inform students of the date, place, and time of the hearing reasonably in advance of the hearing.

▪ The student *must* be afforded a full and fair opportunity to present evidence relevant to the issue raised. The student may be assisted or represented at the hearing by one or more persons of his/her choice, including an attorney, at the student's expense. However, note that this is not a legal hearing and formal Rules of Evidence or due process do not apply.

▪ The hearing may be conducted by any individual, including an official of the institution, provided such person does not have a direct interest in the outcome of the hearing.

▪ Decisions of the colleges and universities *must* be in writing, *must* be based solely on the evidence presented at the hearing(s), and *must* include a summary of the evidence and the reasons for the decision. The decision should be delivered to all parties concerned who have a legitimate educational interest.

  ▶ The institution will amend or destroy the education record in accordance with the decision of the hearing if the decision is in favor of the student, and inform the student of the action in writing.

  ▶ Should the educational agency or institution decide not to amend the record in accordance with the student's request, the appropriate official *must* inform the student that:

   ▷ The student has the opportunity to place with the education record a statement commenting on the information in the record, or a statement setting forth any reason for disagreeing with the decision of the hearing.

   ▷ The statement placed in the education record by the student will be maintained as part of the record for as long as the record is held by the institution.

   ▷ The record, when disclosed to an authorized party, *must* include the statement filed by the student.

A FERPA Hearing Request: Policy and Procedures

As an example of how an institution can comply with a student's request to change or delete education record information, the following information will be helpful.

Found below are relevant sections of a university's FERPA policy related to complying with a student request to challenge the contents of his/her education records:

RIGHT TO CHALLENGE INFORMATION IN RECORDS

Students have the right to challenge the content of their education records if they consider the information within to be inaccurate, misleading, or inappropriate.

This process includes an opportunity for amendment of the records or insertion of written explanations by the student into such records.

Note: The right to challenge grades does not apply under The Act unless the grade assigned was inaccurately recorded, in which case the record will be corrected.

HEARINGS TO CHALLENGE RECORDS

Students challenging information in their records must submit, in writing, a request for a hearing to the appropriate office maintaining the record, listing the specific information in question and the reasons for the challenge.

Hearings will be conducted by a university official who has no direct interest in the outcome of the hearing.

Students shall be afforded a full and fair opportunity to present evidence relevant to the reasons for the challenge.

The hearing officer will render a decision, in writing, noting the reason and summarizing all evidence presented within a reasonable time frame after the challenge is filed.

Should the hearing be in favor of the student, the record shall be amended accordingly. Should the request be denied, an appeal *may* be made, in writing, and submitted to the university registrar within 10 days of the student's notification of the decision of the hearing officer. The appeal shall be heard by an appeals board of three disinterested senior university officials and a decision rendered, in writing, within a reasonable period of time.

Should the appeal be in favor of the student, the record shall be amended accordingly. Should the request be denied, the student *may* choose to place a statement with the record commenting on the accuracy of the information in the record and/or setting forth any basis for inaccuracy. When disclosed to an authorized party, the record will always include the student's statement and notice of the board's decision, as long as the student's record is maintained by the university.

Records of Requests and Disclosures (§99.32, §99.33)

All institutions, subject to the provisions of The Act, are required to maintain records of requests for, and disclosures of, certain personally identifiable information.

The records of disclosures and requests for disclosures are considered a part of the students' education records; therefore, they *must* be retained as long as the education records to which they refer are retained by the institutions.

The records of requests and disclosures *must* include:

- The parties who have requested or obtained personally identifiable information from the education records of a student.
- The legitimate interests these parties had in requesting or obtaining the information.

These records *must* be made available for inspection to students, institutional officials responsible for the record, state and federal auditors, and others, as prescribed by law.

Records of requests and disclosures do not have to be maintained for:

- Requests made by students for their own education records.
- Disclosures made with the written consent of the student.
- Disclosures made to school officials under the conditions that allowed such disclosures (§99.31.a.1).
- Disclosures made to a party seeking directory information.
- Disclosures made in compliance with a subpoena or court order issued for a law enforcement purpose that includes an order that the subject of the subpoena not be notified.

§99.33 generally requires that institutions notify third parties to whom student education records have been released that they cannot redisclose that information to another party without the consent of the student. See the sample form, "Agent/Contractor Agreement." on page 126.

FERPA TIPS

FERPA was not intended to provide a process to be used to question substantive decisions that are correctly recorded. The rights of challenge are not intended to allow students to contest, for example, a grade in a course because they felt a higher grade should have been assigned. FERPA is intended to ensure the factual and accurate nature of the information in students' education records and students' rights to verify that information.

Chapter Four

FERPA Issues:
Analysis & Application

Since the passage of FERPA, a number of issues have arisen from changes in technology, interpretations of the Act by the Family Policy Compliance Office (FPCO), regulatory changes, institutional practices, and an increasing interest in, and pressure from, a societal "desire to know." This chapter will cover some of these issues. The discussion of these issues, including analysis and application, is based on the most recent information available and should not be considered legal interpretation or legal guidance.

Academic Standing

A student's current academic standing—such as "in good standing" or "eligible to return"—should not be designated as directory information under FERPA. By process of elimination, those who are "not in good standing" could be identified, which would be considered an improper disclosure under FERPA. However, "standing" as in freshman, sophomore, junior or senior can be designated as directory information.

Access to Education Records

Student

Students have the right to inspect and review their own education records. You don't need to provide immediate access to records, but must permit the student to access them within a reasonable period of time (45 calendar days within FERPA legislation, but the time frame may be shorter based on state open records laws for public institutions). Forty-five days provides time to reasonably pull together records and address any records clean-up issues (*e.g.*, redacting information about other students), but this time frame is not intended to encourage a delay in responding to a student request.

Third Party

Except in a few specific circumstances specified by law, third parties (*e.g.*, parents, spouses, employers) may be given access to student education records only with the signed and dated written permission of the student. The office releasing the information should keep a copy of the consent. In addition, unless a student has opted out, directory information can be released to anyone.

School Officials

School officials with a legitimate educational interest may access student education records within the scope of performing their job duties. Most employees of an institution will not have access to all records, and simply being an employee does not convey a "legitimate educational interest" on a school official. The 2009 regulations contain new requirements concerning school official access. (*See* §99.31 (a)(1) in Appendix B, on page 155).

Admissions Files

Under FERPA, an admitted student has the right to access the information in his/her admissions file, once in attendance at the institution. Under many state open records laws, rights to access admissions files likely begin when the institution creates the record.

Student admissions files for all admitted students should be reviewed in order to destroy items which have fulfilled their admissions—related purpose, and no longer need to be maintained.

One category of items which should be considered for removal, particularly at selective institutions, are notes written by admissions counselors during the admissions process, and any voting records which formed the basis of an admissions decision. Once a student enrolls, all the admissions records that have not been removed and destroyed in accordance with the institution's records retention plan become part of the student's education record—and are covered by FERPA. As such, they can be reviewed by the student. (*See* the FPCO "Letter to Harvard University," on page 183.)

Admitted vs. Enrolled/In Attendance Students

Individuals who applied for admission but were not accepted have no rights under FERPA. Admitted students are covered by FERPA only within the component unit to which they are admitted, and once they have enrolled at the institution. The institution should have a definition of "enrolled" or "in attendance" since that determines when a student's FERPA rights begin. Each institution may determine when a student's FERPA rights begin after being admitted. If the institution does not identify when a student is considered enrolled/in attendance, the student's FERPA rights begin on the day the student begins attending class. (*See* the FPCO "Letter to University of New Mexico," on page 181).

FERPA | TIPS

Institutions should have a definition of "enrolled"/ "in attendance" since that determines when a student's FERPA rights begin. Unless defined otherwise, FERPA rights begin on the day the student begins attending class.

Individuals who are denied admission to a program of study or component unit are not entitled by FERPA to have access to materials relating to the denied application, even if the individual is subsequently admitted into and enrolled in another course of study as an auditor. However, these individuals may be permitted access to these records under a state's open records law.

Agents/Contractors

(*See* "Contractors/Agents" on page 24.)

Alumni Records

Alumni records are those records created or received by an educational agency or institution after an individual is no longer a student in attendance and that are not directly related to the individual's attendance as a student (§99.3.5). Records that pertain to a student's time as a student, even if created after he or she left or graduated, such as an investigative report, are still education records and are covered by FERPA. The 2009 regulations clarify this distinction concerning alumni records.

Annual Notification and FERPA Policy

FERPA requires institutions to provide an annual notification to students regarding their FERPA rights. While educational institutions were previously required to have a FERPA policy, the 1996 amendments to the regulations removed this provision and clarified what must be included in the annual notification of rights to students.

The required annual notification must include several specific items: (1) the right of students to access their education records, (2) the right for a student to request a change to an education record believed to contain inaccurate or misleading information, (3) the right to a hearing if the request to correct an alleged inaccuracy is denied, (4) the right to consent to certain disclosures of information, and (5) the right to file a complaint with the Family Policy Compliance Office. Additionally, the institution, *if it has a practice of releasing education records or information from education records to school officials without the student's written permission*, must: (1) notify students of the conditions under which this information will be released, (2) identify those "school officials" who will have access to students' records, and (3) note the "educational interests" that permit these school officials to gain access to the records (*see* "Legitimate Educational Interest/School Officials," on page 31 and note that the 2009 regulations added specific requirements under the "school official" exception in 99.31 (a)(1)).

Thus, the annual notification provides an avenue for the institution to include many significant items that reflect the institution's direction in complying with FERPA. A model for an institutional FERPA annual notification to students is found in Appendix D (on page 177). Your institution's annual notification should be reviewed and updated on a regular basis.

Note that a specific format or communication vehicle is not required. However, the notice must reasonably inform students of their specific rights. The notice can be included in registration instructions, the student handbook, student newspaper, or other medium available to all students.

Even though not required, having a campus policy may serve several useful purposes:

- ⊞ It is a valuable training and reference tool for faculty and staff.
- ⊞ It provides clear and consistent responses to questions from students and others about FERPA-related issues.
- ⊞ It provides a history of your campus' FERPA policies.

Athletes (Student-Athletes)

FERPA does not apply any differently to student-athletes than it does to students in general. Institutions often list certain information about student-athletes (*e.g.*, "height and weight") as directory information, and student-athletes often sign waivers for the institution to release certain other information, particularly to external media and the NCAA. Beyond those provisions, their records should be treated as you would all student records. *See* the three "Letter[s] to NCAA" (beginning on page 281); *see also* the NCAA waiver form, "Student Athlete's Authorization to Disclose Information in Education Records Pursuant to FERPA," on page 132.

Campus Security/Police Records

In order to remain exempt from FERPA, law enforcement records must have been created by the institution's law enforcement unit, for a law enforcement purpose, and maintained separately from education records. If a copy of a law enforcement record is given to a school official, and that copy is maintained by the institution outside the law enforcement office, that copy becomes an education record subject to FERPA. If more than one student is identified in the copied law enforcement record, an institution must redact information about other students before allowing the student access to the record. For example, if Isaac and Craig were caught damaging institutional property and the law enforcement record about the incident was provided to the campus judicial office, the record in the judicial office is an educational record and if either Isaac or Craig wanted to review the record, any information pertaining to the other person must be redacted.

Challenging Student Records

Under FERPA, students have the right to challenge a record the student believes to be inaccurate or misleading. While the institution may not agree with the student's assessment, the institution must have a process to address the challenge. If, after all levels of review of the challenge have been considered, there is still a lack of agreement between the institution and the student, the institution must provide an opportunity for the student to place a statement in the record regarding the student's position.

Charging a Fee for Copying/Search/Retrieval

FERPA allows for the assessment of a fee for copies of education records provided to students unless its imposition "effectively prevents a parent or eligible student from exercising the right to inspect and review the student's education records" (§99.11). Such fees are limited to copying/postage charges. The institution cannot charge the student a fee to search for or retrieve his/her records, nor pass along the charge from a vendor who performs the search/retrieval for its work on behalf of the institution.

The regulations are silent on charging fees for valid third-party requests for students' education records. Consequently, the Family Policy Compliance Office has stated that nothing in FERPA prevents an institution from charging a search and retrieval fee along with other administrative fees to third parties who request information from students' records.

Computer Access to Records

Institutions must provide training to potential users regarding FERPA before granting access to education record information. The 2009 regulations require an institution to use "reasonable methods" to ensure that school officials have access only to records in which they have a legitimate educational interest. (*See* §99.31). After training, users should be required to sign a form indicating they understand student privacy, particularly legitimate educational interest, and the subsequent implications of a violation on their part (*see* sample form, "Code of Responsibility...," on page 119). Only then should system access be assigned or renewed.

It should also be easy for a user to determine that a student has placed a block/non-disclosure on his or her directory information.

The preamble to the 2009 regulations also include safeguarding recommendations applicable to an electronic environment.

Conducting Studies

FERPA allows an institution to disclose personally identifiable information from education records, without consent, to organizations conducting studies "for, or on behalf of" the institution. The information released must be protected so that only representatives of the organization conducting the study have access, and the data must either be destroyed or returned when no longer needed for the study. The 2009 regulations require that there be a written agreement between the institution and the organization conducting the study, and that the agreement specify the terms under which student identifiable information can be used. (*See* §99.31(a)(6)). The 2009 regulations also clarify that the institution is not required to initiate the study or agree with the outcome of the study.

Contractors/Agents

Institutions sometimes contract with an external agency or company to perform some service or business that it could perform itself. In most cases, the agreement/contract establishes that the external agency is acting in place of the institution—and is thus serving as a legal agent of the institution. Within the scope of the agreement/contract, the agency can perform as the institution would and access and use student information necessary to carry out the contract. Under FERPA, safeguarding measures must be included in the contract such that the agent is required to use the student data only for the purposes intended, destroys or returns the information when the work is concluded, and does not provide access to the data by any other third party unless otherwise legally able to do so. (*See* §99.31 and "Legitimate Educational Interest" [on page 31] for additional information regarding contractors).

Deceased Students

Under common law regarding privacy rights, the privacy interests of an individual expire with that individual's death. Accordingly, the FPCO has determined that the disposition of records held by an institution pertaining to a deceased eligible student is not a FERPA issue but a matter of institutional policy and/or state law. From a practical perspective, many institutions will simply substitute the "next of kin" for the deceased student in the decision-making process.

Destruction and Retention of Records

FERPA does not include a records retention plan. Which records should be kept, and for how long, are institutional decisions. Each institution should establish a regular process to decide which records to keep and for how long, keeping in mind that other federal or state laws or institutional policy could impact any such plan.

An institution may not purge any education records if there is an outstanding request to inspect and review those records. Furthermore, the institution shall maintain a record of each request for access to and disclosure of personally identifiable information from education records as long as the institution maintains the records. It is, therefore, strongly recommended that each institution establish a records retention schedule following the AACRAO guidelines found in *AACRAO's Retention of Records Guide.*

Directory Information

Directory information is defined as information contained in an education record of a student "that would not generally be considered harmful or an invasion of privacy if disclosed." (*See* §99.3.) Regulations specify that directory information includes, but is not limited to:

student's name, address, telephone number, date and place of birth, major field of study, participation in officially recognized activities and sports, weight and height of members of athletic teams, dates of attendance, degrees and awards received, the most recent educational institution attended by the student, and other similar information.

The list in the regulations is merely a list of examples. Within the parameters from the definition noted above, the institution should decide what it considers to be directory information for its students.

The 2009 regulations clarified that a social security number (SSN), or part of an SSN, cannot be designated as directory information. In addition, the revised regulations state that, in general, a Student Identification Number (SIN) can also not be directory information, with one noted exception: a "student ID number, user ID, or other unique personal identifier used by the student for purposes of accessing or communicating in electronic systems," can be directory information, "but only if the identifier cannot be used to gain access to education records" with non-directory information without an additional factor. (*See* the FPCO "Letter to University of Wisconsin–River Falls," on page 196.) Grades, GPA, race, gender, religion and national origin are also items that cannot be designated as directory information.

Under FERPA, a school may not comply with a request to disclose or confirm "directory information" that is linked to *non*-directory information such as a social security number. For instance, if someone calls the institution to verify the SSN from an application that states the applicant attended your institution, you cannot validate the SSN since you would not have been able to release the SSN to begin with. Assuming the student hasn't "opted out" from releasing directory information, you could certainly validate any directory information about that student—*e.g.*, dates of attendance, degree received, etc.

Directory information *may* be disclosed to anyone, and by any means, on those students who did not "opt out" of its release. For example, it could be released over the telephone regardless as to why it is being requested. Again, you are not required to release it, but you *may*. In some states, the interpretation of open records laws suggests that since an institution *may* release directory information, it must do so when requested.

A 2005 AACRAO survey of member institutions revealed that more than 65 percent of all responding institutions consider the following items to be directory information: name, major/field of study, degrees received, dates of attendance, permanent address, permanent phone number, enrollment status (undergraduate/graduate, full-time/part-time), honors and awards received, email address.

Disciplinary Records

Student disciplinary records are education records and are covered by FERPA.

In 2002, a three-judge panel of the United States Court of Appeals for the Sixth Circuit (*United States of America* v. *Miami University; Ohio State University, et al.*) unanimously affirmed a lower court's ruling that university disciplinary records are "education records" under the Family Educational Rights and Privacy Act (FERPA) and that disclosing such records without students' consent, or meeting one of the exceptions to signed consent in §99.31, constitutes a violation of FERPA. "We have believed all along that disciplinary records are protected by FERPA," said

LeRoy Rooker, then-director of the Education Department's Family Policy Compliance Office which administers the Act. The Sixth Circuit concluded that continued release of student disciplinary records "will irreparably harm the United States and the [Department of Education]."

The court reaffirmed the Department's broad reading of the term "education records," and stated that Congress, in amending FERPA in 1998 to allow postsecondary institutions to disclose the final results of disciplinary proceedings, must have intended that disciplinary records be education records or this amendment would be "superfluous."

Releasing Disciplinary Records

The Family Policy Compliance Office, in its 1996 final regulations, stated that an educational agency or institution "may include information in a student's education records concerning disciplinary action taken against the student for conduct that posed a significant risk to the safety or well-being of that student, other students, or other members of the school community." It went further to say that an institution may disclose, without prior consent, information contained in a student's education records concerning disciplinary action taken against the student, described above, to teachers and school officials who have legitimate educational interests (*see* "Legitimate Educational Interest" on page 31) in the behavior of the student.

This means that institutions may disclose, without the student's prior written consent, information about certain disciplinary actions taken against the student to other institutions regardless of level (K–12 to postsecondary) and that the student does not have to be either (1) in attendance at the other institution or (2) seeking or intending to enroll in another institution (see §99.36, Appendix B, on page 160).

In limited circumstances, certain disciplinary information *may* be disclosed under two FERPA exceptions (§99.33 (c&d)).

FERPA was amended in 2000 to provide an exception for release of certain disciplinary information to the victim of an alleged perpetrator of a crime of violence. The disclosure may only include the final results of the disciplinary proceeding conducted by the institution with respect to that alleged crime or offense. The institution may disclose the final results of the disciplinary proceeding, regardless of whether the institution concluded a violation was committed. Note that the Clery Amendment requires the institution to release the results of such a disciplinary hearing to the alleged victim and the institution cannot require the victim to sign a non-disclosure agreement before releasing the results to the alleged victim.

FERPA TIPS

Changing the methods of delivering education to students does not mean that FERPA rules change. We need to ensure that *all* students are annually notified of their FERPA rights and that institutions are fully in compliance with FERPA.

In addition, certain disciplinary information can be released to *any* interested individuals (*i.e.*, the general public). If the disciplinary hearing was related to an alleged crime of violence and if the student was found in violation of rules or policies regarding such crimes, the final results of an institutional disciplinary proceeding can be released to anyone. The final results must include only the name of the student, the violation committed, and any sanction imposed by the institution against the student.

The institution can release information to parents regarding the student's violation of any federal, state, or local law, or of any institutional policy or rule governing the use of alcohol or a controlled substance *if* the institution has determined that the student has committed a disciplinary violation with respect to that use or possession, and the student is under the age of 21. This disclosure can be made regardless of whether or not the student is a dependent student under FERPA. Institutions should verify that their state open records law permits this disclosure, because it is prohibited in some states.

Disciplinary Information on a Transcript

FERPA does not address what information a school may or may not maintain or print on a transcript. Thus, the institution can decide whether or not to include behavioral issues on a student's transcript. Any information appearing on a transcript must be protected and/or disclosed in compliance with FERPA.

Distance Education; Using Technology in the Classroom Setting

The high tech revolution that has occurred in the past 20 years has permitted educational institutions to explore alternate ways of providing an education to students.

As many institutions explore these alternatives, it is best to keep in mind that, whether we are dealing with high tech or low tech issues, one education records law (FERPA) governs student privacy issues.

This means that, for FERPA purposes, it is of no consequence how education is delivered to students or where they are when they are participating in a course. Whether they are on-campus attending classes in traditional classrooms or half way around the world taking courses via the Web, students have the same FERPA rights and are to be accorded equal treatment under the law.

Therefore, institutions must plan to annually notify all of its students of their FERPA rights no matter where the student is living or taking courses. This also applies to the student's right to access their records and any other right accorded to the students by FERPA. FERPA rights also apply to non-credit experiences offered by the institution if the institution maintains personally identifiable information about those students and their experience.

This added dimension to providing education creates challenges for an institution in complying with FERPA in a distributed environment. However, changes in technology also assist each institution with its task of complying with FERPA. For example, the annual notification can be sent via email to each student who is taking courses via the Web anywhere in the world.

Sharing Email Addresses, Grades and Other Personally Identifiable Information Among Students in the Same Class

Faculty who utilize electronic teaching tools such as WebCT or Blackboard may wish to share students' email addresses in a class with others in the same class. The 2009 amendments clarified that a student cannot be "anonymous" in class, even in a distance learning setting. While grades and other personally identifiable information that relates to the student's progress in the class cannot be disclosed, it is appropriate that contact information be shared if the class includes online discussions.

It is also important to consider access to class information in a broader sense. For example, some classes have a Web site to support the class instruction. If that Web site is available to the general public it cannot contain any non-directory information for *any* student in the class, and cannot contain *any* information for students who have a directory information non-disclosure in place on their record. So, it is recommended that such a Web site be behind a security protocol which can be accessed only by those directly involved with the class (*e.g.*, the students and instructors).

Dual-Enrolled Students

Students who are enrolled in both high school and courses at a postsecondary institution provide a unique situation. While the rights under FERPA belong to the parents with respect to the high school records, they would also belong to the student with respect to the postsecondary records. In this case, FERPA's provisions allowing disclosure of information to parents of students who are dependents for income tax purposes would apply, allowing the postsecondary institution to share grades and other information from the student's education records with parents. (*See* discussion under "Parental Access to a Student's Education Records," on page 36.) Further, the high school and postsecondary institution may share information from records of dual-enrolled students under the exception to the consent provision which allows §99.34(b). (*See* FPCO "Letter to Virginia Commonwealth University" [on page 192] and "Letter to University of Medicine & Dentistry of New Jersey" [on page 194]).

Electronic Signatures

FERPA is technology-neutral with respect to how to meet disclosure and signature requirements. In cases where FERPA requires a signed and dated written consent under §99.30 for a disclosure such as issuance of a transcript to a third party, the amended regulations specify that "an agency or institution *may* accept electronic consents and signatures when reasonable security is provided for the process."

The rule stipulates that allowable electronic consent must:

- ▣ Establish a reasonable way to identify the individual and authenticate the identity of the particular eligi-

ble student or parent as the source of the electronic message or record requesting access or consenting to the disclosure of education records;
- ▣ Attribute the electronic signature to the unaltered message or document to prevent repudiation by the sender;
- ▣ Verify the integrity of the signed message or document in transmission and upon receipt; and
- ▣ Document and record the signed electronic message.

FPCO has been careful to point out that §99.30 constitutes only general guidance for the use of electronic communications in meeting certain FERPA requirements and does not specify desired methods. It further states that while agencies and institutions are not limited to any particular technology or method, the Department of Education considers electronic signature standards established under the federal student loan programs to satisfy the written consent requirement in FERPA. While schools are not required by FERPA to follow the Federal Student Aid (FSA) "safe harbor" standards for electronic signatures, FPCO has determined that those standards do "satisfy the written consent requirement in FERPA." In response to commenters who argued that it was confusing to apply the FSA safe harbor standards to FERPA, FPCO stated: "We agree that some circumstances within the FSA Standards do not relate directly to FERPA. While schools are not required by FERPA to follow the FSA Standards, we believe that schools may use the set-up and security measures described in the FSA Standards, particularly sections 3 through 7 [U.S. Department of Education, Standards for Electronic Signatures in Electronic Student Loan Transactions, April 30, 2001], as guidance for security measures in a system using electronic records and signatures under FERPA." (*See* Appendix I, on page 321, for the full text of the guidelines.)

Implementing Institutional Electronic Signatures—Helpful Hints & Resources

It is highly recommended that schools establish an institutional electronic signature policy prior to rolling out self-service electronic submissions to their students and alumni. Additional electronic signature resources are available at:

- ▣ *Family Educational Rights and Privacy Act: Final Rule* 34 C.F.R. 99 (69 F.R. 21670–21672) located at www.ed.gov/news/fedregister or www.ed.gov/policy/gen/guid/fpco/index.html.

- U.S. Department of Education "Standards for Electronic Signatures in Electronic Student Loan Transactions" located at http://ifap.ed.gov/dpclet ters/gen0106.html—see attached document to this letter—http://ifap.ed.gov/dpcletters/attachments/gen0106Arevised.pdf.
- AACRAO Compliance Web site at: www.aacrao.org/compliance/.
- Federal Policy Compliance Office Web site "Online Library" at www.ed.gov/policy/gen/guid/fpco/ferpa/library/index.html
- Regist-L Colleagues—search on "electronic signatures." Register for the listserv via www.aacrao.org/useful_links/listserv.cfm
- Also see Chapter 5, "Training Materials," Chapter 6, "Sample Forms," and on AACRAO's Web site at www.aacrao.org/compliance/ferpa/.

A final recommendation, for schools interested in implementing online self-service transactions utilizing electronic signature consent is that you work with the Family Policy Compliance Office (FPCO) to ensure that your proposed policy, electronic signatures, and safe harbor standards are "FERPA compliant."

FERPA | **TIPS**

Written requests that permit institutions to release non-directory information to third parties on a continuing basis, e.g., sending grades to employers at the end of each semester of attendance, are acceptable under FERPA as long as the request includes all the information required under FERPA. Although these requests are acceptable, each institution may decide if it wishes to honor such requests.

Electronic Transmission of Student Data

FERPA requires institutions to prevent the unauthorized release of personally identifiable, non-directory information from student education records without the permission of the student. When student data is transmitted electronically, the sender must require the same written authorization from the student as it does for a paper document (*see* "Disclosure of Education Record Information," on page 16).

Emailing Grades

There is no guarantee of confidentiality in transmitting information electronically, particularly when it is done through the Internet. Faculty who wish to send grades to students via email need to understand that, if there is an unauthorized release of grades to someone who is not a school official, the institution could be found to be in violation of FERPA if the Family Policy Compliance Office conducted an investigation. (*See also* "Posting of Grades," on page 38.)

Email Transcript Requests

An email transcript request would not contain a student's signature and the receiver cannot be confident about the identity of the sender. Therefore, such requests should not be honored. Although FERPA requires a student's written permission to release a transcript, it is silent on how that permission is transmitted to the office issuing the transcript. Therefore, transcript requests received via fax that include the student's signature, or a scanned document attached to an email message authorizing release of a transcript that includes the student's written permission on the document, are acceptable methods of providing the written permission required under FERPA. (*See also* "Facsimile Records," on page 29.)

Also, if a student has submitted written permission to send a transcript, or end-of-term grades or any other non-directory information on the student, on a regular basis to a third party, the institution may send the requested information upon receipt of an email message from the student. The institution needs to take reasonable steps to ensure that the request did, in fact, come from the student. The institution does not have to obtain written permission every time non-directory information is to be released as long as the institution has on file written permission from the student to release such information to a specific third party. Such written permission must include: the party to whom the information is to be released, the information to be released, the purpose for the release, and the signature of the student. Although students may submit such standing letters to release non-directory information, *it is still the institution's prerogative to honor such requests.*

Emergency Situations

(*See* "Health or Safety Emergency" on page 30.)

Enforcement Procedures and Penalties (§99.60–99.67)

The Family Policy Compliance Office (FPCO) reviews and investigates specific alleged instances of violations of FERPA, or institutional policies or practices that may be in violation of FERPA. Investigations may be initiated by the student, or when otherwise brought to the attention of FPCO (*see* changes in §99.64(b) of the 2009 regulations).

FPCO will notify the institution of the alleged violation and direct it to respond within a set period of time. Information that may be requested includes: a written response, reports, information on policies and procedures, annual notifications, training materials, and other information necessary to conduct the investigation. The finding(s) of the investigation will be reported to the school and the complainant (if any).

If the Office finds that there has indeed been a failure to comply with FERPA, it will notify the institution about the corrections that need to be made to bring the institution into compliance, including any changes to policy or practice of the institution that may be in violation of FERPA. The Office will establish a reasonable period of time for the institution to voluntarily accomplish the specified changes.

If the Secretary of Education finds, after this reasonable period of time, that the institution has failed to comply with FERPA and determines that compliance cannot be secured by any means, the secretary can, among other options, direct that the Department of Education may take any legally available enforcement action, including but not limited to withholding payments of funds, issuing a cease and desist order, or terminating eligibility to receive funding.

Further, in *United States of America v. Miami University; Ohio State University, et al.*, 294 F.3d 797 (6th Cir. 2002), the Court ruled that the Department was within its rights to seek an injunctive relief to enforce compliance because none of the administrative remedies authorized by FERPA would have stopped the violations in that case. In effect, the court held that the Department can take preemptive actions in enforcing FERPA, rather than only after violations occur. In the court's own words, "once personally identifiable information has been made public, the harm cannot be undone."

Facsimile Records (Fax)

The use of fax technology involves two issues: receiving requests and sending information.

Receiving Requests

It is acceptable to use a fax as a signed, dated request from the student to release information to a third party. FERPA requires that the student's written permission, under most circumstances, be obtained before releasing a non-direc-

tory education record (for example, a transcript) to a third party. The receipt of a written request to release an education record via fax satisfies this requirement of FERPA. The FPCO recommends that institutions have "sufficient information to convince the responsible official at the institution that the signed document is a *bona fide* copy of an original consent." (Rooker 1989).

Sending Information

Sending information via a fax machine is acceptable under FERPA, however, the sending institution should have solid security measures and validation procedures established. AACRAO has found that most institutions that accept fax transcripts will do so for advising purposes, but require that the student subsequently provide an official copy.

Financial Aid

§99.31 of the regulations provides an exception regarding the release of education records information without the consent of the student when the release is related to financial aid. The disclosure is permitted if the information is necessary to:

> **FERPA TIPS**
>
> An institution that receives a request from the student to fax an education record to the student should require that the student provide a written request which includes the fax number. Thus if someone other than the student retrieves the fax, the institution has the signed consent directing that it be faxed to that number.

- ✚ Determine eligibility for the aid,
- ✚ Determine the amount of the aid,
- ✚ Determine the conditions for the aid, and/or
- ✚ Enforce the terms and conditions of the aid.

FERPA is straightforward when considering access by faculty or staff on campus who are working with financial aid issues, decisions and questions. They have a legitimate educational interest in accessing information needed to perform their responsibilities.

Questions frequently arise with regard to providing access to people more loosely affiliated with the university or third parties involved with making financial aid decisions. For example, what records information should appropriately be provided to a group of alumni from an alumni group providing a scholarship to a student at an institution?

At the very least, it is appropriate to provide enough information to establish basic eligibility to receive the aid, *e.g.,* "Does the student have at least the minimum GPA required to be considered?" In fact, if the student applied for the aid and had any reasonable notice that his/her records information might be necessary to make a decision regarding the financial aid, then this exception should provide enough flexibility to support the release of records information necessary to make the decision.

From a practical perspective, make sure that the application process includes notice to the student regarding release of records information as a part of the evaluation process. Their sign-off to the application process will then provide the needed flexibility.

Former Students' Rights

Students who have ceased attendance or have graduated from an institution of higher education have the same FERPA rights as students currently attending a college or university, including the right to (1) inspect their education records, (2) have a hearing to amend an education record, and (3) have their education record privacy protected by the institution. Former students may request non-disclosure of directory information, however, it would be at the institution's discretion whether or not to honor such a request. But if a student has requested non-disclosure of directory information in his or her last term of attendance, that request must be honored until that student requests its removal.

Health or Safety Emergency

If non-directory information is needed to resolve an emergency situation, an educational institution may release that information if the institution determines that it is "necessary to protect the health or safety of the student or other individuals" (§99.36). This includes releasing information to school officials at another institution. A record must be made of the disclosure (*see* "Records of Requests and Disclosures," on page 19). The 2009 regulations require the institution to document the "articulable and significant threat" that is the reason for releasing the information.

Factors to be considered or questions to be asked in making a decision to release such information in these situations are: (1) the severity of the threat to the health or safety of those involved; (2) the need for the information; (3) the time required to deal with the emergency; and (4) the ability of the parties to whom the information will be given to deal with the emergency.

The 2009 regulations stipulate:

"An educational agency or institution may take into account the totality of the circumstances pertaining to a threat to the health or safety of a student or other individuals. If the educational agency or institution determines that there is an articulable and significant threat to the health or safety of a student or other individuals, it may disclose information from education records to any person whose knowledge of the information is necessary to protect the health or safety of the student or other individuals. If, based on the information available at the time of the determination, there is a rational basis for the determination, the Department will not substitute its judgment for that of the educational agency or institution in evaluating the circumstances and making its determination."

Additionally,

"an educational agency or institution must record the following information when it discloses personally identifiable information from education records under the health or safety emergency exception in §99.31(a) (10) and §99.36:
* *The articulable and significant threat to the health or safety of a student or other individuals that formed the basis for the disclosure; and*
* *The parties to whom the agency or institution disclosed the information."*

Contacting a Student for an Emergency

The institution may want to develop some procedures that balance the student's privacy with a potential emergency situation. For example, rather than releasing a student's schedule to a third party, a representative of the institution could deliver an emergency message to the student and the student could respond accordingly.

HIPAA and FERPA

The Health Insurance Portability and Accountability Act (HIPAA) was enacted to establish a national standard for the protection of personally identifiable information relating to health care. The HIPAA privacy rule establishes standards and imposes requirements to protect the privacy of individually identifiable health information. However, records that are subject to FERPA are *not* subject to the HIPAA Privacy Rule (*see* page 82483, *Federal Register*, December 28, 2000). Other HIPAA rules may apply, and educational institutions that provide health or medical services to students may qualify as "covered entities" under the HIPAA Privacy Rule. However, the HIPAA Privacy Rule specifically excludes from its coverage those records that are protected by FERPA. The definition of "Protected health information" in 45 C.F.R. 160.103, states, in relevant part, the following:

(2) Protected health information excludes individually identifiable health information in:

(i) Education records covered by the *Family Educational Rights and Privacy Act*, as amended, 20 U.S.C. 1232g; [and]

(ii) Records described at 20 U.S.C. 1232g (a)(4)(B)(iv) ["treatment records"]. (*See* Appendix H, on page 309, for additional information regarding HIPAA and FERPA.)

IRS Summons

For purposes of FERPA, an IRS summons, or "any other subpoena issued for a law enforcement purpose," should be assessed as to its validity and, if found to be lawfully issued, treated as any other "lawfully issued subpoena" (§99.31(a)(9)(ii)(B)). Information from a student's education records can be disclosed without the student's written consent to comply with the summons. A reasonable attempt to notify the student is required prior to releasing the information. (*See* "Subpoenas," on page 46; *see also* the FPCO "Letter to the Internal Revenue Service," on page 251.)

Law Enforcement Records

Congressional legislation passed in 1992 exempts from FERPA's definition of education records those "records maintained by a law enforcement unit of the educational agency or institution that were created by that law enforcement unit for the purpose of law enforcement." Thus, records that meet the law enforcement unit definition are not covered by FERPA and could be disclosed by the law enforcement unit without the written permission of the students involved.

Institutional law enforcement records must be kept separate from education records. Such separation of records not only further protects the privacy of the student's education records but also facilitates timely and appropriate access to personal and sensitive information by authorized school officials.

Although law enforcement unit records are not subject to FERPA *if kept separate from education records at the institution*, a law enforcement unit record will become an education record, subject to FERPA, if the original or copy is maintained by a school official outside of the law enforcement unit or is kept in an area where it is accessible to other school officials.

Law enforcement officials of the institution or others contracted to perform a law enforcement service for the institution must be identified as "school officials" in the institution's annual FERPA notification if they are permitted access to student education records. Campus law enforcement agencies accessing student records are bound by all of the requirements of FERPA. Thus, while they may have access to student education records, information from those records (such as attendance) cannot be included in any law enforcement records.

Legitimate Educational Interest/School Officials

In order for a school official at the institution to have access to student education records, the official must have a legitimate educational interest in the records being accessed. Legitimate educational interest means that the official has a need to access student education records for the purpose of performing an appropriate educational, research or administrative function for the institution.

One of the main emphases of FERPA is that personally identifiable information in an education record may not generally be disclosed without prior written consent from the student. FERPA, however, provides several exceptions to this consent requirement, which allows institutions to disclose personally identifiable information from a student's education record without the written consent.

It is important to note that although these exceptions exist, FERPA does not *require* an institution to disclose such information from the education record to any party, except to the student.

One of the primary exceptions is that an institution may disclose personally identifiable information, without the student's written consent, to school officials whom the institution has determined have a legitimate educational interest. The regulations implementing FERPA, however, do not establish criteria for determining the limits of what may be considered a legitimate educational interest.

There are several important factors to consider if an institution is to exercise prudence in releasing education record information under the aegis of legitimate educational interest:

- Although FERPA makes it clear that an institution may release personally identifiable information to school officials, an institution must state the institution's intention to allow school officials to access this information in its annual notification.
- The criteria for determining who is a "school official" must also be specified in the annual notification.
- Criteria must be formulated for determining legitimate educational interest.

"School Officials"

It would be impractical to list, in specific terms, every person or group who might be considered a "school official." The institution's criteria should be broad enough to include anyone who may reasonably fall within that category. Sample criteria for determining a "school official" might be:

- A person employed by the institution in an administrative, supervisory, academic or research, or support staff position.
- A person serving on an institutional governing body.
- A person employed by, or under contract to, the institution to perform a special task, such as an attorney or an auditor.
- A person or organization acting as an official agent of the institution, and performing a business function or service on behalf of the institution (the function or service must be one that the institution normally would perform itself).
- A member of the law enforcement unit or health staff.

- A student serving on a committee.
- A student assisting another school official in fulfilling their professional responsibilities (work study).

Although an individual has been designated as a "school official," he/she does not have a right of access to student education records. The school official, such as a faculty member, must demonstrate to the records or data custodian a legitimate educational interest, and such a determination must be made on a case-by-case basis.

The 2009 regulations clarified that the "school officials" exception can include contractors, consultants, volunteers, and other outside service providers used by an institution to perform institutional services and functions that the institution would normally do itself. Such individuals may include an outside attorney providing legal services to the institution, an insurance representative, or a collection agency. It is important to understand that these entities must be working directly for the institution and are bound by the same protection and re-disclosure conditions. Institutions should identify outsourcing entities (not necessarily by name, but by stating vendor or contractors may perform services on behalf of the institution) in their annual notification.

If an institution chooses to use outside entities to perform certain functions, the 2009 regulations stipulate that the institution must have "direct control" over that entity's access to and use of the information provided (*e.g.,* a contract that specifies how the service provider is to protect and use the information).

Similarly, it would also be relevant to include "agents" as "school officials" if the nature of the agency relationship is to provide a service that could or would otherwise be performed by the institution. For example, many institutions have established an agency relationship with the National Student Clearinghouse (NSC) to provide student loan verification to loan servicers, including the federal government. In this case, the NSC is acting in place of the institution. Other examples include outsourcing enrollment and/or degree verification information. The agent, whether an individual or an organization, must operate within the same parameters as would the institution, and only for a relevant business purpose. Therefore, it would be a violation of FERPA for the agent to release any personally identifiable information to a third party or to use the information for any purpose other than that for which it was provided.

In its August 30, 2004, letter to Auburn University, regarding the NSC, the Family Policy Compliance Office stated that it was a violation of FERPA for an agent (*i.e.,* NSC), acting on behalf of the university, to use personally identifiable information (*i.e.,* student's social security number), without the student's written consent, to match the SSN with information in the university's database and then subsequently release that information to the requester. In that letter, director of the FPCO, LeRoy Rooker, stated, "The verification of the student's SSN, absent the student's prior written consent, amounts to an improper disclosure of personally identifiable information from education records under FERPA." Finally, it should also be expected that an agent will either return or destroy any student data when the business service function is completed. (*See* the sample "Agent/Contractor Agreement" form on page 126.)

An institution's policy also may include student workers within the category of "school officials." A student worker performing a task or function covered under the institution's definition of legitimate educational interest may then be given access to other students' education records. As with any school official, the student worker needs to be properly trained in the requirements of FERPA. This training should be designed to (1) familiarize student workers with FERPA guidelines and policies, (2) explain the importance of preserving the confidentiality of education records they encounter in their tasks, and (3) require student workers to sign an agreement, similar to that shown in Chapter 6 (on page 120), prior to their employment to emphasize the importance of education record confidentiality and minimize the chance that FERPA will be violated by the unauthorized release of non-directory information.

Articulating Legitimate Educational Interest

Sample language outlining what constitutes legitimate educational interest might include:

A school official is deemed to have a legitimate educational interest if the information requested is necessary for that official to (a) perform appropriate tasks that are specified in his/her position description or by a contract agreement; (b) perform a task related to a student's education; (c) perform a task related to the discipline of a student; (d) provide a service or benefit relating to the student or student's family, such as health care, counseling, job placement or financial aid.

An institution should also make clear in its annual notification to students that disclosure to a school official having a legitimate educational interest does not consti-

tute authorization to share that information with a third party under one of the exceptions to §99.31 or without the student's written permission. Such information, when it has fulfilled its originally specified purpose, should be destroyed or returned to the originating office for appropriate disposition.

The custodian of the education record must decide the legitimacy of each request for information. If there is any doubt or question regarding the request, the record custodian should withhold disclosure absent either written consent of the student, concurrence of appropriate institutional officials, or approval of the immediate supervisor. In all cases, employees in offices containing education records should be instructed to determine legitimate educational interest before an education record is released. This also means that all school officials must have proper FERPA training and be aware of the requirements for determining legitimate educational interest and be prepared to demonstrate their need to know upon request. This will eliminate needless confrontation and provide a better working environment for all concerned.

> **FERPA TIPS**
> The concept of "legitimate educational interest" applies only to officials of the institution or its contractors or agents under its direct control who are identified by the institution as "school officials."

Computer Access and Legitimate Educational Interest

The 2009 regulations at §99.31(a)(1)(ii) stipulate that institutions must

"use reasonable methods to ensure that school officials obtain access to only those education records in which they have legitimate educational interests. An educational agency or institution that does not use physical or technological access controls must ensure that its administrative policy for controlling access to education records is effective and that it remains in compliance with the legitimate educational interest requirements in paragraph 99.31(a)(1)(i)(A)."

The ability of computer systems to provide education record information to an increasing number of institutional officials presents distinct challenges in complying with the FERPA requirement that these officials only access education record data for a legitimate educational interest. Policies and procedures establishing appropriate security measures must be developed and enforced.

FIGURE 4.2 — Sample On-screen Notice #1

I understand that I have access to student records which contain individually identifiable information, the disclosure of which is governed by the Family Educational Rights and Privacy Act (FERPA). I understand that the disclosure of this information to any unauthorized person could subject me to criminal and civil penalties imposed by law and could be cause for disciplinary action including termination of my employment. I understand that by my sign-on (network ID and password) I accept full responsibility for complying with these regulations.

You are attempting to access information that is protected by federal privacy law. Disclosure to unauthorized parties violates FERPA. You should not attempt to proceed unless you are specifically authorized to do so and are informed about FERPA.

When accessing the system, you must access only that information needed to complete your assigned or authorized task. You may communicate the information only to other parties authorized to have access in accordance with the provisions of FERPA.

If you have any questions about these provisions, please contact the office of the registrar.

If you agree to/satisfy the above requirements, click "continue."

CONTINUE   EXIT

Institutions should establish computer access policies and procedures for all of the following:

- Initial instruction of prospective users in FERPA confidentiality requirements.
- Periodic review and update of approved users of all confidentiality protocols.
- Full use of institution's software security assignments to control access to various levels of online users depending on user's need to know and maintenance capabilities.
- Periodic monitoring and system tracking of user access by system officials to guard against abuse.
- Efficient systems to remove user access *immediately* when user leaves the institution or their position.

Institutions should emphasize the importance of instructing school officials concerning FERPA's privacy requirements before they are given access to the student information system. These school officials should also be informed of the institution's criteria for determining legitimate educational interest and their responsibility for assuring that such access is not abused.

As mentioned above, each institution should provide a warning whenever a user logs in to the student information system. An example of a message appears in Figure 4.1, and in sample

FERPA TIPS

It is not a legitimate educational interest for faculty to review a student's previous academic history in other classes prior to assigning a final grade.

forms 20 and 21 starting on page 122.

Letters of Recommendation

Statements made by a person providing a recommendation based on that person's personal observation or knowledge do not require a written release from the student subject of the recommendation. However, if personally identifiable information obtained from a student's education record is included in a letter of recommendation (grades, GPA, etc.), the writer is required to obtain a signed release from the student which 1) specifies the records that may be disclosed, 2) states the purpose of the disclosure, and 3) identifies the party or class of parties to whom the disclosure can be made. (*See* Chapter 5, Slide 58 [on page 71], for a "Sample permission letter to write a letter of recommendation".) Since the letter of recommendation would be part of the student's education record, the student has the right to read it—unless she/he has waived that right of access. (*See* §99.12 (b)(3), in Appendix B, on page 153.)

If asked to investigate a disclosure by a faculty member regarding a letter of recommendation, the Family Policy Compliance Office will seek answers to the following questions to determine whether FERPA has been violated:

- Has the institution established a criterion in its FERPA policy that appears to address disclosures for the purpose in question?
- What does the faculty contract, job description, or other similar document specify regarding the duties and responsibilities of faculty?
- Does, or did, the faculty member teach the student in any course?
- What is the practice regarding recommendations at the institution?
- Does the faculty member otherwise have personal knowledge of the student's abilities?
- Was the faculty member asked by the student to provide the recommendation?
- Is there any state law on this issue?

The Media

Nothing in FERPA allows an institution to discuss a student's education records publicly—even if a lawsuit has made the information a matter of public record. Likewise, a school official may not assume that a student's public discussion of a matter constitutes an implied consent for the school official to disclose anything other than directory information in reply. The school official who wishes to respond to the media under these circumstances should ask the student for a properly executed consent form. (*See* the FPCO "Letter to Towson State University," on page 268).

If the institution lacks written consent to disclose personally identifiable information from a student's record, then the institution should take a cautious approach to releasing redacted information (to the media or any other requester) if the cumulative effect of releasing that information would allow for someone to identify the student with "reasonable certainty." The 2009 regulations uses this new term as it relates to the definition of "personally identifiable information." The point is that even if the data involved doesn't directly relate to the student but if it's reasonable to extrapolate the identity of the student from the information provided, then that constitutes "reasonable certainty;" the institution should be cautious of its disclosure of this data to the media.

Medical Treatment Records

Medical or treatment records at postsecondary institutions are exempt from the definition of education records so long as they are:

- ☒ Made and maintained by a medical professional;
- ☒ Used only in connection with treatment of the student; *and*
- ☒ Disclosed only to individuals providing treatment.

FERPA does not prevent the sharing of these records with other school officials but doing so would make them education records. Also, see HIPAA discussion on page 30 and in Appendix H on page 309.

Non-Disclosure of Directory Information
(Opt Out; FERPA Block)

Under FERPA, a student can request, while still enrolled, that the college/university not release any directory information about him or her. Colleges and universities must comply with this request.

In instances where a student is considering requesting non-disclosure, the student should be advised of the potential problems that may occur as prospective employers and other interested parties make inquiries. With graduating students, the decision to request non-disclosure is particularly important since this decision may have employment, and other, repercussions. The "directory information" disclosure provision is unique in that it is the only one that allows students to opt out of the disclosure. Institutions may disclose information, even if the student requests otherwise, under the other exceptions to FERPA's written consent requirement (*see* "Disclosure of Education Record Information," on page 16; §99.31).

The student has the right to request non-disclosure of directory information only while in attendance. Institutions *must* honor any request from currently enrolled students that directory information not be disclosed. Then, the non-disclosure hold on directory information remains in effect until the student requests the institution to remove it. This is even true after the student has ceased attendance at the institution. While institutions may place a limit on the length of time the request for non-disclosure will remain in effect, it is recommended that non-disclosures remain permanent. While students who have left the institution do not have the right to request non-disclosure of directory information, the institution *may* honor that request if it wishes.

§99.37(c) of the 2009 regulations clarified that a student may not choose to be anonymous within the classroom setting, whether in a traditional or distance learning class, by opting out of "directory information." Disclosure

> **FERPA TIPS**
>
> It is recommended that, prior to providing any access to education record information in any medium, thorough FERPA training be given to any prospective user. At the end of the training, it is also recommended that the user sign an agreement acknowledging that she/he will have access to confidential education records and that such access will only be used in fulfilling his/her professional responsibilities. The consequences of any disclosure not in accordance with FERPA should be included in this agreement. Examples of such agreements are found in chapter 6.

> **FERPA TIPS**
>
> The institutional process of complying with a student's request to block the release of personally identifiable information is called "non-disclosure."

of personally identifiable information, such as the student's name and email address, as required by the instructor and classroom setting for purposes of conducting the class and class activities is permissible under FERPA.

Outsourcing

(*See* "Contractors/Agents" on page 24.)

Parental Access to a Student's Education Records

FERPA applies to education records at all levels of education: primary, secondary and postsecondary. Up to the time the student attains the age of 18 or attends an institution of higher education, regardless of age, FERPA rights reside with the parents. Once the student attains the age of 18 or attends an institution of higher education, regardless of age, FERPA rights transfer to the student. The term "eligible student" is used in the law to denote this transfer of rights to the student. See the definition in Chapter 2.

At the postsecondary level, FERPA rights have transferred to the student and parents have no rights under FERPA to inspect their student's education records. The right to inspect resides solely with the student.

Records may be released to parents without a signed consent from the student or under certain exceptions found in §99.31. These include:

(1) health or safety emergency, (2) where the student has been found in violation of the institution's code of conduct relating to the use of alcohol or a controlled substance if the student is under the age of 21, or (3) by submission of evidence that the parents declare the student as a dependent on their most recent Federal Income Tax form (*see* Appendix G, "Definition of Dependent," on page 305). The release to parents of education records under any of these exceptions is a permissible release. Thus, under FERPA, an institution is not required to disclose information from the student's education records to any parent of a dependent student. It may, however, exercise its discretion to do so. It is strongly recommended that a statement of the institution's policy regarding parental access and disclosure be clearly stated in any FERPA policy.

Biological, Custodial, and Non-Custodial Parents

In cases of divorce, separation or custody, when only one parent claims the student as dependent, an institution may grant equal access to information from the student's education records to the other parent. The institution is not, however, required by FERPA to provide such information to either parent.

State law, however, may require that such a disclosure be made. For example, Virginia recently amended 23–9.2:3 of the Code of Virginia to require that, "...*every public institution of higher education in Virginia shall establish policies and procedures requiring the release of the educational record of a dependent student [as defined by FERPA] to a parent at his request.*" (*See* Appendix L, page 343.) Disclosure to parents of a dependent students is permitted under §99.31(a)(8). Consequently, disclosure pursuant to such a State law is permissible under FERPA.

When access to view or receive information (the parents may not alter the contents of a record, but may simply view the information) is granted to parents under this exception, the file should note that the determination to authorize access was based upon the appropriate documentation demonstrating the student's dependency.

Student Permission to Share Grades with Parents

Does FERPA preclude the institution from notifying parents about the student's academic progress?

The answer is "no." However, FERPA requires that students either provide written permission for the institution to release any non-directory information to parents, or the institution must determine that the student is a dependent of the parents before the information is released. (*See* "Exceptions to Written Consent Requirement," on page 16).

The latter is time consuming. As a general rule, if the institution decided that it wished to notify parents about their student's academic progress or share any non-directory information with the parents, it must obtain the written permission of the student to do so. This written permission should be obtained in a non-coercive environment without the parents present. This could most likely occur during a new student orientation when students and parents are in separate sessions. The institution's administrators could briefly explain FERPA to the students and the institution's policy/practice regarding sharing of information with parents. Each student could then decide whether his or her parents should receive any non-directory information. The choice to provide written permission should be obtained early in the student's academic career at the institution to permit the organized integration of this information into the student information system. An example of such a written permission to release grades to parents is found in Chapter 6.

Additionally, many institutions have established electronic third-party access systems where students can choose to share their information with any third party they choose.

The following statements summarize FERPA regarding parental access to their child's records:

- When a student reaches the age of 18 or begins attending a postsecondary institution, regardless of age, FERPA rights transfer from the parent to the student.
- Parents may obtain non-directory information (grades, GPA, etc.) at the discretion of the institution and only after it has been determined that their child is legally their dependent.
- Parents may also obtain non-directory information by obtaining a signed consent from their child.
- Parents may be provided access to information regarding a finding of a student's violation of campus policy or local, state, or federal law prohibiting the use of alcohol or a controlled substance.
- Parents may be provided information from education records in a health or safety emergency.

Penalties Under FERPA

(*See* "Enforcement Procedures and Penalties," on page 28.)

PINs/Passwords

Institutions may allow students to access their education records electronically (computer, smart phone, etc.) provided the institution has established procedures to ensure that students will obtain access only to their own records. The development of guidelines for restricting access and insuring proper security of data in computer systems is an institutional responsibility. The 2009 regulations at §99.31(c) require that educational institutions use "reasonable methods to authenticate the identity" of the party requesting access, in this case the student. Under the final regulations, institutions may use PINs, passwords, and/or personal security questions; "smart cards" and tokens; biometric indicators; or other factors *known or possessed only by the user,* as appropriate. Note that the Preamble to the 2009 regulations clarifies that social security numbers and date of birth are not "reasonable methods" to authenticate an individual's identity. It is suggested that, at a minimum, institutions use a combination of a student identification number and password, or student network ID and password, to grant students electronic access.

The most acceptable scenario for utilizing the ID number in conjunction with the PIN is for the institution to initially provide a default PIN and allow the user to change that PIN after he or she logs in. This initial PIN should be randomly assigned and communicated to the student in a secure manner. Thus, the student would be able to control and maintain his or her own PIN.

FERPA TIPS

Social security numbers and date of birth are not "reasonable methods" to authenticate an individual's identity.

Because FERPA restricts disclosure of education records to unauthorized parties without the student's prior consent, it is incumbent upon an institution to ensure that computer databases and other systems function so that only authorized parties may obtain access to the records. In these cases, the primary considerations are identification of authorized recipients of information and security of transmissions so that records are disclosed only to authorized parties.

The written consent requirements of FERPA do not apply when a student seeks access to his or her own records. Where an institution provides a secure Web application for a student to request that information from the student's own education records, such as transcripts, be released to them personally, the FPCO has indicated that it would be permissible for the student to log in using their student ID number and PIN, or student network ID and password, and request that transcripts or any non-directory information be released to them. The key word in this procedure is "secure." This means that the information required for the student's transcript and any other non-directory information to be sent to the student must not be accessible to any third parties who are not school officials and that the request be electronically transmitted within the institution's computer infrastructure.

Posting of Grades (§99.3)

The public posting of grades, either by the student's name, institutional student identification number, or social security number, without the student's written permission is a violation of FERPA. This includes the posting of grades to a class/institutional Web site and applies to any public posting of grades for students taking distance education courses.

Even with names obscured, numeric student identifier numbers are considered personally identifiable information. Therefore, the practice of posting grades by social security number (SSN), including posting by the last four digits of the SSN or student identification number violates FERPA.

> **FERPA** | **TIPS**
>
> FERPA applies to all education records created and maintained regardless of the course delivery method.

A student at Hunter College of the City University of New York alleged that one of his professors had posted his examination and final grade on a Web page along with the last four digits of his social security number. In response to an inquiry by FPCO, a college administrator acknowledged that "many [of their] professors posted grades by the last four digits of the student's social security number," but, since "no student names are listed" they did "not consider this practice to be in violation of FERPA." In a letter to Hunter College,[1] Rooker (2001) reaffirmed that while there are certain exceptions within FERPA, "none permit an educational agency or institution to publicly disclose personally identifiable information, including the student's grades and portions of the student's social security number, from the education records of students [without prior written consent from the student]."

FERPA does not prevent an educational agency or institution from posting the grades of students without written consent when it does so in a manner that does NOT disclose personally identifiable information from the student's education record. Thus, while FERPA precludes a school from posting grades by SSNs, student ID numbers, or by names because these types of information are personally identifiable to the students, nothing in FERPA would preclude an instructor from assigning individual numbers to students for the purpose of posting grades as long as those numbers are known only to the student and the school official who assigned them.

The 2009 amended regulations clarify that personally identifiable information includes information that is linked or reasonably linkable to a specific student and which would allow a reasonable person in the school community, who does not have knowledge of the relevant circumstances, to identify the student with reasonable certainty. Therefore, using directory information, such as birth date, to post grades, is not permissible because a student's grade would be linked to information that could reasonably be known by other students. The commentary discussion accompanying those regulations states that "...if a teacher uses a special code known only by the teacher and the student to identify a student, such as for posting grades, this code is not considered personally identifiable information under FERPA because the only reason the teacher can identify the student is because of the teacher's access to personal knowledge of the relevant circumstances, *i.e.*, the key that links the code to the student's name. No one else would reasonably have access to that information."

The bottom line is that instructors and others who post grades should use a system that ensures FERPA requirements are met. This can be accomplished either by obtaining the student's voluntary written permission or by using randomly assigned numbers that only the instructor and individual student know. The order of any such posting, however, should not be alphabetic.

Other Acceptable Methods for Notifying Students of their Grades

- ▣ Prior to official institutional notification of grades, interested students might provide a pre-addressed, stamped envelope to the instructor. The student writes the course and section on the front of the envelope. The instructor records the grade on the inside flap of the envelope, seals the envelope, and mails it to the student when grades have been determined.

---

[1] Downloadable from <www.ed.gov/policy/gen/guid/fpco/ferpa/library/>

- Via email, if it is sent to the institutional account and only contains grade information for the individual student. Non-public educational data should never be sent to non-institutional assigned accounts, since there is no way to verify the authenticity of the end user. The institution would be held responsible if an unauthorized third party gained access to a student's education record through any electronic transmission method where the institution did not take measures to secure that transmission.
- Via a secure network ID and password.

Note: Notification of grades via a postcard violates a student's privacy rights.

Postsecondary Feedback to High Schools

Under normal circumstances, personally identifiable, non-directory information from education records may not be released to a student's high school without the written consent of the student. Aggregate data that does not personally identify the students may be submitted without a release. While some institutions include a statement of consent in their admissions application, which will permit the institution to provide personally identifiable information to high schools, this practice could be challenged if it is seen as coercive or as a requirement for admission to the institution. The institutional statement of consent must specify the records/information to be disclosed and the purpose of the disclosure. The statement of consent should give the student the option of consenting or not consenting to the release.

There may be conditions under which personally identifiable information can be released for postsecondary feedback purposes without students' written permission. Florida, for example, passed the *Postsecondary Feedback Act* in 1991. This *Act* requires postsecondary institutions in Florida to supply certain personally identifiable information from students' education records to the Florida Commissioner of Education. The Commissioner is then required to organize the student records by school district and public high school in which the students were enrolled and report the information to each school district.

The rules of the Florida Board of Education implementing this provision require each postsecondary institution to "report to the school district on the performance of the school district's public high school graduates who are enrolled at the (institution)." The following information must be reported for each student: name of school and county number; student name, social security number, and specified demographic information, date of birth; reporting institution; term of first enrollment; reading, writing, or mathematics courses; test scores below a specified level; enrollment in certain remedial courses; credits attempted and earned toward graduation; grade point average; and courses taken.

In response to a 1992 question to determine if the Florida *Postsecondary Feedback Act* was in conflict with FERPA, the FPCO stated that postsecondary institutions in Florida could release personally identifiable information from student education records without violating FERPA. The office stated:

FERPA generally provides that an educational institution must obtain a student's written consent before disclosing personally identifiable information from the student's education records (20 U.S.C. 1232g (b); 34 C.F.R. 99.4 and 99.30). FERPA does provide that an educational institution may disclose education records or personally identifiable information from such records without prior written consent under certain limited exceptions (20 U.S.C. 1232g(b); 34 C.F.R. 99.31). Under one of the exceptions, an educational institution may disclose information without consent when the disclosure is to authorized representatives of state and local education authorities in connection with an audit or evaluation of federal or state supported education programs. (34 C.F.R. 99.31(a)(3) and 99.35)

Nonconsensual disclosure is also permissible when the disclosure is to organizations conducting studies for, or on behalf of, educational agencies or institutions to improve instruction (34 C.F.R. 99.31(a)(6)). Both the recipients (Commissioner of Education and school districts) and the nature of the information required to be disclosed under this state statute indicate that the purposes of the disclosure include evaluation of state-supported education programs and improvement of instruction. Accordingly, we believe that disclosure without prior written consent is permissible under both sections 99.31(a)(3) and 99.31(a)(6).

FERPA establishes a record keeping requirement that an educational agency or institution must meet in making nonconsensual disclosures from education records. Those conditions are set forth in 34 C.F.R. 99.32. (Rooker, 1993b).

Records Retention

(See "Destruction and Retention of Records," on page 24.)

Record Keeping of Disclosures

According to FERPA, an institution must maintain a record of each request for access to, and each disclosure of, personally identifiable information from student education records, except in those situations listed below. The record of each request for access and each disclosure must contain the name of the parties who have requested or received information and the legitimate interest the parties had in requesting or obtaining the information.

A record does not have to be kept if the request was made by, or disclosure was made to (1) the eligible student, (2) a school official who has been determined to have a legitimate educational interest, (3) a party with written consent from the eligible student, or (4) a party seeking directory information only.

Thus, the record keeping requirement of disclosures of education record information without the student's written consent would include but not be limited to disclo-

FERPA **TIPS**

Institutions are not required to release information to third parties, even when consent of the student has been provided. Remember, "When in doubt, don't give out."

sures: (1) to the parent (either custodial or non-custodial) of an eligible student, (2) in response to a lawfully issued court order or subpoena (except under certain conditions), (3) for external research purposes where individual students have been identified, or (4) in response to a health or safety emergency.

The 2009 regulations require institutions to record specific information when non-public information is released from the student education record in response to a health or safety emergency. Specifically, the institution must record: "the articulable and significant threat to the health or safety of a student or other individuals that formed the basis for the disclosure; and the parties to whom the agency or institution disclosed the information." (§99.32 (a)(5)(i))

These records must be maintained with the education records of the student as long as the institution maintains the records.

Redisclosure

With limited exceptions, a third-party which has appropriately received non-directory student information cannot redisclose any of that information to another third party. The 2009 amendments noted one exception—when a third-party rediscloses information to another third-party that would have had the initial eligibility to have received the data directly—*e.g.*, one state or federal *educational* agency sharing with another state or federal *educational* agency when both are authorized to receive the information. Any such redisclosure must be done "on behalf of" the institution, and recordkeeping requirements apply.

There are specific penalties for inappropriate redisclosures—notably that the third-party cannot receive non-directory student information again for five years.

Releasing Non-Directory Information Over the Phone

To the Student

FERPA does not preclude an institution from disclosing non-directory information from a student's education record to that student by telephone. Institutions must use reasonable methods to authenticate the individual's identity. Note that social security number and date of birth are not considered reasonable. Questions, whose responses would only be known by the student, could be asked by the school official. The identifying questions should be very specific to the student—ones to which only the student should know the answers. These questions should be correctly answered by the student calling before personally identifiable information is provided via the telephone. Remember, however, that a "when in doubt don't give out" policy is always prudent.

To Third Parties

It is risky to release non-directory information to a third party who requests information via the telephone because there are limitations in verifying that the party is indeed someone to whom the information can be disclosed absent written consent. However, if the information requested meets the health or safety emergency exception in FERPA, such a disclosure could be made. School officials should also ensure that directory information is not released over the telephone, including even confirming that a student is enrolled if the student has a "No Release" in place on his or her education record.

Religion as Directory Information

A student's religion or religious preference can never be considered "directory information." Therefore, you should only provide that information to school officials with a legitimate educational interest. If the persons requesting this information do not fall under your institution's definition of school official with a legitimate educational interest, you cannot provide this information unless you obtain the written permission of the student or can justify the release under one of the exceptions to written permission found in §99.31. (*See* "Exceptions to Written Consent Requirement," on page 16).

Institutions may provide (non-suppressed) directory information on all students to any religious organization that requests this information. You may not, however, provide directory information to the religious organization on just those students who have indicated a religious preference for the religious organization since the selection criterion would have been based on non-directory information (religious preference). Also, an institution can send out information on behalf of any organization, thus allowing a student to respond at his/her discretion.

Safeguarding

The 2009 regulations contain non-binding recommendations to assist institutions in addressing challenges inherent in safeguarding education records from unauthorized access and disclosure. Institutions are encouraged to utilize the referenced resources for guidance and to use methods and technologies they determine are reasonable to mitigate the risk of unauthorized access and disclosure. The recommendations also include suggested responses to data breaches and other unauthorized disclosures. (*See* the FPCO "Letter to University of Central Florida," on page 234).

School Officials

(*See* "Legitimate Educational Interest," on page 31.)

SEVIS

SEVIS—The "Student and Exchange Visitor Information System" is an Internet-based system that allows schools and the U.S. Citizenship & Immigration Service to exchange data on the visa status of international students. SEVIS maintains accurate and current information on non-immigrant students (F and M visa), exchange visitors (J visa), and their dependents (F-2, M-2, and J-2). SEVIS enables schools and program sponsors to transmit mandatory information and event notifications via the Internet to the Department of Homeland Security (DHS) or Immigration and Customs Enforcement (ICE) throughout a student's or exchange visitor's stay in the United States. FERPA permits the disclosure of information to ICE, or ICE contractors, in order to certify an institution as eligible to participate in SEVIS. (*See* the FPCO "Letter to AACRAO on SEVIS," on page 337).

Use of the Social Security Number

As a Student Identifier

References in congressional legislation to the social security number (SSN) as a personal identifier are limited. The *Privacy Act of 1974* (not FERPA) states that:

> It shall be unlawful for any federal, state, or local government agency to deny any individual any right, benefit or privilege provided by law because of such individual's refusal to disclose his social security account number. (Sec. 7 (a)(1), Privacy Act of 1974, P.L. 93-579; 5 U.S.C. 552a note)
>
> Any federal, state, or local government agency which requests an individual to disclose his social security account number shall inform that individual whether that disclosure is mandatory or voluntary, by what statutory or other authority such number is solicited, and what uses will be made of it. (Section 7 (a)(2)(B), Privacy Act of 1974, P.L. 93-579; 5 U.S.C. 552a note).

Thus, the federal government recognizes that the SSN can be used for purposes other than an individual's transactions with the Social Security Administration.

The *Privacy Act* does not directly specify public colleges and universities; it has implications for all institutions of higher education. Colleges and universities should not use the student's SSN as an ID number and all institutions must take steps to protect the privacy of the student SSN as required by FERPA.

Some states have passed legislation precluding the use of SSNs as SINs (student identification numbers). For privacy reasons, the Social Security Administration discourages using the SSN as an institution's SIN.

The 2009 regulations clarify that an institution may not confirm directory information "if a student's social security number or other non-directory information is used along or combined with other data elements to identify the student or the student's records." (§99.37 (d)) In addition, the regulations specifically prohibit the designation of a social security number as a directory information item (§99.3 Directory Information.)

Using SSN to Verify Student Information

In a 2004 letter to Auburn University, regarding the National Student Clearinghouse (NSC), the FPCO director LeRoy Rooker stated that it would be a violation of FERPA for an agent, acting on behalf of the university, to use personally identifiable information (*i.e.*, student's social security number), without the student's written consent, in a manner that would match the personal identifier with information in the university's database and then subsequently release that information (*i.e.*, degree and/or enrollment verification data) to the requester. According to Rooker, "The verification of the student's SSN, absent the student's prior written consent, amounts to an improper disclosure of personally identifiable information from education records under FERPA."

FERPA TIPS

Release requirements for "Directory information" under FERPA and "student recruiting information" under Solomon are different, even though there may be a significant overlap between the two sets of data at your institution. Where an institution has discretion in identifying "directory information" and releasing that information, elements of "student recruiting information" are specifically identified by law and the institution must release that information if requested.

FERPA TIPS

An email could not qualify as a "sole possession" record because it has been shared.

"Sole Possession" (Anecdotal) Notes on a Student

All anecdotal notes made about a student that an institution maintains and shares with school officials, regardless of the medium, are included in the definition of education records. They would, therefore, be subject to FERPA. Unless the notes are kept in the "sole possession" of the maker, have not been created with the assistance of anyone else, and are accessible only to a temporary substitute, they are part of the education record and subject to review by the student. This would include all shared paper files as well as notes made about the student on a shared computer record, and includes emails sent by the school officials. If a student has requested access to his/her education record, none of these notes may be destroyed prior to the student review. Examples of "sole possession records" include a reminder to follow up on a topic or question with a student, and notes about a personal experience to help you remember the student.

The Solomon Amendment and FERPA

Under the Solomon Amendment, institutions are required to provide directory-type information on students, at least 17 years of age who are registered for at least one credit, upon request from representatives of the Department of Defense for military recruiting purposes. This information, referred to as "student recruiting information," includes: student name, addresses, telephone listings, age or year of birth, place of birth, level of education or degrees received, academic major, and the most recent previous educational institution in which the student was enrolled.

Most important in this analysis of Solomon and FERPA is that 1) the definitions of the term "directory information" (FERPA) and "student recruiting information" (Solomon) are not synonymous, and 2) a request for student recruiting information under Solomon must be honored unless there is an exception in the law which precludes the institution from providing the requested information. Any one of these exceptions must be applicable to schools seeking *not* to comply with Solomon:

- Certification that the campus has maintained a long-standing policy of pacifism based on historical religious tradition.
- Certification that such information is not collected by the school.
- Certification that each student concerned has formally requested the school to withhold "Directory Information" under FERPA to third parties.

It is important to note that even if an institution has a policy of not releasing "directory information" under FERPA, the institution must still comply with requests for "student recruiting information" to the military (except as noted above).

Institutions are obligated to provide the information only once a term to each branch of the armed services. According to the FPCO, institutions that comply with a Solomon request will not be in violation of FERPA if they honor the request. Also, these sources have indicated that, if an institution discloses "student recruiting information" after a student has requested non-disclosure of information under FERPA, the school will not be in violation of FERPA.

Since race, gender, and veteran status are not "student recruiting information," institutions should not release this information or provide lists for these specific subgroups. It is also important to note that since information is only to be released for students registered for at least one credit in the requested semester/term, "drop out" lists should *not* be provided under Solomon or FERPA.

Regarding the student's right to request non-disclosure of directory information under FERPA, as part of the final Solomon regulations, the Department of Defense will permit the non-disclosure of student recruiting information if a student:

- Has been notified by his/her institution according to the annual notification provision under FERPA that she/he has the right to request non-disclosure of his/her directory information; and
- Subsequently requests non-disclosure of any or all directory information (as identified by the institution under FERPA).

If, however, the student has not exercised his/her right of non-disclosure under FERPA, the rules under Solomon will apply and the student recruiting information required by Solomon must be released. This includes any item of information that is considered "student recruiting information" under Solomon, but may not have been identified as "directory information" by the institution under FERPA. For example, if a Department of Defense representative requests the *places of birth* for all students as part of their request for information under Solomon, that information must be released even though the institution may not have identified that item as "directory information" under FERPA.

Note: On December 6, 2005, the U.S. Supreme Court heard a challenge to the constitutionality of the Solomon Amendment that was brought by a consortium of law schools. On March 6, 2006 the Supreme Court ruled unanimously that colleges that accept federal aid must comply with the requirements of the Solomon Amendment including providing student recruiting information.

More information as well as the final Supreme Court ruling on the Solomon Amendment may be found on AACRAO's Web site: www.aacrao.org/compliance/solomon/index.cfm. Also, regulations passed in 2008 are included in Appendix J on page 327.

State or Federal Program Data Releases

Many states have laws and regulations that require public educational institutions to provide personally identifiable student data to the state educational authority. These agencies are usually charged with state research and reporting responsibilities.

FERPA permits institutions to provide personally identifiable information from education records to authorized representatives of state agencies without consent under certain conditions specified in §99.35 [34 C.F.R. 99.31 (a)(3)]. In general, institutions can provide this data to its state educational authority if it is in connection with audits or evaluations of federal or state-supported education programs. FERPA also allows disclosure to organizations, including state educational authorities, "for conducting studies for, or on behalf of, educational agencies or institutions to develop, validate or administer predictive tests, administer student aid programs, or improve instruction" (Rooker 1991). Paragraph (ii) of §99.31(a)(6) sets forth the conditions that apply to these disclosures.

Institutions that provide personally identifiable student data to its state educational authority, whether in electronic or hard-copy format, should have procedures in place which will protect the confidentiality of this student information. State educational authorities should be advised of the FERPA requirements, especially §99.35, which requires the destruction of this information once it is no longer needed for its original purpose.

In addition, state educational authorities should not, in turn, release personally identifiable student data to a third party, unless on behalf of the originating institution and within the provisions of FERPA that permit redisclosure. For example, a state educational authority could share directory information for students who have not blocked release of such data with another party for the purpose of tracking transfer students. However, that release must only include directory

> **FERPA TIPS**
>
> With the exceptions noted below, institutions MUST release student recruiting information to military recruiters under Solomon. Institutions MAY release "directory information" to anyone under FERPA.

> **FERPA TIPS**
>
> The Solomon Amendment requires institutions to provide "student recruiting information" to military recruiters on currently enrolled students who are 17 years or older. It does not require an institution to provide any information on students not currently enrolled for at least one credit.

information. Non-directory information must not be included in these releases unless written permission of the students is obtained, nor should it include any data for students who have requested non-disclosure of their directory information.

Institutions must record the disclosures in accordance with §99.32 of the regulations. Registrars and other institutional officials with responsibility for the protection of student FERPA rights should take all precautions necessary to ensure security is maintained as the records are transferred from the institution to the state educational agency.

State and federal educational authorities who receive non-directory information must have measures in place to protect against personal identification of the students whose information they received by anyone other than the officials conducting the audit or evaluation for which the information was disclosed.

States' Open Records/Disclosure Laws and FERPA

Often state open records laws appear to conflict with FERPA. Federal law generally supersedes state law when in conflict. However, the open records laws of many, if not most, states defer to FERPA. In those instances when the state open records law affords the student more privacy rights, state law should be followed. When state open records laws are applicable, they cover public institutions.

State open records laws cover more data than that contained in student education record information. For example, they regularly cover information ranging from employment to contracts. If the information being requested qualifies as a student education record, it is covered by FERPA and needs to be treated as such.

The test often reduces to a basic question: "Is the record or issue covered under FERPA?" If the answer is "yes," then the resolution of the situation would fall within the regulations and requirements of FERPA. If the answer is "no," then the resolution of the situation may fall under provisions of the state open records law. Thus, if in your professional judgment you determine that the student record, or part thereof, is not covered by FERPA, the release of or access to that record may then be determined under the state open records law. This has not been any more relevant than with the issue of student disciplinary records (*see* "Disciplinary Records" on page 25).

State Law Conflict with FERPA (§99.61)

Should a state or local law appear to conflict with FERPA, the *Final Regulations* mandate that institutions that can-

not comply with the Act or regulations due to a conflict with state or local law must notify the Family Policy Compliance Office (FPCO) within 45 days, giving the text and citation of the conflicting law (34 C.F.R. 99.61). Notifications should be sent to the Family Policy Compliance Office, U.S. Department of Education, 400 Maryland Avenue, SW, Washington, D.C. 20202-5901; phone: (202) 260-3887, fax: (202) 260-9001.

Student Access to Education Records—Electronic

(*See* "PINs/Passwords" on page 37.)

Student Directories

Release of directory information to any group for publications such as student directories, award or graduation ceremonies, yearbooks, etc. is subject to FERPA restrictions. Any group seeking to publish a student directory at an institution that chooses to release directory information must do so through a supervising school official or office. It must give students who wish to be excluded from the listing the opportunity to notify the group within an appropriate time frame prior to publication.

Student Right-To-Know Act and FERPA

The *Student Right-to-Know Act of 1990* (SRTK) requires institutions to publish and distribute, among other things, graduation rates to current and prospective students.

Discussion of this topic in the 1995 edition of this Guide was relatively brief. It affirmed that, since data was to be reported in aggregate form (with no personally identifiable information disclosed), no conflict with FERPA existed. In the interest of student privacy, institutions do not have to report their SRTK graduation rates for any cohort/sub-cohort with five or fewer students. It is advised that a notation be made to this effect on your SRTK report whenever appropriate.

On August 2, 1999, the Family Policy Compliance Office determined that it would be acceptable for the National Student Clearinghouse (NSC) to assist institutions in complying with SRTK as long as only directory information was used. In addition, as clarified in a March 28, 2006 letter from FPCO to the Los Angeles Unified School District, it was made clear that the NSC could not use the student's social security number in any directory information search. (*See* the FPCO letter on page 249).

FERPA contains an exemption to the prior written consent requirement when the disclosure is made to other school officials, including teachers, within the agency or institution whom the agency or institution has determined to have legitimate educational interests. (§99.31(a)(1)) An organization such as NSC, by virtue of a contractual relationship with an educational agency or institution, may be considered a school official with legitimate educational interests under §99.31(a)(1). This is particularly true when the organization needs to review the institution's education records in order to provide verification services on behalf of the educational agency or institution.

Under the regulations at §99.7(a)(3)(iii), an educational agency or institution must include in its annual notification of rights under FERPA a statement indicating whether it has a policy of disclosing personally identifiable information under §99.31(a)(1) and, if so, a specification of the criteria for determining who constitutes a school official and what constitutes a legitimate educational interest. Accordingly, if an educational institution or agency has included in its annual notification criteria that support the designation of an organization such as NSC as a school official with a legitimate educational interest, then FERPA would permit the educational institution to disclose personally identifiable information from education records to an organization like NSC without first obtaining the signed and dated written consent of the student.

When a school verifies or relies on education records to confirm or verify or match a social security number, the school is in fact making a "disclosure" of information from the student's education records. Rooker (2004a) explained that, "In the [Auburn] case, NSC as an agent of the University was not permitted under FERPA to match the student's social security number with information in the University's database, which in turn, produced the directory information that was ultimately disclosed to the requester—(Mr. X) via EdVerify—without the student's prior written consent. Although a school may disclose education records to an organization such as NSC as discussed above, NSC may not disclose by matching personally identifiable information, such as a social security number, from a student's education records without the student's prior written consent."

In response to Auburn University, NSC president Daniel R. Boehmer (2004) agreed to adjust the procedures utilized by NSC on behalf of Auburn. Specifically, "when a requestor comes to the [NSC] Web verification page to verify degree/enrollment information, the requestor will not be provided a place to enter a social security number," thereby eliminating the possibility of utilizing the social security number as a verifier.[2]

Students' Right to Review Records

Students have the right to review their education records regardless of the location or medium of the record. Once a student has submitted a request to inspect his or her records, the institution must comply within 45 calendar days; however, state law or institutional policy may require access in a shorter period of time.

When the student has an outstanding financial debt or other hold on his/her record, the student still maintains the right to review the education records. FERPA does not require an institution to provide the student with copies of those records unless failure to do so would effectively deny the student the opportunity to inspect and review the records. Also, an institution is not required to provide a third party access to education records even when the student has provided the consent required under §99.30. This would, for example, allow the institution to decline to provide a transcript to such a third party if the student has an outstanding financial obligation. Note, however, that the institution could not communicate to the third party why the request is being denied. It is important that institutions familiarize themselves with their state's open records law with regards to copies, as some do have copying requirements.

In cases where a student is not within reasonable commuting distance (50 miles) of campus, and therefore is physically unable to be present to view the record on campus, the institution must make arrangements for the student to obtain access for review of these records. The institution may do so either (a) by making copies of the requested records and sending them to the student by mail or other means; or (b) by making arrangements with an appropriate third party, such as another institution or an attorney's office located in the vicinity of the student, to act as an agent. Such individuals would agree to abide by the institution's instructions to allow the student to review but not copy the records. This method would be used particularly in instances where the student has an outstanding financial debt or other obligation to the college.

[2] Boehmer, Daniel R. 2004. October 6 letter to Dr. John T. Fletcher, Assistant Vice President, Student Affairs at Auburn University. Not published.

When providing a copy of a student record to authorized parties, a reasonable fee may be assessed. Regulations allow for the assessment of a fee unless its imposition "effectively prevents a parent or eligible student from exercising the right to inspect and review the student's education records" (§99.11). Under normal circumstances, it is recommended that the fee assessed be based upon a reasonable determination of the cost of providing the copies and postage. Colleges and universities may not charge the student a fee for searching for or retrieving their records since this is considered part of accepted and normal business *(see* "Charging a Fee...," on page 23).

Students as Members of Institutional Committees

If students serving in certain official capacities are designated as school officials in the institution's annual notification, they can access student education records to fulfill those duties.

Often, student scholarships, for example, are awarded by committees, which may include students. If the review is made only by school officials (including students, if the annual notice identifies them as a school official) who have been determined to have a "legitimate educational interest," no student release is necessary. If, however, such a review includes a person or persons not identified as "school officials" in the institution's annual FERPA notification, a signed written consent from the student must be obtained before any review of the student's education record may take place. Alternately, the third party can be designated as a "school official" in the institution's FERPA annual notice for the specific purposes for which the scholarship committee is responsible.

In the case of student committee members, the institutional FERPA annual notice could identify a student serving on a committee as a "school official" while performing their responsibilities as a committee member. This would then permit the student to view other students' education records without prior written consent of those students.

If students serve on a committee that will have access to the records of other students, the student committee members should clearly understand their responsibility with that access—in the same manner as other "school officials."

Subpoenas

A subpoena is a command from a court to require the person named in the subpoena to appear at a stated time and place to provide testimony or evidence.

There are two main types of subpoenas. The subpoena *duces tecum* requires the production of documents, papers, or other tangible items to the court. The subpoena *ad testificandum* requires a person to testify in a particular court case.

A bench warrant issued by a judge, and also considered a court order, requires a person to produce something to, or testify before, a court. Likewise, an *ex parte* order is an order issued by a court of competent jurisdiction without notice to an adverse party.

What FERPA Says About Subpoenas

According to FERPA, non-directory, personally identifiable information from education records can be released "to comply with a judicial order or lawfully issued subpoena" provided that the "institution makes a reasonable effort to notify the student of the order or subpoena in advance of compliance." [§99.31(a)(9)(i)(ii); Appendix B, page 156].

FERPA exempts institutions from the notification requirements in the case of a federal grand jury subpoena, or any other subpoena issued for a law enforcement purpose, that specifically orders that notification not be made in the subpoena [§99.31(a)(9)(ii)(A)(B)].

If an institution initiated legal action against a student, or vice versa, no subpoena for the relevant education records of a student would be required for the institution to either proceed with legal action as plaintiff or defend itself [§99.31 (a)(9)(iii)(A)(B); Appendix B, page 156].

In his April 12, 2002 *Dear Colleague* letter, FPCO director, LeRoy Rooker wrote,

> *"FERPA permits educational agencies and institutions to disclose, without consent, information from a student's education records in order to comply with a 'lawfully issued subpoena or court order' in three contexts. 20 U.S.C. 1232g(b)(1)(J)(i) and (ii), (b)(2)(B); 34 C.F.R. 99.31(a)(9). These three contexts are:*
>
> *1. Grand Jury Subpoenas—Educational agencies and institutions may disclose education records to the entity or persons designated in a federal grand jury subpoena. In addition, the court may order the institution not to disclose to anyone the existence or contents of the subpoena or the institution's response. If the court so orders, then neither the prior notification requirements of §99.31(a)(9) nor the recordation requirements at 34 C.F.R. 99.32 would apply.*

2. *Law Enforcement Subpoenas—Educational agencies and institutions may disclose education records to the entity or persons designated in any other subpoena issued for a law enforcement purpose. As with federal grand jury subpoenas, the issuing court or agency may, for good cause shown, order the institution not to disclose to anyone the existence or contents of the subpoena or the institution's response. In the case of an agency subpoena, the educational institution has the option of requesting a copy of the good cause determination. Also, if a court or an agency issues such an order, then the notification requirements of §99.31(a)(9) do not apply, nor would the recordation requirements at 34 C.F.R. 99.32 apply to the disclosure of education records issued pursuant to the law enforcement subpoena.*

3. *All other Subpoenas—In contrast to the exception to the notification and record keeping requirements described above, educational agencies or institutions may disclose information pursuant to any other court order or lawfully issued subpoena only if the school makes a reasonable effort to notify the parent or eligible student of the order or subpoena in advance of compliance, so that the parent or eligible student may seek protective action. Additionally, schools must comply with FERPA's record keeping requirements under 34 C.F.R. 99.32 when disclosing information pursuant to a standard court order or subpoena."* (Rooker, 2002)

Ex Parte Court Orders

In response to the September 11, 2001 terrorist attacks on the United States, Congress passed the *USA Patriot Act*, which amended FERPA to allow the release of information from the student's education records to the Attorney General of the United States or to his designee in response to an *ex parte* order in connection with the investigation or prosecution of terrorism crimes specified in sections 2332b (g)(5)(B) and 2331 of title 18, U.S. Code. An *ex parte* order is an order issued by a court of competent jurisdiction without notice to an adverse party. In addition to allowing disclosure without prior written consent or prior notification, this provision amends FERPA's record keeping requirements (20 U.S.C. 1232g (b)(4); §99.32). As a result, FERPA, as amended, does not require a school official to record a disclosure of information from a student's education record when the school makes that disclosure pursuant to an *ex parte* order. Further, an educational agency or

institution that, in good faith, produces information from education records in compliance with an *ex parte* order issued under the amendment "shall not be liable to any person for that production." [20 U.S.C. 1232g (j)(4)].

The *Federal Rules of Civil Procedure* state that every Federal subpoena shall: state the name of the court from which the subpoena is issued; state the title of the action, the name of the court in which the action is pending, and its civil action number; and command each person named in the subpoena to appear and either give testimony or produce documentary evidence at a time and place specified in the subpoena.

Jurisdiction

The *Federal Rules of Civil Procedure* require that a subpoena be issued from the court for the district in which the hearing or trial is to be held. If the subpoena orders the production or inspection of documents, the subpoena must be issued from the court in which the production or inspection is to be made. (The West Group 2000, p. 200).

A court cannot act upon a person over which it has no jurisdiction. State courts have jurisdiction only within the boundaries of the state. However, federal district courts effectively have jurisdiction in all 50 states since attorneys who are permitted to represent a client in a federal court can issue a subpoena from any federal court for the district in which the subpoena is to be served. "In authorizing attorneys to issue subpoenas from distant courts, the rule effectively authorizes service of a subpoena anywhere in the United States by an attorney representing any party." (If a subpoena is served on an individual that requires the individual to testify personally [*ad testificandum*] as opposed to providing documents only [*duces tecum*], the deposition/hearing must be conducted no more than 100 miles from the site of the deposition. The individual is not compelled to travel further. [The West Group 2000, p. 204]).

What to Do When Presented with a Subpoena

FERPA does not mandate that an institution of higher education automatically comply with a subpoena. To determine if the institution should comply with a subpoena, the following information should be considered:

☒ **DETERMINE IF IT IS A SUBPOENA.** It is the responsibility of the person served with the subpoena, or his/her institution, to determine if the piece of paper presented has the validity of a legal subpoena. Consult with your institution's legal counsel if you are not sure you have received a real subpoena.

☒ **DETERMINE IF THE COURT ISSUING THE SUBPOENA HAS JURISDICTION.** The subpoena powers of a court, federal district, state, or county, are limited. In order for the subpoena to be binding upon the institution on which the subpoena is served, an officer of a court that has jurisdiction over the institution must have issued it. As stated earlier, a federal district subpoena has validity in all 50 states as long as the 100-mile rule is observed. However, at the state level, a subpoena issued from a state court in Michigan has no validity in Texas.

The person served with a subpoena should determine whether a subpoena received is jurisdictionally valid before complying. If the court issuing the subpoena does not have jurisdiction, the person upon whom the subpoena was served, or the institution's legal counsel, must inform the maker of this fact. It is then up to the maker to determine if the information is important enough to seek a subpoena from a court which has jurisdiction. Once served with a jurisdictionally valid subpoena, the institution should comply with the request rather than face possible contempt of court charges.

☒ **DETERMINE WHAT IS REQUESTED.** Part of the subpoena identifies what the maker is requesting. In many instances, the wording of what is requested is overly broad. Whenever confronted with such wording in a subpoena, it is in the institution's best interest to request that the issuer of the subpoena be more specific with the request. With more specificity, it may be determined that the need can be met by providing either directory information or simply a transcript—therefore potentially saving significant time and effort.

☒ **DETERMINE IF WHAT IS REQUESTED IS COVERED BY FERPA AND MEETS THE PROCESS REQUIREMENTS OUTLINED IN FERPA** In some subpoenas, the maker of the subpoena commands the person served to refrain from notifying the subject that the person served will comply with the subpoena. Unless the subpoena meets the guidelines mentioned earlier (*e.g.*, a federal grand jury subpoena, a law enforcement subpoena, etc.), the recipient of the subpoena

cannot comply with that portion of the subpoena. Other than those instances noted above, despite a command in a subpoena to the contrary, the requirement that the person served with a subpoena notify the student of the receipt of a subpoena and the institution's probable intent to comply must be upheld. In most cases where this occurs, no judge has reviewed the subpoena before it was issued.

When the subpoena orders the recipient not to notify the student (and the subpoena is not a federal grand jury subpoena or one issued for law enforcement purposes, as mentioned above), it is best to contact the person who issued the subpoena and advise that person of the FERPA notification requirement. If the issuer insists that the student not be notified, the person served with a subpoena should seek advice of counsel. Legal counsel should advise the court regarding FERPA requirements since the court may not understand those requirements.

The "prior notification" requirement within FERPA regarding subpoenas is intended to alert the student to possible court action and allow him/her to determine if he/she wishes to seek counsel if he/she feels that the subpoena is unwarranted. The student's counsel can make a motion to quash the subpoena in the court from which the subpoena was issued. This was successfully demonstrated in the case of *Goldman* v. *Goldman*, Family Court of the State of New York, County of Rockland, V–852/91.

The judge of a court from which a subpoena was issued can order the quashing, or modification, of a subpoena if the subpoena fails to allow reasonable time for compliance or requires disclosure of privileged or other protected matter and no exception or waiver applies.

Rights of a Person When Served with a Subpoena

A person served with a subpoena should not feel intimidated or threatened if he/she is making an honest effort to comply with the requirements within FERPA. The most important first step is not to panic if served with a subpoena; you do not need to, and should not, respond immediately despite some of the strong language in the subpoena.

Keep in mind, if the person served with a subpoena is commanded to produce, permit inspection and copy documents, that person does not have to appear in person, unless specifically ordered to do so. (The West Group 2000, p. 201.)

Also, as indicated above, if the subpoena is issued from a federal district court having jurisdiction, the person served with a subpoena does not have to travel more than 100 miles to provide the deposition or produce documents. The person served with a subpoena may also submit a written objection (see instances below which may apply) to the issuer of the subpoena. This must be done within 14 calendar days after being served or before the time specified for compliance if such time is less than 14 days after service.

If objection is made, the party who served the subpoena is not entitled to inspect the materials specified unless an order of the court permitting inspection is issued. If objection has been made, upon notifying the person served with the subpoena, the party serving the subpoena may move to compel the production of the materials in the original subpoena.

In some cases, the institution may have legal or policy reasons for wishing to object to a subpoena. The institution should have a protocol in place for identifying any such cases. The protocol should require that the institution's attorneys be notified whenever all subpoenas or subpoenas of special types are received. The attorneys can then take responsibility for objecting to the subpoena and/or having it quashed.

Notifying the Student

The subpoena must give the person served with a subpoena a "reasonable time to respond." "Reasonable time" is normally considered 14 calendar days or 10 working days.

If a subpoena mandates a response in fewer than 14 calendar days, the person served with the subpoena, or the institution's legal counsel, should contact the attorney and explain the notification requirements under FERPA.

Unless explicitly directed in the subpoena not to notify the student, FERPA requires the institution to notify the student on the receipt of a subpoena. (*See* "What FERPA Says about Subpoenas," on page 46.) The record custodian served with a subpoena should promptly notify the student of the receipt and that the institution intends to comply (if it does) on a particular date (realistically 14 days from the date the subpoena is received). The notice should inform the student that a motion to quash the subpoena must be filed before that date with a copy to the institution. The notice to the student should ordinarily be sent by certified mail, return receipt. A copy should also be sent to the court, attorney, judge or other official who caused the subpoena to be issued.

In the case of an alumnus with no current address, the institution should do its best to locate him/her within reason and document what was done. Best efforts to notify students/alumni whose addresses, maintained by the institution, may not be current would include: any special delivery that provides a record of receipt, email, fax, or telephone with the call noted in the file with a memo. Attorneys involved in the case may also be an appropriate source for obtaining current addresses. (*See* the sample "Notice of Intent to Comply with a Subpoena," on page 125; and FPCO "Letter to Youngstown State University," on page 245.)

Complying with the Subpoena

Once the person served with a subpoena is satisfied that: he/she has been served with a valid subpoena from a court having jurisdiction over the institution; a reasonable attempt has been made to notify the student of the institution's intent to comply with the subpoena; and a reasonable amount of time has elapsed for the student to react to this notification, the person served with a subpoena can then provide official copies (never the originals) of the documents requested to the issuer of the subpoena or the agency which collects such documents for court hearings/trials. In certain jurisdictions, it may be possible to submit the requested records to the attention of the presiding judge of the court having jurisdiction in the case.

Chapter Five

Training Materials

This chapter provides helpful information/tools that will assist the FERPA practitioner in training other school officials regarding their responsibilities under FERPA. As an added benefit, all of the training materials located in this chapter are also available on AACRAO's Web site at www.aacrao.org/compliance/ferpa/. You are encouraged to adapt these materials and use them at your institution.

Frequently Asked Questions

These are the more commonly asked questions regarding FERPA. Answers to all of these questions are found in this publication. You might want to use some of these as teaser questions to stimulate interest in FERPA on your campus.

- What is FERPA? How does it affect me as a school employee? Am I considered a school official according to FERPA's criteria?
- When are parents allowed to see their child's education records?
- What rights do students have under FERPA?
- What obligations do colleges have under FERPA?
- Where is the best place to post the annual notification to students?

From Parents

- Why can't I get my son/daughters' grades/schedule? I'm paying the bills!
- How can I pay my son/daughter's account if you can't even tell me how much he/she still owes?
- Can you send me a letter certifying that my child is enrolled as a full-time student at your institution?
- I used to be able to see my student's information and now I can't. What happened?

From Students

- How I can let my friends get my address/phone number on campus, without giving it out indiscriminately?

- Why do I always get junk mail from insurance companies, credit card companies, auto agencies, etc. that want to sell me something? Can't you keep these vultures from getting my name/address, etc.?
- I've forgotten my PIN. Can you tell me what it is?
- How can I let my parents see the information I want them to see, but not all of it?

From Faculty

- Why can't I post grades by the last four digits of a student's SSN?
- Why can't I have access to *all* our students, not just my advisees or students in my classes?
- May I include a student's GPA in a letter of recommendation that the student has asked me to write? What can I include in the recommendation? What can't I include?
- What do I have to do to comply with FERPA in returning examinations and term papers?
- A father has called me about his daughter's performance in my class. What can I tell him?
- Can I pass around a class list to take attendance?
- The student has a "no release" on his or her record; can I contact him or her about class related matters?

> **FERPA TIPS**
>
> AACRAO Consulting Services provides FERPA compliance training for individual institutions. Check the AACRAO Web site for additional information or email consulting@aacrao.org.

■ What is the big deal about photos? If they're not defined as public information can I share them with my TAs for students in my class?

From Registrars

■ Can I change "directory information" for my campus?

■ Is it okay for me to not release student information to anybody?

■ How can my staff and I comply with FERPA and, at the same time, be a customer service-focused office?

■ How can I make sure that all student information users on my campus abide by FERPA?

■ Can I confirm to someone (other than the student) over the phone that a student did or did not receive a degree without getting the student's permission first?

■ A third party calls and wants to confirm the date of a student's degree. Can I confirm to that person that the student did not receive a degree if the student has requested that we not disclose that information? What would be the proper response?

■ I employ work-study students in my office. Can they look at other students' records?

■ When can I release information to police or others in the event of an emergency?

Key Terms/Concepts in FERPA

Anyone who wishes to have a working knowledge of FERPA needs to understand the following key terms and concepts. These are all discussed in this publication. (*See* Table 5.1.)

If you have a working knowledge of these concepts and terms, you will be well on your way to understanding what FERPA is all about.

How Do You Determine What is an Education Record?

The following guidelines can assist in determining whether the record is an education record and covered under FERPA. An education record subject to FERPA is:

■ Maintained by your institution;

Table 5.1: Key FERPA Concepts and Terms

	Source in the Code of Federal Regulations (CFR)	Source in 2010 *AACRAO FERPA Guide*
Concepts		
Required annual notification	34 C.F.R. 99.7	Page 151
Written permission of student required to disclose	§ 99.30	Page 154
The exceptions to written permission	§ 99.31	Page 154
Student's right to access his/her records	§ 99.10	Page 147
The "musts" and "mays" in FERPA	(throughout); notably § 99.31	Page 147
Parents/parental disclosure	§ 99.31(a)(8) [a]	Page 156
Legitimate educational interest	§ 99.31(a)(1)	Page 155
Terms		
Education Record	§ 99.3	Page 148
Directory Information	§ 99.3	Page 148
School Official	§ 99.7(a)(3)(iii)	Page 151
Personally Identifiable	§ 99.3	Page 148
Eligible Student	§ 99.3	Page 148

[a] Note: Remember this is in a "may" section.

■ Personally identifiable to a student (directly related to a student or from which a student can be identified); and/or

■ Not one of the excluded categories of records (*see* definition of "Education Records" on page 9).

What Does FERPA Say About Parents?

■ When a student reaches the age of 18 or begins attending a postsecondary institution regardless of age, FERPA rights transfer to the student.

■ Parents, like any other third party, may obtain directory information at the discretion of the institution.

■ Parents may obtain non-directory information (grades, GPA, etc.) only at the discretion of the institution and after it has been determined that their child is legally their dependent.

■ If there is an emergency or safety situation, appropriate non-directory information may be released to parents.

■ If the student is under the age of 21 and has been found in violation of a substance abuse law or regulation, information about these circumstances may be released to the parents.

■ Parents may also be provided non-directory information by obtaining a signed consent from their child.

Written Authorization by Student to Share Grades with Parents

For examples see the sample "Authorization of Grade Disclosure," on page 106, "Permission to Release Education Record Information" on page 103, and

"Authorization to Release Grades/Transcript," on page 127.

The Student's Rights of Non-Disclosure Under FERPA

▣ A student has the right to request non-disclosure of directory information. Other information from an education record can only be disclosed with a signed consent from the student, unless it meets one of the exceptions to signed consent in §99.31.

▣ A student does *not* have the right to limit disclosures that are otherwise permitted by FERPA in §99.31.

▣ A student does *not* have the right to request non-disclosure to a particular person or group of persons to whom disclosures are permitted under FERPA, but the institution may honor that request if it wishes.

▣ An institution may honor a student's request to withhold non-directory information but is not compelled to do so if the disclosure is permitted under FERPA.

▣ The student has the right to request non-disclosure of directory information only while in attendance.

▣ Students who have left the institution do not have the right to request non-disclosure of directory information, but the institution may honor that request if it wishes.

▣ Institutions must honor a request that directory information not be disclosed for currently enrolled students.

▣ The non-disclosure hold on directory information remains in effect until the student requests the institution to remove it. This is even true after the student has ceased attendance at the institution.

FERPA-Related College/Registrar Web Sites

Table 5.2 provides a great deal of information regarding FERPA, as well as examples of institutional approaches to providing FERPA information to the campus community. The first set includes Web sites with general information/FAQs. The second set lists tutorials.

Table 5.2: Institution-provided FERPA Information and Tutorials Available Online

Institution	Web Address (URL)
General Information/FAQs	
AACRAO Web site	www.aacrao.org/compliance/ferpa/
Auburn University	www.auburn.edu/student_info/student_affairs/registrar/helpful-resources/your-rights-and-records.html
George Mason University	http://registrar.gmu.edu/privacy/
Maricopa Community Colleges	www.maricopa.edu/legal/ferpa/index.htm (general information and tutorial)
Michigan State University	www.reg.msu.edu/ROInfo/Notices/PrivacyGuidelines.asp
Ohio State University	www.ureg.ohio-state.edu/ourweb/more/Content/ferpa_pg1.html
Penn State University	www.registrar.psu.edu/confidentiality/confidentiality_index.cfm
Seattle Pacific University	www.spu.edu/depts/sas/resources/ferpa.asp
University of Missouri	http://registrar.missouri.edu/policies/ferpa.php
University of Nebraska at Omaha	www.ses.unomaha.edu/registrar/ferpa.php
University of North Carolina at Chapel Hill	http://regweb.unc.edu/faculty/ferpa_training.php
University of Oregon	http://registrar.uoregon.edu/records_privacy
University of Puget Sound	www.pugetsound.edu/academics/academic-offices/academic-advising-registrar/know-educational-rights/
University of Southern California	www.usc.edu/dept/ARR/ferpa/
University of Texas at Austin	www.utexas.edu/student/registrar/ferpa/
Washington and Lee University	www.wlu.edu/x36022.xml
Tutorials	
Catholic University of America	http://enrollmentservices.cua.edu/facultystaffinfo/Facultystaffinfo.cfm
Maricopa Community Colleges	www.maricopa.edu/legal/ferpa/ferpa_tutorial/ferpatutorial.htm
Ohio State University	www.ureg.ohio-state.edu/ourweb/more/Content/ferpa_tutorial/main.htm
University of Arizona	www.registrar.arizona.edu/ferpacourse/default.htm
University of Maryland	www.sis.umd.edu/ferpa/
University of Nebraska at Kearney	www.unk.edu/offices/registrar/ferpa/index.php?id=425
University of Southern California	https://lunyudaxue.usc.edu/FERPA.aspx
University of Wisconsin–Madison	http://registrar.wisc.edu/ferpa/faculty/
Texas A&M University	http://admissions.tamu.edu/forms/registrarForms/WebFERPA.ppt

A FERPA Brochure

The next two pages provide an example of an institutional FERPA brochure. It was designed as a one-page, 8½ x 11", double-sided, tri-fold handout to be used by employees of the institution, students, and other interested parties. It was not designed to be a substitute for the annual notification to students, but, with a little work and thought, it could turn into that.

The Family Educational Rights and Privacy Act Informational Guidelines

What is FERPA?

The *Family Educational Rights and Privacy Act of 1974* helps protect the privacy of student education records. The Act provides eligible students the right to inspect and review education records, the right to seek to amend those records and to limit disclosure of information from the records. The intent of the legislation is to protect the rights of students and to ensure the privacy and accuracy of education records. The Act applies to all institutions that are the recipients of federal aid administered by the Secretary of Education.

What rights does FERPA afford students with respect to their education records?

▣ The right to inspect and review their education records within 45 days of the day the university receives a request for access.

Students should submit written requests to the Office of Student Records and identify the record(s) they wish to inspect. The staff of the office will make arrangements for access and notify the student of the time and place where the records may be inspected. If the requested records are not maintained in the Office of Student Records, the student will be notified of the correct official to whom the request should be addressed.

▣ The right to request an amendment to the student's education records that the student believes are inaccurate or misleading.

Students may ask the university to amend a record that they believe is inaccurate or misleading. They should write the Office of Student Records or the specific office involved with the record in question (*e.g.* a department office regarding a grade), clearly identify the part of the record they want changed, and specify why it is inaccurate or misleading.

If the university decides not to amend the record as requested by the student, the university will notify the student of the decision and advise the student of his or her right to a hearing regarding the request for amendment. Additional information regarding the hearing will be provided to the student when notified of the hearing.

▣ The right to consent to disclosures of personally identifiable information contained in the student's education records, except to the extent that FERPA authorizes disclosure without consent.

One exception which permits disclosure without consent is disclosure to school officials with legitimate educational interests. A school official is: a person employed by the university in an administrative, supervisory, academic or research, or support staff position (including law enforcement unit personnel and health staff); a person or company with whom the university has contracted (such as an attorney, auditor, or collection agent); a person serving on the Board of Trustees; or a student serving on an official committee, such as a disciplinary or grievance committee, or assisting another school official in performing his or her tasks.

A school official has a legitimate educational interest if the official needs to review an education record in order to fulfill his or her professional responsibilities.

▣ The right to file a complaint with the U.S. Department of Education concerning alleged failures by the College to comply with the requirements of FERPA. The name and address of the Office that administers FERPA is:

Family Policy Compliance Office
U.S. Department of Education
400 Maryland Ave., SW
Washington DC 20202–5901

Who is protected under FERPA?

FERPA protects the education records of students who are currently enrolled or formerly enrolled regardless of their age* or status with regard to parental dependency. The education records of students who have applied to but have not attended an institution are not subject to FERPA guidelines, nor are deceased students.

Parents of a student termed as "dependent" for income tax purposes may have access to the student's education records. A copy of their parent's most recent Federal Income Tax return, where the parents declared the student as a dependent, must be submitted to the Office of Student Records to document "dependency."

What are education records?

With certain exceptions (noted below), an education record is any record (1) which contains information that is personally identifiable to a student, and (2) is maintained by the university. With the exception of information about other students, financial records of parents and confidential letters of reference to which the student has waived access, a student has the right of access to his or her education records.

Education records include any records in whatever medium (handwritten, print, email, magnetic tape, film, diskette, etc.) that are in the possession of any school official. This includes transcripts or other records obtained from a school in which a student was previously enrolled.

What information is not considered part of an education record?

- Sole possession records or private notes held by school officials that are not accessible or released to other personnel.
- Law enforcement or campus security records that are solely for law enforcement purposes and maintained solely by the law enforcement unit.
- Records relating to individuals who are employed by the institution (unless contingent upon attendance).
- Records relating to treatment provided by a physician, psychiatrist, psychologist or other recognized professional or paraprofessional and disclosed only to individuals providing treatment.
- Records of an institution that contain only information about an individual obtained after that person is no longer a student at that institution, *i.e.*, alumni records.

What is directory information?

Institutions may disclose information about a student without violating FERPA if it has designated that information as "directory information." At University ABC this includes a student's:

- Name
- Address
- Telephone number
- Major field of study
- Dates of attendance
- Current enrollment status (full-time/part-time)
- Class standing
- Receipt or non-receipt of a degree
- Academic awards received (Dean's list, honor roll)

How does a student authorize release of his/her education record in the form of an academic transcript?

Students must authorize the release of their transcripts by written request with signature, by completing and signing a transcript request form available in the Office of Student Records, or by submitting the request online via a secured portal. There is a $5.00 fee for transcripts. The receipt of a written request with signature to release an education record via fax is permissible.

Who may have access to student information?

- The student and any outside party who has the student's written request.
- School officials (as defined by the University) who have "legitimate educational interests."
- Parents of a dependent student as defined by the Internal Revenue Code.
- A person in response to a lawfully issued subpoena or court order, as long as the University makes a reasonable attempt to notify the student first. Normally, the University will comply with a subpoena after two weeks have elapsed from the day of notifying the student.

When is the student's consent not required to disclose information?

When the disclosure is (one or more of the following):
- To school officials (defined in policy) who have a legitimate educational interest.
- To federal, state and local authorities involving an audit or evaluation of compliance with educational programs.
- In connection with financial aid; this includes Veterans' benefits.

- To organizations conducting studies for or on behalf of educational institutions.
- To accrediting organizations.
- To parents of a dependent student.
- To comply with a judicial order or subpoena.
- In a health or safety emergency.
- Releasing directory information.
- Releasing the results of a disciplinary hearing to an alleged victim of a crime of violence.

FERPA Basics for Faculty/Instructional Staff

The following document is intended to serve as a "one-page," double-sided summary of FERPA, particularly focused toward faculty and instructional staff. It can be used as a handout as well as a training tool.

The Essence

- Federal law designed to protect the privacy of education records. It also provides guidelines for appropriately using and releasing student education records.
- It is intended that students' rights be broadly defined and applied. Therefore, consider the student as the "*owner*" of the information in his or her education record, and the institution as the "*custodian*" of that record.

Key Terms/Definitions

"EDUCATION RECORDS" include any record maintained by the institution that contains information that is personally identifiable to a student (in whatever format or medium) with some narrowly defined exceptions:

- Records in the "sole possession of the maker" (*e.g.,* private advising notes).
- Law enforcement records created and maintained by a law enforcement agency for a law enforcement purpose.
- Employment records (unless the employment is based on student status). The employment records of student employees (*e.g.,* work-study, wages, graduate teaching associates) are part of their education records.
- Medical/psychological treatment records (*e.g.,* from a health or counseling center).
- Alumni records (*i.e.,* those created after the student graduated or left the institution).

"DIRECTORY INFORMATION:" Those data items that are generally not considered harmful or an invasion of privacy if publicly available. This information cannot be released if student has a "no release" on his or her record. Each institution establishes what it considers to be directory information. Common examples include: name, address (local, home and email), telephone (local and home), academic program of study, dates of attendance, date of birth, most recent educational institution attended, and degrees and awards received.

- Directory information *cannot* include: race, gender, SSN (or part of an SSN), grades, GPA, country of citizenship, or religion. Except in very specific circumstances, a student ID number (SIN) also cannot be considered directory information.
- Every student must be given the opportunity to have directory information suppressed from public release. This process is often referred to as a "no release," "opt out" or "suppression." When a student makes this request, everyone within the institution must abide by a student's request that no information be released about the student.
- It is important to understand, that a "no release" does *not* mean that a school official within the institution who has a demonstrated legitimate educational interest (*e.g.,* a faculty member teaching the student in class) is precluded from using the information to perform that official's job duties.

"PARENT:" With reference to FERPA, the term "parent" refers to either parent (including custodial and non-custodial, if divorced).

When do FERPA rights begin?

A FERPA-related college education record begins for a student when he or she enrolls in a higher education institution. At a postsecondary institution, rights belong to the student in attendance, regardless of the student's age.

Basic Rights of Students under the Act

- Be notified of their FERPA rights at least annually.
- Inspect and review their records.
- Amend an incorrect record.
- Consent to disclosure (with exceptions).

Annual Notification

Every institution must notify students of their FERPA rights at least annually.

Inspection and Review

Students have the *right* to see everything in their "education record," except:

- Information about other students;
- Financial records of parents; and
- Confidential letters of recommendation if they waived their right of access.

FERPA does not prescribe what records are created or how long they are to be kept; however, you cannot destroy a record if there is a request to inspect and review. It is important to know and understand your institution's records retention policy.

Right to Consent to Disclosure

Start with the premise that the student has the right to control to whom his or her education record is released. Then, there are several exceptions when that permission is not required.

In those instances where a signed release is required, regulations now provide the flexibility to accept an electronic signature.

WHEN IS PRIOR CONSENT NOT REQUIRED?

The institution may disclose records without consent if certain requirements are met, but it is not required to do so.

Some examples of the exceptions to the release requirement include:

- "School officials" with a "legitimate educational interest." Employees and legal agents have access to education records in order to perform their official, educationally-related duties.
- Disclosure to organizations conducting studies to improve instruction, or to accrediting organizations.
- Disclosure to parents of *dependent students* (IRS definition); Check to see how your institution expects parents to demonstrate student dependent status.

- To comply with a judicial order or lawfully issued subpoena.
- Disclosure for a health/safety emergency (must document what the emergency was and to whom the information was released).
- Disclosure of directory information, provided the student has not requested "no release."

Some Specific Issues for Faculty and Instructional Staff

- **POSTING GRADES:** Since grades can never be directory information, it is inappropriate to post grades in a public setting. An instructor may, however, post grades if the grades are posted in such a manner that only the instructor and the individual student can identify the individual and his or her grade. Grades should never be posted by any portion of the SSN. Additionally, it is recommended that such a posted list should not be in the same order as the class roster or in alphabetical order.

- **WEB-BASED TOOLS TO SUPPORT CLASSES:** Courses supported by class Web sites and/or discussion groups must take extra precautions to not inadvertently release non-directory student information. Only directory information can be available to the general public and other class members, so it is recommended that such Web-based tools employ a security layer so that only class members and instructors can access appropriate information.

- **STUDENTS OPTING FOR NO RELEASE IN THE CLASSROOM SETTING:** Students cannot choose to be anonymous in the classroom setting. If a student has chosen "no release" for his or her directory information, that does not mean that an instructor cannot call on him or her by name in class or that the student's email address cannot be displayed on an electronic classroom support tool such as a discussion board, blog, or chat feature.

FERPA Basics for Staff

The following document is intended to serve as a "one-page," double-sided summary of FERPA, particularly focused toward staff in an office that regularly works with student education records. It can be used as a handout as well as a training tool.

The Essence

- Federal law designed to protect the privacy of education records. It also provides guidelines for appropriately using and releasing student education records.
- It is intended that students' rights be broadly defined and applied. Therefore, consider the student as the *"owner"* of the information in his or her education record, and the institution as the *"custodian"* of that record.

Key Terms/Definitions

"EDUCATION RECORDS" include any record maintained by the institution that contains information that is personally identifiable to a student (in whatever format or medium) with some narrowly defined exceptions:

- Records in the "sole possession of the maker" (*e.g.*, private advising notes).
- Law enforcement records created and maintained by a law enforcement agency for a law enforcement purpose.
- Employment records (unless the employment is based on student status). The employment records of student employees (*e.g.*, work-study, wages, graduate teaching associates) are part of their education records.
- Medical/psychological treatment records (*e.g.*, from a health or counseling center).
- Alumni records (*i.e.*, those created after the student graduated or left the institution).

"DIRECTORY INFORMATION:" Those data items that are generally not considered harmful or an invasion of privacy if publicly available. Cannot be released if student has a "no release" on his or her record. Each institution establishes what it considers to be directory information. Common

examples include: name, address (local, home and email), telephone (local and home), academic program of study, dates of attendance, date of birth, most recent educational institution attended, and degrees and awards received.

- Directory Information *cannot* include: race, gender, SSN (or part of an SSN), grades, GPA, country of citizenship, or religion. Except in very specific circumstances, a student ID number (SIN) also cannot be considered directory information.
- Every student must be given the opportunity to have directory information suppressed from public release. This process is often referred to as a "no release," "opt out" or "suppression." Everyone within the institution must abide by a student's request that no information be released about the student.
- It is important to understand, that a "no release" does *not* mean that a school official within the institution who has a demonstrated legitimate educational interest (*e.g.*, faculty member teaching the student in class) is precluded from using the information to perform that official's job duties.

"PARENT:" With reference to FERPA, the term "parent" refers to either parent (including custodial and non-custodial, if divorced).

When do FERPA rights begin?

A FERPA-related college education record begins for a student when he or she enrolls in a higher education institution. At a postsecondary institution, rights belong to the student in attendance, regardless of the student's age.

Basic Rights of Students under the Act:

- Be notified of their FERPA rights at least annually.
- Inspect and review their records.
- Amend an incorrect record.
- Consent to disclosure (with exceptions).

Annual Notification

Every institution must notify students of their FERPA rights at least annually.

Inspection and Review

Students have the *right* to see everything in their "education record," except:

- Information about other students.
- Financial records of parents.
- Confidential letters of recommendation if they waived their right of access.

FERPA does not prescribe what records are created or how long they are to be kept; however, you cannot destroy a record once there is a request to inspect and review. It is important to know and understand your institution's records retention policy.

Right to Consent to Disclosure

Start with the premise that the student has the right to control to whom his or her education record is released. Then, there are several exceptions when that permission is not required.

In those instances where a signed release is required, regulations now provide the flexibility to accept an electronic signature.

WHEN IS PRIOR CONSENT NOT REQUIRED?

The institution may disclose records without consent if certain requirements are met, but it is not required to do so. Some examples of the exceptions to the release requirement include:

- "School officials" with a "legitimate educational interest." Employees and legal agents have access to education records in order to perform their official, educationally-related duties.
- Disclosure to another institution where the student seeks to enroll or is enrolled.
- Disclosure to DOE, state/local education authorities.
- Disclosure in connection with the receipt of financial aid.
- Disclosure to state/local officials in conjunction with legislative requirements.

- Disclosure to organizations conducting studies to improve instruction, or to accrediting organizations.
- Disclosure to parents of *dependent students* (IRS definition). Check to see how your institution expects parents to demonstrate student dependent status.
- To comply with a judicial order or lawfully issued subpoena.
- Disclosure for a health/safety emergency (must document what the emergency was and to whom the information was released).
- Disclosure of directory information provided the student has not requested "no release."
- Disciplinary information:
  - ▶ Disclosure to the alleged victim of a crime of violence, such as information from disciplinary proceedings.
  - ▶ *Only* when found in violation, and *only* for crimes of violence—release of name, sanction and outcome can be made to anyone.
- Disclosure to parents of any student under the age of 21, a violation of federal, state, local or institutional laws/regulations related to substance abuse (provided that other laws governing the institution, such as state law, do not preclude such disclosures).

FERPA rights at a postsecondary institution end with a student's death. However, state law may provide for a continued right to privacy in your state. Students have a formal right to file a complaint with the Department of Education.

Key Resources for Additional Information:

- Your campus registrar
- AACRAO (Compliance)—www.aacrao.org/compliance/ferpa/
- Family Compliance Office of the Department of Education (administers FERPA compliance)—www.ed.gov/policy/gen/guid/fpco/

A FERPA Workshop/Presentation

The following slides are designed to form the basis of a FERPA workshop and may be found as a PowerPoint presentation on AACRAO's Web site at www.aacrao.org/compliance/ferpa/. There are explanatory notes with most of the slides.

Slide № 1 TRAINING FACULTY AND STAFF ON FERPA

AACRAO Federal Compliance Committee
February 2010

Notes: The following slides are designed to form the basis of a FERPA workshop/presentation and may be found on AACRAO's Web site at www.aacrao.org/compliance/ferpa/. There are notes with most of the slides explaining what is covered in the slide. The title may be changed to reflect the content you wish to include; the catchier the title, the better.

Slide № 2 FAMILY EDUCATIONAL RIGHTS AND PRIVACY ACT OF 1974

"A Federal Law designed to protect the privacy of education records, to establish the right of students to inspect and review their education records, and to provide guidelines for the correction of inaccurate and misleading data through informal and formal hearings."

Notes: Congress enacted FERPA for the three main purposes shown in this slide. In this presentation, the first two purposes are covered. The third has not become a major factor in our study of FERPA. Although important to the overall understanding of the intent of Congress in protecting the privacy of education records and providing for corrections to erroneous information found in education records, the hearing process has not emerged as an important part of this legislation since few hearings have resulted from a FERPA complaint within an institution.

Slide № 3 FAMILY EDUCATIONAL RIGHTS AND PRIVACY ACT OF 1974

FERPA is enforced by the Family Policy Compliance Office, U.S. Department of Education, Washington, D.C.

Notes: The Family Policy Compliance Office is the office within the Department of Education that administers FERPA and is responsible for providing technical assistance to educational institutions on FERPA. FERPA is applicable to both K–12 and higher education. The Family Policy Compliance Office is responsible for both levels of education. The main difference in FERPA between these two levels of education is that the rights that are ascribed to the "student" at the higher education level are ascribed to the parents at the K–12 level. As will be made clear in subsequent slides, FERPA rights are granted to parents until their son/daughter reaches the age of 18 or begins attending an institution of higher education regardless of age.

Slide № 4 THE ESSENCE OF THE ACT

- College students must be permitted to inspect their own education records.
- School officials may not disclose personally identifiable information about students nor permit inspection of their records without written permission unless such action is covered by certain exceptions permitted by the Act.

Slide № 5 KEY CONCEPTS

- Required annual notification
- Written permission required for disclosure of student education record
- The exceptions to written permission of student
- Students' right to access their records
- The "musts" and "mays" in FERPA
- Parents'/parental disclosure
- Legitimate educational interest

Notes: These are important concepts that all faculty and staff who regularly work with FERPA issues need to master. This and the next slide are shown twice in this presentation. The first time introduces participants to concepts and terms emphasized in this presentation. This slide is then shown toward the end of the presentation to reemphasize FERPA's key terms and concepts.

Slide № 6 KEY TERMS

- Education Record
- Personally Identifiable
- Directory Information
- School Official

Notes: Throughout the presentation, these terms will be highlighted in a different color. The participant should understand what these key terms and concepts are; they are important to understanding FERPA.

Slide № 7 WHAT IS AN "EDUCATION RECORD?"

- Any record, with certain exceptions, maintained by an institution that is directly related to a student or students. This record can contain a student's name(s) or information from which an individual student can be personally (individually) identified.

◨ These records include: files, documents, and materials in whatever medium (handwriting, print, email, tapes, disks, film, microfilm, microfiche) which contain information directly related to students and from which students can be personally (individually) identified.

Notes: This is the FERPA definition of an "education record." It is important to start with this definition since you must determine if a piece of information is an "education record." If the record can be identified as an "education record," it is subject to FERPA. Notice how broad the definition is, not only in the information covered but also in the variety of media in which such a record can be found. This definition basically tells us that an education record is not just a record that can be identified by a student's name, nor is it limited to paper documents found in the registrar's office. This is a pervasive definition that draws all academic and administrative offices of an institution under the FERPA umbrella.

Slide № 8   "PERSONALLY IDENTIFIABLE"

◨ The name of the student, the student's parent, or other family members;

◨ The student's campus or home address;

◨ A personal identifier (such as a social security number or student number);

◨ A list of personal characteristics or other information which would make the student's identity known with "reasonable certainty."

Notes: To determine what is "personally identifiable," FERPA provides these guidelines. Note that "personally identifiable" includes more than just a student's name; it includes a "personal identifier" such as a social security number. This is why the posting of grades by ID or Social Security Number without obtaining the student's written permission is not permitted under FERPA.

Slide № 9   GRADES POSTED ON BULLETIN BOARD OUTSIDE OF INSTRUCTOR'S OFFICE

Grade Posting: Sample 1
Instructor Summary December 15, 2009 Grade Book
(Unregistered Copy) MKT 227 Fall 09

A = 90.0, B = 80.0, C = 70.0, D = 60.0

ID	Rg Avg % 100.00	Ext Cr % 5.6	Grade
2949	93.8	2.1	A
4532	84.5	4.2	B
5599	83.1	0.7	B
1197	71.0	0.7	B
7463	72.6	0.7	C
6115	66.2	5.6	C
7692	66.9	4.2	C
2342	68.1	1.4	D
1543	62.9	0.7	D
6748	61.8	0.7	D

Notes: The next two slides are taken from two instructors' web pages. Both slides show grades, etc. of their students in one of the sections of the classes they are teaching. The identifying numbers in the left hand column show the last four digits of the students' social security numbers. According to the Family Policy Compliance Office, this is not permitted without obtaining the students' written permission. If an instructor wants to post grades in any public way, he or she should use a code known only to the instructor and each individual student.

For example, each student could have a random number assigned at the beginning of the term. The alphabetical order of the list must be rearranged so that students cannot be personally identified.

Slide № 10   WHAT IS NOT AN EDUCATION RECORD?

◨ "Sole possession notes"

◨ Law enforcement unit records

◨ Records maintained exclusively for individuals in their capacity as employees

◨ Records of individuals who are employed as a result of their status as students (work-study) are education records.

◨ Medical & treatment records

◨ Alumni records

Notes: These are the categories of information that are not subject to FERPA. "Sole possession notes" will be covered shortly. Law enforcement unit records are those records created by a law enforcement unit for a law enforcement purpose and maintained by the law enforcement unit. Any of these records that are shared with another school official become subject to FERPA. Employee records: If a student is also an employee of the institution, those employment records of that person are not subject to FERPA. However, records created for an employment purpose by the fact that the person is a student are education records. The most common examples of these kinds of records are work-study records. Doctor-patient privilege records: Those records made or maintained by a physician, psychiatrist, psychologist, or other recognized professional or paraprofessional acting in their professional capacity or assisting in a paraprofessional capacity in the treatment of a student; such records are only to be disclosed to those providing treatment to the student. "Treatment" does not include any remedial educational activities or activities that are part of the educational program of the institution disclosed for accommodation purposes. Alumni records are those records created by an institution after the student has left the institution unrelated to his/her time as a student.

Slide № 11   "SOLE POSSESSION NOTES"

Are made by one person as an individual observation or recollection, are kept in the possession of the maker, and are only shared with a temporary substitute.

◨ This term has always been narrowly defined.

◨ Notes taken in conjunction with any other person are not sole possession notes (counselor's notes, interview notes).

◨ Sharing these notes with another person, or placing them in an area where they can be viewed by others makes them "education records" and subject to FERPA.

◨ Emails can never be sole possession.

◨ Best advice: If you don't want it reviewed, don't write it down.

Notes: There has been some confusion over what constitutes a "sole possession" record and many within higher education attribute a broader definition to a sole possession record than what is legally correct. The points in this slide will show how limited the definition of a sole possession record can be. Follow this slide up with Story #1 to reinforce the limited nature of "sole possession notes."

Slide № 12   "SOLE POSSESSION NOTES"

OK, folks...

It's story time!!!!

Story #1

Notes: Prior to reading this story, you should have reviewed the characteristics of a "sole possession note" according to the law. You could give an example such as a notation of a "knee jerk observation to a behavior of a student in a class that a temporary substitute might need to know."

Story #1—At an institution in the Midwest, the Affirmative Action Officer (subsequently referred to as the AAO) was investigating a complaint filed by a student with the State's Department of Human Rights. The student alleged that she had been sexually harassed by a faculty member. In the investigation, the AAO interviewed all students who may have observed the alleged incident. The AAO interviewed each student individually and privately, and while interviewing, wrote notes of each student's observation and recollection. The AAO did not ask each student to review the notes for accuracy and did not share the notes with anyone. The interview notes were maintained in the AAO's office in a locked cabinet. No other person had access to the notes. The AAO did review the notes when preparing a response to the State Department of Human Resources, but did not disclose the notes themselves to anyone. Several years later, the student who had made the accusation of sexual harassment discovered that the notes existed and asked to see them since, under FERPA she said: "a student has the right to examine education records." The AAO was advised by legal counsel that the notes were "sole possession" records, and thus were not education records and not subject to review by the student. The student then filed a complaint with the Family Policy Compliance Office, claiming that her "right to access" under FERPA had been denied. Was her "right to access" improperly denied? The Family Policy Compliance Office determined that since the notes had been "...prepared with the assistance or participation of others, such as the students interviewed...", the notes are education records and the student must be provided access to these records under FERPA. Therefore, the notes in question are not sole possession notes. The notes were redacted to protect the privacy of the students who had been interviewed and the notes were provided to the complainant (student).

Slide № 13   WHAT IS AN EDUCATION RECORD? (SUMMARY)

If you have a record that is:

- ▣ Maintained by your institution
- ▣ Personally identifiable to a student (directly related to a student and from which a student can be identified)
- ▣ Not one of the excluded categories of records...

...then, you have an education record and *it is subject* to FERPA.

Notes: This is the end of the beginning of the presentation. This slide presents the steps in the test to determine if there is an education record. Ask the three questions below:
① Is it personally identifiable to a student?
② Is it maintained by the institution?
③ Can it be excluded from all of the categories of records that are not education records (law enforcement unit records, employment records, etc.)? If you can answer "yes" to all three questions, you have an education record and it is subject to FERPA.

Slide № 14   REQUIREMENTS FOR COMPLIANCE

What we must do...

- ▣ Provide annual notification to students of their FERPA rights

- ▣ Provide students access to their education records

Notes: This is the beginning of the second part of the presentation: What we must do to comply with FERPA. There are two main FERPA requirements with which each institution must comply.

Slide № 15   REQUIREMENTS FOR COMPLIANCE

▣ Provide annual notification to students of their right to:

① Inspect and review their education records
② Request an amendment to their education records
③ A hearing if the request for an amendment is unsatisfactory
④ Request that the institution not disclose directory information items about them
⑤ File a complaint with the U.S. Department of Education

Notes: There are six main points that must be included in the annual notification to students regarding their FERPA rights. The first five are self explanatory and are easily disposed of. The sixth point is more complex and must be dealt with separately on subsequent slides. The seventh point presented in this presentation, student notification regarding directory information, is not legally required to be included in the annual notification. However, since FERPA requires us to notify students about what items of information an institution identifies as directory information, we, along with the Family Policy Compliance Office, recommend that this notification be included in the annual notification to students. Also, it would be helpful to download the Model Annual Notification from the Family Policy Compliance Office's Web site to study how these seven points are included in the annual notification. The URL for the Family Policy Compliance Office's Web site is www2.ed.gov/policy/gen/guid/fpco/index.html.

Slide № 16   REQUIREMENTS FOR COMPLIANCE

▣ Provide annual notification to students of their right to know:

⑥ 1) that school officials within the institution may obtain information from education records without obtaining prior written consent, 2) the criteria for determining who will be considered school officials and 3) what legitimate educational interest will entitle school officials to have access to education records.

Notes: Point six is a mouthful!!! Within this point lie three key terms that are at the foundation of understanding what FERPA directs regarding how education records should be treated by school officials within the institution. This point, intertwined with the key terms, provides the legal underpinning for establishing the necessity of demonstrating a professional need to know prior to accessing an education record. Simply because a person is employed by the institution does not mean that that person has an implied right to go on a "fishing expedition" among students' education records. There must be a professional need to know and that concept is identified as a "legitimate educational interest." This is an important part of the annual notification to students. FERPA stipulates that students must be informed of who within the institution will have access to their education records and the conditions under which this access will occur.

Slide № 17   REQUIREMENTS FOR COMPLIANCE

⚁ Provide annual notification to students of their right to:

⑦ Know which information the institution has designated as public or directory information.

Note: This notification of directory information is *not* required to be included in the annual notification.

Notes: As this slide indicates, notification to students about what the institution has designated as directory information is not required to be included in the annual FERPA notification. (However, FERPA does require that each institution notify students of what it considers to be directory information at some point; see next slide). The Family Policy Compliance Office has recommended that this notification be included in the annual notification.

Slide № 18 ⋯⋯⋯ **REQUIREMENTS FOR COMPLIANCE**

⚁ Directory Information
  ▶ Although not required to be included in the institution's annual notification, the institution must notify students of what information the institution has designated as directory information.
  ▶ The Family Policy Compliance Office has recommended that this notification be part of the institution's annual FERPA notification to students.

Notes: These are the three key points in FERPA regarding directory information. Probably the most misunderstood point is that the student's right to non-disclosure applies only to directory information. An institution may still disclose directory information under any of the exceptions to student written permission noted later in the presentation (this encapsulates all of the exceptions to written permission found in the FERPA regulations at §99.31). Also, a student may request non-disclosure at any time, whether they are a currently enrolled student or former student. The institution MUST honor the non-disclosure request from a currently enrolled student. It does not have to honor a non-disclosure request from a former student who left without a non-disclosure request in place, but it may do so if it wishes. Non-disclosures that have been honored by the institution remain in effect until the student removes it. The institution may require the student to renew the non-disclosure as long as the student is still in attendance. However, if the student has requested non-disclosure during the last term of attendance, the non-disclosure must be honored by the institution until the (now) former student informs the institution otherwise.

Slide № 19 ⋯⋯⋯ **REQUIREMENTS FOR COMPLIANCE**

⚁ Directory Information
  ▶ Information not normally considered a violation of a person's privacy
  ▶ Students must be notified of the items of directory information
  ▶ Students must be given the opportunity to request that directory information not be released. This right of non-disclosure applies to directory information only.

Slide № 20 **WHAT CAN DIRECTORY INFORMATION INCLUDE?**

⚁ Student's name
⚁ Addresses, including email
⚁ Telephone number
⚁ Date/place of birth
⚁ Major; Fields of study
⚁ Participation in officially recognized activities and sports
⚁ Height/weight of athletic team members
⚁ Dates of attendance
⚁ Degrees and awards received
⚁ Most recent educational institution attended
⚁ Photographs

Notes: These are just examples of directory information that are specifically found in FERPA or acknowledged by the Family Compliance Office to be examples. Note the use of the word MAY. In other words, institutions have a choice of selecting any, all or none of these items as directory information. What would be the implications of NOT designating anything as directory information?

Slide № 21 **WHAT CAN DIRECTORY INFORMATION NEVER INCLUDE?**

⚁ Race
⚁ Gender
⚁ Social security number (or part of an SSN)
⚁ Grades
⚁ GPA
⚁ Country of citizenship
⚁ Religion

Notes: The Family Policy Compliance Office has determined that releasing these items would be a violation of a student's privacy if released without the student's written permission.

Slide № 22 **DIRECTORY INFORMATION COLLEGE XYZ STYLE**

XYZ College has designated directory information according to the *Family Educational Rights and Privacy Act of 1974* to be the student's:

⚁ Name
⚁ Local and permanent address/telephone number
⚁ Major field of study
⚁ Participation in officially recognized activities/sports
⚁ Weight/height of members of athletic teams
⚁ Dates of attendance
⚁ Degrees and awards received and dates
⚁ Most recent previous educational institution attended
⚁ Academic level
⚁ Enrollment status (FT/PT)

Notes: At this point, with the proper foundation laid, you can now display on this slide what your institution identifies as directory information. This is a good "post-it" for future reference. Have this available as a separate handout or advise session participants to copy it and post it close to their phone.

Slide № 23 DIRECTORY INFORMATION

- ☒ It is important to remember that directory information be defined as such.
- ☒ If a data element isn't defined as directory information *it isn't* directory information and can only be released if the student's written permission is obtained or the release meets the requirements under one of the exceptions to student's written permission found in FERPA.

Notes: This slide emphasizes the importance of not releasing an item of information if it has not been identified as directory information. It also reinforces one of the two statements in the slide titled "The Essence of the Act." The exceptions to students' written permission are found in §99.31.

Slide № 24 DIRECTORY INFORMATION

- ☒ Student ID numbers (SINs)
  - ▶ The 2009 regulations made it clear that SIN's cannot be directory information unless they are being used as electronic personal identifiers (*e.g.*, as a user name), and
  - ▶ If used to access data systems, they must be used in conjunction with a secondary authentication factor, such as a secret password or PIN.

Notes: The basic recommendation is never to have SIN's considered directory information. However, because some institutions have made their SIN's user names and part of the authentication process for students to access student records systems, the 2009 regulations include a narrow exception to the directory information exclusion.

Slide № 25 REQUIREMENTS FOR COMPLIANCE

- ☒ Provide annual notification to students of their right to know:
  - ⑥ 1) that school officials within the institution may obtain information from education records without obtaining prior written consent, 2) the criteria for determining who will be considered school officials and 3) what "legitimate educational interests" will entitle school officials to have access to education records.

Notes: Now back to the point 6 mouthful! The first part of point 6 informs the student that "school officials" can have access to their education records without written permission. Seems obvious; but it is important to have this included as part of the law. The next two slides clarify who is a school official. Note the word "may" in the first line of part 6.

Slide № 26 "SCHOOL OFFICIALS"

A school official can be a person:

- ☒ Employed by the college in an administrative, supervisory, academic, research, or support staff position (including law enforcement and health staff personnel),
- ☒ Elected to the Board of Trustees,
- ☒ [Or a company] Employed by or under contract to the college to perform a specific task, such as, an agent, an attorney, an auditor, or an outsourced service provider.
- ☒ Serving as a student representative on an official committee, such as a disciplinary or grievance committee, or assisting another school official in performing his or her tasks.

Notes: There is no definition in FERPA for "school official." All that FERPA says regarding "school official" is that each institution must specify the "criteria for determining who constitutes a school official...." 34 CFR 99.7 (a)(2)(iii). Therefore it is up to each institution to identify who the "school officials" are for their institution and include those individuals or groups in the annual notification. This slide identifies the typical individuals and groups who can be identified as school officials. Note that individuals other than the institution's faculty and staff may be included as "school officials." Also, if an institution has graduate assistants and/or work-study students or has students serving on committees that have access to other students' education records, the institutional definition of "school official" must be broad enough to include these students for their specified tasks. It is not necessary to require these students to sign an agreement regarding the confidentiality of these records. Generally, students who are informed of the importance of their responsibilities regarding the privacy of education records under FERPA present little, if any, threat to the violation of that privacy. Train them on FERPA and then treat them as intelligent adults. Your trust will be amply rewarded. The 2009 regulations contain some specific accountability and contractual expectations for agents and contractors with the institution.

Slide № 27 AT XYZ COLLEGE, A SCHOOL OFFICIAL IS A PERSON

- ☒ Employed by the University in an administrative, supervisory, academic or research, or support staff position (including law enforcement unit personnel and health staff).
- ☒ [Or company] With whom the University has contracted, *e.g.*, attorney, auditor, collection agency.
- ☒ Serving on the Board of Trustees.
- ☒ [Or student] Serving on an official committee, such as a disciplinary or grievance committee, or assisting another school official in performing his or her tasks.

Notes: This slide illustrates a typical institutional statement regarding who is considered to be school officials. For this slide, substitute your institutional statement on who are school officials at your institution.

Slide № 28   REQUIREMENTS FOR COMPLIANCE

⊡ Provide annual notification to students of their right to know:

⑨ 1) that school officials within the institution may obtain information from education records *without obtaining prior written consent*, 2) the criteria for determining who will be considered school officials and 3) what legitimate educational interest will entitle school officials to have access to education records.

Notes: The term "legitimate educational interest" is coupled with the definition/identification of "school officials." It is important for these two terms to be associated with one another, *e.g.*, a "school official" must have a "legitimate educational interest" to have access to a student's education record. In other words, a school official cannot be on a fishing expedition when s/he reviews a student's records. There must be a purpose and that purpose must be covered in the institution's statement on "legitimate educational interest" and included in the annual notification to students.

Slide № 29   "LEGITIMATE EDUCATIONAL INTEREST"

⊡ The demonstrated need to know by those officials of an institution who act in the student's educational interest, including faculty, administrators, clerical and professional employees, and other persons who manage student record information.

⊡ Although FERPA does not define "legitimate educational interest", it states that institutions must specify the criteria for determining it.

Notes: Like the term "school officials", FERPA is silent on what constitutes a "legitimate educational interest." 34 CFR 99.7(a)(3)(iii). Therefore, each institution must articulate what this term means and include it in its annual notification. The definition in this slide came from an earlier *AACRAO FERPA Guide*. This provides another way of explaining/introducing "legitimate educational interest" to the group.

Slide № 30   "LEGITIMATE EDUCATIONAL INTEREST" AT XXX COLLEGE

A school official has a legitimate educational interest if the official needs to review an education record in order to fulfill his or her professional responsibility.

Notes: This slide is similar to the slide on "school official." You will want to substitute your institutional definition of "legitimate educational interest" here. An "educational need to know," or something similar, is sometimes used synonymously with "legitimate educational interest." The legal term used in FERPA is "legitimate educational interest." This term most commonly requires that, in order to view a student's record, a "school official" must be performing a duty or service related to a professional responsibility outlined in his/her contract. This statement may also be expanded to include designated agents that are performing duties that school officials would normally be performing.

Slide № 31   "LEGITIMATE EDUCATIONAL INTEREST"

Time for another story...
Story #2

Notes: Story #2 is a letter addressed to the Assistant Registrar of a major university. If this incident can happen at one institution, it can happen at any institution.
Dear Ms. XXXXXX:
I am writing concerning the release of information about my educational record to my ex-husband, XXXX, the Director of XXXX at XYZ University. I refer to the unofficial grade transcript that I gave to you during our meeting last week. I was separated from him in December, 2007 and divorced from him in October, 2008. We are currently involved in a court decision concerning custody of our two children. In his answers to interrogatories filed with my attorney on February 11, 2009, my ex-husband wrote that he would submit the "educational record" of me as evidence at the trial. My attorney said that he didn't know how my ex-husband would be able to supply the court with a copy of my transcript, since that information is protected. On March 3, his lawyer gave my lawyer several documents he intended to use as exhibits in court, including my grade transcript. The hearing date was March 4. At the hearing, his attorney did not submit my transcript itself, but he submitted a sheet showing a set of bar graphs representing my academic progress at XYZ University as opposed to his progress at Yale and Harvard. This sheet had been prepared by his new wife, a faculty member in the Statistics Department. In his testimony, my ex-husband also referred to my grades since the divorce, and to the fact that I had completed the required number of hours for an M.A., but had not yet completed my thesis. My ex-husband has obtained my unofficial transcript to further his case against me as a custodial parent. I am angry that he has gotten this personal information about me, and has shared it with his lawyer, my lawyer, his wife, and perhaps other people as well. I am proud of my academic record, but it is my record to disclose..." We, of course, would agree that this is a violation of a student's FERPA rights. It is also an example of a school official (the ex-husband) obtaining an education record without a legitimate educational interest. This was a serious violation of FERPA that could have had serious legal implications for the university. The lesson to be learned is that there needs to be a continuous attempt to inform all school officials, new and old, of their FERPA responsibilities. FERPA is a law that involves any employee who comes in contact with education records at any institution.

Slide № 32   REQUIREMENTS FOR COMPLIANCE

⊡ Provide annual notification to students of their FERPA rights

⊡ Provide students' access to their education records

Notes: This is a transition slide between part 1 (the annual notification requirement to students of their rights under FERPA) and part 2 (providing students access to their records). In other words, we're going to be looking into what FERPA says about how we permit students to look at their records and under what conditions that review can take place.

Slide № 33   REQUIREMENTS FOR COMPLIANCE

Provide students access to their education records

They have the right to:

① Inspect and review within 45 days of the request to inspect.

Notes: This slide emphasizes one of the major rights of students under FERPA: their right to review (access) their records. FERPA allows an institution 45 days to comply with a student's request to review their records. 45 days provides sufficient time if it is necessary to pull together education records from different sources, redact information about other students or research specific records questions raised by the student. It is not intended to encourage institutions to be unresponsive to records requests from students. Note: The hearing process (another FERPA right of the student) is not covered in this presentation due to time constraints and because FERPA hearings have not become prevalent happenings on college campuses. Some general guidelines in conducting FERPA hearings are found in this AACRAO FERPA Guide.

Slide № 34   REQUIREMENTS FOR COMPLIANCE

Limitations to the right to inspect
- Parental financial information
- Confidential letters and recommendations to which the student has waived his/her right of inspection
- Education records containing information about more than one student
  - ▶ The institution *must permit access* to that part of the record which pertains only to the inquiring student

Notes: There are three main areas of education records that students do not have the right to view. They are shown in this slide. If you come from a selective institution, you may want to find out how the admissions office handles confidential letters of recommendation. Some selective institutions request the applicant to indicate whether they waive, or do not waive, their right to inspect a confidential letter or recommendation prior to providing the form to the person requested to write the letter. Thus, the counselor, headmaster, principal, clergy, etc. knows before writing the letter If the student has waived the right to subsequently review the letter of recommendation. Remember that the confidential letter of recommendation becomes an "education record" if maintained by the institution after the student has begun attending the institution. Therefore, if the student has not waived his/her right to review the letter, or has not been given the opportunity to waive his/her right, it is subject to review by the student. You may want to find out if the individuals writing the letters of recommendations are assuming that these letters are confidential when, in fact, these letters may legally be reviewed by the student after the student is attending the institution. You may want to get an example of an admissions packet if you are from an institution that requires written recommendations from applicants. You will either find that the institution is not asking the student to waive their rights to subsequent review (therefore, the recommendation will be subject to review by the student after they are admitted) or there is a section where the "applicant" can indicate whether they have waived their right to subsequent review of the recommendation. This is probably a slide that should be included in presentations to both faculty and staff.

Slide № 35   PROCEDURES AND STRATEGIES FOR COMPLIANCE

- Disclosure of educational record information
  - ① Institutions shall obtain written consent from the student before disclosing any personally identifiable information from their education records (with the exceptions as noted in sections 2 and 3 below). The written consent must:
    - Ⓐ Specify the records to be released;
    - Ⓑ State the purpose of the disclosure;
    - Ⓒ Identify the party or parties to whom disclosure may be made; and
    - Ⓓ Be signed and dated by the student.

Notes: This is a summary slide regarding one of the basic rights in FERPA: a student's written permission is required to release information unless the release is permitted under one of the exceptions to written consent found in the law. Using a transcript request as an example, we normally get three of the four criteria specified in this slide: a. (the records to be released), c. (party/parties to whom

disclosure is to be made), and d. (signature of student and date). We often do not obtain b. (the purpose of the disclosure) particularly with a transcript request. Although this may be a technical violation of FERPA by not obtaining the purpose for the release, we must balance legal requirements against the realities of the amount of time it might take to obtain this information from the student if it was not provided initially. The most important of the criteria specified are: a. the records to be released, c. to whom, and d. the signature of the student whose records are to be released and date of the signature.

Slide № 36   PROCEDURES AND STRATEGIES FOR COMPLIANCE

- Disclosure of educational record information
  - ② Institutions *must* disclose education records *without written consent* of students *only to* students who request to see information from their own records

Notes: This is the only example in FERPA where we MUST release information about a student. All of the other releases are in the MAY category, and appear on later slides. The VA law authorizing payment to veterans for educational purposes requires education records to be made available to VA representatives.

Slide № 37   PROCEDURES AND STRATEGIES FOR COMPLIANCE

- Disclosure of educational record information
  - ③ Institutions *may* disclose education records *without written consent* of students to the following:
    - Ⓐ School officials, as discussed earlier.
    - Ⓑ Authorized representatives of the following for audit, evaluation, or enforcement of federal and state supported programs:
      - ▶ Comptroller General of the United States
      - ▶ Secretary, U.S. Department of Education
      - ▶ U.S. Attorney General (law enforcement only)
      - ▶ State educational authorities

Notes: The following nine slides are at the heart of where we spend most of our time as records keepers in interpreting FERPA. These slides show why and/or to whom education records may be released without the student's written permission. If you are a subscriber to regist-L, count how many FERPA questions fall into the "exceptions" category. In one survey of questions from registrar-l (regist-L) covering a period of three months in 2000, 8 out of every 10 questions on FERPA focused on "exceptions." Note the differences in these slides between the words "may" and "must". These words have a significant impact on how institutions comply with FERPA. It also means that institutions don't have to be consistent but may decide to release information based on an individual situation.

Slide № 38   PROCEDURES AND STRATEGIES FOR COMPLIANCE

- Disclosure of educational record information
  - ③ Institutions *may* disclose education records *without written consent* of students to the following:
    - Ⓒ Personnel within the institution determined by the institution to have a legitimate educational interest

Ⓓ Officials of other institutions in which the student seeks to enroll, on condition that the issuing institution makes a reasonable attempt to inform the student of the disclosure

Notes: A continuation of the exceptions-to-written-permission topic. Item c. permits institutions to send any non-directory information to institutions where the student is seeking to enroll. Note the notification requirement. Anecdotal: Shortly after FERPA was passed in 1974, a registrar received a call from the Dean of the Marshall University College of Education. The Dean said he had received a transcript from the registrar's institution from an applicant who was seeking admission to the graduate program in education at Marshall. The Dean said he believed the transcript had been forged and wanted assistance from the registrar to verify the forgery. Based on exception c. shown in this slide, the registrar was able to discuss the student's record with the Dean. They concluded that the applicant had given herself two additional years of credit and a bachelor's degree. The registrar notified the student of the disclosure and informed her that any transcripts that she requested to be sent in the future would have to be sent directly to a *bona fide* third party and not to herself. The registrar never heard from the student again.

Slide № 39 — PROCEDURES AND STRATEGIES FOR COMPLIANCE

✚ Disclosure of educational record information
③ Institutions *may* disclose education records *without written consent* of students to the following:
Ⓔ Persons or organizations providing to the student financial aid programs, or determining financial aid decisions
Ⓕ Organizations conducting studies to develop, validate, and administer predictive tests, to administer student aid programs, or to improve instruction

Notes: Under e., the definition of financial aid does not extend to parents. Institutions could however release grades to companies who are providing tuition reimbursement to their employees without obtaining written permission from the student. Remember an institution MAY do this. They do not have to. The intent of f. is to provide institutions with the ability to cooperate in regional, state, national standardized testing activities or studies that can be of benefit to the institution without obtaining the students' written permission first. This is the section that some registrars have used in justifying the release of personally identifiable information to doctoral students who are working on research related to their dissertation. This latter instance may be a "stretch," but as long as the researcher understands FERPA and agrees to keep the information confidential and destroy the information when finished, it is probably worth the risk. Again, this is a situational matter. You may approve one research request for personally identifiable information and not approve others. Or, you may decide to reject all requests.

Slide № 40 — PROCEDURES AND STRATEGIES FOR COMPLIANCE

✚ Disclosure of educational record information
③ Institutions *may* disclose education records *without written consent* of students to the following:
Ⓖ Accrediting organizations carrying out their accrediting functions

Ⓗ Parents of a student who have established that student's status as a dependent as defined by the IRS code

Notes: Under g., there have been times when accrediting groups have requested a random set of records to be reviewed by an accreditation team either prior to the on-site visit or during the on-site visit. This exception permits school officials to provide this information to members of the accrediting team without obtaining the student's written permission as long as the release is to comply with part of the accreditation process. Under h., this is where an institution may release non-directory information to parents. This also identifies the conditions under which parents qualify. IRS Code of 1986, Section 152 basically says that, in the last and most-recent federal income tax return of the parent, the student has been identified as a dependent. Institutions must determine that dependency first before releasing information to parents. If the dependency cannot be established, the parents are not entitled to non-directory information under this exception to written permission. A summary slide is provided later about what FERPA says about parents.

Slide № 41 — PROCEDURES AND STRATEGIES FOR COMPLIANCE

✚ Disclosure of educational record information
③ Institutions *may* disclose education records *without written consent* of students to the following:
Ⓘ Persons in compliance with a judicial order or a lawfully issued subpoena, provided that the institution first make a reasonable attempt to notify the student. *Exception:* If the subpoena is issued from a federal grand jury, or for a law enforcement purpose, and orders the institution *not* to notify the student.

Notes: This is the subpoena exception. Refer to the *AACRAO FERPA Guide* for more information on responding to subpoenas. The "Exception" in this slide was added in 1996 in response to law enforcement officials' requests that the student notification requirement in this section was hindering their law enforcement efforts (drug busts, etc.; if the student is notified, they have more of a tendency to disappear if they have broken the law). An IRS summons is similar to a subpoena.

Slide № 42 — PROCEDURES AND STRATEGIES FOR COMPLIANCE

✚ Disclosure of educational record information
③ Institutions *may* disclose education records *without written consent* of students to the following:
Ⓙ A court if the student has initiated legal action against the institution or the institution has initiated legal action against the student

Notes: This is a more recent addition to the list of written exceptions. This exception removes the necessity of an institution having to get into an awkward situation with a student regarding presenting the student's records in court. Prior to the inclusion of this exception, the institution would either have had to obtain the student's written permission to produce the records in court or issue a subpoena upon itself to produce the records.

Slide № 43 — PROCEDURES AND STRATEGIES FOR COMPLIANCE

- ▣ Disclosure of educational record information
  - ③ Institutions *may* disclose education records *without written consent* of students to the following:
    - Ⓚ Persons in an emergency, if it is determined that there is a rational basis to believe there is a significant threat to a student or other persons

Notes: This slide includes any kind of an emergency. Based on the tragedies at Virginia Tech and Northern Illinois, this exception is discussed significantly in the 2009 regulations. There is a relaxed standard for making a judgment of an emergency situation and an acknowledgement that if the decision-maker was acting reasonably in making his or her assessment of the situation, there will not be any liability incurred even if the situation does not turn out to be an emergency.

Slide № 44 — PROCEDURES AND STRATEGIES FOR COMPLIANCE

- ▣ Disclosure of educational record information
  - ③ Institutions *may* disclose education records *without written consent* of students to the following:
    - Ⓛ An alleged victim of any crime of violence of the results of any institutional disciplinary proceeding against the alleged perpetrator of that crime with respect to that crime

Notes: Basically this translates: The victim of a crime of violence should be informed of the results of an institutional hearing against the alleged perpetrator of that crime. That's true regardless of the outcome. The 2009 regulations clarified that the limits on redisclosure found in §99.33 do not apply to this release to the victim.

Slide № 45 — PROCEDURES AND STRATEGIES FOR COMPLIANCE

- ▣ Disclosure of educational record information
  - ③ Institutions *may* disclose education records *without written consent* of students to the following:
    - Ⓜ The public regarding the *final results* of an institutional disciplinary proceeding so long as the student has been determined to be the alleged perpetrator of a crime of violence or non-forcible sex offense.

Notes: This is another 2000 addition to the exceptions to written permission section of FERPA. It permits institutions to release the final results of an institutional disciplinary hearing after it has been determined that the student is the alleged perpetrator of a crime of violence or non-forcible sex offense. In other words, the institution may release this information to a newspaper if it wishes. It does not have to. "Final results" includes the initial finding of a violation and does not have to wait for any appeal outcome.

Slide № 46 — WHAT DO THE "FINAL RESULTS" INCLUDE?

- ▣ Must include only: the name of the student, violation committed, and any sanction imposed by the institution against the student.
- ▣ The institution may not disclose the name of any other student, including a victim or witness, without prior written consent of the other student.

Notes: These are two important provisions within this exception that relate to the "final results" of a disciplinary hearing and to the protection of the privacy of individuals other than the alleged perpetrator of the crime.

Slide № 47 — PROCEDURES AND STRATEGIES FOR COMPLIANCE

- ▣ Disclosure of educational record information
  - ③ Institutions *may* disclose education records *without written consent* of students to the following:
    - Ⓝ Parents of a student under the age of 21 regarding a violation of any law, at any level, or institutional policy or rule governing the use of alcohol or a controlled substance

Does not supersede any state law that prohibits disclosure of this information.

Slide № 48 — PROCEDURES AND STRATEGIES FOR COMPLIANCE

- ▣ Disclosure of educational record information
  - ④ Institutions *may* disclose information about students to their parents by any of four procedures:
    - ▶ By obtaining the student's written consent
    - ▶ By having the parents establish the student's dependency as defined by Internal Revenue Code
    - ▶ By exercising its disclosure option on any students under age 21 regarding a violation of an institutional rule or federal, state, or local law regarding the use of alcohol or controlled substance as long as state law permits
    - ▶ In a health or safety emergency

Notes: These next two slides relate to parents. This slide identifies what FERPA specifically says about how we can, if we wish, release information to parents. Institutions are not required to release any information to parents. Many faculty have questions about what to discuss with parents regarding their child's academics. They should know that they just can't talk about anything with the parents. If this hasn't occurred at your institution already, you might want to propose a policy regarding what to say to parents, or at least how to handle parental requests, about their child's records/academic performance.

Slide № 49   WHAT ABOUT PARENTS?

⊠ When a student reaches the age of 18 or begins attending a postsecondary institution regardless of age, FERPA rights transfer to the student.

⊠ Parents may obtain directory information at the discretion of the institution.

⊠ Parents may obtain non-directory information (grades, GPA, etc.) at the discretion of the institution *and* after it has been determined that their child is legally their dependent.

⊠ Parents may also obtain non-directory information by obtaining a signed consent from their child.

Notes: This summarizes in simple terms what FERPA says about parents. This is a good "post-it" for quick reference.

Slide № 50   PROCEDURES AND STRATEGIES FOR COMPLIANCE

⊠ Disclosure of educational record information

⑤ Institutions *may* release *without written consent* those records identified as public or directory information for students who are currently enrolled with the following conditions:

▶ That the institution inform the students of those categories designated as directory information

▶ That students be given the opportunity to refuse disclosure of any or all categories

▶ That the students be given a reasonable period of time in which to state such refusals in writing

Notes: This slide covers the responsibilities of institutions regarding directory information. Note that students must be given the opportunity to inform the institution that they don't want directory information released. Students do have the right to request that only one piece of directory information not be released. If this is difficult for your institution to handle, you may inform the student of this fact and tell the student that you will not disclose any directory information. The student then has the choice on what to do. Because release of directory information is permissible, not required, this is an acceptable alternative according to the Family Policy Compliance Office. From here on, except for the slides on the key terms and concepts, the slides may not be of interest to faculty attending the workshop.

Slide № 51   PROCEDURES AND STRATEGIES FOR COMPLIANCE

⊠ Disclosure of educational record information

⑥ Institutions may release *without written consent* those items identified as public or directory information on any students not currently enrolled.

⑦ Institutions may release *without written consent* information on any student found by a campus disciplinary body to have committed a crime of violence or non-violent sexual offense. The information that may be released is limited to the following: name, violation committed, sanction imposed by the institution.

⑧ Institutions are responsible for informing parties to whom personally identifiable information is released that recipients are *not* permitted to disclose the information to others *without written consent of the students*.

Notes: These are some additional points that staff would be more interested in than faculty. You can show an example of Item 8 from any transcript you have received from another institution. The "third party notification" should be found on all of these transcripts you have received.

Slide № 52   PROCEDURES AND STRATEGIES FOR COMPLIANCE

⊠ Records of requests and disclosures

① All institutions are required to maintain records of requests and disclosures of education records

▶ These records will include the names and addresses of the requestor and his/her indicated interest in the records.

Notes: Institutions are required to keep records of disclosures. However, as this and the next slides indicate, this requirement is minor and not burdensome.

Slide № 53   PROCEDURES AND STRATEGIES FOR COMPLIANCE

⊠ Records of requests and disclosures

② Records of requests and disclosure *do not* have to be kept for:

Ⓐ Requests from students for their own use

Ⓑ Disclosures in response to written requests from students

Ⓒ Requests made by school officials

Ⓓ Those specified as directory information

Ⓔ What's left?

Notes: The answer to e. is: Any release of non-directory information made to a third party who is not a school official. A common example is a release based on the receipt of a subpoena. While complying with the subpoena, simply make a copy of the appropriate documentation and file it in the student's folder, attached it to the student's digitized folder (if no paper folder exists), or file or digitize it within an administrative "folder" labeled "FERPA Releases." Create an alphabetical index of student names that are included in the "folder." Another example is release of a transcript. Most institutions require students to complete a transcript request, either online or with a paper form, so that request serves as the record.

Slide № 54   PROCEDURES AND STRATEGIES FOR COMPLIANCE

⊠ Records of requests and disclosures

③ These records of requests and disclosures are part of the student's education records and must be retained as long as the education records to which they refer are maintained by the institution.

KEY CONCEPTS REVISITED

- Required annual notification
- Written permission required for disclosure of student education record
- The exceptions to written permission of student
- Students' right to access their records
- The "musts" and "mays" in FERPA
- Parents/parental disclosure
- Legitimate educational interest

Notes: This is the second time this slide has been shown and is presented here to begin a summary of the presentation. These are the key concepts that one has to know to understand FERPA.

KEY TERMS RESVISTED

- Education Record
- Personally Identifiable
- Directory Information
- School Official

Notes: Again, these are the key terms within FERPA that are important for a working knowledge of FERPA.

CRITERIA TO BE USED IN DETERMINING A LEGITIMATE EDUCATIONAL INTEREST WHEN WRITING RECOMMENDATIONS

- Has the school established a criterion in its FERPA policy that appears to address disclosures for the purpose at issue?
- What does the faculty contract specify regarding the duties of faculty members? Does or did the faculty member teach the student in any course?
- What is the practice regarding recommendations at the school?
- Does the faculty member otherwise have personal knowledge of the student's abilities?
- Was the faculty member asked by the student to provide the recommendation?
- Is there any state law on this issue?

Notes: You probably won't want to include this in the presentation but this is a set of questions that the Family Policy Compliance Office would use to determine if there was a FERPA violation in writing a letter of recommendation.

SAMPLE PERMISSION LETTER TO WRITE A LETTER OF RECOMMENDATION

I give permission to Prof. Kostal to write a letter of recommendation to:

Annie's Catering
344 Willow Dr.
Lynchburg VA 24502

Prof. Kostal has my permission to include my grades, GPA, and class rank in this letter.

I waive/do not waive my right to review a copy of this letter at any time in the future.

_____
    Signature   Date

Notes: This is an example of a form that school officials (this includes faculty, of course) can use with students who wish for the school official to write a letter of recommendation that includes non-directory information that is maintained by the institution such as grades, GPA, class rank. If any non-directory information is included in a letter of recommendation, the student's written permission is required to include any of these items. This slide was added because a student filed a complaint with the Family Policy Compliance Office after a faculty member had included a grade and GPA in a letter of recommendation without obtaining the student's permission to do so. The Family Policy Compliance Office determined that the faculty member violated FERPA.

BALANCE POINTS/CHALLENGES

- The public's right to know vs. individual privacy rights
- Providing service vs. protecting access to information
- FERPA vs. state's open records laws

FERPA INFORMATION SOURCES

Family Policy Compliance Office
U.S. Department of Education
400 Maryland Ave., SW
Washington, D.C. 20202–5901
202–260–3887 (phone)
202–260–9001 (fax)
ferpa@ed.gov
www2.ed.gov/policy/gen/guid/fpco/index.html
Or
ferpa@aacrao.org

Notes: And, if all else fails, this is the information you need to obtain assistance with your FERPA queries.

FERPA Case Studies with Answers

Pick and choose case studies based on your audience and time allotted. Using case studies provides an opportunity for hands-on exposure to practical FERPA-related issues. Consider breaking into small groups for discussion of possible solutions, and then come back together for analysis and sharing.

Sole Possession Notes

Joe Student is assigned to Annie Adviser. At one point during the year, he asks if he may view his education record, including everything that Annie has written about him. He is concerned about what personal information Annie has included. Does FERPA allow access to all of his record? If not, can he still see his record? A year later, Joe is now assigned to Bill Adviser, who "inherited" Joe (and his record) from Annie. If Joe asks to see his record again, would there be any limitations? How should the institution respond?

Records "within the exclusive control of the maker" do not need to be released, although the concept of "sole possession" records is that they are memory-jogging types of notes, not a means by which to "hide" important student records information. The rest must be released after removing references to other students. Once given to Bill Adviser, the entire record becomes an education record, accessible to Joe.

Talking with Parents

You are an adviser in a college office. You receive a call from Dave and Kathy Smith, the parents of one of your former students. Their son, Kevin, was dismissed over a year ago. Dave and Kathy live in Florida and have been paying Kevin to attend your college for every term during the last three years, including room and board and out-of-state tuition. They called to see how things were going since they don't hear much from Kevin about school. How do you handle this conversation?

FERPA permits disclosure of information from education records to parents of students in a few different circumstances:

* *A health or safety emergency situation.*
* *When the student has been found in violation of conduct related to a controlled substance or alcohol and is under the age of 21.*
* *When the student is dependent based on the IRS definition of "dependency."*
* *When you have written permission from the student.*

Here, prior consent is required to release anything but directory information. However, so long as Kevin has not opted out of directory information, the school official could inform the parent that Kevin is not a student at the institution. You cannot tell the parents he was dismissed. Also, consider practical tips for talking with the parents. Find out what they already know and then build from it. If appropriate, discuss use of the dependency exception for providing access to Kevin's record.

Access by Divorced Parents

Frank's parents are divorced. By agreement, his mother claims him as dependent, but his father is required to pay his way through college. Frank and his mother have both refused to tell Frank's father anything about his academic progress at State College. Frank's father turns to the institution for help. Can the institution give him the information?

The regulations allow release of information to either parent if the student is claimed as a dependent on either parent's taxes. The institution should obtain a copy of the tax return validating dependency prior to disclosing the information. The father may need to resort to court action to gain access to the education records information.

Parents who are Employed at the Institution/ "Legitimate Educational Interest"

Stephanie Student attends Cole College as an undergraduate. Her father is a faculty member in the medical school there. He wants to find out how Stephanie is doing in school, so he calls the registrar's office to find out. How should the office respond?

The father does not have a legitimate "need to know" Stephanie's record even though he is on the faculty. You need to get a signed consent from Stephanie or show dependency.

Talking with Parents or Third Parties

Following commencement, you are helping to distribute diplomas to students who did not attend the ceremony. Cindy Student and her parents come up to get her diploma. You check the student's record and discover that Cindy was dismissed a year ago. How would you handle this situation in light of FERPA?

It would be advisable to receive written consent from the student, even if agreeing to meet with the student and parents together. If the student refuses, you can release only directory information, unless the parents can provide proof that the student has been claimed as a dependent on the most recent tax submission.

Responding to Subpoenas

State University in Michigan received a subpoena for Gene Student's academic record. The subpoena is from a State court in California and the materials are due tomorrow. How should the institution respond? What if the subpoena specifically stated that the student is not to be informed?

Since the court is in California, and does not have jurisdiction over your institution, do you care? If you decide to comply, then make sure that you follow the procedures in §99.31 (see page 154). You always need to provide time for the student to get included in the "loop," unless it is an ex parte, Grand Jury or law enforcement subpoena that specifically states otherwise. Just because a subpoena states you shouldn't inform the student doesn't mean that you are not obligated to do so.

State Databases

Your State Board of Higher Education is establishing a centralized database for student data, and your institution is a state school. They are asking for detailed records information concerning every student enrolled at any state institution. This data will be used to review academic programs across the state, conduct studies regarding educational trends, and provide data regarding articulation among the institutions. You work in the Enrollment Services Office and have been asked to prepare this data for the Board. Should you have any FERPA concerns?

As it relates to analysis within the state agency, the regulations provide for the release of personally identifiable information to a state or federal agency for this purpose. It is the responsibility for the agency to take the appropriate steps to protect the integrity of the data once received, and ensure that it is used solely for the purposes intended. In general, data should only be publicly released by the agency in the aggregate, and once no longer needed, the personally identifiable information should be destroyed. However, as this request applies to release of student information to other institutions, any disclosure would need to be limited to directory information. For example, it would be appropriate to share the names of students who have transferred, but not their social security numbers.

Admissions Records

Jan Student applied to be a graduate student at State University and was denied. She demands to see her admissions file, including all her reference letters. Does she have a right to access this information? What are the issues to address in making that decision? What if she later enrolls to audit a course since she had been denied regular admission? Same result? Could State University have destroyed her admission file, thus denying her access? What if she attended State University as an undergraduate? How should the institution respond?

Tarka v. Franklin (5th Cir., 1989). Student was not admitted as a regular student and the University of Texas did not have to release the information under FERPA since the student was not "enrolled." Enrolling as an auditor was also not sufficient to provide access to the admissions record related to the Graduate School. Since there is no records retention plan within FERPA, the institution could have destroyed the record within its established records retention plan. The records, however, may be accessible by the student under the state's open records law. In fact, that happened with this case in Texas.

Private Cause of Action under FERPA

Ralph Student feels that his college records have been released inappropriately. Can Ralph use FERPA to bring a suit against the college? Why or why not? What other options might he have as well? How should the institution respond?

There is no private cause of action under FERPA. This issue was recently confirmed by the U.S. Supreme Court in Gonzaga University and Robert S League v. John Doe, a 2002 decision. The student might want to pursue action under a Common Law remedy, such as libel or slander.

Use of Technology in Transferring Education Records

Sally Student has applied to your institution as a transfer student and you want to receive a transcript of her previous education record. Can you request to have the information sent to you electronically? Do you need to get written permission from the student in order to receive Sally's transcript from her previous school?

FERPA does not address how a record is transmitted, so you just need to address the procedural and security issues that you always have with the release of transcripts. The regulations provide the opportunity for an institution to release student records information to another institution when one of its students has enrolled or applied to enroll at the second institution. However, the fact that the initial institution follows this approach must be clearly stated in the institution's FERPA annual notification so that students have reasonable notice of this procedure. If the institution's annual notice does not state that you forward records, the student must be notified when his or her record is disclosed under this exception. It should also be noted that many applications for admission include a statement for the student to sign which permits the first institution to send the student record, upon request, to the second institution. Regardless of the manner in which the education record is transferred, most institutions ask students to submit a transcript request (either in writing or via a secured electronic application) to forward the record. That way there is both a record of the permission and the records transfer.

Sending Transcripts

Debbie Student needs transcripts sent immediately to a prospective employer in Illinois. She is currently attending graduate school in Michigan, but graduated from a university in Ohio last year. She calls you in the Registrar's Office at the Ohio school. What are your options?

Option 1: Debbie could fax written consent for you to release a transcript.

Option 2: Ask whether or not the Michigan institution would send both the current and previous transcripts. While most institutions would not be willing to forward a copy of a previous intsitution's transcript, some might.

Option 3: Send the request using express mail.

Option 4: Electronic request, utilizing an e-signature.

Posting Grades

John Faculty is tired of taking phone calls from students to find out their grades after every examination, so he decided to post their grades on the wall outside his office door. Should he do this? If yes, are there any limitations to the manner in which he posts them?

In general this is not a good practice since many institutions have electronic means for students to view their grades in near real-time. If the faculty member insists on this practice he/she can do so; however the grades must be posted in such a manner known only to the individual student and the instructor. For example, a code established at the beginning of the term could work. Grades should not be posted in the same order as a class roster or in alphabetical order.

Students as Student Employees/Disciplinary Records

Sue Student works in the registrar's office. She has an ax to grind with her ex-boyfriend, Ken, so she tells his fraternity brothers that he was recently placed on academic probation and is in danger of being dismissed. She knows that Ken cannot continue to hold his office position in the fraternity if they know that his grades are bad. She viewed Ken's grades while working in the registrar's office. Obviously, Ken and his parents are very upset, and have hired an attorney to address this situation. Can Ken's attorney use FERPA or the state's open records law to determine if any disciplinary action can be taken by the university against Sue? Would it make a difference if the university was private or public? Would it make a difference if Sue was a regular employee rather than a student? How should the institution respond?

Sue should not have looked at nor released the information from Ken's record. If the office knows she did so, the institution should take disciplinary action. That said, FERPA precludes release of Sue's employment information since because she holds her position as a student, Sue's employment records are "education records." FERPA trumps the typical state's open records law, and thus a state's open records law might not be applicable. However, even if it were, a state's open records law would probably apply only to state (public) institutions, rather than to private ones. If Sue was a regular employee, then FERPA would not apply and the typical state open records law might require release of the information.

Disciplinary Records, Scenario 1

Paul Student was assaulted on campus a few weeks ago. Campus security was able to track down the alleged assailant based on Paul's description. It turned out to be another student. Paul filed charges with the local police department, and also with the campus judicial office. He knows that a hearing was held on campus, but he hasn't been able to find out what the outcome was because the hearing was confidential. Does Paul have the right to know what happened at the hearing?

Since this was a "crime of violence," the institution may release the hearing results to the alleged victim regardless of the outcome and to the general public if the student perpetrator was found in violation of the institution's code of conduct.

Disciplinary Records, Scenario 2

"University Gossip," the student newspaper at State University in Ohio asks the judicial affairs office for details about judicial cases on campus. They believe it is their First Amendment right to have access to the information, and that students across campus have a right to know about campus crime and other judicial actions. Is this a FERPA issue? What should be released to them?

Disciplinary records are education records, and therefore covered by FERPA. Federal Court decisions have affirmed this Department of Education interpretation. In 2000, the Federal District Court in Columbus, Ohio held that disciplinary records were, in fact, education records and permanently enjoined the institutions involved from releasing personally identifiable information from those records. That decision was

affirmed on appeal by the 6th Circuit Court of Appeals in 2002. However, note that FERPA now allows certain limited release of the outcome of disciplinary hearings related to "crimes of violence."

Access by Campus Law Enforcement Officials

Detective Sanders from campus security calls your office to get the address for a student. In the same conversation he asks for the class schedule for that student. Do you give it to him? What if Detective Sanders says that he has a warrant for his arrest?

FERPA regulations consider campus security officials as employees with a "legitimate educational interest" if they are designated as "school officials" and operating within the scope of their employment. The warrant would not be necessary. It is advisable for institutions to include campus law enforcement personnel as school officials in the annual notification to students.

Alumni Records

Tom Terrific graduated from State University several years ago. He has been very involved as an alumnus. A journalism student wants to write a story about his involvement at the university, both as a student and as an alumnus. What can be released to the student?

Alumni records are generally open to the public because they are not "education records" under FERPA. However, that does not mean that Tom's education records information from when he was a student is releasable. You can release only directory information regarding education records from when Tom was a student. If the journalism program has a way to contact Tom Terrific and get his permission to release non-directory information, you can accept a signed release from him. Also, since this is a state school, the state's open records law may apply to any "alumni records" since FERPA does not.

Student Loan Clearinghouse/Agents

Your institution is very excited about the possibility of participating in the National Student Clearinghouse. Rather than your institution having to verify enrollment information separately to each lending agency, most of this process would occur through the one, centralized clearinghouse. To participate, your institution would need to provide enrollment information about all its students to the Clearinghouse. What FERPA considerations are there?

The Department of Education says that the Clearinghouse is acting as a legal agent of the institutions contracting with the NSC. Therefore, you may release information about non-loan students. The financial aid exception in the regulations allows access for all the students receiving aid. It is advised that all schools that intend to release information to agents or contractors include these entities in the annual notification to students. They do not need to be enumerated by name, but rather a statement that the institution may release non-directory information to agencies with whom it contracts for services.

Records of Deceased Former Students

George is doing some family background research. He discovers that his deceased great grandmother attended Goodman State University many years ago. He asked the registrar's office at Goodman State for any records they have for his great grandmother. What should they provide?

FERPA rights, and, in general, the right to privacy, end at death. State law may dictate some parameters for dealing with records for deceased persons, but this is fundamentally an institutional policy decision. Many institutions tend to treat records for deceased students as they would for living students, except that the "next of kin" is viewed as the "owner" of the record since the student is deceased. It is also appropriate to ask for proof of death if not already recorded in the institution's data files.

Violation of Substance Abuse Records

John Student was caught smoking marijuana in his residence hall room at State University. The residence hall director wonders whether or not it is appropriate or even allowed for him to contact John's parents since John is 20 years old and is no longer dependent on his parents.

FERPA provides flexibility for the institution to contact parents of students under the age of 21—regardless of whether or not they are dependent for tax purposes (and therefore within the FERPA definition)—if a student has been found in violation of institutional policy or any laws/regulations related to substance abuse. Note

that there is no affirmative requirement for the institution to do so. Note also that state law may prohibit such disclosure without permission from the student.

Class Web-based Discussion Sites

Fred Faculty teaches a course that has a Web-based discussion component. Class members can see each other's email addresses and name. It is not open to the public for view or use. Are there any FERPA issues?

Since the discussion site is only accessible to students in the class, there is no FERPA issue. It is advisable for the faculty member to remind class members that the discussion threads should not be shared with others outside the class without permission from the author to do so. No non-directory information should be displayed on the site. The 2009 FERPA regulations specifically state that student usernames can be displayed to others in a class, even if the students in question have chosen "no release" for their directory information.

Class Web-based Discussion Sites, Part 2

Instructor Ivana wants to make her online course management (*i.e.*, Moodle) pages publicly accessible to anyone. Are there FERPA implications for making this information available to individuals beyond the course?

Yes. Specific course registrations and personally identifiable class materials from students are not directory information. Therefore, they should not be publically accessible. Additionally, there may be students in the course who have chosen "no release" for their directory information; displaying their information effectively disregards this request. The instructor can offer a voluntary "public" version of her course but cannot compel students to participate.

Podcasting Classes

Professor Pendergast wants to publicly podcast the entire content of his courses. This includes class discussion. He decides this shortly before the term begins and hasn't notified registered students that this will be occurring. What are the FERPA implications for this practice?

Student participation in class discussions should not be made public without their express written permission.

Grades and Honors

Prestigious Engineering Firm has asked you, the Registrar, for a list of the names and addresses of engineering students in the top 10% of the senior class so that they can send them information regarding a tremendous employment opportunity. How should you respond?

The institution should establish a policy about release of information to third parties. Grades/GPA can never be directory information. It is OK to release directory information, but the designation of top 10% is not typically directory information, and is more likely to be considered "too close" to releasing actual grades information. However, it should be OK to release the "Dean's List" without consent, if that honor is included in your directory information. You could also offer to have the firm provide you their recruiting materials which the institution could forward on to students who meet their qualifications.

Financial Aid Issues

You work in the financial aid office. You are talking with a member of an alumni group. They are establishing a new scholarship to be offered to students from their local area who are attending your institution. The evaluation of the applications will be done by a scholarship board from the alumni group. The alumnus has asked you for the names, addresses and GPAs for all the currently-enrolled students from that area. What should you give them?

Since the alumni are not employees of the institution, they could not generally be provided personally identifiable information from student records. Therefore, you should only release directory information to them. However, if students applying for financial aid have given written permission to release information to third parties in reviewing all their financial aid opportunities, you could release their information.

Class Announcements

You hear that George Professor requested aloud to his class that any disabled students in the room identify themselves, by holding up their hands, if they need special accommodations for the class or for tests. Was this approach appropriate according to FERPA? What suggestions would you give to the faculty member?

This is certainly not an ethical approach, even if it doesn't directly violate FERPA. Consider options, such as asking the student to call, visit during office hours, or meet after class.

Change in Record

Jeff Student graduated from State University last year. It was recently discovered that he plagiarized some of the work on his dissertation and his Ph.D. was revoked. You receive an inquiry over the telephone from a potential employer about his academic record. What should you say? Should you do anything else since his degree was revoked?

Degree information would typically be considered directory information; however, before confirming whether or not Jeff has a degree you must check if he has requested a non-release. If he has not, you can confirm that the student does not have a degree from your institution. Don't say that the Ph.D. was revoked; simply say that he has not received one from your institution. You might want to consider contacting others who have requested an official transcript since the Ph.D. was awarded to give them a "corrected" copy.

Emergency Situation, #1

Mom calls the registrar's office, looking for information about her son, Travis. She has not heard from him in three days and he does not answer his cell phone. She is worried. She wants the names, phone numbers and emails of her son's instructors to verify with them if he has been coming to class. Should you provide that information?

Under routine circumstances, you would not release course information to Mom since course enrollment information is not likely considered directory information. You could contact the faculty members on behalf of Mom to inquire about Travis' attendance, or you could send someone from your office or the university police to the class to talk with the student. If you felt that this was a genuine health or safety emergency, you would have more flexibility to release information, but here you have a very reasonable alternative. If it turns out that Travis has recently not been attending class, it would then be advisable to contact the police and let Mom know. In addition, if you or others have recently seen Travis you could communicate that information to Mom since it is not information from an education record.

Emergency Situation, #2

Cindy, a student at your campus, has attempted suicide. An adviser from her college office calls asking about whether or not they can initiate a withdrawal for the student per the parent's request. The student is coherent, but still very shaky. What would you tell the adviser? Does it make a difference if the student has a no release on her record? Does it matter if this occurs earlier or later in the semester?

If you are able to obtain the student's permission to begin withdrawal procedures, you should do so. If not, you will need to use your professional judgment.

Implied Consent and FERPA

Ted Student is a very outspoken and well-known student-athlete at Barrett University. In a recent news conference he discussed a great deal of information about his academic and disciplinary record. A nosy reporter calls you in the registrar's office to confirm the information and to get some more details. What should you tell him?

You can only give out directory information (assuming Ted does not have a "no release"). Even though the student made the information public, you still need a student release in order to release or, in this case, confirm it. There is no implied consent with FERPA. An effective strategy would be to provide the reporter with a consent form and suggest getting the student's signature on it. This places the burden on the student to decide whether or not to release the information to the reporter.

FERPA and the Solomon Amendment

You are new in the registrar's office and are responsible for responding to data requests. You just received a request from the local Marine recruiter, asking for a long list of information about most of your students. The recruiter based the request on the Solomon Amendment. What should you give him?

The Department of Education has determined that the Solomon Amendment supersedes most elements of FERPA. An institution is therefore obligated to release data included in the list of "Student Recruiting Information," which may or may not match the FERPA directory information list you have published for your students. However, it has also been interpreted that the "No Release" code placed on student records for FERPA directory information can also be applied to

release of information under the Solomon Amendment because the student has asked that no information be released to any third party. Therefore, data regarding those students can be removed from any data released to the recruiter.

Consortia/Exchange Programs

You have developed an exchange program with an institution in Russia. The president of this Russian university wants to stay current with the academic progress of all the Russian students, so would like to receive their grades each term. As the students' advisor, you hear that some of the students would prefer that you not forward the grades to the Russian school authorities. What do you do?

Two possible solutions to consider:
* *Is the program realistically considered a joint-enrollment program between both institutions? If so, then does the president of the Russian school have a legitimate "need to know" the student information? If yes, then the information can be forwarded, even without the students' consent. If this will be the normal course of business for the program, you may want to consider notifying participants of this in advance.*
* *Consider asking the students when they apply or register for the program for permission to exchange this information with the "home" school. That way, they have not only been notified in advance, they have authorized the release of the data.*

Research Exception for Disclosure to Another Institution

A high school guidance counselor at a local high school contacts your office seeking student level course and grade information on students who previously attended her high school and are now enrolled at your institution. The counselor goes on to say that the reason she wants the data is to evaluate the success of the college prep and advanced placement courses that are taught at the high school. She was assigned this research project by the principal of her high school. How do you respond?

The research exception within FERPA applies only to studies or research done on behalf of the institution where the student is currently enrolled. Since this is not the case here, then the information cannot be released. One option would be for the counselor to obtain releases from each student whose record she wishes to evaluate. Also, assuming the number of students is large enough, you might be able to at least provide some non student identifiable summative outcome information or aggregate data.

Student ID Numbers (SINs) as Directory Information

Your institution is reviewing whether or not your list of directory information items should be updated. It was proposed that student ID numbers should be included so that it could be listed in the online Student Directory. Are there any FERPA considerations?

The 2009 regulations establish that student ID numbers cannot be considered directory information items unless expressly necessary as electronic identifiers, and only in conjunction with other security protocols. The amendments also confirmed that social security numbers can never be directory information nor used in confirming directory information without a signed consent.

Distance Education Course Enrollment

Your institution is increasingly enrolling students in online coursework. A student in one of those classes asked you if her educational record was covered by FERPA in the same manner as students taking classes in the traditional way. What do you tell her?

The 2009 regulations clarify that education records on students in non physical presence circumstances are subject to FERPA.

Definition of "Personally Identifiable"

You have been asked to provide information about student-athletes at your institution, including their graduation success rate, and sorted out by sport and race. The names of the individual athletes would not be included. Clearly, race is not a directory information item, but should you be concerned about anything else from a FERPA perspective in releasing the data?

Releasing student information in the aggregate is permissible under FERPA so long as the identity of an individual student cannot reasonably be extrapolated from the aggregate data. The 2009 regulations replaced the term "easily traceable" with "identifiable with reasonable certainly" to apply to these circumstances.

Validating a Transcript

You receive a call from the Registrar at Distant University. A former student from your institution has submitted a transcript from your institution to Distant U. The Registrar is concerned that the transcript has been falsified. What can you tell him?

The 2009 regulations clarify that it is appropriate for the purported source of an education record to be able to validate the authenticity of that record to the recipient.

"Legitimate Educational Interest" Access to Educational Records

You are helping to design security protocols for your new student information system. You heard that you can allow access only to those faculty and staff with a clear "legitimate educational interest" for individual student records. How detailed does your online security system need to be to meet expectations?

The 2009 regulations clarify that institutions are expected to use "reasonable methods" to ensure that an official is given access to only those education records in which the official has a legitimate educational interest. These reasonable methods can include systems functionality, institutional policies and institutional business practices or a combination of those. However, the institution must be able to demonstrate that any such methods are effective in keeping it in compliance with the legitimate educational interest requirements in §99.31(a)(1)(i)(A).

Data Breach

Professor Paulson calls you in the registrar's office to tell you that his laptop was stolen. There were student record files on the machine, including grades. Are there any FERPA issues? Other legal issues? What advice might you give the professor?

It would be a violation of FERPA, albeit completely unintended, if the thief was able to access the "student identifiable information" beyond any directory information. This would constitute inappropriate release of information to a "third party."

The 2009 regulations to FERPA outline some guidelines and recommendations for safeguarding and responding to data breaches. Suggested responses for data breaches and other unauthorized disclosures include:

* Reporting the incident to law enforcement authorities. Depending on the nature of the breach, you may also have state or federal legal obligations. For example, if the data files contained SSNs, many states have reporting and notification requirements.
* Taking steps to retrieve data and prevent further disclosures.
* Identifying all affected records and students. It may be appropriate—even required—for you to notify the students affected.
* Determining how the incident occurred. How can you prevent similar future exposures?
* Determining whether institutional policies and procedures were breached. Do you have policies related to breaches, encrypting student data on laptops, the appropriateness of student data on laptops, etc.?
* Conducting a risk assessment.

Non-Credit Courses

Janet Adviser from your continuing education division asks you whether or not the records for students in the non-credit classes offered by CED are covered under FERPA. Are they?

If the records contain personally identifiable information about students and are maintained in any way by the institution, then the fact that they are non-credit is not relevant. They are education records and are covered by FERPA.

High School Dual Enrollment Students

Melanie is a senior in high school and is also taking classes at LCC, the local community college. The classes she is taking at LCC count both for high school and college credit. How does FERPA apply to her education records?

FERPA applies to both primary/secondary and college/university records, but in different ways. For post-secondary enrollment, the "ownership" of the education record is vested with the student, regardless of his or her age. However, until a student begins college work or turns 18, whichever occurs first, the "ownership" of a student's education record is considered held by the student's parents or legal guardians. Thus, the typical record for a high school student is managed by the student's parents. That is why grades and other education records information for high school students are routinely released to parents.

However, that is not true for a college student. Unless the student has signed a consent form or the parents have established the student's dependency status with the institution, grades are not routinely released to parents.

In this scenario, Melanie is both a high school and a college student. The university should treat her as it would any other college student and her records are treated accordingly as well. Most state provisions for postsecondary enrollment option (dual enrollment students) contain reporting requirements, including grades, back to the high school or secondary school district. Since it is routine for most high schools to communicate grade information to parents, the likely result is that LCC releases grades to Melanie, and to Melanie's high school. In turn, the high school likely releases grade information to Melanie's parents.

Faculty Access to Admissions Records

Fred Faculty wants to review the admissions file, including transcripts for students currently in his program. Is this permissible?

In general, faculty members do not have a legitimate need-to-know to access admissions files once an admissions decision has been made.

Access to Student Records Information by Student Organizations

The Smart Student Honor Society requests a list of students with 3.85 cumulative GPAs or higher. Can you comply with their request?

Student organizations, including honor societies, can generally be provided only directory information. If your institution has designated honors as directory information you may provide this list, after first removing students who have opted for no-release of their directory information. Alternatively, the honor society can provide you with their membership materials and you can distribute them to students who meet their stated criteria.

Access to Student Records Information by Third-Party Financial Supporter

Phil Student has education benefits from the company for whom he works. After the completion of a term, a representative from the company contacts the registrar's office to validate Phil's enrollment and academic progress. What can you tell them?

You can certainly verify enrollment and anything that is directory information (assuming Phil has a "Y" release on his record). Beyond that, you would need to have written permission from Phil to release additional information. Many, if not most, employer-sponsored education programs require the employee to authorize release of certain education records information as part of the program's application process. So, the company may, in fact, already have a waiver they can forward to you. If the student applied for financial aid, the financial aid exception might also apply to this case.

Student Athlete Transferring to Another School

Sally Student Athlete is transferring to another school. The school she is intending to attend requests that you complete a transfer form, certifying the student is still eligible to compete at your institution. Can you complete this form? Can you include information on GPA, disciplinary issues, or financial issues?

The 2009 FERPA regulations clarify that an institution can provide information, including grades and disciplinary records, to institutions where a student seeks or intends to enroll. So, yes, you can provide the requested information.

True/False Quiz

The following tool might be used as a "teaser" to provide a sense of a person's familiarity/comfort level with FERPA, as well as a training tool. Pick and choose items based on time available and/or how the instrument is being utilized.

Answers to this quiz can be found at the end of this chapter on page 97.

1. ___ "Education records" include only those records contained in a student's permanent file.

2. ___ Students must be given the opportunity to inspect and review their education records within 10 days of a request.

3. ___ Faculty has the right to inspect and review the education records of any student.

4. ___ If a student discloses in an open forum that he has been suspended and that he feels the suspension is unwarranted, the school may infer that he has given implied consent for openly discussing the issue.

5. ___ An adviser does not have to allow a student to inspect and review her personal notes about the student that are held in a file in the desk of the adviser's office.

6. ___ The institution doesn't need to provide access to the educational records of a student to a noncustodial parent if the custodial parent submits a notarized statement that he or she does not consent to the disclosure.

7. ___ A school does not have to send education records to another school in which a student seeks or intends to enroll if the student has an outstanding balance to the current institution.

8. ___ A student has the right to inspect and review an essay submitted by the student, even if the teacher does not intend to return it to the student or to permanently maintain it.

9. ___ Health records, maintained at the student health center, are education records, subject to FERPA.

10. ___ A college newspaper has the right of access to detailed information about disciplinary hearings for students at the institution.

11. ___ A state institution in Ohio must respond to a subpoena received from the Supreme Court of California.

12. ___ An institution should provide data to an engineering firm which asks for a list of all the College of Engineering students who are in the top 10 percent of the senior class.

13. ___ Tom Faculty has posted the grades of all the students in his class on the wall outside his office. This is a violation of FERPA.

14. ___ Sally Student, who is not a dependent student, has been found in violation of the university's residence halls' alcohol policies. Her hall director could contact her parents to discuss the violation without her permission.

15. ___ Admissions records are "education records," therefore covered under FERPA.

16. ___ A student's social security number (SSN) could be verified to a caller who received a document with the student's SSN on it.

17. ___ Ralph Student feels that his college records have been released inappropriately. Ralph can use FERPA to bring a suit against the college.

18. ___ Tom Terrific graduated from State University several years ago. He has been very involved as an alumnus. A journalism student wants to write a story about his involvement at the university, both as a student and as an alumnus. The university should release only his alumni information.

19. ___ Using the institutional student ID number (SIN), Tom Faculty has posted the grades of all the students in his class on the wall outside his office. This is violation of FERPA.

20. ___ "Student recruiting information" under the Solomon Amendment is the same as "directory information" under FERPA.

A FERPA Final Exam

This examination is designed to test your knowledge of the *Family Educational Rights and Privacy Act of 1974 as Amended* (FERPA). An electronic version of this exam is downloadable from AACRAO's Web site at www.aacrao.org/compliance/ferpa/.

You may also consider using part of the exam (*e.g.*, just the T/F questions) as a "teaser" or introduction to a FERPA training session or presentation. Answers to this quiz can be found at the end of this chapter on page 98.

CONFIDENTIALITY AND STUDENT EDUCATION RECORDS

The answers to the first section are either *True* or *False*. Mark either a "T" or "F" on each line next to the statement.

1. ___ A student's degree can be confirmed to some external (outside of your college) source without first obtaining the permission of the student as long as the institution identifies "degree" as directory information.

2. ___ A student has a right to inspect information in his or her file in the registrar's office and in his or her major department.

3. ___ It is permissible for a professor to post student grades on an office door if only a student's social security number (or portion) is used.

4. ___ The registrar may release information about a student without the student's written permission upon receipt of a properly issued subpoena.

5. ___ Parents may obtain confidential information from their student's academic record if the student is financially dependent under IRS standards.

6. ___ Your college must annually notify students of their rights under the FERPA.

7. ___ In a legal separation or divorce situation, biological parents have equal standing as custodial parents to gain access to the student's education records.

8. ___ Faculty has a right to inspect education records of any student attending your college without giving a reason.

9. ___ Student representatives on committees (*e.g.*, honors, curriculum, etc.) have the right to see other students' education records during the deliberations of that committee if they have been designated as school officials.

10. ___ An institution must give its students the opportunity to withhold the release of any or all designated items of directory information.

11. ___ It is permissible to distribute graded examinations by placing them on a table for students to pick up after class.

12. ___ Email addresses can be considered directory information.

13. ___ "Student recruiting information" under the Solomon Amendment is the same as "directory information" under FERPA.

14. ___ In writing a letter of recommendation, it is permissible for a faculty member to include a student's grades and GPA without obtaining the student's written permission since the student requested the faculty member to write the recommendation and provided a copy of her resume with the requested information to the faculty member.

15. ___ Former students of an institution of higher education have the right to request that their education records not be disclosed and the institution must comply.

16. ___ Currently attending students of an institution of higher education have the right under FERPA to request that all of their education records not be disclosed and the institution must comply.

17. ___ A student's written permission is required before an institution releases information to a national research organization conducting a study on the advantages and disadvantages of selective admissions.

18. __ An institution must release any information identified as directory information by the institution to anyone upon request.

19. __ It is permissible for an employment agency not connected with your institution to share a student's transcript with a prospective employer as long as the student has given written permission to the institution to provide the transcript to the employment agency.

20. __ A former student has the same right to inspect and review his record as a student who is currently attending the institution.

....

MULTIPLE CHOICE
Place the letter of the most accurate response on the line to the left of the number.

....

21. __ An institution must permit a student to review his records within how many days from the day the student requests the review?
a) 10 days
b) 20 days
c) 25 days
d) 30 days
e) none of these

22. __ Which of the following is not identified in the original FERPA Act as being an example of "directory information"? The student's
a) name
b) date of birth
c) email address
d) dates of attendance

23. __ Directory information may include all of the following except the student's
a) photograph
b) major
c) class schedule
d) country of citizenship

24. __ You receive a phone call asking you to verify 1) that a currently enrolled student attended your institution, 2) what his address was at the time of attendance, 3) his date of birth, and 4) the student's GPA. According to FERPA, you can verify all of these except the student's
a) attendance at the institution
b) address during the time of attendance
c) date of birth
d) GPA

Bonus: Before you respond to the caller in question 24, what must you determine about the student?

_____

_____

_____

25. __ A faculty member comes into your office and asks one of the staff for the names of all of the graduates in his program since its beginning in 1980. Which of the following statements is true?
a) The faculty member can legally obtain this information under FERPA as long as he has written permission from the dean or designee.
b) The faculty member cannot legally obtain this information since it is excluded from FERPA.
c) The faculty member must provide a valid reason before obtaining the information.
d) The faculty member is not entitled to all of the information since FERPA does not permit release of this information on students not currently attending the institution.

26. __ Question 25 is an example of:
a) legitimate educational interest
b) eminent domain
c) permissible exclusion
d) informational exclusivity
e) non-disclosure
f) implied consent

27. __ FERPA requires institutions to obtain which of the following from the student before releasing any directory information:

a) written permission

b) verbal permission

c) certified permission

d) consensual permission

e) none of the above

28. __ A transcript request form completed by a student:

a) must be kept by the institution indefinitely.

b) does not have to be kept by the institution for any specific period of time.

c) does not have to be kept by the institution for more than one year from the date of the request.

d) must be kept by the institution if the transcript is sent to a third party, which the student has identified in the transcript request.

29. __ "Legitimate educational interest" refers to:

a) a school official's need to review a student's education records to perform his or her job duties.

b) a student's right to review his education records.

c) the need to provide education records in child custody cases.

d) the delegation of authority to the Trustees' to determine educational records policy for the institution.

30. __ As defined in FERPA, "legitimate educational interest" refers to:

a) a faculty member's need to provide feedback to students in the form of grades/evaluations.

b) the registrar's need to obtain education record information from faculty to produce a student's transcript.

c) a school official's right to obtain information only about students he is advising or teaching during the current year.

d) a school official's need to review student education record information to fulfill a responsibility as part of her contract.

31. __ Which of the following would not be acceptable under FERPA?

a) releasing the title of a congressman's degree to the local newspaper

b) the provost having access to all students' education records

c) notifying students of their FERPA rights via the student handbook

d) a faculty member announcing to his class that they can pick up their graded term papers after class in the chair outside of his office

32. __ According to FERPA, students may request that institutions not disclose which of the following about them:

a) directory information

b) non-directory information

c) both directory information and non-directory information

d) incidental information

e) education record information

33. __ At the K–12 level, parents:

a) have the same FERPA rights given to students attending an institution of higher education.

b) cannot review their child's records without first receiving permission from their child.

c) have no FERPA rights since FERPA only applies to higher education.

d) can only review test scores of their children.

34. __ Which of the following is not an "education record" under FERPA?

a) a student's traffic violation

b) a student's email address

c) the women soccer team's roster showing home town, height, weight, and current class of team members

d) a work study student's work record

35. __ At the college level, parents:

a) have the same rights of access and review as their child.

b) can only see their child's records after receiving permission from the Dean of Students or designee.

c) may receive tuition bills about their child sent directly to them from the institution.

d) may review their child's grades if they can prove that the student is legally their dependent.

36. __ FERPA rights:

a) pass from parents to student when the student attains the age of 18.

b) pass from parents to student when the student begins attending an institution of higher education.

c) are shared equally by parents and student at the higher education level.

d) apply only to parents of students attending colleges and universities.

e) apply only to students attending institutions of higher education.

f) a and b only

g) a and e only

h) b and e only

37. ___ "Parent" is to "eligible student" as "K–12" is to:

a) college

b) legitimate educational interest

c) FERPA

d) personally identifiable

e) K–9

38. ___ The FERPA rights of a student begin:

a) when the application for admission is received.

b) when the student is formally admitted.

c) when the student pays his first tuition bill.

d) when the student is "in attendance" as defined by the institution.

39. ___ To be an "education record", a piece of information must be:

a) personally identifiable to a student.

b) maintained by the institution.

c) kept in the registrar's office.

d) made available to the law enforcement unit.

e) a and b only

f) a, b, c only

g) a and d only

40. ___ FERPA:

a) permits institutions, through the "implied consent" rule, to disclose non-directory information about a student if the student has publicly disclosed non-directory information about himself.

b) permits disclosure of non-directory information to the press based on the *Privacy Act.*

c) permits disclosure of non-directory information to other school officials through the "implied consent" rule.

d) permits disclosure of non-directory information to a representative of an insurance company who has been designated by the institution to recommend a new student health insurance policy.

41. ___ Which of the following is required from students by FERPA before releasing information about them?

a) verbal consent to release the information

b) written permission unless the release is covered by any exception listed in FERPA

c) verbal consent from the student's advisor

d) written consent from the parents of a dependent student

42. ___ Institutions may release information to parents:

a) by obtaining the student's written permission.

b) by having the parents establish the student's dependency according to the current IRS code.

c) through a legally issued subpoena.

d) all of the above

e) a and b only

43. ___ Records of disclosures of student information must be kept for requests from, and releases to:

a) students for their own use.

b) school officials.

c) members of the Board of Trustees.

d) individuals seeking directory information.

e) work study students who have a need to access other students' records as a result of their employment in an office of the institution.

f) none of the above

g) all of the above (a,b,c,d,e)

44. ___ FERPA applies to the following educational institutions:

a) public

b) private

c) religious

d) all of the above

45. ___ In publishing a student directory that includes students' home addresses, is the institution in violation of FERPA?

a) yes

b) no

c) depends

If you chose c., what is your reason?

_____

_____

_____

_____

_____

_____

46. ___ Upon receiving a subpoena, you must:

a) notify the student in all cases that you have received the subpoena.

b) determine if the subpoena has jurisdiction over your institution before complying.

c) notify the server of the subpoena that you will comply within ten working days.

d) notify the student's parents that you have received it.

47. ___ A student has the right to review which of the following information about him that is maintained by the institution:

a) parental financial information

b) letters of recommendation for which the student has not signed a waiver

c) law enforcement unit records

d) admissions records related to the denial of his application into another college of the institution

e) all of the above

48. ___ Which of the following is not a student's right under FERPA?

a) the right to request that the institution discontinue the use of the social security number as a personal identifier

b) the right to limit disclosure of directory information

c) the right to request an amendment to their education record

d) the right to inspect and review their education records

49. In general, which of the following would likely be an acceptable release of student information without the student's written permission? (Place an "X" in the appropriate box.) 1 point each.

Type of Release	Acceptable?	
	Yes	No
To the student		
To the State Controller's office in relation to an audit of a state-funded program		
To the student's advisor		
To potential employers attempting to verify grades, class rank, and degree received		
To a custodial parent who is paying the student's tuition		
To an officer of a court in response to a legally issued subpoena		
To parents of a student regarding an alcohol violation of the student at the institution		
To the student newspaper regarding the final results of a student disciplinary hearing for a crime of violence		
To an institution in which the student intends to enroll and the request is for the student's GPA		
To the town's local law enforcement office inquiring about whether the student is in attendance this semester		

50. All items below are found in various offices of the institution. Would they be considered education records? (Enter "Y" for yes or "N" for no next to each.)

a. ____ a class roster with all students' names on it

b. ____ a traffic violation of a student kept in the institution's security office

c. ____ the honor roll list

d. ____ the annual giving record of an ex-student

e. ____ a note made in the student record by a faculty member of an advising session with a student

f. ____ notes taken by the institution's Affirmative Action Officer when interviewing students regarding a sexual harassment charge made against a faculty member

g. ____ student photographs on a department's bulletin board identifying the majors in that department

h. ____ medical records made and maintained by the university's contracted doctor related to the treatment of a student

i. ____ the employment records of an individual who is a full-time employee of the institution and is also a part-time student

j. ____ scores of a student who took the Test of English as a Foreign Language (TOEFL)

k. ____ test scores of a group of students identified only by ID# and kept in a faculty member's office files only

l. ____ a faculty member's note about a student having an epileptic seizure in one of his classes and kept in his locked office files

m. ____ financial information on a student's parents filed in the financial aid office

Bonus: Why is it important to identify what is and is not an education record?

_____

_____

_____

_____

_____

_____

51. Which of the following requests made by students are specifically granted by FERPA? Place an "X" in the space if FERPA allows you to comply with the request.

	Granted to	
Type of Student Request	Currently-enrolled Student?	Former Student?*
Inspect their education records		
A copy of any education record		
Amend an education record		
Non-disclosure of directory information		
Non-disclosure of non-directory information		
Have a hearing to amend an education record		
Prevent parents from viewing education records		
Forward any subpoenas received by the college for his education records to his attorney.		

* i.e., no longer attending

And now some brain stretchers to conclude this part of the exam...

For each of the situations below, answer the questions thoroughly and completely using your knowledge of FERPA. You will be best served if you use specifics within FERPA to make your conclusions.

52. In a "Release of Student Information" policy at one institution, the following statements appear:

"Public information" is limited to name; address; phone; major field of study; dates of attendance; admission or enrollment status; campus; school; college, or division; class standing; degrees and awards; activities; sports; and athletic information....

Public information shall be released freely unless the student files the appropriate form requesting that certain public information not be released....

Public information that cannot be restricted includes the name, enrollment status, degrees, and dates of attendance.

What is wrong with this last statement? How should this statement be changed to make it FERPA compliant?

_____

_____

_____

53. The following statement appears in one University's FERPA policy:

The following information will be released to those requesting it unless the student specifically requests otherwise on the form provided, or by submitting written notification to the registrar's office:

- ▶ *Student's Name*
- ▶ *Local Address*
- ▶ *Local Phone Number*
- ▶ *Enrollment Status*
- ▶ *Major*
- ▶ *Dates of Attendance*

All other information will not be released without written consent of the student."

What would be another FERPA-acceptable way to restate the sentence in bold above to allow your institution more flexibility in complying with requests for student information?

_____

_____

_____

_____

Cite the section of FERPA to which your new statement would now apply.

_____

_____

_____

_____

54. A faculty member at University A has suggested that she wants to provide email addresses of all students in her class to every student so that they can communicate among themselves.

   As the registrar, you know that email addresses are not identified as directory information at your institution.

   What would need to occur for this professor to share email addresses among her students?

   Your answer should include a discussion of directory information as it pertains to FERPA, non-disclosure, the annual notification to students, as well as any other pertinent information you deem appropriate.

_____
_____
_____
_____
_____
_____
_____
_____

SHORT ANSWER OR YOUR DAILY FERPA IN-BASKET

You are the Registrar/Director of Admissions and Records for your institution. You have direct daily responsibility for academic records. You are asked to provide a solution to each in-basket item and cite the FERPA reason(s) that justify(s) your decision. Remember: there may be more than one correct response. Your reasoning and FERPA justification are most important here. Whether directly asked or not, you are expected to give at least one reason for your answer. A simple "yes" or "no" is not sufficient. Short answers please; not essays.

In-basket Item #1

The Dean of the Graduate School calls you and relates the following:

I have a question about FERPA. I am familiar with the idea of the law, but I am wondering if you can give me an interpretation for the following scenario. That is, is what I'm about to describe a violation of the student's right to review records, or merely bad pedagogy?

One of our Ph.D. students took the qualifying examination in January and was told shortly thereafter she had failed. Her department informed her that she would have another chance to take the examination in the summer. The student wanted to see her graded examination, since she wanted to learn from any mistakes she may have made and also because she truly believed she performed sufficiently well to pass. She informed her advisor, the department chair, and the graduate committee chair in writing of her wish to inspect the graded exam. After a month had passed, she reminded the graduate committee chair verbally of her desire to inspect her graded exam. He acknowledged this request but was not certain that it could be granted; a couple weeks later, he suggested she try to reconstruct the exam and her responses from memory and then discuss them with her advisor.

About two months after her initial request (having repeated it again a couple times in the interim) her advisor informed her that the department policy is NOT to let students inspect graded qualifying examinations. Furthermore, the graduate committee has objected to her request-in-advance to review the grading for the second examination she is to take in the summer.

At this point, nearly three months have passed since she first asked to inspect her graded test paper. She has come to me to appeal the decision of the department. What should I do?

What do you advise?

_____
_____
_____

In-basket Item #2

You overhear a registrar from another institution saying:

We do verification of attendance over the phone. And we will give name, year and semesters attended, degree(s) earned and majors. We require a written release from the student or former student for anything else. Also, if a student has signed to withhold directory information in the last semester of attendance, we will *never release information, even if the student later asks us to change it. It is a binding decision.*

Is this a FERPA-correct statement? Why or Why not?

_____

_____

_____

In-basket Item #3

Currently, your Admissions office is the owner of all the information that is on the student's application. A copy of all this information is given to you, the registrar, *after* the student has matriculated. (Admissions keeps a copy of the data for their reference).

Ⓐ Career Services requests this data in order to help place the students in jobs. Are you in compliance with FERPA if you give Career Services access to all this admissions data? Why?

_____

_____

_____

Ⓑ Do you need any waiver or header or notification to the applicant that you are doing this?

_____

_____

_____

Ⓒ Can Admissions share its database information with other departments/individuals without advising the applicants?

_____

_____

_____

Ⓓ Without advising the student if they matriculate?

_____

_____

_____

Ⓔ Without providing FERPA training/reference to the individuals who are accessing the data?

_____

_____

_____

In-basket Item #4

At a meeting of the college's academic administrators, the question of providing class rolls (rosters) on a timely basis comes up. One department head indicates that these class rolls are already on the Web, but each faculty member has access to all of the class rolls—not just to his/her own. He thinks this isn't appropriate and asks you whether something can be done.

You reply, "Our current system doesn't allow us to make these very specific measures a reality. If it was more sophisticated, we might consider it. We do send out an email to all faculty and staff at the beginning of the year asking them to look at just their own class rolls due to privacy issues." One dean suggests, "If we put a heading on the beginning class roll page informing faculty about FERPA, would that be acceptable and not require us to limit access to individual class rolls only to the faculty/staff member who teaches the course? Our academic secretaries need access to a number of different class rolls because they work for multiple faculty. Would that be OK?"

Ⓐ How would you respond?
Ⓑ Can you suggest what the heading might say?
Ⓒ If that won't work, any other suggestions?

_____

_____

_____

In-basket Item #5

The director of financial aid comes to you and asks for your interpretation of when parents can/cannot see a student's education record.

She says that she had just attended a financial aid workshop where FERPA had been discussed. The college lawyer who made the presentation told them that dependency "had nothing to do with it unless the student is under 18. If the student is over 18, s/he has the right to the educational record, not the parents. If the student chooses to waive that right and let college administrators release that information, that's up to the student. Otherwise, we cannot disclose anything from the educational record without the student's permission."

How would you respond to your colleague?

_____

_____

In-basket Item #6

Currently, your institution does not include birthdates as directory information. There is some discussion that the student's birth date should be added as directory information. Some on campus are reluctant to agree to include this item since they feel that the student may not want this information released.

In order to resolve this problem, your Dean comes to you and asks what can be done. He is the designated official at your institution that chairs the committee that decides issues related to FERPA. He has no strong feelings one way or the other on this but knows that it will come before his committee sooner or later. Since he considers you to be the FERPA expert on campus, he asks, "If we do decide to include birthdates, do we have the option of releasing birthdates on some requests, and denying their release on other requests? If it is directory information are we obligated to release it to everyone?"

How do you respond?

_____

_____

_____

_____

In-basket Item #7

You have a foreign national over age 18 that was placed on academic probation. The father who lives in another country has requested a copy of the student's grades, a report from each teacher on performance in each class and a report of dormitory activities.

Your institution's policy is to provide the student with a copy of the transcript for parents' use. The student has not given said transcript to the parent.

You believe under FERPA that the student still falls under U.S. law and you cannot, therefore, release anything but directory information without the student's written permission.

What do you tell the parent?

_____

_____

_____

In-basket Item #8

A graduate from ten years back calls your office and says that she has lost many of her "educational records." While she still has her transcript from your institution, she is requesting that we send her copies of her transcripts from previous schools that are in her folder. Can you comply with her request and still be in compliance with FERPA?

_____

_____

In-basket Item #9

You receive a phone call from a parent for a copy of her son's transcript. She states that he had been in a car accident and had head injuries. She is now his legal guardian and needs a copy of his academic record for his rehab center to continue rehabilitation. You also find out that this is a former student who is 27 years old and last attended your institution in 1997. You ask her for a written release and a copy of guardianship papers.

After thinking about it, you realize that you are not aware of the extent of his injuries and possibly he is capable of requesting or denying a release of his records. So, you phone mom. She indicates that he is capable of issuing the release but asks again if you can comply with the request because of her guardianship.

What issues are involved? What do you decide?

_____

_____

_____

In-basket Item #10

It is final grades time and grades are due from faculty in five hours. You see a faculty member come in to the front desk and ask one of the staff if he can look at some student academic records. The staff member asks why he wants to look at them. He replies that he only wants to look at the records of students in his class and, before he assigns a grade in his class to those students, he wants to get a "feel" for which grades were assigned to those students in the past.

Should you grant his request? Why? Why not?

_____

_____

In-basket Item #11

The wife of one of your students comes in to the office and hands one of the staff a piece of paper which is written and signed permission for the wife to pick up his transcript. Is this permissible? Would you permit it?

In-basket Item #12

Your boss asks you what information you can release over the phone. How do you reply?

_____

_____

_____

In-basket item #13

Jill from the human resources office emails that she has just received a call from Food Services and she needs some help with a "FERPA question," as she puts it. Earlier that morning an FBI agent had visited the manager of Food Services and asked to see work records of a Food Service employee who was hired under a work-study contract. Jill wants to know if the manager should show the records to the agent. What should you first ask her? What do you tell her?

_____

_____

_____

In-basket item #14

An officer from a police department in a nearby town calls. The officer states that they have arrested a person who claims to be a student of your college. He is calling to verify this. You know that this police department has the policy of releasing students for minor infractions (which is involved in this case) if it can be verified that the person is a student. You check your records and find that this person is a student. There is, however, a signed statement from the student that he wants no information released on him.

Do you verify to the officer that this person is a student? Why or Why not?

_____

_____

_____

_____

_____

_____

_____

_____

_____

A FERPA Audit

Do you wonder if your campus is meeting general expectations regarding FERPA? Use the following questions/checklist to do a basic self-assessment of your office and/or your campus.

Who on your campus is responsible for FERPA compliance?

Typically, this responsibility falls to the registrar's office, but Legal Affairs or Academic Affairs might also hold it.

If you are the "point person" for FERPA on your campus, have you received appropriate training?

- ⊞ AACRAO sponsors FERPA workshops throughout the year at various locations across the country. Visit the AACRAO Web site (www.aacrao.org) for details.
- ⊞ FERPA is always a topic of several sessions at national AACRAO meetings.
- ⊞ AACRAO Consulting Services provides FERPA compliance training for individual institutions. Check the AACRAO Web site for additional information or email consulting@aacrao.org.
- ⊞ Other professional organizations (e.g., state/regional divisions of AACRAO) sponsor FERPA-related sessions or presentations each year.
- ⊞ Have you read this publication and understand the important concepts and terms within FERPA that are found here?

What resources can you utilize in addressing FERPA issues on your campus?

- ⊞ Do you have a legal affairs or general counsel resource (with someone on staff who is knowledgeable about FERPA)?
- ⊞ Professional colleagues, professional associations, e.g., AACRAO, the National Association of College and University Attorneys (NACUA), CLHE, and publications from those entities are excellent resources. For example, NACUA has published an outstanding complement to this publication: *The Family Educational Rights and Privacy Act: A Legal Compendium* by Stephen McDonald.

- ⊞ The Family Policy Compliance Office in the U.S. Department of Education—particularly given its expanding Web site materials—is an excellent resource for information and answers to problem situations. The Web site is www.ed.gov/policy/gen/guid/fpco/.
- ⊞ The federal guidelines (known as the regulations) regarding FERPA are also helpful. (*See* Appendix B, on page 147.)

Do you have a records retention plan?

While FERPA does not include a records retention plan, it does have direct impact on access to and use of existing records. Having an up-to-date records retention plan is good policy for any office that regularly works with important institutional records. For example, under FERPA, if students request access to their education records, you can't destroy those records, if they still exist, until after the students have seen them. You can, however, tell a student who has requested to see his education records that those records have been destroyed (if that has occurred), as long as they were destroyed in accordance with the institution's records retention plan. *AACRAO's Retention of Records Guide* is an excellent resource.

What security policies and protocols do you have in place on your campus?

- ⊞ This is a critical area related to FERPA, particularly in this age of greater reliance on technology. The 2009 regulations place specific expectations for institutions to have "reasonable methods" in place to appropriately manage access to education records.
- ⊞ Who is responsible for security controls and policy decisions regarding security in your networked/electronic environment?
- ⊞ Ideally, you should establish security controls which limit access to those who should/need to have access in order to do their jobs. This refers to the FERPA concept of "legitimate educational interest" or the "educational need to know." These controls relate to records regardless of what media is involved. For example, you may have specific controls for paper records that are different from controls for electronic records. In many older

student information systems, student database maintenance is more tightly controlled than providing users viewing access to student records; therefore, consider both viewing and maintenance capabilities.

⊡ Perform an analysis of roles and security-related decision-making procedures on your campus. For example, you are likely to have "sets" of common security protocols for staff advisers, faculty, office processing staff, student staff, etc. Once established, such "sets" make it easier to administer and manage security issues.

What training requirements and policies do you have in place regarding FERPA and student records?

⊡ Do you have mandatory training for persons who will have access to student records—particularly via technology?

⊡ If so, must/should that training occur prior to receiving access (*e.g.*, the staff person doesn't receive a password until after he or she has completed training)?

⊡ Who is responsible for training? Is it a centralized (*e.g.*, the registrar's office) or decentralized function (*e.g.*, every department that has access to student data)?

⊡ Consider all the options available for training and education: videotapes, workshops, documentation (both for training and for reference), and use of case studies. Some examples of training materials are included in this manual.

⊡ Consider tailoring training for the audience involved—make it relevant for them. The needs and issues for faculty are very different from those for frontline staff in the registrar's office.

⊡ What steps do you take to provide ongoing training and/or updates to the campus community? There will always be staff and faculty new to your campus, and others who change roles. As technology and other means of access evolve, reminders about FERPA, particularly for those who don't regularly deal with security issues, are very important.

What expectations of accountability do you have for those who have access to student data?

⊡ Do you have any written "sign-off" of responsibility by staff? Such a document is useful to clarify expectations, set appropriate limits, and give notice of consequences if the expectations are not met. Be sure to include an expectation to report violations.

⊡ Ensure that you tie access directly to each staff person. For example, don't structure your security access so

that multiple people use the same ID/password/pass code, and actively discourage anyone from sharing their pass code with others—even on a temporary basis.

⊡ Do you have tracking capabilities within the system—an "audit trail," particularly for maintenance? This capability will be very important when researching problems or alleged violations of security.

Do (or should) you have a FERPA policy on your campus?

⊡ An amendment to the FERPA regulations removed the requirement that every institution have a policy.

⊡ You are still required to annually notify students about FERPA. What must be included in the annual notification?

▶ The right to inspect and review their records (and how to do that);

▶ The right to seek amendments to their records (and how to do that);

▶ The right to consent to disclosure (with exceptions);

▶ The right to obtain a copy of the institution's policy (if there is one); and

▶ The right to file a complaint.

Other elements in your notification should include:

⊡ Definition of "school officials" and "legitimate educational interest" (educational need to know);

⊡ Whether it is the institution's policy to release records information without the student's written consent to another school at which the student is enrolled or seeks to enroll;

⊡ Which items the institution defines as directory information; and

⊡ A student's option to request "no release" (non-disclosure) of directory information. You are encouraged to include the consequences of choosing this option (*e.g.*, the student's name won't appear in an institutional directory).

See Appendix D of this publication (on page 177) for a Model Annual Notification to Students prepared by the Family Policy Compliance Office. It can also be viewed at www.ed.gov/policy/gen/guid/fpco/ferpa/ps-officials. html

Students must receive notification of this information at least annually. The mechanism of distribution is not specified—therefore it could be included with registration materials, included in a student handbook, or sent via email if that is a regular means for communication with your students.

Why your campus might still want to have a FERPA policy: It is excellent documentation

- ▪ for educational and training purposes with staff and faculty.
- ▪ to use when someone—particularly a student, family members, and others in the campus community—have questions about data access and security. It also provides for consistency in responding to those questions.
- ▪ to prove institutional policies in the event that a FERPA-related problem does arise—and it helps protect institutional "memory."

Are you meeting the record-keeping requirements under FERPA?

Under FERPA, you must record certain requests for and releases of personally identifiable records information. You are responsible to collect the following:

- ▪ The date the information was released;
- ▪ To whom it was released;
- ▪ What records were released; and
- ▪ The purpose of the request.

You do not have to keep records for releases:

- ▪ To the student;
- ▪ To school officials (with the appropriate "educational need to know");
- ▪ With the written consent from the student;
- ▪ Of directory information (assuming the student does not have a "no release"/requested non-disclosure).

Do you have appropriate institutional policies and every-day practices in place?

This is a practical encouragement for you and the appropriate people on your campus to discuss, then implement, FERPA-related policies and practices related to situations/issues that might result in FERPA violations. It is always best to be proactive in minimizing the risk of a FERPA violation by providing the training and identifying potential illegal releases of student information. This is particularly relevant with regard to the release of information to third parties.

Here are just a few examples:

- ▪ In a practical sense, how do you balance appropriate access to information with the legitimate protection of a student's privacy? Have you created procedures for people to get information they need to conduct their business, without compromising the student's privacy? For example, can someone in the business community easily confirm the attendance or degree for one of your students (assuming the student has not requested you to withhold directory information/"no release")?
- ▪ What does your institution consider to be "directory information?" The list included in the regulations is not intended to be absolute. So long as you do not include data elements that would be considered an invasion of a student's privacy, e.g., religion, citizenship, grades, SSN, etc., you may choose additional data items. Likewise, you do not have to include everything on the list of examples in the regulations. One common misconception is that students may request that an institution block the disclosure of all information about them. This is not correct and it is incumbent on you to clarify this misconception.
- ▪ What are your institution's non-disclosure ("no release") practices? Can a student have some elements suppressed (e.g., a telephone number), without necessarily suppressing all directory information? How do you receive a non-disclosure ("no release") request from your students? Do they understand the ramifications of making that decision? How does a staff person know that a student has a non-disclosure request on his or her records? Is it easy to discern that within your electronic records? How does a student reverse the decision to withhold directory information?
- ▪ How does a student gain access to their record (the right to inspect and review)? Will you routinely provide a copy, if requested? Will you charge for that copy (and, if so, how much)? Do you have an expectation for how quickly you will respond to such a request?
- ▪ How does a student request an amendment to his or her record? The regulations contain a very basic protocol, which focuses on the issues of timing and notification, but does your campus have a more specific policy in this area?
- ▪ What procedures do you have in place for releasing information to the parents of dependent students? This is a common question, so you should have a protocol in place that can be consistently followed across campus. In this area, what is the student development philosophy of your institution? How do you balance the role of the parents with the desire to

regard the students as independent adults? How do you ask parents to validate dependency? How do you build the student into the notification loop? Do you have "pre-waivers" by students—general (all records that the student would have access to), or specific (*e.g.*, financial information only)? Have you examined this issue at your institution?

■ What do you consider to be a valid signature or authorization for release of information? A faxed signature can be considered valid—but is that in your policies? The Federal Electronic Signatures in Global and National Commerce Act, as well as FERPA §99.30(d), permit the use of electronic signatures as authorization for releasing information. Again, does your institutional policy address electronic signatures?

■ Do you have an established procedure to respond to subpoenas? Unless the subpoena, on its face, legally prohibits you from doing so, you must inform the student as part of the process.

■ Do you routinely release results of disciplinary proceedings to alleged victims?

■ How do you treat the records for deceased students? FERPA rights, and the right to privacy, legally end at death, so this is an institutional policy decision.

■ Another amendment to FERPA permits institutions to inform the parents of a student under the age of 21 (even if he/she is not dependent) that their child has violated laws or rules related to the use of alcohol or drugs. However, you are not required to do so. Does (or should) your institution routinely do this?

These are just some of the issues you may want to address in your planning, policymaking, and implementation of procedures. This manual includes examples of training materials, solutions to potential problem situations, and a wealth of other practical information. Utilize these materials to help you and your campus identify the issues you want to address as you evaluate your institution's FERPA compliance.

True/False Quiz Answer Key

Question	Answer	Notes
1	F	With specific exceptions, "education records" are those maintained by the institution in any format that is identifiable to the student.
2	F	While institutions legally have 45 days to respond, consider whether you prefer and are able to fulfill the request in a more timely fashion, and whether your state open records law identifies a more abbreviated time frame for response.
3	F	All faculty and staff must show a "legitimate educational interest/need to know" within the context of their role to have appropriate access to education records.
4	F	There is no implied consent in FERPA, so you need to follow regular guidelines for releasing this student record information.
5	T	"Sole possession" records are an exception to the definition of "education records," and are therefore not accessible by the student.
6	F	If the student is legally financially dependent on either parent, then either parent can submit a request to access the student's record. If the institution would provide access for one parent, it may do so for either parent.
7	T	While the institution must provide access to the student, it is not required to do so for any third party.
8	T	So long as the record currently exists, it would be part of the student's "education record" and the student has the right to access it.
9	F	Medical treatment records are not covered by FERPA, so long as they are shared only with other medical service providers.
10	F	If the student is found in violation of the institution's conduct code related to a "crime of violence," then the student's name, violation and result of the disciplinary hearing are public information—releasable to anyone. Detailed disciplinary records are never public information, and the names of any victims or witnesses cannot be disclosed without consent.
11	F	A state court has legal jurisdiction only within that state. However, it is permissible for the institution in Ohio to respond to the California subpoena as a matter of professional courtesy. All the FERPA requirements regarding responding to subpoenas must be followed.
12	F	There are three issues here. First, grades and GPAs can never be directory information. Academic honors (e.g., Dean's List) can be directory information if the school has so designated academic honors to fall in that category. The question of top 10% of grades falls into a somewhat gray area, since it does not directly provide access to grade information for an individual student, but also does not meet the definition of directory information. In fact, it may come close to identifying grade information. Our recommendation is that schools not release the names of students in a top category of grades if that category is not designated as an academic honor in directory information.
13	D	It depends on HOW he posted the grades. If by name, Student ID Number, SSN (or part thereof), or something that can be fairly easily interpreted by a third party, then "yes," it's a violation. However, if the grades were posted by some "code" known only by the student and instructor, then that's OK.
14	T	This is true for any student under the age of 21—regardless of whether or not the student is financially dependent on his or her parent. Note that some state laws prohibit sharing this information without permission.
15	D	If the student is not yet "in attendance," then records related to the admission would generally not be an "education record." This is also true if the student is never admitted. However, if admitted and enrolled, all admissions records the institution continues to maintain become education records. It is also important that institutions familiarize themselves with state law and when education records start under those provisions since some begin once an institution begins creating a record.
16	F	A student's social security number can never be directory information, and therefore cannot be disclosed or even confirmed as public information.
17	F	There is no private cause of action under FERPA. This issue was confirmed by the U.S. Supreme Court in Gonzaga University v. John Doe, a 2002 decision. The student might want to pursue action under a Common Law or state law remedy, such as libel or slander.
18	F	The 2009 regulations clarified that records created after the student was enrolled are considered Alumni Records and are generally open to the public because they are not "education records" under FERPA. Since this is a state school, the state's open records law may apply if FERPA does not. Unless the student has a "No Release" on his record, you could also release directory information about Tom from when he was a student.
19	T	Posting grades in any personally identifiable format, such as with a name, SSN or SIN, would be a violation under FERPA.
20	F	"Student Recruiting Information" is a set of data defined within the Solomon Amendment. "Directory information" is a set of data defined by each institution. While there MAY be substantial overlap among the data items at any specific institution, they are not the same.

T=True, F=False, D=Depends

FERPA Final Exam Answer Key

True/False Section

1.	T	6.	T	11.	F	16.	F
2.	T	7.	T	12.	T	17.	F
3.	F	8.	F	13.	F	18.	F
4.	T	9.	T	14.	F	19.	F
5.	T	10.	T	15.	F	20.	T

Multiple Choice Section

21.	e [1]	32.	a	43.	f	50e.	Y
22.	c	33.	a	44.	d	50f.	Y
23.	d	34.	a	45.	c [3]	50g.	Y
24.	d [2]	35.	d	46.	b	50h.	N
25.	c	36.	f	47.	b	50i.	N
26.	a	37.	a	48.	a	50j.	Y
27.	e	38.	d	49.	See Table K1 below	50k.	Y
28.	b	39.	e	50a.	Y	50l.	N
29.	a	40.	d	50b.	N	50m.	N
30.	d	41.	b	50c.	Y	50.	Bonus [4]
31.	d	42.	d	50d.	N	51.	See Table K2 below

Table K1

Type of Release	Acceptable?	
	Yes	No
To the student	X	
To the State Controller's office in relation to an audit of a state-funded program	X	
To the student's advisor	X	
To potential employers attempting to verify grades, class rank, and degree received		X
To a custodial parent who is pay-ing the student's tuition	X [5]	
To an officer of a court in response to a legally issued subpoena	X [6]	
To parents of a student regarding an alcohol violation of the student at the institution	X	
To the student newspaper regarding the final results of a student disciplin-ary hearing for a crime of violence	X	
To an institution in which the student intends to enroll and the request is for the student's GPA	X [7]	
To the town's local law enforcement office inquiring about whether the stu-dent is in attendance this semester	X [8]	

Table K2

Type of Student Request	Granted to	
	Currently-enrolled Student?	Former Student?*
Inspect their education records	X	X
A copy of any education record		
Amend an education record	X	X
Non-disclosure of directory information	X	
Non-disclosure of non-directory information		
Have a hearing to amend an education record	X	X
Prevent parents from viewing education records		
Forward any subpoenas received by the college for his education records to his attorney		

* i.e., no longer attending

---

[1] The correct answer is 45 days.

[2] Whether he has requested that any directory information not be disclosed, and that items a, b, and c are considered directory information by your institution.

[3] Reason for choosing answer c: If a student's home address is not designated as directory information, the institution must obtain each student's written permission to include it in the student directory.

[4] If it is not an "education record," FERPA does not apply or FERPA only applies to "education records."

[5] If the student is legally financially dependent.

[6] If the court has appropriate jurisdiction.

[7] If this is the way your institution routinely does business and students have notice of such.

[8] Assuming "in attendance" is directory information and the student has a "Y" release on his/her record.

Brain Stretchers

52. An institution cannot tell a student which items of directory information can and cannot be subject to non-disclosure. The right of non-disclosure is the student's right exclusively. The institution may identify items of directory information but it may not place any conditions on a student's right to block any directory information.

53. The institution may release other information on students without written permission of the student if the release can be justified under one of the exceptions to written permission found in FERPA. The section of FERPA to which your new statement would now apply is 34 C.F.R. 99.31.

54. Two possibilities...

  ▶ Obtain written permission of each student in the class to share their email addresses with other students in the class.

  ▶ A better long-term solution would be for the institution to identify email address as directory information. Before doing so, however, it would have to notify students of that intent first. Students would then have to be given a period of time to request that their email address not be disclosed (right of non-disclosure).

  The institution needs to answer the question on when to notify students about adding an item to its directory information list. If it is in the middle of the academic year, this would necessitate a special notification to all students with the attendant period for them to request that their email addresses not be disclosed. If the decision to notify students could wait until the institution annually notified students of their FERPA rights, this would save the time and effort of the special, mid-year notification and make the notification process more efficient.

  Even if email addresses were included as directory information, a special procedure would have to be created to identify any student in any class not wishing to share email addresses with all students in the class. This procedure would identify any student in the class who had requested non-disclosure of their email address. The student could then be notified of the implications of their non-

disclosure for that class, and could decide if he or she wished to keep the non-disclosure active.

In-basket Items

1. The student has the right under FERPA to review the examination since it meets the definition of "education record," *i.e.*, personally identifiable to the student, maintained by the institution, and not one of the excluded categories from FERPA. (45 days have elapsed from the first request to review the record and the institution is in violation of FERPA.)

2. Yes. The institution may release any directory information on a case-by-case basis as long as the student (while still a student) has not requested non-disclosure. A non-disclosure request can only be removed by a current student unless the institution agrees to honor a similar request from an alumnus.

3a. Yes. At most institutions, this would be considered a valid exercise of "legitimate educational interest." However, each institution determines what is legitimate educational interest.

3b. No. This should be part of the annual notification to students required by FERPA.

3c. Yes. Same reason as above in 3a.—legitimate educational interest.

3d. Yes. Students are annually notified re: legitimate educational interest.

3e. Yes. FERPA does not require any training but training is strongly recommended for all users of "education records."

4a. "It is probably not a FERPA violation to continue the *status quo* but all users need to be trained on their responsibilities under FERPA."

4b. "Federal law (FERPA) requires that you must have a valid professional reason for viewing this class roll."

4c. (Open ended) Given the current situation, the academic administrators should take the initiative and formulate a policy regarding access to the screens and notify everyone of this policy. It is better to have something in writing than to merely make a decision and verbally communicate that decision to those who need to know. You may also want to consider making adjustments with your student system to better accommodate your security needs.

5. The lawyer is partially correct. FERPA rights pass to the student at age 18 or when s/he begins attending a college/university. Parents have only those rights of access that the student or institution gives to the parents. In general, if the parents prove legal dependency (IRS standard, not financial aid standards), the institution may provide access to the parents.

6. The institution is not obligated to release directory information to anyone since FERPA states an institution "may" release. It doesn't have to.

7. Our institution's policy is to release student information directly, and only to students. We would consider releasing information to you if we receive 1) written permission from your child, or 2) proof of your child's dependency (not applicable in this case since you do not pay federal income taxes and, therefore, you cannot provide a federal income tax return), or 3) a legally issued subpoena itemizing specific information you wish to review.

8. FERPA only requires institutions to provide access to education records. It does not require that you make copies of any records unless geographic distance precludes personal inspection. Professional courtesy and the fact that another institution's records on that student may have changed are two reasons for not copying other institutions' transcripts for students.

9. Dependency, legal guardianship, written permission of the student, power of attorney.

   (*Emergency situation*—probably give to mom after her submission of legal guardianship papers. Of course, obtaining the student's written permission has the highest priority if at all possible.)

10. No. This is not a valid exercise of legitimate educational interest and you should call the dean after denying access to the faculty member. Grades are independent evaluative judgments made by a faculty member regarding a student's performance in one class. They should be assigned without any intervening external variables such as past academic performance.

11. It is permissible. You have the student's written permission to release the transcript to the spouse and that is what FERPA requires. You must verify that the signature is that of the student's. You may, however, deny the release to the wife if your policy indicates release to the student only, or if you question the validity of the signature of the student.

12. Without the student's written permission you can only release what you identify as "directory information;" and you can release this information at your discretion. Even directory information can be released only if the student has a "Y" release on his or her record.

   Non-directory information can be released without written permission of the student if the release falls under one of the exceptions to written permission in FERPA. (34 C.F.R. 99.31)

13. First question—does the agent have a signed release (written permission) from the student indicating that the agent can see the records requested?

   If "yes", the food services manager may provide the information to the agent although FERPA does not require it.

   If "no", the food services manager should not release the information (work study employment records are subject to FERPA).

14. No. The student has placed a non-disclosure on this information and you are honoring this request. (This example is based on an actual occurrence.)

Chapter Six

Sample Forms

The following 31 sample forms are also available from AACRAO's Web site at www.aacrao.org/compliance/ferpa/, and can be adapted to fit your institution.

Sample Form 1:   Permission to Release Education Record Information—Version A 103

Sample Form 2:   Permission to Release Education Record Information—Version B 104

Sample Form 3:   Permission to Release Education Record Information—Version C... 105

Sample Form 4:   Authorization of Grade Disclosure 106

Sample Form 5:   Consent to Send Grades to Parents.. 107

Sample Form 6:   Authorization to Disclose Education Records to Parents/Opt Out of Directory Information....108

Sample Form 7:   Consent to Return Graded Assignments in a Public Manner.. 109

Sample Form 8:   Request to Opt Out of Directory Information—Version A... 110

Sample Form 9:   Request to Opt Out of Directory Information—Version B 111

Sample Form 10: Request to Opt Out of Directory Information—Version C.. 112

Sample Form 11: Request for Revocation of Non-Disclosure of Directory Information.. 113

Sample Form 12: Request to Review Education Records.. 114

Sample Form 13: Request to Inspect and Review Education Records... 115

Sample Form 14: Request to Amend or Remove Education Records... 116

Sample Form 15: Request for Formal Hearing to Amend or Remove Education Records—Version A 117

Sample Form 16: Request for Formal Hearing to Amend or Remove Education Records—Version B..................... 118

Sample Form 17: Code of Responsibility for Security and Confidentiality of Data 119

Sample Form 18: Student Worker—Statement of FERPA Understanding...120

Sample Form 19: Request for Computer Access to Student Records in the Student Information System (SIS)...... 121

Sample Form 20: Agreement for Accessing Private Electronic Student Data by Staff 122

Sample Form 21: Staff Login Notice for Accessing Private Electronic Student Data.. 123

Sample Form 22: Request to Change SSN to Another Personal Identifier 124

Sample Form 23: Notice of Intent to Comply with a Subpoena.. 125

Sample Form 24: Agent/Contractor Agreement 126

Sample Form 25: Authorization to Release Grades/Transcripts for Dual-Enrolled Students 127

Sample Form 26: Notification of Student Privacy Rights under FERPA (Email Version) 128

Sample Form 27: Transcript Notice of FERPA Redisclosure Limitation.. 129

Sample Form 28: Student Dependent Status/Consent to Disclosure to Parents 130

Sample Form 29: Student Dependent Status... 131

Sample Form 30: Student-Athlete's Authorization to Disclose Information in Education Records
Pursuant to FERPA.. 132

Sample Form 31: NCAA Student-Athlete Statement.. 133

Office of University Registrar
University Name
Street Address
Phone

Permission to Release Education Record Information

Requested By (Student):   **Release To (Recipient):**

LAST NAME	FIRST NAME

LAST NAME	FIRST NAME

STUDENT IDENTIFICATION NUMBER

ORGANIZATION/SCHOOL

DATE

ADDRESS

CITY, STATE, ZIP

Education record information to be released:

_____

Purpose of release:

_____

I give permission for _____ to release the specified information to the recipient listed above.

STUDENT SIGNATURE

OFFICE USE ONLY

Action taken: ☐ Completed ☐ Filed ☐ Held ☐ Other:

DATE   BY WHOM

Office of University Registrar
University Name
Street Address
Phone

Student Information Release Authorization

In compliance with the federal *Family Educational Rights and Privacy Act of 1974* and the Regents' Policy on Access to and Release of Student Education Records, the University is prohibited from providing certain information from your student records to a third party, such as information on grades, billing, tuition and fees assessments, financial aid (including scholarships, grants, work-study, or loan amounts) and other student record information. This restriction applies, but is not limited, to your parents, your spouse, or a sponsor.

You may, at your discretion, grant the University permission to release information about your student records to a third party by submitting a completed Student Information Release Authorization. You must complete a separate form for each third party to whom you grant access to information on your student records. The specified information will be made available only if requested by the authorized third party. The University does not automatically send information to a third party.

Submit your completed form to _{Office}_, _{University of X}_, at the address given below for your campus. Please note that your authorization to release information has *no expiration date*; however, you may revoke your authorization at any time by sending a written request to the same address. This form allows third parties to access student record information from any _{University of X}_ campus. **NOTE**: For the third party designee you name on this form, this release overrides all FERPA directory suppression information that you have set up in your student record. *However, it is University policy not to release certain aspects of student records (e.g., registration, grades, GPA) over the phone or via email.*

This information release authorization is intended for use only by the offices listed below:

{Office List}

A. Student Information

NAME (LAST, FIRST, MIDDLE INITIAL)   SSN (LAST 4 DIGITS)   STUDENT ID NUMBER

CURRENT ADDRESS (STREET/PO, APT, CITY, STATE & ZIP)   DAYTIME PHONE

B. Third-party Designee

NAME (LAST, FIRST, MIDDLE INITIAL)   SSN (LAST 4 DIGITS)

CURRENT ADDRESS (STREET/PO, APT, CITY, STATE & ZIP)   DAYTIME PHONE

RELATION TO STUDENT   EMAIL ADDRESS

- ☐ Grades/GPA, demographic, registration, student ID number, academic progress status, and/or enrollment information
- ☐ Billing statements, charges, credits, payments, past due amounts, and/or collection activity
- ☐ Financial aid awards, application data, disbursements, eligibility, and/or financial aid satisfactory academic progress
- ☐ University-maintained loan disbursements, billing and repayment history (including credit reporting history), communication history, balances, and/or collection activity
- ☐ Access to student records maintained by the Office of the Registrar and the Office of Student Finance, including all of the above examples

INFORMATION TYPES ALLOWED (CHECK ONE OR MORE OF THE BOXES ABOVE TO GRANT AUTHORIZATION)

C. Certification

STUDENT'S SIGNATURE   DATE

Sample Form 3: Permission to Release Education Record Information—Version C

Office of University Registrar
University Name
Street Address
Phone

Student Information Release Authorization

{Office List}

Student Information

NAME (LAST, FIRST, MIDDLE INITIAL) | SSN (LAST 4 DIGITS) | STUDENT ID NUMBER

Third-party Information

NAME (LAST, FIRST, MIDDLE INITIAL) | EMAIL ADDRESS

CURRENT ADDRESS (STREET/PO, APT, CITY, STATE & ZIP) | DAYTIME PHONE

PURPOSE OF RELEASE

☐ Academic ☐ Financial ☐ All ☐ Other (Enter Other)

INFORMATION TO BE RELEASED

Authentication

Online Students

When the party named above contacts _{University of X's}_ online campus, he/she will be asked to authenticate his/her identity by providing a a special identifier code. You, the student, should create this identifier and provide it to your third party contact. Do not choose an identifier that could easily be guessed. If your third party contact is not able to correctly provide the five digit identifier, _{University of X}_ will not release any information from your record. If you forget or misplace your five digit identifier, _{University of X}_ can only provide it to you by sending it to your email address on file, upon request.

IDENTIFIER CODE

Identifier Code Requirements:
{Code Format, e.g.: The identifier must include exactly two (2) letters and three (3) numbers (e.g. HT515)}

On-Campus Students

When the party named above contacts _{University of X's}_ campus, he/she will be asked to authenticate his/her identity by providing at least one personal security question answer. **You, the student, should choose at least one personal security question and provide it to your third party contact.** Do not choose a question that could easily be guessed. If your third party contact is not able to correctly provide the correct answer to the personal security question, _{University of X}_ will not release any information from your record. If you forget or misplace your personal security question, _{University of X}_ can provide it to you by sending it to your email address on file, or you may come to the registrar's office on campus to make changes or get a reminder.

ELEMENTARY SCHOOL | FAVORITE TEACHER'S NAME | FAVORITE PET'S NAME | FIRST AUTOMOBILE

Authorization

In accordance with The Family Educational Rights and Privacy Act (FERPA) of 1974, _{University of X}_ will only disclose confidential information from the education records of students to parents or other third parties provided the University has written consent from the student on file. Please sign below and return to the Office of the Registrar if you consent for the University to release your education records to your parents or any other third-party. *Please Note: This release form will remain valid through the student's enrollment at _{University of X}_ unless specifically revoked by this student.*

By signing below, I consent that _{University of X}_ may disclose and discuss confidential information from my education record with the individuals listed above in reference to the purpose of release:

STUDENT'S SIGNATURE | DATE

Revoke Authorization (To revoke a prior Authorization to Release only)

By signing below, I hereby revoke any prior authorization for _{University of X}_ to disclose my education record information with the individuals listed above, effective immediately.

STUDENT'S SIGNATURE | DATE

Office of University Registrar
University Name
Street Address
Phone

Authorization of Grade Disclosure

I hereby authorize University of X to release my grade reports, both midterm and final, for the _____ academic year, to my parents(s), or other named individuals or entities. NOTE: If parents live at different addresses, please list them both.

LAST NAME	FIRST NAME		LAST NAME	FIRST NAME

ADDRESS		ADDRESS

CITY, STATE, ZIP		CITY, STATE, ZIP

If person(s) named above are not your parents(s), how are they related to you?

_____

The released reports will be used for the purpose of

_____

I understand that by signing this authorization, I am consenting to the release of the education records listed to the persons specifically listed. This release does not permit the disclosure of these records to any other persons or entities without my written consent or as permitted by law.

DATE	STUDENT NAME

– –

SOCIAL SECURITY NUMBER

STUDENT SIGNATURE

Office of University Registrar
University Name
Street Address
Phone

Consent to Send Grades to Parents

IMPORTANT—PLEASE READ CAREFULLY

Disclosure of Directory Information

University of X, in compliance with the *Family Educational Rights and Privacy Act of 1974*, has designated the following items as *directory information*: student's name, address, telephone number; parents' names, address, telephone number; major field of study, class, enrollment status, anticipated degree date, participation in officially recognized activities, degree and awards received, most recent previous educational agency or institution attended by the student. University of X may disclose any of the above listed items without the student's prior written consent, unless the registrar's office is notified in writing to the contrary.

All other student academic information is considered confidential and will not be released, with certain exceptions, without the student's written permission.

A student's grades are considered confidential information. Therefore, if you wish to have your grades sent to your parents at the end of each semester, you need to sign this form and return it to the registrar's office to authorize the college to do so.

I authorize University of X to send my grades to my parents at the end of each semester.

LAST NAME (STUDENT)	FIRST NAME		DATE
STUDENT IDENTIFICATION NUMBER			STUDENT SIGNATURE

FORM ID##

Office of University Registrar
University Name
Street Address
Phone

Authorization to Disclose Education Records to Parents/ Opt Out of Directory Information

LAST NAME (STUDENT)	FIRST NAME	STUDENT IDENTIFICATION NUMBER

Annual Notice to Students

Annually, University of X informs students of the *Family Educational Rights and Privacy Act of 1974* (FERPA), as amended. This *Act*, with which the institution intends to comply fully, was designated to protect the privacy of educational records, to establish the rights of students to inspect and review the educational records, and to provide guidelines for the correction of inaccurate or misleading data through informal and formal hearings. Students also have the right to file complaints with The Family Policy Compliance Office concerning alleged failures by the institution to comply with the *Act*.

Local policy explains in detail the procedures to be used by University of X for compliance with the provisions of the *Act*. Copies can be obtained from the Office of Student Affairs and Office of the Registrar. It is also printed in the student handbook and the university bulletins. Questions concerning the *Family Educational Rights and Privacy Act* may be directed to these offices.

AUTHORIZATION TO DISCLOSE ACADEMIC INFORMATION TO PARENTS

In accordance with FERPA, the University will disclose to parents information from the academic records of a student provided the University has on file written consent of the student. Please sign below and return to the Office of the Registrar if you consent for the University to release to your parents your educational records.

DATE	STUDENT SIGNATURE

AUTHORIZATION TO WITHHOLD DIRECTORY INFORMATION

The following is considered *directory information* at University of X and will be made available to the general public unless the student notifies the Office of the Registrar in person or in writing before the last day to add classes.

> Student's name, telephone number, date and place of birth, college, major, honors, awards, photo, class standing, dates of enrollment, degrees conferred, dates of conferral, graduation distinctions and the institution attended immediately prior to admission.

Under the provisions of the *Family Educational Rights and Privacy Act of 1974* you have the right to withhold disclosure of such directory information. University of X will honor your request to withhold directory information.

Please consider carefully the consequences of any decision to withhold such directory information. Should you decide not to release any of this information, any requests for such information from University of X will be refused.

This signed request must be received in the Office of the Registrar by 4:45 p.m. on the last day to add classes as listed in the academic calendar. This authorization is valid until a written request to rescind is received by the Office of the Registrar.

I hereby request University of X not release any directory information from my academic records. I have read the above paragraphs and understand the consequences of my action.

DATE	STUDENT SIGNATURE

Office of University Registrar
University Name
Street Address
Phone

Consent to Return Graded Assignments in a Public Manner
Academic Department FERPA Waiver

In compliance with the *Family Educational Rights and Privacy Act* (FERPA), it is the policy of the Department of _{Department Name}_ at _{University of X}_ to maintain the confidentiality of student's records.

I understand that the record of my academic performance at the university is confidential. However, in an effort to maximize instruction time and limit time expended passing back thousands of assignments during the semester, I authorize the instructor of the course listed below to place my exams and assignments out for pick-up immediately before, during or after class time (or during other appropriate group meetings of class members), or to pass them around during the class period. Only other members of the class could potentially see my name and scores, and only during the restricted time frame specified above.

I understand that I may rescind this waiver, in writing to the instructor, at any time during the academic term.

LAST NAME (STUDENT) FIRST NAME	DATE
STUDENT IDENTIFICATION NUMBER	SEMESTER COURSE NAME
STUDENT SIGNATURE	

If you **do not** wish to waive your FERPA rights, please sign below. If you sign below, the exams and assignments for the course listed below will be returned directly to you, and will not be accessible to other students.

LAST NAME (STUDENT) FIRST NAME	DATE
STUDENT IDENTIFICATION NUMBER	SEMESTER COURSE NAME
STUDENT SIGNATURE	

Office of University Registrar
University Name
Street Address
Phone

Request to Suppress Public Information

First, please read the following paragraph. **Then**, if you still wish to suppress public information, check **one** box below and return the completed form to one of the offices listed below. You may complete this form on the Web at _{Web Location}_. Go to the section called _{Section, e.g.: "Changing Your Name or Address"}_ and click on _{Form Link}_ (online).

The _{University X}_ has designated some information about you as public information. This information includes: name, address, email address, phone number, dates of enrollment, enrollment status, major, adviser, college, class, academic awards and honors, and degrees received. This means that the University can release this information to anyone who requests it. You have the opportunity to suppress parts or all of this information from public release.

Suppression might have undesirable consequences. With some options individuals at the University might be unable to contact you about assignments, or you might not receive notice of some services. A suppression does not limit access to your file by authorized individuals nor does it apply to employment information. Information can be released by subpoena, to parents of dependent children with appropriate documentation, etc. The following five options are available for suppression; please choose one:

☐ Suppress my phone number

☐ Suppress my address

☐ Suppress my address and phone number

☐ Suppress my address, phone number, and email

(No information about you will appear in the University's electronic directory or in the next edition of the printed directory, and your address, phone number, and email address will not be released to third parties.)

☐ Suppress all public information about me

(No information about you will be released to third parties without your signature. You will not be able to call and receive your own information over the phone. The fact of your attendance will not be released; prospective employers, financial institutions, or others offering services will be unable to have the University verify your attendance.)

☐ Remove suppression

(Any current suppression will be removed.)

STUDENT NAME (LAST, FIRST, MIDDLE INITIAL)	STUDENT ID OR SSN
STUDENT SIGNATURE	DATE

Records Offices:

{Records Office 1}
{Records Office 1 Address 1}
{Records Office 1 Address 2}
{Records Office 1 Phone}

{Records Office 2}
{Records Office 2 Address 1}
{Records Office 2 Address 2}
{Records Office 2 Phone}

{Records Office 3}
{Records Office 3 Address 1}
{Records Office 3 Address 2}
{Records Office 3 Phone}

Office of University Registrar
University Name
Street Address
Phone

Request to Opt Out of Directory Information

LAST NAME (STUDENT)	FIRST NAME		STUDENT IDENTIFICATION NUMBER

SEMESTER/QUARTER	YEAR

At University of X the following information about a student can, by law, be released to the general public and may be listed in the campus directory:

> permanent address and telephone number, local address and telephone number, confirmation that you are enrolled here.

No other student information is released to non-university personnel without your written permission. By completing this form, you will be requesting that information **not** be released to non-university personnel or listed in the campus directory.

Some of the effects of your decision to request confidential status will be that you must make all address changes with a signed authorization or in person with a form of ID; friends or relatives trying to reach you will not be able to do so through the University; information that you are a student here will be suppressed, so that if a loan company, perspective employer, family member, etc., inquire about you, they will be informed that we have no record of your attendance here.

Once you have designated a confidential classification, it will not be removed until you submit a signed authorization requesting that it be removed.

DATE		STUDENT SIGNATURE

Office of University Registrar
University Name
Street Address
Phone

Request to Opt Out of Directory Information

To: All Students

These items listed below are designated as *directory information* and may be released for any purpose at the discretion of our institution.

Under the provisions of the *Family Educational Rights and Privacy Act of 1974, as Amended*, you have the right to withhold the disclosure of any or all of the categories of directory information listed below.

Please consider very carefully the consequences of any decision by you to withhold any category of directory information. Should you decide to inform the institution not to release any or all of this directory information, any future requests for such information from non-institutional persons or an organization will be refused.

The institution will honor your request to withhold any of the categories listed below but cannot assume responsibility to contact you for subsequent permission to release them. Regardless of the effect upon you, the institution assumes no liability for honoring your instructions that such information be withheld.

Please mark the appropriate boxes and affix your signature below to indicate your disapproval for the institution to disclose the following public or directory information.

Category I	**Category II**	**Category III**
☐ *ALL of this category*	☐ *ALL of this category*	☐ *ALL of this category*
☐ name	☐ previous institution(s) attended	☐ Past and present participation in officially recognized sports and activities
☐ address	☐ major field of study	
☐ telephone number	☐ awards	
☐ dates of attendance	☐ honors (includes Dean's list)	☐ physical factors (height, weight of athletes)
☐ class	☐ degree(s) conferred (including dates)	☐ date and place of birth

LAST NAME (STUDENT)   FIRST NAME   SEMESTER/QUARTER   YEAR

STUDENT IDENTIFICATION NUMBER   DATE

                                                                STUDENT SIGNATURE

If this form is not received in [Campus Office] prior to [Due Date], it will be assumed that the above information may be disclosed for the remainder of the current academic year. A new form for non-disclosure must be completed each academic term.

Office of University Registrar
University Name
Street Address
Phone

Request for Revocation of Non-Disclosure of Directory Information

University of X does not normally disclose *directory information*. However, at its discretion, it may provide directory information in accordance with the *Family Educational Rights and Privacy Act of 1974* (FERPA), as amended. At University of X, directory information is limited to:

> student's name, address, telephone number, email address, major field of study, dates of attendance, admission or enrollment status, campus, school, college, division, class standing, degrees earned, awards, activities, sports, athletic information, and the most recent previous educational agency or institution attended.

Under the provisions of FERPA, students have the right to withhold the disclosure of directory information. Student requests for non-disclosure may be made in the registrar's office any time during the semester.

University of X will honor your request to withhold any directory information item but cannot assume responsibility to contact you for subsequent permission to release them. Your request for non-disclosure will remain in effect until rescinded in writing (see below). Please consider very carefully the consequences of any decision by you to withhold directory information.

Please Note: Non-disclosure of directory information does not prevent University of X from disclosing personally identifiable information from a student's record to authorized representatives of federal, state and local agencies when that disclosure is in connection with financial aid for which the student has applied or which the student has received, or any of the other exceptions to signed consent found in §99.31 of the FERPA regulations.

> I hereby authorize the Office of the Registrar at University of X to remove the non-disclosure block from my education record. Effective immediately, directory information may once again be released to the public, at the discretion of University of X.

LAST NAME (STUDENT)   FIRST NAME   DATE

STUDENT IDENTIFICATION NUMBER   STUDENT SIGNATURE

OFFICE USE ONLY

To be filled out by Student Records Representative:

DATE OF REVOCATION   LAST NAME (REP)   FIRST NAME

                                       SIGNATURE (REP)

Office of University Registrar
University Name
Street Address
Phone

Request to Review Education Records

Student

DATE

LAST NAME   FIRST NAME

STUDENT IDENTIFICATION NUMBER

Requestor

LAST NAME   FIRST NAME

REQUESTOR'S AFFILIATION

Purpose of review:

_____

_____

Item(s) of information requested:

_____

_____

Office to which request was made:

_____

_____

I hereby agree to keep the information disclosed to me confidential according to applicable legislation and regulations.

DATE

SIGNATURE

OFFICE USE ONLY

Disposition of request: ☐ Approved ☐ Disapproved

Specify materials reviewed (records, types of information):

_____

_____

NAME OF OFFICIAL SUPERVISING REVIEW

DATE

TITLE

SIGNATURE OF OFFICIAL APPROVING REQUEST

Office of University Registrar
University Name
Street Address
Phone

Request to Inspect and Review Education Records

Student   **Record Custodian**

LAST NAME	FIRST NAME

LAST NAME	FIRST NAME

STUDENT IDENTIFICATION NUMBER

LOCATION OF RECORD (OFFICE)

ADDRESS (LOCAL / ON-CAMPUS)

REQUEST RECEIVED (DATE)

CITY, STATE, ZIP

DATE AVAILABLE

TELEPHONE

CUSTODIAN SIGNATURE

I wish to inspect the following education record(s):

_____

_____

DATE   STUDENT SIGNATURE

Office of University Registrar
University Name
Street Address
Phone

Request to Amend or Remove Education Records

LAST NAME (STUDENT)	FIRST NAME		STUDENT IDENTIFICATION NUMBER

ADDRESS			TELEPHONE (LOCAL/ON-CAMPUS)

CITY, STATE, ZIP

I have reviewed my education records held within [Office] at University of X. I am not satisfied with the accuracy and/or completeness of these records. Specifically, I request that these records be amended in the following way(s). (Use next page if additional space is needed):

_____

_____

I request that the following document(s) be removed from my file:

_____

DATE		STUDENT SIGNATURE

....

Record Custodian Reviewing Request to Amend Education Record

LAST NAME (CUSTODIAN)	FIRST NAME		DISPOSITION OF REQUEST

TITLE		DATE

Reason for Approval/Disapproval (use next page if additional space is needed):

_____

_____

DATE		CUSTODIAN SIGNATURE

Appeals of the Record Custodian's decision may be made by completing a "Student Request for Formal Hearing" form. This form is available from _____.

The Records Custodian must send a copy of this form to the student making the request and to _____.

Office of University Registrar
University Name
Street Address
Phone

Request for Formal Hearing to Amend or Remove Education Records

LAST NAME (STUDENT)	FIRST NAME	STUDENT IDENTIFICATION NUMBER

ADDRESS	TELEPHONE (LOCAL/ON-CAMPUS)

CITY, STATE, ZIP

I request a formal hearing concerning correction or removal of what I believe to be inaccurate or misleading information contained in my education records. The following education record(s) is/are being contested:

_____

_____

I am contesting the information because (please use next page if additional space is needed):

_____

_____

Please notify me of the date, time, and place of the hearing.

DATE	STUDENT SIGNATURE

First Endorsement

The decision of the Hearing Panel is as follows (please use next page if additional space is needed):

_____

_____

_____

LAST NAME (CHAIRPERSON)	FIRST NAME	DATE

	CHAIRPERSON'S SIGNATURE

Note: If the student disagrees with the Hearing Panel's decision, he/she has the right to place in his/her record a written statement commenting on the information in the record and/or stating his/her reasons for disagreeing with the decision. This explanation will become part of the student's education record as long as this record is maintained and whenever a copy of this record is sent to any party, the explanation will accompany it.

The chairperson of the Hearing Panel must send copies of the Panel's decision to the student requesting the hearing, and to _____.

Student: Please return this form to the executive director of Academic Records.

Office of University Registrar
University Name
Street Address
Phone

Request for Formal Hearing to Amend or Remove Education Records

| LAST NAME (STUDENT) | FIRST NAME | | STUDENT IDENTIFICATION NUMBER |

| ADDRESS | | TELEPHONE (LOCAL/ON-CAMPUS) |

| CITY, STATE, ZIP |

I request a formal hearing concerning correction or removal of what I believe to be inaccurate or misleading information contained in my education records, as described below:

Education Record(s)

_____

_____

_____

_____

Contested Information

_____

_____

_____

_____

Please notify me of the date, time, and place of the hearing.

| DATE | | STUDENT SIGNATURE |

....

First Endorsement

The decision of the Hearing Panel is as follows:

_____

_____

_____

| LAST NAME (CHAIRPERSON) | FIRST NAME | | DATE |

| | CHAIRPERSON'S SIGNATURE |

Student: Please return this form to the Hearing Panel chairperson named above.

Office of University Registrar
University Name
Street Address
Phone

Code of Responsibility for Security and Confidentiality of Data

Both federal law (the *Family Educational Rights and Privacy Act of 1974*, as amended) and state law (The State Revised Code Section _____) are in effect to ensure the security and confidentiality of information used in our operations. Thus, security and confidentiality is a matter of concern for all employees within the Office of the University Registrar and any other persons who have access to our data systems or physical facilities. Each person working in the Office of the University Registrar or who has direct access to student records information holds a position of trust relative to this information and must recognize the responsibilities entrusted to them and this office in preserving the security and confidentiality of this information. Therefore, each employee of this department, and any person authorized access to any information through the facilities of this department is:

1. Not to make or permit unauthorized use of any information.
2. Not to seek personal benefit or permit others to benefit personally by any confidential information which has come to them by virtue of their work assignment and in accordance with University and office policies.
3. Not to exhibit or divulge the contents of any record or report to any person except in the conduct of their work assignment in accordance with University and office policies.
4. Not to knowingly include or cause to be included in any record or report a false, inaccurate or misleading entry.
5. Not to remove any official record (or copy) or report from the office where it is kept except in the performance of their duties.
6. Not to operate or request others to operate any University equipment for purely personal business.
7. Not to aid, abet, or act in conspiracy with another to violate any part of this code.
8. To immediately report any violation of this code to his or her supervisor.

While your supervisor can assist you in understanding these policies and how we must operate within them, you should become familiar with its provisions, particularly those regarding required consent to release information, the list of information which can be released for currently enrolled students without consent, and how information is designated when the student has indicated that it cannot be released.

When the student has chosen to indicate information is not to be released, the requestor should be advised "that we are unable to release any information" and be given no indication of whether or not you may have any information on the person. You are advised to refer any questions or requests for information that you are unsure of to your supervisor.

As custodians of official University records, we all share the responsibility for ensuring the security and privacy of the records and data we maintain. Please study the attached document and, after you have read it, sign the statement below. This acknowledgement will be retained in your personnel file.

A violation of this policy may lead to reprimand, suspension, dismissal or other disciplinary action, consistent with the general personnel policies of the University, and the Code of Student Conduct for student employees.

In addition, the State Revised Code specifies:

> *"No present or former public official or employee shall disclose or use, without an appropriate authorization, any information acquired by him in the course of his official duties which is confidential because of statutory provisions, or which has been clearly designated to him as confidential when such confidential designation is warranted because of the status of the proceedings or the circumstances under which the information was received and preserving its confidentiality is necessary to the proper conduct of government business."*

Conviction for violation of this statute is a first degree misdemeanor (up to 6 month imprisonment and/or $1,000 fine).

I hereby affirm that I have read the University of X policy statement on Student Rights Under the *Family Educational Rights and Privacy Act, of 1974 as Amended*, and the foregoing statement. I understand the obligations imposed by these documents and will comply with the standards and requirements contained therein. I have retained in my possession a copy of the document for future reference.

| LAST NAME | FIRST NAME | DATE |

| TITLE | SIGNATURE |

Office of University Registrar
University Name
Street Address
Phone

Student Worker—
Statement of FERPA Understanding

LAST NAME (STUDENT) FIRST NAME	STUDENT IDENTIFICATION NUMBER

ADDRESS	CITY, STATE, ZIP

I understand that by the virtue of my employment with [Office] at University of X, I may have access to records which contain individually identifiable information, the disclosure of which is prohibited by the *Family Educational Rights and Privacy Act of 1974*. I acknowledge that I fully understand that the intentional disclosure by me of this information to any unauthorized person could subject me to criminal and civil penalties imposed by law. I further acknowledge that such willful or unauthorized disclosure also violates University of X's policy and could constitute just cause for disciplinary action including termination of my employment regardless of whether criminal or civil penalties are imposed.

DATE	STUDENT WORKER SIGNATURE

Office of University Registrar
University Name
Street Address
Phone

Request for Computer Access to Student Records in the Student Information System (SIS)

Please sign and date the bottom of this form and return to the Office of the Registrar.

LAST NAME (EMPLOYEE) FIRST NAME	POSITION

EMAIL	DEPARTMENT

TELEPHONE	

Approved by supervisor:

DATE	IMMEDIATE SUPERVISOR'S SIGNATURE (REQUIRED)

Computer Center Access

Access Area (Check One):   **Individual Screens:**

☐ Student Worker Access (Inquiry Only)   _____   _____
☐ Advisor Access (Standard Advisor Access)   _____   _____
☐ Dean Access (Standard Dean Access)   _____   _____

Confidentiality Statement

Along with the right to access the transcripts of students at University of X comes the responsibility to maintain the rights of students particularly as outlined in the *Family Educational Rights and Privacy Act* (FERPA). The university catalog, semester bulletins and student handbook state the policy regarding student records at University of X. Student records are open to members of the faculty and staff who have a legitimate need to know their contents; however, you do have a responsibility to maintain confidentiality. Under the terms of FERPA, University of X established the following as directory information: student's name, local address/telephone number, permanent address/telephone number, email address, date and place of birth, hometown, degrees and awards received and dates, dates of attendance (current and past), full or part-time enrollment status, participation in officially recognized activities, participation in officially recognized sports, weight/height of member of athletic teams, most recently attended educational institution, major field of study, academic levels, residency status, and photographs. All other information may not be released without written consent of the student. Grades, social security numbers, ethnicity, and student schedules should not be released to anyone other than the student under discussion and not over the phone.

I have read the above and agree to maintain the confidentiality of student records.

DATE	EMPLOYEE SIGNATURE

OFFICE USE ONLY

Notes:

COLLEAGUE LOGIN ID	DATE

LAST NAME (REGISTRAR) FIRST NAME	SIGNATURE (REGISTRAR)

Office of University Registrar
University Name
Street Address
Phone

Staff Agreement for Accessing Private Electronic Student Data

Appropriate Use Agreement for Accessing Private Student Data in the Student Information System

In order to gain access to the _{Resource Site}_, you must continue through the Appropriate Use Agreement screens and agree to use _{Resource Name}_ according to the relevant university policies (even if you don't personally have access to private data and intend to use only the public reports). If you do not agree to abide by university policy, you will not be allowed into the _{Resource Site}_.

As a member of the university community you are granted access to information technology resources to facilitate your university-related academic, research, and job activities. The _{ Policy Name, e.g.: "Regents Policy on Academic Freedom"}_ extends to information resources that are available electronically. By using these resources you agree to abide by all relevant _{University of X}_ policies and procedures, as well as all current federal, state, and local laws.

You have rights and responsibilities related to university information/data, systems and resources. This includes liability related to acceptable use, personal communications, privacy, and security issues. Prior to gaining access, you will be asked to certify that you understand and agree to comply with university policy.

The _{Internal Access to Information Policy}_ applies to any and all information the university has, regardless of who created it or how it is distributed or maintained. The policy describes how access to university information is authorized based on job responsibilities, and it outlines the penalties for a security breach, up to and including termination of employment.

The _{Policy Name, e.g.: "Acceptable Use of Information Technology Policy"}_ describes how systems resources are managed to ensure their integrity, security, and availability for appropriate educational and business activities. The policy includes sections on _{Section List, e.g.: "User Rights and Responsibilities" and "Guidelines for Using Information Technology Resources"}_. A policy violation may result in loss of access privileges, university disciplinary action, and/or criminal prosecution.

Any student may request suppression of his or her _{University of X}_ records. According to FERPA regulations, you may not release any information about this student to a third party. The Office of the Registrar's complete policy statement concerning student records, including what is considered public and private information, can be found at _{ Policy Name, e.g.: "Policies on Access to Student Records"}_.

By clicking *I Agree* below, I understand and agree to comply with university policies, including _{Policy List, e.g.: "Internal Access to University Information, Acceptable Use of Information Technology Resources" and "Policies on Access to Student Records," etc}_.

By clicking *I Agree*, you will gain access to _{Resource Name}_. _{Department Name}_ will maintain a record of all users who agree to the above statement. Users will be prompted to agree to this statement on an annual basis.

☑ **AGREE**

Office of University Registrar
University Name
Street Address
Phone

Staff Login Notice for Accessing Private Electronic Student Data

NOTICE

You are attempting to access information that is protected by federal privacy law. Disclosure to unauthorized parties violates the *Family Educational Rights and Privacy Act* (FERPA). You should not attempt to proceed unless you are specifically authorized to do so and are informed about FERPA. When accessing the system, you must access only that information needed to complete your assigned or authorized task. You may communicate the information only to other parties authorized to have access in accordance with the provisions of FERPA. If you have any questions about those provisions, please contact __{Contact Info}__ .

Please enter the following information:

LAST NAME	FIRST NAME	NAME OF THE FILE YOU ARE ACCESSING
TODAY'S DATE		PURPOSE CODE

§99.31(a)(1) School Officials

Reminder: Information about a student that is maintained by an educational institution on a computer database is part of the student's education record and thus protected by FERPA. Access to such information should be limited to those individuals who are "school officials" with a "legitimate educational interest" in the information.

Office of University Registrar
University Name
Street Address
Phone

Request to Change SSN to Another Personal Identifier

LAST NAME (STUDENT)	FIRST NAME	SOCIAL SECURITY NUMBER

All of the computerized information which University of X holds on you in the student records, financial aid, business, housing, and dining service computer systems, whichever are applicable, and any reports generated from those systems which utilize ID numbers, will use the new number.

University of X will not release your old ID number to any outside agencies, but will make a note of what your old ID number was on your academic record for internal use only. By signing this form, you also understand and affirm that:

- You will use the new ID number in any future transactions involving University of X which require an ID number.

- Certain problems may arise if we receive information requests from outside agencies which only contain your old ID number. You will not hold University of X responsible for any such problems which may arise due to this change in ID numbers.

- You are not receiving any type of financial aid from the state or federal governments.

Upon this request, I understand that University of X will assign a new identification number to replace my current ID number (SSN).

DATE	STUDENT SIGNATURE

OFFICE USE ONLY

Status of request: ☐ Completed ☐ Student Notified of New ID

NEW STUDENT IDENTIFICATION NUMBER	DATE ACTIVE

Office of University Registrar
University Name
Street Address
Phone

Notice of Intent to Comply with a Subpoena

March 28, 2010

[Student First Name] [Student Last Name]
[Street Address]
[City], [ST] [Zip Code]

Dear Mr./Ms. [Student Last Name]:

Enclosed please find a copy of a subpoena we have received for your records. According to the *Family Educational Rights and Privacy Act of 1974*, we are required to notify you that we intend to comply with this subpoena on Tuesday, June 1, 2010.

If you plan to obtain the services of an attorney to attempt to quash this subpoena, we would appreciate notification prior to Saturday, May 1, 2010.

Sincerely Yours,

[Registrar's Full Name]
[Title]
cc: [cc Recipient 1]
[cc Recipient 2]

Office of University Registrar
University Name
Street Address
Phone

Agent/Contractor Agreement

The University agrees to provide the following student information:

_____

to _____ for the sole purpose of

_____

and for the time period of

_____

In the course of performing this function for the University, _____ is acting as a legal agent ("school official") of the University and will release information only in the following circumstances:

_____

_____

and only to the following persons/organizations

_____

The student information submitted to _____ by the University is confidential information and shall be used only for the purposes stated in this agreement. _____ agrees not to share or disclose this data with any third-party outside of the purposes stated in this agreement, unless required to do so by law or other agency regulations. Failure to comply with the requirement not to release information, except for the sole purpose stated above, will result in cancellation of this agreement and the eligibility for _____ to receive any student information from the University for a period of not less than five (5) years. In addition, _____ agrees to indemnify and hold the University harmless for any loss, cost, damage or expense suffered by the University as a direct result of _____ failure to comply with the requirement not to release information, except for the sole purpose stated above.

_____ agrees to either destroy the student information in a manner that completely protects the confidentiality of the student information or return the information to the University upon the expiration of this agreement.

| LAST NAME (AGENT REP) | FIRST NAME | | LAST NAME (UNIVERSITY REP) | FIRST NAME |

| DATE | | DATE |

| SIGNATURE (AGENT REPRESENTATIVE) | | SIGNATURE (UNIVERSITY REPRESENTATIVE) |

Office of University Registrar
University Name
Street Address
Phone

Authorization to Release Grades/Transcripts for Dual-Enrolled Students

LAST NAME (STUDENT)	FIRST NAME		STUDENT IDENTIFICATION NUMBER

STUDENT'S HIGH SCHOOL		STUDENT'S UNIVERSITY

I hereby authorize the registrar's office at University of X to send an official copy of my

☐ Fall   ☐ 1st Quarter
☐ Spring   ☐ 2nd Quarter
☐ Summer I   ☐ 3rd Quarter
☐ Summer II   ☐ 4th Quarter

grades and/or transcript to my high school at the conclusion of the academic year. I understand that my high school counselor and/or principal require this official documentation of my college work in order to determine its applicability towards my high school graduation requirements.

I understand that this authorization is good for one official copy of my grades and/or transcript each semester and that the grade report or transcript must be sent from University of X, **directly** to the high school. I further understand that any additional copies that I may want for my own personal use must be requested in person and be accompanied by a $_____ payment.

DATE		STUDENT SIGNATURE

....

Authorized Recipient:

HIGH SCHOOL		CITY, STATE, ZIP

LAST NAME	FIRST NAME		TELEPHONE

TITLE

Once completed and signed by the dual-enrolled student, mail this form to:

Sample Form 26: Notification of Student Privacy Rights under FERPA (Email Version)

FROM: "DOE, JOHN" <DOEJ@UNIVERSITYOFX.EDU>
DATE: MARCH 27, 2006 10:50:29 AM EST
TO: "STUDENT" <STUDENT@SOMEADDRESS.COM>
SUBJECT: NOTIFICATION OF STUDENT PRIVACY RIGHTS UNDER FERPA

Dear Student:

We want to take this opportunity to give you a brief summary of your rights under the *Family Educational Rights and Privacy Act* (FERPA), the federal law that governs release of and access to student education records. These rights include:

1. The right to inspect and review your education record within a reasonable time after the University receives a request for access. If you want to review your record, contact the University office that maintains the record to make appropriate arrangements.

2. The right to request an amendment of your education record if you believe it is inaccurate or misleading. If you feel there is an error in your record, you should submit a statement to the University official responsible for the record, clearly identifying the part of the record you want changed and why you believe it is inaccurate or misleading. That office will notify you of their decision and advise you regarding appropriate steps if you do not agree with the decision.

3. The right to consent to disclosure of personally identifiable information contained in your education records, except to the extent that FERPA authorizes disclosure without consent. One exception which permits disclosure without consent is disclosure to school officials with "legitimate educational interests." A school official has a legitimate educational interest if the official has a "need to know" information from your education record in order to fulfill his or her official responsibilities. Examples of people who may have access, depending on their official duties, and only within the context of those duties, include: university faculty and staff, agents of the institution, students employed by the institution or who serve on official institutional committees, and representatives of agencies under contract with the University.

4. The right to file a complaint with the U.S. Department of Education concerning alleged failures by the University to comply with the requirements of FERPA.

Release of student record information is generally not done at University of X without the expressed, written consent of the student. There are, however, some exceptions.

For example, directory information includes the following, and may be released without the student's consent: name, local address, home address, email address, local telephone number, home telephone number, college of enrollment, major, campus attended, status (including current enrollment, dates of attendance, full-time/part-time, withdrawn), honors received (*e.g.*, Dean's List recognition), participation in officially recognized activities and sports, weight and height of members of athletic teams. Please note that you have the right to withhold the release of directory information. To do so, you must complete a "Request for Non-Disclosure of Directory Information" form, which is available from the Office of the Registrar, or your college/extended campus office. Please note two important details regarding placing a "No Release" on your record:

1. The University receives many inquiries for directory information from a variety of sources outside the institution, including friends, parents, relatives, prospective employers, the news media and honor societies. Having a "No Release" on your record will preclude release of such information, even to those people.

2. A "No Release" applies to all elements of directory information on your record. University of X does not apply a "No Release" differentially to the various directory information data elements.

A copy of the *Act*, more details about your rights, and any University policies related to the *Act* are available from the Office of the Registrar, at [http://www.universityofx.edu].

Questions concerning FERPA should be referred to the Office of the Registrar.

John Doe
University Registrar
University of X
[doej@universityofx.edu]

Official Transcript

{School Name}
{School Address 1}
{School Address 2}
{School Address 3}

Print Date: _{Student Name}_
Student Name: _{Student Name}_
Student ID: _{Student ID}_
Birthdate: _{Student Birthdate}_
Student Address: _{Student Address}_

NOTICE

In accordance with USC 438(6(4)(8)(The Family Educational Rights and Privacy Act of 1974) you are hereby notified that this information is provided upon the condition that you, your agents or employees, will not permit any other party access to this record without consent of the student. Alteration of this transcript may be a criminal offense.

-----Beginning of Credit Record-----

Course/Description			Attempted/Earned/Points			
2008 Fall						
GOL 105	Physical Geology		4.00	4.00	A	16.000
Term >>>	GPA:	4.00	TOTALS: 4.00	4.00		16.000
2009 Spring						
GOL 106	Historical Geology		4.00	4.00	A	16.000
Term >>>	GPA:	4.00	TOTALS: 4.00	4.00		16.000
2009 Fall						
HIS 122	U.S. History II		3.00	3.00	A	12.000
MTH 163	Pre-calculus I		3.00	3.00	A	12.000
SPA 101	Beginning Spanish I		5.00	5.00	A	20.000
Term >>>	GPA:	4.00	TOTALS: 11.00	11.00		44.000
Credit Career Totals						
CUM >>>	GPA:	4.00	TOTALS: 19.00	19.00		76.000

For manual calculations of students GPA, credits for "P" grades must be subtracted from credits attempted.

REGISTRAR NAME (PRINT)

REGISTRAR SIGNATURE

Office of University Registrar
University Name
Street Address
Phone

Student Dependent Status/Consent to Disclosure to Parents

Under the *Family Educational Rights and Privacy Act* (FERPA), _{University of X}_ is permitted to disclose information from your education records to your parents if your parents (or one of your parents) claim you as a dependent for federal tax purposes. Please indicate whether your parents claim you as a tax dependent.

A. Student Information

Please click the appropriate answer:

LAST NAME   FIRST NAME   MI

⦿ Yes. I certify that my parents claim me as a dependent for federal income tax purposes

ADDRESS

○ No. I certify that my parents do not claim me as a dependent for federal income tax purposes

CITY, STATE, ZIP   CERTIFICATION OF TAX STATUS

SIGNATURE   DATE

If you are not claimed as a dependent or you do not know whether you are claimed as a dependent for federal income tax purposes, but you agree that _{University of X}_ may disclose information from your education records to your parents, please sign the following consent:

I consent to the disclosure of any personally identifiable information from my education records to my parent(s), for reasons determined by _{University of X}_ as appropriate. This authorization will remain in effect for the _{Academic Year}_ school year.*

SIGNATURE   DATE

B. Parent Information (If parents live at the same address, please list both in the first column)

NAME(S)   NAME(S)

ADDRESS   ADDRESS

CITY, STATE, ZIP   CITY, STATE, ZIP

TELEPHONE   TELEPHONE

*Students cannot be denied any educational services from _{University of X}_ if they refuse to provide consent.

Office of University Registrar
University Name
Street Address
Phone

Student Dependent Status

Under the *Family Educational Rights and Privacy Act* (FERPA), _{University of X}_ is permitted to disclose information from your education records to your parents if your parents (or one of your parents) claim you as a dependent for federal tax purposes. Please indicate whether your parents claim you as a tax dependent.

A. Student Information

Please click the appropriate answer:

LAST NAME   FIRST NAME   MI

⊙ Yes. I certify that my parents claim me as a
    dependent for federal income tax purposes

ADDRESS

○ No. I certify that my parents do not claim me as a
    dependent for federal income tax purposes

CITY, STATE, ZIP   CERTIFICATION OF TAX STATUS

SIGNATURE   DATE

B. Parent Information (If parents live at the same address, please list both in the first column)

NAME(S)   NAME(S)

ADDRESS   ADDRESS

CITY, STATE, ZIP   CITY, STATE, ZIP

TELEPHONE   TELEPHONE

Office of University Registrar
University Name
Street Address
Phone

Student-Athlete's Authorization to Disclose Information in Education Records Pursuant to FERPA

I understand that my education records are protected by the *Family Educational Rights and Privacy Act of 1974*, and they may not be disclosed without my consent. I hereby consent to the disclosure of the following education records pertaining to me to the persons and for the purposes as stated below:

I hereby authorize the following:
1.   The _{University of X Office of University Registrar}_; and
2.   Faculty members teaching courses in which I am currently (or was) enrolled

to disclose the following:
1.   any and all information contained in my official permanent academic record;
2.   copies of my official permanent academic record; and
3.   specific information regarding my academic progress (attendance, attitude, grades, etc.) prior to the final determination of grade

to the following persons:
1.   the Student-Athlete Support Services Office;
2.   the Athletic Compliance Office; and
3.   any other person within the University who the University, in good faith, determines has a legitimate "need to know"

for the following purposes:
1.   to monitor, assist and determine eligibility for intercollegiate athletic practice and/or competition;
2.   to monitor and assist with respect to my athletic grant-in-aid.

I recognize that my parent(s) and/or legal guardian(s) may request to receive information about my academic progress (attendance, attitude, grade, etc.) prior to and after the final determination of grade for the purpose of determining and maintaining my academic eligibility for athletic participation, practice and grant-in-aid. My choice is marked below:

◉ Yes

I do authorize my Athletic Academic Counselor to disclose the above-referenced information to my parent(s) and/or legal guardian(s) upon their request for the above-referenced purpose. Such information may be released to the following person(s) [provide the names of your parent(s) and/or legal guardian(s) who may receive such information:

{Authorized Recipients} _____

○ No

I do NOT authorize my Athletic Academic Counselor to disclose the above-referenced information to my parent(s) and/or legal guardian(s) upon their request for the above-referenced purpose.

I understand further: (1) that such records may be disclosed only on the condition that the party to whom the information is disclosed will not redisclose the information to any other party without my written consent unless specifically allowed by law; (2) that I have the right not to consent to this release of my education records; (3) that I recognize that a copy of such records must be provided to me upon my request; and 4) that this Authorization remains in effect unless revoked by me in writing.

By signing this form, I certify that I agree to the disclosure of the records referenced above.

A copy of this authorization shall be considered as effective and valid as the original.

SIGNATURE _____   DATE _____

Athletic Compliance Office
University Name
Street Address
Phone

NCAA Student-Athlete Statement

This form has seven parts. You must sign all seven parts to participate in intercollegiate competition. Before you sign this form, you should read the Summary of NCAA Regulations provided by your director of athletics or read the bylaws of the NCAA Division I Manual that deal with your eligibility. If you have any questions, you should discuss them with your director of athletics or you may contact the NCAA at (317) 917-6222. The conditions that you must meet to be eligible and the requirement that you sign this form are indicated in the following bylaws of the Division I Manual: Bylaws 10, 12, 13, 14, 15 and 16; Bylaws 14.1.3.1, 18.4 and 31.2.3:

Part I: Student-Athlete Information

NAME (LAST, FIRST, MIDDLE INITIAL)   DATE OF BIRTH

HOME ADDRESS (STREET/PO, APT, CITY, STATE & ZIP)   AGE

SPORT(S)

Part II: Statement Concerning Eligibility

By signing this part of the form:

1. You affirm that to the best of your knowledge you are eligible to compete in intercollegiate competition.
2. You affirm that your institution has provided you a copy of the summary of NCAA regulations or the relevant sections of the NCAA Division I Manual and that your Director of Athletics (or his/her designee) gave you the opportunity to ask questions about them.
3. You affirm that you meet the NCAA regulations for student-athletes regarding eligibility, recruitment, financial aid, amateur status and involvement in organized gambling.
4. You affirm that all information provided to the NCAA, the Eligibility Center and the institution's admissions office is accurate and valid, including SAT or ACT scores, high school attendance, completion of coursework and high school grades, as well as the student athlete's amateur status.
5. You affirm that you have reported to the Director of Athletics (or his/her designee) of your institution any violations of NCAA regulations involving you and your institution.
6. You affirm that you understand that if you sign this statement falsely or erroneously, you violate NCAA legislation on ethical conduct and you will further jeopardize your eligibility.

STUDENT ATHLETE'S SIGNATURE   DATE

PAGE 1 OF 3

Part III: Buckley Amendment Consent

By signing this part of the form, you certify that you agree to disclose your educational records. You understand that this entire form and the results of any NCAA drug test you may take are part of your educational records. These records are protected by the Family Educational Rights and Privacy Act of 1974, and they may not be disclosed without your consent. You give your consent to disclose only to authorized representatives of this institution, its athletic conference and the NCAA, **except as permitted in the Drug-Testing Consent form,** the following documents:

1. This form
2. Results of NCAA drug tests
3. Results of positive drug tests done by non-NCAA national or international athletics organizations
4. Any transcript from your high school, this institution, or any junior college or any other four-year institutions you have attended
5. Pre-college test scores, appropriately related information and correspondence (e.g., testing sites, dates and letters of test-score certification or appeal), and where applicable, information relating to eligibility for or conduct of nonstandard testing
6. Graduation status
7. Race and gender identification
8. Records concerning your financial aid
9. Any other papers or information pertaining to your NCAA eligibility

You agree to disclose these records only to determine your eligibility for intercollegiate athletics, your eligibility for athletically related financial aid, for evaluation of school and team academic success, for purposes of inclusion in summary institutional information reported to the NCAA (and which may be publicly released by it), for NCAA longitudinal research studies and for activities related to NCAA compliance reviews. You will not be identified by name by the NCAA in any such published or distributed information. You also agree that information regarding any infractions matter in which you may be involved may be published or distributed to third parties as required by NCAA policies, bylaws or programs.

STUDENT ATHLETE'S SIGNATURE	DATE

Part IV: Promotion of NCAA Championships, Events, Activities, or Programs

You authorize the NCAA [or a third party acting on behalf of the NCAA (e.g., host institution, conference, local organizing committee)] to use your name or picture to generally promote NCAA Championships or other NCAA events, activities, or programs:

STUDENT ATHLETE'S SIGNATURE	DATE

Part V: Results of Drug Tests

If you have not tested positive for a banned substance by the NCAA and/or by a non-NCAA national or international athletics organization or any athletics conference or institution, sign A and C. If you have tested positive, complete B and C.

A. No Positive Drug Test. You affirm that you have not tested positive for a banned substance by the NCAA and/or by a non-NCAA national or international athletics organization.

STUDENT ATHLETE'S SIGNATURE	DATE

B. Positive Drug Test. If you have ever tested positive for a substance banned by the NCAA and/or by a non-NCAA national or international athletics organization, the results must be declared here. Further, the results will be reported by your director of athletics to NCAA Educational Services. Should you consequently transfer, you are obligated to report NCAA positive drug-test results to the respective institution.

Are you currently under such a drug testing suspension?   ○ Yes   ⦿ No

SUBSTANCE	ORGANIZATION CONDUCTING TEST	DATE OF TEST

STUDENT ATHLETE'S SIGNATURE	DATE

PAGE 2 OF 3

C. Subsequent Positive Test. Should you test positive for a substance banned by the NCAA and/or by a non-NCAA national or international athletics organization at any time after you sign this statement, as described in the above paragraph, you must report the results to your director of athletics, who must then report the results to the NCAA. You will be subject to future NCAA drug-testing in which failure of the drug test could lead to the possible loss of eligibility.

STUDENT ATHLETE'S SIGNATURE   DATE

Part VI: Previous Involvement in NCAA Rules Violations

Are you aware of any NCAA violations you were involved in while attending your previous institution?

○ Yes   ◉ No

Were you required to be withheld from competition while attending your previous institution?

○ Yes   ◉ No

Part VII: Affirmation of Status as an Amateur Athlete

You affirm that you have read and understood the NCAA amateurism rules. By signing this part of the form, you affirm that, to the best of your knowledge, you have not violated any amateurism rules since you requested a final certification from the clearinghouse or since the last time you signed a Division I student-athlete statement, whichever occurred later. You affirm that since requesting a final certification from the Eligibility Center, you have not provided false or misleading information concerning your amateur status to the NCAA, the NCAA clearinghouse and the institution's athletics department, including administrative personnel and coaching staff.

STUDENT ATHLETE'S SIGNATURE   DATE

Part VIII: Incoming Freshman—Affirmation of Valid SAT or ACT

You affirm that, to the best of your knowledge, you have received a validated ACT and/or SAT score. You agree that, in the event you are or have been notified by ACT or SAT of the possibility of an invalidated test score, you will immediately notify the director of athletics at your institution.

STUDENT ATHLETE'S SIGNATURE   DATE

Appendix A

The Family Educational Rights and Privacy Act of 1974 as Amended

Taken from http://uscode.house.gov/uscode-cgi/fastweb.exe?getdoc+uscview+t17t20+4095+1++%28%29%20%20A

20 USC Sec. 1232g

Title 20	Education
Chapter 31	General Provisions Concerning Education
Subchapter III	General Requirements And Conditions Concerning Operation And Administration Of Education Programs: General Authority Of Secretary
Part 4	Records; Privacy; Limitation on Withholding Federal Funds
Sec. 1232g	Family Educational and Privacy Rights

(a) Conditions for availability of funds to educational agencies or institutions; inspection and review of education records; specific information to be made available; procedure for access to education records; reasonableness of time for such access; hearings; written explanations by parents; definitions

(1)(A) No funds shall be made available under any applicable program to any educational agency or institution which has a policy of denying, or which effectively prevents, the parents of students who are or have been in attendance at a school of such agency or at such institution, as the case may be, the right to inspect and review the education records of their children. If any material or document in the education record of a student includes information on more than one student, the parents of one of such students shall have the right to inspect and review only such part of such material or document as relates to such student or to be informed of the specific information contained in such part of such material. Each educational agency or institution shall establish appropriate procedures for the granting of a request by parents for access to the education records of their children within a reasonable period of time, but in no case more than forty-five days after the request has been made.

(B) No funds under any applicable program shall be made available to any State educational agency (whether or not that agency is an educational agency or institution under this section) that has a policy of denying, or effectively prevents, the parents of students the right to inspect and review the education records maintained by the State educational agency on their children who are or have been in attendance at any school of an educational agency or institution that is subject to the provisions of this section.

(C) The first sentence of subparagraph (A) shall not operate to make available to students in institutions of postsecondary education the following materials:

(i) financial records of the parents of the student or any information contained therein;

(ii) confidential letters and statements of recommendation, which were placed in the education records prior to January 1, 1975, if such letters or statements are not used for purposes other than those for which they were specifically intended;

(iii) if the student has signed a waiver of the student's right of access under this subsection in accordance with subparagraph (D), confidential recommendations—

(I) respecting admission to any educational agency or institution,

(II) respecting an application for employment, and

(III) respecting the receipt of an honor or honorary recognition.

(D) A student or a person applying for admission may waive his right of access to confidential statements described in clause (iii) of subparagraph (C), except that such waiver shall apply to recommendations only if

(i) the student is, upon request, notified of the names of all persons making confidential recommendations and

(ii) such recommendations are used solely for the purpose for which they were specifically intended. Such waivers may not be required as a condition for admission to, receipt of financial aid from, or receipt of any other services or benefits from such agency or institution.

(2) No funds shall be made available under any applicable program to any educational agency or institution unless the parents of students who are or have been in attendance at a school of such agency or at such institution are provided an opportunity for a hearing by such agency or institution, in accordance with regulations of the Secretary, to challenge the content of such student's education records, in order to insure that the records are not inaccurate, misleading, or otherwise in violation of the privacy rights of students, and to provide an opportunity for the correction or deletion of any such inaccurate, misleading or otherwise inappropriate data contained therein and to insert into such records a written explanation of the parents respecting the content of such records.

(3) For the purposes of this section the term "educational agency or institution" means any public or private agency or institution which is the recipient of funds under any applicable program.

(4)(A) For the purposes of this section, the term "education records" means, except as may be provided otherwise in subparagraph (B), those records, files, documents, and other materials which—

(i) contain information directly related to a student; and

(ii) are maintained by an educational agency or institution or by a person acting for such agency or institution.

(B) The term "education records" does not include—

(i) records of instructional, supervisory, and administrative personnel and educational personnel ancillary thereto which are in the sole possession of the maker thereof and which are not accessible or revealed to any other person except a substitute;

(ii) records maintained by a law enforcement unit of the educational agency or institution that were created by that law enforcement unit for the purpose of law enforcement;

(iii) in the case of persons who are employed by an educational agency or institution but who are not in attendance at such agency or institution, records made and maintained in the normal course of business which relate exclusively to such person in that person's capacity as an employee and are not available for use for any other purpose; or

(iv) records on a student who is eighteen years of age or older, or is attending an institution of postsecondary education, which are made or maintained by a physician, psychiatrist, psychologist, or other recognized professional or paraprofessional acting in his professional or paraprofessional capacity, or assisting in that capacity, and which are made, maintained, or used only in connection with the provision of treatment to the student, and are not available to anyone other than persons providing such treatment, except that such records can be personally reviewed by a physician or other appropriate professional of the student's choice.

(5)(A) For the purposes of this section the term "directory information" relating to a student includes the following: the student's name, address, telephone listing, date and place of birth, major field of study, participation in officially recognized activities and sports, weight and height of members of athletic teams, dates of attendance, degrees and awards received, and the most recent previous educational agency or institution attended by the student.

(B) Any educational agency or institution making public directory information shall give public notice of the categories of information which it has designated as such information with respect to each student attending the institution or agency and shall allow a reasonable period of time after such notice has been given for a parent to inform the institution or agency that any or all of the information designated should not be released without the parent's prior consent.

(6) For the purposes of this section, the term "student" includes any person with respect to whom an educational agency or institution maintains education records or personally identifiable information, but

does not include a person who has not been in attendance at such agency or institution.

(b) Release of education records; parental consent requirement; exceptions; compliance with judicial orders and subpoenas; audit and evaluation of federally-supported education programs; recordkeeping

(1) No funds shall be made available under any applicable program to any educational agency or institution which has a policy or practice of permitting the release of education records (or personally identifiable information contained therein other than directory information, as defined in paragraph (5) of subsection (a) of this section) of students without the written consent of their parents to any individual, agency, or organization, other than to the following—

(A) other school officials, including teachers within the educational institution or local educational agency, who have been determined by such agency or institution to have legitimate educational interests, including the educational interests of the child for whom consent would otherwise be required;

(B) officials of other schools or school systems in which the student seeks or intends to enroll, upon condition that the student's parents be notified of the transfer, receive a copy of the record if desired, and have an opportunity for a hearing to challenge the content of the record;

(C)(i) authorized representatives of

(I) the Comptroller General of the United States,
(II) the Secretary, or
(III) State educational authorities, under the conditions set forth in paragraph (3), or

(ii) authorized representatives of the Attorney General for law enforcement purposes under the same conditions as apply to the Secretary under paragraph (3);

(D) in connection with a student's application for, or receipt of, financial aid;

(E) State and local officials or authorities to whom such information is specifically allowed to be reported or disclosed pursuant to State statute adopted—

(i) before November 19, 1974, if the allowed reporting or disclosure concerns the juvenile justice sys-

tem and such system's ability to effectively serve the student whose records are released, or

(ii) after November 19, 1974, if—

(I) the allowed reporting or disclosure concerns the juvenile justice system and such system's ability to effectively serve, prior to adjudication, the student whose records are released; and

(II) the officials and authorities to whom such information is disclosed certify in writing to the educational agency or institution that the information will not be disclosed to any other party except as provided under State law without the prior written consent of the parent of the student.[1]

(F) organizations conducting studies for, or on behalf of, educational agencies or institutions for the purpose of developing, validating, or administering predictive tests, administering student aid programs, and improving instruction, if such studies are conducted in such a manner as will not permit the personal identification of students and their parents by persons other than representatives of such organizations and such information will be destroyed when no longer needed for the purpose for which it is conducted;

(G) accrediting organizations in order to carry out their accrediting functions;

(H) parents of a dependent student of such parents, as defined in section 152 of title 26;

(I) subject to regulations of the Secretary, in connection with an emergency, appropriate persons if the knowledge of such information is necessary to protect the health or safety of the student or other persons; and

(J)(i) the entity or persons designated in a Federal grand jury subpoena, in which case the court shall order, for good cause shown, the educational agency or institution (and any officer, director, employee, agent, or attorney for such agency or institution) on which the subpoena is served, to not disclose to any person the existence or contents of the subpoena or any information furnished to the grand jury in response to the subpoena; and

(ii) the entity or persons designated in any other subpoena issued for a law enforcement purpose, in which case the court or other issuing agency may order, for good cause shown, the educational agency or institution (and any officer, director, employee, agent, or attorney for such agency or institution) on which the subpoena is served, to not disclose to any person the existence or contents of the subpoena or any information furnished in response to the subpoena.

Nothing in subparagraph (E) of this paragraph shall prevent a State from further limiting the number or type of State or local officials who will continue to have access thereunder.

(2) No funds shall be made available under any applicable program to any educational agency or institution which has a policy or practice of releasing, or providing access to, any personally identifiable information in education records other than directory information, or as is permitted under paragraph (1) of this subsection, unless—

(A) there is written consent from the student's parents specifying records to be released, the reasons for such release, and to whom, and with a copy of the records to be released to the student's parents and the student if desired by the parents, or

(B) except as provided in paragraph (1)(J), such information is furnished in compliance with judicial order, or pursuant to any lawfully issued subpoena, upon condition that parents and the students are notified of all such orders or subpoenas in advance of the compliance therewith by the educational institution or agency.

(3) Nothing contained in this section shall preclude authorized representatives of

(A) the Comptroller General of the United States,

(B) the Secretary, or

(C) State educational authorities from having access to student or other records which may be necessary in connection with the audit and evaluation of Federally-supported education programs, or in connection with the enforcement of the Federal legal requirements which relate to such programs: Provided, That except when collection of personally identifiable information is specifically authorized by Federal law, any data collected by such officials shall be protected in a manner which will not permit the personal identification of students and their parents by other than those officials, and such personally identifiable data shall be destroyed when no longer needed for such audit, evaluation, and enforcement of Federal legal requirements.

(4)(A) Each educational agency or institution shall maintain a record, kept with the education records of each student, which will indicate all individuals (other than those specified in paragraph (1)(A) of this subsection), agencies, or organizations which have requested or obtained access to a student's education records maintained by such educational agency or institution, and which will indicate specifically the legitimate interest that each such person, agency, or organization has in obtaining this information. Such record of access shall be available only to parents, to the school official and his assistants who are responsible for the custody of such records, and to persons or organizations authorized in, and under the conditions of, clauses (A) and (C) of paragraph (1) as a means of auditing the operation of the system.

(B) With respect to this subsection, personal information shall only be transferred to a third party on the condition that such party will not permit any other party to have access to such information without the written consent of the parents of the student. If a third party outside the educational agency or institution permits access to information in violation of paragraph (2)(A), or fails to destroy information in violation of paragraph (1)(F), the educational agency or institution shall be prohibited from permitting access to information from education records to that third party for a period of not less than five years.

(5) Nothing in this section shall be construed to prohibit State and local educational officials from having access to student or other records which may be necessary in connection with the audit and evaluation of any federally or State supported education program or in connection with the enforcement of the Federal legal requirements which relate to any such program, subject to the conditions specified in the proviso in paragraph (3).

(6)(A) Nothing in this section shall be construed to prohibit an institution of postsecondary education from disclosing, to an alleged victim of any crime of violence (as that term is defined in section 16 of title 18), or a nonforcible sex offense, the final results of any disciplinary proceeding conducted by such institution against the alleged perpetrator of such crime or offense with respect to such crime or offense.

(B) Nothing in this section shall be construed to prohibit an institution of postsecondary education from disclosing the final results of any disciplinary proceeding conducted by such institution against a student who is an alleged perpetrator of any crime of violence (as that term is defined in section 16 of title 18), or a nonforcible sex offense, if the institution determines as a result of that disciplinary proceeding that the student committed a violation of the institution's rules or policies with respect to such crime or offense.

(C) For the purpose of this paragraph, the final results of any disciplinary proceeding—

(i) shall include only the name of the student, the violation committed, and any sanction imposed by the institution on that student; and

(ii) may include the name of any other student, such as a victim or witness, only with the written consent of that other student.

(7)(A) Nothing in this section may be construed to prohibit an educational institution from disclosing information provided to the institution under section 14071 of title 42 concerning registered sex offenders who are required to register under such section.

(B) The Secretary shall take appropriate steps to notify educational institutions that disclosure of information described in subparagraph (A) is permitted.

(c) Surveys or data-gathering activities; regulations

Not later than 240 days after October 20, 1994, the Secretary shall adopt appropriate regulations or procedures, or identify existing regulations or procedures, which protect the rights of privacy of students and their families in connection with any surveys or data-gathering activities conducted, assisted, or authorized by the Secretary or an administrative head of an education agency. Regulations established under this subsection shall include provisions controlling the use, dissemination, and protection of such data. No survey or data-gathering activities shall be conducted by the Secretary, or an administrative head of an education agency under an applicable program, unless such activities are authorized by law.

(d) Students' rather than parents' permission or consent

For the purposes of this section, whenever a student has attained eighteen years of age, or is attending an institu-

tion of postsecondary education, the permission or consent required of and the rights accorded to the parents of the student shall thereafter only be required of and accorded to the student.

(e) Informing parents or students of rights under this section

No funds shall be made available under any applicable program to any educational agency or institution unless such agency or institution effectively informs the parents of students, or the students, if they are eighteen years of age or older, or are attending an institution of postsecondary education, of the rights accorded them by this section.

(f) Enforcement; termination of assistance

The Secretary shall take appropriate actions to enforce this section and to deal with violations of this section, in accordance with this chapter, except that action to terminate assistance may be taken only if the Secretary finds there has been a failure to comply with this section, and he has determined that compliance cannot be secured by voluntary means.

(g) Office and review board; creation; functions

The Secretary shall establish or designate an office and review board within the Department for the purpose of investigating, processing, reviewing, and adjudicating violations of this section and complaints which may be filed concerning alleged violations of this section. Except for the conduct of hearings, none of the functions of the Secretary under this section shall be carried out in any of the regional offices of such Department.

(h) Disciplinary records; disclosure

Nothing in this section shall prohibit an educational agency or institution from—

(1) including appropriate information in the education record of any student concerning disciplinary action taken against such student for conduct that posed a significant risk to the safety or well-being of that student, other students, or other members of the school community; or

(2) disclosing such information to teachers and school officials, including teachers and school officials in other schools, who have legitimate educational interests in the behavior of the student.

(i) Drug and alcohol violation disclosures

(1) In general

Nothing in this Act or the Higher Education Act of 1965 [20 U.S.C. 1001 et seq.] shall be construed to prohibit an institution of higher education from disclosing, to a parent or legal guardian of a student, information regarding any violation of any Federal, State, or local law, or of any rule or policy of the institution, governing the use or possession of alcohol or a controlled substance, regardless of whether that information is contained in the student's education records, if—

(A) the student is under the age of 21; and

(B) the institution determines that the student has committed a disciplinary violation with respect to such use or possession.

(2) State law regarding disclosure

Nothing in paragraph (1) shall be construed to supersede any provision of State law that prohibits an institution of higher education from making the disclosure described in subsection (a) of this section.

(j) Investigation and prosecution of terrorism

(1) In general

Notwithstanding subsections (a) through (i) of this section or any provision of State law, the Attorney General (or any Federal officer or employee, in a position not lower than an Assistant Attorney General, designated by the Attorney General) may submit a written application to a court of competent jurisdiction for an ex parte order requiring an educational agency or institution to permit the Attorney General (or his designee) to—

(A) collect education records in the possession of the educational agency or institution that are relevant to an authorized investigation or prosecution of an offense listed in section 2332b(g)(5)(B) of title 18, or an act of domestic or international terrorism as defined in section 2331 of that title; and

(B) for official purposes related to the investigation or prosecution of an offense described in paragraph (1)(A), retain, disseminate, and use (including as evidence at trial or in other administrative or judicial proceedings) such records, consistent with such guidelines as the Attorney General, after consultation with the Secretary, shall issue to protect confidentiality.

(2) Application and approval

(A) In general.—An application under paragraph (1) shall certify that there are specific and articulable facts giving reason to believe that the education records are likely to contain information described in paragraph (1)(A).

(B) The court shall issue an order described in paragraph (1) if the court finds that the application for the order includes the certification described in subparagraph (A).

(3) Protection of educational agency or institution

An educational agency or institution that, in good faith, produces education records in accordance with an order issued under this subsection shall not be liable to any person for that production.

(4) Record-keeping

Subsection (b)(4) of this section does not apply to education records subject to a court order under this subsection.

Footnotes

[1] Sc in original. The period probably should be a semicolon.

(Pub. L. 90-247, title IV, Sec. 444, formerly Sec. 438, as added Pub. L. 93-380, title V, Sec. 513(a), Aug. 21, 1974, 88 Stat. 571; amended Pub. L. 93-568, Sec. 2(a), Dec. 31, 1974, 88 Stat. 1858; Pub. L. 96-46, Sec. 4(c), Aug. 6, 1979, 93 Stat. 342; Pub. L. 101-542, title II, Sec. 203, Nov. 8, 1990, 104 Stat. 2385; Pub. L. 102-325, title XV, Sec. 1555(a), July 23, 1992, 106 Stat. 840; renumbered Sec. 444 and amended Pub. L. 103-382, title II, Secs. 212(b)(1), 249, 261(h), Oct. 20, 1994, 108 Stat. 3913, 3924, 3928; Pub. L. 105-244, title IX, Secs. 951, 952, Oct. 7, 1998, 112 Stat. 1835, 1836; Pub. L. 106-386, div. B, title VI, Sec. 1601(d), Oct. 28, 2000, 114 Stat. 1538; Pub. L. 107-56, title V, Sec. 507, Oct. 26, 2001, 115 Stat. 367; Pub. L. 107-110, title X, Sec. 1062(3), Jan. 8, 2002, 115 Stat. 2088.)

References in Text

This Act, referred to in subsec. (i)(1), is Pub. L. 90-247, Jan. 2, 1968, 80 Stat. 783, as amended, known as the Elementary and Secondary Education Amendments of 1967. Title IV of the Act, known as the General Education Provisions Act, is classified generally to this chapter. For complete classification of this Act to the Code, see Short Title of 1968 Amendment note set out under section 6301 of this title and Tables.

The Higher Education Act of 1965, referred to in subsec. (i)(1), is Pub. L. 89-329, Nov. 8, 1965, 79 Stat. 1219, as amended, which is classified principally to chapter 28 (Sec. 1001 et seq.) of this title. For complete classification of this Act to the Code, see Short Title note set out under section 1001 of this title and Tables.

Prior Provisions

A prior section 444 of Pub. L. 90-247 was classified to section 1233c of this title prior to repeal by Pub. L. 103-382.

Amendments

2002—
Subsec. (a)(1)(B). Pub. L. 107-110, Sec. 1062(3)(A), realigned margins.

Subsec. (b)(1). Pub. L. 107-110, Sec. 1062(3)(C), substituted "subparagraph (E)" for "clause (E)" in concluding provisions.

Subsec. (b)(1)(J). Pub. L. 107-110, Sec. 1062(3)(B), realigned margins.

Subsec. (b)(7). Pub. L. 107-110, Sec. 1062(3)(D), realigned margins.

2001—*Subsec.* (j). Pub. L. 107-56 added subsec. (j).

2000—*Subsec.* (b)(7). Pub. L. 106 386 added par. (7).

1998—
Subsec. (b)(1)(C). Pub. L. 105-244, Sec. 951(1), amended subpar. (C) generally. Prior to amendment, subpar. (C) read as follows: "authorized representatives of (i) the Comptroller General of the United States, (ii) the Secretary, or (iii) State educational authorities, under the conditions set forth in paragraph (3) of this subsection;".

Subsec. (b)(6). Pub. L. 105-244, Sec. 951(2), designated existing provisions as subpar. (A), substituted "or a nonforcible sex offense, the final results" for "the

results", substituted "such crime or offense" for "such crime" in two places, and added subpars. (B) and (C).

Subsec. (i). Pub. L. 105-244, Sec. 952, added subsec. (i).

1994—
Subsec. (a)(1)(B). Pub. L. 103-382, Sec. 249(1)(A)(ii), added subpar. (B). Former subpar. (B) redesignated (C).

Subsec. (a)(1)(C). Pub. L. 103-382, Sec. 249(1)(A)(i), (iii), redesignated subpar. (B) as (C) and substituted "subparagraph (D)" for "subparagraph (C)" in cl. (iii). Former subpar. (C) redesignated (D).

Subsec. (a)(1)(D). Pub. L. 103-382, Sec. 249(1)(A)(i), (iv), redesignated subpar. (C) as (D) and substituted "subparagraph (C)" for "subparagraph (B)".

Subsec. (a)(2). Pub. L. 103-382, Sec. 249(1)(B), substituted "privacy rights" for "privacy or other rights".

Subsec. (a)(4)(B)(ii). Pub. L. 103-382, Sec. 261(h)(1), substituted semicolon for period at end.

Subsec. (b)(1)(A). Pub. L. 103-382, Sec. 249(2)(A)(i), inserted before semicolon ", including the educational interests of the child for whom consent would otherwise be required".

Subsec. (b)(1)(C). Pub. L. 103 382, Sec. 261(h)(2)(A), substituted "or (iii)" for "(iii) an administrative head of an education agency (as defined in section 1221e-3(c) of this title), or (iv)".

Subsec. (b)(1)(E). Pub. L. 103-382, Sec. 249(2)(A)(ii), amended subpar. (E) generally. Prior to amendment, subpar. (E) read as follows: "State and local officials or authorities to whom such information is specifically required to be reported or disclosed pursuant to State statute adopted prior to November 19, 1974;".

Subsec. (b)(1)(H). Pub. L. 103-382, Sec. 261(h)(2)(B), substituted "the Internal Revenue Code of 1986" for "the Internal Revenue Code of 1954", which for purposes of codification was translated as "title 26" thus requiring no change in text.

Subsec. (b)(1)(J). Pub. L. 103-382, Sec. 249(2)(A)(iii)–(v), added subpar. (J).

Subsec. (b)(2). Pub. L. 103-382, Sec. 249(2)(B)(i), which directed amendment of matter preceding subpar. (A) by substituting ", unless—" for the period, was executed by substituting a comma for the period before "unless—" to reflect the probable intent of Congress.

Subsec. (b)(2)(B). Pub. L. 103-382, Sec. 249(2)(B)(ii), inserted "except as provided in paragraph (1)(J)," before "such information".

Subsec. (b)(3). Pub. L. 103-382, Sec. 261(h)(2)(C), substituted "or (C)" for "(C) an administrative head of an education agency or (D)" and "education programs" for "education program".

Subsec. (b)(4). Pub. L. 103-382, Sec. 249(2)(C), inserted at end "If a third party outside the educational agency or institution permits access to information in violation of paragraph (2)(A), or fails to destroy information in violation of paragraph (1)(F), the educational agency or institution shall be prohibited from permitting access to information from education records to that third party for a period of not less than five years."

Subsec. (c). Pub. L. 103-382, Sec. 249(3), substituted "Not later than 240 days after October 20, 1994, the Secretary shall adopt appropriate regulations or procedures, or identify existing regulations or procedures, which" for "The Secretary shall adopt appropriate regulations to".

Subsec. (d). Pub. L. 103-382, Sec. 261(h)(3), inserted a comma after "education".

Subsec. (e). Pub. L. 103-382, Sec. 249(4), inserted "effectively" before "informs".

Subsec. (f). Pub. L. 103-382, Sec. 261(h)(4), struck out ", or an administrative head of an education agency," after "The Secretary" and substituted "enforce this section" for "enforce provisions of this section", "in accordance with" for "according to the provisions of", and "comply with this section" for "comply with the provisions of this section".

Subsec. (g). Pub. L. 103-382, Sec. 261(h)(5), struck out "of Health, Education, and Welfare" after "the Department" and "the provisions of" after "adjudicating violations of".

Subsec. (h). Pub. L. 103-382, Sec. 249(5), added subsec. (h).

1992—

Subsec. (a)(4)(B)(ii). Pub. L. 102-325 amended cl. (ii) generally. Prior to amendment, cl. (ii) read as follows: "if the personnel of a law enforcement unit do not have access to education records under subsection (b)(1) of this section, the records and documents of such law enforcement unit which (I) are kept apart from records described in subparagraph (A), (II) are maintained solely for law enforcement purposes, and (III) are not made available to persons other than law enforcement officials of the same jurisdiction;".

1990—*Subsec.* (b)(6). Pub. L. 101-542 added par. (6).

1979—*Subsec.* (b)(5). Pub. L. 96-46 added par. (5).

1974—

Subsec. (a)(1). Pub. L. 93-568, Sec. 2(a)(1)(A)-(C), (2)(A)-(C), (3), designated existing par. (1) as subpar. (A), substituted reference to educational agencies and institutions for reference to state or local educational agencies, institutions of higher education, community colleges, schools, agencies offering preschool programs, and other educational institutions, substituted the generic term education records for the enumeration of such records, and extended the right to inspect and review such records to parents of children who have been in attendance, and added subpars. (B) and (C).

Subsec. (a)(2). Pub. L. 93-568, Sec. 2(a)(4), substituted provisions making the availability of funds to educational agencies and institutions conditional on the granting of an opportunity for a hearing to parents of students who are or have been in attendance at such institution or agency to challenge the contents of the student's education records for provisions granting the parents an opportunity for such hearing, and inserted provisions authorizing insertion into the records a written explanation of the parents respecting the content of such records.

Subsec. (a)(3) to (6). Pub. L. 93-568, Sec. 2(a)(1)(G), (2)(F), (5), added pars. (3) to (6).

Subsec. (b)(1). Pub. L. 93-568, Sec. 2(a)(1)(D), (2)(D), (6), (8)(A)-(C), (10)(A), in provisions preceding subpar. (A), substituted "educational agency or institution which has a policy of permitting the release of education records (or personally identifiable information contained therein other than directory information, as defined in paragraph (5) of subsection (a) of this section)" for "state or local educational agency, any institution of higher education, any community college, any school, agency offering a preschool program, or any other educational institution which has a policy or practice of permitting the release of personally identifiable records or files (or personal information contained therein)", in subpar. (A), substituted "educational agency, who have been determined by such agency or institution to have" for "educational agency who have", in subpar. (B), substituted "the student seeks or intends to" for "the student intends to", in subpar. (C), substituted reference to "section 408(c)" for reference to "section 409 of this Act" which for purposes of codification has been translated as "section 1221e-3(c) of this title", and added subpars. (E) to (I).

Subsec. (b)(2). Pub. L. 93-568, Sec. 2(a)(1)(E), (2)(E), substituted "educational agency or institution which has a policy or practice of releasing, or providing access to, any personally identifiable information in education records other than directory information, or as is permitted under paragraph (1) of this subsection" for "state or local educational agency, any institution of higher education, any community college, any school, agency offering a preschool program, or any other educational institution which has a policy or practice of furnishing, in any form, any personally identifiable information contained in personal school records, to any persons other than those listed in subsection (b)(1) of this section".

Subsec. (b)(3). Pub. L. 93-568, Sec. 2(a)(8)(D), substituted "information is specifically authorized by Federal law, any data collected by such officials shall be protected in a manner which will not permit the personal identification of students and their parents by other than those officials, and such personally identifiable data shall be destroyed when no longer needed for such audit, evaluation, and enforcement of Federal legal requirements" for "data is specifically authorized by Federal law, any data collected by such officials with respect to individual students shall not include information (including social security numbers) which would permit the personal identification of such students or their parents after the data so obtained has been collected".

Subsec. (b)(4). Pub. L. 93-568, Sec. 2(a)(9), substituted provisions that each educational agency or institution maintain a record, kept with the education records of each student, indicating individuals, agencies, or organizations who obtained access to the student's record and the legitimate interest in obtaining such information, that such record of access shall be available only to parents, school officials, and their assistants having responsibility for

the custody of such records, and as a means of auditing the operation of the system, for provisions that with respect to subsecs. (c)(1), (c)(2), and (c)(3) of this section, all persons, agencies, or organizations desiring access to the records of a student shall be required to sign forms to be kept with the records of the student, but only for inspection by the parents or the student, indicating specifically the legitimate educational or other interest of the person seeking such information, and that the form shall be available to parents and school officials having responsibility for record maintenance as a means of auditing the operation of the system.

Subsec. (e). Pub. L. 93-568, Sec. 2(a)(1)(F), substituted "to any educational agency or institution unless such agency or institution" for "unless the recipient of such funds".

Subsec. (g). Pub. L. 93-568, Sec. 2(a)(7), (10)(B), struck out reference to sections 1232c and 1232f of this title and inserted provisions that except for the conduct of hearings, none of the functions of the Secretary under this section shall be carried out in any of the regional offices of such Department.

Effective Date of 2002 Amendment

Amendment by Pub. L. 107-110 effective Jan. 8, 2002, except with respect to certain noncompetitive programs and competitive programs, see section 5 of Pub. L. 107-110, set out as an Effective Date note under section 6301 of this title.

Effective Date of 1998 Amendment

Amendment by Pub. L. 105-244 effective Oct. 1, 1998, except as otherwise provided in Pub. L. 105-244, see section 3 of Pub. L. 105-244, set out as a note under section 1001 of this title.

Effective Date of 1992 Amendment

Section 1555(b) of Pub. L. 102-325 provided that: "The amendment made by this section [amending this section] shall take effect on the date of enactment of this Act [July 23, 1992]."

Effective Date of 1979 Amendment

Amendment by Pub. L. 96-46 effective Oct. 1, 1978, see section 8 of Pub. L. 96-46, set out as a note under section 930 of this title.

Effective Date of 1974 Amendment

Section 2(b) of Pub. L. 93-568 provided that: "The amendments made by subsection (a) [amending this section] shall be effective, and retroactive to, November 19, 1974."

Effective Date

Section 513(b)(1) of Pub. L. 93-380 provided that: "The provisions of this section [enacting this section and provisions set out as a note under section 1221 of this title] shall become effective ninety days after the date of enactment [Aug. 21, 1974] of section 438 [now 444] of the General Education Provisions Act [this section]."

Family Educational Rights and Privacy Act Regulations

Amendments made in 2009 have been highlighted for the convenience of readers.

34 CFR Part 99

Subpart A—General

Section

99.1 To which educational agencies or institutions do these regulations apply?

99.2 What is the purpose of these regulations?

99.3 What definitions apply to these regulations?

99.4 What are the rights of parents?

99.5 What are the rights of students?

99.7 What must an educational agency or institution include in its annual notification?

99.8 What provisions apply to records of a law enforcement unit?

Subpart B—What Are the Rights of Inspection and Review of Education Records?

Section

99.10 What rights exist for a parent or eligible student to inspect and review education records?

99.11 May an educational agency or institution charge a fee for copies of education records?

99.12 What limitations exist on the right to inspect and review records?

Subpart C—What Are the Procedures for Amending Educating Records?

Section

99.20 How can a parent or eligible student request amendment of the student's education records?

99.21 Under what conditions does a parent or eligible student have the right to a hearing?

99.22 What minimum requirements exist for the conduct of a hearing?

Subpart D—May an Educational Agency or Institution Disclose Personally Identifiable Information from Education Records?

Section

99.30 Under what conditions is prior consent required to disclose information?

99.31 Under what conditions is prior consent not required to disclose information?

99.32 What recordkeeping requirements exist concerning requests and disclosures?

99.33 What limitations apply to the redisclosure of information?

99.34 What conditions apply to disclosure of information to other educational agencies or institutions?

99.35 What conditions apply to disclosure of information for federal or state program purposes?

99.36 What conditions apply to disclosure of information in health and safety emergencies?

99.37 What conditions apply to disclosing directory information?

99.38 What conditions apply to disclosure of information as permitted by state statute adopted after November 19, 1974 concerning the juvenile justice system?

99.39 What definitions apply to the nonconsensual disclosure of records by postsecondary educational institutions in connection with disciplinary proceedings concerning crimes of violence or nonforcible sex offenses?

Subpart E—What Are the Enforcement Procedures?

Section

99.60 What functions has the Secretary delegated to the Office and to the Office of Administrative Law Judges?

99.61 What responsibility does an educational agency or institution have concerning conflict with state or local laws?

99.62 What information must an educational agency or institution submit to the Office?

99.63 Where are complaints filed?

99.64 What is the investigation procedure?

99.65 What is the content of the notice of investigation issued by the Office?

99.66 What are the responsibilities of the Office in the enforcement process?

99.67 How does the Secretary enforce decisions?

Appendix A To Part 99—Crimes of Violence Definitions

Subpart A—General

§ 99.1 To which educational agencies or institutions do these regulations apply?

(a) Except as otherwise noted in § 99.10, this part applies to an educational agency or institution to which funds have been made available under any program administered by the Secretary, if—

  (1) The education institution provides educational services or instruction, or both, to students; or

  (2) The educational agency is authorized to direct and control public elementary or secondary, or postsecondary educational institutions.

(b) This part does not apply to an educational agency or institution solely because students attending that agency or institution receive non-monetary benefits under a program referenced in paragraph (a) of this section, if no funds under that program are made available to the agency or institution.

(c) The Secretary considers funds to be made available to an educational agency or institution if funds under one or more of the programs referenced in paragraph (a) of this section—

  (1) Are provided to the agency or institution by grant, cooperative agreement, contract, subgrant, or subcontract; or

  (2) Are provided to students attending the agency or institution and the funds may be paid to the agency or institution by those students for educational purposes, such as under the Pell Grant Program and the Guaranteed Student Loan Program (Titles IV-A-1 and IV-B, respectively, of the *Higher Education Act of 1965*, as amended).

(d) If an educational agency or institution receives funds under one or more of the programs covered by this section, the regulations in this part apply to the recipient as a whole, including each of its components (such as a department within a university).

[Authority: 20 u.s.c. 1232g]

§ 99.2 What is the purpose of these regulations?

The purpose of this part is to set out requirements for the protection of privacy of parents and students under section 444 of the *General Education Provisions Act*, as amended.

[Authority: 20 u.s.c. 1232g]

§ 99.3 What definitions apply to these regulations?

The following definitions apply to this part:

"ACT" means the *Family Educational Rights and Privacy Act of 1974*, as amended, enacted as section 444 of the *General Education Provisions Act*.

[Authority: 20 u.s.c. 1232g]

"ATTENDANCE" includes, but is not limited to:

  (a) Attendance in person or by paper correspondence, videoconference, satellite, Internet, or other electronic information and telecommunications technologies for students who are not physically present in the classroom; and

  (b) The period during which a person is working under a work-study program.

[Authority: 20 u.s.c. 1232g]

"BIOMETRIC RECORD," as used in the definition of "personally identifiable information," means a record of one or more measurable biological or behavioral characteristics that can be used for automated recognition of an individual. Examples include fingerprints; retina and iris patterns; voiceprints; DNA sequence; facial characteristics; and handwriting.

[Authority: 20 U.S.C. 1232g]

"DATES OF ATTENDANCE." (a) The term means the period of time during which a student attends or attended an educational agency or institution. Examples of dates of attendance include an academic year, a spring semester, or a first quarter.

(b) The term does not include specific daily records of a student's attendance at an educational agency or institution.

[Authority: 20 u.s.c. 1232g(a)(5)(A)]

"DIRECTORY INFORMATION" means information contained in an education record of a student that would not generally be considered harmful or an invasion of privacy if disclosed.

(a) Directory information includes, but is not limited to, the student's name, address, telephone listing, electronic mail address, photograph, date and place of birth, major field of study, dates of attendance, grade level, enrollment status (*e.g.*, undergraduate or graduate; full-time or part-time), participation in officially recognized activities and sports, weight and height of members of athletic teams, degrees, honors and awards received, and the most recent educational agency or institution attended.

(b) Directory information does not include a student's:

(1) Social security number; or
(2) Student identification (ID) number, except as provided in paragraph (c) of this section.

(c) Directory information includes a student ID number, user ID, or other unique personal identifier used by the student for purposes of accessing or communicating in electronic systems, but only if the identifier cannot be used to gain access to education records except when used in conjunction with one or more factors that authenticate the user's identity, such as a personal identification number (PIN), password, or other factor known or possessed only by the authorized user.

[Authority: 20 u.s.c. 1232g(a)(5)(A)]

"DISCIPLINARY ACTION OR PROCEEDING" means the investigation, adjudication, or imposition of sanctions by an educational agency or institution with respect to an infraction or violation of the internal rules of conduct applicable to students of the agency or institution.

"DISCLOSURE" means to permit access to or the release, transfer, or other communication of personally identifiable information contained in education records to any party, by any means, including oral, written, or electronic means. Disclosure means to permit access to or the release, transfer, or other communication of per-

sonally identifiable information contained in education records by any means, including oral, written, or electronic means, to any party except the party identified as the party that provided or created the record.

[Authority: 20 u.s.c. 1232g(b)(1) and (b)(2)]

"EDUCATIONAL AGENCY OR INSTITUTION" means any public or private agency or institution to which this part applies under § 99.1(a).

[Authority: 20 u.s.c. 1232g(a)(3)]

"EDUCATION RECORDS" (a) The term means those records that are:

(1) Directly related to a student; and
(2) Maintained by an educational agency or institution or by a party acting for the agency or institution.

(b) The term does not include:

(1) Records that are kept in the sole possession of the maker, are used only as a personal memory aid, and are not accessible or revealed to any other person except a temporary substitute for the maker of the record.

(2) Records of the law enforcement unit of an educational agency or institution, subject to the provisions of § 99.8.

(3)(i) Records relating to an individual who is employed by an educational agency or institution, that:

(A) Are made and maintained in the normal course of business;
(B) Relate exclusively to the individual in that individual's capacity as an employee; and
(C) Are not available for use for any other purpose.

(ii) Records relating to an individual in attendance at the agency or institution who is employed as a result of his or her status as a student are education records and not excepted under paragraph (b)(3)(i) of this definition.

(4) Records on a student who is 18 years of age or older, or is attending an institution of postsecondary education, that are:

(i) Made or maintained by a physician, psychiatrist, psychologist, or other recognized professional or paraprofessional acting in his or her professional capacity or assisting in a paraprofessional capacity;

(ii) Made, maintained, or used only in connection with treatment of the student; and

(iii) Disclosed only to individuals providing the treatment. For the purpose of this definition, "treatment" does not include remedial educational activities or activities that are part of the program of instruction at the agency or institution; and

(5) Records created or received by an educational agency or institution after an individual is no longer a student in attendance and that are not directly related to the individual's attendance as a student.

(6) Grades on peer-graded papers before they are collected and recorded by a teacher.

[Authority: 20 u.s.c. 1232g(a)(4)]

"ELIGIBLE STUDENT" means a student who has reached 18 years of age or is attending an institution of postsecondary education.

[Authority: 20 u.s.c. 1232g(d)]

"INSTITUTION OF POSTSECONDARY EDUCATION" means an institution that provides education to students beyond the secondary school level; "secondary school level" means the educational level (not beyond grade 12) at which secondary education is provided as determined under state law.

[Authority: 20 u.s.c. 1232g(d)]

"PARENT" means a parent of a student and includes a natural parent, a guardian, or an individual acting as a parent in the absence of a parent or a guardian.

[Authority: 20 u.s.c. 1232g]

"PARTY" means an individual, agency, institution, or organization.

[Authority: 20 u.s.c. 1232g(b)(4)(A)]

"PERSONALLY IDENTIFIABLE INFORMATION" includes, but is not limited to:

(a) The student's name;

(b) The name of the student's parent or other family members;

(c) The address of the student or student's family;

(d) A personal identifier, such as the student's social security number or student number, or biometric record;

(e) Other indirect identifiers, such as the student's date of birth, place of birth, and mother's maiden name;

(f) Other information that, alone or in combination, is linked or linkable to a specific student that would allow a reasonable person in the school community, who does not have personal knowledge of the relevant circumstances, to identify the student with reasonable certainty; or

(g) Information requested by a person who the educational agency or institution reasonably believes knows the identity of the student to whom the education record relates.

[Authority: 20 u.s.c. 1232g]

"RECORD" means any information recorded in any way, including, but not limited to, handwriting, print, computer media, video or audio tape, film, microfilm, and microfiche.

[Authority: 20 u.s.c. 1232g]

"SECRETARY" means the Secretary of the U.S. Department of Education or an official or employee of the Department of Education acting for the Secretary under a delegation of authority.

[Authority: 20 u.s.c. 1232g]

"STUDENT," except as otherwise specifically provided in this part, means any individual who is or has been in attendance at an educational agency or institution and regarding whom the agency or institution maintains education records.

[Authority: 20 u.s.c. 1232g(a)(6)]

§ 99.4 What are the rights of parents?

An educational agency or institution shall give full rights under the *Act* to either parent, unless the agency or institution has been provided with evidence that there is a court order, state statute, or legally binding document relating to such matters as divorce, separation, or custody that specifically revokes these rights.

[Authority: 20 u.s.c. 1232g]

§ 99.5 What are the rights of students?

(a)(1) When a student becomes an eligible student, the rights accorded to, and consent required of, parents under this part transfer from the parents to the student.

(2) Nothing in this section prevents an educational agency or institution from disclosing education records, or personally identifiable information from education records, to a parent without the prior written consent of an eligible student if the disclosure meets the conditions in §99.31(a)(8), §99.31(a)(10), §99.31(a)(15), or any other provision in §99.31(a).

(b) The *Act* and this part do not prevent educational agencies or institutions from giving students rights in addition to those given to parents.

(c) An individual who is or has been a student at an education institution and who applies for admission at another component of that institution does not have rights under this part with respect to records maintained by that other component, including records maintained in connection with the student's application for admission, unless the student is accepted and attends that other component of the institution.

[Authority: 20 u.s.c. 1232g(d)]

§ 99.7 What must an educational agency or institution include in its annual notification?

(a)(1) Each educational agency or institution shall annually notify parents of students currently in attendance, or eligible students currently in attendance, of their rights under the *Act* and this part.

(2) The notice must inform parents or eligible students that they have the right to—

(i) Inspect and review the student's education records;

(ii) Seek amendment of the student's education records that the parent or eligible student believes to be inaccurate, misleading, or otherwise in violation of the student's privacy rights;

(iii) Consent to disclosures of personally identifiable information contained in the student's education records, except to the extent that the *Act* and § 99.31 authorize disclosure without consent; and

(iv) File with the Department a complaint under § 99.63 and § 99.64 concerning alleged failures by the educational agency or institution to comply with the requirements of the act and this part.

(3) The notice must include all of the following:

(i) The procedure for exercising the right to inspect and review education records.

(ii) The procedure for requesting amendment of records under § 99.20.

(iii) If the educational agency or institution has a policy of disclosing education records under § 99.31(a)(1), a specification of criteria for determining who constitutes a school official and what constitutes a legitimate educational interest.

(b) An educational agency or institution may provide this notice by any means that are reasonably likely to inform the parents or eligible students of their rights.

(1) An educational agency or institution shall effectively notify parents or eligible students who are disabled.

(2) An agency or institution of elementary or secondary education shall effectively notify parents who have a primary or home language other than English.

(Approved by the Office of Management and Budget under control number 1880–0508)

[Authority 20 u.s.c. 1232g(e) and (f)]

§ 99.8 What provisions apply to records of a law enforcement unit?

(a)(1) "Law enforcement unit" means any individual, office, department, division, or other component of an educational agency or institution, such as a unit of commissioned police officers or non-commissioned security guards, that is officially authorized or designated by that agency or institution to—

(i) Enforce any local, state, or federal law, or refer to appropriate authorities a matter for enforcement of any local, state, or federal law against any individual or organization other than the agency or institution itself; or

(ii) Maintain the physical security and safety of the agency or institution.

(2) A component of an educational agency or institution does not lose its status as a "law enforcement unit" if it also performs other, non-law enforcement functions for the agency or institution, including

investigation of incidents or conduct that constitutes or leads to a disciplinary action or proceedings against the student.

(b)(1) Records of law enforcement unit means those records, files, documents, and other materials that are—

(i) Created by a law enforcement unit;

(ii) Created for a law enforcement purpose; and

(iii) Maintained by the law enforcement unit.

(2) Records of law enforcement unit does not mean—

(i) Records created by a law enforcement unit for a law enforcement purpose that are maintained by a component of the educational agency or institution other than the law enforcement unit; or

(ii) Records created and maintained by a law enforcement unit exclusively for a non-law enforcement purpose, such as a disciplinary action or proceeding conducted by the educational agency or institution.

(c)(1) Nothing in the *Act* prohibits an educational agency or institution from contacting its law enforcement unit, orally or in writing, for the purpose of asking that unit to investigate a possible violation of, or to enforce, any local, state, or federal law.

(2) Education records, and personally identifiable information contained in education records, do not lose their status as education records and remain subject to the *Act*, including the disclosure provisions of § 99.30, while in possession of the law enforcement unit.

(d) The *Act* neither requires nor prohibits the dis-closure by any educational agency or institution of its law enforcement unit records.

[Authority: 20 u.s.c. 1232g(a)(4)(B)(ii)]

Subpart B—What Are the Rights of Inspection and Review of Education Records?

§ 99.10 What rights exist for a parent or eligible student to inspect and review education records?

(a) Except as limited under § 99.12, a parent or eligible student must be given the opportunity to inspect and review the student's education records.

This provision applies to—

(1) Any educational agency or institution; and

(2) Any state educational agency (SEA) and its components.

(i) For the purposes of subpart B of this part, an SEA and its components constitute an educational agency or institution.

(ii) An SEA and its components are subject to subpart B of this part if the SEA maintains education records on students who are or have been in attendance at any school of an educational agency or institution subject to the *Act* and this part.

(b) The educational agency or institution, or SEA or its component, shall comply with a request for access to records within a reasonable period of time, but not more than 45 days after it has received the request.

(c) The educational agency or institution, or SEA or its component, shall respond to reasonable requests for explanations and interpretations of the records.

(d) If circumstances effectively prevent the parent or eligible student from exercising the right to inspect and review the student's education records, the educational agency or institution, or SEA or its component, shall—

(1) Provide the parent or eligible student with a copy of the records requested; or

(2) Make other arrangements for the parent or eligible student to inspect and review the requested records.

(e) The educational agency or institution, or SEA or its component, shall not destroy any education records if there is an outstanding request to inspect and review the records under this section.

(f) While an education agency or institution is not required to give an eligible student access to treatment records under paragraph (b)(4) of the definition of "Education records" in § 99.3, the student may have those records reviewed by a physician or other appropriate professional of the student's choice.

[Authority: 20 u.s.c. 1232g(a)(1)(A) and (B)]

§ 99.11 May an educational agency or institution charge a fee for copies of education records?

(a) Unless the imposition of a fee effectively prevents a parent or eligible student from exercising the right to inspect and review the student's education records, an educational agency or institution may charge a fee for a copy of an education record which is made for the parent or eligible student.

(b) An educational agency or institution may not charge a fee to search for or to retrieve the education records of a student.

[Authority: 20 u.s.c. 1232g(a)(1)]

§ 99.12 What limitations exist on the right to inspect and review records?

(a) If the education records of a student contain information on more than one student, the parent or eligible student may inspect and review or be informed of only the specific information about that student.

(b) A postsecondary institution does not have to permit a student to inspect and review education records that are:

(1) Financial records, including any information those records contain, of his or her parents;

(2) Confidential letters and confidential statements of recommendation placed in the education records of the student before January 1, 1975, as long as the statements are used only for the purposes for which they were specifically intended; and

(3) Confidential letters and confidential statements of recommendation placed in the student's education records after January 1, 1975, if:

(i) The student has waived his or her right to inspect and review those letters and statements; and

(ii) Those letters and statements are related to the student's:

(A) Admission to an education institution;

(B) Application for employment; or

(C) Receipt of an honor or honorary recognition.

(c)(1) A waiver under paragraph (b)(3)(i) of this section is valid only if:

(i) The educational agency or institution does not require the waiver as a condition for admission to or receipt of a service or benefit from the agency or institution; and

(ii) The waiver is made in writing and signed by the student, regardless of age.

(2) If a student has waived his or her rights under paragraph (b)(3)(i) of this section, the education institution shall:

(i) Give the student, on request, the names of the individuals who provided the letters and statements of recommendation; and

(ii) Use the letters and statements of recommendation only for the purpose for which they were intended.

(3)(i) A waiver under paragraph (b)(3)(i) of this section may be revoked with respect to any actions occurring after the revocation.

(ii) A revocation under paragraph (c)(3)(i) of this section must be in writing.

[Authority: 20 u.s.c. 1232g(a)(1)(A), (B), (C), and (D)]

Subpart C—What Are the Procedures for Amending Education Records?

§ 99.20 How can a parent or eligible student request amendment of the student's education records?

(a) If a parent or eligible student believes the education records relating to the student contain information that is inaccurate, misleading, or in violation of the student's rights of privacy, he or she may ask the educational agency or institution to amend the record.

(b) The educational agency or institution shall decide whether to amend the record as requested within a reasonable time after the agency or institution receives the request.

(c) If the educational agency or institution decides not to amend the record as requested, it shall inform the parent or eligible student of its decision and of his or her right to a hearing under § 99.21.

[Authority: 20 u.s.c. 1232g(a)(2)]

§ 99.21 Under what conditions does a parent or eligible student have the right to a hearing?

(a) An educational agency or institution shall give a parent or eligible student, on request, an opportunity for a hearing to challenge the content of the student's education records on the grounds that the information contained in the education records is inaccurate, misleading, or in violation of the privacy rights of the student.

(b)(1) If, as a result of the hearing, the educational agency or institution decides that the information is inaccurate, misleading, or otherwise in violation of the privacy rights of the student, it shall:

(i) Amend the record accordingly; and

(ii) Inform the parent or eligible student of the amendment in writing.

(2) If, as a result of the hearing, the educational agency or institution decides that the information in the education record is not inaccurate, misleading, or otherwise in violation of the privacy rights of the student, it shall inform the parent or eligible student of the right to place a statement in the record commenting on the contested information in the record or stating why he or she disagrees with the decision of the agency or institution, or both.

(c) If an educational agency or institution places a statement in the education records of a student under paragraph (b)(2) of this section, the agency or institution shall:

(1) Maintain the statement with the contested part of the record for as long as the record is maintained; and

(2) Disclose the statement whenever it discloses the portion of the record to which the statement relates.

[Authority: 20 u.s.c. 1232g(a)(2)]

§ 99.22 What minimum requirements exist for the conduct of a hearing?

The hearing required by § 99.21 must meet, at a minimum, the following requirements:

(a) The educational agency or institution shall hold the hearing within a reasonable time after it has received the request for the hearing from the parent or eligible student.

(b) The educational agency or institution shall give the parent or eligible student notice of the date, time, and place, reasonably in advance of the hearing.

(c) The hearing may be conducted by any individual, including an official of the educational agency or institution, who does not have a direct interest in the outcome of the hearing.

(d) The educational agency or institution shall give the parent or eligible student a full and fair opportunity to present evidence relevant to the issues raised under § 99.21. The parent or eligible student may, at their own expense, be assisted or represented by one or more individuals of his or her own choice, including an attorney.

(e) The educational agency or institution shall make its decision in writing within a reasonable period of time after the hearing.

(f) The decision must be based solely on the evidence presented at the hearing, and must include a summary of the evidence and the reasons for the decision.

[Authority: 20 u.s.c. 1232g(a)(2)]

Subpart D—May an Educational Agency or Institution Disclose Personally Identifiable Information from Education Records?

§ 99.30 Under what conditions is prior consent required to disclose information?

(a) The parent or eligible student shall provide a signed and dated written consent before an educational agency or institution discloses personally identifiable information from the student's education records, except as provided in § 99.31.

(b) The written consent must:

(1) Specify the records that may be disclosed;
(2) State the purpose of the disclosure; and
(3) Identify the party or class of parties to whom the disclosure may be made.

(c) When a disclosure is made under paragraph (a) of this section:

(1) If a parent or eligible student so requests, the educational agency or institution shall provide him or her with a copy of the records disclosed; and

(2) If the parent of a student who is not an eligible student so requests, the agency or institution shall provide the student with a copy of the records disclosed.

(d) "Signed and dated written consent" under this part may include a record and signature in electronic form that—

(1) Identifies and authenticates a particular person as the source of the electronic consent; and

(2) Indicates such person's approval of the information contained in the electronic consent.

[Authority: 20 u.s.c. 1232g(b)(1) and (b)(2)(A)]

§ 99.31 Under what conditions is prior consent not required to disclose information?

(a) An educational agency or institution may disclose personally identifiable information from an education record of a student without the consent required by § 99.30 if the disclosure meets one or more of the following conditions:

(1)(i)(A) The disclosure is to other school officials, including teachers, within the agency or institution whom the agency or institution has determined to have legitimate educational interests.

(B) A contractor, consultant, volunteer, or other party to whom an agency or institution has out-sourced institutional services or functions may be considered a school official under this paragraph provided that the outside party—

(1) Performs an institutional service or function for which the agency or institution would otherwise use employees;

(2) Is under the direct control of the agency or institution with respect to the use and maintenance of education records; and

(3) Is subject to the requirements of §99.33(a) governing the use and redisclosure of personally identifiable information from education records.

(ii) An educational agency or institution must use reasonable methods to ensure that school officials obtain access to only those education records in which they have legitimate educational interests. An educational agency or institution that does not use physical or technological access controls must ensure that its administrative policy for controlling access to education records is effective and that it remains in compliance with the legitimate educational interest requirement in paragraph (a)(1)(i)(A) of this section.

(2) The disclosure is, subject to the requirements of § 99.34, to officials of another school, school system, or institution of postsecondary education where the student seeks or intends to enroll , or where the student is already enrolled so long as the disclosure is for purposes related to the student's enrollment or transfer.

Note: Section 4155(b) of the No Child Left Behind Act of 2001, 20 U.S.C. 7165(b), requires each State to assure the Secretary of Education that it has a procedure in place to facilitate the transfer of disciplinary records with respect to a suspension or expulsion of a student by a local educational agency to any private or public elementary or secondary school in which the student is subsequently enrolled or seeks, intends, or is instructed to enroll.

(3) The disclosure is, subject to the requirements of § 99.35, to authorized representatives of—

(i) The Comptroller General of the United States;
(ii) The Attorney General of the United States;
(iii) The Secretary; or
(iv) State and local educational authorities.

(4)(i) The disclosure is in connection with financial aid for which the student has applied or which the student has received, if the information is necessary for such purposes as to:

(A) Determine eligibility for the aid;
(B) Determine the amount of the aid;
(C) Determine the conditions for the aid; or
(D) Enforce the terms and conditions of the aid.

(ii) As used in paragraph (a)(4)(i) of this section, "financial aid" means a payment of funds provided to an individual (or a payment in kind of tangible or intangible property to the individual) that is conditioned on the individual's attendance at an educational agency or institution.

[Authority: 20 U.S.C. 1232g(b)(1)(D)]

(5)(i) The disclosure is to state and local officials or authorities to whom this information is specifically-

(A) Allowed to be reported or disclosed pursuant to a state statute adopted before November 19, 1974, if the allowed reporting or disclosure concerns the juvenile justice system and the system's ability to effectively serve the student whose records are released;or

(B) Allowed to be reported or disclosed pursuant to a state statute adopted after November 19, 1974, subject to the requirements of § 99.38.

(ii) Paragraph (a)(5)(1) of this section does not prevent a state from further limiting the number or type of state or local officials to whom disclosures may be made under that paragraph.

(6)(i) The disclosure is to organizations conducting studies for, or on behalf of, educational agencies or institutions to:

(A) Develop, validate, or administer predictive tests;

(B) Administer student aid programs; or

(C) Improve instruction.

(ii) An educational agency or institution may disclose information under paragraph (a)(6)(i) of this section only if:

(A) The study is conducted in a manner that does not permit personal identification of parents and students by individuals other than representatives of the organization that have legitimate interests in the information;

(B) The information is destroyed when no longer needed for the purposes for which the study was conducted.

(C) The educational agency or institution enters into a written agreement with the organization that—

(1) Specifies the purpose, scope, and duration of the study or studies and the information to be disclosed;

(2) Requires the organization to use personally identifiable information from education records only to meet the purpose or purposes of the study as stated in the written agreement;

(3) Requires the organization to conduct the study in a manner that does not permit personal identification of parents and students, as defined in this part, by anyone other than representatives of the organization with legitimate interests; and

(4) Requires the organization to destroy or return to the educational agency or institution all personally identifiable information when the information is no longer needed for the purposes for which the study was conducted and specifies the time period in which the information must be returned or destroyed.

(iii) An educational agency or institution is not required to initiate a study or agree with or endorse the conclusions or results of the study.

(iv) If this Office determines that a third party outside the educational agency or institution to whom information is disclosed under this para-

graph (a)(6) violates paragraph (a)(6)(ii)(B) of this section, the educational agency or institution may not allow that third party access to personally identifiable information from education records for at least five years.

(v) For the purposes of paragraph (a)(6) of this section, the term "organization" includes, but is not limited to, federal, state, and local agencies, and independent organizations.

(7) The disclosure is to accrediting organizations to carry out their accrediting functions.

(8) The disclosure is to parents, as defined in § 99.3, of a dependent student, as defined in section 152 of the Internal Revenue Code of 1986.

(9)(i) The disclosure is to comply with a judicial order or lawfully issued subpoena.

(ii) The educational agency or institution may disclose information under paragraph (a)(9)(i) of this section only if the agency or institution makes a reasonable effort to notify the parent or eligible student of the order or subpoena in advance of compliance, so that the parent or eligible student may seek protective action, unless the disclosure is in compliance with—

(A) A federal grand jury subpoena and the court has ordered that the existence or the contents of the subpoena or the information furnished in response to the subpoena not be disclosed;

(B) Any other subpoena issued for a law enforcement purpose and the court or other issuing agency has ordered that the existence or the contents of the subpoena or the information furnished in response to the subpoena not be disclosed; or

(C) An *ex parte* court order obtained by the United States Attorney General (or designee not lower than an Assistant Attorney General) concerning investigations or prosecutions of an offense listed in 18 U.S.C. 2332b(g)(5)(B) or an act of domestic or international terrorism as defined in 18 U.S.C. 2331.

(iii)(A) If an educational agency or institution initiates legal action against a parent or student, the educational agency or institution may disclose to the court, without a court order or subpoena, the education records of the student that are relevant for the educational agency or institution to proceed with the legal action as plaintiff.

(B) If a parent or eligible student initiates legal action against an educational agency or institution, the educational agency or institution may disclose to the court, without a court order or subpoena, the student's education records that are relevant for the educational agency or institution to defend itself.

(10) The disclosure is in connection with a health or safety emergency, under the conditions described in § 99.36.

(11) The disclosure is information the educational agency or institution has designated as "directory information," under the conditions described in § 99.37.

(12) The disclosure is to the parent of a student who is not an eligible student or to the student.

(13) The disclosure, subject to the requirements in § 99.39, is to a victim of an alleged perpetrator of a crime of violence or a non-forcible sex offense. The disclosure may only include the final results of the disciplinary proceeding conducted by the institution of postsecondary education with respect to that alleged crime or offense. The institution may disclose the final results of the disciplinary proceeding, regardless of whether the institution concluded a violation was committed.

(14)(i) The disclosure, subject to the requirements in § 99.39, is in connection with a disciplinary proceeding at an institution of postsecondary education. The institution must not disclose the final results of the disciplinary proceeding unless it determines that—

(A) The student is an alleged perpetrator of a crime of violence or non-forcible sex offense; and

(B) With respect to the allegation made against him or her, the student has committed a violation of the institution's rules or policies.

(ii) The institution may not disclose the name of any other student, including a victim or witness, without the prior written consent of the other student.

(iii) This section applies only to disciplinary proceedings in which the final results were reached on or after October 7, 1998.

(15)(i) The disclosure is to a parent of a student at an institution of postsecondary education regarding the student's violation of any federal, state, or local law, or of any rule or policy of the institution, governing the use or possession of alcohol or a controlled substance if—

(A) The institution determines that the student has committed a disciplinary violation with respect to that use or possession; and

(B) The student is under the age of 21 at the time of the disclosure to the parent.

(ii) Paragraph (a)(15) of this section does not supersede any provision of state law that prohibits an institution of postsecondary education from disclosing information.

(16) The disclosure concerns sex offenders and other individuals required to register under section 170101 of the Violent Crime Control and Law Enforcement Act of 1994, 42 U.S.C. 14071, and the information was provided to the educational agency or institution under 42 U.S.C. 14071 and applicable federal guidelines.

(b)(1) De-identified records and information. An educational agency or institution, or a party that has received education records or information from education records under this part, may release the records or information without the consent required by §99.30 after the removal of all personally identifiable information provided that the educational agency or institution or other party has made a reasonable determination that a student's identity is not personally identifiable, whether through single or multiple releases, and taking into account other reasonably available information.

(2) An educational agency or institution, or a party that has received education records or information from education records under this part, may release de-identified student level data from education records for the purpose of education research by attaching a code to each record that may allow the recipient to match information received from the same source, provided that—

(i) An educational agency or institution or other party that releases de-identified data under paragraph (b)(2) of this section does not disclose any information about how it generates and assigns a record code, or that would allow a recipient to identify a student based on a record code;

(ii) The record code is used for no purpose other than identifying a de-identified record for purposes of education research and cannot be used to ascertain personally identifiable information about a student; and

(iii) The record code is not based on a student's social security number or other personal information.

(c) An educational agency or institution must use reasonable methods to identify and authenticate the identity of parents, students, school officials, and any other parties to whom the agency or institution discloses personally identifiable information from education records.

(d) Paragraphs (a) and (b) of this section do not require an educational agency or institution or any other party to disclose education records or information from education records to any party except for parties under paragraph (a)(12) of this section.

[Authority: 20 u.s.c. 1232g(a)(5)(A), (b), (h), (i), and (j)]

§ 99.32 What recordkeeping requirements exist concerning requests and disclosures?

(a)(1) An educational agency or institution must maintain a record of each request for access to and each disclosure of personally identifiable information from the education records of each student , as well as the names of State and local educational authorities and Federal officials and agencies listed in §99.31(a)(3) that may make further disclosures of personally identifiable information from the student's education records without consent under §99.33(b).

(2) The agency or institution shall maintain the record with the education records of the student as long as the records are maintained.

(3) For each request or disclosure the record must include:

(i) The parties who have requested or received personally identifiable information from the education records; and

(ii) The legitimate interests the parties had in requesting or obtaining the information.

(4) An educational agency or institution must obtain a copy of the record of further disclosures maintained under paragraph (b)(2) of this section and make it available in response to a parent's or eligible student's request to review the record required under paragraph (a)(1) of this section.

(5) An educational agency or institution must record the following information when it discloses personally identifiable information from education records under the health or safety emergency exception in §99.31(a)(10) and §99.36:

(i) The articulable and significant threat to the health or safety of a student or other individuals that formed the basis for the disclosure; and

(ii) The parties to whom the agency or institution disclosed the information.

(b)(1) Except as provided in paragraph (b)(2) of this section, if an educational agency or institution discloses personally identifiable information from education records with the understanding authorized under §99.33(b), the record of the disclosure required under this section must include:

(i) The names of the additional parties to which the receiving party may disclose the information on behalf of the educational agency or institution; and

(ii) The legitimate interests under §99.31 which each of the additional parties has in requesting or obtaining the information.

(2)(i) A State or local educational authority or Federal official or agency listed in §99.31(a)(3) that makes further disclosures of information from education records under §99.33(b) must record the names of the additional parties to which it discloses information on behalf of an educational agency or institution and their legitimate interests in the information under §99.31 if the information was received from:

(A) An educational agency or institution that has not recorded the further disclosures under paragraph (b)(1) of this section; or

(B) Another State or local educational authority or Federal official or agency listed in §99.31(a)(3).

(ii) A State or local educational authority or Federal official or agency that records further disclosures of information under paragraph (b)(2)(i) of this section may maintain the record by the student's class, school, district, or other appropriate grouping rather than by the name of the student.

(iii) Upon request of an educational agency or institution, a State or local educational authority or Federal official or agency listed in §99.31(a)(3) that maintains a record of further disclosures under paragraph (b)(2)(i) of this section must provide a copy of the record of further disclosures to the educational agency or institution within a reasonable period of time not to exceed 30 days.

(c) The following parties may inspect the record relating to each student:

(1) The parent or eligible student.
(2) The school official or his or her assistants who are responsible for the custody of the records.
(3) Those parties authorized in § 99.31 (a)(1) and (3) for the purposes of auditing the recordkeeping procedures of the educational agency or institution.

(d) Paragraph (a) of this section does not apply if the request was from, or the disclosure was to:

(1) The parent or eligible student;
(2) A school official under § 99.31 (a)(1);
(3) A party with written consent from the parent or eligible student;
(4) A party seeking directory information; or
(5) A party seeking or receiving the records in accordance with §99.31(a)(9)(ii)(A) through (C).

(Approved by the Office of Management and Budget under control number 1880–0508)
[Authority: 20 u.s.c. 1232g(b)(1) and (b)(4)(A)]

§ 99.33 What limitations apply to the rediscloscure of information?

(a)(1) An educational agency or institution may disclose personally identifiable information from an education record only on the condition that the party to whom the information is disclosed will not disclose the information to any other party without the prior consent of the parent or eligible student.

(2) The officers, employees, and agents of a party that receives information under paragraph (a)(1) of this section may use the information, but only for the purposes for which the disclosure was made.

(b)(1) Paragraph (a) of this section does not prevent an educational agency or institution from disclosing personally identifiable information with the understanding that the party receiving the information may make further disclosures of the information on behalf of the educational agency or institution if:

(i) The disclosures meet the requirements of § 99.31; and
(ii)(A) The educational agency or institution has complied with the requirements of § 99.32(b); or

(B) A State or local educational authority or Federal official or agency listed in §99.31(a)(3) has complied with the requirements of §99.32(b)(2).

(2) A party that receives a court order or lawfully issued subpoena and rediscloses personally identifiable information from education records on behalf of an educational agency or institution in response to that order or subpoena under §99.31(a)(9) must provide the notification required under §99.31(a)(9)(ii).

(c) Paragraph (a) of this section does not apply to disclosures under §§99.31(a)(8), (9), (11), (12), (14), (15), and (16), and to information that postsecondary institutions are required to disclose under the Jeanne Clery Disclosure of Campus Security Policy and Campus Crime Statistics Act, 20 u.s.c. 1092(f) (Clery Act), to the accuser and accused regarding the outcome of any campus disciplinary proceeding brought alleging a sexual offense.

(d) An educational agency or institution must inform a party to whom disclosure is made of the requirements of paragraph (a) of this section except for disclosures made under §§99.31(a)(8), (9), (11), (12), (14), (15), and (16), and to information that postsecondary institutions are required to disclose under the Clery Act to the accuser and accused regarding the outcome of any campus disciplinary proceeding brought alleging a sexual offense.

(e) If this Office determines that a third party outside the educational agency or institution improperly rediscloses personally identifiable information from education records in violation of this section, or fails to provide the notification required under paragraph (b)(2) of this section, the educational agency or institution may not allow that third party access to personally identifiable information from education records for at least five years.

[Authority: 20 u.s.c. 1232g(b)(4)(B)]

§ 99.34 What conditions apply to disclosure of information to other educational agencies or institutions?

(a) An educational agency or institution that discloses an education record under § 99.31(a)(2) shall:

(1) Make a reasonable attempt to notify the parent or eligible student at the last known address of the parent or eligible student, unless:

(i) The disclosure is initiated by the parent or eligible student; or

(ii) The annual notification of the agency or institution under § 99.7 includes a notice that the agency or institution forwards education records to other agencies or institutions that have requested the records and in which the student seeks or intends to enroll or is already enrolled so long as the disclosure is for purposes related to the student's enrollment or transfer:

(2) Give the parent or eligible student, upon request, a copy of the record that was disclosed; and

(3) Give the parent or eligible student, upon request, an opportunity for a hearing under Subpart C.

(b) An educational agency or institution may disclose an education record of a student in attendance to another educational agency or institution if:

(1) The student is enrolled in or receives services from the other agency or institution; and

(2) The disclosure meets the requirements of paragraph (a) of this section.

[Authority: 20 u.s.c. 1232g(b)(1)(B)]

§ 99.35 What conditions apply to disclosure of information for federal or State program purposes?

(a)(1) Authorized representatives of the officials or agencies headed by officials listed in §99.31(a)(3) may have access to education records in connection with an audit or evaluation of federal or state supported education programs, or for the enforcement of or compliance with federal legal requirements that relate to those programs.

(2) Authority for an agency or official listed in §99.31(a)(3) to conduct an audit, evaluation, or compliance or enforcement activity is not conferred by the Act

or this part and must be established under other Federal, State, or local authority.

(b) Information that is collected under paragraph (a) of this section must:

(1) Be protected in a manner that does not permit personal identification of individuals by anyone other than the officials or agencies headed by officials referred to in paragraph (a) of this section, except that those officials and agencies may make further disclosures of personally identifiable information from education records on behalf of the educational agency or institution in accordance with the requirements of §99.33(b); and

(2) Be destroyed when no longer needed for the purposes listed in paragraph (a) of this section.

(c) Paragraph (b) of this section does not apply if:

(1) The parent or eligible student has given written consent for the disclosure under § 99.30; or

(2) The collection of personally identifiable information is specifically authorized by federal law.

[Authority: 20 u.s.c. 1232g(b)(3)]

§ 99.36 What conditions apply to disclosure of information in health and safety emergencies?

(a) An educational agency or institution may disclose personally identifiable information from an education record to appropriate parties, including parents of an eligible student, in connection with an emergency if knowledge of the information is necessary to protect the health or safety of the student or other individuals.

(b) Nothing in the *Act* or this part shall prevent an educational agency or institution from-

(1) Including in the education records of a student appropriate information concerning disciplinary action taken against the student for conduct that posed a significant risk to the safety or well-being of that student, other students, or other members of the school community;

(2) Disclosing appropriate information maintained under paragraph (b)(1) of this section to teachers and school officials within the agency or institution who the agency or institution has determined have legitimate educational interests in the behavior of the student; or

(3) Disclosing appropriate information maintained under paragraph (b)(1) of this section to teachers and school officials in other schools who have been determined to have legitimate educational interests in the behavior of the student.

(c) In making a determination under paragraph (a) of this section, an educational agency or institution may take into account the totality of the circumstances pertaining to a threat to the health or safety of a student or other individuals. If the educational agency or institution determines that there is an articulable and significant threat to the health or safety of a student or other individuals, it may disclose information from education records to any person whose knowledge of the information is necessary to protect the health or safety of the student or other individuals. If, based on the information available at the time of the determination, there is a rational basis for the determination, the Department will not substitute its judgment for that of the educational agency or institution in evaluating the circumstances and making its determination.

[Authority: 20 u.s.c. 1232g(b)(1)(I) and (h)]

§ 99.37 What conditions apply to disclosing directory information?

(a) An educational agency or institution may disclose directory information if it has given public notice to parents of students in attendance and eligible students in attendance at the agency or institution of:

(1) The types of personally identifiable information that the agency or institution has designated as directory information;

(2) A parent's or eligible student's right to refuse to let the agency or institution designate any or all of those types of information about the student as directory information; and

(3) The period of time within which a parent or eligible student has to notify the agency or institution in writing that he or she does not want any or all of those types of information about the student designated as directory information.

(b) An educational agency or institution may disclose directory information about former students without meeting the conditions in paragraph (a) of this section. However, the agency or institution must continue to honor any valid request to opt out of the disclosure of

directory information made while a student was in attendance unless the student rescinds the opt out request.

(c) A parent or eligible student may not use the right under paragraph (a)(2) of this section to opt out of directory information disclosures to prevent an educational agency or institution from disclosing or requiring a student to disclose the student's name, identifier, or institutional email address in a class in which the student is enrolled.

(d) An educational agency or institution may not disclose or confirm directory information without meeting the written consent requirements in §99.30 if a student's social security number or other non-directory information is used alone or combined with other data elements to identify or help identify the student or the student's records.

[Authority: 20 u.s.c. 1232g(a)(5)(A) and (B)]

§ 99.38 What conditions apply to disclosure of information as permitted by State statute adopted after November 19, 1974 concerning the juvenile justice system?

(a) If reporting or disclosure allowed by state statute concerns the juvenile justice system and the system's ability to effectively serve, prior to adjudication, the student whose records are released, an educational agency or institution may disclose education records under § 99.31(a)(5)(i)(B).

(b) The officials and authorities to whom the records are disclosed shall certify in writing to the educational agency or institution that the information will not be disclosed to any other party, except as provided under state law, without the prior written consent of the parent of the student.

[Authority: 20 u.s.c. 1232g(b)(1)(J)]

§ 99.39 What definitions apply to the nonconsensual disclosure of records by postsecondary educational institutions in connection with disciplinary proceedings concerning crimes of violence or non-forcible sex offenses?

As used in this part:

ALLEGED PERPETRATOR OF A CRIME OF VIOLENCE is a student who is alleged to have committed acts that would, if proven, constitute any of the following offenses or attempts to commit the following offenses that are defined in appendix A to this part:

* Arson
* Assault offenses

- ⊞ Burglary
- ⊞ Criminal homicide—manslaughter by negligence
- ⊞ Criminal homicide—murder and nonnegligent manslaughter
- ⊞ Destruction/damage/vandalism of property
- ⊞ Kidnapping/abduction
- ⊞ Robbery
- ⊞ Forcible sex offenses

ALLEGED PERPETRATOR OF A NONFORCIBLE SEX OFFENSE means a student who is alleged to have committed acts that, if proven, would constitute statutory rape or incest. These offenses are defined in Appendix A to this part.

FINAL RESULTS means a decision or determination, made by an honor court or council, committee, commission, or other entity authorized to resolve disciplinary matters within the institution. The disclosure of final results must include only the name of the student, the violation committed, and any sanction imposed by the institution against the student.

SANCTION IMPOSED means a description of the disciplinary action taken by the institution, the date of its imposition, and its duration.

VIOLATION COMMITTED means the institutional rules or code sections that were violated and any essential findings supporting the institution's conclusion that the violation was committed.

[Authority: 20 u.s.c. 1232g(b)(6)]

Subpart E—What Are the Enforcement Procedures?

§ 99.60 What functions has the Secretary delegated to the Office and to the Office of Administrative Law Judges?

(a) For the purposes of this subpart, "Office" means the Family Policy Compliance Office, U.S. Department of Education.

(b) The Secretary designates the Office to:

(1) Investigate, process, and review complaints and violations under the *Act* and this part; and

(2) Provide technical assistance to ensure compliance with the *Act* and this part.

(c) The Secretary designates the Office of Administrative Law Judges to act as the Review Board required under the *Act* to enforce the *Act* with respect to all applicable programs. The term "applicable program" is defined in section 400 of the *General Education Provisions Act*.

[Authority: 20 u.s.c. 1232g(f) and (g), 1234]

§ 99.61 What responsibility does an educational agency or institution have concerning conflict with State or local laws?

If an educational agency or institution determines that it cannot comply with the *Act* or this part due to a conflict with state or local law, it shall notify the Office within 45 days, giving the text and citation of the conflicting law.

[Authority: 20 u.s.c. 1232g(f)]

§ 99.62 What information must an educational agency or institution submit to the Office?

The Office may require an educational agency or institution to submit reports, information on policies and procedures, annual notifications, training materials, and other information necessary to carry out its enforcement responsibilities under the Act or this part.

[Authority: 20 u.s.c. 1232g(f) and (g)]

§ 99.63 Where are complaints filed?

A parent or eligible student may file a written complaint with the Office regarding an alleged violation under the *Act* and this part. The Office's address is: Family Policy Compliance Office, U.S. Department of Education, 400 Maryland Avenue, SW, Washington, D.C. 20202–4605.

[Authority: 20 u.s.c. 1232g(g)]

§ 99.64 What is the investigation procedure?

(a) A complaint filed under § 99.63 must contain specific allegations of fact giving reasonable cause to believe that a violation of the *Act* or this part has occurred. A complaint does not have to allege that a violation is based on a policy or practice of the educational agency or institution.

(b) The Office investigates a timely complaint filed by a parent or eligible student, or conducts its own investigation when no complaint has been filed or a complaint has been withdrawn, to determine whether an educational agency or institution has failed to comply with a provision of the Act or this part. If the Office determines that an educational agency or institution has failed to comply with a provision of the Act or this part, it may also determine whether the failure to comply is based on a policy or practice of the agency or institution.

(c) A timely complaint is defined as an allegation of a violation of the *Act* that is submitted to the Office within 180 days of the date of the alleged violation or of the date that the complainant knew or reasonably should have known of the alleged violation.

(d) The Office may extend the time limit in this section for good cause shown.

[Authority: 20 u.s.c. 1232g(f)]

§ 99.65 What is the content of the notice of investigation issued by the Office?

(a) The Office notifies the complainant, if any, and the educational agency or institution in writing if it initiates an investigation of a complaint under § 99.64(b). The notice to the educational agency or institution-

  (1) Includes the substance of the alleged violation; and
  (2) Directs the agency or institution to submit a written response and other relevant information, as set forth in §99.62, within a specified period of time, including information about its policies and practices regarding education records.

(b) The Office notifies the complainant if it does not initiate an investigation of a complaint because the complaint fails to meet the requirements of § 99.64.

[Authority: 20 u.s.c. 1232g(g)]

§ 99.66 What are the responsibilities of the Office in the enforcement process?

(a) The Office reviews the complaint, if any, information submitted by the educational agency or institution, and any other relevant information. The Office may permit the parties to submit further written or oral arguments or information.

(b) Following its investigation, the Office provides to the complainant, if any, and the educational agency or institution a written notice of its findings and the basis for its findings.

(c) If the Office finds that an educational agency or institution has not complied with a provision of the *Act* or this part, it may also find that the failure to comply was based on a policy or practice of the agency or institution. A notice of findings issued under paragraph (b) of this section to an educational agency or institution that has not complied with a provision of the Act or this part:

  (1) Includes a statement of the specific steps that the agency or institution must take to comply; and
  (2) Provides a reasonable period of time, given all of the circumstances of the case, during which the educational agency or institution may comply voluntarily.

[Authority: 20 u.s.c. 1232g(f)]

§ 99.67 How does the Secretary enforce decisions?

(a) If an educational agency or institution does not comply during the period of time set under § 99.66(c), the Secretary may take any legally available enforcement action in accordance with the Act, including, but not limited to, the following enforcement actions available in accordance with part E of the *General Education Provisions Act*—

  (1) Withhold further payments under any applicable program;
  (2) Issue a complaint to compel compliance through a cease-and-desist order; or
  (3) Terminate eligibility to receive funding under any applicable program.

(b) If, after an investigation under § 99.66, the Secretary finds that an educational agency or institution has complied voluntarily with the *Act* or this part, the Secretary provides the complainant and the agency or institution written notice of the decision and the basis for the decision.

(Note: 34 C.F.R. Part 78 contains the regulations of the Education Appeal Board.)

[Authority: 20 u.s.c. 1232g(f); 20 u.s.c. 1234]

[Updated January 2009.]

Appendix A to Part 99—Crimes of Violence Definitions

ARSON: Any willful or malicious burning or attempt to burn, with or without intent to defraud, a dwelling house, public building, motor vehicle or aircraft, personal property of another, etc.

ASSAULT OFFENSES: An unlawful attack by one person upon another.

Note: By definition there can be no "attempted" assaults, only "completed" assaults.

  (a) *Aggravated Assault.* An unlawful attack by one person upon another for the purpose of inflicting severe or aggravated bodily injury. This type of assault usually is accompanied by the use of a weapon or by means likely to produce death or great bodily harm. (It is not necessary that injury result from an aggravated assault when a gun, knife, or other weapon is used which could and probably would result in serious injury if the crime were successfully completed.)

(b) *Simple Assault.* An unlawful physical attack by one person upon another where neither the offender displays a weapon, nor the victim suffers obvious severe or aggravated bodily injury involving apparent broken bones, loss of teeth, possible internal injury, severe laceration, or loss of consciousness.

(c) *Intimidation.* To unlawfully place another person in reasonable fear of bodily harm through the use of threatening words or other conduct, or both, but without displaying a weapon or subjecting the victim to actual physical attack.

Note: This offense includes stalking.

BURGLARY: The unlawful entry into a building or other structure with the intent to commit a felony or a theft.

CRIMINAL HOMICIDE—MANSLAUGHTER BY NEGLIGENCE: The killing of another person through gross negligence.

CRIMINAL HOMICIDE—MURDER AND NONNEGLIGENT MANSLAUGHTER: The willful (nonnegligent) killing of one human being by another.

DESTRUCTION/DAMAGE/VANDALISM OF PROPERTY: To willfully or maliciously destroy, damage, deface, or otherwise injure real or personal property without the consent of the owner or the person having custody or control of it.

KIDNAPPING/ABDUCTION: The unlawful seizure, transportation, or detention of a person, or any combination of these actions, against his or her will, or of a minor without the consent of his or her custodial parent(s) or legal guardian.

Note: Kidnapping/Abduction includes hostage taking.

ROBBERY: The taking of, or attempting to take, anything of value under confrontational circumstances from the control, custody, or care of a person or persons by force or threat of force or violence or by putting the victim in fear.

Note: Carjackings are robbery offenses where a motor vehicle is taken through force or threat of force.

SEX OFFENSES, FORCIBLE: Any sexual act directed against another person, forcibly or against that person's will, or both; or not forcibly or against the person's will where the victim is incapable of giving consent.

(a) *Forcible Rape* (Except "Statutory Rape"). The carnal knowledge of a person, forcibly or against that person's will, or both; or not forcibly or against the person's will where the victim is incapable of giving

consent because of his or her temporary or permanent mental or physical incapacity (or because of his or her youth).

(b) *Forcible Sodomy.* Oral or anal sexual intercourse with another person, forcibly or against that person's will, or both; or not forcibly or against the person's will where the victim is incapable of giving consent because of his or her youth or because of his or her temporary or permanent mental or physical incapacity.

(c) *Sexual Assault with an Object.* To use an object or instrument to unlawfully penetrate, however slightly, the genital or anal opening of the body of another person, forcibly or against that person's will, or both; or not forcibly or against the person's will where the victim is incapable of giving consent because of his or her youth or because of his or her temporary or permanent mental or physical incapacity.

Note: An "object" or "instrument" is anything used by the offender other than the offender's genitalia. Examples are a finger, bottle, handgun, stick, etc.

(d) *Forcible Fondling.* The touching of the private body parts of another person for the purpose of sexual gratification, forcibly or against that person's will, or both; or not forcibly or against the person's will where the victim is incapable of giving consent because of his or her youth or because of his or her temporary or permanent mental or physical incapacity.

Note: Forcible Fondling includes "Indecent Liberties" and "Child Molesting."

NONFORCIBLE SEX OFFENSES (EXCEPT "PROSTITUTION OFFENSES"): Unlawful, nonforcible sexual intercourse.

(a) *Incest.* Nonforcible sexual intercourse between persons who are related to each other within the degrees wherein marriage is prohibited by law.

(b) *Statutory Rape.* Nonforcible sexual intercourse with a person who is under the statutory age of consent.

[Authority: 20 u.s.c. 1232g(b)(6) and 18 u.s.c. 16]

These regulations were current at the time of publication of this guide. The reader should always check to see if the Department of Education has issued any amendments to these regulations, since publication of this Guide, through the Family Policy Compliance Office (the DOE office that has responsibility for administering FERPA) Web site at: www. ed.gov/policy/gen/guid/fpco/index.html.

FERPA Section-by-Section Analysis

When the 2009 Amendments to the Family Educational Rights and Privacy Act (FERPA) regulations were published in December 2008, the Department of Education (Department) sent a Dear Colleague letter to school officials advising them of the changes. A portion of the letter included an analysis of each section of the regulations that were impacted by the amendments. Below is a version of that section-by-section document, modified so that the focus is on the impact of the changes on postsecondary institutions.

Under FERPA, 20 U.S.C. § 1232g, a student has a right to inspect and review the student's education records and to seek to have them amended in certain circumstances. A student must also provide a signed and dated written consent before an educational agency or institution discloses personally identifiable information from education records. Exceptions to this requirement are set forth in § 99.31(a).

FERPA applies to any "educational agency or institution" that receives funds under any program administered by the Department through the Family Policy Compliance Office (FPCO). See 34 CFR § 99.1(a). This includes virtually all postsecondary institutions, public or private. For ease of reference, this document uses the terms institution, college, institution of higher education, and postsecondary institution, as appropriate, in place of "educational agencies and institutions." Changes from the Notice of Proposed Rulemaking (NPRM) that was published in the *Federal Register* on March 24, 2008 (73 FR 15574) are noted. For the purposes of this document, the term "previous regulations" means the FERPA regulations that were in effect until January 8, 2009.

§ 99.3 Definitions

ATTENDANCE was previously defined to include attendance in person or by correspondence. (A "student" is defined as an individual who is or has been "in attendance" at an educational agency or institution and regarding whom the agency or institution maintains education records.) The final regulations add other situations in which students "attend" classes but are not physically present, including attendance by videoconference, satellite, Internet, or other electronic information and telecommunications technologies. This change will ensure that individuals who receive instruction through distance learning and other contemporary modalities are covered as "students" and, therefore, that their records are protected under FERPA.

DIRECTORY INFORMATION is defined as information that would not generally be considered harmful or an invasion of privacy if disclosed. Postsecondary institutions may disclose directory information without consent if they have given the student notice of the kinds of information they designate as directory information and an opportunity to opt out of directory information disclosures. The statute and regulations specifically list some items that can be identified as directory information, including a student's name; address; telephone number; email address; photograph; date and place of birth; enrollment status; and major field of study. Neither the statute nor previous regulations lists any items that may not be designated and disclosed as directory information.

SSNS AND STUDENT ID NUMBERS. Previous regulations specify that a student's Social Security Number (SSN) and student ID number are "personally identifiable information" (*see* below) but did not indicate whether these personal identifiers may be designated and disclosed as directory information. The final regulations specifically prohibit the disclosure of a student's SSN, or part of an SSN, as directory information; however, based on public comments, the FPCO modified the rule to allow student ID numbers to be disclosed as directory information if they qualify as electronic personal identifiers (discussed below). This is designed to: prevent institutions from attaching these identifiers to students' names on sign-in sheets in classrooms, health clinics, etc.; prevent institutions from disclosing lists with these identifiers attached to students' names, addresses, and other directory information; and prevent instructors from using them to post grades. This change is intended to help reduce the risk of unauthorized access to personal information and identity theft by ensuring that institutions do not make these identifiers available publicly. School officials will still be able to use class lists with ID numbers but cannot make them available to students. Instructors that still post grades publicly will have to use a code known only to the instructor and the student.

ELECTRONIC PERSONAL IDENTIFIERS. Many of the authentication applications that support electronic information systems used to deliver certain student services, such as Web-based class registration, access to academic records and library resources, etc., require disclosure of the user name or other personal identifier used by a student to gain access to these systems. Public key infrastructure (PKI) technology for encryption and digital signatures also requires wide dissemination of the sender's public key, which is an identifier. The final regulations allow postsecondary institutions to designate these electronic personal identifiers as directory information, including student ID numbers, but only if the identifier functions essentially as a name, *i.e.*, it is not used by itself to authenticate identity and cannot be used by itself to gain access to education records. A unique electronic identifier disclosed as directory information may be used to provide access to education records, but only when the identifier is combined with other authentication factors known only to the user, such as a secret password or personal identification number (PIN), or some other method or combination of methods to authenticate the user's identity and ensure that the user is, in fact, a person authorized to access the records. This change allows institutions to use advanced technologies to deliver student services and access to education records. (*See* the FPCO "Letter to University of Wisconsin–River Falls," on page 196, for more details on student account identifiers.)

DISCLOSURE is defined to mean permitting access to or the release, transfer, or other communication of personally identifiable information from education records to any party by any means. The new regulations exclude from

"disclosure" returning an education record, or information from an education record, to the party identified as the provider or creator of the record. This will accomplish two things. First, a state-consolidated record system can allow a postsecondary institution to have access to information that the institution provided to the system without violating the statutory prohibition on redisclosure, 20 U.S.C. 1232g(b)(3). Second, it will help institutions deal with falsified transcripts, letters of recommendation, and other documents they receive by allowing an institution that has received a questionable document to return it to the ostensible sender for verification. (This second problem is also addressed in changes to § 99.31(a)(2), discussed below.) The Department clarified in the preamble to the 2009 regulations that it has no authority to exclude from the term "disclosure" an institution's release or transfer of personally identifiable information from education records to its state longitudinal data system or to parties that agree to keep the information confidential, and that the final regulations do not authorize the release or transfer of education records to a student's previous institution that is not identified as the source of those records.

EDUCATION RECORDS are defined as records that are directly related to a "student" and maintained by an "educational agency or institution" or by a party acting for the agency or institution. (The term "student" excludes individuals who have not been in attendance at the agency or institution.)

POST-ENROLLMENT RECORDS. The regulations exclude records that only contain information about an individual after he or she is no longer a student at that institution. This was intended to apply to fundraising and similar types of records related to alumni. Some schools, however, have on occasion mistakenly interpreted this provision to mean that any record created or received by the institution after a student is no longer enrolled, regardless of the subject matter, is not an "education record" under FERPA. For example, under this interpretation, a settlement agreement maintained by an institution related to a discrimination, wrongful death, or other lawsuit brought by a parent after the student is no longer enrolled is not an "education record" under FERPA and, therefore, could be subject to mandatory disclosure under an open records law or otherwise released without consent to anyone. The 2009 regulations clarify that records that pertain to an individual's previous attendance as a student are "education records" under

FERPA regardless of when they were created or received by the institution.

PEER-GRADING (*Owasso Indep. Sch. Dist. No. I-011 v. Falvo*, 534 U.S. 426 (2002)). Under FERPA a school generally may not disclose a student's grades to another student without the prior written consent of the eligible student. "Peer-grading," however, is an educational practice in which teachers require students to exchange homework assignments, tests, and other papers, grade one another's work, and then either call out the grade or turn in the work to the teacher for recordation. Even though peer-grading results in students finding out each other's grades, the U.S. Supreme Court in 2002 issued a narrow holding in Owasso that this practice does not violate FERPA because grades on students' papers are not "maintained" under the definition of "education records" and, therefore, would not be covered under FERPA at least until the teacher has collected and recorded them in the teacher's grade book, a decision consistent with the Department's longstanding position on peer-grading. Since this practice is generally used at the elementary and secondary level, it has limited application at the postsecondary level. The final regulations create an exception to the definition of "education records" that excludes grades on peer-graded papers before they are collected and recorded by a teacher. This change clarifies that peer-grading does not violate FERPA.

PERSONALLY IDENTIFIABLE INFORMATION. This is discussed below under § 99.31(b).

§ 99.5 Disclosures to Parents and Rights of Students

Under the FERPA regulations, all rights of parents under FERPA, including the right to inspect and review education records, to seek to have education records amended in certain circumstances, and to consent to the disclosure of education records, transfer to the student once the student has reached 18 years of age or attends a postsecondary institution and thereby becomes an "eligible student." The regulations also provide that even after a student has become an "eligible student" under FERPA, postsecondary institutions (and high schools, for students over 18 years of age) may allow parents to have access to their child's education records, without the student's consent, in the following circumstances: the student is a dependent for federal income tax purposes (§ 99.31(a)(8)); the disclosure is in connection with a health or safety emergency under the conditions specified in § 99.36 (*i.e.*, if knowledge of

the information is necessary to protect the health or safety of the student or other individuals [§ 99.31(a)(10)]); and, for postsecondary students, if the student has violated any federal, state or local law, or any rule or policy of the institution, governing the use or possession of alcohol or a controlled substance, if the institution determines that the student has committed a disciplinary violation regarding that use or possession and the student is under 21 at the time of the disclosure (§ 99.31(a)(15)).

There was a concern at the Department that some colleges and other postsecondary institutions did not fully understand their options with regard to disclosing education records (or personally identifiable information from education records) of eligible students to their parents and continue to believe mistakenly that FERPA prevents them from releasing this information to parents under any circumstances, including a health or safety emergency. The final regulations clarify that disclosures to parents are permissible without the student's consent under any of these three exceptions. That is, an institution may disclose education records to a parent of a dependent student under any circumstance; this exception to the consent requirement is likely to cover the vast majority of traditional college students. Even if a student is not a dependent, a postsecondary institution may disclose education records to a student's parent under the alcohol or controlled substance exception (§ 99.31(a)(15)) or in connection with a health or safety emergency (§ 99.31(a)(10)) under the circumstances set forth in § 99.36, discussed below. The change is intended to clarify for institutions that while they may choose to follow a policy of not disclosing information to the parents of eligible students, FERPA does not prevent them from doing so in certain circumstances.

§ 99.31(a)(1) School Officials

Under the FERPA regulations, postsecondary institutions may allow "school officials, including teachers, within the agency or institution" to have access to students' education records, without consent, if they have determined that the official has "legitimate educational interests" in the information. Under § 99.7, a postsecondary institution that discloses information under this exception must include in its annual FERPA notification to eligible students a specification of criteria for determining who constitutes a school official and what constitutes a legitimate educational interest. Disclosures to school officials with legitimate educational interests are not subject to the recordation requirements in § 99.32. (*See* the "FPCO

Letter of Finding," on page 231, for more details on authentication/records security.)

§ 99.31(a)(1)(i)(B) Outsourcing

Neither the statute nor the regulations addresses disclosure of education records without consent to non-employees retained to perform institutional services and functions. The new regulations, however, expand the "school officials" exception to include contractors, consultants, volunteers, and other outside service providers used by a postsecondary institution to perform institutional services and functions. A contractor or other outside service provider, such as an attorney or insurance company, that is given access to education records under this provision must be under the direct control of the disclosing institution with respect to the use of those education records and subject to the same conditions on use and redisclosure of education records that govern other school officials (see § 99.33). In particular, the institution is required to ensure that the contractor has procedures in place to ensure that only individuals with legitimate educational interests (as determined by the institution) obtain access to personally identifiable information from education records it maintains (or creates) on behalf of the institution. The information may only be used for the purpose for which it has been disclosed, and must be destroyed or returned to the institution once the service for the institution has been completed. Further, in accordance with § 99.33(a) and (b), the contractor may not redisclose personally identifiable information without consent unless the institution has authorized the redisclosure under a FERPA exception and the district or institution records the subsequent disclosure.

An institution may not disclose education records to an outside service provider under this exception unless it has specified in its annual FERPA notification that it uses contractors, consultants, volunteers, etc. as school officials to provide certain institutional services and functions. An institution's recordation of a disclosure to an outside service provider will not waive its failure to comply with the annual notification requirements for outside service providers. Additionally, institutions should be aware that a memorandum of understanding is an agreement between equals and thus does not establish direct control by the institution over the agent's use of the information from education records as is required under this provision. This change is consistent with the Department's longstanding guidance that FERPA does not require postsecondary institutions to provide all institutional services and func-

tions on an in-house basis. As institutions have expanded the range of services they outsource, from traditional legal and debt collection services to fundraising, enrollment and degree verification, transcript distribution, and information technology (IT) services and more, the need to establish in regulations the conditions for these non-consensual disclosures has become critical. In addition to requiring the disclosing institution to have direct control over its outside service providers' maintenance and use of education records, the new regulations explain that disclosure is permitted under this exception only if the institution is outsourcing a service it would otherwise provide using employees. For example, postsecondary institutions may not use this exception to disclose education records, without consent, to a financial institution or insurance company that provides a good student discount on services that the institution would not otherwise provide. This prevents uncontrolled designation of outside parties as "school officials" for marketing and other purposes for which non-consensual disclosure of education records is not authorized by statute. (See the FPCO "Letter to Clark County School District (NV)," on page 211, for more details on disclosure of education records to outside service providers.)

The preamble to the final regulations explains that state educational authorities that operate state longitudinal data systems are not "school officials" under this exception and that disclosures to these state systems generally fall under the "audit or evaluation" exception. The preamble also explains how an institution may disclose education records without consent to its own law enforcement unit under the school officials' exception but not to outside police officers. The new regulations also clarify that the "direct control" requirement means control of the outside service provider's maintenance and use of information from education records and is not intended to affect the outside party's status as an independent contractor or render that party an employee under state or federal law.

§ 99.31(a)(1)(ii) Controlling Access to Education Records by School Officials

The previous FERPA regulations did not specify what steps, if any, a postsecondary institution must take to enforce the "legitimate educational interests" requirement in the school officials' exception. Parents and students have complained about school officials having unrestricted access to the education records of all students in a district's or institution's system, particularly in districts and institutions where records are maintained electronically. Additionally, institutions themselves have expressed uncertainty about what methods they should use to comply with this requirement when establishing or upgrading their recordkeeping systems.

The new regulations require postsecondary institutions to use "reasonable methods" to ensure that instructors and other school officials (including outside service providers) obtain access to only those education records—paper or electronic—in which they have legitimate educational interests. Many districts and postsecondary institutions already use physical or technological controls to protect education records against unauthorized access, such as locks on filing cabinets for paper records and software applications with role-based access controls for electronic records. Under the new regulations, while institutions may forego physical or technological controls and rely instead on administrative policies for controlling access to education records by school officials, those that choose this method must ensure that their administrative policy is effective and that they remain in compliance with the legitimate educational interest requirement for accessing records. In particular, if a student alleges that a school official obtained access to the student's records without a legitimate educational interest, the burden is on the district or institution to show that the school official had a legitimate educational interest in the information. The preamble to the new regulations explains that the requirement for using "reasonable methods" applies whether an institution uses physical, technological, or administrative controls to restrict access to education records by school officials.

The preamble to the NPRM suggested that institutions should consider restricting or tracking access to education records by school officials to ensure that they remain in compliance with this requirement. (Recommendations for safeguarding education records from unauthorized access and disclosure outside the institution itself are discussed below.)

In terms of assessing the reasonableness of methods used to control access to education records by school officials, the preamble to the final regulations explains that the risk of unauthorized access means the likelihood that records may be targeted for compromise and the harm that could result. Methods are considered reasonable if they reduce the risk to a level commensurate with the likely threat and potential harm. The greater the harm that would result, the more protections an institution must use to ensure that its methods are reasonable. For example, high-risk records, such as SSNs and other information that could be used for identity theft, should generally receive greater and more immediate protection than medium- or low-risk records, such as those containing only publicly available directory information. What is reasonable depends ultimately on the usual and customary good business practices of similarly situated institutions, which, in turn, requires ongoing review and modification of methods and procedures as standards and technologies change.

Many institutions use software with role-based security features that limit an individual's access to electronic records based on their professional responsibilities and, therefore, already comply with the final regulations. Those institutions that are not currently in compliance in this regard now have specific guidance for updating or upgrading the security of their recordkeeping systems as appropriate.

§ 99.31(a)(2) Student's New School

Under FERPA, a postsecondary institution may disclose education records, without consent, to officials of another school, or postsecondary institution where a student "seeks or intends to enroll." There has been uncertainty over the years within the education community about the scope of the "seeks or intends to enroll" language and whether it permits an institution to send education records to a student's new school after the student has actually enrolled. The new regulations clarify that the authority to disclose or transfer education records to a student's new school does not cease automatically the moment a student has enrolled and continues to any future point in time so long as the disclosure is for purposes related to the student's enrollment or transfer. As explained in the preamble to the final regulations, this means that an institution may disclose any records or information, including health and disciplinary records, that the institution could have disclosed when the student was seeking or intending to enroll in the new school.

The preamble to the final regulations also explained that there are other federal laws, such as the *Individuals with Disabilities Education Act* (IDEA), §504 of the *Rehabilitation Act of 1973*, and Title II of the *Americans with Disabilities Act of 1990* (ADA), with different requirements that may affect the release of student information. For example, §504 generally prohibits postsecondary institutions from making pre-admission inquiries about an applicant's disability status. However, after admission,

§504 and Title II of the ADA do not prohibit institutions from obtaining information concerning a current student, including those with disabilities, from any school previously attended by the student in connection with an emergency and as necessary to protect the health or safety of the student or other persons under FERPA.

The clarification regarding the nature of the disclosure authority under §99.31(a)(2) will allow a student's previous school to supplement, update, or correct any records it sent during the student's application or transfer period. Combined with the changes to the definition of "disclosure" (described earlier) that allow a student's new school to return a transcript or other document to the purported sender or creator of the record, this change will also allow a student's previous school to identify any falsified or fraudulent records and explain the meaning of any records disclosed previously to the new school.

§ 99.31(a)(6) Organizations Conducting Studies

The FERPA regulations restate the statutory provision that allows a postsecondary institution to disclose personally identifiable information from education records, without consent, to organizations conducting studies "for, or on behalf of" the disclosing institution for purposes of developing, validating, or administering predictive tests; administering student aid programs; or improving instruction. (Note that under changes to §99.35(b), discussed below, this exception now applies also to state educational agencies (SEAs) and state higher education authorities that receive education records without consent from postsecondary institutions under §99.31(a)(3) for audit, evaluation, or enforcement purposes.) Information disclosed under this exception must be protected so that students and their parents cannot be personally identified by anyone other than representatives of the organization conducting the study, and must be destroyed when no longer needed for the study. Failure to destroy information in accordance with this requirement could lead to a five-year ban on the disclosure of information to that organization.

The phrase "for, or on behalf of" is not defined in the FERPA regulations. Organizations seeking to conduct independent research have asked for clarification about the circumstances in which personally identifiable information from education records may be disclosed without consent under this exception, and districts and institutions have asked whether they may use this exception even if they have no particular interest in the proposed study.

The new regulations require a postsecondary institution that uses this exception to enter into a written agreement with the recipient organization that specifies the purposes of the study. The written agreement must specify that information from education records may only be used to meet the purposes of the study stated in the written agreement and must contain the current requirements in §99.31(a)(6) on redisclosure and destruction of information, as described above. The regulations also require that the written agreement must specify the purpose, scope, and duration of the study and the information to be disclosed; require the organization to destroy or return all personally identifiable information when no longer needed for the purposes of the study; and specify the time period during which the organization must either destroy or return the information. In addition, the written agreement must require the organization to conduct the study in a manner that does not permit personal identification of parents and students by anyone other than representatives of the organization with legitimate interests.

A new provision in the regulations states that an institution is not required to initiate research requests or agree with or endorse the conclusions or results of the study when disclosing information under this exception. However, the statutory language "for, or on behalf of" indicates that the disclosing district or institution agrees with the purposes of the study and retains control over the information from education records that is disclosed. The written agreement required under the regulations will help ensure that information disclosed under this exception is used only to meet the purposes of the study as stated in the agreement and that all redisclosure and destruction requirements are met.

Although disclosure of personally identifiable information without consent is allowed for studies under this exception, the Department recommends in the preamble to the final regulations that whenever possible agencies and institutions either release de-identified information or remove students' names and SSNs to reduce the risk of unauthorized disclosure of personally identifiable information.

Applicability of this provision to SEAs and state higher educational authorities that redisclose personally identifiable information from education records on behalf of postsecondary institutions is discussed below under §99.35(b).

§ 99.31(a)(9)(ii) Ex parte Court Orders Under USA PATRIOT Act

The previous regulations did not address amendments to FERPA under the USA PATRIOT Act, P.L. 107-56, which authorizes the U.S. Attorney General (or designee) to apply for an *ex parte* court order that allows the Attorney General to collect education records from an educational institution, without the consent or knowledge of the student, that are relevant to an investigation or prosecution of an offense listed in 18 U.S.C. 2332b(g)(5)(B) or an act of domestic or international terrorism specified in 18 U.S.C. 2331. Under the statutory amendment and final regulations, postsecondary institutions are allowed to make these disclosures without consent or notice to the student that would otherwise be required under §99.31(a)(9) of the regulations and without recording the disclosure under §99.32(a). Note that the court order itself may instruct the district or institution not to notify the student or record the disclosure of education records, or disclose the existence of the *ex parte* order to any party.

The district or institution that is served by the Attorney General with an *ex parte* court order under this exception should ensure that the order is valid, just as it does when determining whether to comply with other judicial orders and subpoenas under §99.31(a)(9). It is not, however, required or authorized to examine the underlying certification of facts that the Attorney General is required to present to the court in the Attorney General's application for the order. (*See* Appendix K, Anti-Terrorism Related Amendments on page 333).

§ 99.31(a)(16) Registered Sex Offenders

The Campus Sex Crimes Prevention Act (CSCPA), which is §1601(d) of the *Victims of Trafficking and Violence Protection Act of 2000*, P.L. 106-386, created a new exception to the consent requirement in FERPA that allows postsecondary institutions to disclose information concerning registered sex offenders provided under state sex offender registration and campus community notification programs for institutions of higher education required under the Wetterling Act, 42 U.S.C. 14071. Under the Wetterling Act, States must require certain sex offenders to register their name and address with the state authority where the offender lives, works, or is enrolled as a student. States are also required to release relevant information necessary to protect the public concerning persons required to register under what are known as "community notification programs."

CSCPA contains registration and notice requirements designed specifically for higher education campus communities, including a requirement that states collect information about a registered offender's enrollment or employment at an institution of higher education, along with any change in enrollment or employment status at the institution, and make this information available promptly to a campus police department or other appropriate law enforcement agency. CSCPA also amended the *Higher Education Act of 1965* (HEA) by requiring institutions of higher education to advise the campus community where it can obtain information about registered sex offenders provided by the state under the Wetterling Act, such as a campus law enforcement office, a local law enforcement agency, or a computer network address.

The regulations add a new exception that allows a postsecondary institution to disclose without consent information it has received from a state under the Wetterling Act about a student who is required to register as a sex offender in the state. The Department removed the sentence included in the 2008 NPRM that stated that nothing in FERPA requires or encourages an institution to collect or maintain information about registered sex offenders because it could be confusing and could discourage institutions from disclosing relevant information about a registered sex offender in appropriate circumstances. Note that disclosures under this exception are required to comply with guidelines issued by the U.S. Attorney General for state community notification programs, which were published in the *Federal Register* on Jan. 5, 1999 (64 FR 572) and Oct. 25, 2002 (67 FR 65598).

§ 99.31(b) De-identification of Information

Education records may be released without consent under FERPA if all personally identifiable information has been removed. The final regulations provide objective standards under which postsecondary institutions, state higher education authorities, and any other party may release, without consent, education records, or information from education records, that has been de-identified through the removal of all "personally identifiable information" taking into account unique patterns of information about the student, whether through single or multiple releases, and other reasonably available information. The new standards apply to both individual, redacted records and statistical information from education records in both student level or microdata and aggregate form.

Under previous regulations, *personally identifiable information* (PII) includes a student's name and other direct personal identifiers, such as the student's SSN or student number. PII also includes indirect identifiers, such as the name of the student's parent or other family members; the student's or family's address, and personal characteristics or other information that would make the student's identity easily traceable. The new regulations add biometric records to the list of personal identifiers that constitute PII, and add other indirect identifiers, such as date and place of birth and mother's maiden name, as examples of identifiers that should be considered in determining whether information is personally identifiable. The new regulations define "biometric record" to mean a record of one or more measurable biological or behavioral characteristics that can be used for automated recognition of an individual, including fingerprints, retina and iris patterns, voiceprints, DNA sequence, facial characteristics, and handwriting. The definition is based on National Security Presidential Directive 59 and Homeland Security Presidential Directive 24.

The new regulations remove from the definition of PII the reference to "other information that would make the student's identity easily traceable" because the phrase lacked specificity and clarity, and possibly suggested a fairly low standard for protecting education records. In its place, the regulations add that PII includes "other information that, alone or in combination, is linked or linkable to a specific student that would allow a reasonable person in the school community, who does not have personal knowledge of the relevant circumstances, to identify the student with reasonable certainty." This change brings the definition more in line with recent Office of Management and Budget (OMB) guidance to federal agencies, with modifications tailored to the educational community. (*See* OMB M-07-16, "Safeguarding Against and Responding to the Breach of Personally Identifiable Information" at footnote 1: www.whitehouse.gov/omb/memoranda/fy2007/m07-16.pdf.) Under the new regulations, PII also includes "information requested by a person who the educational institution reasonably believes knows the identity of the student to whom the education record relates."

The definition of PII provides objective standards for institutions, state higher education authorities, and other parties that release information, either at will or in response to an open records request, to use in determining whether they may release information, including in special cases such as those involving well-known students or records that concern highly publicized incidents. The preamble to the final regulations notes that the disclosing party must look to local news, events, and media coverage in the "school community" in determining whether "other information" (*i.e.*, information other than direct and indirect identifiers listed in the definition of PII), would make a particular record personally identifiable even after all direct identifiers have been removed. In regard to so-called targeted requests, the final regulations clarify that a party may not release information from education records if the requester asks for the record of a particular student, or if the party has reason to believe that the requester knows the identity of the student to whom the requested records relate. (For more details, see the following FPCO letters to: Miami University [on page 237]; University of Oklahoma [on page 257]; Kennesaw University [on page 260]; and the Georgia Board of Regents [on page 263].)

These standards for determining whether records contain PII also apply to the release of statistical information from education records, in particular small data cells that may identify students. The potential for identification through small cells varies from situation to situation. It is the institution's responsibility to ensure that data from education records to be disclosed in small statistical cells cannot be linked to specific students. If the potential exists, the information should not be disclosed.

Under the new regulations a party that releases either redacted records or statistical information should also consider other information that is linked or linkable to a student, such as law enforcement records, published directories, and other publicly available records that could be used to identify a student, and the cumulative effect of disclosure of student data. In all cases, the disclosing party must determine whether the other information that is linked or linkable to an education record would allow a "reasonable person in the school community" to identify the student "with reasonable certainty." The regulations recognize that the risk of avoiding the disclosure of PII cannot be completely eliminated and is always a matter of analyzing and balancing risk so that the risk of disclosure is very low. The reasonable certainty standard in the new definition of PII requires such a balancing test.

In regard to statistical information from education records, the final regulations recognize that it is not possible to prescribe a single disclosure limitation method to apply in every circumstance to minimize the risk of disclosing PII. The preamble to the final regulations does, however, provide several examples of the kinds of statistical, scientific, and technological concepts used by the federal statistical agencies that can assist parties in developing a sound approach to de-identifying information for release depending on what information has already been released and what other information is publicly available.

The new regulations also codify the Department's November 18, 2004, guidance to the Tennessee Department of Education (*see* FPCO letter on page 241) by allowing a disclosing party to attach a code to properly de-identified student level information for education research, which would allow the recipient to match information received from the same source. However, the recipient may not have access to any information about how the disclosing party generates and assigns a record code, or that would allow the recipient to identify a student based on the record code; certain other conditions apply. A party that releases data under this provision must ensure that the identity of any student cannot be determined with reasonable certainty in this "coded data," including assurances of sufficient cell and subgroup size, and the linking key that connects the code to student information cannot be shared with the requesting party. These standards establish an appropriate balance that facilitates educational research and accountability while preserving the privacy protections in FERPA. As noted above, the Department cannot specify in general which disclosure limitation methods should be used in any particular case. However, parties are directed to monitor releases of coded microdata to ensure that overlapping or successive releases do not result in data sets in which PII is disclosed.

§ 99.31(c) Identification and Authentication of Identity

The new regulations require a postsecondary institution to use reasonable methods to identify and authenticate the identity of parents, students, school officials, and any other parties to whom they disclose education records. The previous regulations did not address this issue. Authentication of identity is more complex for disclosure of electronic records as new methods and technologies are developed. Under the final regulations, districts and institutions may use: PINs, passwords, personal security questions; "smart cards" and tokens; biometric indicators; or other factors known or possessed only by the user, as appropriate.

§ 99.32 Recordkeeping Requirements

Previous regulations required an educational institution to maintain a record of redisclosures it has authorized

under § 99.33(b) (*see* below for an explanation of changes to this section), including the names of the additional parties to which the receiving party may further disclose the information on behalf of the institution and their legitimate interests under § 99.31 in receiving the information. The regulations now also require a state or federal official that rediscloses education records on behalf of an institution to comply with these recordation requirements if the institution does not currently do so, and to make the record available to an educational institution upon request within a reasonable period of time not exceeding 30 days. An educational institution is required to obtain a copy of the state or federal official's record of further disclosures and make it available in response to a student's request to review the student's record of disclosures. The regulations also allow a state or federal official to maintain the record by the student's class, school, or other grouping rather than by the name of the student. The Department made this modification in order to ease the administrative burdens of recordkeeping.

§ 99.33 Redisclosure of Education Records

The previous regulations prohibited recipients of education records, without prior written consent, from redisclosing personally identifiable information from the records *unless* 1) the institution disclosed the information with the understanding that the recipient may make further disclosures on the institution's behalf under one of the exceptions in § 99.31 and 2) the institution records the redisclosure.

§ 99.33(b)(1) By Federal and State Officials

The new FERPA regulations permit federal and state officials that receive education records under §§ 99.31(a)(3) and 99.35 for audit, evaluation, and compliance and enforcement purposes to redisclose education records under the conditions of § 99.33(b). While not previously allowed, a state higher education authority that obtained education records for audit, evaluation, or compliance and enforcement purposes may now redisclose the records for other qualifying purposes under § 99.31 so long as it is on behalf of the institution. These include forwarding records to a student's new school within the state's university system and to another official listed in § 99.31(a)(3) (such as the Secretary, or state higher education authority) for another qualifying audit, evaluation, or compliance and enforcement purpose. This will facilitate the development of consolidated state data systems used for accountability and research purposes. The final regulations also allow state and federal officials to redisclose education records under other exceptions listed in § 99.31(a), including disclosures: to an accrediting agency; in connection with a health or safety emergency; and in compliance with a court order or subpoena.

§ 99.33(b)(2) Under Court Order or Subpoena

The final regulations require a state higher education authority or other party that rediscloses education records on behalf of an institution in compliance with a court order or subpoena to comply with the notification requirements in § 99.31(a)(9)(ii) before it responds to the order or subpoena. The five-year penalty rule in § 99.33(e) was revised so that if the Department determines that a third party, such as a state higher education authority, does not notify the eligible student as required, the institution may not allow that third party access to education records for at least five years.

§ 99.33(c) Clery Act

The new regulations provide that disclosures made under the *Jeanne Clery Disclosure of Campus Security Policy and Campus Crimes Statistics Act* (Clery Act) in the HEA are not subject to the prohibition on redisclosure in § 99.33(a), and that institutions may not require a victim to execute a non-disclosure or confidentiality agreement in order to receive information that the institution is required to disclose under the Clery Act. While previous regulations permitted a postsecondary institution to disclose the outcome of a disciplinary proceeding to a victim of an alleged perpetrator of a crime of violence or a non-forcible sex offense, regardless of the outcome, only on the condition that the institution notify the recipient that he or she may not redisclose the information without the student-perpetrator's consent, the Department has determined that the statutory prohibition on redisclosure does *not* apply to information required to be released under the Clery Act.

§ 99.36 Health and Safety Emergencies

Previous regulations stated, in part, that an educational institution may disclose personally identifiable information from education records to appropriate parties in connection with an emergency if knowledge of the information is necessary to protect the health or safety of the student or other individuals. The regulations also stated that the health and safety emergencies provisions must be "strictly construed."

The new regulations remove the language requiring strict construction of this exception and add a provision that says that, in making a determination under § 99.36, an educational institution may take into account the totality of the circumstances pertaining to a threat to the safety or health of the student or other individuals. If the institution determines that there is an articulable and significant threat to the health or safety of a student or other individuals, it may disclose information from education records to appropriate parties whose knowledge of the information is necessary to protect the health and safety of the student or other individuals. The recordkeeping requirements in § 99.32(a)(5) were revised to require an educational institution to record the articulable and significant threat that formed the basis for the disclosure and the parties to whom the information was disclosed. If there is a rational basis for the determination, the Department will not substitute its judgment for that of the educational institution in deciding to release the information. Section 99.36 also provides that "appropriate parties" include "parents of an eligible student." The preamble to the final regulations also clarifies the circumstances under which an educational institution may release without consent an eligible student's "treatment records" for purposes other than treatment.

These changes were made as a result of issues that were raised after the Virginia Tech tragedy in April 2007. In the first instance, the Department determined that greater flexibility and deference should be afforded to administrators so that they can bring appropriate resources to bear on circumstances that threaten the health or safety of individuals. With regard to the second amendment adding "parents" to those considered an "appropriate party," this change clarifies to colleges and universities that parents may be notified when there is a health or safety emergency involving their son or daughter, notwithstanding any FERPA provision that might otherwise prevent such a disclosure.

§ 99.37 Directory Information

FERPA regulations permit the disclosure of properly designated directory information without meeting FERPA's written consent requirement. An institution must designate the categories to be disclosed and permit students the opportunity to opt out before making such disclosures.

§ 99.37(b) Former Students

FERPA regulations permit institutions to disclose directory information on former students without providing notice as otherwise required or an additional opt-out opportunity. The regulations require institutions to honor a former student's opt-out request made while in attendance unless it has been specifically rescinded by the former student. This makes clear that institutions may not disclose the directory information of a former student if the student opted out of the disclosure while the student was in attendance.

§ 99.37(c) Student Identification and Communication in Class

The previous regulations did not address whether a student who opts out of directory information disclosures may prevent school officials from identifying the student by name or from disclosing the student's electronic identifier or institutional email address in class. The final regulations provide specifically that an opt out of directory information disclosures does not prevent an institution from identifying a student by name or from disclosing a student's electronic identifier or institutional email address in class. This change clarifies that a right to opt out of directory information disclosures does not include a right to remain anonymous in class, and may not be used to impede routine classroom communications and interactions, whether class is held in a specified physical location or online through electronic communications.

§ 99.37(d) Use of SSNs

The previous regulations did not specifically prohibit the use of SSNs to identify students when disclosing or confirming directory information. The final regulations prohibit the use of an SSN or part of an SSN as an identification element when disclosing or confirming directory information unless the student has provided written consent for the disclosure. Some institutions and vendors providing services such as degree verifications on behalf of the institution may be using a student's SSN as a means of confirming identity. Unless the student has provided prior written consent to confirm the SSN, this implicit confirmation of the SSN is not permitted under FERPA.

§ 99.62, § 99.64, § 99.65, § 99.66, § 99.67 Enforcement Provisions

The FERPA regulations contain a number of provisions that address the Department's authority, through the Family Policy Compliance Office (FPCO), to investigate a postsecondary institution when a student files a complaint. The final regulations enhance and clarify the

Department's enforcement responsibilities as described in *Gonzaga University* v. *Doe*, 536 U.S. 273 (2002). In particular, the new regulations clarify that FPCO may investigate allegations that FERPA has been violated made by a school official or some other party that is not a student, including information that has been brought to the attention of the Department by media reports. The new regulations also clarify that a complaint does not have to allege that an institution has a policy or practice of violating FERPA in order for the Department to initiate an investigation or find the institution in violation. The Department removed a provision in the proposed rules that would have required FPCO to find that an educational institution has a policy or practice in violation of FERPA in order to take any enforcement action, because it unnecessarily limited the Department's enforcement authority.

Safeguarding Recommendations

The preamble to the NPRM and final regulations contain non-binding recommendations to help institutions navigate the significant challenges inherent in safeguarding education records from unauthorized access and disclosure. These challenges include inadvertent posting of students' grades or financial information on publicly available Web servers; theft or loss of laptops and other portable devices that contain education records; computer hacking; and failure to retrieve education records at termination of employment. Agencies and institutions are encouraged to review the National Institute of Standards and Technology (NIST) Special Publication (SP) 800-100, "Information Security Handbook: A Guide for Managers," and NIST SP 800-53, "Recommended Security Controls for Federal Information Systems" for guidance and to use any methods or technologies they determine are reasonable to mitigate the risk of unauthorized access and disclosure taking into account the likely harm that would result. The recommendations also include suggested responses to data breaches and other unauthorized disclosures, such as: reporting the incident to law enforcement authorities; taking steps to retrieve data and prevent further disclosures; identifying all affected records and students; determining how the incident occurred; determining whether institutional policies and procedures were breached; and conducting a risk assessment. Notification of students is not required but recommended. Following these safeguarding recommendations will undoubtedly help prevent unauthorized disclosures at an institution. Additionally, if, despite adopting these safeguards, an institution finds that such an unauthorized disclosure has occurred, the institution may be well-positioned to respond to any Department investigation that might result. (*See* the FPCO "Letter to University of Central Florida," on page 234, for more details on safeguarding of student records .)

Appendix D

Model Notification of Rights under FERPA for Postsecondary Institutions

The *Family Educational Rights and Privacy Act* (FERPA) affords students certain rights with respect to their education records. These rights include:

☒ The right to *inspect and review* the student's education records within 45 days of the day the University receives a request for access.

A student should submit to the registrar, dean, head of the academic department, or other appropriate official, a written request that identifies the record(s) the student wishes to inspect. The University official will make arrangements for access and notify the student of the time and place where the records may be inspected. If the records are not maintained by the University official to whom the request was submitted, that official shall advise the student of the correct official to whom the request should be addressed.

☒ The right to request the *amendment* of the student's education records that the student believes are inaccurate, misleading, or otherwise in violation of the student's privacy rights under FERPA.

A student who wishes to ask the University to amend a record should write the University official responsible for the record, clearly identify the part of the record the student wants changed, and specify why it should be changed.

If the University decides not to amend the record as requested, the University will notify the student in writing of the decision and the student's right to a hearing regarding the request for amendment. Additional information regarding the hearing procedures will be provided to the student when notified of the right to a hearing.

☒ The right to provide *written consent* before the University discloses personally identifiable information from the student's education records, except to the extent that FERPA authorizes disclosure without consent.

The University discloses education records without a student's prior written consent under the FERPA exception for disclosure to school officials with legitimate educational interests. A school official is a person employed by the University in an administrative, supervisory, academic or research, or support staff position (including law enforcement unit personnel and health staff); a person or company with whom the University has contracted as its agent to provide a service instead of using University employees or officials (such as an attorney, auditor, or collection agent); a person serving on the Board of Trustees; or a student serving on an official committee, such as a disciplinary or grievance committee, or assisting another school official in performing his or her tasks.

A school official has a legitimate educational interest if the official needs to review an education record in order to fulfill his or her professional responsibilities for the University.

[*Optional*] Upon request, the University also discloses education records without consent to officials of another school in which a student seeks or intends to enroll. [NOTE TO UNIVERSITY: FERPA requires an institution to make a reasonable attempt to notify each student of these disclosures unless the institution states in its annual notification that it intends to forward records on request.]

☒ The right to *file a complaint* with the U.S. Department of Education concerning alleged failures by the

University to comply with the requirements of FERPA. The name and address of the Office that administers FERPA is:

Family Policy Compliance Office
U.S. Department of Education
400 Maryland Avenue, SW
Washington, DC 20202-5901

[*Note*: In addition, an institution may want to include its directory information public notice, as required by § 99.37 of the regulations, with its annual notification of rights under FERPA.]

Available for download at: www2.ed.gov/policy/gen/guid/fpco/ferpa/ps-officials.html.

Appendix E
FPCO Letters

In Attendance

Letter #01. Letter to University of New Mexico..177

Letter #02. Letter to Harvard University 179

Letter #03. Letter to Drinker, Biddle & Reath..183

Dual Enrollment

Letter #04. Letter to Virginia Commonwealth University 188

Letter #05. Letter to University of Medicine & Dentistry of New Jersey 190

Directory Information

Letter #06. Letter to University of Wisconsin-River Falls 192

Letter #07. Letter to Los Angeles Unified School District..196

Unauthorized Access to Education Records

Letter #08. Letter to Tazewell County (VA) School Board..198

Letter #09. Letter to Strayer University 200

Contractors

Letter #10. Letter to Clark County School District (NV) 207

Medical Interns and Residents

Letter #11. Letter to University of Arkansas 210

Teaching Assistants

Letter #12. Letter to the American Federation of Teachers 212

Letter #13. Letter to the University of Massachusetts 216

Disability Records

Letter #14. Letter to University of North Alabama 218

Financial Aid

Letter #15. Letter to Yale University 221

Posting Grades by Social Security Number

Letter #16. Letter to Hunter College 223

Authentication/ Safeguarding

Letter #17. Letter to Cornell University...225

Letter #18. FPCO Letter of Finding 227

Letter #19. Letter to University of Central Florida 230

Disclosure of Data

Letter #20. Letter to Miami University (OH) 233

Letter #21. Letter to Tennessee Department of Education 237

Letter #22. Letter to Nebraska Coordinating Commission 239

Subpoenas

Letter #23. Letter to Youngstown University (OH) 241

Letter #24. Letter to Los Angeles Unified School District 245

Letter #25. Letter to the Internal Revenue Service 247

Letter #26. Letter to Shelton State Community College (AL) 249

Registered Sex Offenders

Letter #27. Family Policy Compliance Office Guidelines to the Educational Community:
Disclosure of Education Records Concerning Registered Sex Offenders 251

Open Records Requests

Letter #28. Letter to University of Oklahoma 253

Letter #29. Letter to Kennesaw State University 256

Letter #30. Letter to Georgia Board of Regents 259

Disclosure to Media

Letter #31. Letter to Mohave Community College 262

Letter #32. Letter to Towson State University 264

Conflict with State Law

Letter #33. Letter to Clark County School District (NV) 273

Letter #34. Letter to Grossmont-Cuyamaca Community College District (CA) 275

NCAA

Letter #35. Letter to NCAA 277

Letter #36. Letter to NCAA 287

Letter #37. Letter to NCAA 289

Letter #38. Letter to University of Mississippi 292

Solomon Amendment

Letter #39. Letter to Senator Charles E. Grassley 294

Deceased Student

Letter #40. Letter to University of Notre Dame 296

UNITED STATES DEPARTMENT OF EDUCATION
OFFICE OF HUMAN RESOURCES AND ADMINISTRATION

Mr. Robert E. Bienstock   OCT 29 1993
Associate University Counsel
The University of New Mexico
Scholes Hall 150
Albuquerque, New Mexico 87131-0056

Dear Mr. Bienstock:

This is in response to your letter, dated September 2, 1993, addressed to Ms. Frances Moran, regarding the Family Educational Rights and Privacy Act (FERPA). Your letter was referred to this Office for response because we administer FERPA. Specifically, you ask "at what point in the process of application, acceptance, mailing in a deposit, attendance at orientation sessions, matriculation, and attendance at classes" is a student considered "in attendance" for the purposes of FERPA. In your letter, you also state the following:

Because we are constantly inundated with requests for communication by parents of student-applicants and admittees, for assistance in making arrangements for orientation, student housing, registration, and the like, and because we prefer to continue communicating with these parents as long as possible in order to assist high school students in making the transition to college, it is imperative that we know precisely when we may no longer communicate to the parents without specific written consent from the students...

As you are aware, FERPA affords parents and eligible students certain rights with respect to the student's education records. When a student has reached the age of 18 or is attending an institution of postsecondary education, the student becomes an "eligible student" and all rights afforded by FERPA transfer from the parent to the student. Prior to that time, all FERPA rights belong to the parents. FERPA defines the term "student" as any individual who is or has been in attendance at an educational agency or institution.

With regard to your specific question as to when a student would be considered "in attendance" for the purposes of FERPA, neither the statute nor the regulations offer guidance which would provide further clarification. Historically, the Department has left it to each institution to determine when a student is considered to be "in attendance" at the particular institution.

However, such a determination should be justified by some reasonable basis of fact. Please note that the Department reserves the right ultimately to conclude whether, as a matter of federal law, the facts on which the determination is based are relevant and reasonable and that such determination is applied consistently.

With regard to your concern that the University be able to continue communication with parents for as long as possible, you may wish to consider the following alternative. As you know, FERPA limits an educational agency or institution's ability to release personally identifiable information from a student's education records without the student's prior written consent. However, FERPA also provides certain exceptions to this general limitation on disclosure under section 99.31. One of these exceptions permits a school to disclose information from a student's education records to that student's parent if the student is claimed as a dependent for income tax purposes. Specifically, FERPA states that a school can disclose education records without prior written consent if:

The disclosure is to parents of a dependent student, as defined in section 152 of the Internal Revenue Code of 1954.

34 CFR 99.31 (a)(8)

While FERPA does not offer guidance on what may be considered adequate documentation of a student's status as a dependent, this Office would support a policy of documenting a student's dependency status by requiring a parent seeking access to his or her child's education records to supply a copy of the parent's most recent federal income tax form, as was the University's previous policy.

Additionally, nothing in FERPA would preclude a university from requiring students to identify their status at the time of registration or even application for incoming freshmen and transfer students. If an institution elects to adopt such a requirement, we believe that students should be advised of the reason why they are asked about their tax status as dependents and suggest the following or similar statement to students:

Under FERPA, the University may disclose to parents information from the education records of a student who is "dependent" under the federal tax laws without the student's consent. Have you been claimed by your parents as a dependent for federal tax purposes?

Thereafter, if a parent were to request access to information from a student's education records and those records have been identified as the records of a *non-dependent student*, the record custodian could then ask that the parent supply a copy of his or her most recent federal income tax form before access to those records would be given. In this way, the burden on a university of obtaining proof of a student's dependent status from a parent would be removed in many instances and colleges and universities could more readily distinguish those students who are dependent students from those who are not.

I trust the above information is responsive to your inquiry. Should you have any further questions about FERPA, please feel free to contact this Office again.

Sincerely,

LeRoy S. Rooker, Director
Family Policy Compliance Office

UNITED STATES DEPARTMENT OF EDUCATION

Mr. Neil Rudenstein
President, Harvard University
Cambridge, Massachusetts 02138

AUG 22 1991
Complaint No. [REDACTED]
Family Educational Rights and Privacy Act (FERPA)

Dear Mr. Rudenstein:

This is to inform you of the finding in the complaint filed with this Office by Mr. [REDACTED], an undergraduate student in Harvard College. Mr. [REDACTED] alleged that the College denied him access to his education records in violation of the Family Educational Rights and Privacy Act (FERPA). Specifically, he alleged that the University denied him access to a summary sheet that was prepared by the Admissions Committee in connection with his application for admission to the University. This Office informed your predecessor, Dr. Derek Bok, of the allegation by letter dated May 13, 1991. By letter dated July 12, 1991, Ms. Marianna C. Pierce, attorney, responded on behalf of the University. Following is a discussion of the allegation, the University's response, and the results of our investigation.

In support of his allegation, Mr. [REDACTED] submitted a copy of a letter dated March 8, 1991, addressed to him by the director of admissions, Ms. Marlyn McGrath Lewis, in which she informed Mr. Gerstein as follows:

> *Let me explain how the College compiles a student's file. Once a student is admitted to the College, all admissions related documents not prepared by the Admissions Committee, such as the application itself and various recommendations, are placed in a folder which then becomes the student's file. It is sent to the Freshman Dean's Office, and later documents relating to the student are placed in it. It then will travel to the House where the student lives as an upperclassman, and similarly grows as new materials are placed in it. The student has full access to this file, other than to confidential letters to which he or she has waived access. I understand that you reviewed this file, and presumably inspected all materials other than those to which you waived access.*
>
> *The summary sheets (which contain the readers' comments) that you request are prepared by and kept in the Admissions Office. Summary sheets are, of course, made before the students enroll; by the time they enroll, those records have no further significance to them. The summary sheets are therefore deliberately kept separate from the student files. [Emphasis added.]*
>
> *As you may know, the Buckley Amendment was enacted to ensure student access to educational records that the institution may use in making decisions that affect a student's future, and to give the student the opportunity to challenge and correct inaccurate information. Since the summary sheets have no significant to enrolled students, they are not documents for which the opportunity that the Buckley Amendment affords to challenge and correct information would be meaningful. We therefore have concluded that summary sheets are not covered by the Buckley Amendment. [Emphasis added.]*
>
> *Moreover, the summary sheet you request is heavily derivative of the confidential materials to which you waived access; indeed, it excerpts them directly. We therefore believe that [it] is also confidential and that we have no legal obligation to make it available to you. Indeed, we feel strongly that we have an obligation not to do so.*

In his letter to this Office, Mr. [REDACTED] stated that he had waived his FERPA right of access to confidential letters of recommendation. However, with respect to the summary sheets, he stated:

> *Even if the exemption for certain confidential recommendations is stretched to include information on application summary sheets, it does not follow that Harvard must deny students access to those sheets in their entirety.*

Harvard's interpretation has the unacceptable result of allowing the university to exempt any document from FERPA simply by jotting down a margin note on it which contains something taken from a confidential recommendation.

If necessary, Harvard could redact derivative information from the summary sheets. Of course, this process would be fraught with danger because Harvard would inevitably attempt to exaggerate the presence of derivative data. However, such a redaction would allow students to have access to the vast majority of summary sheet information, which has no relation to any recommendations.

In its response to the complaint the University confirms that it denied Mr. [REDACTED] access to the summary sheet. The University argues, however, that the denial of access does not violate FERPA because (1) the summary sheet is not "used by the institution in making decisions that affect the life of the student" (120 Cong. Rec. 39858-9 (1974)) and, therefore, does not fall within the scope of FERPA, and (2) the summary sheet is "heavily derivative of the teacher recommendations to which [Mr. [REDACTED]] waived access [and if] Harvard were to release Mr. [REDACTED]'s sheet to him, it would in effect be releasing parts of those confidential recommendations [a result which] is not compelled by the statute."

The University states that the summary sheets "include candid evaluations of the candidate by the initial readers." It states further:

The Admissions Office has considered simply destroying the sheets after their use and may decide to do so [but] has not yet done so because the summary sheets are useful in explaining in our processes in the case of a complaint by a disappointed applicant, or in the case of review initiated by an outside agency [e.g., to see whether Harvard's practices are discriminatory].... [Emphasis added.]

[I]f it is determined by the Department that the summary sheet must be disclosed, we believe that it should be redacted.... Indeed, Mr. [REDACTED] suggests redaction as a possible solution.

As discussed more fully below, based on our review of Mr. [REDACTED]'s allegations and the University's response, this Office finds that the University has denied Mr. [REDACTED] access to the summary sheet in violation of FERPA. We also find that the University is not required by FERPA to give Mr. [REDACTED] access to any portion of the summary sheet that is excerpted from or identifiably derived from a particular confidential letter or statement of recommendation—unless the University has used the letter, or the portion of the summary sheet that is excerpted from or derived from the letter, for a purpose other than the purpose for which it was intended.

Analysis

The issue to be decided in this complaint is whether the University violated FERPA when the Admissions Office denied Mr. [REDACTED] access to a summary sheet that was "created by [a]dmissions officers to help condense the material in Mr. [REDACTED]'s application folder," "is heavily derivative of ...teacher recommendations to which he waived access," and includes "candid evaluations of the candidate by the initial readers."

FERPA defines the term "education records" as

[T]hose records, files, documents, and other materials which (i) contain information directly related to a student; and (ii) are maintained by an educational agency or institution, or by a person acting for such agency or institution.

20 U.S.C. 1232g(a)(4)(A); See also 34 CFR 99.3

Because the summary sheet at issue relates to a student (Mr. [REDACTED]) and is maintained by the University Admissions Office, it is an "education record" subject to FERPA. The University takes the position that because "the University's policy is not to use the summary sheet for any purpose after the applicant enrolls and becomes a 'student,' [and because] it is …not used by the institution in making decisions that 'affect the life of a student[,]' …it is not …protected by FERPA." However, the University also states that the reason it maintains the summary sheets on "students" after completion of the admissions process and does not destroy them is that "the summary sheets are useful in explaining out processes in the case of …review initiated by an outside agency." Thus, it appears the University does use the summary sheets after the applicants enroll and become "students." Even if the University does not use them, however, the sheets are nevertheless subject to FERPA because they contain information related to students and are maintained by the University. Therefore, it is not necessary to consider the University's position further. Clearly, the summary sheets fall within the FERPA definition of "education records."

FERPA requires that an educational institution afford students the right to "inspect and review" the student's "education records." 20 U.S.C. 1232g(a)(1)(A). See also 34 CFR 99.10. There are certain limitations on the student's right to inspect and review "education records." The University proposes that one of those limitations applies in this case. 20 U.S.C. 1232g(a)(1)(B)(iii) and (C). See also 34 CFR 99.12(b) and (c). That limitation, as stated in 34 CFR 99.12, provides that

> (b) A postsecondary institution does not have to permit a student to inspect and review *education records* that are—
>
> (3) Confidential letters and confidential statements of recommendation placed in the student's education records after January 1, 1975, if—
>
> (i) *The student has waived his or her right to inspect and review those letters and statements*; and
>
> (ii) Those letters and statements are related to the student's—
>
> (A) *Admission to an educational institution*;
>
> (B) Application for employment; or
>
> (C) Receipt of an honor or honorary recognition.
>
> (c)(2) If a student has waived his or her rights under paragraph (b)(3)(i) of this section, the educational institution shall—
>
> (ii) *Use the letters and statements of recommendation only for the purpose for which they were intended*
>
> (iii) Give the student, on request, the names of the individuals who *provided* the letters and statements of recommendation [.] [Emphasis added.]

Under this provision, the limitation of a student's right to inspect and review applies to letters and statements of recommendation "provided" by individuals that are "related to the student's …[a]dmission to an educational institution" if the student has "waived his or her right" of access to the documents. The limitation does not apply to a summary sheet that is "created by [a]dmissions officers to …condense the material in [an] application folder" and that includes "candid evaluations of the candidate by the initial readers." [Emphasis added.] Therefore, Mr. [REDACTED] was entitled by FERPA to inspect and review the summary sheet that is related to him. However, the University was not required by FERPA to allow Mr. [REDACTED] to inspect and review any portions of the summary sheet that are excerpted or specifically derived from a confidential letter or statement to which Mr. [REDACTED] clearly waived his right of access.

Finding

Based on Mr. [REDACTED]'s allegation and the response provided by the University as discussed above, this Office finds that the summary sheet at issue is an "education record" subject to FERPA. This Office finds further that the University violated FERPA when it denied Mr. [REDACTED] the right to inspect and review those portions of the summary sheet that were not excerpts from, or specifically derived from, confidential letters and statements of recommendations to which he had waived his right to inspect and review under 34 CFR 99.12.

Action Required

This Office will close the investigation of Mr. [REDACTED]'s complaint upon receipt of a written assurance that Mr. [REDACTED] has been afforded the right to inspect and review the summary sheet at issue in accordance with the provisions of FERPA discussed above. The University should also inform appropriate University personnel of the pertinent FERPA provisions.

Please provide the requested assurance within four weeks from your receipt of this letter. Thank you for the University's cooperation in resolving Mr. [REDACTED]'s complaint.

Sincerely,

LeRoy S. Rooker, Director
Family Policy Compliance Office

cc: [REDACTED]

Mr. Jonathan D. Tarnow   AUGUST 16, 2007
Drinker, Biddle & Reath, LLP
1500 K Street, NW
Suite 1100
Washington, DC 20005-1209

Dear Mr. Tarnow:

This is in response to your February 16, 2007, letter in which you request guidance on the applicability of the Family Educational Rights and Privacy Act (FERPA) to the Commonwealth of Virginia's recently enacted sex offender reporting statute. This Office administers FERPA and provides technical assistance to educational agencies and institutions to ensure compliance with the statute and regulations, which are codified at 20 U.S.C. § 1232g and 34 CFR Part 99 respectively.

Issues

You explain that, in 2006, the Virginia General Assembly amended a number of provisions related to the state's Sex Offender and Crimes Against Minors Registry. You state:

One provision of the law, codified at Virginia Code Annotated § 23-2.2:1, requires both two-year and four-year institutions in Virginia to report to the Virginia State Police the following information for all applicants that are accepted for admission: (1) name; (2) social security number [SSN] or other identifying number; (3) date of birth; and (4) gender. This information is to be reported after acceptance for admission, but prior to the applicant becoming a "student in attendance." Specifically, according to guidelines jointly issued by the State Council on Higher Education for Virginia, the Virginia State Police, and the Virginia Community College System, institutions are to report this information within seven working days of granting an applicant acceptance or enrolling him or her in the institution. See Guidelines for Compliance with § 23-2.2:1. Reporting of enrollment information to Sex Offender and Crimes Against Minors Registry at 1 (hereinafter the "Guidelines" or "Guidance"), attached.

Although the Virginia statute requires institutions to report information before applicants become students in attendance, the Guidelines anticipate that [it] may not be possible for some institutions with continuous enrollments. Hence, the Guidelines require reporting within seven business days of either granting acceptance or enrolling the student. See id. at 1, 5. The Guidelines also provide that "if an institution plans to transmit data after students are in attendance, it should consult with its legal counsel about designating data to be reported as 'directory information' under FERPA, by revising the institution's definition of directory information." Id. at 5.

This data is to be compared with information contained in the Virginia Criminal Information Network and the National Crime Information Center Convicted Sexual Offender Registry File.

You state that for your client, an institution of higher education in Virginia, and for other institutions that admit students on an on-going basis, "the Virginia statute and the interpretations provided in the Guidelines appear to create a significant dilemma." In this regard, you explain:

An institution that enrolls students on a continuing basis, such as our client, will always have new students beginning classes. In order to satisfy Virginia's reporting requirement, our client would thus have to provide the information required under the Virginia statute on a daily basis. Such a system is not operationally practical. Therefore, whenever our client reports the required data to Virginia, it will be reporting on some number of students that are already in attendance and will thus be implicating FERPA.

You also note that the Guidelines do not appear to recognize that FERPA does not require educational agencies and institutions to have a "directory information" policy, nor do the Guidelines account for the fact that FERPA permits students to "individually opt-out of an institution's directory information designations." Please note that we are providing guidance on the applicability of FERPA to these requirements. Concerns about the requirements imposing an administrative burden on institutions should be addressed to appropriate officials of the Commonwealth.

Applicable FERPA Provisions

Postsecondary institutions subject to FERPA may not have a policy or practice of permitting the disclosure of "education records, or personally identifiable information contained therein" without the written consent of eligible students. 20 U.S.C. § 1232g(b)(1) and (b)(2); 34 CFR § 99.30(a). (An "eligible student" is one who is at least 18 years of age or attends a postsecondary institution. See 34 CFR § 99.3.) Under FERPA, "education records" means those records that are:

(a) Directly related to a student; and
(b) Maintained by an educational agency or institution or by a party acting for the agency or institution.

34 CFR § 99.3 "Education records"

The term "personally identifiable information" is defined in the regulations as:
(a) The student's name;
(b) The name of the student's parent or other family member;
(c) The address of the student or student's family;
(d) A personal identifier, such as the student's social security number or student number;
(e) A list of personal characteristics that would make the student's identity easily traceable; or
(f) Other information that would make the student's identity easily traceable.

34 CFR § 99.3

"Disclosure" means "to permit access to or the release, transfer, or other communication of personally identifiable information contained in education records to any party, by any means, including oral, written, or electronic means." See 34 CFR § 99.3.

One of the exceptions to FERPA's general consent requirement permits the disclosure of certain information that has been appropriately designated as "directory information" by the educational agency or institution, in accordance with § 99.37 of the regulations. FERPA defines directory information as information contained in an education record of a student which would not generally be considered harmful or an invasion of privacy if disclosed. Directory information could include information such as name, address, telephone listing, electronic mail address, date and place of birth, major field of study, dates of attendance, grade level, enrollment status, participation in officially recognized activities and sports, weight and height of members of athletic teams, degrees, honors and awards received, and the most recent educational agency or institution attended.

In contrast, SSNs, also listed as "personally identifiable information" under FERPA, are often used to obtain a variety of sensitive, non-public information about individuals, such as employment, credit, financial, health, motor vehicle, and educational information, that would be harmful or an invasion of privacy if disclosed. For these reasons, this Office has routinely advised that a student's SSN is the kind of personally identifiable information that may not be designated and disclosed as directory information. We have generally included "student ID numbers" in the same category because these numbers have historically been used much like SSNs, that is, as unique identifiers used by themselves to obtain access to non-directory information about a student, such as education records (or educational services). This Office has also historically advised that information such as race or gender may not be designated as "directory information" under FERPA.

A postsecondary institution may disclose directory information to third parties without consent if it has given public notice to students in attendance of the types of information which it has designated as "directory information," of the student's right to restrict the disclosure of such information, and of the period of time within which a student has to notify the school in writing that he or she does not want any or all of those types of information designated as "directory information." The means of notification could include publication in various sources, including in a newsletter, in a local newspaper, or in the student handbook. A school is not required to individually notify students regarding directory information.

It is important to understand the definition of "student" in this context of your questions. The term "student"

includes any person with respect to whom an educational agency or institution maintains education records or personally identifiable information, but does not include a person who has not been in attendance at such agency or institution.

20 U.S.C. § 1232g(a)(6)

The FERPA regulations define the term "student" in this manner:

*"Student," except as otherwise specifically provided in this part, means any individual who is or has been **in attendance** at an educational agency or institution and regarding whom the agency or institution maintains education records."*

34 CFR § 99.3 ("Student")(Emphasis added)

Neither the statute nor the regulations offer guidance which would provide further clarification as to when a student would be considered "in attendance" for the purposes of FERPA. Historically, the Department has left it to each institution to determine when a student is considered to be "in attendance" at that particular institution. However, such a determination should be justified by some reasonable basis of fact, and the Department reserves the right ultimately to conclude whether, as a matter of federal law, the facts on which the determination is based are relevant and reasonable and that such determination is applied consistently. Generally, a student should be considered "in attendance" no later than the first day of class.

Accordingly, applications of individuals who are not attending an educational agency or institution are generally not "education records" because the individuals are not "students" at the educational agency or institution. However, please note that an institution that receives information (such as a transcript) on an applicant from a high school or from another postsecondary institution is required to protect that information and may not redisclose the information except in accordance with § 99.33 of the FERPA regulations.

Discussion

With regard to the Commonwealth of Virginia's recently enacted sex offender reporting statute, you specifically ask these two questions:

* *Can the Virginia statute's reporting requirements be reconciled with the FERPA provisions (specifically 20 U.S.C. §§ 1232g(a)(5), (b)(1)) that permit but do not require institutions to designate student information as directory information for purposes of disclosure?*

* *Assuming that an institution chooses (or can be compelled by state statute) to designate certain items as directory information under FERPA, can the Virginia statute's reporting requirements be reconciled with 20 U.S.C. § 1232g(a)(5)(B), which allows students to opt-out of directory information disclosure?*

While the implementation of a "directory information" policy under FERPA (20 U.S.C. §§ 1232g(a)(5), (b)(1) and 34 CFR §§ 99.31(a)(11) and 99.37) is *permitted* but not *required* under the federal law, a state statute can require educational agencies and institution[s] to implement and disclose "directory information" under certain conditions. However, FERPA would not permit a state to require that information that is considered harmful or an invasion of privacy—such as students' SSNs, race, or gender—be designated and disclosed as "directory information." Also, any state requirement concerning "directory information" would have to honor "opt-outs" by parents and eligible students at K-12 agencies and institutions and by eligible students at postsecondary institutions. That is, under FERPA, parents and eligible students have the right to refuse to let an educational agency or institution designate any or all of the types of information about the student designated as "directory information." *See* 34 CFR § 99.37(a)(1)-(2). Therefore, any requirement that institutions disclose "directory information" must take into account the fact that students have to be provided notice of the items designated as "directory information," be advised of their right to refuse the[sic] let the institution disclose "directory information," and be told the period of time that the student has to notify the institution in writing that he or she does not want the information disclosed ("opt-out"). It is also important to note that, under FERPA, "directory information" may not be disclosed if a student has opted out of the disclosure of "directory information" items.

While you do not provide a definition for the term "continuous enrollments" used in your inquiry, or the terms used in the Virginia statute ("rolling or instantaneous admissions policy"), we assume for the purposes of this discussion that these terms refer to "students already in attendance," a term that the Guidance uses. For those students already in attendance, FERPA would permit postsecondary institution[s] to disclose only properly designated "directory information," and only on those students who have not opted-out. The Guidance notes, as discussed above, this Office excludes from the definition of "directory information" (34 CFR § 99.3 "Directory information") gender and SSNs. In this regard, the Guidance states:

Thus institutions transmitting data on students already in attendance are unable to transmit gender or social security number, and should transmit "other identifying numbers,["] and "U" in lieu of "M" or "F". The informational items designated by the institution to be directory information would include complete name, date of birth, first date of attendance and the "identifying number" used in lieu of social security number for transmitting the data to the State Police.

See Guidance, page 6. Accordingly, the Commonwealth of Virginia can require that postsecondary institutions designate and disclose certain information that has been properly designated as "directory information" under FERPA on students who have not opted out of the disclosure.

However, the Guidance also states that, for students already in attendance, institutions should use "other identifying number[s]" in lieu of SSNs for transmitting to the State Police. It is not clear from the information provided if this number refers to a student ID number or a randomly assigned number just for the purpose of transmitting the data to the State Police. It is also not clear why the Commonwealth believes that this number can be disclosed as "directory information." We would need further information about this number before we could provide technical assistance on this part of your question.

With regard to applicants who are not yet "students" under FERPA, we note that the Guidance requires that all institutions of higher education located in the Commonwealth of Virginia have a "maximum of seven working days, excluding institutional, state and/or federal holidays, from the time an individual who is seeking academic credit is granted acceptance to, *or enrolled in the institution*, to collect and transmit the [required information] about the student data elements regarding all newly admitted applicants to the Virginia State Police...." (Emphasis added.) Please note that it is not clear what the guidance means by "enrolled in the institution." As explained in our general discussion of FERPA requirements above, each institution must determine when an individual is considered "in attendance" in accordance with its own enrollment procedures. This Office would consider reasonable an institution's determination that an applicant is a student "in attendance" on the date that the applicant accepts an offer of admission. We would also consider reasonable a determination that an applicant who has been accepted is "in attendance" on the first day of classes, or the day that individual begins residency in a campus dormitory. We would not consider reasonable an institution's determination that an individual is not a student "in attendance" beyond the first day of classes.

Finally, 34 CFR § 99.61 requires an educational agency or institution to notify this Office if it determines that it cannot comply with FERPA due to a conflict with state or local law. To the extent that a Virginia institution of higher education determines that it is unable to comply with the requirements of Virginia Code Annotated § 23-2.2:1, it should notify us. Please note that when funding under federal "Spending Clause" legislation is knowingly accepted by a fund recipient, the law imposes enforceable, affirmative obligations on the recipient. See *United States* v. *Miami University*, 294 F.3d 797, 809-810 (6th Cir. 2002). The court explained that educational agencies and institutions are required to comply with all FERPA requirements as a condition for receipt of funding under programs administered by the Department. Once the conditions and funds are accepted, an agency or institution is prohibited from releasing education records without consent. Id.[sic] While it appears that the Commonwealth has attempted to take into consideration FERPA's privacy protections in crafting these reporting requirements, it would appear based on the information you have provided that institutions could not provide the State Police with an "identifying number" in lieu of the student's SSN as "directory information" under FERPA.

I trust this guidance is helpful to you in explaining how FERPA provisions relate to the Virginia statute.

Sincerely,

LeRoy S. Rooker, Director
Family Policy Compliance Office

UNITED STATES DEPARTMENT OF EDUCATION

Mr. David L. Ross   JUN 23 1993
General Counsel
Virginia Commonwealth University
1010 East Marshall Street
MCV, Box 116
Richmond, Virginia 23298-0116

Dear Mr. Ross:

This is in response to your letter dated March 15, 1993, concerning the Family Educational Rights and Privacy Act (FERPA). You ask several questions concerning the FERPA provisions that pertain to the sharing of information from education records between two universities, one of which is public and the other private, in connection with a graduate dual-degree program. You state that students in the program must meet acceptance requirements set by each school and that students "apply some academic credit from each school toward degree requirements of the other school, and the students then receive degrees from each university." You specifically ask whether FERPA would allow the sharing of the records between the schools in accordance with the FERPA provisions that allow disclosure without consent to school officials who have been determined to have a legitimate educational interest. As will be explained more fully below, we do not need to consider whether those provisions apply because it appears the disclosure falls within another exception to FERPA's written consent requirement.

FERPA generally protects a student's privacy interests in "education records." FERPA defines the term "education records" as:

[T]hose records, files, documents, and other materials, which (i) contain information directly related to a student; and (ii) are maintained by an educational agency or institution, or by a person acting for such agency or institution.

20 U.S.C. §1232g(a)(4); See also 34 CFR §99.3 "Education records"

FERPA applies to educational agencies and institutions which receive funding under programs administered by the Secretary of Education. See 34 CFR §99.1. At the postsecondary level, virtually all public and private schools receive such funding. Accordingly, FERPA would apply to both institutions regardless of their status as a public or private school.

FERPA provides that education records, or personally identifiable information from such records, may generally be disclosed by institutions of postsecondary education to third parties only after obtaining prior written consent of the student. 20 U.S.C. § 1232g(b)(1) and (d). See also 34 CFR §99.30. One of the exceptions to FERPA's consent requirement allows disclosure to another school, school system, or institution of postsecondary education where the student seeks or intends to enroll provided certain conditions are met. The exception is set forth at 34 CFR §99.31(a)(2); the conditions at 34 CFR §99.34. Under the conditions at 34 CFR 99.34(a), an institution of postsecondary education may disclose an education record under §99.31(a)(2) if it makes a reasonable attempt to notify the student at the last known address of the (student) or if the provisions of the school's student records policy required under 34 CFR §99.6 "includes a notice that the agency or institution forwards education records to other agencies or institutions that have requested the records and in which the student seeks or intends to enroll [.]" Paragraph (b) of 34 CFR §99.34 states:

(b) An educational agency or institution may disclose an education record of a student in attendance to another educational agency or institution if—

    (1) The student is enrolled in or receives services from the other agency or institution; and

    (2) The disclosure meets the requirements of paragraph (a) of [34 CFR §99.34].

We believe that in the situation you describe, the two universities in which students are enrolled in a dual-degree program may share records under 34 CFR §99.34(B)(1), provided the requirements of 34 CFR §99.34(a) are met.

I trust the above information adequately responds to your inquiry. Enclosed for your reference are a copy of the FERPA regulations and a copy of a model policy for postsecondary institutions to use in developing a student records policy that meets the requirements of 34 CFR §99.6. If you have further questions, please do not hesitate to contact this Office again.

Sincerely,

LeRoy S. Rooker, Director
Family Policy Compliance Office

Enclosures

UNITED STATES DEPARTMENT OF EDUCATION
OFFICE OF INNOVATION AND IMPROVEMENT

Mr. Evan S. Rosenthal   JUL 13 2006
Admissions Coordinator
School of Health Related Professions
University of Medicine & Dentistry of New Jersey
65 Bergen Street, Room 149
PO Box 1709
Newark, New Jersey 07101-1709

Dear Mr. Rosenthal:

This responds to your May 5, 2006, letter, in which you asked for guidance about the disclosure of information from education records under the Family Educational Rights and Privacy Act (FERPA). This Office investigates FERPA complaints and violations and provides technical assistance to educational agencies and institutions to ensure compliance with the statute and regulations, which are codified at 20 U.S.C. § 1232g and 34 CFR Part 99 respectively.

Your letter states that the University of Medicine & Dentistry of New Jersey's School of Health Related Professions (University) has a recognized joint degree program with Thomas Edison State College's School of Applied Science and Technology (College). According to your letter, a school official has proposed that the University ask all incoming students to provide the University registrar with the username and password they use to access their student information system account at the college. You explained that this process would stream-line and expedite the clearance of degree candidates between the two institutions and asked whether it complies with FERPA requirements. We understand your question to be whether the University may require students to provide their username and password at the College so that the University may quickly determine whether a student has met joint degree requirements.

A parent or eligible student (as defined in § 99.3 of the FERPA regulations) must provide a signed and dated written consent in accordance with the requirements of § 99.30) before an educational agency or institution discloses personally identifiable information from education records, except under the conditions set forth in § 99.31. The College may disclose to the University information from the education records of joint degree program students without their consent under § 99.34(b), which provides:

> *An educational agency or institution may disclose an education record of a student in attendance to another educational agency or institution if:*
> *(1) The student is enrolled in or receives services from the other agency or institution; and*
> *(2) The disclosure meets the requirements of paragraph (a) of this section.*

Paragraph (a) of § 99.34 contains notice and copy requirements that apply to these disclosures. Under this exception to the written consent requirement, College officials may disclose to the University (and vice versa) any information that could be disclosed without consent under § 99.31(a), including disclosures to school officials with a legitimate educational interest. This exception would permit school officials in both institutions to share information pertaining to a student's completion of joint degree requirements without meeting the consent requirements in § 99.30.

Requiring students to disclose their usernames and passwords at the College as a means for the University to obtain this information would not be permitted under FERPA because it would allow University officials to obtain access to *any* information maintained by the College which a student can access in student information system[sic], including information in which University officials do not have legitimate educational interests or that may not otherwise be discloseable to them under § 99.31 (a). We note in this regard that an educational agency or institution may not require parents or eligible students to waive their FERPA rights and protections as a condition for acceptance into an educational institution or receipt of educational services, and this principle applies equally to a forced waiver of FERPA rights and protections at another institution.

Finally, your letter indicates that a student's password at the College is defaulted to the last four numbers of the SSN. As this Office has explained previously, widely available information, such as an SSN or last four-digits of an SSN, should not be used to authenticate a student's identity because it may lead to the disclosure of personally identifiable information from education records to unauthorized parties. See our Nov. 5, 2004, letter to the University of Wisconsin available at http://www.ed.gov./policy/gen/guid/fpco/ferpa/library/uwisc.html .

I trust that this information is helpful in explaining the scope of FERPA as it relates to your concerns.

Sincerely,

LeRoy S. Rooker, Director
Family Policy Compliance Office

06 Letter to University of Wisconsin-River Falls

Re: Student ID Numbers as "Directory Information"

Ms. Judy George, Registrar   NOVEMBER 5, 2004
University of Wisconsin-River Falls
410 S. Third Street
River Falls, WI 54022

Gary S. Smith, Ph.D., Chief Information Officer
 & Director of Information Technology Services
Ms. Mary-Alice Muraski, eSIS Project Director
University of Wisconsin-River Falls
410 S. Third Street, North Hall 139
River Falls, WI 54022-5001

Dear Ms. George, Ms. Muraski, and Dr. Smith:

This responds to Ms. George's email dated May 18, 2004, and Ms. Muraski's and Dr. Smith's June 20, 2004, letter and follow-up email dated August 2, 2004. Collectively, you asked whether in the circumstances you described a student's "account ID number" can be disclosed as "directory information" under the Family Educational Rights and Privacy Act (FERPA), 20 U.S.C. § 1232g. This Office administers FERPA and is responsible for investigating complaints and providing technical assistance to ensure compliance with the statute and regulations codified at 34 CFR Part 99.

We have advised previously that a student ID number, like a student's social security number (SSN), may not be designated and disclosed as "directory information" under FERPA. It appears that this has created some confusion or concern on your part about what actually constitutes or defines a "student ID number" for purposes of this guidance. You explained that the problem arises because many commonly used technologies, such as campus portals and single sign-on approaches to information systems, as well as electronic communication systems, require publication of the personal identifier used by students to access the system.

According to your communications, the account ID number in question is a randomly assigned, seven digit number starting with the letter "W" that is not based in any way on an individual's SSN. The University's student information system (known as "eSIS") requires a student user to enter this number and a secret password in order to enter eSIS and access the student's own education records. The University also assigns each student a unique email address. Following the practice of many institutions, the University has ceased using student SSNs for any of these purposes.

The University provides students with an eSIS account ID number when they are accepted for admission, and this number remains assigned to the same student throughout his or her relationship with the University. Students use a web page to activate the number by providing their assigned account ID number, their date of birth, and the last four digits of their SSN. Once authenticated in this manner, the student must choose from a list of randomly generated passwords and establish and answer a security question, such as "What is your mother's maiden name?" Students may change their passwords after logging into the same web page and providing their existing password and the answer to their security question. A student who forgets his or her account ID number can obtain a new one from any of several functional offices, such as Admissions or Registrar.

A school official with an appropriate need to know who wishes to access a student's record must first login to eSIS using his or her own unique account ID and password. Once properly authenticated to the system, the school official may access a student's record by entering the student's account ID number, if known, or the student's name. Dr. Smith indicated that a school official might know a student's eSIS account ID number if the student had provided it or if the number was listed on an internal document. Dr. Smith explained further that the University uses the system's access control features to allow school officials to access a student's records only to an extent consistent with their professional role[s] and responsibilities. For example, a staff person in the Housing Office would only get to see information pertinent to housing matters, whereas someone in the Registrar's office would most likely be allowed to see a greater range of information.

Dr. Smith and Ms. Muraski stated generally that the "directory-based identification and authentication tools that are utilized in these [self-service oriented technological] environments are structured such that it is essentially impossible to effectively hide the logon or access I.D." In response to follow-up questions from this Office, Dr. Smith explained that the eSIS account ID number cannot effectively be made private because it is the key that is used to identify the student in the LDAP (Lightweight Directory Access Protocol) directory server and software. In order for eSIS to return correct information, the account ID number must be verified against the LDAP directory, which in turn is queryable by those with access to the server regardless of their status as school officials with a legitimate educational interest. (Passwords, in contrast, are protected against disclosure through a system query.)

According to Dr. Smith, an eSIS query with the name of a student who has not blocked directory information disclosures under FERPA returns the student's seven-digit, eSIS account ID number along with the student's postal address, telephone number, email address, and affiliation (e.g., student). A system query using the name of a student who has blocked the release of directory information under FERPA returns nothing other than the data that was submitted. While the system is capable of blocking the display of a student's eSIS account ID, those who exercise this option disenfranchise themselves from the conveniences of many self-service activities and may eliminate themselves entirely from participating in certain services where display of this unique electronic identifier is required.

Discussion

FERPA provides that an educational agency or institution may not have a policy or practice of disclosing education records, or personally identifiable information from education records, without the prior written consent of a parent or eligible student, that is, a student who is 18 years of age or attends a postsecondary institution. 20 U.S.C. § 1232g(b)(1) and (b)(2); 34 CFR §§ 99.3 ("Eligible student") and 99.30. The term "education records" is defined as information that is directly related to a student and maintained by an educational agency or institution, or a party acting for the agency or institution. 20 U.S.C. §1232g(a)(4); 34 CFR § 99.3 ("Education records"). Records that are directly related to a student, such as the student's course registration, grades, transcript, housing assignment, and financial assistance, as well as the eSIS account ID number itself, that are maintained by the University constitute "education records" under FERPA.

The term "personally identifiable information" is defined in the regulations as:
(a) The student's name;
(b) The name of the student's parent or other family member;
(c) The address of the student or student's family;
(d) A personal identifier, such as the student's social security number or student number;
(e) A list of personal characteristics that would make the student's identity easily traceable; or
(f) Other information that would make the student's identity easily traceable.

34 CFR § 99.3

"Directory information" is defined as information contained in an education record that would not generally be considered harmful or an invasion of privacy if disclosed and includes a student's name, address, telephone listing, email address, and other types of information about the student. 20 U.S.C. § 1232g(a)(5)(A); 34 CFR § 99.3. An institution that wishes to disclose directory information must comply with the procedural requirements set forth in § 99.37 of the regulations, which allow an eligible student to refuse to allow an institution to disclose directory information about the student.

A student's name and address, which are defined as "personally identifiable information" under FERPA, are also defined as "directory information" because these items are generally made available in public directories outside the school context and otherwise are not considered harmful or an invasion of privacy if disclosed. The legal conclusion in FERPA that these items of personally identifiable information are not considered "harmful or an invasion of privacy if disclosed" is based on an understanding that they generally cannot be used, standing alone, to obtain sensitive, non-public (*i.e.*, non-directory) information about an individual.

In contrast, SSNs, also listed as "personally identifiable information" under FERPA, are often used to obtain a variety of sensitive, non-public information about individuals, such as employment, credit, financial, health, motor vehicle, and educational information, that would be harmful or an invasion of privacy if disclosed. (SSNs may also be used in conjunction with commonly available directory information to establish fraudulent accounts and otherwise steal a person's identity.) For these reasons, as noted above, this Office has routinely advised that a student's SSN is the kind of personally identifiable information that *may not* be designated and disclosed as directory information. We have generally included "student ID numbers" in the same category because these numbers have historically been used much like SSNs, that is, as unique identifiers used by themselves to obtain access to non-directory information about a student, such as education records (or educational services).

Clearly, there are circumstances, such as electronic mail communications, in which institutions must assign each student a unique personal identifier that can be made available publicly. Indeed, the FERPA regulations were amended in 2000 to include a student's email address in the definition of "directory information." Similarly, as you described, many institutions have established or seek to establish portals and single sign-on approaches to student information systems, or use directory-based software and protocols for electronic collaboration by students and teachers, both within and among institutions, that require some form of public dissemination of a unique personal identifier. It is also well-known that public key infrastructure (PKI) technology for encryption and digital signatures requires wide dissemination of the sender's public key. These are the types of circumstances in which institutions may need to publish or disclose a personal identifier other than a student's name and address.

We believe that FERPA allows an institution to designate and disclose as "directory information" a unique personal identifier, such as a student's user or account logon ID (or an email address used as a logon ID), as long as the identifier cannot be used, standing alone, by unauthorized individuals to gain access to non-directory information from education records. In other words, if a student must use a shared secret, such as a PIN or password, or some other authentication factor unique to the student, along with their personal identifier to gain access to their records in the student information system, then that identifier may be designated and disclosed as directory information under FERPA in accordance with the requirements of § 99.37 of the regulations. (Allowance is made for school officials to use the student's published personal identifier alone, just as they use a student's name, to obtain access to the student's education records, provided the school official has a legitimate educational interest in accordance with § 99.31(a)(1) of the regulations.)

Conversely, if an institution allows students to access [their] own education records using a personal identifier but without the use of a password or other factor to authenticate the student's identity (or if the identifier itself is also used to authenticate the student's identity), then that identifier may not be disclosed as directory information under FERPA because it could result in the disclosure of protected information to someone other than the student and thus would be "harmful or an invasion of privacy if disclosed." (Some institutions may continue to use a student's "official ID number" in this manner.) Under this reasoning, an institution that allows a student (or any other party, for that matter) to obtain access to education records by providing just publicly available information, such as a student's name or published email address, without any additional proof or authentication of identity, could have a policy or practice in violation of FERPA because it could lead to the disclosure of education records to unauthorized recipients.

Finally, it should be clear that the standards set forth in this guidance pertain only to the public disclosure of information that identifies a student as part of a computer-based information system that is used to provide directory information on students and allow authorized users to gain access to education records. These standards do not apply to and are not intended to modify in any way the requirements for electronic consent to the disclosure of education records as set forth in § 99.30(d) of the regulations. That is, a student's email address, user ID, logon ID, account number, or any other personal identifier may not be used as an electronic signature unless it meets the specific requirements in 34 CFR § 99.30(d).

In summary, the University may designate and disclose as "directory information" a student's account ID number or other personal identifier used to logon to eSIS provided that it cannot be used, standing alone, by an unauthorized individual to obtain non-directory information from education records.

I trust this responds adequately to your inquiry and thank you for bringing this matter to our attention.

Sincerely,

LeRoy S. Rooker, Director
Family Policy Compliance Office

UNITED STATES DEPARTMENT OF EDUCATION
OFFICE OF INNOVATION AND IMPROVEMENT

Ms. Kelly Rozmus Barnes   JAN 27 2006
Assistant General Counsel
Field Services Legal Team
Los Angeles Unified School District
333 S. Beaudry Avenue, 20th Floor
Los Angeles, California 90017

Dear Ms. Barnes:

This responds to your inquiry of December 14, 2005, and follow-up inquiry of January 4, 2006, regarding the disclosure of certain information from students' education records to the National Student Clearinghouse (NSC) in compliance with the requirements of the Family Educational Rights and Privacy Act (FERPA), 20 U.S.C. § 1232g. This Office administers FERPA and provides technical assistance to ensure compliance with the statute and regulations, which are codified at 34 CFR Part 99.

You indicated that NSC asked the Los Angeles Unified School District (District) to enter into a contract for "StudentTracker" services under which the District would provide NSC with each student's name, high school, and year of graduation, and NSC would use this data to "track" the students in college. You asked whether parents must consent before the District discloses this information, or whether the District could simply inform parents of the disclosure and provide them with an opportunity to opt-out. You also referred to our April 16, 2004, letter to the National Association of Independent Colleges and Universities (NAICU), in which we provided guidance regarding NSC's EnrollmentSearch services, which are now known as "StudentTracker."

A parent (or eligible student, as defined in § 99.3) must provide a signed and dated written consent in accordance with the requirements of § 99.30 of the FERPA regulations before an educational agency or institution discloses personally identifiable information from education records. Exceptions to this requirement are set forth in 34 CFR § 99.31. One of the exceptions permits an educational agency or institution to disclose "directory information," as defined in § 99.3 of the regulations, without prior written consent provided the agency or institution has complied with the conditions in § 99.37 for notifying parents and eligible students of the designation and providing them with an opportunity to opt-out. "Directory information" means information "that would not generally be considered harmful or an invasion of privacy if disclosed" and includes the items you propose to disclose to NSC, *i.e.*, a student's name, high school, and year of graduation (so long as the parent or eligible student has not opted-out of these disclosures). Note that a student's SSN or student identification number may not be designated and disclosed without consent as "directory information."

This Office wrote to NSC on August 2, 1999, when it was known as the National Student Loan Clearinghouse, and explained that an institution that wishes to use EnrollmentSearch to obtain information about the current enrollment or graduation status of its former students, without prior written consent, may disclose to NSC only properly-designated directory information, and only for students who have not[sic] opt-out of directory information disclosures. This letter, available at www.ed.gov/policy/gen/guid/fpco/ferpa/library/herndonva.html), explains in detail that NSC may use only unblocked directory information, and not SSNs, for this type of search of its database because there is no FERPA exception to the consent requirement that allows an institution to disclose non-directory information in order to determine a former student's subsequent enrollment or degree status.

Our review of NSC's Web site indicates that the StudentTracker service operates essentially in the same manner as EnrollmentSearch and purports to use only unblocked directory information for determining "Subsequent

Enrollment for Previously Enrolled Students," as required under our August 2, 1999, letter. In that regard, however, we note that data record layout forms for this particular StudentTracker service permit an institution to submit "any data that you want returned with this record (*e.g.*, cohort identification, unique student ID, etc.), which will assist you in processing the Clearinghouse response file." Similarly, the StudentTracker response file layouts for this service include "your unique ID," this is, the "Student Identifier provided in your request file." An institution may not use these forms or any other means to disclose a student's SSN or student identification number for purposes of determining subsequent enrollment (or degree status) without prior written consent.

In summary, FERPA permits the District (or educational institutions in the District) to designate a student's name, high school, and year of graduation as "directory information," and disclose this information to NSC (or any other party) without a parent's or eligible student's prior written consent, provided the District or institution has complied with the notice and opt-out procedures designated "directory information" for the StudentTracker service described above unless a parent or eligible student has provided prior written consent.

You also asked whether the District is required to designate NSC as its "agent," as described in our April 16, 2004, letter to NAICU. The District (or its educational institutions) must enter into an agreement establishing NSC as its agents only if its wishes NSC serve as an outside "school official," and disclose education records *other than unblocked directory information,* such as SSNs or student identification numbers, to NSC without prior written consent. Educational agencies and institution[sic] may use the "school official exception" in § 99.31(a)(1) to disclose education records to contractors and other outside parties, such as NSC, only if the contractor or other outside party provides services that would otherwise have to be performed by employees; the contractor would have "legitimate educational interests" in the information if the service[sic] were performed in-house; and the contractor provides services as an agent under the direct control of the educational agency or institution that discloses the information. FERPA does not require the District to enter into this type of principal-agent agreement with NSC in order to disclose unblocked directory information to under[sic] StudentTracker service, as described above.

Finally, you asked whether the District may release information without prior written consent under a state law provision analogous to the exception in § 99.31(a)(6) of the FERPA regulations for disclosures without consent to organizations conducting studies for or on behalf of an educational agency or institution to develop, validate, or administer predictive tests; administer student aid programs; or improve instruction. StudentTracker is able to provide information about a student's subsequent enrollment or degree status because other educational institutions have agreed to allow NSC to maintain this information in its database and provide it in response to an inquiry under the StudentTracker service. The so-called "studies" exception in § 99.31(a)(6) of the FERPA regulations would not apply because even if the District entered into an agreement with NSC to conduct a study for the District, other institutions whose data is maintained in NSC's database would not be parties to that agreement as "organizations conducting studies for or on behalf of" the District and, therefore, NSC could not disclose to the District information from the education records in[sic] maintains for those other institutions. This is a reason why, as noted above, the StudentTracker service for determining subsequent enrollment or degree status of former students must be based solely on the use of unblocked directory information.

I trust that the above information is helpful in explaining the scope and limitations of FERPA as it relates to your concern.

Sincerely,

LeRoy S. Rooker, Director
Family Policy Compliance Office

08   Letter to Tazewell County (VA) School Board

Re: Unauthorized Access to Education Records/ Electronic Records System

B. Alan McGraw, Esq.   OCTOBER 7, 2005
Altizer, Walk & White
209 East Main Street
P.O. Box 30
Tazewell, Virginia 24651

Dear Mr. McGraw:

This responds to your August 12, 2005, request for guidance on behalf of the Tazewell County, Virginia School Board about restricting physical access to education records. This Office is responsible for administering the Family Educational Rights and Privacy Act (FERPA), 20 U.S.C. § 1232g and 34 CFR Part 99. Under that authority we investigate, process and review complaints and violations and provide technical assistance to ensure compliance with the statute and regulations. 34 CFR § 99.60(b).

FERPA provides that no funds administered by the Secretary of Education shall be made available to an educational agency or institution that has a "policy or practice of permitting the release of education records" or "providing access to" any personally identifiable information in education records, without the prior written consent of a parent or eligible student (as defined in § 99.3 of the regulations) except as authorized by law. See 20 U.S.C. § 1232g(b)(1) and (b)(2). Under § 99.30 of the regulations, a parent or eligible student must provide a signed and dated written consent before education records are disclosed, except as provided in § 99.31. "Disclosure" is defined to mean "to permit access to or the release, transfer, or other communication of personally identifiable information contained in education records to any party, by any means, including oral, written, or electronic means." 34 CFR § 99.3.

The term "education records" is defined in FERPA as those records that are directly related to a student; and maintained by an educational agency or institution, or by a party acting for the agency or institution. 34 CFR § 99.3. "Record," in turn, means "any information recorded in any way, including, but not limited to, hand writing, print, computer media, video or audio tape, film, microfilm, and microfiche." 34 CFR § 99.3.

While the law does not prescribe specific methods that should be used to protect education records from unauthorized access or disclosure, the prohibition in FERPA against disclosing or permitting access to education records without consent clearly does not allow an educational agency or institution to leave education records unprotected or subject to access by unauthorized individuals, whether in paper, film, electronic, or any other format. We interpret this prohibition to mean that an educational agency or institution must use physical, technological, administrative and other methods, including training, to protect education records in ways that are reasonable and appropriate to the circumstances in which the information or records are maintained.

Your letter indicates that the Tazewell County Board of Supervisors recently proposed a plan in which various county government offices and agencies would share computer network hardware, software, and personnel resources with the Tazewell County school system. According to your letter,

school system technical support personnel inform us that the county government's "penetration"' of the school system's network resources would be significant, such that electronic student educational records could be accessed by persons or entities not employed by the school system.

You explained that these individuals are not authorized to obtain access to education records, without consent, under § 99.31 of the regulations and you are concerned that the proposal would violate FERPA.

Based on the provisions described above, this Office would consider a record management system that allows unauthorized individuals to have access to education records to constitute a policy or practice of violating FERPA.

In the context of paper records, for example, this means that a school district may not place the report cards of all students in a box on a teacher's or principal's desk and allow parents or students to look through the box to find the student's own record. Similarly, with respect to electronic recordkeeping, a school district may not maintain a system that provides for access to education records by parties that are not parents, students, authorized "school officials," or otherwise permitted to have access as specified in § 99.31 of the regulations.

I trust that the above information is helpful in explaining the scope and limitations of FERPA as it relates to your concern.

Sincerely,

LeRoy S. Rooker, Director
Family Policy Compliance Office

J. Chris Toe, Ph.D.
President
Strayer University
1133 15th Street, NW, Suite 300
Washington, DC 20005

MARCH 11, 2005
Complaint No. [REDACTED}
Family Educational Rights
and Privacy Act

Dear Dr. Toe:

This is to inform you of our finding in the complaint filed by [Student] (Student) alleging that Strayer University (University) violated rights afforded to her under the Family Educational Rights and Privacy Act (FERPA), 20 U.S.C. § 1232g and 34 CFR Part 99. Our letter dated September 8, 2004, notified you that the Student had filed a timely complaint with this Office alleging that [Employee], an employee of the University at its Montgomery County, Maryland campus, accessed the University's computerized database, without the Student's consent, in order to obtain personal information about the Student, such as her name, address, date of birth, height, weight, and drivers license number, for use in filing a personal complaint against the Student with the local police. Your October 4, 2004, response provided the following additional information:

> *[Employee] and the Student had a disagreement on November 17, 2003, regarding student use of the admissions office fax machine. Two days later, on November 19, [Employee] and the Student "exchanged unpleasantries and [Student] allegedly threw a brass business cardholder at [Employee]. [Employee] felt threatened and called the police to report the incident."*
>
> *[REDACTED], Regional Director for the University's Maryland campuses, spoke with the Student on November 19, 2003, and advised her to continue her courses but avoid the admissions office where [Employee] worked. Unfortunately, [Employee] and the Student continued to bother each other and had minor disagreements in early December of 2003.*
>
> *On December 19, 2003, the University convened a meeting to attempt to resolve the situation. In attendance were the Student; [Employee]; [REDACTED], Vice President of Human Resources; [REDACTED], Dean of Student Affairs; [REDACTED]; [REDACTED], Campus Manager of the Montgomery County Campus; [REDACTED], Campus Dean of the Montgomery County Campus; the Student's sister, [REDACTED]; and the Student's attorney. University representatives reviewed all incidents in detail and determined that both [Employee] and the Student demonstrated poor behavior.*
>
> *Shortly after the December 19 meeting, [Employee] dropped the assault charges against the Student. The Student then filed a civil suit against [Employee] in the District Court of Maryland alleging that [Employee] falsely accused her of assault. The Student's civil suit was subsequently dismissed on the merits.*

Included with your October 4, 2004 letter were[sic] a copy of the following documents:

▣ [Employee]'s position description (Admissions Assistant);

▣ Event Report prepared by the Montgomery County, Maryland, Department of Police dated November 20, 2003, summarizing [Employee]'s assault allegations against the Student;

▣ Supplement to the Event Report prepared by the Montgomery County, Maryland, Department of Police dated December 16, 2003, indicating that the Student was charged with second degree assault and trial in district court was set for January 30, 2004;

▣ Excerpts from the University's 2004 Catalog containing its "Notice of Crime on Campus";

▣ Excerpts from the University's 2004 Student Handbook that contains its "Release of Student Information Policy"; and

▣ "Dear Students" email dated October 1, 2003, from the University regarding the same "Release of Student Information Policy."

Your October 4, 2004 letter states that the University did not violate FERPA for the following reasons:

While University policy is to encourage employees to call 911 if they feel unsafe at any time while on campus, [Employee] did not inform the University prior to filing the police report against the Student. [Employee]'s actions with regard to the criminal complaint were her own and not those of the University.

If [Employee] used the University's computer system to assist her in filing this report, these actions were not authorized by the University. However, there is no evidence that [Employee] in fact used the University computer system for this purpose.

Even if [Employee] used the University's computer system and was authorized by the University to do so, this action, along with [Employee]'s subsequent redisclosure of information about the Student to the police department without the Student's consent does not violate FERPA because [Employee] was a "school official" with a "legitimate educational interest" as defined under § 99.31 of the FERPA regulations. In particular, [Employee] served as an admissions assistant for the University, and accessing the University's computer system is specified as one of the duties of this position.

[Employee]'s actions were also authorized under § 99.31(a)(10) of the FERPA regulations because the Student's alleged assault on [Employee] constituted a "health or safety emergency." You explained that "[t]he safety of the University's students and employees is of the utmost importance and criminal behavior of any form on University property is not tolerated. The University does not hesitate to call the police if it has reason to suspect any person poses a danger to the campus community." The police report filed by [Employee] indicates that [Employee] had a bruise on her right chest from the incident. The investigating police officer found the account sufficiently credible to file a report and issue a warrant for the Student, and the University regards disclosure of basic identifying information about the Student to the police in these circumstances to constitute a "textbook case for a 'health or safety emergency.'"

Information that [Employee] provided to the police about the Student was limited to the Student's name; date of birth; estimated height and weight; eye color; hair color; and address. You stated that the University does not maintain information on the height, weight, and eye and hair color of its students and that, therefore, [Employee] likely provided this information based on her own observations.

The Student's driver's license number is not indicated anywhere on the police report, as the Student alleged. Further, the University does not maintain this information on its students.

The University takes its obligations under FERPA very seriously and makes a concerted effort to educate both students and staff regarding this important legislation. FERPA notices are provided to students as required and requests to restrict the release of directory information are processed by the records department and indicated in the University's computer system. Requests for release of student information are approved by either the University's records department or legal counsel.

In response to follow-up questions from this Office, on February 4, 2005, the University provided additional information about its directory information policies and indicated that at some point the Student opted-out of directory information disclosures. The University noted again that the Student's driver's license number does not appear in any police reports concerning this matter and clarified that it does not maintain student driver's license numbers in the computer system to which [Employee] had access. University did not inquire whether [Employee] used the University's computer system to access information about the Student during its December 19, 2003, meeting with the Student, and [Employee] is no longer employed by the University.

FERPA provides that an educational agency or institution may not have a policy or practice of disclosing education records, or personally identifiable information from education records other than directory information, without the prior written consent of a parent or eligible [Student], except as provided in § 99.31 of the regulations. 20 U.S.C. § 1232g(b)(1) and (b)(2); 34 CFR § 99.30(a). (An "eligible student" is one who is at least 18 years of age or attends a postsecondary institution. See 34 CFR § 99.3.) "Education records" are defined as records that are 1) directly related to a student; and 2) maintained by an educational agency or institution or by a party acting for the agency or institution. See 34 CFR § 99.3. "Disclosure" means "to permit access to or the release, transfer, or other communication of personally identifiable information contained in education records to any party, by any means, including oral, written, or electronic means." See 34 CFR § 99.3.

One of the exceptions to the prior written consent requirement in FERPA allows an agency or institution to disclose certain information that has been designated as "directory information" [in] accordance with § 99.37 of the regulations. "Directory information" includes a student's name, address, date of birth, and other information that generally is not considered harmful or an invasion of privacy if disclosed. See 34 CFR § 99.3 ("Directory information"). However, students have a right to block or opt-out of directory information disclosures under § 99.37(a)(2).

The Student alleged that [Employee] accessed the University's database and obtained personal information including the Student's name, address, date of birth, height, weight, and driver's license number for use in filing the police report in question. This information is considered part of the Student's education records to the extent that the University maintains it in its computerized database or elsewhere.

The Event Report and Supplement prepared by the police department contain the Student's name; address; race; sex; date of birth; estimated height; estimated weight; eye color; length and color of hair; description of facial hair; and description of clothing. Neither document contains the Student's driver's license number. The University stated that it does not maintain information on its students' height, weight, and eye and hair color and, therefore, we conclude that if [Employee] provided this information to the police, it was based on [her] own personal knowledge or observations and not the Student's education records. Similarly, we conclude that [Employee] did not obtain the Student's driver's license number from the University's database and disclose it to the police, as alleged, both because that information does not appear on any of the police reports and because it was not maintained in any system to which [Employee] had access. While [Employee] did have access to the Student's name and race in the University's database, we are unable to conclude that [Employee] obtained and disclosed this information from the Student's education records rather than [Employee]'s own personal knowledge and observations.

The only other information about the Student that appears in the police reports is her address and date of birth, which are items that could be disclosed without consent under FERPA as directory information. While we are unable to make a conclusive determination, we think it likely that [Employee] obtained and disclosed the Student's address and date of birth from the University's computerized database, as alleged, because it is undisputed that she had access to that information and because there is no evidence and little likelihood that she got it directly from the Student or some other source. Further, even assuming that directory information could be disclosed without consent for purposes of making a police report, the University is unable to determine whether the Student opted-out of directory information disclosures before or after [Employee]'s alleged disclosures.

As explained below, and apart from any consideration of directory information disclosures, the University's response indicates that it may have a policy or practice of disclosing education records without prior written consent in violation of FERPA. In particular, the University asserted in its defense that:

> [E]ven if one assumes that [Employee] accessed the University's computer system and [Employee]'s actions were authorized by the University, the accessing of [the Student's] information by [Employee] and the release of this information to the police do not constitute violations of § 99.30 of the FERPA regulations because [Employee] was a 'school official' as defined by § 99.31 of the FERPA regulations and the disclosure to law enforcement officials was in the context of a 'health and safety emergency' as provided by § 99.31(a)(10) and § 99.36 of the FERPA regulations.

As you noted in your letter, pursuant to § 99.31(a)(1) of the FERPA regulations, prior consent is not required to disclose education records to "school officials" with "legitimate educational interests." In accordance with 34 CFR § 99.7(a)(3)(iii), the University provides annual notification to its students regarding who constitutes a school official and what constitutes a legitimate educational interest. I have enclosed a copy of the FERPA notification sent to the University's students in 2003. This notice provides in relevant part:

*A school official is a person employed by the University in an administrative, supervisory, academic, research, or support staff position (including law enforcement unit personnel and health staff); a person or company with whom the University has contracted (such as an attorney, auditor, financial aid processing agent, or collection agent); a person serving on the Board of Trustees; or a student serving on an official committee, such as a disciplinary or grievance committee, or assisting another school official in performing his or her tasks. **A school official has a legitimate educational interest if the official needs to review an education record in order to fulfill his or her professional responsibility.***

[Employee] served as an Admissions Assistant for the University. I have enclosed a copy of the University's job description for this position. You will note that accessing the University's computer system is part of these duties. This information should clearly demonstrate that [Employee] was a 'school official' as defined above *and that she had a 'legitimate educational interest' to access [the Student's] educational records.*

(Emphases added.) As noted above, the University asserts that [Employee]'s actions were *also* authorized under § 99.31(a)(10) of the FERPA regulations because the Student's alleged assault on [Employee] constituted a "text-book case for a 'health or safety emergency.'"

As explained below, we reject the University's assertion that [Employee]'s actions were authorized under § 99.31(a)(10) as a "health or safety emergency" because the information it presented does not support a conclusion that there was, in fact, an emergency. FERPA allows an educational agency or institution to disclose personally identifiable information from education records, without prior written consent, "in connection with an emergency [to] appropriate persons if the knowledge of such information is necessary to protect the health or safety of the student or other persons." 20 U.S.C. § 1232g(b)(1)(I); 34 CFR §§ 99.31(a)(10) and 99.36.

Congress added this exception to the written consent requirement when FERPA was first amended, on December 13, 1974. The legislative history demonstrates Congress' intent to limit application of the "health or safety" exception to exceptional circumstances—

Finally, under certain emergency situations it may become necessary for an educational agency or institution to release personal information to protect the health or safety of the student or other students. In the case of the outbreak of an epidemic, it is unrealistic to expect an educational official to seek consent from every parent before a health warning can be issued. On the other hand, a blanket exception for "health or safety" could lead to unnecessary dissemination of personal information. Therefore, in order to assure that there are adequate safeguards on this exception, the amendments provided that the Secretary shall promulgate regulations to implement this subsection. It is expected that he will strictly limit the applicability of this exception.

Joint Statement in Explanation of Buckley/Pell Amendment, 120 Cong. Rec. S21489, Dec. 13, 1974. (These amendments were made retroactive to November 19, 1974, the date on which FERPA became effective.)

Section 99.31(a)(10) of the regulations provides that the disclosure must be "in connection with a health or safety emergency" under the following additional conditions:

An educational agency or institution may disclose personally identifiable information from an education record to *appropriate parties* in connection with *an emergency* if knowledge of the information is necessary to protect the *health or safety* of the student or other individuals.

34 CFR § 99.36(a)(emphases added.) In accordance with Congressional direction, the regulations provide further that these requirements will be strictly construed. 34 CFR § 99.36(c).

The Department has consistently interpreted this provision narrowly by limiting its application to a *specific situation* that presents *imminent danger* to students or other members of the community, or that requires an *immediate need* for information in order to avert or diffuse serious threats to the safety or health of a student or other individuals. While the exception is not limited to emergencies caused by terrorist attacks, the Department's Guidance on "Recent Amendments to [FERPA] Relating to Anti-Terrorism Activities," issued by this Office on April 12, 2002, provides a useful and relevant summary of our interpretation (emphasis added):

> *[T]he health or safety exception would apply to nonconsensual disclosures to appropriate persons in the case of a smallpox, anthrax or other bioterrorism attack. This exception also would apply to nonconsensual disclosures to appropriate persons in the case of another terrorist attach[sic] such as the September 11 attack. However, **any release must be narrowly tailored considering the immediacy, magnitude, and specificity of information concerning the emergency. As the legislative history indicates, this exception is temporally limited to the period of the emergency and generally will not allow for a blanket release of personally identifiable information from a student's education records.***

Under the health and safety exception school officials may share relevant information with "appropriate parties," that is, those parties whose knowledge of the information is necessary to provide immediate protection of the health and safety of the student or other individuals. (Citations omitted.) Typically, law enforcement officials, public health officials, and trained medical personnel are the types of parties to whom information may be disclosed under this FERPA exception....

The educational agency or institution has the responsibility to make the initial determination of whether a disclosure is necessary to protect the health or safety of the student or other individuals. ...

By way of example, in accordance with these principles we concluded in a 1994 letter that a student's suicidal statements, coupled with unsafe conduct and threats against another student, constitute a "health or safety emergency" under FERPA. However, we also noted that this exception does not support a general or blanket exception in every case in which a student utters a threat. More recently, in 2002 we advised that a school district could disclose information from education records to the Pennsylvania Department of Health, without written consent, where six students had died of unknown causes within the previous five months. These facts indicated that the district faced a specific and grave emergency situation that required immediate intervention by the Department of Health to protect the health and safety of students and others in the school district.

With regard to reports required under state law, in 2000 we advised a state senator about a potential conflict between FERPA and a state law that requires a school to notify the appropriate law enforcement agency immediately if it receives a request for the records of a child who has been reported missing, and then notify the requesting school that the child has been reported missing and is the subject of an ongoing law enforcement investigation. Once again noting that the "health and safety emergency" exception generally does not allow a blanket release of personally identifiable, non-directory information from education records, we concluded that FERPA would allow school personnel to comply with this law

> *only if the school has made a case-by-case determination that there is a **present and imminent threat or danger** to the student or that information from education records is needed to avert or diffuse serious threats to the safety or health of a student....In the case of a missing child, we agree that law enforcement officials would constitute an appropriate party for the disclosure **assuming that the school has first determined that a threat or imminent danger to the child exists.***

May 8, 2000, letter to Pennsylvania State Senator Stewart J. Greenleaf (emphases added.)

In summary, an educational agency or institution may disclose personally identifiable, non-directory information from education records under the "health or safety emergency" exception only if it has determined, on a case-by-case basis, that a *specific situation* presents *imminent danger or threat* to students or other members of the community, or requires an *immediate need* for information in order to avert or diffuse serious threats to the safety or health of a student or other individuals. Any release must be *narrowly tailored* considering the immediacy and magnitude of the emergency and must be made only to parties who can address the specific emergency in question. This exception is temporally limited to the period of the emergency and generally does not allow a blanket release of personally identifiable information from a student's education records to comply with general requirements under state law.

The police Event Report states that the alleged incident took place on November 19, 2003, but that [Employee] did not report the matter until the following day, November 20. While the University states that its policy is to encourage employees to call 911 if they feel unsafe on campus, there is no evidence that [Employee] called 911 on November 19, while she was still in the Admissions Office. Rather, documentation shows that she chose instead to file a report with the local police the following day, November 20. Further, as stated above, an educational agency or institution has the responsibility to make the initial determination of whether a disclosure is necessary to protect the health or safety of the student or other individuals. In this case, there is no indication that the University attempted to verify whether [Employee] did indeed disclose information from the Student's education records to the police for "health and safety emergency" purposes and then record the disclosure as required under § 99.32(a)(1) of the regulations. In these circumstances, we decline to find that [Employee]'s disclosure of information from education records, if any, without the Student's written consent was authorized under the health and safety emergency exception.

Another exception to the prior written consent requirement allows "school officials" to have access to a student's education records, without prior written consent, under § 99.31(a)(1) of the regulations, but only if they have a "legitimate educational interest." The University denies that it authorized [Employee] to file a criminal complaint against the Student, and there is no indication that the University was aware of [Employee]'s decision to file the complaint until some time after she had actually done so. However, the University argues that [Employee]'s professional duties as "admissions assistant" include "accessing the University's computer system" and, therefore, even if [Employee] had in fact accessed the Student's records to obtain information about the Student to file a police report, the disclosure would not violate FERPA because of the nature of [Employee]'s professional duties.

The University's own 2003 FERPA notification provides that an official has a legitimate educational interest if the official needs to review an education record *in order to fulfill his or her professional responsibility*. FERPA does not allow teachers and other school officials to use their lawful authority (and actual ability) to access a student's education records for anything other than "legitimate educational interests." Indeed, given that it is virtually impossible to use physical or technological safeguards to prevent authorized users from using their access to education records for unauthorized purposes, it is important that an educational agency or institution establish and enforce policies and procedures, including appropriate training, to help ensure that school officials do not in fact misuse education records for their own purposes.

As discussed above, [Employee] had no legitimate interest in accessing the Student's education records to file a police report given that the circumstances did not rise to the level of a "health or safety emergency" under FERPA. Further, we are concerned that the University appears to have a policy or practice of allowing school officials to obtain access to education records in violation of FERPA because of its assertion that a school official who is authorized to obtain access to students' education records for legitimate educational purposes may use that authority to obtain access and disclose information where no legitimate educational purpose or other FERPA exception applies.

In accordance with § 99.66(c) of the regulations, in order to close this investigation the University must ensure that staff, faculty, and other school officials who have access to education records under § 99.31(a)(1) of the regulations understand the limits imposed by FERPA on their access to and disclosure of education records without a student's prior written consent. The University may inform appropriate school officials through training or a written memorandum. Please notify this Office of the date and manner that the University informed school officials of this FERPA requirement. Your voluntary compliance will allow us to issue you a written decision closing this investigation in accordance with § 99.67(b). You may direct your response to Frances Moran of my staff at:

Family Policy Compliance Office
U.S. Department of Education
400 Maryland Avenue, SW
Washington, DC 20202-5920
(202) 260-3887

Thank you for your continued cooperation with regard to the resolution of this complaint.

Sincerely,

LeRoy S. Rooker, Director
Family Policy Compliance Office

cc: Student

Ms. Jeanne-Marie Pochert   JUNE 28, 2006
Deputy Assistant General Counsel
Clark County School District Legal Department
2832 East Flamingo Road
Las Vegas, Nevada 89121

Dear Ms. Pochert:

This responds to questions raised in your December 30, 2004, email regarding the disclosure of education records to a contractor for the Clark County School District (District). This Office investigates complaints and violations under the Family Educational Rights and Privacy Act (FERPA), 20 U.S.C. §1232g, and provides technical assistance to ensure compliance with the statute and regulations, which are codified at 34 CFR Part 99.

You asked whether FERPA permits the District to disclose education records, without a parent's prior written consent, to Edline, a company that operates an online system that allows parents to access their child's current grades and class attendance reports, as well as school and class news, assignments, calendars, school menus, etc., that have been provided to Edline by District staff. According to your email, Edline provides secure hosting facilities that use encryption, firewall protection, and password codes that parents and students must use to access the student's records. You asked whether Edline is correct in its opinion that the District may disclose education records to Edline, without prior written consent, because it is an agent or contractor of the school and not a third party.

This Office asked you follow-up questions in January 2005, and on February 14, 2005, you forwarded responses provided by Marge Abrams, a representative of Edline. Ms. Abrams explained that Edline has a strict policy against sharing any student information with third parties. Further, according to Ms. Abrams:

> When schools publish private information pertaining to specific students (such as grades) at their Web site hosted by Edline, the school configures exactly who has access to the student information (which is transferred to the school's Web site via secure SSL connection and stored in encrypted format). Thus, the school itself (not Edline) will provide access to student information only to the people it chooses (members of the school staff, parents, etc.) on an individualized basis through password-protected user accounts. No person that doesn't receive a specific account (with specific access) from the school itself will ever have access to student information (public or private) at the school's Edline Web site. Edline never grants third parties access to private reports (such as grades) or any other information, because Edline simply facilitates communication on behalf of the school.
>
> There is no sharing of data between schools (or with any other agency or institution) by Edline. All access to student information, whether by other schools, agencies, or any other third parties - is configured and determined by the school itself.

Under FERPA parents (or "eligible students," as defined in § 99.3 of the regulations) have a right to inspect and review their children's education records and to seek to have them amended in certain circumstances. 34 CFR Part 99, subparts B and C. FERPA provides further that no funds administered by the Secretary of Education shall be made available to an educational agency or institution, such as a public school district, that has a policy or practice of releasing or permitting access to personally identifiable information from education records (other than "directory information") without the prior written consent of a parent (or eligible student) except as authorized by law. 20 U.S.C. §1232g(b)(1) and (b)(2). Accordingly, a parent (or eligible student) must provide a signed and dated written consent in accordance with the requirements of §99.30 of the FERPA regulations before an educational agency or institution discloses education records. Exceptions to this requirement are set forth in 34 CFR §99.31.

"Education records" are defined as records that are directly related to a student and maintained by an educational agency or institution *or by a party acting for the agency or institution.* 34 CFR §99.3 "Education records" (emphasis added). This means that records directly related to a student that are maintained by contractor or other party acting for a school, including records created by that party, are subject to all FERPA requirements.

"Disclosure" in the FERPA regulations means "to permit access to or the release, transfer, or other communication of personally identifiable information contained in education records to any party" by any means and includes access to education records by school officials. Indeed, one of the exceptions to the prior written consent requirement in FERPA allows "school officials, including teachers, within the agency or institution" to obtain access to education records provided the educational agency or institution has determined that they have "legitimate educational interests" in the information. 34 CFR §99.31(a)(1). Although "school official" is not defined in the statute or regulations, this Office has interpreted the term broadly to include a teacher; school principal; president; chancellor; board member; trustee; registrar; counselor; admissions officer; attorney; accountant; human resources professional; information systems specialist; and support or clerical personnel.

In addition, an educational agency or institution may disclose education records without consent to a "school official" under this exception only if it has first determined that the official has "legitimate educational interests" in obtaining the information to perform specified services for the agency or institution. An educational agency or institution that allows school officials to obtain access to education records under this exception must include in its annual notification of FERPA rights a specification of its criteria for determining who constitutes a "school official" and what constitutes "legitimate educational interests" under §99.31(a)(1). See 34 CFR §99.7(a)(3)(iii).

As noted in your email, FERPA does not specifically address disclosure of education records to contractors, consultants, volunteers and service providers who are not employees of an educational agency or institution. However, the statutory definition of "education records" appears to recognize the use of outside service providers in calling for the protection of records maintained by "a person acting for" the agency or institution." Indeed, the Joint Statement in Explanation of Buckley/Pell Amendment (120 Cong. Rec. S39862, Dec. 13, 1974) refers specifically to materials that are maintained by a school "or by one of its agents" when describing the meaning of the new term "education records" in the December 1974 amendments. Accordingly, this Office has advised that agencies and institutions subject to FERPA are not precluded from disclosing education records to parties to whom they have outsourced services so long as they do so under the same conditions applicable to school officials who are actually employed.

Note that an educational agency or institution may not disclose education records without prior written consent merely because it has entered into a contract or agreement with an outside party. Rather, the agency or institution must be able to show that *1) the outside party provides a service for the agency or institution that it would otherwise provide for itself using employees; 2) the outside party would have "legitimate educational interests" in the information disclosed if the service were performed by employees; and 3) the outside party is under the direct control of the educational agency or institution with respect to the use and maintenance of information from education records.* Further, under §99.33(a) of the regulations, any party, including a "school official," that receives education records may use the information only for the purposes for which the disclosure was made and may not redisclose the information to any other party without prior written consent, except as authorized under §99.33(b). As noted above, education records maintained by a party providing services for an educational agency or institution, including records created by that party, are subject to all FERPA requirements. An outside party that does not meet these requirements may not be given access to personally identifiable information from education records without meeting the prior written consent requirements.

Critically, an educational agency or institution must ensure that its service provider does not use or allow anyone to obtain access to personally identifiable information from education records except in strict accordance with the requirements established by the agency or institution that discloses the information. In that vein, the agency or institution that outsources services under these requirements remains completely responsible for its service provider's compliance with applicable FERPA requirements and liable for any misuse of protected information. For that reason, we recommend that these specific protections be incorporated into any contract or agreement between an educational agency or institution and any non-employees it retains to provide institutional services.

The disclosure of education records to school officials without consent under §99.31(a)(1) is ordinarily excepted from FERPA's specific recordation requirements under §99.32(d)(2) because these disclosures are identified in the school's annual FERPA notification. An educational agency or institution that has complied with the notification requirements in §99.7(a)(3)(iii) for disclosure of education records to contractors and other outside service providers retained as "school officials" under the above conditions may exclude these disclosures from the recordation requirements in accordance with §99.32(d)(2). If the agency or institution has not listed contractors and other outside service providers as "school officials" in its annual §99.7 FERPA notification, then it is required to record each disclosure to a qualifying contractor in accordance with §99.32(a).

Based on the information provided, it appears that the arrangement schools within the District have with Edline meets these requirements for disclosing specified information from education records to Edline as a "school official" under this FERPA exception. In particular, 1) Edline provides online hosting services that permit parents to view some of their children's education records, and Edline uses the information from education records to perform those services that would otherwise be provided by school employees; 2) Edline's online access services provide it with "legitimate educational interests" in the information disclosed to Edline by each school; and 3) Edline's use and maintenance of personally identifiable information from education records is subject to the direct control of each school within the District. Each school or the District must ensure that Edline does not redisclose or permit the redisclosure of any personally identifiable information from education records except as specifically authorized by the school or District that is responsible for the contract. The school (or District), in turn, remains responsible for any FERPA violations committed by its service provider. In that regard, we note that Edline takes reasonable and appropriate steps to ensure that information from education records is not disclosed or made available to other parties and does not use the information for any other purpose.

I trust that the above information is helpful in explaining the scope and limitations of FERPA as it relates to your concern.

Sincerely,

LeRoy S. Rooker, Director
Family Policy Compliance Office

11 Letter to University of Arkansas ★

Re: Status of Medical Interns and Residents

UNITED STATES DEPARTMENT OF EDUCATION

Mr. Fred H Harrison   NOV 16 1990
General Counsel
University of Arkansas
University Tower Building, Suite 601
1123 South University
Little Rock, Arkansas 72204

Dear Mr. Harrison:

This is in response to your letter dated September 26, 1990, in which you request information and documents concerning this Department's position that records maintained by teaching hospitals relating to interns and residents are not "education records" as defined by the Family Educational Rights and Privacy Act (FERPA). 20 U.S.C. 1232g(a)(4). (*See* also 34 CFR 99.3) In this regard you refer to a letter that we wrote to Ms. [REDACTED] dated September 18, 1990, informing her of the Department's position on the matter. Ms. [REDACTED], who was seeking information from the records of a resident at the University of Arkansas for Medical Science (WAMS), provided a copy of that letter to you.

In your letter you state that you had previously advised Ms. [REDACTED] that you believed the records to be "education records" under FERPA and you ask whether the following information would affect our opinion: (1) the Appropriation Act for UAMS defines residents as "students engaged in post-graduate clinical training," and (2) the records sought by Ms. [REDACTED] UAMS included not only the contract between UAMS and the resident but also correspondence prior to the initial contract with the resident. You also state that in previous correspondence from Ms. [REDACTED] she had requested "copies of all letters, memoranda or documents regarding the negotiations and subsequent contract agreement between UAMS [and the resident]."

You ask whether the definition of resident and the nature of the documents sought, as discussed above, would affect our position that the records are not subject to FERPA. You state: "It would seem that your determination is based upon your opinion that a resident in a teaching hospital is not a 'student.'"

The conclusion that residents are not students is the single element that is critical to our position that records of residents are not subject to FERPA. This is true whether or not the hospital is a "teaching hospital." It is our understanding that in most States persons who receive a medical degree may not practice medicine independently without supervision, completion of a period of residency, and successful passage of a state licensing exam.

Residents do not take any courses and do not receive education. Instead, they refine their skills and their work is evaluated for the purpose of determining whether they should be licensed for the practice of medicine. The fact that the Appropriation Act for UAMS, in defining the term "residents," qualifies the word "students" with the description "engaged in post-graduate clinical training" is consistent with our position that residents are not "students" as that term would generally be understood—*i.e.*, an individual who is enrolled in an educational agency or institution for the purpose of taking courses and receiving an education.

Concerning your second question, the fact that the records sought by [REDACTED] include documents regarding the negotiations and correspondence prior to the initial contract with the resident would not be a consideration unless those documents contain information disclosed from the "education records" of the former "student" (who is now a resident) to a party other than the former "student," or resident. From the information you have provided, it appears that this is not the case. For your reference in this regard, 34 CFR 99.3(b)(5) exempts from the definition of "education records" those "[r]ecords that only contain information about an individual after he or she is no longer a student at [the] educational agency or institution."

I trust that the above information satisfactorily responds to your inquiry. Enclosed, per your request for other documents concerning the Department's position on the matter, are documents dated June 1, 1979, November 16, 1979, January 30, 1980, May 23, 1990, and September 10, 1990.

Sincerely,

LeRoy S. Rooker, Director
Family Policy Compliance Office

Enclosures

12   Letter to the American Federation of Teachers

Re: Disclosure of Information on Teaching Assistants

Mr. David J. Strom, In-house Counsel   AUGUST 21, 2000
Ms. Stephanie S. Baxter, Senior Associate Counsel
American Federation of Teachers
555 New Jersey Avenue, N.W.
Washington, DC 20001-2079

Dear Mr. Strom and Ms. Baxter:

This is in response to your August 4, 2000 letter, addressed to Deputy Secretary Frank Holleman, in which you asked that the Department interpret the Family Educational Rights and Privacy Act (FERPA) in such a way that universities may disclose to a union representing student graduate assistants who teach undergraduate classes personally identifiable information from the education records of such individuals. I have been asked to respond to your letter to the Deputy Secretary because, as you know, this Office administers FERPA. This also serves to respond to your July 14th letter to this Office, and as a follow-up to our July 19th meeting, on this issue.

You explained in your letter that the University of Oregon (University) and the Graduate Teaching Fellows Federation (GTFF), a union that represents graduate student teaching fellows at the University, have signed an agreement under which the University would disclose certain information regarding graduate teaching fellows to the GTFF. This information includes: name, social security number, department, terms of employment, changes in employment status or rate of pay, home addresses, bargaining unit status, terms of appointment, and major. The agreement provides that addresses disclosed by the University will only be used by GTFF for union business and that social security numbers will only be used for payroll deduction and insurance administration. The agreement further states that "The University will assume no liability for the unauthorized disclosure of information to parties outside the GTFF."

By letter dated April 3, 2000, Melinda W. Grier, general counsel of the University, advised you that based on a September 19, 1999 letter to the University of California from this Office, the University could no longer disclose information from education records of graduate teaching fellows to the GTFF absent prior written consent. In relevant part, we advised in that letter that the records of teaching assistants are education records subject to the provisions of FERPA. We also explained in that letter that when an educational agency or institution chooses to comply with a state law that is in conflict with FERPA, it puts its continued eligibility for federal education funds in jeopardy. That is, FERPA provides that the Department of Education may not make funds available to any educational agency or institution that has a policy or practice of denying students their rights under FERPA. You stated in your letter to this Office that you disagree with "this construction of the statute as it leaves education institutions in the untenable situation of choosing between complying with FERPA and conflicting state and federal law."

You stated that without information about graduate teaching fellows, the GTFF cannot meet its obligations under state and federal law, and such individuals will be "deprived of important rights," such as health enrollment information to eligible non-participants and continuation of benefit notices required under COBRA (the Consolidated Omnibus Budget Reconciliation Act of 1985, Pub.L. 99-272, Apr. 7, 1986, 100 Stat. 82) to teaching fellows who are separated from employment. Additionally, the GTFF would not be able to seek fees to which it is entitled. Finally, you stated that this issue is of concern because such situations exist regarding student graduate teaching assistants and fellows across the country.

You suggested in your letter that this Office interpret FERPA so that the records of graduate teaching fellows/ assistants are employment, and not education, records under FERPA. You state that such individuals "are employed not because they are students, but, instead, because the institution has decided to carry out [its] undergraduate teaching programs using a significant number of graduate teaching fellows rather than professors." You also argued that "the vast majority of public employee relations boards ...have ruled that graduate student employees are 'employees' entitled to organize and bargain collectively," and, as such, their records should not be subject to FERPA. You alternatively suggested in your letter that this Office expand "directory information" to include: graduate employees teaching status, schedule, rate of pay, bargaining unit status and other pertinent employment information. You suggested that this information could not be considered "harmful or an invasion of privacy if disclosed."

FERPA protects privacy interests of parents in their children's "education records," and generally prohibits the disclosure of education records without the consent of the parent. The term "education records" is broadly defined as all records, files, documents and other materials which:

> contain information directly related to a student; and are maintained by the educational agency or institution or by a person acting for such agency or institution.

20 U.S.C. § 232g(a)(4)(A); 34 CFR § 99.3 "Education records."

When a student reaches the age of 18 or attends an institution of postsecondary education, the student is considered an "eligible student" under FERPA and all of the rights afforded by FERPA transfer from the parents to the student.

FERPA provides limited exemptions from the definition of "education records." FERPA states:

> *(B) The term "education records" does not include —*
> *(iii) in the case of persons **who are employed by an educational agency or institution but who are not in attendance at such agency or institution**, records made and maintained in the normal course of business which relate exclusively to such person in that person's capacity as an employee and are not available for use for any other purpose....*

20 U.S.C § 1232g(a)(4)(B)(iii); 34 CFR § 99.3 "Education records" (b)(3)(emphasis added).

The FERPA regulations clarify this provision by explaining that: "records relating to an individual in attendance at the agency or institution who is employed as a result of his or her status as a student are education records and not excepted under paragraph (b)(3)(i) of this definition." 34 CFR § 99.3 "Education records"(b)(3)(ii)(emphasis added).

Thus, FERPA provides a very narrow exemption for records related to an individual's employment from the protections provided by FERPA. This exemption applies to those records related to the employment of individuals who are employed without regard to their status as students. For instance, if a secretary in the president's office takes a course at any given time, her employment records do not become education records because the secretary is not employed as a result of her status as a student. The regulations make clear that if an individual is employed at a school as a result of his or her status as a student, those records are education records under FERPA. While you did contend that graduate fellows/assistants are employed out of necessity for the schools at which they work, you did not contend that graduate fellows would be employed if they were not also enrolled as graduate students in a program at such schools.

You further asked that this Office interpret the records of graduate fellows/assistants as "employment records" rather than as "education records" because some public employee relations boards have ruled that graduate student employees are "employees" entitled to organize and bargain collectively. However, whether graduate student fellows/assistants have the right to organize and bargain collectively as employees does not affect whether records regarding such individuals are education records under FERPA. Further, the fact that certain records may be related to an individual's employment does not prevent such records from also being education records under FERPA. Rather, as discussed above, records regarding an individual's employment at a school *are education records* if the individual's employment is contingent on the fact that he or she is also a student at that school. As stated above, it appears that this is the case with respect to graduate student teaching fellows/assistants.

With regard to your question about directory information, FERPA generally provides that an educational agency or institution may only disclose a student's education records to a third party if the parent or eligible student has given appropriate written consent. 20 U.S.C. § 1232g(b)(1) and (b)(2)(A); 34 CFR § 99.30. FERPA does permit the nonconsensual disclosure of education records in certain limited circumstances that are clearly specified by statute, such as when the information has been appropriately designated as "directory information." 20 U.S.C. § 1232g(b)(1); 34 CFR § 99.31(a)(11). FERPA provides that a school may disclose directory information if it has given public notice of the types of information which it has designated as "directory information," the student's right to restrict the disclosure of such information, and the period of time within which a student has to notify the school in writing that he or she does not want any or all of those types of information designated as "directory information." 20 U.S.C. § 1232g(a)(5)(B); 34 CFR § 99.37(a).

With respect to what information can be considered "directory information," FERPA states:

For the purposes of this section the term "directory information" relating to a student includes the following: the student's name, address, telephone listing, date and place of birth, major field of study, participation in officially recognized activities and sports, weight and height of members of athletic teams, dates of attendance, degrees and awards received, and the most recent previous educational agency or institution attended by the student.

20 U.S.C. § 1232g(a)(5)(A).

In administering FERPA, the Department recognizes that there are other similar types of information that an educational agency or institution may wish to designate and disclose as directory information. In this regard, the FERPA regulations further define directory information as information contained in an education record of a student which would not generally be considered harmful or an invasion of privacy if disclosed. 34 CFR § 99.3 "Directory information." The regulations then specifically list those items set forth as "directory information" in the statute. The recently amended regulations (published in the *Federal Register* on July 6, 2000) also state that electronic mail address, grade level, and student status (part-time, full-time, graduate, undergraduate) can be specified as directory information.

This Office has made determinations on various occasions, in response to specific inquiries from school officials or in connection with the investigation of complaints of alleged violations of FERPA, as to whether a particular type of information can appropriately be considered directory information. In so doing, this Office fully considers the relationship of the potential new type of directory information to those types of information clearly specified by statute. For instance, a photograph or an email address are[sic] very similar to those types of information listed in the statute. They identify the student or provide a means to contact the student, without disclosing to the individual receiving the directory information any additional data that the student would generally expect to be private or that he or she would perceive as harmful if others had access to it.

Much of the information you have specified cannot be designated and disclosed as directory information because it is not similar to those types of information clearly specified by the statute and because it would be an invasion of privacy if disclosed without consent. Specifically, we find that rate of pay and bargaining unit status cannot be designated and disclosed by educational agencies and institutions as directory information.

Additionally, we note that a social security number, or other identification number, is generally linked to significant amounts of other information about an individual. An individual's social security, or other identification, number is a private identification number, the disclosure of which is generally expected to be controlled by the individual. Therefore, the designation and disclosure of a student's social security, or other identification, number as "directory information" is not permitted under FERPA.

However, we agree with your assertion that a graduate fellow's/assistant's status as a graduate fellow/assistant and his/her teaching assignment may be designated as directory information, should an educational agency or institution so choose. This information is similar to those types of information that are specified by the statute under the definition of directory information and are of a nature of being common knowledge to those who are in the individual's class or who pass by the class. We note that if a school publishes and/or posts the names of teaching fellows/assistants with course selection or other registration information, it should be designating these two items as directory information.

With regard to your concern that FERPA's requirement that educational agencies and institutions comply with FERPA even if that means choosing to not comply with conflicting state law, any other interpretation would render FERPA meaningless in the context of any state law that permitted disclosure of education records outside the scope of FERPA's provisions. Further, with regard to your claim that schools are forced to choose between FERPA and conflicting federal statutes, we are not convinced that an irreconcilable conflict exists. Generally, in such cases, we begin with the presumption that Congress does not intend two statutes to conflict. Thus, when determining which of two federal laws controls in an apparent conflict, it is especially important to try to avoid reading them as being in conflict, which Congress presumably does not intend.

The purpose of FERPA is to protect the privacy interests of eligible students in education records. These privacy interests should not be viewed as barriers to be minimized or overcome, but as important public safeguards to be protected and strengthened. Exceptions to the rule of prior written consent under FERPA should be construed narrowly to achieve its statutory purpose — protecting the privacy interests of students. From the circumstances you have presented, a plausible method for sharing personally identifiable information from education records with the union is to obtain the consent of the graduate student fellow/assistant before personally identifiable information is disclosed to the GTFF. Alternatively, the University could provide information to the students on behalf of the GTFF and the graduate student fellows could then submit the required information to the GTFF. Finally, based on the advice we give herein, the GTFF will be able to learn who are graduate teaching fellows through the directory information exception.

As we discussed in our meeting, another option is to seek a legislative amendment to FERPA that would specifically permit the nonconsensual disclosure of information from education records to graduate student teaching fellows/assistants unions. Should you choose to take this step, this Office would, of course, offer any assistance in drafting appropriate language.

Finally, as a matter of note, the agreement between the University and GTFF states: "The University will assume no liability for the unauthorized disclosure of information to parties outside the GTFF." Even if the University could lawfully disclose the information sought by GTFF without consent, this provision in the agreement is not in compliance with FERPA's redisclosure provisions. FERPA provides that a school may disclose personally identifiable information from an education record only on the condition that the party to whom the information is disclosed will not redisclose the information without the prior consent of the parent or eligible student, unless the redisclosure is on behalf of the educational agency or institution and meets the requirements of § 99.31 of the regulations. 20 U.S.C. § 1232(g)(b)(1) and (b)(4)(A); 34 CFR § 99.33. 34 CFR § 99.33(a)(1) and (b). Further, if this Office determines that a third party has improperly redisclosed information from education records, the educational agency or institution may not allow that third party access to personally identifiable information from education records for at least five years. 34 CFR § 99.33(e). The redisclosure provisions do not, however, apply to disclosures of directory information.

I trust that the above information is helpful in explaining the scope and limitations of FERPA as it relates to the issue you have raised. Please let us know if this Office can be of further assistance to you.

Sincerely,

LeRoy S. Rooker, Director
Family Policy Compliance Office

13 Letter to the University of Massachusetts

Re: Disclosure of Information on Teaching Assistants

Mr. Joseph W. Ambash   FEBRUARY 25, 2002
Seyfarth Shaw
World Trade Center East
Two Seaport Lane
Suite 300
Boston, Massachusetts 02210-2028

Dear Mr. Ambash:

This responds to your February 12, 2002, facsimile and recent conversation with Ms. Ingrid Brault of my staff asking for advice regarding the Family Educational Rights and Privacy Act (FERPA) as it relates to a request for information that the University of Massachusetts (University) has received from the Graduate Employee Organization, Local 2322, UAW (Union). As you are aware, this Office administers FERPA and is responsible for providing technical assistance to educational agencies and institutions regarding issues related to education records.

In your letter, you explain that part of the collective bargaining agreement between the Union and the University requires that the University disclose to the Union the following information on its graduate students: student ID number, social security number, waiver type, academic department, work department, employment category, number of hours contracted for, stipend, length of contract, entrance date, home address, phone number, and the fact that they may have been identified for lay-off. You explain that while the Union represents Teaching Assistants, Teaching Associates (graduate students who teach credit courses and whose names are listed in the schedule of courses), and Research Assistants, among others, the University has only defined Teaching Associates in its definition of directory information. You ask, therefore, whether the University may release the above outlined information on its Teaching and Research Assistants and Teaching Associates absent their prior written consent or absent a subpoena for such.

FERPA defines "education records" as "those records, files, documents and other materials which—

(i) contain information directly related to a student; and

(ii) are maintained by an educational agency or institution or by a person acting for such agency or institution.

20 U.S.C. 1232g(a)(4)(i) and (ii)

FERPA specifically includes in the term, those records relating to an individual in attendance at the agency or institution who is employed as a result of his or her status as a student. 34 CFR § 99.3 (b)(3)(ii). Therefore, under FERPA records of Teaching Assistants, Teaching Associates, and Research Assistants whose employment at the University is contingent of their status as students, are "education records," and, as such, are subject to the FERPA provisions authorizing their disclosure or nondisclosure.

With regard to the disclosure of education records, FERPA generally provides that an educational agency or institution may only disclose a student's education record to a third party if the eligible student has given appropriate written consent. 20 U.S.C. § 1232g(b)(1) and (b)(2)(A); 34 CFR § 99.30. FERPA does provide that written consent is not needed if the disclosure concerns information the educational agency or institution has designated as "directory information," under the conditions described in 34 CFR § 99.37. See 34 CFR § 99.31(a)(11). The definition lists items that would not generally be considered harmful or an invasion of privacy if disclosed which includes, but is not limited to: a student's name; address; telephone listing; electronic mail address; photograph; date and place of birth; major field of study; enrollment status (*e.g.* undergraduate or graduate; full-time or part-time); participation in officially recognized activities and sports; weight and height of members of athletic teams;

dates of attendance; degrees and awards received; and the most previous educational agency or institution attended. 34 CFR § 99.3 ("Directory information").

We have advised in the past that a graduate fellow's/assistant's status as a graduate fellow/assistant and his/her teaching assignment may be designated as directory information, should an educational agency or institution so choose. This information is similar to those types of information that are specified by the statute under the definition of directory information and are of a nature of being common knowledge to those who are in the individual's class or who pass by the class. In this regard, if a school publishes and/or posts the names of teaching fellows/assistants with course selection or other registration information, it should be designating these two items as directory information.

You noted that the University has designated Teaching Associates as directory information. Accordingly, the names of those students who are Teaching Associates may be disclosed as directory information. However, as explained above, the records of a Teaching Associate are education records as defined under FERPA. Thus, as with all student education records, FERPA would prevent the University from disclosing information such as the student ID number, social security number, number of hours contracted for, stipend, length of contract, employment category and entrance date to the Union absent another provision that allows for the disclosure. Other information requested by the Union, like home address and phone number, may fit the definition of directory information under FERPA and could, if appropriately designated, be disclosed. As for the fact that a Teaching Associate may have been identified for a lay-off, that information would be protected from disclosure if such information is documented in a record at the University.

I trust that the above information is responsive to your inquiry. Should you have any further questions on FERPA, please feel free to contact this Office again.

Sincerely,

LeRoy S. Rooker, Director
Family Policy Compliance Office

14 Letter to University of North Alabama

Re: Disability Office Records/HIPAA/Faculty Access

Mr. David Cope   NOVEMBER 2, 2004
Assistant Professor
Mathematics Department
University of North Alabama
Florence, AL 35632-0001

Dear Professor Cope:

This responds to your memorandum dated June 18, 2004, in which you asked for guidance regarding the applicability of the Family Educational Rights & Privacy Act (FERPA), 20 U.S.C. § 1232g, to records maintained by the Office of Developmental Services (ODS) at the University of North Alabama (University). This Office administers FERPA and provides technical assistance to educational agencies and institutions to ensure compliance with the statute and regulations codified at 34 CFR Part 99.

You explained that students submit records prepared by a medical or clinical professional to ODS for the purpose of documenting a claim of a disability under federal law and a request for appropriate accommodations. You have occasion to examine these records as a professor from whom disability accommodations are requested. University policy requires that you communicate any concerns you may have about the adequacy of the documentation or the accommodations authorized by ODS to specified administrators in your chain of authority. The University recently announced a policy that prevents a faculty member from sharing information from these records with anyone other than ODS and the student, citing the Americans with Disabilities Act, the Health Insurance Portability & Accountability Act (HIPAA), and FERPA. You expressed concern that this policy has the effect of preventing a faculty member from seeking modifications of accommodations authorized by ODS and asked us to respond to the following questions:

① Do the student's medical or clinical records maintained by ODS qualify as "education records" or "treatment records" under FERPA?

"Education records" are defined as records that are directly related to a student and maintained by an educational agency or institution or by a party acting for the agency or institution. See 34 CFR § 99.3 ("Education records"). The term does not include records on a student who is at least 18 years of age, or who attends a postsecondary institution, that are:

▶ Made or maintained by a physician, psychiatrist, psychologist, or other recognized professional or paraprofessional acting in his or her professional capacity or assisting in a paraprofessional capacity;

▶ Made, maintained, or used only in connection with treatment of the student; and

▶ Disclosed only to individuals providing the treatment. For the purpose of this definition, 'treatment' does not include remedial educational activities or activities that are part of the program of instruction at the agency or institution.

34 CFR § 99.3 ("Education records" (b)(4)). These are sometimes referred to as "treatment" records.

A student's medical or clinical records maintained by ODS qualify as "education records" because they contain information that is directly related to a student and are maintained by the University. There is no exclusion from the definition of "education records" under FERPA for "health" or "medical" records except for "treatment" records that meet the requirements described above.

In order to qualify as treatment records, the record or information may not be made, maintained, or used for any purpose other than treatment by the professionals identified above. The regulations clearly identify medical functions as the focus of "treatment" and exclude educational and other non-medical activities from this concept. As such, we conclude that "treatment" does not include determining appropriate accommodations for a disability and, therefore, these records are not considered "treatment" records excluded from the definition of "education records" under FERPA.

② Are a student's medical or clinical records maintained by ODS exempt from the HIPAA Privacy Rule?

Yes. The HIPAA Privacy Regulations specifically exclude from the definition of "protected health information" individually identifiable health information contained in "education records" covered by FERPA, as well as "treatment" records excluded from the definition of "education records" under FERPA. See 45 CFR § 164.501 ("Protected health information").

③ Does FERPA permit a faculty member from whom accommodations have been requested by a student to inspect the student's medical or clinical records maintained by ODS pursuant to the annual FERPA notification published by the University?

A postsecondary educational agency or institution may not have a policy or practice of disclosing personally identifiable information from education records without the prior written consent of an eligible student except as specified by law. See 34 CFR §§ 99.30 and 99.31. One of the exceptions allows disclosure to "other school officials, including teachers ... whom the agency or institution has determined to have legitimate educational interests." 34 CFR § 99.31(a)(1). An institution that discloses information without consent under this provision must provide in its annual FERPA notification a specification of criteria for determining who constitutes a school official and what constitutes a legitimate educational interest. 34 CFR § 99.7.

The information you provided indicates that the University has adopted the model notification provided by this Office for postsecondary institutions. That notification states that:

A school official is a person employed by the University in an administrative, supervisory, academic or research, or support staff position (including law enforcement unit personnel and health staff); a person or company with whom the University has contracted (such as an attorney, auditor, or collection agent); a person serving on the Board of Trustees; or a student serving on an official committee, such as a disciplinary or grievance committee, or assisting another school official in performing his or her tasks. A school official has a legitimate educational interest if the official needs to review an education record in order to fulfill his or her professional responsibility.

Under this notification, the University could determine that a faculty member from whom accommodations have been requested by a student has a "legitimate educational interest" in inspecting the student's medical or clinical records maintained by ODS. However, FERPA does not require a postsecondary agency or institution to make education records available to anyone other than an eligible student. Therefore, nothing in FERPA would prevent the University from adopting a policy that a faculty member may not have access to these records.

④ Does FERPA permit a faculty member to redisclose a student's medical or clinical records to administrators in the chain of authority who are entitled by University policy to modify the accommodations that were authorized by ODS in response to information contained in the records?

The University's policy on disclosure of education records without consent to teachers and other school officials with legitimate educational interests (quoted above) could permit a faculty member to redisclose the records to other administrators as described in your question. However, as explained above, the University is not required under FERPA to authorize these redisclosures.

I trust that this responds to your questions and appreciate the opportunity to provide assistance.

Sincerely,

LeRoy S. Rooker, Director
Family Policy Compliance Office

15   Letter to Yale University

Re: Letter of Technical Assistance on Financial Aid

Ms. Cathy R. Paul   MAY 26, 1995
Assistant to the General Counsel
Office of the General Counsel
Yale University
451 College Street
P.O. Box 208255
New Haven, Connecticut 06520-8255

Dear Ms. Paul:

This is in response to your May 1, 1995, letter of inquiry and in follow-up to your conversations with me and a member of my staff. You asked whether Yale University (University) could disclose a former student's education records to the state's attorney to assist in the investigation and prosecution of the student for larceny in the first degree. You state that the former student allegedly obtained financial aid, in the form of federal loans and grants and University loans and scholarships, "through fraud and deceit by forging numerous documents in his admissions application." You ask whether the student's education records can be disclosed to the state's attorney under the provision in the Family Educational Rights and Privacy Act (FERPA) which permits the nonconsensual disclosure of education records when the disclosure is in connection with a student's application for, or receipt of, financial aid.

As you are aware, FERPA affords students certain rights with respect to their education records. As relevant here, FERPA generally provides that an educational agency or institution may only disclose a student's education records to a third party if the student has given appropriate written consent. 20 U.S.C. § 1232g(b)(1) and (b)(2)(A); 34 CFR § 99.30. However, FERPA permits the nonconsensual disclosure of education records in certain limited circumstances. As discussed in the telephone conversations, we believe two of the exceptions apply to this situation.

First, FERPA permits the nonconsensual disclosure of education records when the disclosure is made in compliance with a lawfully issued subpoena or court order if the educational agency or institution makes a reasonable attempt to notify the student of the order or subpoena in advance of compliance. 20 U.S.C § 1232g(b)(2)(B). 34 CFR § 99.31(a)(9). While § 99.32 of the FERPA regulations generally requires that an educational agency or institution maintain a record of all requests for access to and disclosures from education records, we have determined that such recordation would not be required when the disclosure was made in compliance with a judicial order or subpoena so long as the school was successful in its attempt to notify the student of the order or subpoena in advance of compliance.

Additionally, we have also determined that the redisclosure provisions at 34 CFR § 99.33 do not apply to records that have been disclosed pursuant to a court order or lawfully issued subpoena. Once an institution determines that the subpoena or judicial order is valid and makes a reasonable attempt to provide advance notice in sufficient time to allow the student to take appropriate action, the institution is not responsible for taking any further action to protect the records against redisclosure, even to the press.

Further, FERPA was recently amended by the Improving America's Schools Act of 1994 so that advance notification is not required when a disclosure of education records is made in compliance with subpoenas or court orders issued for law enforcement purposes. The waiver of the advance notification requirement applies only when the law enforcement subpoena or court order contains language that specifies that the subpoena or court order should not be disclosed. 20 U.S.C. § 1232g(b)(1)(J). (*See* enclosed.) We would like to note here that the recordation requirements at 34 CFR § 99.32 would not apply when disclosure of education records is made in such instances, even though no prior notification will be made when a court order or subpoena prevents disclosure of the fact that it exists.

FERPA also permits the nonconsensual disclosure of education records when the disclosure is "in connection with a student's application for, or receipt of, financial aid." 20 U.S.C. § 1232g(b)(1)(D). The regulations provide that consent is not required when:

[t]he disclosure is in connection with financial aid for which the student has applied or which the student has received, if the information is necessary for such purposes as to—
(A) Determine eligibility for the aid;
(B) Determine the amount of the aid;
(C) Determine the conditions for the aid; or
(D) Enforce the terms and conditions of the aid.

34 CFR § 99.31(a)(4).

When disclosures are made pursuant to this financial aid exception, the record-keeping and redisclosure provisions apply. 34 CFR §§ 99.32 and 99.33.

Based on the circumstances you have presented, the disclosure to the state prosecutor would be permissible under the financial aid exception because the disclosure would be to enforce the terms and conditions of financial aid the student received. 34 CFR § 99.31(a)(4)(d). Additionally, if the record of the disclosure states the legitimate interest as investigating and prosecuting the student for suspected larceny, any redisclosures which are necessary to investigate and prosecute would be permissible. Such redisclosures would be permissible because, unlike the other exceptions to the prior written consent provision, the disclosure of records in connection with financial aid is not limited to a certain party; rather, it is limited only to a certain purpose.

Finally, you stated that the University has disclosed documents to the Department's Office of the Inspector General (OIG) under the financial aid exception. You ask whether OIG could redisclose the information to the state prosecutor for the investigation. As discussed above, when a disclosure is made pursuant to the financial aid exception to the prior written consent provisions, the information disclosed may be redisclosed as necessary to fulfill the purpose for which the disclosure was made. The record-keeping requirements apply and the record of disclosure must state the legitimate interest of OIG and of the state prosecutor in the information.

I trust that the above information is helpful to you. Should you have additional questions regarding this matter or FERPA in general, please do not hesitate to contact this Office again. Please note that our correct address is:

Family Policy Compliance Office
U.S. Department of Education
600 Independence Avenue, SW
Washington, DC 20202-4605

Sincerely,

LeRoy S. Rooker, Director
Family Policy Compliance Office

16 Letter to Hunter College

Re: Posting Grades by Last Four Digits of Social Security Number

Dr. Evangelos J. Gizis
Interim President
Hunter College of the City University of New York
695 Park Avenue
New York, New York 10021

MAY 29, 2001
Complaint No. [REDACTED]
Family Educational Rights
and Privacy Act

Dear Dr. Gizis:

This is to advise you of the finding in the complaint filed with this Office by [Student] who alleged that Hunter College of the City University of New York (College) violated his rights under the Family Educational Rights and Privacy Act (FERPA). Specifically, the Student alleged that Mr. Cullen Schaffer, a computer science professor, posted his exam and final grade on a web page along with the last four digits of his social security number.

This Office advised you of the allegation by letter dated August 21, 2000, and you responded on behalf of the College by letter dated September 25, 2000. You state in your letter that many College professors do post grades by the last four digits of a student's social security number. You state that "no student names are listed" and that this "enables students to easily identify their own grades, yet remain unable to identify any other student's identities." You also state that the College does "not consider this practice to be in violation of FERPA or any other applicable laws."

FERPA protects privacy interests of parents in their children's "education records," and generally prohibits the disclosure of personally identifiable information from education records without the consent of the parent. The term "education records" is broadly defined as all records, files, documents and other materials which:

contain information directly related to a student; and are maintained by the educational agency or institution or by a person acting for such agency or institution.

20 U.S.C. § 1232g(a)(4)(A); 34 CFR § 99.3 "Education records." When a student reaches the age of 18 or attends an institution of postsecondary education, the student is considered an "eligible student" under FERPA and all of the rights afforded by FERPA transfer from the parents to the student.

Under FERPA an eligible student must provide his or her prior written consent before an educational agency or institution discloses personally identifiable information from his or her education records. 20 U.S.C. § 1232g(b); 34 CFR § 99.30. Section 99.3 of the regulations defines the "Personally identifiable information" as information that includes but is not limited to:

(a) the student's name;
(b) the name of the student's parent or other family member;
(c) the address of the student or the student's family;
*(d) a personal identifier, such as the **student's social security number** or student number;*
(e) a list of personal characteristics that would make the student's identity easily traceable; or
(f) other information that would make the student's identity easily traceable.

34 CFR § 99.3 "Personally identifiable information." (Emphasis added.) A student's social security number is, by definition, "personally identifiable information" under FERPA, and may not be disclosed without consent in any form.

FERPA provides that educational agencies and institutions may not disclose personally identifiable, non-directory information from education records unless a parent or eligible student has provided a signed and dated written consent in accordance with the requirements of § 99.30 of the FERPA regulations. While there are certain exceptions to this general prohibition, none permit an educational agency or institution to publicly disclose personally identifiable information, including the student's grades and portions of the student's social security number, from the education records of students.

In this case, the Student's grades were publicly disclosed along with the last four digits of his social security number absent his consent when they were posted on a web page. Because a social security number, or portions thereof, are by definition "personally identifiable information" under FERPA, this Office finds that the College violated the Student's rights under FERPA as alleged. The Student will be advised of this finding by copy of this letter.

We note that FERPA does not prevent an educational agency or institution from posting the grades of students without written consent when it is not done in a personally identifiable manner. Thus, while FERPA precludes a school from posting grades by social security numbers, student ID numbers, or by names because these types of information are personally identifiable or easily traceable to the students, nothing in FERPA would preclude a school from assigning individual numbers to students for the purpose of posting grades as long as those numbers are known only to the student and the school officials who assigned them.

We will close the investigation of the complaint upon receipt of assurance that the College has taken appropriate steps to come into compliance with FERPA. Specifically, please provide this Office with assurance that: 1) The College has taken appropriate steps to revise its policy on posting grades in accordance with the provisions of FERPA as set forth in this letter of finding and 2) appropriate College officials have been advised of FERPA's prohibition on posting grades in personally identifiable form, and that using a student's social security number, or a portion of that number, means a disclosure in personally identifiable form under FERPA. At a minimum, the College should provide a memorandum to all appropriate staff outlining the above requirements of FERPA and provide this Office of such once it has been distributed.

Thank you for your cooperation in the investigation of this complaint. Please provide the requested assurances within two weeks of your receipt of this letter.

Sincerely,

LeRoy S. Rooker, Director
Family Policy Compliance Office

cc: Student

17   Letter to Cornell University   ★

Re: Authentication/ Disclosure of Transcript to Third Party

UNITED STATES DEPARTMENT OF EDUCATION
OFFICE OF HUMAN RESOURCES AND ADMINISTRATION

Dr. David S. Yeh   JUNE 30, 1994
Assistant Vice President and University Registrar
Cornell University
Ithaca, New York 14853-2801

Dr. Dr. Yeh:

This is in response to your letter dated July 26, 1993. You ask whether the Family Educational Rights and Privacy Act (FERPA) allows for the release of a transcript or other information from education records pursuant to an electronic request from the student. You state that the University has developed a computer system that allows students to access their own education records via computer terminals stationed across campus and that the University is currently working toward expanding the system to allow students to request, or authorize, the release of a transcript or other information from education records electronically. In this regard you state:

We are designing a system that requires that when a student first receives his or her unique network identification number and a personal password, he or she must sign a written release form. This document authorizes future releases of that student's transcripts via his or her (and only his or her) electronic request. A student must use a 10-digit electronic password to ... authenticate an electronic request for a transcript. The transcript releases would only occur if the individual student had originally signed the authorization document and then only after the student entered his or her personal password.

FERPA generally requires that students provide signed and dated consent before an institution of postsecondary education discloses education records, or personally identifiable information from such records, to a third party. The written consent must (1) specify the records that may be disclosed; (2) state the purpose of the disclosure; and (3) identify the party or class of parties to whom the disclosure may be made 20 U.S.C. §1232g(b); 34 CFR §99.30. There are several exceptions to the prior written consent provision of FERPA. One of these exceptions allows nonconsensual disclosure to the eligible student to whom the records relate. 34 CFR §99.31 (a)(12).

Another exception to the prior written consent provision allows nonconsensual disclosure, under the conditions set forth in 34 CFR §99.34, to a school, school system, or institution of postsecondary education in which a student seeks or intends to enroll. Section 99.34 provides, in part, that a college can send a student's education records to another college or university in which the student is seeking or intending to enroll without prior written consent or notification if the student initiates the disclosure. Accordingly, if a student requests that his transcript be forwarded to another school, whether that request is made in person, in writing, by telephone, or by electronic transmission, FERPA would not prevent an institution from releasing that student's transcript, or other records specified by the student, without prior written consent meeting the requirements of §99.30(b). However, when such a request is made by a student by telephone or electronic transmission, the school should be reasonably sure that the request was indeed made by the student.

Any other type of disclosures, for instance to a potential employer, which a student may request through electronic transmission, would have to be accompanied by prior written consent as discussed above. An educational institution could afford students an opportunity to provide general written consents for routine use in the event the student later wants to request release by telephone or electronic transmission. With respect to release of transcripts to an employer or prospective employer, the written consent would have to (1) specify "transcripts" (or other records) as the records that my[sic] be disclosed, (2) state that "application for and in connection with employment" is the purpose of the disclosure, and (3) identify "employers or prospective employers" as the class of parties to whom the transcripts may be disclosed. The institution should then use its own judgment in deciding whether to disclose education records pursuant to a student's request which is submitted by telephone or electronic transfer.

This Office, in administering the law, would investigate any complaint which contains specific allegations of fact giving reasonable cause to believe that an educational agency or institution improperly disclosed information from a student's education records in response to a request for the disclosure received by electronic transmission. The institution should implement any procedures it believes necessary to verify a student's identity before disclosing education records pursuant to a student's request made by telephone or electronic transmission. Accordingly, when possible, educational agencies and institutions should require written requests for information.

Finally, we note that an educational agency or institution which releases education records under 34 CFR §99.31(a)(2) and 34 CFR §99.34 must comply with the recordkeeping requirements of 34 CFR §99.32 and the conditions that limit disclosure of information set forth in 34 CFR §99.33. The recordkeeping requirements of 34 CFR §99.32 do not apply if the student has provided a written consent under 34 CFR §99.30 (b).

I trust the above information adequately explains the scope and limitations of FERPA as it pertains to your inquiry. Please feel free to contact this Office with any questions. Enclosed for your reference are a copy of the FERPA regulations and a copy of our recently updated model student records policy for use by postsecondary educational institution [sic].

Sincerely,

LeRoy S. Rooker, Director
Family Policy Compliance Office

Enclosures

UNITED STATES DEPARTMENT OF EDUCATION
OFFICE OF INNOVATION AND IMPROVEMENT

[NAME AND ADDRESS REDACTED]

AUG 15 2007
Complaint No. [REDACTED]
Family Educational Rights
and Privacy Act

Dear [REDACTED]:

This is to advise you of the finding in the complaint filed by [REDACTED] (Student) against [REDACTED] (College) under the Family Educational Rights and Privacy Act (FERPA), 20 U.S.C. §1232g. By letter dated September 22, 2004, the Family Policy Compliance Office informed you of the Student's allegation that the College violated 34 CFR 99.30 of the FERPA regulations by disclosing personally identifiable information from his education records without his prior written consent.

Specifically, the Student alleged that on March 7, 2003, the College disclosed his education records to his father, [REDACTED], without his written consent. The Student stated that he became aware of this disclosure on May 8, 2003, after his mother received a motion packet from her attorney. The information submitted by the father's attorneys, [REDACTED] and [REDACTED] to the New Jersey Superior Court Clerk on May 2, 2003, included information that the Student's father obtained from his son's education records. The Student stated the following regarding his allegation:

[My father] hacked into the [College's] web page by using my social security number, creating a password and representing himself as me. I do not know how many other times he has done this. I contacted [the College], and they informed me that they don't take any position other than to suggest that I change my password.

By letter dated November 2, 2004, [REDACTED], attorney, responded on behalf of the College as follows:

The Student is specifically referring to the [REDACTED] WebAdvisor which can be found by way of the College Web site, or directly on the internet. WebAdvisor became operational in March of 2003 and at that time all students, including the complainant, received a letter from the College Registrar, a copy of which is included herewith Exhibit A. As stated on the second page:

WebAdvisor: "[REDACTED] WebAdvisor is available to all current students and can be found via the [REDACTED] College Web site, or directly at [REDACTED URL ADDRESS]. Your login is on the first page of this mailing. It is your first name, underscore, last name. Your password is the last 6 digits of your social security number (you will be prompted to change this the first time you log on—any difficulty with WebAdvisor access can be addressed to [REDACTED EMAIL ADDRESS]. WebAdvisor can be used to view semester schedules, check grades, view your own schedule, and run program evaluations to ascertain graduation requirements remaining. Some [s]tudents may even register for classes on WebAdvisor, if approved to do so by an advisor." (Emphasis supplied.)

As noted, as soon as a student logs into WebAdvisor, he or she is immediately required to create a new password. Enclosed herewith as Exhibit B is a print screen of what appears when a student logs on for the first time. It appears that the student in this matter must have ignored the letter informing him about WebAdvisor, and he never tried to access it for at least two months. If the student had tried he would have had a problem doing so because of the password created by his father. It is unknown how the student's father became aware that

WebAdvisor became operational in March 2003. Perhaps the father intercepted the letter sent to the student at the time.

Also enclosed herewith are copies of the following:

⬧ Print screen of [REDACTED] Privacy Statement that every student must agree to in order to log in to the data base, Exhibit C.

⬧ [REDACTED] catalog information relating to the Family Educational Rights and Privacy Act of 1974, Exhibit D.

⬧ May 23, 2003, letter from [REDACTED], Esq., representing the student's mother, to [REDACTED], Esq., representing the student's father, Exhibit E. As you will note, the letter states in pertinent part: "Your client utilized the computer system and made up a password since it had not previously been utilized by the child."

As you are aware, FERPA provides that educational agencies or institutions may disclose a student's education records, or personally identifiable information from such records, to third parties only after obtaining the written consent of a minor student's parent, or of a student who has reached the age of `18 or is attending an institution of postsecondary education. 20 U.S.C. 1232g(b)(1) and (d).

"Education records" means those records that are:

(1) Directly related to a student; and

(2) Maintained by an educational agency or institution or by a party acting for the agency or institution.

34 CFR § 99.3 "Education records."

FERPA requires that a consent for disclosure of education records must be signed and dated and must specify the records that may be disclosed; state the purpose of the disclosure; and identify the party or class of parties to whom the disclosure may be made. 20 U.S.C. § 1232g(b); 34 CFR §99.30. "Disclosure" means to permit access to or the release, transfer, or other communication of personally identifiable information contained in education records to any party by any means, including oral, written, or electronic means. 20 U.S.C. § 1232g(b)(1); 34 CFR § 99.30 "Disclosure."

The College admitted that it permits students to access their education records through WebAdvisor by submitting the student's first name, last name, and a password consisting of the last six digits of the student's SSN. An educational agency or institution may not have a policy or practice that allows students (or other individuals) to authenticate their identity and gain access to education records by using information known to other individuals, such as SSNs, thus permitting access to those records by unauthorized individuals. In this instance, the College's procedure for accessing the WebAdvisor allowed the Student's father to gain access to the Student's education records in violation of § 99.30 of the regulations. Requiring the Student to create a new password immediately upon login does not negate the fact that the College allowed the Student's education records to be accessed by anyone in possession of his name and SSN until the password was actually changed into a password of the student's choice. In particular, an educational agency or institution may not shift to students its own responsibility under FERPA for ensuring that it does not permit unauthorized individuals to gain access to education records.

The College states that it is unknown how the Student's father became aware that WebAdvisor became operational in March 2003, indicating that perhaps the father intercepted the letter sent to the student at the time and thus was able to learn how to log into the Student's account. Nonetheless, anyone with knowledge of the WebAdvisor system would have known the routine for the initial accessing the account using widely accessible information such as a student name and SSN.

In order to ensure that it discloses education records only to authorized individuals, an educational agency or institution must authenticate identity using information known or possessed only by the authorized user. For example, when releasing education records to students in person, an institution could ask for a driver's license or other photo ID to confirm the student's identity (if not known personally to the school official releasing the information). When making education records available to students electronically, the institution could mail each student a secret PIN or password known only the student that would be used in combination with a user ID to access the records. These are the kinds of authentication methods that can be used to ensure that education records are disclosed only to the student to whom they relate.

In accordance with § 99.66, in order to close this investigation the College must provide this Office with evidence that it has revised its procedures and allows students to login to WebAdvisor in a manner that does not permit access to unauthorized individuals. Due to the passage of time in the processing and completion of this investigation, the College may have made changes to its login system. In either event, please provide written assurance that the login system has been modified in accordance with the above-outlined requirements.

Finally, a review of the College's annual notification indicates that it needs to be revised to include additional information outlined in our model notification (copy enclosed). Therefore, when the College provides its assurance, please also include a copy of the College's updated annual notification. Ms. Ingrid Brault of my staff is available to provide technical assistance on FERPA and you may contact her at (202) 260-3887.

Sincerely,

LeRoy S. Rooker, Director
Family Policy Compliance Office

Enclosure
cc: Student [REDACTED]

19 Letter to University of Central Florida

Re: Safeguarding of Student Records

UNITED STATES DEPARTMENT OF EDUCATION
OFFICE OF PLANNING, EVALUATION AND POLICY DEVELOPMENT

Dr. John C. Hitt   DEC 19 2008
President
University of Central Florida
P.O. Box 16011
Orlando, Florida 32816-0114

Dear. Dr. Hitt:

This Office is responsible for administration of the Family Educational Rights and Privacy Act (FERPA), which protects the privacy interests of parents and eligible students in students' education records. See 20 U.S.C. §1232g and 34 CFR part 99. Under that authority we investigate, process, and review complaints and violations and provide technical assistance to ensure compliance with all FERPA requirements.

Paul H. Viau, Jr., Associate University Registrar at the University of Central Florida (University) notified this office by letter dated May 13, 2008, that a computer flash drive with graduate student information was missing and presumably stolen from a locked office in the History Department in April 2008. According to Mr. Viau's letter, information on the missing flash drive included each student's full name; email address; mailing address; phone number; entering GPA; University-generated ID number; social security number (SSN); and academic information such as major, courses completed, grades, and currently enrolled courses. Mr. Viau noted correctly that the information on the missing flash drive is protected under FERPA.

Mr. Viau's letter stated that the University Police Department was notified but did not indicate the results of any investigation. The letter reported further that the 77 affected students were notified of the data breach by email on May 1 and advised to change their passwords on email and bank accounts. Mr. Viau's letter described generally protocols that the University's College of Arts and Humanities had in place to protect confidential information, including FERPA training and authorization procedures for faculty and staff who have access to student modules in the University's PeopleSoft student information system. The letter also specified additional steps that the College would implement to improve security, including continuous training on FERPA and other security measures; working with staff to develop additional ways to protect students' confidential information; and collection of SSNs only from students who are admitted to or employed by the University. Mr. Viau asked if this Office could suggest any further steps to address this incident.

Under FERPA, an eligible student must provide a signed and dated written consent before a postsecondary institution discloses personally identifiable information from the student's education records. 34 CFR §§99.5(a); 99.30. Exceptions to the consent requirement are set forth in §99.31(a) of the regulations. "Disclosure" means "to permit access to or the release, transfer, or other communication of personally identifiable information contained in education records to any party, by any means, including oral, written, or electronic means." 34 CFR §99.3. The preamble to the new FERPA regulations explains the necessity for educational agencies and institutions to ensure that adequate controls are in place so that the education records of all students are handled in accordance with FERPA's privacy protections. See 73 *Fed. Reg.* 74806, 74843 (Dec. 9, 2008). The "Department Recommendations for Safeguarding Education Records" (Safeguarding Recommendations) that were published in both the Notice of Proposed Rulemaking (NPRM) and the Final Regulations are intended to provide agencies and institutions additional information and resources to assist them in meeting this responsibility. (The NPRM was published at 73 *Fed. Reg.* 15574, March 24, 2008.)

The FERPA Safeguarding Recommendations recognize that no system for maintaining and transmitting education records, whether in paper or electronic form, can be guaranteed safe from every hacker and thief, technological failure, violation of administrative rules, and other causes of unauthorized access and disclosure. Although FERPA does not dictate requirements for safeguarding education records, the Department encourages the holders of personally identifiable information to consider actions that mitigate the risk and are reasonably calculated to protect such information. Of course, an educational agency or institution may use any reasonable method, combination of methods, or technologies, taking into consideration the size, complexity, and resources available to the institution; the context of the information; the type of information to be protected (such as SSNs or directory information); and methods used by other institutions in similar circumstances. The greater the harm that would result from unauthorized access or disclosure and the greater the likelihood that unauthorized access or disclosure will be attempted, the more protections an agency or institution should consider using to ensure that its methods are reasonable.

As explained in the FERPA Safeguarding Recommendations, one resource for administrators of electronic data systems is "The National Institute of Standards and Technology (NIST) 800-100, Information Security Handbook: A Guide for Managers" (October 2006). See http://csrc.nist.gov/publications/nistpubs/800-100/SP800-100-Mar07-2007.pdf. Another resource is NIST 800-53, Information Security, which catalogs information security controls. See: http://csrc.nist.gov/publications/nistpubs/800-53-Rev2/sp800-53-rev2-final.pdf. Similarly, a May 22, 2007, memorandum to head of federal agencies from the Office of Management and Budget requires executive departments and agencies to ensure that proper safeguards are in place to protect personally identifiable information that they maintain, eliminate the unnecessary use of SSNs, and develop and implement a "breach notification policy." Although directed towards federal agencies, this memorandum may also serve as a resource for educational agencies and institutions. See http://www.whitehouse.gov/omb/memoranda/fy2007/m07-16.pdf.

The Department's FERPA Safeguarding Recommendations specify that an educational agency or institution that has experienced a theft of files or computer equipment, hacking or other intrusion, software or hardware malfunction, inadvertent release of data to Internet sites, or other unauthorized release or disclosure of education records, should consider one or more of the following steps:

- Report the incident to law enforcement authorities
- Determine exactly what information was compromised, *i.e.*, names, addresses, SSNs, ID numbers, credit card numbers, grades, and the like.
- Take steps immediately to retrieve data and prevent any further disclosures.
- Identify all affected records and students.
- Determine how the incident occurred, including which school officials had control of and responsibility for the information that was compromised.
- Determine whether institutional policies and procedures were breached, including organizational requirements governing access (user names, passwords, PINS, etc.); storage; transmission; and destruction of information from education records.
- Determine whether the incident occurred because of a lack of monitoring and oversight.
- Conduct a risk assessment and identify appropriate physical, technological, and administrative measures to prevent similar incidents in the future.
- Notify students that the Department's Office of Inspector General maintains a Web site describing steps students may take if they suspect they are a victim of identity theft at http://www.ed.gov/about/offices/list/oig/misused/idtheft.html; and http://www.ed.gov/about/offices/list/oig/misused/victim.html.

The Safeguarding Recommendations note also that FERPA does not require an educational agency or institution to notify students that information from their education records was stolen or otherwise subject to an unauthorized release, although it does require the agency or institution to maintain a record of each disclosure. 34 CFR §99.32(a)(1). However, student notification may be required in these circumstances for postsecondary institutions under the Federal Trade Commission's Standards for Ensuring the Security, Confidentiality, Integrity and Protection of Customer Records and Information ("Safeguards Rule") in 16 CFR part 314. In any case, direct student notification may be advisable if the compromised data includes student SSNs and other identifying information that could lead to identity theft.

Under FERPA, no funds shall be made available to an educational agency or institution that has a policy or practice of permitting the release of personally identifiable information in education except as authorized by statute. 20 U.S.C. §1232g(b). Failure to take reasonable and appropriate steps to protect education records could result in the release or disclosure of personally identifiable information from education records and may also constitute a policy or practice of permitting the release or disclosure of education records in violation of FERPA requirements. Should this Office investigate a complaint or other indications of noncompliance, we would take into consideration what steps an educational agency or institution has taken in response to a data breach or other unauthorized access to, release, or other disclosure of education records.

We have not received any complaints about the April 2008 incident at the University, and it is not clear whether the student information on the missing flash drive was disclosed in violation of FERPA requirements. However, we do have some concerns based on the limited information that the University has provided. In particular, why were student SSNs and other personal information stored on a flash drive? Was the drive encrypted or otherwise protected against unauthorized access and disclosure? Does the College or University have a policy or procedure addressing this issue? Does the University's policy or procedure apply to contractors and other outside service providers that may have access to student information? What did the University police determine about the incident as a result of their investigation? Was the matter reported to local law enforcement authorities? What further information or guidance was sent to students? Has the University revised its data security procedures or taken other actions in response to the incident?

We would appreciate your review of this matter and ask that you provide this Office with a response to these questions and any additional information regarding your investigation and response to the April 2008 data breach. This information will help us ensure that the University remains in compliance with FERPA requirements.

Sincerely,

LeRoy S. Rooker, Director
Family Policy Compliance Office

Ms. Robin Parker   OCTOBER 19, 2004
General Counsel
Miami University
Roudebush Hall
Oxford, Ohio 45056-3653

Dear Ms. Parker:

This is to respond to your September 15, 2004, letter informing this Office about three requests for student disciplinary information that Miami University (University) has received from Channel 8 Fox News (Channel 8) in Cleveland, Ohio. This Office administers the Family Educational Rights and Privacy Act (FERPA) and is responsible for providing technical assistance to educational agencies and institutions to ensure compliance with the statute and regulations (20 U.S.C. § 1232g; 34 CFR Part 99).

You provided the following information about the three requests from Channel 8:

On April 7, 2004, Channel 8 requested student disciplinary information, from January 1, 1999, to date, under 34 CFR § 99.31(a)(14) and the Ohio Public Records Act. In response to the request, and in accordance with FERPA, the University provided the following information with respect to each student who was an alleged perpetrator of a crime of violence or non-forcible sex offense found responsible for committing a violation of the Miami University Code of Student Conduct:

- Name of the Student,
- Section of the *Code of Student Conduct* violated, and
- Sanction imposed by the institution.

On August 12, 2004, Channel 8 requested "redacted copies of incident reports and victim statements related to all student disciplinary proceedings between January 1, 1999 through the present, in which it was ultimately determined the student violated Section 103 of the *Code of Student Conduct* by perpetrating an act of physical or sexual assault." Under Ohio's Public Records Act (ORC 149.43) and in accordance with both the state and federal court decisions in *The Miami Student* v. *Miami University* lawsuits, the University is required to release student disciplinary records after redacting all personally identifiable information. Your letter indicates that because Channel 8 "had previously received personally identifiable information for some of these records in response to [the reporter's] first request for disciplinary information under 34 C.F.R. 99.31(a)(14), we are taking great care in redacting the records response to [their] August 12, 200[4] request to ensure that all personally identifiable information is redacted." However, it is not clear from your letter how much information you believe needs to be removed in order to protect the identity of the students. You stated that the University expects to produce these redacted records in the near future.

August 26, 2004, Channel 8 sent a request to the University's Police Department, which is a law enforcement unit under FERPA. The request contained a list of the names of students who had been found to have violated the *Code of Student Conduct*, Section 103, *Physical or Mental Abuse or Harm* that the University gave to Channel 8 in response to its first request. Channel 8 requested copies of any and all police reports in which any of the listed students were identified as suspects. The University informed Channel 8 that it would only provide reports of those individuals who had actually been charged with a crime. The University also stated that Police reports regarding uncharged suspects are not public records under Ohio's Public Records Act. These reports are public records once a suspect has been charged with a crime.

Your letter concludes:

Although we have complied with all applicable provisions of FERPA and Ohio's Public Records Act ... the cumulative effect of this compliance is the release of the names of student victims and witnesses that can be easily linked to identified student disciplinary actions. As you know, 34 C.F.R. 99.31(a)(14)(ii) provides that the institution may not disclose the name of any other student, including a victim or witness, without the prior written consent of the other student.... Obviously we must comply with the applicable law and regret that the effect of compliance has been the release of student victim and witness names.

An educational agency or institution subject to FERPA may not have a policy or practice of disclosing education records, or non-directory personally identifiable information from education records, without the prior written consent of the parent or eligible student[1] except as provided by law. 20 U.S.C. § 1232g(b); 34 CFR Subpart D. "Education records" are defined as those records, files, documents, and other materials which—

(1) contain information directly related to a student; and

(2) are maintained by an educational agency or institution or by a person acting for such agency or institution.

20 U.S.C. § 1232g(a)(4)(i) and (ii). See also 34 CFR § 99.3 "Education records."

Excluded from the definition of "education records" are records of the law enforcement unit of an educational agency or institution, but only under the conditions described in § 99.8 of the FERPA regulations. See 20 U.S.C. § 1232g(a)(4)(i) and (ii) and 34 CFR § 99.3 "Education records."

In 1998, Congress amended FERPA as follows to allow postsecondary institutions to disclose without meeting the prior written consent requirements limited information from certain kinds of disciplinary proceedings:

(B) Nothing in this section shall be construed to prohibit an institution of postsecondary education from disclosing the final results of any disciplinary proceeding conducted by such institution against a student who is an alleged perpetrator of any crime of violence (as that term is defined in section 16 of title 18, United States Code), or a nonforcible sex offense, if the institution determines as a result of that disciplinary proceeding that the student committed a violation of the institution's rules or policies with respect to such crime or offense.

(C) For the purpose of this paragraph, the final results of any disciplinary proceeding—

(i) shall include only the name of the student, the violation committed, and any sanction imposed by the institution on that student; and

*(ii) may include the name of any other student, such as a victim or witness, **only with the written consent of that other student.***

Pub. L. No. 105-244, § 951, 105th Cong., 2nd Sess. (October 7, 1998). (Emphasis added.)

Under this amendment, postsecondary institutions may—but are not required by FERPA to—disclose the name of the student who was disciplined and the final results of a disciplinary proceeding in which the institution determines that the student is an alleged perpetrator of a crime of violence or non-forcible sex offense and the student has committed a violation of the institution's rules or policies. See specifically § 99.31(a)(14) and § 99.39 for the regulatory provisions that implement this amendment. In enacting this amendment to FERPA, Congress made it clear that a postsecondary institution may not disclose the name of any other student that might be part of a disciplinary proceeding against a student—such as a victim or witness—unless that other student has provided prior written consent under FERPA.

FERPA also permits an educational agency or institution to disclose education records without meeting the written consent requirements in § 99.30 if it has removed all "personally identifiable information" from the records. "Personally identifiable information" includes, but is not limited to, the following information:

---

[1] "Eligible student" means a student who has reached 18 years of age or is attending an institution of postsecondary institution at any age. See 34 CFR § 99.3 "Eligible student." The rights under FERPA belong to the parents of students under the age of 18 at the elementary/secondary level and transfer to the student when he or she becomes an "eligible student."

(a) the student's name;

(b) the name of the student's parent or other family member;

(c) the address of the student or the student's family;

(d) a personal identifier, such as the student's social security number or student number;

(e) a list of personal characteristics that would make the student's identity easily traceable; or

(f) other information that would make the student's identity easily traceable.

34 CFR § 99.3, "Personally identifiable information." (Emphasis added.)

Thus, FERPA-protected information may not be released in any form that would make the student's identity easily traceable (unless there is a specific exception to the written consent requirement).

Occasionally, a student's identity may be "easily traceable," even after removal or redaction of nominally identifying information from student-level records. This may be the case, for example, with a highly publicized disciplinary action, or one that involved a well-known student, where the student could be easily identified in the community even after the record has been "scrubbed" of identifying data. In these circumstances, FERPA does not allow disclosure of the education record in any form without consent because the irreducible presence of "personal characteristics" or "other information" make[s] the student's identity "easily traceable."

A student's identity may also be "easily traceable" in the release of aggregated or statistical information derived from education records. See, for example, our September 25, 2003, letter to the Board of Regents of the University System of Georgia available at www.ed.gov/policy/gen/guid/fpco/ferpa/library/georgialtr.html. The Board had asked about a newspaper's request for sensitive data about students in aggregate form categorized into specific groupings that the Board believed could be used to identify students, especially through multiple releases. This Office advised the Board that in these circumstances we had insufficient information to determine whether the disclosures would violate FERPA, that the institution itself had to make the determination whether a student's identity would be easily traceable and, if so, they could not disclose the information in that form. This decision was based on our recognition that at least at the outset, agencies and institutions themselves are clearly in the best position to analyze and evaluate this requirement based on their own data, and under FERPA the burden is on the agency or institution not to release either aggregated or de-identified ("redacted") student level data if it believes that personal identity is easily traceable based on the specific circumstances under consideration. We also recognized in the letter to the Board of Regents of the University System of Georgia that FERPA prohibits the disclosure of personally identifiable information from education records without consent even where an individual's personal identity is revealed through *a series or combination of requests that are available to those in possession of the data.*

In the present inquiry, we have not had an opportunity to review and evaluate any of the disclosures you have made or propose to make in response to Channel 8's request. However, we do wish to register our concern regarding your statement that the cumulative effect of your compliance with FERPA and Ohio's Public Record Act is "the release of the names of student victims and witnesses that can easily be linked to identified student disciplinary actions." As explained below, the University would not be in compliance with FERPA if the identities of student victims and witnesses were easily traceable, even after their names and other identifying information had been redacted from incident reports and victim statements, because of the release of other, unredacted disciplinary records and law enforcement unit records.

The University may disclose, without prior written consent, law enforcement unit records because they are excluded from the definition of education records under FERPA. Similarly, the University may disclose, without prior written consent, the final results of disciplinary proceedings in which the student was an alleged perpetrator of a crime of violence or non-forcible sex offense and it was determined that the student violated the University's rules or policies with respect to that allegation because there is a statutory exception in FERPA that permits this disclosure.

However, it appears that your planned decision to release redacted copies of incident reports and victim statements relating to certain disciplinary proceedings in response to Channel 8's August 12th request would not comply with FERPA. Previous state and federal court decisions involving the University discuss the amount of redaction of certain items of information that is required before releasing, pursuant to an open records request, disciplinary records not subject to any statutory exception to the prior written consent requirement under FERPA. While the redaction of these items of information (student's name, social security number, student ID number, and the exact date and time of the incident) may generally be sufficient to remove all "personally identifiable information" under FERPA, and may have been sufficient under the circumstances involved in those cases, the facts are clearly different here because the University has already disclosed other documents to Channel 8 that contain information that you state will make the identities of student victims and witnesses easily traceable. As we have advised previously, redaction of nominally identifying information may not be sufficient to prevent a student's identity from being easily traceable with respect to a highly publicized incident, or with respect to a series of requests for information that make a student's identity easy to trace due to the disclosure of related information.

In sum, where a disclosure of personally identifiable information in education records does not fall within an exception to the prior written consent rule, we believe that the University itself is in the best position to determine, at least at the outset, what information must be removed from education records in order to ensure that a student's identity is not easily traceable. If, because of other records that have been released, the redaction of names, identification numbers, and dates and times of incidents is not sufficient to prevent the identification of a student involved in a disciplinary proceeding, including, but not limited to, student victims and student witnesses, then FERPA prohibits the University from having a policy or practice of releasing the information as such. The University either must remove or redact all of the information in the education record that would make a student's identity easily traceable or refuse to release the requested education record at all.

Thank you for contacting us regarding this matter. I trust this guidance will assist you in complying with FERPA in this regard.

Sincerely,

LeRoy S. Rooker, Director
Family Policy Compliance Office

Mr. Matthew J. Pepper
Policy Analyst
Tennessee Department of Education
Andrew Johnson Tower, 6th Floor
710 James Robertson Parkway
Nashville, Tennessee 37243

NOVEMBER 18, 2004

Dear Mr. Pepper:

This is in response to your November 5, 2004, inquiry in which you ask about the applicability of the Family Educational Rights and Privacy Act (FERPA) to the release of student level records to researchers. You state that the Tennessee Department of Education (TDE) routinely receives requests from researchers for student level data and you are attempting to develop a policy to allow the release of these records. You state that you plan to encrypt the records by changing a student's social security number to a unique student identifier. You state that the "cross-walk" between the social security number and unique student identifier will not be released to researchers. You also ask about the release of small data cells where an individual can be identified by the research. This Office administers FERPA and is responsible for investigating complaints and providing technical assistance to ensure compliance with the statute and regulations. 20 U.S.C. § 1232g; 34 CFR Part 99.

As you know, FERPA generally provides that an educational agency or institution may not have a policy or practice of releasing a student's education records, or personally identifiable information contained within those records, without the prior written consent of the student's parent or parents. 20 U.S.C. § 1232g(b)(1). According to the Department's regulations implementing FERPA, "personally identifiable information" includes a personal identifier, such as the student's social security number or student number. *See* 34 CFR § 99.3. Education records may be released without consent if all personally identifiable information has been removed.

In addition to FERPA, Congress has also recognized that scientifically valid educational research, including applied research, basic research, and field-initiated research, can provide parents, educators, students, researchers, policymakers, and the general public with reliable information about educational practices that improve academic achievement. Such research can also provide important information about the effectiveness of federal and other education programs. *See* sections 102(20) and 111(b) of the Education Sciences Reform Act of 2002. In particular, academic accountability is a central focus of the *No Child Left Behind Act of 2001*, and high-quality research is one of the ways to show whether the achievement gap is closing. A key component of such research is the use of longitudinal studies in which individual student performance is evaluated over a period of time.

To provide appropriate access to data for such studies, and consistent with the privacy protections of FERPA, the Department intends to promulgate regulations in the future defining this type of non-personally identifiable (anonymous) data, thus allowing disclosure, without parental consent, but with appropriate privacy safeguards. While the Department affirms FERPA's requirements, data that cannot be linked to a student by those reviewing and analyzing the data are not "personally identifiable." As such, the data are not "directly related" to any students. Accordingly, a document containing only non-personally identifiable data, even when originally taken from a student's education record, is not a part of the student's education records for purposes of FERPA. Thus, because the document—established or created under the requirements below and given to a researcher—contains no personally identifiable information, it does not constitute a disclosure proscribed by the regulations. However, it should be noted that the establishment or creation of such a document by a district or state is voluntary. Nothing in this letter or the pending regulatory process should be construed to require that such a document be established or created.

Beginning immediately and during the pendency of our rulemaking process, the Department will refrain from any enforcement action under FERPA under circumstances where an educational agency or institution has established or creates an anonymous data file for the purpose of education research, and in which a student is identified *only* by a non-personal identifier *and* the following requirements are met:

- the non-personal identifier itself—
  - ▸ is not a scrambled social security number or student number, unless such identifiers are protected by written agreements reflecting generally accepted confidentiality standards within the research community; and
  - ▸ cannot be linked to an individual student by anyone who does not have access to the linking key;
- the anonymous data file is populated by data from education records in a manner that ensures that the identity of any student cannot be determined, including assurances of sufficient cell and subgroup sizes; and
- the linking key that connects the non-personal identifier to student information is itself an education record subject to the privacy provisions of FERPA. In other words, the linking key must be kept within the agency or institution and must not be shared with the requesting entity.

These requirements do not limit or otherwise modify the FERPA exception for non-consensual disclosure of personally identifiable information from education records to organizations conducting studies for or on behalf of educational agencies or institutions under 34 CFR § 99.31(a)(6).

Please note that if this Office receives a complaint containing specific allegations that the above requirements have not been met and the allegations give reasonable cause to believe that a violation of FERPA has occurred, this Office will initiate an investigation into the matter.

As a reminder, in reporting information, if cell size or other information would make a student's identity "easily traceable," that information would be considered "personally identifiable." *See* 34 CFR § 99.3. The educational agency or institution should use generally accepted statistical

principles and methods to ensure that the data are reported in a manner that fully prevents the identification of students. If that cannot be done, the data must not be reported.

The Department remains strongly committed to enforcing the requirements of FERPA and ensuring that personally identifiable information is protected. Anonymous data procedures will ensure that the data are not traceable to individual students. In addition, the regulations we intend to issue will provide parameters and safeguards to protect the rights of students and parents. In short, the Department's regulations will ensure academic accountability in a framework that protects the identity and privacy of students.

Please feel free to contact me if you have any questions about FERPA in general or this issue in particular.

Sincerely,

LeRoy S. Rooker, Director
Family Policy Compliance Office

22   Letter to Nebraska Coordinating Commission

Re: Data Matching for Reporting Requirement Purpose

Mr. David R. Powers   MARCH 25, 2004
Executive Director
Coordinating Commission for Postsecondary Education
140 N. 8th Street, Suite 300
P.O. Box 95005
Lincoln, Nebraska 68509-5005

Dear Mr. Powers:

This responds to your inquiry in which you described the procedures under which Nebraska's Coordinating Commission for Postsecondary Education (CCPE) meets the reporting requirements of the Federal Workforce Investment Act of 1998 (WIA) on behalf of the state's community, state, private career, and other colleges. You explain that you have revised your contract with the Nebraska Department of Labor to comply with the new guidance issued by William D. Hansen, Deputy Secretary of Education, on January 30, 2003, which rescinded previous guidance on meeting WIA reporting requirements in compliance with the Family Educational Rights and Privacy Act (FERPA). (The January 30, 2003, memorandum indicated that the revised guidance was effective April 30, 2003.) You indicated that you would continue to use the wage matching processes described in your April 24 letter for WIA reporting unless you received written communication from the U.S. Department of Education that the process does not comply with the Department's revised guidance, or unless WIA is amended during reauthorization to change the reporting requirements for postsecondary institutions.

This Office is responsible for administration and enforcement of FERPA, including review of WIA data matching procedures for compliance with the revised guidance issued by the Deputy Secretary on January 30, 2003. We have reviewed the process described in your April 24, 2003, letter and find that it complies with the requirement that a state educational authority (CCPE) maintain direct control over any data matching process and ensure that personally identifiable information, such as student social security numbers, is not disclosed to the labor department or other agency that maintains records for the match. In particular, you explained that

[CCPE] has worked under a continuing contract with our State Department of Labor to match graduates' social security numbers against Labor's UI [unemployment insurance] wage data base. One individual in our office has been designated to perform this function. He has been given limited authority, by our contract with the Labor Department to enter the UI wage data base. This employee has been educated about FERPA limitations and is quite serious about protecting private student information. Thus, an employee of [CCPE] performs the computer match on-site at our agency. Aggregate data showing raw numbers of students who match in various program and industry code categories, with social security numbers and names deleted, is then sent electronically to the Department of Labor, which uses the data to prepare a WIA report for each participating institution.

....

[E]mployees of the Department [of Labor] do not participate in the wage match in the sense that they can actually see student social security numbers. Rather, Labor employees make the UI data for a specific time frame available to a [CCPE] employee who is able to enter the UI data base to conduct the match. All this is handled remotely through electronic communications.

As noted above, we find that this procedure complies with the requirement that CCPE maintain direct control over any data matching process and ensure that personally identifiable information is not disclosed to the labor department or other agency that maintains records for the match.

I trust that this responds to your inquiry and thank you for the opportunity to comment on this matter. Please do not hesitate to contact us again should you have any additional questions.

Sincerely,

LeRoy S. Rooker, Director
Family Policy Compliance Office

Dr. Leslie Cochran
President
Youngstown University
One University Plaza
Youngstown, Ohio 44555-0001

FEBRUARY 16, 1999
Complaint No. [REDACTED]
Family Educational Rights
and Privacy Act

Dear Dr. Cochran:

This is to advise you of the finding in the complaint filed with this Office by Mr. [REDACTED]. Mr. [REDACTED] alleged that Youngstown University (University) violated his rights under the Family Educational Rights and Privacy Act (FERPA) when it disclosed his education records in compliance with a subpoena which he believes was issued without giving him sufficient notice. This Office advised you of the allegation by letter October 20, 1998, and by letter dated December 22, 1998, Ms. Sandra L. Denman, General Counsel, responded on behalf of the University.

Specifically, Mr. [REDACTED] alleged that the University wrote him on June 3, 1998, to advise him of the subpoena for his education records and then released the records nine days later on June 12. He stated that the letter was received at his post office on June 8. Mr. [REDACTED] was out of town on June 8 and did not return until June 16. Nonetheless, he argues that had he been in town on the 8th, he still would not have had sufficient time to move for an order to quash the subpoena in the four days that remained prior to the disclosure of his records. He also alleged that the subpoena was not lawfully issued because it was "served by US Mail without a Certificate of Mailing."

In her response, Ms. Denman explained that the subpoena was lawfully issued and properly served. In this regard, she states that the subpoena was issued in accordance with federal Rules of Civil Procedure (Fed. R. Civ. P.) 45 in that Ms. [REDACTED], the attorney issuing the subpoena, represented the defendant in a civil action pending in a Florida federal court and issued the subpoena out of the federal district court having jurisdiction over the University. She further explains that the subpoena was not served by regular mail and thus a "Certificate of Mailing" was not required. She stated that the subpoena was personally served by a process server, who completed the Affidavit of Service certifying that the subpoena had been served.

Ms. Denman explained that the University was served with the subpoena on June 2, 1998, which requested any and all records that the University maintained on Mr. [REDACTED], including but not limited to his transcript, by June 9, 1998. Because the University was required by FERPA to make a reasonable attempt to notify Mr. [REDACTED] of the subpoena and to allow him sufficient time to object, the University advised Ms. [REDACTED], on June 3, that "the documents would not be produced on the date required by the subpoena." Instead, the University advised that provided "Mr. [REDACTED] made no objection ...the documents would be mailed on June 12th." She states that a letter was sent to Mr. [REDACTED] on June 3 notifying him of the subpoena and that "at the end of the day on June 12th, the University had received no objection from Mr. [REDACTED], his attorney, or any other counsel of record ...," so the University mailed the records.

Ms. Denman provided this Office with a copy of the June 3 letter to Mr. [REDACTED] from Ms. Laurie L. Miraglia, Legal Assistant. That letter states the following:

We intend to comply with this subpoena on June 12, 1998 by providing the records requested, to the extent they exist and may be disclosed, to the individual identified in the subpoena. If you wish to object to the release of your records by the University, you or your attorney must file a motion to that effect in the court from which the subpoena was issued. Please send a copy of any such motion to this Office.

FERPA generally requires that prior written consent be provided by an eligible student[1] before education records are disclosed to a third party. 20 U.S.C. § 1232g(b). 34 CFR § 99.30. There are, however, exceptions to the general prohibition on nonconsensual disclosures. One of the exceptions permits the nonconsensual disclosure of education records when the disclosure is made in compliance with a lawfully issued subpoena or court order if the educational agency or institution makes a *reasonable attempt to notify* the parent or eligible student of the order or subpoena in advance of compliance. 20 U.S.C. § 1232g(b)(2)(B); 34 CFR § 99.31(a)(9). This notification is intended to give the parent or eligible student sufficient time to move for an order to quash the subpoena.

From the information that the University has submitted to us, we see no evidence to suggest that the subpoena for Mr. [REDACTED]'s education records was illegally served, as Mr. [REDACTED] alleges. Mr. [REDACTED] claims that:

> ...*the first clue to the fact that the "Subpoena Duces Tecum was flawed" should have been improper service. The document was served by US Mail without a Certificate of Mailing attached according to the [University]. This is no[t] in accordance with federal Rules of Civil Procedure and constitutes an invalid service.* [Emphasis provided.]

The University explained, however, that the subpoena was personally served by a process server and provided an Affidavit of Service reflecting this. Personal service is a proper means of service under Fed. R. Civ. P. 45.

Turning to Mr. [REDACTED]'s allegation that he was not provided sufficient time to move to quash the subpoena, given the totality of the circumstances in this case, we do not find that the University violated FERPA. Mr. [REDACTED] asserts that "the normal time to respond to a discovery demand is 30 days." However, under Fed. R. Civ. P. 45, a subpoena duces tecum sets forth a time for compliance (which can be far less than 30 days) for the person who is, or the entity that is, commanded to produce documents. Further, under Fed. R. Civ. P. 45, there is a maximum of fourteen days after service of the subpoena for the recipient of the subpoena to serve written objections to the subpoena.

FERPA does not define what constitutes sufficient time to allow a parent or eligible student to move to quash a subpoena and this Office has not issued a per se rule on what is a sufficient amount of time in this context. Whether or not a school makes a reasonable attempt to notify a parent or eligible student in advance of compliance with a subpoena is considered on a case-by-case basis. A reasonable attempt to notify can be a letter via the U.S. mail.

Because we consider each complaint on a case-by-case basis, we look at the totality of the circumstances to determine if the time period provided to the eligible student or parent was reasonable. Factors that we will consider include: (a) the time period that an educational agency or institution was given to comply with the subpoena from the date the subpoena was served; (b) whether this time period for compliance was reasonable, considering the urgency of the issuer's need for the subpoenaed documents and the educational agency's obligation under FERPA to attempt to notify the parent or eligible student;[2] (c) whether the educational agency has made a good faith effort under FERPA in its attempt to notify the eligible student or parent of the subpoena in advance of compliance with it;[3] (d) when and how the educational agency attempted to notify the eligible student or parent of the subpoena duces tecum and whether the parent or eligible student was given sufficient time to move for an order to quash the subpoena.

In this case, we note that the University received the subpoena duces tecum in Ohio at 4:00 p.m. on Tuesday, June 2, 1998, and that the subpoena commanded that the University produce documents in Florida within 7 days,

---

[1] When a student reaches the age of 18 or attends an institution of postsecondary education, that student is deemed "eligible" and all rights afforded by FERPA transfer from the parents to the student. 20 U.S.C. section 1232g(d); CFR 99.3 "Eligible student."

[2] If we conclude that the time period for compliance was insufficient, then we will look at the efforts made by an educational agency to object to or to move to quash the subpoena in order to allow for a sufficient time to notify the eligible student or parent.

[3] If an educational agency learns that an eligible student or parent has moved to quash a subpoena duces tecum, the educational agency would not show good faith if it then produced the subpoenaed records without being ordered to do so.

that is, by 10:00 a.m. on Tuesday, June 9, 1998. In consideration of the second factor, from the evidence presented to us, the University determined that the time period that the party issuing the subpoena gave to the University to produce Mr. [REDACTED]'s education records was too limited. As noted above, the University was given less than seven calendar days both to try to notify Mr. [REDACTED] (a Florida resident) of the subpoena for his education records and to comply with the subpoena. The University has not presented any evidence to this Office showing why compliance with the subpoena in the seven day time period was necessary. In looking at the efforts made by the University to object to that time period for compliance, we note that the University requested from the party issuing the subpoena an additional three business days to comply with the subpoena. On June 3, 1998, the University promptly contacted by fax and regular mail the attorney who had issued the subpoena. The University noted that it had received the subpoena and that it had to make a reasonable effort under FERPA to notify Mr. [REDACTED] of the subpoena. The University stated that if Mr. [REDACTED] did not object to the subpoena, then the University would comply with it on Friday, June 12, 1998. Therefore, on June 3, 1998, the University had nine days both to try to notify Mr. [REDACTED] and to comply with the subpoena. Although the University could have requested even more time before complying with the subpoena, the University did secure some additional time for compliance.

The evidence shows that the University made a good faith effort to comply with FERPA. On June 3, 1998, the University promptly notified Mr. [REDACTED] by US mail that it had been served with a subpoena for his education records. The letter informed Mr. [REDACTED] of the University's intention to comply with the subpoena on June 12, 1998. Additionally, it informed Mr. [REDACTED] that he could move to quash the subpoena in the court that had issued it.

Finally, turning to the fourth factor, the purpose for which the University was required by FERPA, before complying with the subpoena, to attempt to notify Mr. [REDACTED] is so that, in the event that the notification occurred, Mr. [REDACTED] would have had sufficient time to move to quash the subpoena. A reasonable attempt to notify Mr. [REDACTED] was made by the University when on June 3 it mailed Mr. [REDACTED] the letter of notification.

In this case, on Wednesday, June 3, 1998—the day after the University had been served with the subpoena—the University promptly attempted to notify Mr. [REDACTED] of the subpoena duces tecum by regular mail and informed Mr. [REDACTED] that the University would comply with the subpoena on Friday, June 12, 1998. Assuming that the U.S. Mail would take two or three days, the University reasonably could have expected Mr. [REDACTED] to receive the notification by Friday, June 5 or Saturday June 6, 1998, Thus, the University reasonably could have expected that, if Mr. [REDACTED] had received the University's notification letter, he would have had six or seven days in which to file an out-of-state motion to quash the subpoena and to notify the University that he had done so. Significantly, Mr. [REDACTED] did not contact the University during this timeframe. Given these factors, we find this amount of time to be sufficient.

In this regard, Mr. [REDACTED] indicates that the University's letter did not arrive until approximately 2:00 p.m. on June 8, 1998. Furthermore, because Mr. [REDACTED] was on travel until Tuesday, June 16, 1998, his mail was held at the local post office. There is no evidence that the University knew that Mr. [REDACTED] was on travel when it mailed the June 3 letter of notification, and the University is not responsible for Mr. [REDACTED]'s not receiving his mail between June 8 and June 16. Furthermore, the University cannot be held responsible for the fact that the US mail did not deliver the letter to his address until June 8, thus leaving him four days to move to quash the subpoena should he have been in town. Weighing all of the above factors, this Office finds that the University did not violate FERPA as Mr. [REDACTED] has alleged.

Although we do not find that the University violated FERPA in this instance, we encourage educational agencies and institutions to strive to provide a sound and sensible time period to allow a parent or eligible student to take action to quash a subpoena, particularly where a subpoena duces tecum has been issued by a court from a state other than the one in which the parent or eligible student resides. Further, while regular mail is a normal means of notification, we also encourage educational agencies and institutions in an effort to notify students before compliance with a subpoena, to consider using certified mail, telephone, or facsimile as appropriate supplemental means of notification.

Finally, we note that the FERPA regulations were amended in November 1996. The final regulations, a copy of which is enclosed, removed § 99.6—the requirement for a student records policy—and revised the annual notification requirements under § 99.7. This means that while schools must annually notify students currently in attendance of their FERPA rights, they are no longer required to maintain a student records policy. Some of the information required to be in the policy will now appear in the notification. In an effort to assist you with ensuring that the University's notification is in compliance with FERPA, we are enclosing a model notification which meets the new requirements of § 99.7. Additionally, we are closing this complaint and will so notify Mr. [REDACTED] by copy of this letter. Thank you for your cooperation with regard to this investigation.

Sincerely,

LeRoy S. Rooker, Director
Family Policy Compliance Office
Enclosure
cc:
Mr. [REDACTED]
Ms. [REDACTED]

Monique C. Shay   MARCH 28, 2006
Deputy General Counsel
Los Angeles County Office of Education
9300 Imperial Highway
Downey, California 90242-2890

Kelly Rozmus Barnes
Assistant General Counsel
Los Angeles Unified School District
Office of the General Counsel—Field Services
333 S. Beaudry Avenue, 20th Floor
Los Angeles, California 90017

Dear Ms. Shay and Ms. Barnes:

This responds to your requests that this Office clarify whether releasing education records in compliance with the proposed "blanket order" issued by Judge Michael Nash on March 1, 2006, would violate the Family Educational Rights and Privacy Act (FERPA), 20 U.S.C. § 1232g. This Office administers FERPA and provides technical advice to ensure compliance with the statutes and regulations, which are codified at 34 CFR Part 99.

We are very concerned that compliance with the proposed order would not meet FERPA requirements for the following reasons. Section 99.31(a)(9) of the FERPA regulations, 34 CFR § 99.31(a)(9), permits an educational agency or institution to disclose personally identifiable information from students' education records, without parental consent, if "[t]he disclosure is to comply with a judicial order or lawfully issued subpoena," but only if:

the agency or institution makes a reasonable effort to notify the parent or eligible student of the order or subpoena in advance of compliance, so that the parent or eligible student may seek protective action....

(Exceptions to the advance notice requirements are not relevant here.) The regulatory language indicates that this exception applies to a court order to disclose education records needed in connection with a *specific legal proceeding* and not a general or "blanket" order governing a whole segment of the population. For example, the agency or institution is required to notify *the* parent or eligible student rather than parents and eligible students generally. Further, this FERPA exception to the consent requirement states clearly that advance notice is required *so that the parent or eligible student may seek protective action*. We believe that the "ability to seek protective action" contemplated in the regulatory language refers to a motion to quash or other routine action afforded by an ongoing legal proceeding and not an unspecified, generalized ability of an individual to seek to initiate a lawsuit to challenge a general court order.

Our comments focus on the "court order" exception in the FERPA regulations because that is the form of the judge's proposed action in this matter. However, we would point out that other FERPA exceptions to the consent requirement may apply to some of the disclosures under consideration in the proposed court order. For example, 34 CFR § 99.31(a)(2) permits an educational agency or institution to disclose education records, without consent, to another school system where the student seeks or intends to enroll (subject to the requirements of § 99.34). Section 99.31(a)(10) permits disclosure of education records without consent "in connection with a health or safety emergency" (under conditions described in § 99.36).

Section 99.31(a)(5) also permits disclosure or reporting of education records without consent to "state and local officials or authorities" authorized by state statute (enacted after November 19, 1974) where the reporting or disclosure concerns "the juvenile justice system and the system's ability to effectively serve, prior to adjudication, the student whose records are released...." 34 CFR § 99.38(a). Officials and authorities to whom records are disclosed under this exception must "certify in writing to the educational agency or institution" that the information will not be disclosed to any other party, except as provided under state law, without the prior written consent of the parent or student.

The proposed order identifies certain provisions in the California Education and Welfare and Institutions Codes that authorize disclosures that may fall within these or other FERPA exceptions to the written consent requirement. Clearly, to the extent applicable in an individual matter, the Los Angeles Unified School District may comply with those particular disclosures identified in the proposed order that fall within a specified exception to the consent requirement (other than the exception for court orders, discussed above) without violating FERPA.

I trust that the above information is helpful in explaining the scope and limitations of FERPA as it relates to your concern.

Sincerely,

LeRoy S. Rooker, Director
Family Policy Compliance Office

UNITED STATES DEPARTMENT OF EDUCATION
OFFICE OF MANAGEMENT

Mr. James B. Kamieniecki   JUN 10 2002
Internal Revenue Service
Criminal Investigation
600 Arch Street
Room 6224
Philadelphia, Pennsylvania 19106

Dear Mr. Kamieniecki:

This is a follow up to your June 3, 2002, fax and telephone inquiries to this Office. Specifically, you asked whether, under the Family Educational Rights and Privacy Act (FERPA), an IRS summons is considered to be a "lawfully issued subpoena" and, as such, if information from a student's education records may be disclosed pursuant to a summons issued by the Internal Revenue Service (IRS) without prior written consent. This Office administers FERPA and is responsible for providing technical assistance to educational agencies and institutions on the requirements of FERPA.

FERPA generally protects a student's privacy interests in "education records." FERPA defines "education records" as "those records, files, documents, and other materials which—

(i) Contain information directly related to a student; and

(ii) Are maintained by an educational agency or institution or by a person acting for such agency or institution.

20 U.S.C. § 1232g(a)(4)(i) and (ii).

FERPA generally requires that prior written consent be provided by the parent of a minor student or by an eligible student before education records are disclosed to a third party. 20 U.S.C. § 1232g(b)(2)(A). 34 CFR § 99.30. When a student turns 18 years of age or attends an institution of postsecondary education, the student becomes an "eligible student" and all FERPA rights transfer to the student. 34 CFR § 99.3.

FERPA provides a number of exceptions to the general prohibition on nonconsensual disclosures. One of the exceptions permits the nonconsensual disclosure of education records when the disclosure is made in compliance with a lawfully issued subpoena or court order if the educational agency or institution makes a reasonable attempt to notify the parent or eligible student of the order or subpoena in advance of compliance. 20 U.S.C. § 1232g(b)(2)(B); 34 CFR § 99.31(a)(9).

Section 99.32 of the FERPA regulations requires that an educational agency or institution maintain a record of all requests for access to and disclosures from education records. However, this Office has determined that such recordation would not be required when the disclosure was made in compliance with a judicial order or subpoena so long as the school was successful in its attempt to notify the parent or eligible student of the order or subpoena in advance of compliance.

Additionally, we have determined that the redisclosure provisions at 34 CFR § 99.33 do not apply to records that are disclosed pursuant to a court order or lawfully issued subpoena. Once an institution determines that the subpoena or judicial order is valid and makes a reasonable attempt to provide advance notice in sufficient time to allow the parent or eligible student to take appropriate action, the institution is not responsible for taking any further action to protect the records against redisclosure, even to the press.

When subpoenas or court orders are issued for certain law enforcement purposes requesting the disclosure of education records, advance notification is not required before compliance. The waiver of the advance notification requirement applies only when the law enforcement subpoena or court order contains language that specifies that the subpoena or court order should not be disclosed. 20 U.S.C. § 1232g(b)(1)(J); 34 CFR § 99.31(a)(9). Please note that the recordation requirements at 34 CFR § 99.32 would not apply when disclosure of education records is made in such instances, even though no prior notification will be made when a court order or subpoena prevents disclosure of the existence of the order or subpoena.

The Department has historically interpreted an IRS summons to constitute a "lawfully issued subpoena" under FERPA. Enclosed for your reference is this Office's letter of July 3, 1997, that also addresses this matter. Accordingly, an educational agency or institution may, in order to comply with an IRS summons, disclose to agents of the IRS personally identifiable information from education records without a parent or student's written consent, as long as the educational agency or institution has followed the FERPA requirements set forth at 34 CFR § 99.31(a)(9) for response to a court order or subpoena.

I trust this is responsive to your inquiry.

Sincerely,

LeRoy S. Rooker, Director
Family Policy Compliance Office

Enclosure

Ms. Diane Layton   AUGUST 7, 1998
Director of Admissions/Registrar
Shelton State Community College
202 Skyland Boulevard
Tuscaloosa, Alabama 35404

Dear Ms. Layton:

This responds to your February 10, 1997, request for guidance concerning the release of information from a student's education records to the local deputy sheriff who presented a contempt order or warrant for the student's arrest. This office administers the Family Educational Rights and Privacy Act (FERPA), 20 U.S.C. section 1232g and 34 CFR Part 99, and is responsible for providing technical assistance on the law to educational agencies and institutions. I apologize for the amount of time it has taken us to respond to your inquiry. Due to the large amount of correspondence this Office receives, we currently have a backlog that we are working to resolve.

You explained in your letter that the deputy sheriff came to your office seeking to locate a student that he wished to arrest on campus. The deputy sheriff presented you with "an order of contempt from a judge's office" for this student and explained that this was the same as "a warrant for the student's arrest." Nonetheless, because student class schedules are not listed as "directory information" at your campus, you declined to release the information and told the deputy sheriff that you would release the information only if he obtained a subpoena. You further advised the deputy sheriff that if he did not want you to notify the student concerning the subpoena that the subpoena should so specify. You asked this Office specifically whether "this order of contempt and ...warrant for an arrest qualify as a judicial order" for purposes of releasing information to the deputy sheriff without the student's consent under FERPA. You also asked about having subpoenas served on students at school.

As you know, FERPA provides that an educational agency or institution may not disclose personally identifiable information contained in an eligible student's education records without the student's prior written consent except to the extent that FERPA authorizes disclosure without consent. See 34 CFR section 99.31. An institution's record of a student's class schedule constitutes an "education record" subject to FERPA rights and protections.

FERPA authorizes the non-consensual disclosure of information that has been designated as "directory information" in accordance with regulatory requirements. See 34 CFR section 99.31(a)(11). "Directory information" includes information such as a student's name, address, telephone listing, etc., and could include a student's class schedule as information that "would not generally be considered harmful or an invasion of privacy if disclosed." See definition of "directory information" at 34 CFR § 99.3. However, if the institution has not complied with the notice requirements for directory information set forth in 34 CFR § 99.37, then it may not disclose this information without the student's prior written consent.

FERPA also allows the non-consensual disclosure of personally identifiable information from education records if the disclosure is to "comply with a judicial order or lawfully issued subpoena." 34 CFR section 99.31(a)(9)(i). However, the institution must first make a reasonable effort to notify the parent or eligible student of the order or subpoena in advance of compliance, so that the parent or eligible student may seek protective action, unless the disclosure is in compliance with—

(A) [A] federal grand jury subpoena and the court has ordered that the existence or the contents of the subpoena or the information furnished in response to the subpoena not be disclosed; or

*(B) **Any other subpoena issued for a law enforcement purpose** and the court or other issuing agency has ordered that the existence of the contents of the subpoena or the information furnished in response to the subpoena not be disclosed.*

34 CFR section 99.31(a)(9)(ii)(emphasis added).

It is our opinion that the order of contempt or arrest warrant from a judge's office, as you described it in your letter, would not meet the requirements for non-consensual disclosure of information from education records as set forth above. It appears from the information you provided that the document was an order of contempt *against the student* that provided for the student's arrest. The exception for non-consensual disclosure to comply with a "judicial order or lawfully issued subpoena" applies only to orders or subpoenas issued *to the institution* for the purpose of obtaining information or records in the institution's possession.

First, the institution is not legally required to comply with a judicial order or subpoena issued to or against another party. More importantly, the privacy protections at the heart of FERPA would be severely undercut if institutions could release personally identifiable information from a student's education records on the basis of a judicial order or subpoena that was issued to any party for any purpose, rather than an order directing the institution to release specified education records. Otherwise, the deputy sheriff could present this contempt order and demand to see the education records of any student who might be useful in locating the student to be arrested. We do not interpret FERPA to authorize this broad type of non-consensual disclosure. Rather, FERPA contemplates a specific decision by the court or issuing authority to seek information from an institution's education records and not a generalized grant of authority to compel the release of desired information wherever it may be found. The requirement that institutions make a "reasonable effort to notify the parent or eligible student of the order or subpoena in advance of compliance" strongly supports the view that Congress intended this provision to apply only to orders directed at the institution for the purpose of obtaining information from education records.

For these reasons, we agree with the advice that you apparently provided to the deputy sheriff regarding what would be needed in order for the institution to release non-directory information without obtaining the student's prior written consent. You are also correct that the institution is relieved of its obligation to notify the eligible student of the order or subpoena in advance of compliance only if the court or other issuing agency has ordered that the existence or contents of the subpoena not be disclosed. See 34 CFR § 99.31(a)(9)(ii)(A) and (B).

Finally, you asked about having subpoenas served on students at school. If a student's class schedule is listed as directory information, it would be permissible to disclose a student's class schedule to the individual serving the subpoena. If not, then the institution would presumably face the same problems in locating a student as occurred in the situation that prompted your inquiry. Note that FERPA does not prohibit the institution from locating a student for a law enforcement officer or anyone else if a staff member happens to know where the student is and, therefore, does not have to release or retrieve the information from an education record, such as the student's recorded class schedule, in order to do so. Otherwise, there is nothing in FERPA that would prevent law enforcement officials or other persons from serving subpoenas on students at school.

I trust that this responds to your concerns and appreciate the opportunity to assist you with these matters. Please do not hesitate to call upon this office again in the future.

Sincerely,

LeRoy S. Rooker, Director
Family Policy Compliance Office

27 **Family Policy Compliance Office Guidelines to the Educational Community:
Disclosure of Education Records Concerning Registered Sex Offenders**

Appendix E   FPCO LETTERS   [255]

This guidance concerns an amendment to the Family Educational Rights and Privacy Act of 1974 (FERPA), 20 U.S.C. § 1232g, enacted by the Campus Sex Crimes Prevention Act (CSPCA), which is § 1601 of the Victims of Trafficking and Violence Protection Act of 2000 (Pub. L. 106-386). Subsection (d) of the CSCPA amended FERPA to ensure that educational institutions may disclose information concerning sex offenders that they receive under state sex offender registration and community notification programs. See 20 U.S.C. § 1232g(b)(7). This amendment took effect on its enactment date of October 28, 2000.[1] The CSCPA amendment to FERPA directed the Secretary of Education "to take appropriate steps to notify educational institutions" that they may disclose information concerning registered sex offenders provided to them under state registration and community notification programs. See 20 U.S.C. § 1232g(b)(7)(B). In order to notify educational institutions of this amendment to FERPA, the Secretary of Education has issued this guidance.[2]

A federal law, the Jacob Wetterling Crimes Against Children and Sexually Violent Offenders Registration Act (the "Wetterling Act"), provides minimum national standards for state sex offender registration and community notification programs. To comply with the Wetterling Act's standards, States must establish programs that require current address registration by residents of the state who have been convicted of sexually violent offenses or offenses involving sexual abuse or exploitation of minors, as described in the Act. The Wetterling Act's standards also require States to accept registration information from non-resident offenders who have entered the state to work or attend school. The Wetterling Act provides generally that States must release relevant information concerning persons required to register as necessary to protect the public. See 42 U.S.C. § 14071 (Wetterling Act provisions); 64 Fed. Reg. 572 (Jan. 5, 1999)(Attorney General's guidelines for the Wetterling Act).

The CSCPA supplemented the Wetterling Act's general standards for sex offender registration and community notification programs by enacting provisions which are more specifically designed to ensure that the members of campus communities have information available concerning the presence of registered sex offenders. In part, this included an amendment to the Wetterling Act which requires States to obtain information concerning registered sex offenders' enrollment or employment at institutions of higher education, and to make this information available promptly to a campus police department or other appropriate law enforcement agency having jurisdiction where the institution is located. See 42 U.S.C. § 14071(j)(Wetterling Act provisions added by the CSCPA amendment); 67 Fed. Reg. 65598 (October 25, 2002)(Attorney General's guidelines for the amendment).

The CSCPA also enacted two amendments to federal education laws. One of these is an amendment to the Higher Education Act of 1965 which requires institutions of higher education to advise the campus community where it can obtain the information about registered sex offenders provided by the state (pursuant to 42 U.S.C. § 14071(j)), such as the campus law enforcement office, a local law enforcement agency, or a computer network address. See 20 U.S.C. § 1092(f)(1)(I). The other is the FERPA amendment, which makes it clear that FERPA does not prevent educational institutions from disclosing such information:

> *(A) Nothing in this section may be construed to prohibit an educational institution from disclosing information provided to the institution under section 170101 of the Violent Crime Control and Law Enforcement Act of 1994 (42 U.S.C. 14071) concerning registered sex offenders who are required to register under such section.*

---

[1] However, the CSCPA's requirements that (1) registered sex offenders must provide notice, as required under state law, of each institution of higher education where they are employed or enrolled; (2) States must make this information available to a law enforcement agency where the institution of higher education is located; and (3) institutions of higher education must advise the campus community where the information on registered sex offenders can be obtained, do not become effective until October 28, 2002. See Campus Sex Crimes Prevention Act, Pub. L. No. 106-386, § 1601(b) and (c), 114 Stat. 1537, 1538 (to be codified at 20 U.S.C. § 1092(f)(1) and 42 USC § 14071 (j)).

[2] The Secretary of Education also will soon issue a proposed amendment to the FERPA regulations at 34 C.F.R § 99.31 to reflect that prior written consent is not required for these disclosures.

(B) The Secretary shall take appropriate steps to notify educational institutions that disclosure of information described in subparagraph (A) is permitted.

20 U.S.C. § 1232g(b)(7)

The legislative history to the FERPA amendment also confirms that FERPA does not prevent educational institutions from disclosing information about registered sex offenders:

In order to ensure that the information [about registered sex offenders] is readily accessible to the campus community, the Campus Sex Crimes Prevention Act requires colleges and universities to provide the campus community with clear guidance as to where this information can be found, and clarifies that federal laws governing the privacy of educational records do not prevent campus security agencies or other administrators from disclosing such information.

146 Cong. Rec. S10216 (Oct. 11, 2000)(remarks of Senator Kyl, sponsor of the CSCPA); see H. Conf. Rep. No. 939, 106th Cong., 2d Sess. 110 (2000)(conference committee report for the CSCPA)(the CSCPA "[a]mends the Family Educational Rights and Privacy Act of 1974 to clarify that nothing in that Act may be construed to prohibit an educational institution from disclosing information provided to the institution concerning registered sex offenders")

Thus, nothing in FERPA prevents an educational institution from disclosing information provided to the institution under the Wetterling Act concerning registered sex offenders, including personally identifiable, non-directory information from education records that is disclosed without prior written consent or other consent from the person. The authority of educational institutions to make such disclosures extends both to information about registered sex offenders made available by a state in carrying out the specific requirements of the CSCPA (42 U.S.C. 14071(j)), and information about registered sex offenders that may otherwise become available to educational institutions through the operation of state sex offender registration and community notification programs.[3]

While the CSCPA amendments to the Wetterling Act and the Higher Education Act affect only institutions of higher education, both institutions of higher education and other educational institutions are covered by the CSCPA amendment to FERPA. The Family Policy Compliance Office, the Office in the Department that administers FERPA, broadly interprets the term "educational institution" in the amendment to FERPA to be consistent with the use of the term in the Wetterling Act. The Wetterling Act defines the term "student" as "a person who is enrolled on a full-time or part-time basis, in any public or private educational institution, including any secondary school, trade, or professional institution, or institution of higher education." 42 U.S.C. § 14071(a)(3)(G). Thus, because the Wetterling Act broadly applies to students enrolled in any educational institution, the CSCPA amendment to FERPA similarly should be interpreted so as not to prohibit disclosures by an educational institution to which FERPA applies. Further, the Department of Education will not take federal funds away from any local educational agency (LEA) on account of the LEA's policy or practice of releasing information that a state (or any agency authorized by a state) provides to the LEA under the Wetterling Act on a registered sex offender enrolled in an educational institution within the LEA.

In sum, this guidance clarifies that nothing in FERPA prevents educational institutions from disclosing information concerning registered sex offenders provided under the Wetterling Act, including information made available under the CSCPA amendment to that Act and information otherwise made available under state sex offender registration and community notification programs.

This guidance is available on the Family Policy Compliance Office's Web site at: www2.ed.gov/policy/gen/guid/fpco/hottopics/ht10-24-02.html. School officials with questions about FERPA in general, or this issue in particular, may send inquiries to: ferpa@ed.gov.

---

[3] Readers are advised that the United States Supreme Court has granted certiorari to review the constitutionality of sex offender registration and community notification laws in two States. Specifically, the Supreme Court granted certiorari on the question whether Alaska's sex offender registration and community notification law imposes punishment in violation of the Constitution's prohibition of ex post facto legislation. See Glenn G. Godfrey, et. al. v. John Doe I, et al., No. 01-729 (Feb. 19, 2002). The Supreme Court also granted certiorari on whether the Due Process Clause of the Fourteenth Amendment prevents the state of Connecticut from listing convicted sex offenders in a publicly disseminated registry without first affording such offenders individualized hearings on their current dangerousness. See Connecticut Department of Public Safety, et al. v. John Doe, et al., No. 01-1231 (May 20, 2002).

UNITED STATES DEPARTMENT OF EDUCATION
OFFICE OF INNOVATION AND IMPROVEMENT

Ms. Amanda F. Miller   AUG 11 2006
Legal Counsel
Office of Legal Counsel
University of Oklahoma
660 Parrington Oval, Suite 213
Norman, Oklahoma 73019

Dear Ms. Miller:

This is in response to your August 3 and August 7, 2006, inquiries to this Office in which you request guidance on the applicability of the Family Educational Rights and Privacy Act (FERPA) to the disclosure of certain records. You explain that the University of Oklahoma (University) has received numerous requests for all of the investigative material relating to an investigation of certain student athletes in the football program regarding potential violations of National Collegiate Athletic Association (NCAA) rules. You state that you are trying to determine whether, after redacting the student athletes' names from the investigative material, these documents could then be publicly released without violating FERPA. You state that the University is concerned that, due to the small number of student athletes involved, the records would still be easily traceable and identifiable to a particular student athlete, even with redaction of their names.

You explain that the University has received requests for the following information:

☒ Any and all correspondence between the University of Oklahoma [OU] and the NCAA and/or the Big 12 regarding violations or potential violations of NCAA rules by the football program, by OU football coaches and/or football staff, by student athletes in the football program, or by boosters; correspondence between OU and Norman Area automobile dealers regarding violations or potential violations of NCAA rules and correspondence between the OU President's Office and the OU athletic department;

☒ All documents and information relating to the internal university investigation that resulted in the dismissal of Oklahoma football players on August 2, 2006;

☒ A copy of the investigation report involvement the Oklahoma football team and the car dealership;

☒ University Athletic Compliance Office's records pertaining to the student athletes and their employment by a metro area car dealership.

You ask: "If the above documents contain information identifiable to a particular student, (1) would the above records maintained by the University be considered 'education records' within the meaning of FERPA; and (2) If so, may the University provide any responsive documents which, even after the students' names and other personal identifiers have been removed, may still be easily traceable to the students, even if the majority of the public is aware of the students' identities?"

Any educational agency or institution subject to FERPA may not have a policy or practice of disclosing education records, or non-directory personally identifiable information from education records, without the prior written consent of the parent or eligible student[1] except as provided by law. 20 U.S.C. § 1232g(b); 34 CFR Subpart D. "Education records" are defined as "those records, files, documents, and other materials which—

---

[1] "Eligible student" means a student who has reached 18 years of age or is attending an institution of postsecondary institution[sic] at any age. See 34 CFR § 99.3 "Eligible student." The rights under FERPA belong to the parents of students under the age of 18 at the elementary/secondary level and transfer to the student when he or she becomes an "eligible student."

(i) Contain information directly related to a student; and

(ii) Are maintained by an educational agency or institution or by a person acting for such agency or institution.

20 U.S.C § 1232g(a)(4)(i) and (ii); See also 34 CFR § 99.3 "Education records"

The information you ask about—correspondence between the University and the NCAA and/or other institutions, documents related to the internal investigation and other investigative reports, and records regarding student athletics employed at a car dealership—would be considered "education records" because these records are directly related to a student and maintained by the University.

FERPA also permits an educational agency or institution to disclose education records without meeting the written consent requirements in § 99.30 if it has removed all "personally identifiable information" from the records. "Personally identifiable information" includes, but is not limited to, the following information:

(a) The student's name;

(b) The name of the student's parent or other family member;

(c) The address of the student or the student's family;

(d) A personal identifier, such as the student's social security number or student number;

(e) A list of personal characteristics that would make the student's identity easily traceable; or

(f) Other information that would make the student's identity easily traceable.

34 CFR § 99.3 "Personally identifiable information" (Emphasis added)

Thus, FERPA-protected information may not be released in any form that would make the student's identity easily traceable (unless there is a specific exception to the written consent requirement).

Occasionally, a student's identity may be "easily traceable." Even after removal or redaction of nominally identifying information from student-level records. This may be the case, for example, with a highly publicized disciplinary action, or one that involved a well-known student, where the student could be easily identified in the community even after the record has been "scrubbed" of identifying data. In these circumstances, FERPA does not allow disclosure of the education record in any form without consent because the irreducible presence of "personal characteristics" or "other information" make[sic] the student's identity "easily traceable."

A student's identity may also be "easily traceable" in the release of aggregated or statistical information derived from education records. See, for example, our September 25, 2003, letter to the Board of Regents of the University System of Georgia available at www.ed.gov/policy/gen/guid/fpco/ferpa/library/georgialtr.html. The Board had asked about a newspaper's request for sensitive data about students in aggregate form categorized into specific groupings that the Board believed could be used to identify students, especially through multiple releases. This Office advised the Board that in these circumstances we had insufficient information to determine whether the disclosures would violate FERPA, that the institution itself had to make the determination whether a student's identity would be easily traceable and, if so, they could not disclose the information in that form. This decision was based on our recognition that at least at the outset, agencies and institutions themselves are clearly in the best position to analyze and evaluate this requirement based on their own data, and under FERPA the burden is on the agency or institution not to release either aggregated or de-identified ("redacted") student level data if it believes that personal identity is easily traceable based on the specific circumstances under consideration. We also recognized in the letter to the Board of Regents of the University System of Georgia that FERPA prohibits the disclosure of personally identifiable information from education records without consent even where an individual's personal identity is revealed through a series or combination of requests that are available to those in possession of the data.

As previously noted, redaction of nominally identifying information (student's name, social security number, and the exact date and time of the incident) may not be sufficient to prevent a student's identify from being easily traceable with respect to a highly publicized incident, or with respect to a series of requests for information that make a student's identity easy to trace due to the disclosure of related information.

In sum, where a disclosure of personally identifiable information in education records does not fall within an exception to the prior written consent rule, we believe that the University itself is in the best position to determine, at least at the outset, what information must be removed from education records in order to ensure that a student's identity is not easily traceable. If, because of other records that have been released or the notoriety of certain events, the redaction of names, identification numbers, and dates and times of incidents is not sufficient to prevent the identification of a student involved in an investigation or proceeding, then FERPA prohibits the University from having a policy or practice of releasing the information as such. The University either must remove or redact all of the information in the education record that would make a student's identity easily traceable or refuse to release the requested education record at all.

Thank you for contacting us regarding this matter. I trust this guidance will assist you in complying with FERPA in this regard.

Sincerely,

LeRoy S. Rooker, Director
Family Policy Compliance Office

29 Letter to Kennesaw State University

Re: State Open Records Request (GA)/ Disciplinary Records

Ms. Diane Walker   SEPTEMBER 27, 2002
Director
Judiciary Programs
Kennesaw State University
1000 Chastain Road MB # 0506
Kennesaw, Georgia 30144-5591

Dear Ms. Walker:

This is in response to your email of September 26, 2002, in which Kennesaw State University (University) seeks clarification on certain provisions of the Family Educational Rights and Privacy Act (FERPA). 20 U.S.C. § 1232g; 34 CFR Part 99. You ask whether certain education records can be disclosed pursuant to a state open records request. Specifically, you state that you have received a media request under the Georgia open records act for disciplinary records relating to incidents that occurred in student housing. You state that the campus law enforcement unit has incident reports, which are open to the public, and that any information relating to disciplinary proceedings, such as sanctions, could be compared to the law enforcement unit records and, thus, reveal the identity of individual students.

FERPA protects eligible students'[1] privacy interests in "education records," which are defined as "those records, files, documents, and other materials which –

(i) contain information directly related to a student; and

(ii) are maintained by an educational agency or institution or by a person acting for such agency or institution.

20 U.S.C. § 1232g(a)(4)(i) and (ii); See also 34 CFR § 99.3 "Education records"

Excluded from the definition of "education records" are records of the law enforcement unit of an educational agency or institution, but only under the conditions described in § 99.8 of the FERPA regulations. Records on a student regarding violations of housing or other regulations maintained by school officials outside of the University's law enforcement unit are protected as "education records" under FERPA because the records are "directly related" to students and maintained by the institution and do not fall under the law enforcement unit exemption to "education records." See 20 U.S.C. § 1232g(a)(4)(i) and (ii) and 34 CFR § 99.3 "Education records."

FERPA prohibits a recipient of U.S. Department of Education funds from having a policy or practice of non-consensually disclosing personally identifiable information derived from education records, except in certain statutorily specified circumstances. 20 U.S.C. § 1232g(b); 34 CFR § 99.31. While there are specific statutory exceptions to the prohibition that personally identifiable information from education records may not be released without consent, the FERPA statute does not include a *general* exception for the public disclosure of student disciplinary records. Accordingly, these records may not be disclosed without the prior written consent of the student or students about whom the records relate. 20 U.S.C. § 1232g(b)(1) and (d). See also 34 CFR § 99.30.

In 1998, Congress amended FERPA to, in relevant part, provide the following:

(B) Nothing in this section shall be construed to prohibit an institution of postsecondary education from disclosing the final results of any disciplinary proceeding conducted by such institution against a student who is an alleged perpetrator of any crime of violence (as that term is defined in section 16 of title 18, United States

---

[1] "Eligible student" means a student who has reached 18 years of age or is attending an institution of postsecondary institution at any age. See 34 CFR § 99.3 "Eligible student." The rights under FERPA belong to the parents of students under the age of 18 at the elementary/secondary level and transfer to the student when he or she becomes an "eligible student."

Code), or a nonforcible sex offense, if the institution determines as a result of that disciplinary proceeding that the student committed a violation of the institution's rules or policies with respect to such crime of offense.
(C) For the purpose of this paragraph, the final results of any disciplinary proceeding—
   (i) shall include only the name of the student, the violation committed, and any sanction imposed by the institution on that student; and
   (ii) may include the name of any other student, such as a victim or witness, only with the written consent of that other student.

Pub. L. No. 105-244, § 951, 105th Cong., 2nd Sess. (October 7, 1998)

Under this amendment, postsecondary institutions may—but are not required by FERPA to—disclose the final results of a disciplinary proceeding in which the institution determines that the student perpetrator committed a crime of violence or non-forcible sex offense. On July 6, 2000, the Department published in the *Federal Register* regulations implementing this change to FERPA. See specifically § 99.31(a)(14) and § 99.39. Enclosed is a copy of those regulations. You did not indicate whether the University believes that the violations constitute offenses that would, if proven, constitute a crime of violence. If the University believes that the offense would rise to the level of a crime of violence, then FERPA would not prohibit the disclosure of the final results of the disciplinary proceeding. (*See* the definition of "final results" under § 99.39.)

With regard to the disclosure of a disciplinary record (assuming that the request is *not* within the purview of the amendments to FERPA involving crimes of violence), the school may not disclose the information, even in redacted form, if the information could be traced to the individual student. "Personally identifiable information" includes, but is not limited to, the following information:
   (a) the student's name;
   (b) the name of the student's parent or other family member;
   (c) the address of the student or the student's family;
   (d) a personal identifier, such as the student's social security number or student number;
   (e) a list of personal characteristics that would make the student's identity easily traceable; or
   *(f) other information that would make the student's identity **easily traceable**.*

34 CFR § 99.3, "Personally identifiable information" (emphasis added)

FERPA does not specifically define the term "easily traceable," and whether or not the release of information might be considered easily traceable must be analyzed on a case-by-case basis. If a school reasonably believes that release of information would make the student's identity "easily traceable," then the school should not disclose the information to the requesting party. Where a request asks for a specific student's disciplinary records, then it is reasonable to conclude that the student's identity would be obvious to the requester. However, if the institution of postsecondary education receives a general request for disciplinary records, as long as personally identifiable information (including information that is easily traceable to a student) is redacted, such a release would not be prohibited by FERPA.

Your email indicated that the editor of the school newspaper indicated that a decision of the Georgia Supreme Court supported his position. We are aware that in 1993, the Supreme Court of Georgia concluded that records of disciplinary proceedings of the University of Georgia were "not the type" of records FERPA was "intended to protect." *Red & Black Publishing Company* v. *Board of Regents*, 427 S.E. 2d 257, 261 (Ga. 1993). We believe that decision is inapposite for several reasons.

---

[1] Specifically, the requested records were those of the "Organization Court," which "hears and adjudicates cases involving alleged University rule and regulation violation on the part of fraternities and sororities." 427 S.E. 2d at 260.

On its face, the records sought in that case pertained to organizations, not individual students.[2] Moreover, the United States Supreme Court recently decided the case of *Gonzaga University v. Doe*, No. 01-679 (June 20, 2002). There, the disclosure at issue pertained to allegations of "sexual misconduct." While the Court ultimately held that FERPA's nondisclosure provisions create no rights enforceable under 42 U.S.C. § 1983, there was no dispute that records regarding student misconduct are subject to FERPA. Since disciplinary records pertain to student misconduct, the United States Supreme Court has, in effect, overturned the decision in *Red & Black*. Further, as noted above, *Red & Black,* which was decided in 1993, was overtaken by Congressional action in 1998 through the enactment of section 951 of Pub.L. No. 105-244. Finally, we note that on June 27, 2002, the United States Court of Appeals for the Sixth Circuit unanimously affirmed a lower court's ruling that university disciplinary records are "education records" under FERPA and that disclosing such records without students' consent constitutes a violation of FERPA. *United States of America* v. *Miami University; Ohio State University, et al.*, 294 F.3d 797 (6th Cir. 2002). Although we realize that Georgia is not in the Sixth Circuit, this decision is consistent with the Supreme Court's decision in *Gonzaga* and would be highly persuasive to the federal courts in Georgia.

I trust that this explains the scope and limitations of FERPA as it pertains to your inquiry. Should you have any additional questions, please do not hesitate to contact this Office again.

Sincerely,

LeRoy S. Rooker, Director
Family Policy Compliance Office

Enclosure

Ms. Corlis P. Cummings   SEPTEMBER 25, 2003
Senior Vice Chancellor for Support Services
Board of Regents of the University System of Georgia
270 Washington Street, S.W.
Atlanta, Georgia 30334

Dear Ms. Cummings:

This responds to your letter of September 19, 2003, in which you asked for an official opinion whether the Family Educational Rights and Privacy Act (FERPA), 20 U.S.C. § 1232g, permits the Board of Regents of the University System of Georgia (Board) to release certain information from education records to the *Atlanta Journal-Constitution*. You asked for expedited consideration because the newspaper submitted its request pursuant to Georgia's Open Records Act. This Office administers FERPA and provides technical assistance to educational agencies and institutions to ensure compliance with the statute and regulations codified at 34 CFR Part 99.

Inquiry: The Journal-Constitution asked the Board to provide the following information for every student who completed an application for federal student aid for the past two academic years: Georgia HOPE scholarship eligibility, Pell Grant eligibility, Pell Grant amount, and federal expected family contribution. The information must also be categorized by the student's secondary institution, college or university, and county of residence. The newspaper has not asked for the student's name, social security number, or other personally identifiable information and has agreed to allow the Board to follow its policy of not releasing information in cohorts of 10 or fewer students. However, the newspaper insists that the information must be released in student-level rather than aggregated form.

The Board believes that FERPA precludes it from releasing the information in the format requested because a recipient would be able to identify individual students and their families with relative ease by cross-referencing information provided in the listings by secondary school, college, and county. The Board asks whether it may provide the information as requested by the newspaper consistent with its obligations under FERPA.

Discussion: An educational agency or institution subject to FERPA may not have a policy or practice of disclosing education records, or non-directory, personally identifiable information from education records, without the written consent of the parent or eligible student, except as provided by law. 20 U.S.C. §1232g(b); 34 CFR Subpart D. "Education records" are defined as

records that are directly related to a student, and maintained by an educational agency or institution or by a party acting for the agency or institution. 34 CFR § 99.3 ("Education records"). The information requested by the newspaper (each student's Georgia HOPE scholarship eligibility, Pell Grant eligibility, Pell Grant amount, and federal expected family contribution) clearly falls within the definition of "education records" under FERPA.[1]

Under the FERPA regulations, "disclosure" means "to permit access to or the release, transfer, or other communication of *personally identifiable information* contained in education records to any party, by any means, including oral, written, or electronic means." 34 CFR § 99.3 ("Disclosure")(emphasis added). The regulations define "personally identifiable information" so that it includes, but is not limited to:

(a) The student's name;

(b) The name of the student's parent or other family member;

(c) The address of the student or student's family;

---

[1] Information submitted by an individual who is applying to an educational agency or institution and who does not become a student at that educational agency or institution is not protected by FERPA. However, other laws, such as § 501 of the Gramm-Leach-Bliley Act (Public Law 106-102, November 12, 1999), might apply to the financial information contained in these applications. See 67 Fed. Reg. 36484 (May 23, 2002).

(d) A personal identifier, such as the student's social security number or student number;

*(e) A list of personal characteristics that would make the student's identity **easily traceable**; or*

*(f) Other information that would make the student's identity **easily traceable**.*

34 CFR § 99.3 ("Personally identifiable information")(emphases added)

That is, FERPA-protected information may not be released in any form that would make the student's identity easily traceable. *E.g.*, September 27, 2002, letter from this Office to Kennesaw State University at page 2-3. Conversely, student-level information from education records may be disclosed, without consent, if "personally identifiable information," as defined above, has been removed. This has been referred to as deidentified or anonymous data.

In the case of standardized tests, this requirement can usually be met by removing the student's name, address, identification numbers, and "other information that would make the student's identity easily traceable," such as the alphabetical or other testing order. Courts have affirmed these procedures in cases such as *Bowie v. Evanston Community Consolidated School District #65*, 522 N.E.2d 669 (Ill. App. I Dist. 1988), *aff'd*, 538 N.E.2d 557 (Ill. 1989) and *Kryston v. Board of Education, East Ramapo Central School District*, 77 A.D.2d 896, 430 N.Y.S.2d 688 (App.Div. 2nd Dept. 1980). Similarly, in a case involving disciplinary records, Miami University redacted not only the student's name and student ID number but also the exact date and time of the alleged incident. The Court of Appeals later observed that these court-imposed redactions rendered the disclosure compliant with FERPA requirements. *State ex rel. Miami Student v. Miami University,* 680 N.E.2d 956, 959 (Ohio 1997), cited in *United States v. Miami University, Ohio State University*, 294 F.3d 797, (6th Cir. 2002).

Occasionally a student's identity may be "easily traceable" even after removal of nominally identifying data. This may be the case, for example, with a highly publicized disciplinary action, or one that involved a well-known student, where the student would be identified in the community even after the record has been "scrubbed" of identifying data. In these circumstances, FERPA does not allow disclosure of the record in any form without consent because the irreducible presence of "personal characteristics" or "other information" make[s] the student's identity "easily traceable."

These principles apply equally to the disclosure of aggregated information. That is, the FERPA prohibition on disclosure of "personally identifiable information" allows agencies and institutions to aggregate data and disclose statistical information from education records, without consent, so long as the student's identity is not "easily traceable." Just as the removal of names and identification numbers is not always adequate to protect against personal identification with student level data, there are circumstances, such as those described in your letter, in which the aggregation of anonymous or de-identified data into various categories could render personal identity "easily traceable." *In those cases, FERPA prohibits disclosure of the information without consent.* This is true whether personal identity is revealed through a single request or through a series or combination of requests that are available to those in possession of the data.

Because of the wide variety of data compilations, configurations, search requests, and other factors related to the disclosure of anonymous data, it is neither possible nor desirable for this Office to take a categorical approach regarding the minimum size of cohorts or other restrictions applicable to the release of aggregated or student-level information necessary to avoid personal identification of an individual. However, any agency or institution that releases aggregated or anonymous student-level information from education records must first review the details of the resulting datasets to ensure that personal identity is not easily traceable. Clearly, agencies and institutions themselves are in the best position to analyze and evaluate these requirements based on their own data, and under FERPA the burden is on the agency or institution not to release aggregated or de-identified student level data if it believes that personal identity is easily traceable based on the specific circumstances under consideration. Indeed, this Office will initiate an investigation of any complaint that provides specific allegations of fact giving reasonable cause to believe that FERPA is violated by the release of aggregated or deidentified student level information.

In summary, based on the information you provided, we are unable to conclude that the disclosure in question would not render a student's identity easily traceable and, therefore, would not violate FERPA. Further, under FERPA, the Board should not disclose anonymous or de-identified data in aggregation that it believes could make a student's identity easily traceable.

Sincerely,

LeRoy S. Rooker, Director
Family Policy Compliance Office

UNITED STATES DEPARTMENT OF EDUCATION
OFFICE OF INNOVATION AND IMPROVEMENT

Dr. Thomas C. Henry   DEC 22 2006
Chancellor
Mohave Community College
1971 Jagerson Avenue
Kingman, Arizona 86409

Dear Dr Henry:

This responds to your letter of August 1, 2006, in which you reported possible violation of the Family Educational Rights and Privacy Act (FERPA) by a school official of Mohave Community College (College). This Office investigates complaints and violations of FERPA and provides technical assistance to ensure compliance with the statute and regulations, which are codified at 20 U.S.C. § 1232g and 34 CFR part 99 respectively.

You stated that on July 14, 2006, a former dental hygiene student (Student) issued a letter to the College's Board of Governors and also disseminated her letter to some media outlets along with other entities and individuals. The College's directory of dental hygiene (Director) prepared a response to the Student's letter on July 26, 2006, for the Board of Governors. You indicated that the Director's response letter, which contained some student information likely to be protected under FERPA, was also sent to the additional original recipients listed in the Student's letter. You asked what other steps, including remedial action, should the College take at this point.

An eligible student must provide a signed and dated written consent in accordance with § 99.30 of the FERPA regulations before a postsecondary institution, such as the College, discloses any personally identifiable information from the student's education records. Exceptions to this requirement are set forth in § 99.31(a). One of the exceptions permits an institution to disclose properly designated "directory information," such as the student's name, address, dates of attendance, etc., provided that the student has not opted out of directory information disclosures. See 34 CFR §§ 99.31(a)(II) and 99.37. There is no exception to the consent requirement that permits an institution to disclose anything other than directory information from a student's education records in response to charges against the institution made by that student to the media. In those circumstances, if the student refuses to provide written consent, the institution should notify the media that it is unable to respond fully to the allegations because of the privacy protections afforded to the student under FERPA.

You indicated that the Director's response contained "some student information that we believe is likely protected by FERPA." The term "education records" is defined as records that are:

1. Directly related to a student and maintained: and

2. Maintained by an educational agency or institution or by a party acting for the agency or institution.

34 CFR § 99.3

This generally includes all written information maintained [by] an institution, including a school official or other party acting for the institution, that personally indentifies the student.

The College violated FERPA if the Director's letter to the media and other parties contained personally identifiable information from the Student's education records. If the Student filed a timely complaint with this Office, we would initiate an investigation under § 99.65 of the regulations and ask the College to submit additional information about the matter, including a specific description of the information about the Student that the Director disclosed and the parties who received the Director's letter. If we found the College in violation of FERPA, we would seek voluntary compliance, as required under § 99.66(c).

This Office does not have sufficient information at this time to make a definitive finding that the College violated FERPA when the Director issued his letter. In order to ensure that the College remains in compliance, however, we ask you to take the steps that we would require were we to make a finding that the Director's conduct violated FERPA. In particular, please provide this Office within four weeks of your receipt of this letter written documentation that all appropriate school officials, including the Director, have been notified that school officials may not disclose personally identifiable information from a student's education records, without consent, to the media or other members of the public in response to charges against the institution made by that student. School officials should also be advised that they may not disclose to the media the fact that a student has refused to provide consent for the disclosure.

I trust that the above information is helpful in explaining the scope and limitations of FERPA as it relates to your concern.

Sincerely,

LeRoy S. Rooker, Director
Family Policy Compliance Office

32 Letter to Towson State University ★

Re: Disclosure to the Media/ Implied Consent

UNITED STATES DEPARTMENT OF EDUCATION
OFFICE OF MANAGEMENT

Dr. Hoke Smith
President
Towson State University
Towson, Maryland 21204-7097

JUN 22 1998
Complaint No. [REDACTED]
Family Educational Rights
and Privacy Act

Dear Dr. Smith:

This is to advise you of the partial finding in the complaint filed with this Office by Ms. [REDACTED] under the Family Educational Rights and Privacy Act (FERPA). Ms. [REDACTED] alleged that Towson State University (University) violated her rights under FERPA when it disclosed information from her education records to the *Baltimore Sun* and when it denied her access to certain of her education records. By letter dated February 18, 1998, this Office advised you of the allegations and by letter dated March 27, 1998, Mr. Michael A. Anselmi, University Counsel, responded on behalf of the University. Each allegation is discussed separately below.

Allegation 1

Ms. [REDACTED] alleged in her December 20, 1997, letter to this Office that the University violated her rights under FERPA when Mr. Anselmi disclosed without her consent her education records and medical records to Ms. Suzanne Loudermilk, a reporter for the *Baltimore Sun*. She stated that the article came out on or before Thanksgiving 1997 and that she learned of it on December 1, 1997. She explained that Mr. Anselmi provided Ms. Loudermilk with a consent for her to sign prior to disclosing information from her education records, but that upon seeing the consent she "had second thoughts about doing the article at all." She stated that when she next spoke with Ms. Loudermilk, she was advised that Mr. Anselmi had already disclosed information from her education records based on "the recent Family Policy Compliance Office ruling that allowed Johns Hopkins University to release information to a third party without written consent."

Mr. Anselmi responded to this allegation by asserting that the University had not violated FERPA as alleged when it disclosed information from Ms. [REDACTED]'s education records to the *Baltimore Sun* because Ms. [REDACTED] "impliedly waived her right to consent." Mr. Anselmi cited in support of his claim February 19, 1997, letter of finding issued by this Office in which we ruled that Johns Hopkins University has not violated FERPA when it disclosed information from a student's education records to the student's employer, the National Cancer Institute (NCI). Mr. Anselmi stated the following:

Although FERPA regulations do not address waiver, the Department has ruled that students can impliedly waive the right to consent to disclosure. Specifically, in the November 21, 1996 Final Rule, the Department ruled that a student who sues a school impliedly waives the right to consent to disclosure before the school releases information in its defense. *See* 61 FR 59292, 59294. Thereafter, by letter of ruling of February 19, 1997 ...the Department extended the reach of the implied waiver rule and said that universities may release information from student records, without consent where (1) "a student has taken an adversarial position against an institution"; (2) "made written allegations of wrongdoing against the institution"; and (3) "shared this information with third parties". As more particularly shown below, [REDACTED] has a long history of filing charges of wrongdoing against the University. This history, coupled with the seriousness of the charges she made to the *Baltimore Sun*, fully supports a finding of waiver in this matter.

Mr. Anselmi further stated that Ms. [REDACTED] had previously sought to involve third parties in her dispute with the University by contacting them in writing about her concerns. He provided a list of those parties, which includes accrediting associations, state legislators, the Maryland Higher Education Commission, the Attorney General of Maryland, the Chancellor of the University of Maryland System, the Maryland State Treasurer, and the University's newspaper. He asserts that Ms. [REDACTED]'s history in contacting third parties with "convenient and purposeful disclosure of her educational records ...clearly weakens her claim of confidentiality in these records." He further stated the following:

*Apparently, as a last resort, [REDACTED] wrote the **Baltimore Sun** in late 1997 ...Following review of the charges, Suzanne Loudermilk, a **Sun** reporter, telephoned the University's attorney in late November 1997 asking for information about [REDACTED's] charges. Ms. Loudermilk said [REDACTED] provided her a number of documents to support her claims ...During the phone call, Ms. Loudermilk verbally summarized [REDACTED's] allegations ...Ms. Loudermilk informed the University that she would report on these charges and she requested a timely University response. Ms. Loudermilk said she spoke to [REDACTED] and that [REDACTED] would consent to the University's reference to educational records in its response to the charges. By letter dated November 20, 1997 ...the University provided Ms. Loudermilk the written consent form for [REDACTED] to sign. Shortly thereafter, Ms. Loudermilk informed the University that [REDACTED] would not sign the consent. Nonetheless, Ms. Loudermilk wished to proceed with the article and again provided the University an opportunity to respond. Given the seriousness of [REDACTED's] charges, the University reasonably could assume it would be harmed if it did not answer them.*

Mr. Anselmi then stated that "neither the public nor the University's interest are[sic] served by an article that reports only the student's allegations of wrongdoing." He also stated that the University sought to obtain the student's consent, but that she refused. He contended that:

[c]learly, [REDACTED] cannot be permitted to charge the University in a public forum with serious misconduct and then, knowingly and intentionally, seek to deprive the University from using the very information it needs to defend itself. Fairness required that the University be permitted to respond without [REDACTED] consent; accordingly, finding a waiver of the right to consent in these circumstances is entirely appropriate and fully supported.

Mr. Anselmi stated that the information from Ms. [REDACTED]'s education records that was disclosed was directly and solely limited to that information that was necessary to respond to the charges made to Ms. Loudermilk by Ms. [REDACTED]. He further stated that Ms. Loudermilk was not permitted to view nor was she provided copies of Ms. [REDACTED]'s education records, but that he did reference the education records to refute the charges that Ms. [REDACTED] made to the *Baltimore Sun.*

Mr. Anselmi provided this Office with a copy of his November 20, 1997, letter to Ms. Loudermilk in which he provided her with a consent form for Ms. [REDACTED] to sign. Mr. Anselmi also provided Ms. Loudermilk with a copy of the Department's February 19, 1997, letter to Johns Hopkins University (which he refers to as the "Ruling") and stated:

While I believe the Ruling applies to the [REDACTED] allegations, it is always best to obtain a student's written consent; accordingly, I would appreciate you having Ms. [REDACTED] execute the attached original before we speak on Friday Morning.... [I]f [REDACTED] elects not to sign the Consent, I will rely on the Ruling in our discussions.

The consent form, a copy of which he also provided this Office, states:

I, [REDACTED], consent to the release, inspection, copying or other disclosure, including the discussion of, any and all student records (whether academic, disciplinary, financial, scholarship, degree or otherwise) to Suzanne Loudermilk or other journalists employed by the Baltimore Sun Newspaper, or parties associated with that paper, in connection with their review and report on recent allegations I made against Towson University. This autho-

rization may only be revoked by a subsequent writing signed by me, and any person or entity presented with an original or copy of this authorization shall be duty bound promptly to release the information referred to above.

The consent includes a signature line for [REDACTED] to sign her name.

Discussion

FERPA generally prohibits the nonconsensual disclosure of education records. The term "education records" is defined as those records which contain information directly related to a student and which are maintained by an educational agency or institution or by a party acting for the agency or institution. 34 CFR § 99.3 "Education records." "Disclosure" means to permit access to or the release, transfer or other communication of personally identifiable information contained in education records to any party, by any means, including oral, written, or electronic means. 34 CFR § 99.3 "Disclosure."

FERPA generally requires that a student provide written consent before an educational agency or institution discloses a student's education records. 20 U.S.C. § 1232g(b); 34 CFR §§ 99.30 and 99.31. While there are several statutory exceptions to the written consent provision, none permits the nonconsensual disclosure in circumstances such as the subject of this complaint. 20 U.S.C. § 1232(b); 34 CFR § 99.31. Moreover, neither the statute nor the regulations specifically permit an educational agency or institution to infer an implied waiver of the right to consent.

As Mr. Anselmi referenced in his letter, the Department stated in the "Analysis of Comments and Changes" section of the November 21, 1996, publication of the FERPA Final Rule issued to implement certain changes made to FERPA by the Improving America's Schools Act of 1994 that this Office has a policy of permitting a school to infer an implied waiver of the right to consent to disclosures of information from education records if the parent or student has sued the institution. The rationale for this policy is based on the belief that a student or parent should not be permitted to use rights afforded them under FERPA to prevent an educational agency or institution from defending itself in a court of law when the parent or student has initiated legal action and seeks damages against the agency or institution. In such circumstances, the educational agency or institution must be able to defend itself. The Department has maintained a consistent position on this issue, and advises educational institutions that any disclosure of personally identifiable information from a student's education records to a court of law in response to a lawsuit filed against the institution by the student must be limited to that information necessary to defend itself against the specific charges made.

Mr. Anselmi also correctly notes in his letter that this Office extended its policy permitting educational agencies and institutions to infer an implied waiver of the right to consent in other specific circumstances. However, the policy was extended based on the narrow set of facts present in that particular case, although our February 14, 1997, finding did not explicitly state this. In that case, a student copied his letter to a dean at Johns Hopkins University in which he had made allegations concerning Johns Hopkins University and a professor therein to his then employer, the National Cancer Institute (NCI). The dean responded to the student's letter, and sent a copy of the response to NCI, which was an organization with which Johns Hopkins has a special grantor-grantee relationship. The student requested that NCI, based on his allegations, take a particular action to assist him outside Johns Hopkins, and Johns Hopkins disclosed the information believing that, as such, NCI should be fully aware of the facts and have information from the perspective of Johns Hopkins on the matter.

In an August 14, 1995, letter, this Office issued its finding that Johns Hopkins had violated FERPA as alleged, based on the policy of this Office to permit a school to infer an implied waiver of the right to consent only in limited situations, specifically where a student files a lawsuit against a school and a school cannot defend itself without reference to information from the student's education records. In so doing, this Office took into consideration the fact that NCI was not rendering a decision affecting Johns Hopkins based on the student's allegations.

In a July 10, 1996, letter, Johns Hopkins requested that this Office reconsider the complaint and our policy of allowing a school to infer an implied waiver of the right to consent in extremely limited circumstances. We did so, and as a result issued the February 14, 1997, finding in which we stated:

Based on the additional information provided by the University in its July 10 letter, we have determined that this complaint is analogous to an educational institution inferring a student's implied waiver of the right to consent to the release of information from his education records when the student has sued the institution. In both instances the student had requested the involvement of an entity outside of the institution, and it is logical and appropriate that the institution would respond on the record.

Therefore, we believe that if a student has taken an adversarial position against an institution, made written allegations of wrongdoing against the institution, and shared this information with third parties, the institution must be able to defend itself. In order to defend itself, it would be difficult for an institution to provide a response without referring to the student's education records.

While the policy statement made in the Johns Hopkins finding was general and suited toward a broad application, the extension of the policy on implied waiver of the right to consent was based on a narrow set of facts. In retrospect, this Office believes that it should have more clearly delineated guidelines in the Johns Hopkins ruling that would have better clarified those situations, other than those in which the student has sued the agency or institution, where it is appropriate for an educational agency or institution to infer an implied waiver of the right to consent. We therefore set forth clearer guidelines in this decision today. However, we also wish to emphasize that any educational agency or institution that faces a question about disclosure with respect to an implied waiver of the right to consent should contact this Office with details about the particular situation it is facing for guidance before the agency or institution releases any education records.

As a matter of clarification of the Department's policy on permitting an educational agency or institution to infer an implied waiver of the right to consent to disclosure of personally identifiable information from a student's education records in a non-litigation context, we offer the following guidelines:

The Department will support an educational agency or institution that has inferred an implied waiver of the student's right to consent to disclosure when:

- The student has taken an adversarial position against the educational agency or institution;
- The student has initiated the involvement of the third party by contacting that party in writing, and, in so doing:
  - ▶ Set forth specific allegations against the educational agency or institution; and,
  - ▶ Requested that action be taken against the educational agency or institution or that the third party assist the student in circumventing decisions made about the student by the educational agency or institution;

The third party's special relationship[1] with the educational agency or institution:

- Gives the third party authority to take specific action against the educational agency or institution; or
- Reasonably could be significantly adversely affected if the educational agency or institution cannot refute the allegations; and
- The disclosure is as limited as is necessary for the educational agency or institution adequately to defend itself from the student's charges or complaint. The third party should follow the procedures set forth in 34 CFR § 99.33 on limitations that apply to the redisclosure of information derived from education records.

---

[1] Examples include: an educational agency or institution's grantor/grantee relationships; an educational agency or institution's relationship with a state or federal legislator; or an educational agency or institution's relationship with a state or federal commission charged with looking into allegations made by a student.

In formulating and establishing a policy that is not directly addressed by FERPA and is being implied, the Department seeks to ensure that the basis for such policy is strong enough to outweigh the potential harm. In this circumstance, the strong policy consideration behind the waiver of the right to consent doctrine is that an educational agency or institution should be able to defend itself against an adversarial position that has been taken against it by a student where the student has shared this information in writing with a third party that has a special relationship with the educational agency or institution in a way that could significantly adversely affect the educational agency or institution. The potential harm is the dissemination of personally identifiable information from education records without the appropriate written consent. The above guidelines are our effort to minimize the harm, while at the same time to protect the strong policy consideration that gives rise to the doctrine of the waiver of the right consent.

The widespread dissemination that occurred with [REDACTED]'s records is not permissible under the implied waiver of the right to consent for two reasons. First, the harm to [REDACTED] from the disclosure to the *Baltimore Sun* was too great. In this respect, the harm to the student differs from a disclosure in a lawsuit or a disclosure to a discrete third party that has a special relationship with the educational agency or institution and has been asked by the student to assist the student in an adversarial situation with the educational agency or institution. With respect to the University's disclosure to the *Baltimore Sun*, there can be no effective limitation on the widespread dissemination of the information from [REDACTED]'s education records. Unlike a situation where the student has sued the school, the student cannot seek an order of protection from further disclosure when a school has disclosed records to the general public. Similarly, unlike a situation where information is disclosed to a discrete third party that has a special relationship with the educational agency or institution and has been asked by the student to assist the student in an adversarial situation against the educational agency or institution, the disclosure of information in this case was to the general public, and there can be no limitation on redisclosure. The harm to the student's privacy interest under FERPA is simply too great where the disclosure of personally identifiable information in education records is to the general public.

Second, unlike situations in which an educational agency or institution would be unable to defend itself in litigation brought by the student, or in which the educational agency or institution's special relationship with a third party could be significantly adversely affected, or the third party might take specific action against the educational agency or institution unless the agency or institution could refute the charges made against it by the student, the media and the general public cannot take such specific actions. Nothing in FERPA prevents an educational agency or institution from responding to a request for information or an interview with a statement to the effect that FERPA prohibits the disclosure of information from the student's education records which would be necessary to respond. If information is published which is inaccurate and misleading, FERPA does not prohibit an educational agency or institution from filing suit for libel.[2]

With regard to Mr. Anselmi's assertion that [REDACTED]'s history of writing third parties with her allegations against the University "weakens her claim to confidentiality," FERPA does not protect the confidentiality of information, per se. Rather, FERPA affords students a right to privacy of information contained in their education records, in particular, the right to consent to most disclosures of personally identifiable information derived from their education records. With respect to Mr. Anselmi's reference to previous occasions where [REDACTED] sought the involvement of third parties with respect to her complaints against the University, it is possible that some of those sets of circumstances would have met the criteria for inferring an implied waiver of the right to consent, as outlined above. However, because any such disclosures by the University that may have occurred in such instances where [REDACTED] contacted other third parties regarding her complaints against the University

---

[1] When a school sues a parent or student, it may disclose personally identifiable information from the student's education records to the court absent a court order or subpoena so long as it first notifies the parent or student in accordance with 34 CFR § 99.31 (a)(9)(i). 34 CFR § 99.31 (a)(9)(iii).

are not subject to the investigation of this complaint, further comment or analysis of such circumstances is immaterial to this letter of finding.

Finally, with regard to the consent which Mr. Anselmi drafted and provided to Ms. Loudermilk for [REDACTED], FERPA requires that a student's consent for disclosure of education records must:

- ⚊ Specify the records that may be disclosed;
- ⚊ state the purpose of the disclosure; and
- ⚊ Identify the party or class of parties to whom the disclosure may be made.

The consent must also be signed and dated.

The consent prepared for [REDACTED]'s signature appropriately specified the records that could be disclosed, stated the purpose of disclosure and identified the parties to whom the disclosure could be made. However, we note that FERPA does not require that an educational agency or institution disclose education records when a student has consented to the disclosure, as implied by the last sentence of the consent that Mr. Anselmi drafted. We further note that should a student revoke consent, such action would not affect disclosures made prior to the date the student does so.

Finding

While Mr. Anselmi stated that he neither permitted Ms. Loudermilk to review [REDACTED]'s records nor sent Ms. Loudermilk copies of them, Mr. Anselmi orally disclosed information from [REDACTED]'s education records to Ms. Loudermilk. In so doing, the University assumed that an implied waiver of [REDACTED]'s right to consent to disclosures from her education records could be inferred. We find that this assumption incorrectly went beyond the limited scope of those circumstances in which such an inference is appropriate. We find this because [REDACTED] had not sued the University and because the disclosure was not to a third party with a special relationship with the University that would allow the third party to take specific action against the University. Also, we do not believe that the *Baltimore Sun* and the University's relationship would have been significantly adversely affected had the University not refuted [REDACTED]'s allegations.

However, in recognition of the facts that University met the three prongs of the test that we set forth in our February 14, 1997, finding involving Johns Hopkins University and that our guidance on the special relationship prong of the doctrine of implied waiver of the right to consent under FERPA did not clearly delineate that the rule was based on the narrow set of facts present in that case, we do not find that the University committed a FERPA violation. However, we set forth clearer guidance today and encourage University officials to contact this Office for technical assistance, prior to the release of education records without the student's written consent, when guidance is needed in applying FERPA to a particular set of facts.

Allegation 2

[REDACTED] alleged that the University violated her rights under FERPA when it failed to provide her access to her education records within 45 days. Specifically, [REDACTED] alleged that Dr. Frederick Arnold informed her on December 19, 1997, that "there was hardly anything left in [her] file" and that while she could have copies of her own letters regarding her appeals. "Mr. Anselmi would not let [her] have information that was presented before the Graduate Studies Committee that was presented by 'the other side' because that was considered privileged."

In our February 18, 1998, letter to the University, we set forth the position of this Office on permitting an educational agency or institution to deny a student access to education records that are subject to the attorney-client privilege and we asked that the University provide specific information for each document [REDACTED] had been denied based on that privilege. Our analysis of [REDACTED]'s allegation that she has been denied access to her education records is considered in two parts—records subject to her general allegation and records which the University claims are protected by the attorney-client privilege.

Records Subject to General Allegation

Mr. Anselmi explained in his response the following:

Dr. Arnold, Associate Dean of the Graduate School, recalls that [REDACTED] called him on December 16, 1997 and made a request to "look at her file". Dr. Arnold informed [her] of the information typically maintained by the Graduate School on former students. Dr. Arnold did not tell [her] she could not have access to certain information. Rather, to avoid misunderstanding regarding her request, Dr. Arnold asked [her] to put her request in writing identifying the information she wished to see. [REDACTED], however, continued to call Dr. Arnold, and each time she called he asked that she put her request in writing. On December 23, 1998, [she] did so.... That letter requested "a copy of all [her] undergraduate and graduate student records," including "(academic, disciplinary, financial, scholarship, degree, or otherwise)."

Mr. Anselmi explained that after a series of contact between the University and [REDACTED], the University "express mailed to [REDACTED] the records she requested" on January 30, 1998. By letter dated March 12, 1998, [REDACTED] alleged that she had not been provided access to "copies of audiograms done at [the University] on campus Speech and Hearing Clinic." She stated that "these audiograms would document [her] hearing over [a] long period of time." She stated that in response to a phone call to his office regarding these records, Mr. Anselmi wrote her a February 23, 1998, letter but that he did not provide her with the audiograms. She provided a copy of the February 23, 1998, letter, which does not appear to address her request for access to the audiograms. She also provided a copy of a February 20, 1998, summary of the questions [REDACTED] raised in her telephone call. Item one on that list is that [REDACTED] "wants to know if the University has copies of the audiograms that were performed on her here at the University, and, if so, would like copies of them."

Finally, by letter dated April 27, 1998, Mr. Anselmi wrote this Office and explained the following:

In preparing the University's response to the above complaint, the University conducted an extensive and thorough search of all University records that pertain to [REDACTED]. Because of [REDACTED] 10 year history of filing complaints against the University, several files were established in a number of different University departments. To assure that [REDACTED] has received all the documents to which she is entitled, my administrative assistant and I personally reviewed each file and every University record relating or pertaining to [REDACTED]. This review resulted in the identification of certain documents that may not have been disclosed to [REDACTED]. The university mailed these documents to [REDACTED] and the attached letter.

In his April 27, 1998, letter to [REDACTED], a copy of which he provided to this Office, Mr. Anselmi stated:

After we expressed mailed the records to you on January 28, 1998, my assistant and I again reviewed University records to prepare a response to the complaint you filed with the Department of Education. To assure completeness, I am providing you these additional documents. While you may have received some of these documents, and some may be duplicates, there are documents included in this response that inadvertently may not have been provided to you in the University's January 28, 1998, response.

In order for this Office to make a determination as to whether the University fully complied with FERPA with respect to [REDACTED]'s request for access, we will need additional information from you. In particular, please advise this Office whether the University maintains "copies of audiograms" completed on [REDACTED], and if so, whether (and when) she was provided access to them. Additionally, we will need clarification as to whether the University believes that the copies of records sent to [REDACTED] on April 27 definitely included records that had not previously been provided to [REDACTED] in compliance with her December 1997 request for access. We are also requesting that [REDACTED] provide additional information relative to this allegation (*see* copy of enclosed letter to [REDACTED])."

Records for which the University Has Claimed Attorney-Client Privilege

Finally, in Mr. Anselmi's March 27, 1998, response to the complaint, he explains that the University denied [REDACTED] access to 12 documents on the grounds that the documents are covered by the attorney-client privilege. He explains that for each document, the privilege is held by Towson State University, the communication is between the University and its attorney (himself) for the purpose of obtaining a legal opinion or legal services and not for the purpose of obtaining a legal opinion or legal services and not for the purpose of committing an illegal act or tort, and the communication is confidential and the privilege has not been waived. He identified the documents as:

- Letter dated September 29, 1987 from Michael A. Anselmi to Dr. Vic S. Gladstone regarding Complaint of [REDACTED] confirming their previous discussions and requesting information needed for legal advice.
- Letter dated October 13, 1987 from Bill L. Wallace, Ph.D. to Michael A. Anselmi regarding Complaint of [REDACTED] providing the information requested in the September 29, 1987 letter above.
- Letter dated March 31, 1988 from Michael A. Anselmi to Bill L. Wallace, Ph.D. regarding Complaint of [REDACTED] requesting additional information needed for legal advice.
- Letter dated April 7, 1988 from Bill L. Wallace, Ph.D. to Mr. Michael A. Anselmi regarding Complaint of [REDACTED] in response to Mr. Anselmi's March 31, 1988 letter.
- Letter dated July 25, 1988 from Bill L. Wallace, Ph.D. to Mr. Michael A. Anselmi regarding Complaint of [REDACTED] requesting legal advice on Complainant's allegations.
- Memorandum dated March 13, 1990 from Dr. Vic. S. Gladstone to Michael A. Anselmi providing information needed for legal advice.
- Memorandum dated May 18, 1990 from Dr. Vic S. Gladstone to Michael A. Anselmi requesting legal review of letter dated May 18, 1990 to Clinical Certification Board.
- Memorandum dated May 18, 1990 from Michael A. Anselmi to Vic Gladstone advising him that [REDACTED] threatened litigation and providing legal advice on University obligations.
- Memorandum dated May 17, 1990 from Michael A. Anselmi to Vic Gladstone regarding Complaint of [REDACTED] and commenting on letter dated May 15, 1990 from Peter Taliaferro.
- Memorandum dated May 4, 1990 from Michael A. Anselmi to Vic Gladstone regarding draft letter prepared by Mr. Anselmi for Dr. Gladstone's review and signature.
- Memorandum dated March 22, 1990 from Michael A. Anselmi to Dr. Vic Gladstone regarding University's legal position on [REDACTED]'s request for certification.
- Memoranda dated May 16, 1990, May 10, 1990 and May 16, 1990 from Michael A. Anselmi to his file regarding discussion with Dr. Gladstone and [REDACTED]'s attorney on the legal obligations, if any, that Dr. Gladstone may have to complete certification forms.

As discussed in our February 18, 1998, letter, FERPA requires educational agencies and institutions to provide eligible students an opportunity to inspect and review their education records within 45 days of receipt of a request. 20 U.S.C. § 1232g(a)(1)(A) ; 34 CFR § 99.10 (a). As noted above, FERPA broadly defines the term "education records." 20 U.S.C. § 1232g (a)(4)(A); 34 CFR § 99.3 "Education records." While FERPA does exempt certain types of records from the definition of education records, neither the statute nor the implementing regulations specifically provides for denying a student's right to inspect and review an education record based on attorney-client privilege or work product privilege grounds. Nonetheless, an educational institution may deny a request to inspect and review on these grounds in certain circumstances. In particular, an educational institution's ability under FERPA to assert the privilege against a student seeking access to education records may be inferred by the institution's need to obtain confidential legal advice in certain circumstances. That is, when an educational institution needs to obtain confidential legal advice, and in so doing creates "education records," the institution may decline to permit inspection and review of those records, or portions of those records, on attorney-client privilege rounds, provided that all the below conditions are met. In order for an attorney to invoke the attorney-client privilege for the client, he or she must establish that:

- the asserted holder of the privilege is or sought to become a client;
- the communication is between a client and a member of the bar, or his or her subordinate, who is acting as a lawyer in connection with the communication;
- the communication relates to facts disclosed by the client to the attorney for the purpose of securing either an opinion of law or legal services, and not for the purpose of committing an illegal act or tort;
- the communication is in fact confidential and not made in the presence of anyone outside the particular attorney-client relationship; and
- the privilege has been claimed and not waived.

After reviewing the above-delineated information about the letters in question, this Office has determined that the letters are [REDACTED]'s education records. However, the University has provided this Office with facts showing that each of the above-delineated requirements for invoking attorney-client privilege has been met with regard to each of the identified documents. This Office finds that the University did not violate FERPA when it withheld from [REDACTED] those education records of hers which are subject to the attorney-client privilege, and, accordingly, this Office is closing its investigation of this aspect of this allegation. Consequently, the University will not be required to provide [REDACTED] with access to these documents.

Thank you for your continued cooperation with regard to the investigation of this complaint. Please provide the additional information requested under the general discussion of allegation two within three weeks of your receipt of this letter.

Sincerely,

LeRoy S. Rooker, Director
Family Policy Compliance Office

Enclosure
cc: Ms. [REDACTED]
Mr. Michael A. Anselmi

Ms. Jeanne-Marie Pochert   JANUARY 27, 2005
Deputy Assistant General Counsel
Clark County School District Legal Department
2832 East Flamingo Road
Las Vegas, Nevada 89121

Dear Ms. Pochert:

This is to respond to your August 25, 2004, email message on behalf of the Clark County School District (District), stating that you believe there is a conflict between Nevada law and the Family Educational Rights and Privacy Act (FERPA), 20 U.S.C. § 1232g. This Office administers FERPA and is responsible for providing technical assistance to educational agencies and institutions to ensure compliance with the statute and regulations found at 34 CFR Part 99.

Section 99.61 of the regulations provides that an educational agency or institution that determines that it cannot comply with FERPA due to a conflict with state or local law shall notify this Office within 45 days and include the text and citation of the conflicting law. You stated that Nevada law requires the release of certain education records to the Clark County Child Death Review Team (Team). The Team is a multi-disciplinary committee that assesses and evaluates selected cases of deaths of children 17 years of age and younger. The Team exists as the result of a statutory mandate (NRS 432B.403 to 432B.409, inclusive). Its purpose and mission is to evaluate and analyze the circumstances involved in selected cases of deaths of children in order to make recommendations for improvements to laws, policies and practice, support the safety of children, and prevent future deaths. You add that at the Team meetings, there are often questions regarding student health issues, discipline, and attendance of the deceased student/child.

You also provided the following information about Nevada law:

NRS 432B.406 provides that a multi-disciplinary team to review the death of a child that is organized by an agency which provides child welfare services must include, among others, a representative of any school that is involved with the case under review. NRS 432B.407 further provides that: "Each organization represented on a multidisciplinary team to review the death of a child shall share with other members of the team information in its possession concerning the child who is the subject of the review, any siblings of the child, any person who was responsible for the welfare of the child and any other information deemed by the organization to be pertinent to the review." NRS 432B.407(2). Section 432B.407 also provides that a team may petition the district court for the issuance of, and the district court may issue, a subpoena to compel the production of any books, records, or papers relevant to the cause of any death being investigated by the team.

FERPA provides that a parent must provide signed and dated written consent before an educational agency or institution discloses personally identifiable information from education records. 34 CFR § 99.30. Exceptions to this general rule are set forth in

§ 99.31. The term "education records" is defined as records, files, documents, and other materials that contain information directly related to a student and that are maintained by an educational agency or institution or by a person acting for the agency or institution. 20 U.S.C. § 1232g(a)(4)(A); 34 CFR § 99.3 "Education records." Based on these provisions, and assuming that public school districts in Nevada receive funds from the U.S. Department of Education, records maintained by the District that contain the names of students and information concerning their health, disciplinary matters, or attendance constitute "education records" under FERPA.

A FERPA exception permits disclosure without prior consent to comply with a judicial order or lawfully issued subpoena so long as the District makes a reasonable effort to notify the parent of the order or subpoena in advance of compliance, so the parent may seek protective action. 34 CFR § 99.31(a)(9). It should also be noted that FERPA permits disclosure to a Team if a parent provides prior written consent. 34 CFR § 99.30.

In general, an actual conflict of laws arises if it is impossible for a party to comply with both federal and state law, or when a state law stands as an obstacle to the accomplishment and execution of the full purposes and objectives of a federal law. *Taubman Realty Group Ltd. Partnership v. Norman Mineta*, 198 F.Supp 2d 744, 761 (E.D. Va. 2002), citing *English v. General Electric*, 496 U.S. 72 (1990). Based upon our review of the information you have provided and applicable law, we have determined that Nevada law does not conflict with FERPA in that it is possible for the Teams that assess and evaluate the deaths of children to comply with both laws when they investigate student deaths. Specifically, Nevada law provides that the Teams may review selected cases of deaths of children, and that a Team may petition the district court for the issuance of, and the district court may issue, a subpoena to compel the production of any books, records or papers relevant to the cause of any death being investigated by the Team.

In summary, we find that there is no conflict between state law regarding Child Death Review Teams and FERPA. A parent may provide prior written consent for the disclosure of education records to a Team, or the Team may petition a court to issue a subpoena or court order to compel the District to provide it with education records and the District may provide those records, without prior written consent, in accordance with § 99.31(a)(9) of the FERPA regulations.

I trust this information is responsive to your inquiry. Should you have additional questions regarding this or other FERPA issues, please do not hesitate to contact this Office again.

Sincerely,

LeRoy S. Rooker, Director
Family Policy Compliance Office

cc: Mr. Keith W. Rheault
Superintendent
Nevada Department of Education

Dr. Omero Suarez
Chancellor
Grossmont-Cuyamaca Community
College District
8800 Grossmont College Drive
El Cajon, California 92020-1799

JANUARY 16, 2004

Dear Dr. Suarez:

This is in response to your letter, dated June 2, 2003, regarding a possible conflict between the Family Educational Rights and Privacy Act (FERPA)(20 U.S.C. § 1232g) and California Education Code § 76031. As you know, this Office administers FERPA and is responsible for providing technical assistance to educational agencies and institutions to ensure compliance with the statute and regulations found at 34 CFR Part 99.

You stated that you submitted your letter pursuant to FERPA requirements. Specifically, you noted that § 99.61 of the regulations provides that an educational agency or institution that determines that it cannot comply with FERPA due to a conflict with state or local law shall notify this Office within 45 days and include the text and citation of the conflicting law. California Education Code § 76031 states, in relevant part:

> *Whenever a minor is suspended from a community college, the parent or guardian shall be notified in writing by the president or the president's designee.*

You explained that the Grossmont-Cuyamaca Community College District (the College) enrolls a number of minors in its programs, either as high school graduates, holders of equivalency diplomas or certificates, or as specially enrolled part-time students. Occasionally, such students are suspended for misconduct and the suspension is part of the students' education records. You state that under FERPA this information from a student's education records "may not be disclosed to a parent of a student enrolled in a postsecondary institution." As explained more fully below, the California law would conflict with FERPA in some circumstances but under other limited circumstances the College would be able to disclose information on minors to their parents.

An educational agency or institution subject to FERPA may not have a policy or practice of disclosing education records, or non-directory, personally identifiable information from education records, without the written consent of the parent or eligible student, except as provided by law. 34 CFR Part 99, Subpart D. When a student reaches the age of 18 or attends an institution of postsecondary education, the student is considered an "eligible student," and all of the rights afforded by FERPA transfer from the parents to the student. 34 CFR § 99.3 "Eligible student." The term "education records" is defined as records, files, documents, and other materials that contain information directly related to a student and that are maintained by an educational agency or institution or by a person acting for the agency or institution. 20 U.S.C. § 1232g(a)(4)(A); 34 CFR § 99.3 "Education records." Clearly, a record on a student concerning a disciplinary action is "a protected 'education record' within the meaning of FERPA." See, *United States of America v. Miami University, Ohio State University*, 294 F.3d 797 (6th Cir. 2002).

Generally, FERPA provides that an educational agency or institution may not disclose education records, or personally identifiable information from education records, without the prior written consent of an eligible student. 20 U.S.C. § 1232g(d); 34 CFR § 99.30. An exception to this rule permits disclosure of the education records of an eligible student to a parent if the student is a dependent for federal income tax purposes. 34 CFR § 99.31(a)(8). You state that in some instances these FERPA provisions do not permit disclosure because the student will not provide consent and is not a dependent.

Another FERPA disclosure exception, set forth in § 99.31(a)(14) of the regulations, permits an institution of postsecondary education to disclose the final results of a disciplinary proceeding, if it determines that:

1. the student is an alleged perpetrator of a crime of violence or non-forcible sex offense; and

2. with respect to the allegation made against him or her, the student has committed a violation of the institution's rules or policies.

When an institution determines that an accused student is an alleged perpetrator and has violated the institution's rules, then there are no restrictions on disclosure or redisclosure of the final results of a disciplinary proceeding.

Based on the California law and circumstances that you describe, it appears that California law requires disclosures in some circumstances where FERPA does not permit disclosure. Specifically, if a student does not provide prior written consent, is not a dependent under the FERPA disclosure exception, and the § 99.31(a)(14) FERPA exception does not apply, then FERPA would not generally permit the disclosure of a suspension action, notwithstanding California law. An institution would be in violation of FERPA to the extent that it has a policy or practice of disclosing education records in circumstances where FERPA does not permit disclosure. Where there is such a violation, the Department of Education may withhold further payments under any applicable Department program, issue a complaint to compel compliance, terminate an institution's eligibility to receive funding, or take any other action authorized by law. 34 CFR § 99.67; 20 U.S.C. 1232g(f); 20 U.S.C. 1234c. These FERPA provisions have been reaffirmed by the U.S. Court of Appeals in its *U.S. v. Miami University* decision, referenced above.

Thank you for contacting this Office about this important matter. Should you have any questions about the guidance provided herein, please do not hesitate to contact me directly, or Dann Brittenham of my staff, at:

Family Policy Compliance Office
Office of Innovation and Improvement
U.S. Department of Education
400 Maryland Avenue, S.W.
Washington, D.C. 20202-5901

Additionally, the telephone number of this Office is (202) 260-3887.

Sincerely,

LeRoy S. Rooker, Director
Family Policy Compliance Office

Ms. Doris Dixon
National Collegiate Athletic Association
One Dupont Circle, NW
Suite 400
Washington, D.C. 20036

OCTOBER 22, 1998

Dear Ms. Dixon:

This is in response to your May 13, 1997, letter. In your letter, you mentioned several issues that we had previously discussed in a February meeting with you and the President of the National Collegiate Athletic Association (NCAA), Mr. Cedric Dempsey. Using different scenarios as examples, your letter raises additional questions to this Office regarding whether the NCAA can disclose education records of student-athletes in compliance with the redisclosure provisions of the Family Educational Rights and Privacy Act (FERPA).

Scenario One

Actions by student athletes have been brought against the NCAA in administrative or court proceedings on both state and federal levels. In the federal regulations effective December 23, 1996, prior consent is not required when the disclosure is to comply with a judicial order or lawfully issued subpoena or when the educational agency or institution initiates legal action against a parent or student.

Question (a)

Is prior consent of the student required when the NCAA discloses the student's education records for purposes of defending itself against a lawsuit or in an administrative proceeding brought by the student-athlete or his or her parents?

Response

No, if the disclosure is necessary for the NCAA to defend itself. In the preamble to the Department's final rule amending FERPA on November 21, 1996, we stated:

> ...the Department interprets FERPA to allow an educational agency or institution to infer the parent's or student's implied waiver of the right to consent to the disclosure of information from the student's education records if the parent or student has sued the institution.

> 61 Fed. Reg. 59,292, 59,294 (November 21, 1996).

As the preamble states, we have determined that an educational institution may infer a student's implied waiver of the right to consent to the release of information from his or her education records when the student has sued the institution. We believe that if a student sues a school, the school must be allowed to redisclose information to the extent necessary to defend itself.

We further believe that the same principle of implied consent that applies to educational institutions should apply to third parties that receive information from education records, like the NCAA. In short, the NCAA may

---

[1] When a student reaches 18 years of age or attends a postsecondary institution, the student becomes an "eligible student" and all FERPA rights transfer from the parent to the student. 34 CFR § 99.3 ("Eligible student").

also assume the implied consent of a student-athlete that sues the NCAA, and may redisclose the student's education records in court in order to defend itself—whether a student or a parent of the student is the plaintiff.[1]

As to whether the same rationale would apply to a situation where a student or parent has initiated an administrative proceeding against the NCAA, it depends on the nature of the proceeding. While we believe that a law suit and an administrative proceeding to which you refer are comparable, we would need additional information about the types of administrative proceedings that the NCAA is involved in order to answer this question.

Question (b)

If a student refers to other students in such cases and argues that he/she is being treated differently from the other students, is it permissible for the NCAA to defend itself against such accusations by referring to personally identifiable information pertaining to other students.

Response

No. There is no exception in FERPA, or previous interpretation by this Office, that would allow the NCAA to redisclose the education records of other students who have been named in a lawsuit without the other students' prior written consent. However, redaction of all personally identifiable information from an education record may be acceptable, as long as the students' identities would not be easily traceable. In addition, FERPA would not prevent the NCAA from disclosing education records of another student if it received a subpoena for such records.

Scenario Two

State and federal government officials have requested the student files and/or information in the student files. Also, some officials want to discuss personally identifiable information in student's files with NCAA staff persons. There are specific inquiries as well as general inquiries.

Questions (a)(i) and (ii)

For instance, a student-athlete has contacted the governor of her state complaining the NCAA denied her eligibility. The governor's office has contacted an NCAA official or staff person to discuss the individual's case.

   i. Is it permissible for the NCAA to discuss or disclose personally identifiable information from a student's file without first requiring a written consent from the student-athlete?
   ii. By contacting the government official for assistance, does the student-athlete implicitly authorize the NCAA to disclose personally identifiable information from the student-athlete's education records with the government official?

Response

As noted above, we have determined that there are instances where an educational institution must be allowed to defend itself if a student takes an adversarial position against an institution—such as initiating a law suit or administrative hearing. We believe that the implied waiver of the right to consent extends to situations where a parent or student attempts to enlist the assistance of an entity that will possibly intervene in the matter against the school.

In other words, if the student or parent asks a third party, in writing,[2] to take action against a school, we believe that the institution must be allowed to defend itself, and that it may release a student's education records without the consent of the student. Because the student has asked a third party to take action against the institution, the student has attempted to use a "special relationship" to his or her advantage, and common sense dictates that the school must be allowed to respond. In sum, the "special relationship" test applies if the student has taken an adver-

---

[1] FERPA provides that in order to be valid, any consent given by the parent or eligible student must be in writing. 20 U.S.C. § 1232g(b)(1); 34 CFR § 99.30(a). We have concluded that in order for the implied waiver of consent to apply, the initial request by the parent or eligible student must also be in writing.

sarial position against the school, the allegations of wrongdoing are in writing, and the allegations have been shared with the entity whose assistance is being sought.

We have determined that this same principle also applies to the NCAA. In short, the NCAA, like any postsecondary institution, must be able to defend itself if a student-athlete has taken an adversarial position, written the governor of his or her state, complained that the NCAA denied him or her eligibility and asked the governor to intervene.

Questions (b)(i)(ii)(iii) and (iv)

Another instance, which the Department of Education's Family Policy Compliance Office may be aware of, is that the Department of Justice has informally requested that NCAA produce to them entire student files for all disabled student-athletes who applied for a waiver of the initial eligibility requirements of the 1996–1997 school year. The Department of Justice will allow NCAA to redact the names and addresses of the student. These files may include other personally identifiable information including the high school attended by the student, the university the student attended, the type of sport the student participates in, the name of the student's treating physicians and other similar information.

I. In this situation, does the NCAA or the government agency make the determination as to what information is personally identifiable?

ii. Does personally identifiable information have to be determined on a case-by-case review of each student's file? That is, in some high-profile cases, even a description of the type of disability might make the student-athlete easily traceable or personally identifiable. In these situations, how much discretion does NCAA have to redact this information?

iii. Does the NCAA need to obtain a written consent from and/or provide notification to each student-athlete whose file is sent to a government agency in response to a formal or informal inquiry or investigation?

[iv.] If the NCAA releases student files to the government agency under the good faith belief that it does not contain personally identifiable information, what is the extent of NCAA's liability?

Response

It is our understanding that Congress has introduced legislation to amend FERPA to allow for the nonconsensual disclosure of information from student education records maintained by postsecondary institutions, or third parties that maintain education records, such as the NCAA, to authorized representatives of the Attorney General for law enforcement purposes. Assuming that this language is enacted into law, the NCAA would be able to rerelease personally identifiable information from a student's education record in response to a Department of Justice investigation without violating FERPA. This proposed change is currently found in section 951 of the Higher Education Amendments of 1998, and we would be happy to provide a copy of the provision to you once the bill becomes law.

Scenario/Question Three

Can the NCAA release information to an eligible student-athlete's parents or attorney without first obtaining written consent from the student-athlete?

Response

The NCAA may redisclose information from a student's education records to the student's attorney because an attorney would be acting as a legal representative for the student. We recommend that you obtain a written designation of the attorney by the student in these circumstances. However, this is not necessarily the case with the student's parents.

When a student reaches the age of 18 or attends an institution of postsecondary education, that student is deemed "eligible" and all of the rights afforded by FERPA transfer from the parents to the student. The statute provides:

For the purposes of this section, whenever a student has attained eighteen years of age, or is attending an institution of postsecondary education the permission or consent required of and the rights accorded to the parents of the student shall thereafter only be required of and accorded to the student.

20 U.S.C. § 1232g(d)

Accordingly, the rights afforded by FERPA transfer to students in attendance at a college or university, whether or not they have reached the age of 18. However, FERPA states that a school can disclose an eligible student's education records to his or her parents without prior written consent if:

The disclosure is to parents of a dependent student, as defined in section 152 of the Internal Revenue Code of 1954.

34 CFR § 99.31(a)(8)

Therefore, the NCAA may not redisclose education records to a student-athlete's parents without written consent of the eligible student unless the redisclosure is to parents of a "dependent student" and the redisclosure is made on behalf of the postsecondary institution. See 34 CFR § 99.33(a)(2)(b).

Scenario Four

There are many instances where a student-athlete or her parents publicly disclose personally identifiable information such as grades or test scores to the media as well as to state and federal government officials usually in whole or in part. For instance, a student-athlete who does not meet the NCAA core course requirement for eligibility may publicize to the media that he/she had a 3.9 grade point average and was denied eligibility. Often, the student-athlete or the parents do not reveal the entire story or may even provide false or misleading information. The result is that the media publishes a story that is not true or is misleading and the NCAA bears the wrath of the public.

Question (a)

In these situations, to what extent may the NCAA publicly disclose personally identifiable information from a student's education records in order to correct or to clarify information provided by the student-athlete or the parents?

Response

As you are aware, FERPA generally protects students' privacy interests in "education records" by generally prohibiting the disclosure of education records absent the student's prior written consent. The term "education records" is defined as:

[T]hose records, files, documents, and other materials, which (i) contain information directly related to a student; and (ii) are maintained by an educational agency or institution, or by a person acting for such agency or institution.

20 U.S.C. § 1232g(a)(4); See also 34 CFR § 99.3 "Education records"

In addition, the general prohibition on the disclosure of information from education records extends to the third party maintaining the records. Consequently, FERPA restricts the "redisclosure" of education records or information from education records by third parties, except under certain conditions.

FERPA provides that education records, or personally identifiable information from such records, may be disclosed by institutions of postsecondary education to third parties only after the student has provided his or her prior written consent. 20 U.S.C. § 1232g(b)(1) and (b)(2)(A); 34 CFR § 99.30. In the case of the NCAA, postsecondary institutions may disclose information from the education records of student-athletes to the NCAA if the student has signed a copy of the NCAA's Student Athlete Statement. This Office has previously determined that the Student Athlete Statement meets FERPA's prior written consent requirement.

Because FERPA limits the redisclosure of information from education records by third parties, information from an education record that the NCAA receives from an institution cannot generally be redisclosed without the student's prior written consent. See 34 CFR § 99.33(a). In this regard, the FERPA regulations state that officers, employees, and agents of a party that receives information from education records may use the information, but only for the purposes for which the disclosure was made. Section 99.33(a)(2)(b) further states:

> *Paragraph (a) of this section does not prevent an educational agency or institution from disclosing personally identifiable information with the understanding that the party receiving the information may make further disclosures of the information **on behalf of the educational agency or institution** if:*
> *(1) The disclosures meet the requirements of § 99.31; and*
> *(2) The educational agency or institution has complied with the requirements of § 99.32(b).*

(Emphasis added)

Section 99.31 lists the 13 exceptions under which schools may disclose education records absent prior written consent of the student. Section 99.32(b) requires that schools keep a record of disclosure of information from education records that includes the name of the party receiving the information and the legitimate interest of the requesting party.

Further, the statute states:

> *If a third party outside the educational agency or institution permits access to information in violation of paragraph (2)(A), or fails to destroy information in violation of paragraph (1)(F), the educational agency or institution shall be prohibited from permitting access to information from education records to that third party for a period of not less than five years.*

20 U.S.C. § 1232g(b)(4)(B); See 34 CFR § 99.31(a)(6)(iii)

Therefore, if the NCAA improperly redisclosed information from a student's education record that it received from a particular institution, that institution could be precluded by FERPA from making further disclosures to the NCAA for a minimum of five years. We also note that the institution has the initial responsibility of notifying a party (*i.e.*, the NCAA) receiving education records under §§ 99.30 and 99.31 of the FERPA requirements relating to any rerelease of information from those records. See 34 CFR § 99.33(d). This requirement does not apply if the disclosure of education records is to an eligible student, a disclosure of directory information, or to disclosures made pursuant to lawfully issued subpoenas or to comply with a judicial order. 34 CFR § 99.33(c).

Turning to your question regarding whether the NCAA can redisclose "inaccurate" or "incomplete" information from education records, this Office has determined that the NCAA cannot make a statement concerning inaccurate or incomplete information because the NCAA would have to rely on information from education records. For example, if the media claims that a student-athlete has a 3.5 Grade Point Average (GPA) and the student's education records indicate a 3.0 GPA, a statement from the NCAA that the 3.5 GPA is inaccurate would be based on information derived from the student's education record.

While you have expressed to this Office the need for the NCAA to be able to correct inaccurate information, the only way in which the NCAA could do so without violating FERPA would be to have the student-athlete provide his or her written consent for the NCAA to redisclose publicly information from his or her education records. Accordingly, in a situation where the NCAA wishes to correct inaccurate information, the NCAA should indicate that FERPA restricts the redisclosure of information from education records, and in order to discuss any details from such records, the student would have to provide his or her prior written consent. The NCAA may want to add that it would be free to discuss information in education records[3] after it receives the student's written consent to do so.

Furthermore, information created by the NCAA that does not contain information from education records is not protected by FERPA. For example, an NCAA decision to investigate a student-athlete for an NCAA rules violation that is created and maintained by the NCAA, and not derived from education records, would not be protected by FERPA.[4]

Question (b)

Does the student-athlete (or parents) waive the privacy protections of the Buckley Amendment by either the filing of a lawsuit contesting the NCAA's eligibility determination or by discussing personally identifiable information with the media?

Response

As discussed above in scenario one, question (a), the NCAA may disclose information from an education record for the limited purpose of defending itself in a lawsuit. The student-athlete, however, does not waive his or her privacy rights by talking to the media. Even if a lawsuit is brought against the NCAA by a student-athlete, the NCAA cannot redisclose education records to the media regarding the case. Rather, the NCAA could direct the media to certain information from education records revealed in court documents[sic] filings.

Question (c)

Are there situations, other than the written consent, when the student or the parents can waive their rights under the Buckley Amendment with regards to disclosure of personally identifiable information?

Response

Those situations are discussed above.

Scenario Five

There is a common question among many NCAA staffers with regards to dealing with the media in light of the Buckley Amendment. NCAA actions and decisions receive wide media attention. Some of these actions and decisions are made upon personally identifiable information in a student's education records. Staff members are contacted on a daily basis by members of the media concerning high profile cases involving individual student athletes. NCAA staff members have been instructed to inform the media and other interested persons that they cannot discuss individual cases because of the Buckley Amendment's requirements. However, rather than asking about a case, the creative media people pose hypotheticals that have one or two key facts similar to the individual cases. Our policy at this point is to explain the NCAA bylaws and rules applicable to the situation and NCAA's interpretation of these rules based on precedent. Of course, some members of the media may take this explanation out of context.

---

[3] FERPA only protects information contained in education records. FERPA does not protect the confidentiality of information in general, and, therefore, does not apply to the disclosure of information derived from a source other than education records, even if education records exist which contain such information. As a general rule, information that is obtained through personal knowledge or observation, and not from an education record, is not protected from disclosure under FERPA. Cf. Kline v. Department of Health & Human Services, 927 F.2d 522 (10th Cir. 1991)(Privacy Act); Thomas v. Department of Energy, 719 F.2d 342 (10th Cir. 1983)(Privacy Act); Savarese v. Harris, 620 F.2d 298 (5th Cir. 1980)(Privacy Act), cert. denied, 449 U.S. 1078 (1982).

[4] For the record, we do not believe that the NCAA is a recipient of federal funds as provided for by FERPA. FERPA applies to any "educational agency or institution to which funds have been made available under any program administered by the Secretary…" 34 CFR § 99.1(a). We are not aware of any Department program that provides federal funding directly to the NCAA. Therefore, we have concluded that the 3rd Circuit's recent holding that the NCAA is a "recipient" for purposes of Title IX is distinguishable because FERPA's regulatory framework for determining who is a recipient is much narrower than Title IX's. See Smith v. NCAA, 139F.3d 180, 189 (3rd. Cir. 1998), cert. granted, 67 U.S.L.W. 3187 (U.S. Sept. 29, 1998)(No. 98-84)(Title IX definition of recipient includes entities that benefit indirectly from receipt of federal funds.)

Question (a)

Is the NCAA's policy in conformance with the requirements of the Buckley Amendment?

Response

As long as information from education records is not redisclosed or *relied upon* during discussions with the media about how NCAA bylaws and rules apply to a particular situation, these types of discussions would not violate FERPA regardless whether members of the media take the explanation out of context. The NCAA could also explain that if the media wants facts about a particular student's education records, it simply needs to provide the NCAA with a written consent from the student allowing for the redisclosure of information from education records to the media. FERPA neither prevents the NCAA from discussing its own rules and bylaws with the public, nor does it address conclusions drawn by the media as a result of these discussions.

Question (b)

Can we confirm or deny reports or rumors if the information is provided by the member of the media, *e.g.* can you confirm that John Doe is ineligible because he did not have the requisite minimum grade point average?

Response

No. In order to confirm or deny a student-athlete's status, an NCAA staff member would have to generally rely on information from an education record. As such, we believe an improper disclosure would take place, even if the NCAA does not release the student's exact GPA. Therefore, we suggest that the NCAA explain that it cannot comment unless it receives the student's prior written consent to do so.

Question (c)

Do you have other suggestions for dealing with the media given the nature of the NCAA and its functions?

Response

Because FERPA does not allow for the redisclosure of a student-athlete's education records to the media, we again suggest that the NCAA rely on FERPA's prior written consent provision that would allow the redisclosure of such information. The NCAA should indicate to the media that if it receives prior written consent of the student, it would be free to comment on information from education records.

Scenario Six

As an essential part of the investigation and enforcement proceedings, NCAA needs to share information such as transcripts, test results and other data from a student's educational records with involved individuals who may be named in an allegation. As part of the due process measure set forth in the Enforcement Procedure, any individual against whom an allegation has been alleged has the right to review all pertinent evidentiary materials involving him/her. We may also need to discuss personally identifiable information with relatives or friends of the student-athlete for purposes of investigating the validity of allegations.

Question (a)

Is the NCAA required to obtain a written consent from the student-athlete prior to disclosing and/or discussing this information with such individuals in its investigation of violations?

Response

Yes, except for information that is not obtained from education records.

Question (b)

If so, is it possible to use a standard consent form such that the student consents to the disclosure of this information during the infraction investigation to the above-described individuals? Can we incorporate this type of consent into the student-athlete statement without affecting the enforceability of said consent?

Response

FERPA requires that specific written consent be provided prior to disclosure of education records. The consent must be signed and dated. In addition, the written consent must specify the records that may be disclosed, state the purpose of the disclosure, and identify the party or class of parties to whom the disclosure may be made. 34 CFR § 99.30.

As we discussed at our meeting, one possibility would be for the NCAA to provide a form to student-athletes that includes a waiver allowing for the redisclosure of information from education records in certain situations. The NCAA could determine in what particular situations redisclosure may be important or necessary. For example, the NCAA could draft a consent form allowing for the redisclosure of education records to specified individuals during an infraction investigation. The NCAA must ensure that the consent form meets the above outlined requirements. Additionally, the NCAA could incorporate such a prior written consent into its Student Athlete Disclosure form. This Office would be glad to review any proposed disclosure form.

Scenario Seven

The NCAA publishes information regarding its infraction cases and certain eligibility appeals in the *NCAA News Register*. This release excludes the student-athlete's name and the name of the member institution. The categories reported include: 1) how reported; 2) the type of sport(s); 3) citation to the NCAA bylaws and rules; 4) description of the facts; 5) description of the action taken by the member institution; 6) description of the action taken by the NCAA. The purpose of publishing this information is to inform and educate member institutions, institutional staff members and student-athletes of NCAA rules and their application to certain facts.

Question (a)

Does this type of information constitute personally identifiable information when the student's name and the name of the member institution is not revealed?

Response

FERPA defines "personally identifiable information" as including, but not limited to, the following:

(a) The student's name;

(b) The name of the student's parent or other family member;

(c) The address of the student or student's family;

(d) A personal identifier, such as the student's social security number or student number;

(e) A list of personal characteristics that would make the student's identity easily traceable;

(f) Other information that would make the student's identity easily traceable.

34 CFR § 99.3 ("Personally identifiable information")

Therefore, information would be considered easily traceable if sufficient details are disclosed to allow a reasonable person to determine the identity of the student-athlete and thus easily trace the record to that individual. Based on the categories you have mentioned above, we do not believe that the information disclosed in the *NCAA News Register* would constitute personally identifiable information under FERPA as long as the NCAA did not mention the name of the student-athlete, the name of institution, and the factual description was brief and nonspecific. We note that in high profile cases, the description of facts in nonpersonally identifiable form may be such that reasonable persons could determine the identity of the student-athlete. In such cases, a detailed listing of the facts may need to be omitted.

Question (b)

Is this type of release acceptable under the Buckley Amendment?

Response

If the information from education records is not easily traceable to a student-athlete, then FERPA would permit this type of release. Of course, if challenged each disclosure would have to be examined on a case-by-case basis.

Question (c)

After the Committee on Infractions' hearings, the Committee's report is released to the media with the names of individuals deleted. Is this permissible?

Response

See answers to questions (a) and (b), and the discussion of "easily traceable."

Scenario/Question Eight

The NCAA often recognizes student-athletes who excel in the areas of academics, intercollegiate competition and extracurricular activities. Would the Department of Education consider it a violation of the Buckley Amendment if the NCAA publishes the grade-point average, *i.e.* 3.9 GPA, of an outstanding academic All-American student-athlete without first obtaining the student's written consent?

Response

As mentioned previously, there are 13 exceptions that permit a school to disclose personally identifiable information from a student's education records without the prior consent of the student. One exception allows for the disclosure of "directory information"—information contained in an education record of a student that would not generally be considered harmful or an invasion of privacy if disclosed.

More specifically, directory information includes, but is not limited to, information such as: "a student's name, address, telephone listing, date and place of birth, major field of study, participation in officially recognized activities and sports, weight and height of members of athletic teams, dates of attendance, degrees and awards received, and the most previous educational agency or institution attended." 34 CFR § 99.3 ("directory information"). FERPA further provides that prior consent before disclosure is not required if the information to be disclosed is information the educational agency or institution has designated as "directory information" under the conditions described in § 99.37.[5] 34 CFR § 99.31(a)(11).

We have previously determined that the type of information you describe is information that postsecondary institutions may designate as "directory information." For example, schools may publish as directory information "top 10% of the class" because it is similar to receiving an award or honor. Please note, however, that schools could not disclose the actual grades or GPA of a student who was in the top 10% of his or her class. We believe that—provided the disclosing institution has appropriately designated "degrees and awards received" in its directory information—the NCAA could redisclose this type of information under FERPA's directory information exception without the student's prior consent.

---

[1] Section 99.37 requires postsecondary institutions to give public notice of the types of information it has designated as directory information, allow students the opportunity to opt out of the disclosure of this type of information, and provide students a time period in which they must submit in writing to the institution the fact that they does not want their directory information disclosed.

I trust that this letter is helpful in responding to your questions. We apologize for the amount of time it took to respond. Please do not hesitate to contact this Office again if you have further questions or need additional clarification for any of the answers in this letter.

Sincerely,

LeRoy S. Rooker, Director
Family Policy Compliance Office

Ms. Doris Dixon   MARCH 12, 1999
National Collegiate Athletic Association
One Dupont Circle, NW, Suite 400
Washington, D.C. 20036

Dear Ms. Dixon:

This letter is written in follow-up to our meeting of January 13, 1999, in which you and other participants expressed concern on behalf of the National Collegiate Athletic Association (NCAA) regarding the limitations that the Family Educational Rights and Privacy Act (FERPA) places on certain disclosures of education records. Also, this responds to a February 4, 1999, letter from Mr. John Morris relative to our meeting. In particular, the NCAA is concerned about the "easily traceable" aspect of FERPA as it applies to the release of NCAA investigative reports, waivers, and denial decisions.

While we are considering the scope of "easily traceable" information within the definition of "personally identifiable information," we wanted to provide to you, in writing, our suggestion that a prospective student-athlete provide to the NCAA prior written consent to disclose education records. Specifically, we suggest that if the NCAA added the following language to its Student Athlete Statement, it would permit the NCAA to release the investigative reports and respond to any subsequent questions regarding those reports in compliance with FERPA:

I allow the NCAA to disclose personally identifiable information from my education records to any third party, including but not limited to the media, for the purpose of reporting or verifying compliance/accuracies with regard to the NCAA Constitution and Bylaws, to investigate alleged violations of the Constitution and Bylaws, and/or to issue student infraction reports.

Additionally, we suggest that if the NCAA added the following language to its Student Athlete Statement, it would permit the NCAA to release waiver and denial decisions and respond to any subsequent questions regarding those waivers or decisions:

I allow the NCAA to disclose personally identifiable information from my education records to any third party, including but not limited to the media, for the purpose of reporting or verifying compliance/accuracies with regard to a waiver or denial decision.

As we have previously informed you, FERPA requires that specific written consent be provided prior to disclosure of education records. The consent must be signed and dated. In addition, the written consent must specify the records that may be disclosed, state the purpose of the disclosure, and identify the party or class of parties to whom the disclosure may be made. 34 CFR § 99.30. The above statements meet the prior written consent requirement for the purpose of FERPA.

Also, even if a student-athlete were to sign the above consent, the NCAA would be under no obligation to change its policy of disclosing information from education records in nonpersonally identifiable form. Rather, the NCAA could continue its disclosure in the same manner but the signed consent would alleviate any FERPA implications where a student's identity might be easily traceable.

Although we have typically advised schools that an easily traceable analysis must be made, at least in part, by the school on a case-by-case basis, we have concluded that if a reasonable person in the community can identify the subject of the report based on the information provided, then that release will violate FERPA. While we recognize that this conclusion may cause some difficulty for current NCAA reporting procedures, we believe that the legislative history and purpose of FERPA require the balance be struck in favor of the protection of privacy of a student-athlete's identity. We also have concluded that the caselaw in a non-privacy context (Freedom of Information Act) supports this decision as well. *Whitehouse v. United States Dep't of Labor,* 997 F. Supp. 172 (D. Mass. 1998).

We enjoyed meeting with you and would be interested in having the NCAA's thoughts regarding such a modification of your consent agreement. Please do not hesitate to contact this Office if you have any questions.

Sincerely,

LeRoy S. Rooker, Director
Family Policy Compliance Office

37   Letter to NCAA

Re: Letter of Technical Assistance Concerning Student-Athlete Records

Ms. Doris Dixon   SEPTEMBER 27, 1999
Director of Federal Relations
National Collegiate Athletic Association
One Dupont Circle, NW, Suite 400
Washington, D.C. 20036

Dear Ms. Dixon:

This is in response to your August 25, 1999, letter written in follow-up to the March 12, 1999, letter of advice we gave the National Collegiate Athletic Association (NCAA) on the Family Educational Rights and Privacy Act (FERPA) as it relates to written consent that student-athletes must provide before the NCAA can disclose information from their education records. You provided this Office with three separate consent proposals that the NCAA is considering for use in its application and eligibility forms for student-athletes. You ask that we review the proposed language and submit to you any suggestions or recommendations. You explain that you plan on presenting the proposed language to the NCAA governance bodies at an executive meeting scheduled for this October.

As you know, FERPA generally protects privacy rights with respect to "education records." "Education records" are records that contain information directly related to a student and that are maintained by an educational agency or institution or by a party acting for the agency or institution. 34 CFR § 99.3 "Education records." The rights afforded under FERPA rest with a student's parents until the student reaches the age of 18 or attends an institution of postsecondary education. 34 CFR §§ 99.3 "Eligible student" and 99.5(a). Generally, in order to disclose information from student education records, a parent or eligible student must provide his or her prior written consent. FERPA's consent provisions require a *specification* of 1) the records that may be disclosed; 2) the purpose of the disclosure; and 3) the identity of the party or class of parties to whom the records may be disclosed. 34 CFR § 99.30. In our recommendations on the NCAA's proposed language, we have addressed each consent separately for the purpose of clarity.

Proposed Language for Initial Eligibility Waiver Application (both self-filed and institutional)

Additionally, I give my consent to the NCAA to disclose personally identifiable information from my educational records to a third party, including but not limited to the media, for the purpose of correcting inaccuracies or reporting about this waiver, without such disclosure constituting a violation of my rights under the Family Educational Rights and Privacy Act.

- ✚ At the term, "personally identifiable information," we believe that the consent form should point out "*the necessary* personally identifiable information." This gives a more specific indication of the records that will be disclosed.
- ✚ Remove the term "reporting" which is confusing and change "correcting inaccuracies about this waiver" to "correcting any inaccuracies related to this waiver."
- ✚ Correct the term "educational records" to "education records."

With our above suggested changes, the consent form would read:

Additionally, I give my consent to the NCAA to disclose the necessary personally identifiable information from my education records to a third party, including but not limited to the media, for the purpose of correcting any inac-

curacies related to this waiver, without such disclosure constituting a violation of my rights under the Family Educational Rights and Privacy Act.

Proposed Language for the Student-Athlete Statement

Further, you agree to authorize the NCAA to disclose personally identifiable information from your education records, including any NCAA violations that you engage in while you are a student-athlete, to a third party, including but not limited to the media, for the purpose of correcting inaccurate statements related to the processing of a student-athlete reinstatement case, infractions case or waiver request. You also agree that case information may be published or distributed to third parties but that you will no[sic] be identified by name in any such published or distributed data.

- ✚ At the term "personally identifiable information" we believe that the consent form should point out "*the necessary* personally identifiable information." This gives a more specific indication of the records that will be disclosed.
- ✚ In the last sentence, specify what records are comprised in "case information," include the term "necessary" before case information, and state the purpose of this type of release, for example, specify the NCAA bylaw(s) that requires such publication or distribution.
- ✚ Correct the term "no" to "not"

With our above suggested changes, the consent form would read:

Further, you agree to authorize the NCAA to disclose the necessary personally identifiable information from your education records, including any NCAA violations that you engage in while you are a student-athlete, to a third party, including but not limited to the media, for the purpose of correcting inaccurate statements related to the processing of a student-athlete reinstatement case, infractions case or waiver request. You also agree that necessary case information, that is, information from your student-athlete reinstatement case, infractions case or waiver request to be published or distributed to third parties as required by NCAA bylaws. You will not be identified by name in any such published or distributed data.

Proposed Language for the NCAA Initial-Eligibility Clearinghouse Student Release Form

I understand and agree to abide by the procedures in the NCAA Guide for the College-Bound Student-Athlete. I authorize the high schools listed to release to the NCAA Initial-Eligibility Clearinghouse my transcripts, including ACT and SAT scores, proof of graduation, and any other academic information or records, as requested by the Clearinghouse for determining my athletic eligibility. I further authorize the release of information or records obtained by the Clearinghouse, including this release form and resulting certification decisions, to the NCAA, to any testing service whose test scores are included in my records (e.g. ACT or ETS), to my current high school, and to all NCAA member institutions requesting my eligibility information. I authorize the NCAA to disclose personally identifiable information from my education records (without such disclosure constituting a violation of my rights under the Family Educational Rights and Privacy Act) to a third party, including but not limited to the media, for the purpose of correcting inaccuracies or reporting about my preliminary or final certification decision. I understand and agree that the information provided to the Clearinghouse also may be used for research concerning athletic eligibility, the academic preparation and performance of student-athletes, and related issues. I also understand and agree that the research may be published or distributed to third parties but that I will not be identified in any such published or distributed data.

- ✚ For clarity, change "for determining" to "for the purpose of determining."

⊞ Regarding the second sentence, in consideration of the breadth of the education records that will be disclosed and parties that will receive it, the NCAA should specify the purpose of the disclosure. For instance, the Clearinghouse will be able to release any education records it obtains to the NCAA, testing services whose scores are in the student's records, the student's current high school, and all NCAA member institutions. The NCAA should clarify the limitations of this provision by specifying the purpose of these disclosures.

⊞ We believe the sentence "the release of information or records" should state "the release of *necessary* personally identifiable information from education records" and the sentence that begins "I authorize the NCAA to disclose personally identifiable information from my education records" should also include the term, *necessary*.

⊞ Remove the term "reporting" which is confusing and change "correcting inaccuracies about this waiver" to "correcting any inaccuracies related to my preliminary or final certification decision."

⊞ In the forth[sic] sentence, after the word Clearinghouse, the NCAA should add "for the purpose of determining my athletic eligibility."

⊞ In the last sentence, it appears that the NCAA is informing students that the information from their education records (that is disclosed by schools to the Clearinghouse) will be subsequently published in nonpersonally identifiable form for the purpose of studying academic preparation and student performance statistics. If that is the case, then the NCAA does not need to amend this sentence. However, if the NCAA believes that a student can be identified when certain information is published in this manner, then the last sentence should be reworked to meet FERPA's prior written consent requirement. That is, state the specific records that will be disclosed, the purpose of the disclosure and to whom the disclosure will be made.

With our above suggested changes, the consent form would read:

I understand and agree to abide by the procedures in the NCAA Guide for the College-Bound Student-Athlete. I authorize the high schools listed to release to the NCAA Initial-Eligibility Clearinghouse my transcripts, including ACT and SAT scores, proof of graduation, and any other academic information or records, as requested by the Clearinghouse for the purpose of determining my athletic eligibility. For the purpose of ..., I further authorize the release of necessary personally identifiable information from my education records obtained by the Clearinghouse, including this release form and resulting certification decisions, to the NCAA, to any testing service whose test scores are included in my records (e.g. ACT or ETS), to my current high school, and to all NCAA member institutions requesting my eligibility information. I authorize the NCAA to disclose the necessary personally identifiable information from my education records (without such disclosure constituting a violation of my rights under the Family Educational Rights and Privacy Act) to a third party, including but not limited to the media, for the purpose of correcting any inaccuracies related to my preliminary or final certification decision. I understand and agree that the information provided to the Clearinghouse for the purpose of determining my athletic eligibility also may be used for research concerning athletic eligibility, the academic preparation and performance of student-athletes, and related issues. I also understand and agree that the research may be published or distributed to third parties but that I will not be identified in any such published or distributed data.

A final note, if the prospective student-athlete is not an eligible student under FERPA, that is, he or she is under 18 years of age or is not yet in attendance at the postsecondary institution, then it is the student's parents who must sign the consent forms.

I trust that the above information is helpful. If you have further questions, please do not hesitate to contact this Office again.

Sincerely,

LeRoy S. Rooker, Director
Family Policy Compliance Office

38 Letter to University of Mississippi

Re: On National Collegiate Athletic Association (NCAA) Records

Mr. L. Lee Tyner, Jr.   FEBRUARY 12, 2002
Associate University Attorney
The University of Mississippi
209 Lyceum
P.O. Box 1848
University, Mississippi 38677-1848

Dear Mr. Tyner:

This is in response to your January 25, 2002, letter to this Office in which you request our opinion concerning an application of the Family Educational Rights and Privacy Act (FERPA). Specifically, you "request an opinion … regarding whether certain documents are" education records under FERPA. You enclosed a copy of a letter from the University of Mississippi (University) to the Southeastern Conference (SEC) and a redacted self-report to the National Collegiate Athletic Association (NCAA) as examples of the documents you wish us to review. In your letter, you explain that you previously released similar documents after removing "the names of current or former students and any other personally identifiable information" in response to a request for the documents from *The Clarion-Ledger*, a daily newspaper in Mississippi. You state you are requesting guidance on whether you may, under FERPA, disclose the example and similar documents in personally identifiable form in response to a request from *The Clarion-Ledger* for an unredacted version of the documents. This Office administers FERPA, which addresses issues that pertain to education records.

FERPA is a federal law that gives parents the right to have access to their children's education records, the right to seek to have the records amended, and the right to have some control over the disclosure of information from the records. When a student reaches 18 years of age or attends a postsecondary institution, he or she becomes an "eligible student" and all rights under FERPA transfer from the parent to the student. FERPA defines "education records" as "those records, files, documents, and other materials which—

(i) contain information directly related to a student; and

(ii) are maintained by an educational agency or institution or by a person acting for such agency or institution.

20 U.S.C. 1232g(a)(4)(i) and (ii)

In using the term "education records," the Department refers to materials that are preserved or retained by an educational agency or institution, or someone acting for such agency or institution, as an institutional or official record of the student. In other words, the term does not include student work that is created, used, or kept in the classroom and does not become part of the student's institutional record.[1]

FERPA generally prohibits the disclosure of personally identifiable information derived from education records without the prior written consent of the eligible student, except in certain specified circumstances. Based on the information you have provided this Office, none of the exceptions to the prior written consent provision in § 99.31 applies to *The Clarion-Ledger's* request for unredacted documents. 34 CFR § 99.30 and 99.31.

Please note that section 99.3 of the regulations defines "personally identifiable information" as information that includes but is not limited to:

---

[1] This interpretation of "education records" is the position of the United States as set out in more detail in an amicus curiae brief supporting petitioners in *Owasso Independent School District No. I-011 v. Falvo No. 00-1073* (S. Ct.). The Supreme Court may rule on the scope of the term "education records" in the above-captioned matter. The Department will review the Court's ruling in this case, and may issue additional guidance or regulations to further clarify the scope of the term "education records."

(a) the student's name;

(b) the name of the student's parent or other family member;

(c) the address of the student or the student's family;

(d) a personal identifier, such as the student's social security number or student number;

*(e) a list of personal characteristics that would make the student's identity **easily traceable**; or*

*(f) **other information that would make the student's identity easily traceable.***

(Emphasis added)

Based on our review of the letter and sample report you submitted, this Office has determined that the documents at issue are education records. We have determined that the documents, in unredacted form, are education records because they are directly related to the student—they contain specific information such as the name of the student and his high school—and because the documents are maintained by the University, and are institutional in nature (they relate to the school's responsibility to self-report violations to the NCAA).[2]

FERPA does not specifically define "easily traceable," and situations regarding disclosures of information that could be considered easily traceable must be analyzed on an individual basis. For example, a university is in the best position to determine whether a redacted version of an education record would be easily traceable if disclosed by the institution. In making this determination, an institution should take into consideration a number of factors. First, the school should consider whether the party seeking access to the records has prior knowledge of the students listed in the education record. In examining the prior knowledge of a potential recipient, the standard the school official should apply is whether the individual can trace the identity of the student without significant amounts of additional searching for information. Thus, our focus has been on whether the school official reasonably could have concluded, at the time of the disclosure, that the disclosure would not make the student's identity easy to trace. If an institution determines that an education record remains easily traceable to a student even after it has been redacted, the institution would be prohibited from disclosing the record without the prior written consent of the student.

I trust that the above is responsive to your inquiry.

Sincerely,

LeRoy S. Rooker, Director
Family Policy Compliance Office

---

[2] In an unreported decision, the Chancery Court of the 1st Judicial district of Hinds County rules on this issue in 1996. *Gannett River States Publishing Corporation v. Mississippi State University*, Case G95-1795 (July 5, 1996). The court held that the records at issue in that case—correspondence from the NCAA to the university—were subject to disclosure under the judicial order exception in FERPA. In order to apply the exception, the court had to have concluded that the records were "education records" under FERPA. To the extent the holding contradicts the notion that correspondence to or from the NCAA is an education record, the Department disagrees with the ruling.

39 **Letter to Senator Charles E. Grassley** ★

Re: Solomon Amendment

UNITED STATES DEPARTMENT OF EDUCATION
OFFICE OF MANAGEMENT

Honorable Charles E. Grassley   DEC 18 1998
United States Senate
Washington, D.C. 20510-1501

Dear Senator Grassley:

This is in response to your letter, dated November 2, 1998, to former Assistant Secretary Kay Casstevens, regarding an Email from Sergeant Jon M. Borseth, USAF Recruiter. In his Email to you, Sergeant Borseth raises a concern that Walhert High School, a private school in Iowa, has refused to provide him with a list of high school seniors for recruiting purposes. Sergeant Borseth asserts that Walhert High School receives federal funds and asks whether the school is required "by law" to release the list to the military. I have been asked to respond to your letter because this Office administers the Family Educational Rights and Privacy Act (FERPA), which addresses issues relating to education records. 20 U.S.C. § 1232g; 34 CFR Part 99.

As you are aware, FERPA is a federal law which affords parents the right to have access to their children's education records, the right to seek to have the records amended, and the right to have some control over the disclosure of information from the records. Once a student reaches 18 years of age or attends a postsecondary institution, he or she becomes an "eligible student," and all rights under FERPA transfer from the parent to the student. FERPA applies only to educational institutions to which funds are made available under any federal program for which the Secretary of the U.S. Department of Education has administrative responsibility. Private and parochial schools at the elementary and secondary levels generally do not receive such funding and are, therefore, not required to comply with the law.

With regard to disclosure of information about students to military recruiters, the Solomon Amendment to the Omnibus Appropriations Bill of 1996 provides for the disclosure of certain personally identifiable information from education records to the U.S. Armed Services for recruiting purposes. Specifically, the Solomon Amendment requires that postsecondary institutions provide access to student names, addresses, and telephone listings, and if known, student ages, level of education, and majors, if requested by a military recruiter. (*See* The Omnibus Consolidated Appropriations Act for fiscal year 1997, P.L. 104-208, § § 514 and 515.) As written, the Solomon Amendment does not require the consent of the student in order to make such a release. Because the Solomon Amendment to the Omnibus Consolidated Appropriations Act is a newer enacted statute than FERPA, it would supersede any protections afforded by FERPA in this regard.

The Department of Defense (DOD) issued a final rule implementing the Solomon Amendment, "Military Recruiting and Reserve Officer Training Corps Program Access to Institutions of Higher Education" on October 23, 1998 (63 FR 56819-56824). Should you or your constituent have further questions about the Solomon Amendment, you may contact:

Mr. William J. Carr
Office of the Under Secretary of Defense, Personnel and Readiness
Force Management Personnel
Military Personnel Policy (AP)
Room 2B-271, 4000 Defense Pentagon
Washington, D.C. 20301-4000

Should you have further questions relating to FERPA, please do not hesitate to contact this Office directly. The name and address is as follows:

Family Policy Compliance Office
U.S. Department of Education
400 Maryland Avenue, SW
Washington, D.C. 20202-4605

I trust that the above adequately explains the scope and limitations of FERPA as it relates to your inquiry.

Sincerely,

LeRoy S. Rooker, Director
Family Policy Compliance Office

cc: Mr. William J. Carr

UNITED STATES DEPARTMENT OF EDUCATION
OFFICE OF HUMAN RESOURCES AND ADMINISTRATION

Ms. Susan Faccenda   MAR 9 1993
Assistant Vice President and Counsel
University of Notre Dame
Notre Dame, Indiana 46556

Dear Mrs. Faccenda:

This is in response to your letter on February 17, 1993, in which you request written confirmation from this Office regarding rights of deceased students under the Family Educational Rights and Privacy Act (FERPA). You provided a copy of a document entitled The Academic Archivist which indicates that personally identifiable information from education records could become public in census records seventy-two years after creation. The document also accurately states that such time period does not appear in FERPA. You ask for confirmation that the protections afforded by FERPA expire upon the death of the student and that FERPA does not allow the disclosure of education records based exclusively on the amount of time that has passed.

FERPA generally protects an "eligible student's" privacy interests in "education records." Under FERPA an individual becomes an "eligible student" when he or she is 18 years of age or attends an institution of postsecondary education. The term "education records" is defined as records that are directly related to a student and maintained by an educational agency or institution or a party acting for such agency or institution.

FERPA does not address the issue of education records of deceased students. However, based on common law principles relating to privacy rights, the privacy rights of an individual generally expire with the individual's death. Accordingly, we have determined that the education records of a deceased "eligible student" are not protected by FERPA and that an institution may disclose those records at its discretion.

As noted in The Academic Archivist, FERPA does not make reference to a time period of seventy-two years after which education records could become public. While it may be reasonable to assume that after a certain number of years, a former student is no longer living and that education records relating to that individual would no longer be protected by FERPA, this may not necessarily be the case. In the event this Office received a complaint containing specific allegations of fact giving reasonable cause to believe that an institution improperly disclosed information from education records, we would initiate an investigation based on that complaint.

I trust that the above information is helpful in explaining FERPA as it relates to the education records of deceased students. If you have further questions, please do not hesitate to contact this Office again.

Sincerely,

LeRoy S. Rooker, Director
Family Policy Compliance Office

Appendix F

FPCO Guidance Brochures

FPCO FERPA Brochure 1 for Colleges[4]

Balancing Student Privacy and School Safety: A Guide to the Family Educational Rights and Privacy Act for Colleges and Universities

Postsecondary officials are regularly asked to balance the interests of safety and privacy for individual students. While the *Family Educational Rights and Privacy Act* (FERPA) generally requires institutions to ask for written consent before disclosing a student's personally identifiable information, it also allows colleges and universities to take key steps to maintain campus safety. Understanding the law empowers school officials to act decisively and quickly when issues arise.

Health or Safety Emergency

In an emergency, FERPA permits school officials to disclose without student consent education records, including personally identifiable information from those records, to protect the health or safety of students or other individuals. At such times, records and information may be released to appropriate parties such as law enforcement officials, public health officials, and trained medical personnel. See 34 C.F.R. 99.31 (a)(10) and 99.36. This exception to FERPA's general consent rule is limited to the period of the emergency and generally does not allow for a blanket release of personally identifiable information from a student's education records. In addition, the Department interprets FERPA to permit institutions to disclose information from education records to parents if a health or safety emergency involves their son or daughter.

Disciplinary Records

While student disciplinary records are protected as education records under FERPA, there are certain circumstances in which disciplinary records may be disclosed without the student's consent. A postsecondary institution may disclose to an alleged victim of any crime of violence or non-forcible sex offense the final results of a disciplinary proceeding conducted by the institution against the alleged perpetrator of that crime, regardless of whether the institution concluded a violation was committed. An institution may disclose to anyone—not just the victim—the final results of a disciplinary proceeding, if it determines that the student is an alleged perpetrator of a crime of violence or non-forcible sex offense, and with respect to the allegation made against him or her, the student has committed a violation of the institution's rules or policies. See 34 C.F.R. 99.31 (a)(13) and (14).

The Clery Act

The *Jeanne Clery Disclosure of Campus Security Policy and Campus Crime Statistics Act* requires postsecondary institutions to provide timely warnings of crimes that represent a threat to the safety of students or employees and to make public their campus security policies. It also requires that crime data be collected, reported and disseminated to the campus community and to the Department annually. The *Clery Act* is intended to provide students and their families with accurate, complete and timely information about safety on campuses so that they can make informed decisions. Such disclosures are permitted under FERPA.

---

[4] Available for download in brochure form at <www2.ed.gov/policy/gen/guid/fpco/brochures/elsec.html>.

The following Web site provides more information about these and other provisions about campus safety: www.ed.gov/admins/lead/safety/campus.html.

Law Enforcement Unit Records

Many colleges and universities have their own law enforcement units to monitor safety and security in and around campus. Institutions that do not have specific law enforcement units may designate a particular office or school official to be responsible for referring potential or alleged violations of law to local police authorities. Investigative reports and other records created and maintained by these law enforcement units are not considered education records subject to FERPA. Accordingly, institutions may disclose information from law enforcement unit records to anyone, including outside law enforcement authorities, without student consent. *See* 34 C.F.R. 99.8.

While an institution has flexibility in deciding how to carry out safety functions, it must also indicate in its policy or in information provided to students which office or school official serves as the college or university's "law enforcement unit." (The institution's notification to students of their rights under FERPA can include this designation. As an example, the Department has posted a model notification on its Web site at http://www.ed.gov/policy/gen/guid/fpco/ferpa/ps-officials.html.)

Law enforcement unit officials who are employed by the college or university should be designated in the institution's FERPA notification as "school officials" with a "legitimate educational interest." As such, they may be given access to personally identifiable information from students' education records. The institution's law enforcement unit officials must protect the privacy of education records it receives and may disclose them only in compliance with FERPA. For the reason, it is advisable that law enforcement unit records be maintained separately from education records.

Disclosure to Parents

When a student turns 18 years old or enters a postsecondary institution at any age, all rights afforded to parents under FERPA transfer to the student. However, FERPA also provides ways in which schools may share information with parents without the student's consent. For example:

- Schools may disclose education records to parents if the student is a dependent for income tax purposes.
- Schools may disclose education records to parents if a health or safety emergency involves their son or daughter.
- Schools may inform parents if the student who is under age 21 has violated any law or its policy concerning the use or possession of alcohol or a controlled substance.
- A school official may generally share with a parent information that is based on that official's personal knowledge or observation of the student.

FERPA and Student Health Information

Postsecondary institutions that provide health or medical services to students may share student medical treatment records with parents under the circumstances described above. While these records may otherwise be governed by the *Health Insurance Portability and Accountability Act of 1996* (HIPAA), the HIPAA Privacy Rule excludes student medical treatment records and other records protected by FERPA. The Department plans to issue further guidance on the interplay between FERPA and HIPAA.

FERPA and Student and Exchange Visitor Information System (SEVIS)

FERPA permits institutions to comply with information requests from the Department of Homeland Security (DHS) and its Immigration and Customs Enforcement Bureau (ICE) in order to comply with the requirements of SEVIS. Officials who have specific questions about this and other matters involving international students should contact the U.S. Department of Education's Family Policy Compliance Office.

Transfer of Education Records

Finally, FERPA permits school officials to disclose any and all education records, including disciplinary records, to another institution at which the student seeks or intends to enroll. While student consent is not required for transferring education records, the institution's annual FERPA notification should indicate that such disclosures are made. In the absence of information about disclosures in the annual FERPA notification, school officials must make a reasonable attempt to notify the student about the disclosure, unless the student initiates the disclosure. Additionally, upon request, the institution must provide a copy of the information disclosed and an opportunity for a hearing. *See* 34 C.F.R. 99.31(a)(2) and 99.34(a).

Contact Information

For further information about FERPA, please contact the Family Policy Compliance Office or visit its Web site.

> Family Policy Compliance Office
> U.S. Department of Education
> 400 Maryland Ave., S.W.
> Washington, DC 20202-5901
> 202-260-3887

For quick, informal responses to routine questions about FERPA, school officials may email the Family Policy compliance Office at ferpa@ed.gov.

For inquiries about FERPA compliance training, contact ferpa.client@ed.gov.

Additional information and guidance may be found at FPCO's Web site at: http://www.ed.gov/policy/gen/guid/fpco/index.html.

FPCO FERPA Brochure 2 for Parents[5]

Parents Guide to the Family Educational Rights and Privacy Act: Rights Regarding Children's Education Records

What is FERPA?

The *Family Educational Rights and Privacy Act* (FERPA) is a federal privacy law that gives parents certain protections with regard to their children's education records, such as report cards, transcripts, disciplinary records, contact and family information, and class schedules. As a parent, you have the right to review your child's education records and to request changes under limited circumstances. To protect your child's privacy, the law generally requires schools to ask for written consent before disclosing your child's personally identifiable information to individuals other than you.

The following questions and answers are intended to help you understand your rights as a parent under FERPA. If you have further questions, please contact the U.S. Department of Education's Family Policy Compliance Office using the contact information provided below.

My child's school won't show me her or his education records. Does the school have to provide me with a copy of the records if I request them?

Schools must honor your request to review your child's education records within 45 days of receiving the request. Some states have laws similar to FERPA that require schools to provide access within a shorter period of time. FERPA requires that schools provide parents with an opportunity to inspect and review education records, but not receive copies, except in limited circumstances.

Parents whose children receive services under the *Individuals with Disabilities Education Act* (IDEA) may have additional rights and remedies with regard to their children's education records. The school district, local special education director, or state special education director can answer questions about IDEA.

Who else gets to see my child's education records?

To protect your child's privacy, schools are generally prohibited from disclosing personally identifiable information about your child without your written consent. Exceptions to this rule include:

- Disclosures made to school officials with legitimate educational interests;
- Disclosures made to another school at which the student intends to enroll;
- Disclosures made to state or local education authorities for auditing or evaluating federal- or state-supported education programs, or enforcing federal laws that relate to those programs; and
- Disclosures including information the school has designated as "directory information."

---

[5] Available for download in brochure form at <www2.ed.gov/policy/gen/guid/fpco/brochures/parents.html>.

What is directory information?

FERPA defines "directory information" as information contained in a student's education record that generally would not be considered harmful or an invasion of privacy if disclosed. Directory information could include:

- Name, address, telephone listing, electronic mail address, date and place of birth, dates of attendance, and grade level;
- Participation in officially recognized activities and sports;
- Weight and height of members of athletic teams;
- Degrees, honors, and awards received; and
- The most recent school attended.

A school may disclose directory information to anyone, without consent, if it has given parents: general notice of the information it has designated as "directory information;" the right to opt out of these disclosures; and the period of time they have to notify the school of their desire to opt out.

Does FERPA give me a right to see the education records of my son or daughter who is in college?

When a student turns 18 years old or enters a postsecondary institution at any age, all rights afforded to you as a parent under FERPA transfer to the student ("eligible student"). However, FERPA provides ways in which a school may—but is not required to—share information from an eligible student's education records with parents, without the student's consent. For example:

- Schools may disclose education records to parents if the student is claimed as a dependent for tax purposes.
- Schools may disclose education records to parents if a health or safety emergency involves their son or daughter.
- Schools may inform parents if the student, if he or she is under age 21, has violated any law or policy concerning the use or possession of alcohol or a controlled substance.
- A school official may generally share with a parent information that is based on that official's personal knowledge or observation of the student.

Contact Information

For further information about FERPA, please contact the Department's Family Policy Compliance Office or visit its Web site.

Family Policy Compliance Office
U.S. Department of Education
400 Maryland Ave. S.W.
Washington, DC 20202-5901
202-260-3887

For quick, informal responses to routine questions about FERPA, parents may also email the Family Policy compliance Office at ferpa.customer@ed.gov.

Additional information and guidance may be found at FPCO's Web site at: http://www.ed.gov/policy/gen/guid/fpco/index.html.

Definition of Dependent

Internal Revenue Code of 1954, Section 152

(Including amendments and applicable sections of the *Tax Reform Act of 1976*)

Because both the "*Final Regulations*" and "the *Act*" make references to the Internal Revenue Code of 1954, Section 152, it is reproduced here in its entirety from the 1976 edition of the Internal Revenue Code of 1954, with permission from Prentice Hall, Inc., Englewood Cliffs, N.J. 07632.

Sec. 152. Dependent Defined.

(a) General Definition—For purposes of this subtitle, the term "dependent" means any of the following individuals over half of whose support, for the calendar year in which the taxable year of the taxpayer begins, was received from the taxpayer (or is treated under subsection (c) or (e) as received from the taxpayer):

(1) A son or daughter of the taxpayer, or a descendant of either,

(2) A stepson or stepdaughter of the taxpayer,

(3) A brother, sister, stepbrother, or stepsister of the taxpayer,

(4) The father or mother of the taxpayer, or an ancestor of either,

(5) A stepfather or stepmother of the taxpayer,

(6) A son or daughter of a brother or sister of the taxpayer,

(7) A brother or sister of the father or mother of the taxpayer,

(8) A son-in-law, daughter-in-law, father-in-law, mother-in-law, brother-in-law, or sister-in-law of the taxpayer.

(9) An individual (other than an individual who at any time during the taxable year was the spouse, determined without regard to section 153, of the taxpayer) who, for the taxable year of the taxpayer, has as his principal place of abode the home of the taxpayer and is a member of the taxpayer's household, or

(10) An individual who—

(A) is a descendant of a brother or sister of the father or mother of the taxpayer,

(B) for the taxable year of the taxpayer receives institutional care required by reason of a physical or mental disability, and

(C) before receiving such institutional care, was a member of the same household as the taxpayer.

Last amendment—Sec. 152(a) appears above as amended by § [1](b) of Public Law 90-78, Aug. 31, 1967, effective (Sec. 2 of Public Law 90-78, Aug. 31, 1967) with respect to taxable years beginning after Dec. 31, 1966.

Prior amendment—Sec. 152(a) was previously amended by Sec. 4(a) of Public Law 85-866, Sept. 2, 1958 (qualified effective date rule in Sec. 1(c)(1) of Public Law 85-866, Sept. 2, 1958). Sec. 152(a) as so amended is in P-H Cumulative Changes.

(b) Rules Relating to General Definition—For purposes of this section—

(1) The terms "brother" and "sister" include a brother or sister by the half-blood.

(2) In determining whether any of the relationships specified in subsection (a) or paragraph (1) of this subsection exists, a legally adopted child of an individual (and a child who is a member of an individual's household, if placed with such individual), or a foster child of an individual (if such child satisfies the requirements of subsection (a)(9) with respect to such individual), shall be treated as a child of such individual by blood.

Last amendment—Sec. 152(b)(2) appears above as amended by Sec. 912(a) of Public Law 91-172, Dec. 30, 1969, effective (Sec. 912(b) of Public Law 91-172, Dec. 30, 1969) with respect to taxable years beginning after Dec. 31, 1969.

Prior amendment—Sec. 152(b)(2) was previously amended by Sec. [1](a) of Public Law 86-376, Sept. 23, 1959, effective (Sec. [1](b) of Public Law 86-376, Sept. 23, 1959) for taxable years beginning after Dec. 31, 1958. Sec. 152(b)(2) as so amended is in P-H Cumulative Changes.

(3) The term "dependent" does not include any individual who is not a citizen or national of the United States unless such individual is a resident of the United States, of a country contiguous to the United States, of the Canal Zone, or of the Republic of Panama. The preceding sentence shall not exclude from the definition of "dependent" any child of the taxpayer—

(A) born to him, or legally adopted by him, in the Philippine Islands before January 1, 1956, if the child is a resident of the Republic of the Philippines, and if the taxpayer was a member of the Armed Forces of the United States at the time the child was born to him or legally adopted by him, or

(B) legally adopted by him, if, for the taxable year of the taxpayer, the child has as his principal place of abode the home of the taxpayer and is a member of the taxpayer's household, and if the taxpayer is a citizen or national of the United States.

Last amendment—Sec. 152(b)(3) appears above as amended by Sec. [1](a) of Public Law 92-580, Oct. 27, 1972, effective (Sec. [1](c) of Public Law 92-580, Oct. 27, 1972) with respect to taxable years beginning after Dec. 31, 1971.

Prior amendments—Sec. 152(b)(3) was previously amended by the following: Sec. 4(b) of Public Law 85-866, Sept. 2, 1958, effective (Sec. 4(d) of Public Law 85-866, Sept. 2, 1958) for taxable years beginning after Dec. 31, 1957.* Sec. 2 of Public Law 333, Aug. 9, 1955 (qualified effective date rule in Sec. 3(b) of Public Law 333, Aug. 9, 1955).*

*Sec. 152(b)(3) as so amended is in P-H Cumulative Changes.

(4) A payment to a wife which is includible in the gross income of the wife under section 71 or 682 shall not be treated as a payment by her husband for the support of any dependent.

(5) An individual is not a member of the taxpayer's household if at any time during the taxable year of the taxpayer the relationship between such individual and the taxpayer is in violation of local law.

Addition—Sec. 152(b)(5) was added by Sec. 4(c) of Public Law 85-866, Sept. 2, 1958 (qualified effective date rule in Sec. 1(c)(1) of Public Law 85-866, Sept. 2, 1958).

(c) Multiple Support Agreements—For purposes of subsection (a), over half of the support of an individual for a calendar year shall be treated as received from the taxpayer if—

(1) no one person contributed over half of such support;

(2) over half of such support was received from persons each of whom, but for the fact that he did not contribute over half of such support, would have been entitled to claim such individual as a dependent for a taxable year beginning in such calendar year;

(3) the taxpayer contributed over 10 percent of such support; and

(4) each person described in paragraph (2) (other than the taxpayer) who contributed over 10 percent of such support files a written declaration (in such manner and form as the Secretary or his delegate may by regulations prescribe) that he will not claim such individual as a dependent for any taxable year beginning in such calendar year.

(d) Special Support Test in Case of Students—For purposes of subsection (a), in the case of any individual who is—

(1) a son, stepson, daughter, or stepdaughter of the taxpayer (within the meaning of this section), and

(2) a student (within the meaning of section 151(e)(4)), amounts received as scholarships for study at an education institution (as defined in section 151(e)(4)) shall not be taken into account in determining whether such individual received more than half of his support from the taxpayer.

(e) Support Test in Case of Child of Divorced Parents, etc.

(1) General rule—If—

(A) a child [as defined in section 151(e)(3)] receives over half of his support during the calendar year from his parents who are divorced or legally separated under a decree of divorce or separate maintenance, or who are separated under a written separation agreement, and

(B) such child is in the custody of one or both of his parents for more than one-half of the calendar year; such child shall be treated, for purposes of subsection (a), as receiving over half of his support during the calendar year from the parent having custody for a greater portion of the calendar year unless he is treated, under the provisions of paragraph (2), as having received over half of his support for such year from the other parent (referred to in this subsection as the parent not having custody).

(2) Special rule—The child of parents described in paragraph (1) shall be treated as having received over half of his support during the calendar year from the parent not having custody if—

(A)(i) the decree of divorce or of separate mainte-nance, or a written agreement between the par-ents applicable to the taxable year beginning in such calendar year, provides that the parent not having custody shall be entitled to any deduction allowable under section 151 for such child, and

(ii) such parent not having custody provides at least $600 for the support of such child during the calendar year, or

(B)(i) the parent not having custody provides $1,200 or more for the support of such child (or if there is more than one such child, $1,200 or more for all of such children) for the calendar year, and

(ii) if the parent having custody of such child does not clearly establish that he provided more for the support of such child during the calen-dar year than the parent not having custody.

For the purposes of this paragraph, amounts expended for the support of a child or children shall be treated as received from the parent not having custody to the extent that such parent provided amounts for such support.

(3) Itemized statement required—If a taxpayer claims that paragraph (2)(B) applies with respect to a child for a calendar year and the other parent claims that paragraph (2)(B)(i) is not satisfied or claims to have provided more for the support of such child during such calendar year than the taxpayer, each parent shall be entitled to receive, under regulations to be prescribed by the Secretary or his delegate, an item-

ized statement of the expenditures upon which the other parent's claim of support is based.

(4) Exception for multiple-support agreement—The provisions of this subsection shall not apply in any case where over half of the support of the child is treated as having been received from a taxpayer under the provisions of subsection (c).

(5) Regulations—The Secretary or his delegate shall prescribe such regulations as may be necessary to carry out the purposes of this subsection.

Addition—Sec. 152(e) was added by Sec. [1](a) of Public Law 90-78, Aug. 31, 1967, effective (Sec. 2 of Public Law 90-78, Aug. 31, 1967) with respect to tax-able years beginning after Dec. 31, 1966.

Tax Reform Act of 1976

[§ 484] Code Sec. 152. Dependent Defined.

* * * * * *

(e) Support Test in Case of Child of Divorced Parents, etc—

* * * * * *

(2) Special rule—The child of parents described in paragraph (1) shall be treated as having received over half of his support during the calendar year from the parent not having custody if—

(A)(i) the decree of divorce or of separate mainte-nance, or a written agreement between the par-ents applicable to the taxable year beginning in such calendar year, provides that the parent not having custody shall be entitled to any deduction allowable under section 151 for such child, and

(ii) such parent not having custody provides at least $600 for the support of such child during the calendar year, or

(B)(i) the parent not having custody provides $1,200 or more for the support of such child (or if there is more than one such child, $1,200 or more for each of such children) for the calendar year, and

(ii) the parent having custody of such child does not clearly establish that he provided more for the support of such child during the calendar year than the parent not having custody.

For the purposes of this paragraph, amounts expended for the support of a child or children shall be treated as received from the parent not having custody to the extent that such parent provided amounts for such support.

* * * * * *

[Footnote 484] Matter in italics in Sec. 152(e)(2)(B)(i) added by section 2139(a), *'76 Tax Reform Act*, which struck out (1) "all"

Effective date (Sec. 2139(b), *'76 Tax Reform Act*)—Applies to taxable years beginning after the date of enactment of this *Act*.

Title 38, United States Code—Veterans' Benefits

Examination of Records

Section 1790 (c) Notwithstanding any other provision of law, the records and accounts of educational institutions pertaining to eligible veterans or eligible persons who received educational assistance under this chapter or chapter 31, 32, 34, or 35 of this title, as well as the records of other students which the Administrator determines necessary to ascertain institutional compliance with the requirements of such chapters, shall be available for examination by duly authorized representatives of the Government. (Added p.l. 92-540, § 316(2), amended p.l. 94-502, § 510).

Appendix H

HIPAA/FERPA Guidance

[309]

Guidance Resource 1:

Joint Guidance on the Application of the Family Educational Rights and Privacy Act (FERPA) and the Health Insurance Portability and Accountability Act of 1996 (HIPAA) To Student Health Records[6]

Introduction

The purpose of this guidance is to explain the relationship between the Family Educational Rights and Privacy Act (FERPA) and the Health Insurance Portability and Accountability Act of 1996 (HIPAA) Privacy Rule, and to address apparent confusion on the part of school administrators, health care professionals, and others as to how these two laws apply to records maintained on students. It also addresses certain disclosures that are allowed without consent or authorization under both laws, especially those related to health and safety emergency situations. While this guidance seeks to answer many questions that school officials and others have had about the intersection of these federal laws, ongoing discussions may cause more issues to emerge. Contact information for submitting additional questions or suggestions for purposes of informing future guidance is provided at the end of this document. The Departments of Education and Health and Human Services are committed to a continuing dialogue with school officials and other professionals on these important matters affecting the safety and security of our nation's schools.

Overview of FERPA

FERPA is a federal law that protects the privacy of students' "education records." (*See* 20 U.S.C. § 1232g; 34 CFR Part 99). FERPA applies to educational agencies and institutions that receive funds under any program administered by the U.S. Department of Education. This includes virtually all public schools and school districts and most private and public postsecondary institutions, including medical and other professional schools. If an educational agency or institution receives funds under one or more of these programs, FERPA applies to the recipient as a whole, including each of its components, such as a department within a university. See 34 CFR § 99.1(d).

Private and religious schools at the elementary and secondary level generally do not receive funds from the Department of Education and are, therefore, not subject to FERPA. Note that a private school is not made subject to FERPA just because its students and teachers receive services from a local school district or state educational agency that receives funds from the Department. The school itself must receive funds from a program administered by the Department to be subject to FERPA. For example, if a school district places a student with a disability in a private school that is acting on behalf of the school district with regard to providing services to that student, the records of that student are subject to FERPA, but not the records of the other students in the private school. In such cases, the school district remains responsible for

---

Originally published November 2008 by U.S. Department of Health and Human Services, U.S. Department of Education. Also downloadable from <www.hhs.gov/ocr/privacy/hipaa/understanding/coveredentities/hipaaferpajointguide.pdf>.

complying with FERPA with respect to the education records of the student placed at the private school.

An educational agency or institution subject to FERPA may not have a policy or practice of disclosing the education records of students, or personally identifiable information from education records, without a parent or eligible student's written consent. See 34 CFR § 99.30. FERPA contains several exceptions to this general consent rule. See 34 CFR § 99.31. An "eligible student" is a student who is at least 18 years of age or who attends a postsecondary institution at any age. See 34 CFR §§ 99.3 and 99.5(a). Under FERPA, parents and eligible students have the right to inspect and review the student's education records and to seek to have them amended in certain circumstances. See 34 CFR §§ 99.10—99.12 and §§ 99.20—99.22.

The term "education records" is broadly defined to mean those records that are: (1) directly related to a student, and (2) maintained by an educational agency or institution or by a party acting for the agency or institution. See 34 CFR § 99.3. At the elementary or secondary level, a student's health records, including immunization records, maintained by an educational agency or institution subject to FERPA, as well as records maintained by a school nurse, are "education records" subject to FERPA. In addition, records that schools maintain on special education students, including records on services provided to students under the Individuals with Disabilities Education Act (IDEA), are "education records" under FERPA. This is because these records are (1) directly related to a student, (2) maintained by the school or a party acting for the school, and (3) not excluded from the definition of "education records."

At postsecondary institutions, medical and psychological treatment records of eligible students are excluded from the definition of "education records" if they are made, maintained, and used only in connection with treatment of the student and disclosed only to individuals providing the treatment. See 34 CFR § 99.3 "Education records." These records are commonly called "treatment records." An eligible student's treatment records may be disclosed for purposes other than the student's treatment, provided the records are disclosed under one of the exceptions to written consent under 34 CFR § 99.31(a) or with the student's written consent under 34 CFR § 99.30. If a school discloses an eligible student's treatment records for purposes other than treatment, the records are no longer excluded from the definition of "education records" and are subject to all other FERPA requirements.

The FERPA regulations and other helpful information can be found at: http://www.ed.gov/policy/gen/guid/fpco/index.html.

Overview of HIPAA

Congress enacted HIPAA in 1996 to, among other things, improve the efficiency and effectiveness of the health care system through the establishment of national standards and requirements for electronic health care transactions and to protect the privacy and security of individually identifiable health information. Collectively, these are known as HIPAA's Administrative Simplification provisions, and the U.S. Department of Health and Human Services has issued a suite of rules, including a privacy rule, to implement these provisions. Entities subject to the HIPAA Administrative Simplification Rules (see 45 CFR Parts 160, 162, and 164), known as "covered entities," are health plans, health care clearinghouses, and health care providers that transmit health information in electronic form in connection with covered transactions. See 45 CFR § 160.103. "Health care providers" include institutional providers of health or medical services, such as hospitals, as well as non-institutional providers, such as physicians, dentists, and other practitioners, along with any other person or organization that furnishes, bills, or is paid for health care in the normal course of business. Covered transactions are those for which the U.S. Department of Health and Human Services has adopted a standard, such as health care claims submitted to a health plan. See 45 CFR § 160.103 (definitions of "health care provider" and "transaction") and 45 CFR Part 162, Subparts K–R.

The HIPAA Privacy Rule requires covered entities to protect individuals' health records and other identifiable health information by requiring appropriate safeguards to protect privacy, and setting limits and conditions on the uses and disclosures that may be made of such information without patient authorization. The rule also gives patients rights over their health information, including rights to examine and obtain a copy of their health records, and to request corrections.

Where FERPA and HIPAA May Intersect

When a school provides health care to students in the normal course of business, such as through its health clinic, it is also a "health care provider" as defined by HIPAA. If a school also conducts any covered transactions electronically in connection with that health care, it is then a covered entity under HIPAA. As a covered entity, the school must comply with the HIPAA Administrative Simplification Rules for Transactions and Code Sets and Identifiers with respect to its transactions. However, many schools, even those that are HIPAA covered entities, are not required to comply with the HIPAA Privacy Rule because the only health records maintained by the school are "education records" or "treatment records" of eligible students under FERPA, both of which are excluded from coverage under the HIPAA Privacy Rule. See the exception at paragraph (2)(i) and (2)(ii) to what is considered "protected health information" (PHI) at 45 CFR § 160.103. In addition, the exception for records covered by FERPA applies both to the HIPAA Privacy Rule, as well as to the HIPAA Security Rule, because the Security Rule applies to a subset of information covered by the Privacy Rule (*i.e.*, electronic PHI). Information on the HIPAA Privacy Rule is available at: http://www.hhs.gov/ocr/HIPAA/. Information on the other HIPAA Administrative Simplification Rules is available at: http://www.cms.hhs.gov/HIPAAGenInfo/.

Frequently Asked Questions and Answers

▨ *Does the HIPAA Privacy Rule apply to an elementary or secondary school?*

Generally, no. In most cases, the HIPAA Privacy Rule does not apply to an elementary or secondary school because the school either: (1) is not a HIPAA covered entity or (2) is a HIPAA covered entity but maintains health information only on students in records that are by definition "education records" under FERPA and, therefore, is not subject to the HIPAA Privacy Rule.

▶ **THE SCHOOL IS NOT A HIPAA COVERED ENTITY.** The HIPAA Privacy Rule only applies to health plans, health care clearinghouses, and those health care providers that transmit health information electronically in connection with certain administrative and financial transactions ("covered transactions"). See 45 CFR § 160.102. Covered transactions are those for which the U.S. Department of Health and Human Services has adopted a standard, such as health care claims submitted to a health plan. See the definition of "transaction" at 45 CFR § 160.103 and 45 CFR Part 162, Subparts K–R. Thus, even though a school employs school nurses, physicians, psychologists, or other health care providers, the school is not generally a HIPAA covered entity because the providers do not engage in any of the covered transactions, such as billing a health plan electronically for their ser-

vices. It is expected that most elementary and secondary schools fall into this category.

▶ **THE SCHOOL IS A HIPAA COVERED ENTITY BUT DOES NOT HAVE "PROTECTED HEALTH INFORMATION."** Where a school does employ a health care provider that conducts one or more covered transactions electronically, such as electronically transmitting health care claims to a health plan for payment, the school is a HIPAA covered entity and must comply with the HIPAA Transactions and Code Sets and Identifier Rules with respect to such transactions. However, even in this case, many schools would not be required to comply with the HIPAA Privacy Rule because the school maintains health information only in student health records that are "education records" under FERPA and, thus, not "protected health information" under HIPAA. Because student health information in education records is protected by FERPA, the HIPAA Privacy Rule excludes such information from its coverage. See the exception at paragraph (2)(i) to the definition of "protected health information" in the HIPAA Privacy Rule at 45 CFR § 160.103. For example, if a public high school employs a health care provider that bills Medicaid electronically for services provided to a student under the IDEA, the school is a HIPAA covered entity and would be subject to the HIPAA requirements concerning transactions. However, if the school's provider maintains health information only in what are education records under FERPA, the school is not required to comply with the HIPAA Privacy Rule. Rather, the school would have to comply with FERPA's privacy requirements with respect to its education records, including the requirement to obtain parental consent (34 CFR § 99.30) in order to disclose to Medicaid billing information about a service provided to a student.

▨ *How does FERPA apply to health records on students maintained by elementary or secondary schools?*

At the elementary or secondary school level, students' immunization and other health records that are maintained by a school district or individual school, including a school-operated health clinic, that receives funds under any program administered by the U.S. Department of Education are "education records" subject to FERPA, including health and medical records maintained by a school nurse who is employed by or under contract with a school or school district. Some schools may receive a grant from a foundation or government agency to hire a nurse. Notwithstanding the source of the funding, if the nurse is hired as a school official (or contractor), the records maintained by the nurse or clinic are "education records" subject to FERPA.

Parents have a right under FERPA to inspect and review these health and medical records because they are "education records" under FERPA. See 34 CFR §§ 99.10—99.12. In addition, these records may not be shared with third parties without written parental consent unless the disclosure meets one of the exceptions to FERPA's general consent requirement. For instance, one of these exceptions allows schools to disclose a student's health and medical information and other "education records" to teachers and other school officials, without written consent, if these school officials have "legitimate educational interests" in accordance with school policy. See 34 CFR § 99.31(a)(1). Another exception permits the disclosure of education records, without consent, to appropriate parties in connection with an emergency, if knowledge of the information is necessary to protect the health or safety of the student or other individuals. See 34 CFR §§ 99.31(a)(10) and 99.36.

■ *Does FERPA or HIPAA apply to elementary or secondary school student health records maintained by a health care provider that is not employed by a school?*

If a person or entity acting on behalf of a school subject to FERPA, such as a school nurse that provides services to students under contract with or otherwise under the direct control of the school, maintains student health records, these records are education records under FERPA, just as they would be if the school maintained the records directly. This is the case regardless of whether the health care is provided to students on school grounds or off-site. As education records, the information is protected under FERPA and not HIPAA.

Some outside parties provide services directly to students and are not employed by, under contract to, or otherwise acting on behalf of the school. In these circumstances, these records are not "education records" subject to FERPA, even if the services are provided on school grounds, because the party creating and maintaining the records is not acting on behalf of the school. For example, the records created by a public health nurse who provides immunization or other health services to students on school grounds or otherwise in connection with school activities but who is not acting

on behalf of the school would not be "education records" under FERPA. In such situations, a school that wishes to disclose to this outside party health care provider any personally identifiable information from education records would have to comply with FERPA and obtain parental consent. See 34 CFR § 99.30.

With respect to HIPAA, even where student health records maintained by a health care provider are not education records protected by FERPA, the HIPAA Privacy Rule would apply to such records only if the provider conducts one or more of the HIPAA transactions electronically, *e.g.*, billing a health plan electronically for his or her services, making the provider a HIPAA covered entity.

■ *Are there circumstances in which the HIPAA Privacy Rule might apply to an elementary or secondary school?*

There are some circumstances in which an elementary or secondary school would be subject to the HIPAA Privacy Rule, such as where the school is a HIPAA covered entity and is not subject to FERPA. As explained previously, most private schools at the elementary and secondary school levels typically do not receive funding from the U.S. Department of Education and, therefore, are not subject to FERPA.

A school that is not subject to FERPA and is a HIPAA covered entity must comply with the HIPAA Privacy Rule with respect to any individually identifiable health information it has about students and others to whom it provides health care. For example, if a private elementary school that is not subject to FERPA employs a physician who bills a health plan electronically for the care provided to students (making the school a HIPAA covered entity), the school is required to comply with the HIPAA Privacy Rule with respect to the individually identifiable health information of its patients. The only exception would be where the school, despite not being subject to FERPA, has education records on one or more students to whom it provides services on behalf of a school or school district that is subject to FERPA. In this exceptional case, the education records of only those publicly placed students held by the private school would be subject to FERPA, while the remaining student health records would be subject to the HIPAA Privacy Rule.

■ *Where the HIPAA Privacy Rule applies, does it allow a health care provider to disclose protected health information (PHI) about a troubled teen to the parents of the teen?*

In most cases, yes. If the teen is a minor, the HIPAA Privacy Rule generally allows a covered entity to disclose PHI about the child to the child's parent, as the minor child's personal representative, when the disclosure is not inconsistent with state or other law. For more detailed information, see 45 CFR § 164.502(g) and the fact sheet regarding personal representatives at: http://www.hhs.gov/ocr/HIPAA/guidelines/personalrepresentatives.pdf. In some cases, such as when a minor may receive treatment without a parent's consent under applicable law, the parents are not treated as the minor's personal representative. See 45 CFR § 164.502(g)(3). In such cases where the parent is not the personal representative of the teen, other HIPAA Privacy Rule provisions may allow the disclosure of PHI about the teen to the parent. For example, if a provider believes the teen presents a serious danger to self or others, the HIPAA Privacy Rule permits a covered entity to disclose PHI to a parent or other person(s) if the covered entity has a good faith belief that: (1) the disclosure is necessary to prevent or lessen the threat and (2) the parent or other person(s) is reasonably able to prevent or lessen the threat. The disclosure also must be consistent with applicable law and standards of ethical conduct. See 45 CFR § 164.512(j)(1)(i).

In addition, the Privacy Rule permits covered entities to share information that is directly relevant to the involvement of a family member in the patient's health care or payment for care if, when given the opportunity, the patient does not object to the disclosure. Even when the patient is not present or it is impracticable, because of emergency circumstances or the patient's incapacity, for the covered entity to ask the patient about discussing his or her care or payment with a family member, a covered entity may share this information with the family member when, in exercising professional judgment, it determines that doing so would be in the best interest of the patient. See 45 CFR § 164.510(b).

☆ *Where the HIPAA Privacy Rule applies, does it allow a health care provider to disclose protected health information (PHI) about a student to a school nurse or physician?*

Yes. The HIPAA Privacy Rule allows covered health care providers to disclose PHI about students to school nurses, physicians, or other health care providers for treatment purposes, without the authorization of the student or student's parent. For example, a student's primary care physician may discuss the student's medi-cation and other health care needs with a school nurse who will administer the student's medication and provide care to the student while the student is at school.

☆ *Does FERPA or HIPAA apply to records on students at health clinics run by postsecondary institutions?*

FERPA applies to most public and private postsecondary institutions and, thus, to the records on students at the campus health clinics of such institutions. These records will be either education records or treatment records under FERPA, both of which are excluded from coverage under the HIPAA Privacy Rule, even if the school is a HIPAA covered entity. See the exceptions at paragraphs (2)(i) and (2)(ii) to the definition of "protected health information" at 45 CFR § 160.103.

The term "education records" is broadly defined under FERPA to mean those records that are: (1) directly related to a student and (2) maintained by an educational agency or institution or by a party acting for the agency or institution. See 34 CFR § 99.3, "Education records."

"Treatment records" under FERPA, as they are commonly called, are:

records on a student who is eighteen years of age or older, or is attending an institution of postsecondary education, which are made or maintained by a physician, psychiatrist, psychologist, or other recognized professional or paraprofessional acting in his professional or paraprofessional capacity, or assisting in that capacity, and which are made, maintained, or used only in connection with the provision of treatment to the student, and are not available to anyone other than persons providing such treatment, except that such records can be personally reviewed by a physician or other appropriate professional of the student's choice.

See 20 U.S.C. § 1232g(a)(4)(B)(iv); 34 CFR § 99.3, "Education records." For example, treatment records would include health or medical records that a university psychologist maintains only in connection with the provision of treatment to an eligible student, and health or medical records that the campus health center or clinic maintains only in connection with the provision of treatment to an eligible student. (Treatment records also would include health or medical records on an eligible student in high school if the records otherwise meet the above definition.)

"Treatment records" are excluded from the definition of "education records" under FERPA. However, it is important to note, that a school may disclose an eligible student's treatment records for purposes other than the student's treatment provided that the records are disclosed under one of the exceptions to written consent under 34 CFR § 99.31(a) or with the student's written consent under 34 CFR § 99.30. If a school discloses an eligible student's treatment records for purposes other than treatment, the treatment records are no longer excluded from the definition of "education records" and are subject to all other FERPA requirements, including the right of the eligible student to inspect and review the records.

While the health records of students at postsecondary institutions may be subject to FERPA, if the institution is a HIPAA covered entity and provides health care to nonstudents, the individually identifiable health information of the clinic's nonstudent patients is subject to the HIPAA Privacy Rule. Thus, for example, postsecondary institutions that are subject to both HIPAA and FERPA and that operate clinics open to staff, or the public, or both (including family members of students) are required to comply with FERPA with respect to the health records of their student patients, and with the HIPAA Privacy Rule with respect to the health records of their nonstudent patients.

☒ *Under FERPA, may an eligible student inspect and review his or her "treatment records"?*

Under FERPA, treatment records, by definition, are not available to anyone other than professionals providing treatment to the student, or to physicians or other appropriate professionals of the student's choice. However, this does not prevent an educational institution from allowing a student to inspect and review such records. If the institution chooses to do so, though, such records are no longer excluded from the definition of "education records" and are subject to all other FERPA requirements.

☒ *Under FERPA, may an eligible student's treatment records be shared with parties other than treating professionals?*

As explained previously, treatment records, by definition, are not available to anyone other than professionals providing treatment to the student, or to physicians or other appropriate professionals of the student's choice. However, this does not prevent an educational institution from using or disclosing these records for other purposes or with other parties. If the institution

chooses to do so, a disclosure may be made to any party with a prior written consent from the eligible student (*see* 34 CFR § 99.30) or under any of the disclosures permitted without consent in 34 CFR § 99.31 of FERPA.

For example, a university physician treating an eligible student might determine that treatment records should be disclosed to the student's parents. This disclosure may be made if the eligible student is claimed as a dependent for federal income tax purposes (*see* 34 CFR § 99.31(a)(8)). If the eligible student is not claimed as a dependent, the disclosure may be made to parents, as well as other appropriate parties, if the disclosure is in connection with a health or safety emergency. See 34 CFR §§ 99.31(a)(10) and 99.36. Once the records are disclosed under one of the exceptions to FERPA's general consent requirement, the treatment records are no longer excluded from the definition of "education records" and are subject to all other FERPA requirements as "education records" under FERPA.

☒ *Under what circumstances does FERPA permit an eligible student's treatment records to be disclosed to a third-party health care provider for treatment?*

An eligible student's treatment records may be shared with health care professionals who are providing treatment to the student, including health care professionals who are not part of or not acting on behalf of the educational institution (*i.e.*, third-party health care provider), as long as the information is being disclosed only for the purpose of providing treatment to the student. In addition, an eligible student's treatment records may be disclosed to a third-party health care provider when the student has requested that his or her records be "reviewed by a physician or other appropriate professional of the student's choice." See 20 U.S.C. § 1232g(a)(4)(B)(iv). In either of these situations, if the treatment records are disclosed to a third-party health care provider that is a HIPAA covered entity, the records would become subject to the HIPAA Privacy Rule. The records at the educational institution continue to be treatment records under FERPA, so long as the records are only disclosed by the institution for treatment purposes to a health care provider or to the student's physician or other appropriate professional requested by the student.

If the disclosure is for purposes other than treatment, an eligible student's treatment record only may be disclosed to a third party as an "education record," that is, with the prior written consent of the eligible student or if one of the exceptions to FERPA's general consent requirement is met. See 34 CFR §99.31. For example, if a university is served with a court order requiring the disclosure of the mental health records of a student maintained as treatment records at the campus clinic, the university may disclose the records to comply with the court order in accordance with the provisions of §99.31(a)(9) of the FERPA regulations. However, the mental health records that the university disclosed for non-treatment purposes are no longer excluded from the definition of "education records" and are subject to all other FERPA requirements as "education records" under FERPA.

▣ *Are all student records maintained by a health clinic run by a postsecondary institution considered "treatment records" under FERPA?*

Not all records on eligible students that are maintained by a college- or university-run health clinic are treatment records under FERPA because many such records are not made, maintained, or used only in connection with the treatment of a student. For example, billing records that a college- or university-run health clinic maintains on a student are "education records" under FERPA, the disclosure of which would require prior written consent from the eligible student unless an exception applies. See 34 CFR §99.30. In addition, records relating to treatment that are shared with persons other than professionals providing treatment to the student are "education records" under FERPA. Thus, to the extent a health clinic has shared a student's treatment information with persons and for purposes other than for treatment, such information is an "education record," not a treatment record under FERPA.

▣ *Does FERPA or HIPAA apply to records on students who are patients at a university hospital?*

Patient records maintained by a hospital affiliated with a university that is subject to FERPA are not typically "education records" or "treatment records" under FERPA because university hospitals generally do not provide health care services to students on behalf of the educational institution. Rather, these hospitals provide such services without regard to the person's status as a student and not on behalf of a university. Thus, assuming the hospital is a HIPAA covered entity, these records are subject to all of the HIPAA rules, including the

HIPAA Privacy Rule. However, in a situation where a hospital does run the student health clinic on behalf of a university, the clinic records on students would be subject to FERPA, either as "education records" or "treatment records," and not subject to the HIPAA Privacy Rule.

▣ *Where the HIPAA Privacy Rule applies, does it permit a health care provider to disclose protected health information (PHI) about a patient to law enforcement, family members, or others if the provider believes the patient presents a serious danger to self or others?*

The HIPAA Privacy Rule permits a covered entity to disclose PHI, including psychotherapy notes, when the covered entity has a good faith belief that the disclosure: (1) is necessary to prevent or lessen a serious and imminent threat to the health or safety of the patient or others and (2) is to a person(s) reasonably able to prevent or lessen the threat. This may include, depending on the circumstances, disclosure to law enforcement, family members, the target of the threat, or others who the covered entity has a good faith belief can mitigate the threat. The disclosure also must be consistent with applicable law and standards of ethical conduct. See 45 CFR §164.512(j)(1)(i). For example, consistent with other law and ethical standards, a mental health provider whose teenage patient has made a credible threat to inflict serious and imminent bodily harm on one or more fellow students may alert law enforcement, a parent or other family member, school administrators or campus police, or others the provider believes may be able to prevent or lessen the chance of harm. In such cases, the covered entity is presumed to have acted in good faith where its belief is based upon the covered entity's actual knowledge (*i.e.*, based on the covered entity's own interaction with the patient) or in reliance on a credible representation by a person with apparent knowledge or authority (*i.e.*, based on a credible report from a family member or other person). See 45 CFR §164.512(j)(4).

For threats or concerns that do not rise to the level of "serious and imminent," other HIPAA Privacy Rule provisions may apply to permit the disclosure of PHI. For example, covered entities generally may disclose PHI about a minor child to the minor's personal representative (*e.g.*, a parent or legal guardian), consistent with state or other laws. See 45 CFR §164.502(b).

⊞ *Does* FERPA *permit a postsecondary institution to disclose a student's treatment records or education records to law enforcement, the student's parents, or others if the institution believes the student presents a serious danger to self or others?*

An eligible student's education records and treatment records (which are considered education records if used or made available for any purpose other than the eligible student's treatment) may be disclosed, without consent, if the disclosure meets one of the exceptions to FERPA's general consent rule. See 34 CFR § 99.31. One of the permitted disclosures is to appropriate parties, which may include law enforcement or parents of a student, in connection with an emergency if knowledge of the information is necessary to protect the health or safety of the student or other individuals. See 34 CFR §§ 99.31(a)(10) and 99.36.

There are other exceptions that apply to disclosing information to parents of eligible students that are discussed on the "Safe Schools & FERPA" Web page, as well as other information that should be helpful to school officials, at: http://www.ed.gov/policy/gen/guid/fpco/ferpa/safeschools/index.html.

⊞ *Are the health records of an individual who is both a student and an employee of a university at which the person receives health care subject to the privacy provisions of* FERPA *or those of* HIPAA?

The individual's health records would be considered "education records" protected under FERPA and, thus, excluded from coverage under the HIPAA Privacy Rule. FERPA defines "education records" as records that are directly related to a student and maintained by an educational agency or institution or by a party acting for the agency or institution. 34 CFR § 99.3 ("education records"). While FERPA excludes from this definition certain records relating to employees of the educational institution, to fall within this exclusion, such records must, among other things, relate exclusively to the individual in his or her capacity as an employee, such as records that were created in connection with health services that are available only to employees. Thus, the health or medical records that are maintained by a university as part of its provision of health care to a student who is also an employee of a university are covered by FERPA and not the HIPAA Privacy Rule.

⊞ *Can a postsecondary institution be a "hybrid entity" under the* HIPAA *Privacy Rule?*

Yes. A postsecondary institution that is a HIPAA covered entity may have health information to which the Privacy Rule may apply not only in the health records of nonstudents in the health clinic, but also in records maintained by other components of the institution that are not education records or treatment records under FERPA, such as in a law enforcement unit or research department. In such cases, the institution, as a HIPAA covered entity, has the option of becoming a "hybrid entity" and, thus, having the HIPAA Privacy Rule apply only to its health care unit. The school can achieve hybrid entity status by designating the health unit as its "health care component." As a hybrid entity, any individually identifiable health information maintained by other components of the university (*i.e.*, outside of the health care component), such as a law enforcement unit, or a research department, would not be subject to the HIPAA Privacy Rule, notwithstanding that these components of the institution might maintain records that are not "education records" or treatment records under FERPA.

To become a hybrid entity, the covered entity must designate and include in its health care component all components that would meet the definition of a covered entity if those components were separate legal entities. (A covered entity may have more than one health care component.) However, the hybrid entity is not permitted to include in its health care component other types of components that do not perform the covered functions of the covered entity or components that do not perform support activities for the components performing covered functions. That is, components that do not perform health plan, health care provider, or health care clearinghouse functions and components that do not perform activities in support of these functions (as would a business associate of a separate legal entity) may not be included in a health care component. Within the hybrid entity, most of the HIPAA Privacy Rule requirements apply only to the health care component, although the hybrid entity retains certain oversight, compliance, and enforcement obligations. See 45 CFR § 164.105 of the Privacy Rule for more information.

Conclusion

The HIPAA Privacy Rule specifically excludes from its coverage those records that are protected by FERPA. When making determinations as to whether personally identifiable information from student health records maintained by the educational agency or institution may be disclosed, school officials at institutions subject to FERPA should refer to FERPA and its requirements. While the educational agency or institution has the responsibility to make the initial, case-by-case determination of whether a disclosure meets the requirements of FERPA, the Department of Education's Family Policy Compliance Office is available to offer technical assistance to school officials in making such determinations.

For quick, informal responses to routine questions about FERPA, school officials may email the Department at ferpa@ed.gov. For more formal technical assistance on the information provided in this guidance in particular or FERPA in general, please contact the Family Policy Compliance Office at the following address:

Family Policy Compliance Office
U.S. Department of Education
400 Maryland Ave. S.W.
Washington, D.C. 20202-8520

You may also find additional information and guidance on the Department's Web site at: http://www.ed.gov/policy/gen/guid/fpco/index.html.

For more information on the HIPAA Privacy Rule, please visit the Department of Health and Human Services' HIPAA Privacy Rule Web site at: http://www.hhs.gov/ocr/HIPAA/. The Web site offers a wide range of helpful information about the HIPAA Privacy Rule, including the full text of the Privacy Rule, a HIPAA Privacy Rule summary, over 200 frequently asked questions, and both consumer and covered entity fact sheets.

In addition, if you would like to submit additional questions not covered by this guidance document or suggestions for purposes of informing future guidance, please send an email to ocrprivacy@hhs.gov and ferpa@ed.gov.

Guidance Resource 2:
Don't Tie Yourself in FERPA/HIPAA Knots

The former heads of FERPA and HIPAA Compliance, LeRoy Rooker and Richard M. Campanelli, unravel misconceptions that can interfere with safety on college and university campuses.[7]

Recent outbreaks of violence affecting higher education campuses are a reminder that college and university communities must be prepared to confidently respond when concerns arise about the behavior of a student who could pose a threat to his or her own safety or the safety of or others. Unfortunately, confusion about FERPA and HIPAA[8] and how they interact, can unnecessarily impede appropriate and legal responses to a threat to safety or health, and endanger both the student and the community. Here are some common myths and facts about FERPA and HIPAA, and some practical advice on steps to make sure that safety *and* privacy are protected.

MYTH 1: *Under FERPA, a university employee is not allowed to share observations about a student's behavior with a school administrator, campus police, local law enforcement, or the student's parents.*

REALITY: Mere observations about a student's behavior are not covered by FERPA because personal knowledge and observations are not derived from an "education record" subject to FERPA. As discussed below, even if the information is committed to an education record, such as in an email to a school official, FERPA provides certain important exceptions that can allow the information to be shared.

MYTH 2: *Anything written down becomes an "education record" under FERPA and thus cannot be shared.*

REALITY: Not all records are "education records" under FERPA. In the context of public safety, for instance, when records are made and maintained by "law enforcement units" of educational institutions for law enforcement purposes, they are not education records, and they are not subject to FERPA. And while "treatment records"—made, maintained and used only in connection with treatment of the student and shared only with those who provide treatment—are subject to FERPA, they are not education records. In both cases, the records can be shared with administrators or others, consistent with FERPA and any ethical or legal obligations that otherwise exist.

MYTH 3: *Assuming a record is an education record under FERPA, the law says the information in it cannot be shared even if it demonstrates that a student may harm himself or others.*

REALITY: There are a number of circumstances where FERPA allows disclosure of education records. In this context, for instance, information in an education record can be shared under the "health or safety emergency" exception: If the institution determines that there is an articulable and significant threat to health or safety of a student or others, the information can be shared with parents or anyone else whose knowledge is necessary to protect the health or safety of a student or others.

MYTH 4: *Sharing information in an education record based on the "health and safety exception" can be a big risk for an educational institution, because whether the threat is "significant" comes down to a judgment call. Someone at the Department of Education will always second-guess our decision to share the information.*

REALITY: The Department of Education specifically changed its regulations in 2008 to give institutions greater confidence in making these determinations. Now, as long as the educational institution can show, based on the information available at the time, that it had a rational basis for determining there was an articulable and significant threat of harm to the student or others, the preamble

---

[7] This resource originally was published in newsletter format; intended for information only and is not to be considered legal advice.

About the Authors: LeRoy Rooker, ferpa@aacrao.org, was Director of the U. S. Department of Education's Family Policy Compliance Office from 1988 to 2009, and is a Senior Fellow at AACRAO. Richard M. Campanelli, Esq., richard.campanelli@bakerd.com, was Director of the Office for Civil Rights, responsible for HIPAA compliance, at the U.S. Department of Health & Human Services, 2002–2005. He is of Counsel with Baker & Daniels LLP and Senior Advisor to B&D Consulting.

[8] The Family Educational Rights and Privacy Act (FERPA), and the Health Information Portability and Accountability Act (HIPAA), specifically the HIPAA Privacy Rule.

to the regulations explained that the Department won't substitute its judgment for that of the institution.

MYTH 5: *FERPA is confusing enough, but then we have to worry about HIPAA. Even in potentially dangerous situations, it is best just not to share any information.*

REALITY: HIPAA and FERPA are structured to minimize overlap.[9] In many cases HIPAA will not apply to the records, and when it does apply, HIPAA also provides exceptions that allow safety concerns to be addressed.

Student education records or treatment records covered by FERPA are specifically excluded from coverage under the HIPAA Privacy Rule and HIPAA Security Rule. For instance, where the only health records maintained by the school are education records or treatment records subject to FERPA, the school is not required to comply with the HIPAA Privacy or Security Rules with respect to those records, even if the school otherwise is subject to HIPAA.

Further, HIPAA only applies to certain types of entities—HIPAA "covered entities"—and their "business associates." HIPAA covered entities include health plans, health care clearinghouses, and health care providers that transmit heath information in electronic form using certain standards adopted by the federal government. A typical example of a HIPAA-covered entity is a university-related hospital that provides medical services and bills a health plan electronically for its services. If, together with its components, an educational institution does not meet the legal definition of a HIPAA covered entity, it is not subject to the HIPAA requirements. School administrators or legal counsel can advise whether HIPAA applies to the institution or any of its components.

Finally, even if HIPAA protections apply to the information (because the institution is a covered entity or business associate of a covered entity, and the information is not an education or treatment record under FERPA), HIPAA provisions contain exceptions that permit disclosures in cases of serious and imminent threat to the health or safety of the patient or others. Under HIPAA, a covered entity can disclose protected health information, including psychotherapy notes, when it has a good faith belief that the disclosure is necessary to prevent or lessen the threat to the health or safety of the patient or others, and

it is disclosed to persons reasonably able to prevent or lessen the threat. (The disclosure must also be consistent with any other applicable law and standards of ethical conduct.) This means that depending on the circumstances and the need, these disclosures could be made to law enforcement, family members, the target of the threat, school administrators, campus police or others if the covered entity has a good faith belief that the person to whom it is disclosed is reasonably able to prevent or lessen the threat. Further, the entity will be presumed to have acted in good faith where it acts on the basis of its own knowledge, or reliance on a credible report from a family member or anyone else.

* * * * * * *

Of course individuals—or their parents, representatives or guardians when they are empowered to do so under law—can also give permission under FERPA or HIPAA to share information that would otherwise be protected. Other laws and requirements, such as professional and ethical requirements and state law, should also be reviewed to determine how they may align with FERPA and HIPAA and impact how information is protected and shared.

* * * * * * *

Educational institutions must be confident that they can both protect privacy as required by law, and protect the health and safety of students and the community. As a practical matter, our experience suggests that staff will be in the best position to address both privacy and security needs if they have adequate training with respect to FERPA and HIPAA concepts, and if a "go-to" person is identified for times of crisis or confusion who knows how information must be protected, and how and with whom it can be shared. *The most important thing to remember is that there are pathways, under both FERPA and HIPAA, to appropriately address privacy concerns and meet the safety needs of students and the larger college and university community.*

---

[9] After the Virginia Tech tragedy, the U. S. Department of Health & Human Service and U.S. Department of Education published joint guidance to specifically clarify how—under both laws—safety needs can be met while complying with privacy requirements.

Electronic Signature Regulations

Federal Guidelines for Accepting "Signed and Dated Written Consent" in Electronic Format

FR DOC 04-9054

Federal Register: April 21, 2004 (Volume 69, Number 77)

Rules and Regulations

From the Federal Register Online via GPO Access at wais.access.gpo.gov.

[DOCID: fr21ap04-11]

* * * * * * *

DEPARTMENT OF EDUCATION

34 CFR Part 99

RIN 1855-AA00

Family Educational Rights and Privacy Act

Agency: Office of Innovation and Improvement; Department of Education.

Action: Final regulations.

* * * * * * *

SUMMARY: The Secretary amends 34 CFR part 99 to implement the Department's interpretation of the Family Educational Rights and Privacy Act (FERPA) identified through administrative experience as necessary for proper program operation. These final regulations provide general guidelines for accepting "signed and dated written consent" under FERPA in electronic format.

DATES: These regulations are effective May 21, 2004.

SUPPLEMENTARY INFORMATION: On July 28, 2003, the Secretary published a notice of proposed rulemaking (NPRM) for this amendment in the Federal Register (68 FR 44420). In the preamble to the NPRM, we invited interested persons to submit comments concerning the proposed change. We proposed to add Sec. 99.30(d) in order to provide general guidelines for educational agencies and institutions that choose to meet the requirements of Sec. 99.30 with records and signatures in electronic format.

We reviewed guidance for electronic signatures recently published by a variety of federal government sources, including the Office of Management and Budget (OMB), the General Services Administration, and the National Institute for Standards and Technology. Based on that review and comments received from school officials, we believe it is necessary to modify these final regulations. We modified these regulations to reflect the definition of "electronic signature" established in the Government Paperwork Elimination Act (GPEA), Public Law 105-277, Title XVII, Section 1710.

Electronic signatures are an area of rapidly evolving technology. These modified regulations provide more fluid and flexible standards for schools that choose to implement a process for accepting electronic signatures. These modified regulations permit schools to take advantage of changing technology as it may become available, whether the change concerns additional security provisions or enhanced customer service.

Analysis of Comments and Changes

In response to the Secretary's invitation in the NPRM, 16 parties submitted comments on the proposed regulations. We publish an analysis of the comments and of the changes in the regulations since publication of the NPRM as an appendix at the end of these final regulations. We discuss substantive issues under the sections of the regulations to which they pertain. Generally, we do not address technical and other minor changes and suggested changes the law does not authorize the Secretary to make. However, we have reviewed these regulations since publication of the NPRM and have made changes as follows:

Acceptance of signature in electronic form (Sec. 99.30)

COMMENTS: None.

DISCUSSION: Electronic formats for signatures and documents are changing rapidly and substantially in response to evolving technologies and public acceptance. We wish to provide the widest possible flexibility for schools to adapt to such changes yet retain a methodology that operates within FERPA's requirements for proper disclosure of education records. Because FERPA applies to educational agencies and institutions at all levels, we do not want these regulations to inadvertently impose standards on elementary and secondary schools that may be valid only for postsecondary schools under federal student aid programs.

Based on our review of standards acceptable to other areas of the federal government, including OMB circulars and Federal Student Aid (FSA) guidance for electronic student loan transactions, as well as standards established by laws such as the Electronic Signatures in Global and National Commerce Act (E-Sign) and GPEA, we believe these modified regulations will more easily permit schools to adapt to changing standards in the areas of electronic signatures and documents.

CHANGES: We have revised these regulations to be consistent with other federal government standards for "electronic signatures."

Executive Order 12866

We have reviewed these final regulations in accordance with Executive Order 12866. Under the terms of the order we have assessed the potential costs and benefits of this regulatory action.

The potential costs associated with these final regulations are those resulting from statutory requirements and those we have determined to be necessary for administering this program effectively and efficiently.

In assessing the potential costs and benefits—both quantitative and qualitative—of these final regulations, we have determined that the benefits of the regulations justify the costs.

Summary of Potential Costs and Benefits

We summarized the potential costs and benefits of these final regulations in the preamble to the NPRM (68 FR 44421).

Paperwork Reduction Act of 1995

These regulations do not contain any information collection requirements.

Assessment of Educational Impact

In the NPRM we requested comments on whether the proposed regulations would require transmission of information that any other agency or authority of the United States gathers or makes available.

Based on the response to the NPRM and on our review, we have determined that these final regulations do not require transmission of information that any other agency or authority of the United States gathers or makes available.

Electronic Access to This Document

You may view this document, as well as all other Department of Education documents published in the Federal Register, in text or Adobe Portable Document Format (PDF) on the Internet at the following site: www.ed.gov/news/fedregister.

To use PDF you must have Adobe Acrobat Reader, which is available free at this site. If you have questions about using PDF, call the U.S. Government Printing Office (GPO), toll free, at 1-888-293-6498; or in the Washington, DC, area at (202) 512-1530.

You may also find these regulations, as well as additional information about FERPA, on the following Web site: *http://www.ed.gov/policy/gen/guid/fpco/index.html*.

Note: The official version of this document is the document published in the Federal Register. Free Internet access to the official edition of the Federal Register and the Code of Federal Regulations is available on GPO Access at: *http://www.gpoaccess.gov/nara/index.html*.

(Catalog of Federal Domestic Assistance Number does not apply.)

List of Subjects in 34 CFR Part 99

Administrative practice and procedure, Education, Information, Parents, Privacy, Records, Reporting and recordkeeping requirements, Students.

Dated: April 2, 2004.

Rod Paige,
Secretary of Education.

For the reasons discussed in the preamble, the Secretary amends part 99 of title 34 of the Code of Federal Regulations as follows:

1. The authority citation for part 99 continues to read as follows:

    Authority: 20 U.S.C. 1232g, unless otherwise noted.

2. Section 99.30 is amended by adding a new paragraph (d) to read as follows:

§ 99.30 Under what conditions is prior consent required to disclose information?

* * * * * * *

(d) "Signed and dated written consent" under this part may include a record and signature in electronic form that—

(1) Identifies and authenticates a particular person as the source of the electronic consent; and

(2) Indicates such person's approval of the information contained in the electronic consent.

Appendix

Analysis of Comments and Changes

Note: The following appendix will not appear in the Code of Federal Regulations.

Use at Multiple School Levels

COMMENTS: One commenter asked whether the proposed regulations apply only to eligible students at postsecondary institutions.

DISCUSSION: FERPA gives the right to consent to disclosure of education records to parents of minor children at the elementary and secondary school levels, and to parents of children with disabilities who receive services under Part B or Part C of the Individuals with Disabilities Education Act (IDEA). When a student turns 18 years of age or attends a postsecondary institution at any age, the student is considered an "eligible student" under FERPA.

The right to consent under FERPA transfers under either of those two conditions from the parent to the eligible student. Although the term "eligible student" will be used throughout this document, educational agencies and institutions at all levels may use these regulations to accept electronic signatures.

CHANGE: None.

Specific Methodologies

COMMENTS: Several commenters asked for more specific guidance on authentication methods and technologies that may be used.

DISCUSSION: As explained in the preamble to the NPRM, the regulations are purposefully narrow in scope and intended to be technology-neutral (page 44420). While we will issue additional guidance that will include further examples

of an acceptable process, we do not want to limit the flexibility of schools in this area of rapid technological change.
CHANGE: None.

Safe Harbor

COMMENTS: Several commenters support the use of the FSA standards for electronic signatures in electronic student loan transactions (FSA Standards) as a "safe harbor" provision for acceptance of electronic signatures in FERPA. Several other commenters objected to the FSA Standards as being too rigorous for the perceived level of risk of improper disclosure. The FSA Standards may be viewed on the Internet at the following site: *http://www.ifap.ed.gov/dpcletters/gen0106.html.*

DISCUSSION: The preamble to the NPRM stated (page 44421) that the FSA Standards would be the "safe harbor" provision. A "safe harbor" is not set at the minimally acceptable level of security. Due to the nature of the information that may be disclosed and the potential harm a student may suffer from an unauthorized disclosure, we believe the "safe harbor" provision is not unduly rigorous. Schools retain the flexibility to choose to implement a system that meets the "safe harbor" provisions or to choose to implement another system to meet the new FERPA provisions.

However, schools should be reminded that Congress has also, through the Gramm-Leach-Bliley Act (GLB) (Pub.L. 106-102, November 12, 1999), imposed additional privacy restrictions on financial institutions, which include postsecondary institutions, requiring institutions to protect against unauthorized access to, or use of, consumer records. The Federal Trade Commission's (FTC) rule on the privacy of consumer financial information provides that postsecondary institutions that are complying with FERPA to protect the privacy of their student financial aid records will be deemed in compliance with the FTC's rule. (65 FR 33646, 33648 (May 24, 2000)). This exemption applies to notice requirements and the restrictions on a financial institution's disclosure of nonpublic personal information to nonaffiliated third parties in Title V of GLB. However, postsecondary institutions are not exempt from the FTC final rule implementing section 501 of GLB on Safeguarding Customer Information. (67 FR 368484 (May 23, 2002)). Financial institutions, including postsecondary institutions, are required to have adopted an information security program by May 23, 2003, under the FTC rule.

Thus, while schools have the maximum flexibility in choosing a system that meets FSA's "safe harbor" provisions or another process for authenticating Personal

Identification Number (PIN) numbers under FERPA, post-secondary institutions should keep these other federal requirements in mind when implementing such systems.
CHANGE: None.

Applicability of FSA Standards

COMMENTS: One commenter stated that it was confusing to apply the situations and terminology in the FSA Standards to FERPA. The commenter suggested that we issue a separate guide on FERPA standards.

DISCUSSION: The FSA Standards do not apply directly to FERPA because some actions are imposed only on lenders or borrowers of financial aid. For example, the FSA Standards require that paper copies of transactions be provided to a student borrower at no cost in some circumstances, and lenders are required to obtain a borrower's specific consent to conduct loan transactions electronically. Neither of those circumstances has parallels within FERPA.

We agree that some circumstances within the FSA Standards do not relate directly to FERPA. While schools are not required by FERPA to follow the FSA Standards, we believe that schools may use the set-up and security measures described in the FSA Standards, particularly sections 3 through 7, as guidance for security measures in a system using electronic records and signatures under FERPA. We do not plan to issue a separate FERPA standards document, but we will clarify these items in additional guidance.
CHANGE: None.

Use of "Trusted Third Party" in Identification Verification

COMMENTS: A commenter expressed a belief that disclosure by a school of student information without prior written consent to a "trusted third party" as part of an identification verification process may be in violation of FERPA. This commenter stated that the conflict arises because the FSA Standards specify that the third party may not be an agent of the school.

DISCUSSION: FSA authenticates student identification information with the Social Security Administration as a "trusted third party." FERPA's consent provisions do not apply to transactions between a student and FSA.

In situations where a school is disclosing education records to a third party, FERPA's consent provisions apply. When the third party receiving the information from the school is not an agent for the school, FERPA generally requires a school to obtain prior written consent before the disclosure is made. Receipt of the prior consent would then allow a school to disclose personal information for authentication purposes with the records of independent sources such as credit reporting agencies or testing companies.

Schools may also choose to use other processes to authenticate identity. For example, a school may require the eligible student to present photographic identification issued by a government agency. Such photographic identification includes, but is not limited to, a state-issued driver's license, a federally-issued passport, [Page 21672] and other Military, federal, or state-issued identification cards.
CHANGE: None.

Issuing a PIN or Password

COMMENTS: One commenter stated that schools that issue a PIN to students as outlined in the FSA Standards can result in a PIN that is recorded and accessible to school officials. The commenter is concerned that this conflicts with FERPA policy that a PIN is not acceptable for use under FERPA if persons other than the student have access to the PIN.

DISCUSSION: The process described in the FSA Standards does not permit school officials to access a student's PIN or password. In addition, the FSA Standards permit an eligible student to change an assigned password or PIN to one of their own choosing. Under the FSA Standards, all of the passwords or PINs, whether assigned or student-selected, are maintained in a secure database in an encrypted manner that is not generally accessible to school officials or other parties.

A school that uses a similar methodology would remain in compliance with requirements for the acceptance of an electronic signature under FERPA. However, a school may not use a PIN or password process that results in a PIN or password that is visible and easily accessible to persons other than the eligible student because that type of process results in an insecure PIN or password. Schools retain the maximum flexibility to implement any appropriate methodology.
CHANGE: None.

Use of Current Systems

COMMENTS: Several commenters asked whether it is acceptable to use existing systems that include sign-on capability, such as campus email, admissions, enrollment, and fee payment systems. Several commenters also asked if it is acceptable to permit eligible students to provide notice of directory information opt outs by use of electronic signatures.

DISCUSSION: As explained in the preamble to the NPRM, the requirements for an electronic signature apply in circumstances where a signed and dated written consent is required under FERPA (page 44420). Such consent is generally required under FERPA when information from education records is to be disclosed to a third party, as in the issuance of a transcript to a prospective employer. Consent is not a requirement for disclosure of an eligible student's own records to the student. A school that wishes to use its current system for situations where FERPA consent is required must determine whether it provides the required level of security.

The majority of the systems mentioned by the commenters are designed for communication between a school and an eligible student. Systems that permit eligible students to view, alter, or update the student's own records by electronic means are not the subject of these regulations. A school must ensure that the eligible student and not some other party is the receiver of the information, but the method a school uses to do so is not prescribed by these regulations.

CHANGE: None.

Third-Party Presentation of Electronic Signature

COMMENTS: Several commenters asked whether the proposed regulations are applicable when a third party, not the eligible student, presents the electronic signature claimed to be that of the eligible student. Two commenters expressed strong support for acceptance of electronic signatures presented by third parties, primarily when the third party is a government entity or another educational agency or institution.

DISCUSSION: Educational agencies and institutions are responsible to ensure that education records are disclosed only in accordance with FERPA. Any disclosure of education records to a third party, even in accordance with a student's consent, is permitted but not required under FERPA. Each agency or institution must have the flexibility to decide whether a request for disclosure meets the requirements of FERPA and whether the institution wishes to make the requested disclosure.

The FERPA regulations do not require that an eligible student provide his or her consent directly to the educational agency or institution, and these regulations do not impose a different requirement for electronic signatures. We would support an agency's or institution's decision to only accept electronic signatures presented on behalf of the eligible student by certain third parties, such as federal or state agencies.

CHANGE: None.

Application of Standards of Other Privacy Laws

COMMENTS: One commenter suggested that the standards of the Health Insurance Portability and Accountability Act of 1996 (HIPAA) Privacy Rule for "protected health information" be applied to personally identifiable information contained in students' education records. The commenter was concerned because personally identifiable information from students' education records are disclosed by educational agencies and institutions to outside third parties who have grants to do research. The commenter stated that educational agencies and institutions do not recognize the concern for privacy of such data.

DISCUSSION: The HIPAA Privacy Rule, which is administered by the Department of Health and Human Services, excludes from the definition of "protected health information" two categories of records that are relevant here: "education records" covered by FERPA (34 CFR 99.3 "Education records") and records described under FERPA's medical treatment records provision (34 CFR 99.3 "Education records"). See 45 CFR 160.103(a). The HIPAA Privacy Rule does not cover such records because Congress, through FERPA, specifically has addressed how these records should be protected. As such, FERPA provides ample protections for these records and schools should ensure that health information, as well as other education records on students, are not disclosed to outside third parties without the consent of the student or under one of the exceptions to FERPA's general prior consent rule.

With regard to the commenter's statement that educational agencies and institutions do not recognize the concern for privacy of student information, it has been our experience that the majority of the Nation's schools do comply with FERPA and strive to protect the privacy of information contained in student records. FERPA is not a public open records or freedom of information statute. Rather, the purpose of FERPA is to protect the privacy interests of parents and eligible students in records maintained by educational agencies and institutions on the student. These privacy concerns should not be viewed as barriers to be minimized and overcome but important public safeguards to be protected and strengthened.

CHANGE: None.

Appendix J

Solomon Amendment Regulations

[327]

The original Solomon Rule, published in July 2002, was included in the *2006 FERPA Guide*. New regulations were published on April 28, 2008, and have been included below, the most pertinent information having been highlighted. Also note that on December 6, 2005, the U.S. Supreme Court heard a challenge to the constitutionality of the Solomon Amendment that was brought by a consortium of law schools. On March 6, 2006 the Supreme Court ruled unanimously that colleges that accept federal aid must comply with the requirements of the Solomon Amendment including providing student recruiting information.

More information as well as the final Supreme Court ruling on the Solomon Amendment may be found on AACRAO's Web site: www.aacrao.org/compliance/solomon/.

Title 32—National Defense
Subtitle A—Department of Defense
Chapter I—Office of the Secretary of Defense
Subchapter M—Miscellaneous

Part 216—Military Recruiting and Reserve Officer Training Corps Program Access to Institutions of Higher Education

Section Contents
§ 216.1 Purpose
§ 216.2 Applicability
§ 216.3 Definitions
§ 216.4 Policy
§ 216.5 Responsibilities

AUTHORITY: 10 U.S.C. 983.
SOURCE: 73 FR 16527, Apr. 28, 2008, unless otherwise noted.

§ 216.1 Purpose.

This part:

(a) Implements 10 U.S.C. 983.

(b) Updates policy and responsibilities relating to the management of covered schools that have a policy of denying or effectively preventing military recruiting personnel access to their campuses or access to students on their campuses in a manner that is at least equal in quality and scope to the access to campuses and to students provided to any other employer, or access to student-recruiting information. The term "equal in quality and scope" means the same access to campus and students provided by the school to the any other non-military recruiters or employers receiving the most favorable access. The focus is not on the content of a school's recruiting policy, but instead on the result achieved by the policy and compares the access provided military recruiters to that provided other recruiters. Therefore, it is insufficient to comply with the statute (10 U.S.C. 983) if the policy results in a greater level of access for other recruiters than for the military.

(c) Updates policy and responsibilities relating to the management of covered schools that have an anti-ROTC policy.

§ 216.2 Applicability.

This part applies to the Office of the Secretary of Defense, the Military Departments (including the Coast Guard when it is operating as a Military Service in the Navy), the Chairman of the Joint Chiefs of Staff, the Combatant Commands, the Defense Agencies, and the DoD Field Activities (hereafter referred to collectively as "the DoD Components"). This part also applies, by agreement with the Department of Homeland Security (DHS), to the Coast Guard at all times, including when it is a service in the Department of Homeland Security. The policies herein also affect the Departments of Transportation, Homeland Security, Energy (National Nuclear Security Administration), the Central Intelligence Agency, and any department or agency in which regular appropriations are made in the Departments of Labor, Health and Human Services, Education, and Related Agencies Appropriations Act. The term "Military Services," as used herein, refers to the Army, the Navy, the Marine Corps, the Air Force, and the Coast Guard, including their Reserve or National Guard Components. The term "Related Agencies" as used herein refers to the Armed Forces Retirement Home, the Corporation for National and Community Service, the Corporation for Public Broadcasting, the Federal Mediation and Conciliation Service, the Federal Mine Safety and Health Review Commission, the National Commission on Libraries and Information Science, the National Council on Disability, the National Education Goals Panel, the National Labor Relations Board, the National Mediation Board, the Occupational Safety and Health Review Commission, the Social Security Administration, the Railroad Retirement Board and the United States Institute of Peace.

§ 216.3 Definitions.

(a) **ANTI-ROTC POLICY.** A policy or practice whereby a covered school prohibits or in effect prevents the Secretary of Defense from maintaining, establishing, or efficiently operating a unit of the Senior ROTC at the covered school, or prohibits or in effect prevents a student at the covered school from enrolling in a Senior ROTC unit at another institution of higher education.

(b) **COVERED FUNDS.** "Covered funds" is defined in 10 U.S.C. 983 as any funds made available for the Departments of Defense, Transportation, Homeland Security, or National Nuclear Security Administration of the Department of Energy, the Central Intelligence Agency, or any department or agency in which regular appropriations are made in the Departments of Labor, Health and Human Services, and Education, as well as in Related Agencies Appropriations Act (excluding any federal funds provided to an institution of higher education, or to an individual, to be available solely for student financial assistance, related administrative costs, or costs associated with attendance).

(c) **COVERED SCHOOL.** An institution of higher education, or a subelement of an institution of higher education, subject to the following clarifications:

(1) A determination (§216.5(a)) affecting only a subelement of a parent institution (see §216.3(f)) effects a limitation on the use of funds (see §216.4 (a)) applicable to the parent institution as a whole, including the institution's offending subelement and all of its subelements, if any.

(2) When an individual institution of higher education that is part of a single university system (e.g., University of (State) at (City)—a part of that state's university system) has a policy or practice that prohibits, or in effect prevents, access to campuses or access to students on campuses in a manner that is at least equal in quality and scope to the access to its campus and students as it provides to any other employer, or access to student-recruiting information by military recruiters, or has an anti-ROTC policy, as defined in this rule, it is only that individual institution within that university system that is affected by the loss of federal funds. This limited effect applies even though another campus of the same university system may or may not be affected by a separate determination under §216.5 (a). The funding of a subelement of the offending individual institution of a single university system, if any, will also be withheld as a result of the policies or practices of that offending individual institution.

(d) **ENROLLED.** Students are "enrolled" when registered for at least one credit hour of academic credit at the covered school during the most recent, current, or next term. Students who are enrolled during the most recent term, but who are no longer attending the institution, are included.

(e) **EQUAL IN QUALITY AND SCOPE.** The term means the same access to campus and students provided by the school to the any other nonmilitary recruiters or employers receiving the most favorable access. The focus is not on the content of a school's recruiting policy, but instead on the result achieved by the policy and compares the access provided military recruiters to that provided other recruiters. Therefore, it is insufficient to comply with the statute if the policy results in a greater level of access for other recruiters than for the military. The U.S. Supreme Court further explained that "the statute does not call for an inquiry into why or how the 'other employer' secured its access—[We do not think that the military recruiter has received equal 'access' [when a law firm is permitted on campus to recruit students and the military is not]—regardless of whether the disparate treatment is attributable to the military's failure to comply with the school's nondiscrimination policy."

(f) **INSTITUTION OF HIGHER EDUCATION.** A domestic college, university, or other institution (or subelement thereof) providing postsecondary school courses of study, including foreign campuses of such domestic institutions. The term includes junior colleges, community colleges, and institutions providing courses leading to undergraduate and post-graduate degrees. The term does not include entities that operate exclusively outside the United States, its territories, and possessions. A subelement of an institution of higher education is a discrete (although not necessarily autonomous) organizational entity that may establish policies or practices affecting military recruiting and related actions (*e.g.,* an undergraduate school, a law school, a medical school, other graduate schools, or a national laboratory connected or affiliated with that parent institution). For example, the School of Law of XYZ University is a subelement of its parent institution (XYZ University).

(g) **MILITARY RECRUITERS.** Personnel of DoD whose current assignment or detail is to a recruiting activity of the DoD.

(h) **PACIFISM.** Opposition to war or violence, demonstrated by refusal to participate in military service.

(i) **STUDENT.** An individual who is 17 years of age or older and is enrolled at a covered school.

(j) **STUDENT-RECRUITING INFORMATION.** For those students currently enrolled, the student's name, address, telephone listing, age (or year of birth), place of birth, level of education (*e.g.,* freshman, sophomore, or degree awarded for a recent graduate), most recent educational institution attended, and current major(s).

§ 216.4 Policy.

It is DoD policy that:

(a) Under 10 U.S.C. 983, no covered funds may be provided by contract or grant (to include payment on such contracts or grants previously obligated) to a covered school if the Secretary of Defense determines that the covered school:

(1) Has a policy or practice (regardless of when implemented) that either prohibits or in effect prevents the Secretary of Defense or Secretary of Homeland Security from obtaining, for military recruiting purposes, access to campuses or access to students on campuses that is at least equal in quality and scope, as defined in §216.3(d), to the access to campuses and to students provided to any other employer, or access to directory information on students;

(2) Has failed to disseminate military visit information or alerts at least on par with nonmilitary recruiters since schools offering such services to nonmilitary recruiters must also send emails, post notices, etc., on behalf of military recruiters to comply with the Solomon Amendment;

(3) Has failed to schedule visits at times requested by military recruiters that coincide with nonmilitary recruiters' visits to campus if this results in a greater level of access for other recruiters than for the military (*e.g.,* offering non-military recruiters a choice of a variety of dates for on-campus interviews while only offering the military recruiters the final day of interviews), as schools must ensure that their recruiting policies operate such that military recruiters are given access to students equal to that provided to any other employer;

(4) Has failed to provide military recruiters with a mainstream recruiting location amidst nonmilitary employers to allow unfettered access to interviewees since military recruiters must be given the same access as recruiters who comply with a school's nondiscrimination policy;

(5) Has failed to enforce time, place, and manner policies established by the covered school such that the military recruiters experience an inferior or unsafe recruiting climate, as schools must allow military

recruiters on campus and must assist them in whatever way the school assists other employers;

(6) Has through policy or practice in effect denied students permission to participate, or has prevented students from participating, in recruiting activities; or

(7) Has an anti-ROTC policy or practice, as defined in this rule, regardless of when implemented.

(b) The limitations established in paragraph (a) of this section shall not apply to a covered school if the Secretary of Defense determines that the covered school:

(1) Has ceased the policies or practices defined in paragraph (a) of this section;

(2) Has a long-standing policy of pacifism (see §216.3 (j)) based on historical religious affiliation;

(3) When not providing requested access to campuses or to students on campus, certifies that all employers are similarly excluded from recruiting on the premises of the covered school, or presents evidence that the degree of access by military recruiters is the same access to campuses or to students on campuses provided to the nonmilitary recruiters;

(4) When not providing any student-recruiting information, certifies that such information is not maintained by the covered school; or that such information already has been provided to the Military Service concerned for that current semester, trimester, quarter, or other academic term, or within the past 4 months (for institutions without academic terms); or

(5) When not providing student-recruiting information for a specific student certifies that the student concerned has formally requested, in writing, that the covered school withhold this information from all third parties.

(c) A covered school may charge military recruiters a fee for the costs incurred in providing access to student-recruiting information when that institution can certify that such charges are the actual costs, provided that such charges are reasonable, customary and identical to fees charged to other employers.

(d) An evaluation to determine whether a covered school maintains a policy or practice covered by paragraphs (a)(1) through (a)(6) of this section shall be undertaken when:

(1) Military recruiting personnel are prohibited, or in effect prevented, from the same access to campuses or access to students on campuses provided to non-

military recruiters, or are denied access to student-recruiting information;

(2) Information or alerts on military visits are not distributed at least on par with nonmilitary recruiters since schools offering such services to nonmilitary recruiters must also send emails, post notices, etc., on behalf of the military recruiter to comply with the Solomon Amendment;

(3) Military recruiters are prohibited from scheduling their visits at requested times that coincide with nonmilitary recruiters' visits to its campus if this results in a greater level of access for other recruiters than for the military as schools must ensure their recruiting policy operates in such a way that military recruiters are given access to students equal to that provided to any other employer;

(4) Military recruiters do not receive a mainstream recruiting location amidst nonmilitary employers to allow unfettered access to interviewees since military recruiters must be given the same access as recruiters who comply with the school's nondiscrimination policy;

(5) The school has failed to enforce time, place, and manner policies established by that school such that military recruiters experience an unsafe recruiting climate, as schools must allow military recruiters on campus and must assist them in whatever way the school chooses to assist other employers;

(6) Evidence is discovered of an institution-sponsored policy or practice that in effect denied students permission to participate, or prevented students from participating in recruiting activities;

(7) The costs being charged by the school for providing student-recruiting information are believed by the military recruiter to be excessive, and the school does not provide information sufficient to support a conclusion that such are the actual costs, provided that they are reasonable and customary, and are identical to those costs charged to other employers; or

(8) The covered school is unwilling to declare in writing, in response to an inquiry from a representative of a DoD Component or a representative from the Department of Homeland Security, that the covered school does not have a policy or practice of prohibiting, or in effect preventing, the Secretary of a Military Department or Secretary of Homeland Security from the same access to campuses or access to students on campuses provided to nonmilitary recruiters, or

access to student-recruiting information by military recruiters for purposes of military recruiting.

(e) An evaluation to determine whether a covered school has an anti-ROTC policy covered by paragraph (a)(7) of this section shall be undertaken when:

(1) A Secretary of a Military Department or designee cannot obtain permission to establish, maintain, or efficiently operate a unit of the Senior ROTC; or

(2) Absent a Senior ROTC unit at the covered school, students cannot obtain permission from a covered school to participate, or are effectively prevented from participating, in a unit of the Senior ROTC at another institution of higher education.

§ 216.5 Responsibilities.

(a) The Principal Deputy Under Secretary of Defense for Personnel and Readiness (PDUSD (P&R)), under the Under Secretary of Defense for Personnel and Readiness, shall:

(1) Not later than 45 days after receipt of the information described in paragraphs (b)(3) and (c)(1) of this section:

(i) Inform the Office of Naval Research (ONR) and the Director, Defense Finance and Accounting Service that a final determination will be made so those offices can make appropriate preparations to carry out their responsibilities should a covered school be determined ineligible to receive federal funds.

(ii) Make a final determination under 10 U.S.C. 983, as implemented by this part, and notify any affected school of that determination and its basis, and that the school is therefore ineligible to receive covered funds as a result of that determination.

(iii) Disseminate to federal entities affected by the decision, including the DoD Components and the GSA, and to the Secretary of Education and the head of each other department and agency the funds of which are subject to the determination, the names of the affected institutions identified under paragraph (a)(1)(ii) of this section.

(iv) Notify the Committees on Armed Services of the Senate and the House of Representatives of the affected institutions identified under paragraph (a)(1)(ii) of this section.

(v) Inform the affected school identified under paragraph (a)(1)(ii) of this section that its funding eligibility may be restored if the school provides sufficient new information that the basis for the determination under paragraph (a)(1)(ii) of this section no longer exists.

(2) Not later than 45 days after receipt of a covered school's request to restore its eligibility:

(i) Determine whether the funding status of the covered school should be changed, and notify the applicable school of that determination.

(ii) Notify the parties reflected in paragraphs (a)(1)(i), (a)(1)(iii), and (a)(1)(iv) of this section when a determination of funding ineligibility (paragraph (a)(1)(ii) of this section) has been rescinded.

(3) Publish in the *Federal Register* each determination of the PDUSD (P&R) that a covered school is ineligible for contracts and grants made under 10 U.S.C. 983, as implemented by this part.

(4) Publish in the *Federal Register* at least once every 6 months a list of covered schools that are ineligible for contracts and grants by reason of a determination of the Secretary of Defense under 10 U.S.C. 983, as implemented by this part.

(5) Enter information into the Excluded Parties List System[10] about each covered school that the PDUSD (P&R) determines to be ineligible for contracts and grants under 10 U.S.C. 983 and/or this part, generally within 5 days of making the determination.

(6) Provide ONR with an updated list of the names of institutions identified under paragraph (a)(1)(ii) of this section whenever the list changes due to an institution being added to or dropped from the list, so that ONR can carry out its responsibilities for post-award administration of DoD Components' contracts and grants with institutions of higher education.

(7) Provide the Office of the Deputy Chief Financial Officer, DoD, and the Director, Defense Finance and Accounting Service with an updated list of the names of institutions identified under paragraph (a)(1)(ii) of this section whenever the list changes due to an institution being added or dropped from the

---

[10] The Excluded Parties List System (EPLS) is the system that the General Services Administration maintains for Executive Branch agencies, with names and other pertinent information of persons who are debarred, suspended, or otherwise ineligible for federal procurement and/or covered non-procurement transactions.

list, so those offices can carry out their responsibilities related to cessation of payments of prior contract and grant obligations to institutions of higher education that are on the list.

(8) Publish in the *Federal Register* the list of names of affected institutions that have changed their policies or practices such that they are determined no longer to be in violation of 10 U.S.C. 983 and this part.

(b) The Secretaries of the Military Departments and the Secretary of Homeland Security shall:

(1) Identify covered schools that, by policy or practice, prohibit, or in effect prevent, the same access to campuses or access to students on campuses provided to nonmilitary recruiters, or access to student-recruiting information by military recruiters for military recruiting purposes.

(i) When requests by military recruiters to schedule recruiting visits are unsuccessful, the Military Service concerned, and the Office of the Secretary of Homeland Security when the Coast Guard is operating as a service in the Department of Homeland Security, shall seek written confirmation of the school's present policy from the head of the school through a letter of inquiry. A letter similar to that shown in Appendix A of this part shall be used, but it should be tailored to the situation presented. If written confirmation cannot be obtained, oral policy statements or attempts to obtain such statements from an appropriate official of the school shall be documented. A copy of the documentation shall be provided to the covered school, which shall be informed of its opportunity to forward clarifying comments within 30 days to accompany the submission to the PDUSD (P&R).

(ii) When a request for student-recruiting information is not fulfilled within a reasonable period, normally 30 days, a letter similar to that shown in Appendix A shall be used to communicate the problem to the school, and the inquiry shall be managed as described in §216.5.(b)(1)(ii). Schools may stipulate that requests for student-recruiting information be in writing.

(2) Identify covered schools that, by policy or practice, deny establishment, maintenance, or efficient operation of a unit of the Senior ROTC, or deny students permission to participate, or effectively prevent stu-

dents from participating in a unit of the Senior ROTC at another institution of higher education. The Military Service concerned, and the Office of the Secretary of Homeland Security when the Coast Guard is operating as a service in the Department of Homeland Security, shall seek written confirmation of the school's policy from the head of the school through a letter of inquiry. A letter similar to that shown in Appendix B of this part shall be used, but it should be tailored to the situation presented. If written confirmation cannot be obtained, oral policy statements or attempts to obtain such statements from an appropriate official of the school shall be documented. A copy of the documentation shall be provided to the covered school, which shall be informed of its opportunity to forward clarifying comments within 30 days to accompany the submission to the PDUSD (P&R).

(3) Evaluate responses to the letter of inquiry, and other such evidence obtained in accordance with this part, and submit to the PDUSD (P&R) the names and addresses of covered schools that are believed to be in violation of policies established in §216.4. Full documentation shall be furnished to the PDUSD (P&R) for each such covered school, including the school's formal response to the letter of inquiry, documentation of any oral response, or evidence showing that attempts were made to obtain either written confirmation or an oral statement of the school's policies.

(c) The Heads of the DoD Components and Secretary of Homeland Security shall:

(1) Provide the PDUSD (P&R) with the names and addresses of covered schools identified as a result of evaluation(s) required under §216.4(d) and (e).

(2) Take immediate action to deny obligations of covered funds to covered schools identified under paragraph (a)(1)(ii) of this section, and to restore eligibility of covered schools identified under paragraph (a)(2) of this section.

The above regulations can be found in electronic format at http://ecfr.gpoaccess.gov/cgi/t/text/text-idx?c=ecfr&sid=91ccc26c83776074782f4cf6b87e0aee&tpl=/ecfrbrowse/Title32/32cfr216_main_02.tpl.

Anti-Terrorism Related Amendments & SEVIS Guidance

Note: President Obama signed legislation that extended the *USA Patriot Act* on February 28, 2010.

The following is a reprint of LeRoy Rooker's April 12, 2002 *Dear Colleague* letter, "re: Recent Amendments to Family Educational Rights and Privacy Act Relating to Anti-Terrorism Activities," in its entirety—

Dear Colleague:

The purpose of this guidance is to provide you with an overview of recent changes made by Congress to the *Family Educational Rights and Privacy Act* (FERPA) in response to the September 11 terrorist attacks on the United States. In so doing, we also will provide an overview of the relevant provisions of current law. The changes to FERPA became effective on October 26, 2001, when the President signed into law the *"Uniting and Strengthening America by Providing Appropriate Tools Required to Intercept and Obstruct Terrorism (USA PATRIOT Act) Act of 2001"* (Public Law 107-56; 115 Stat. 272). Section 507 of the *USA PATRIOT Act* amends FERPA, and is attached for your convenience at the end of this letter.

Overview of FERPA

FERPA is a federal law that applies to educational agencies and institutions that receive federal funds under any program administered by the Secretary of Education (20 U.S.C. §1232g; 34 C.F.R. Part 99). Generally, FERPA prohibits the funding of an educational agency or institution that has a policy or practice of disclosing a student's "education record" (or personally identifiable information contained therein) without the consent of the parent. When a student turns 18 years old or attends a postsecondary institution at any age, the rights under FERPA transfer from the parent to the student ("eligible student").

FERPA defines "education records" as

"those records, files, documents and other materials which—

(i) contain information directly related to a student; and

(ii) are maintained by an educational agency or institution or by a person acting for such agency or institution" [20 U.S.C. §1232g(a)(4)(A)(i) and (ii)].

FERPA generally requires prior written consent from the parent or eligible student before an educational agency or institution may disclose personally identifiable information from education records to a third party. However, the law contains 16 exceptions to this general rule. Pertinent exceptions that allow release of personally identifiable information without prior written consent are discussed below.

Ex Parte Orders

Significantly, the recent amendment to FERPA permits educational agencies and institutions to disclose—without the consent or knowledge of the student or parent—personally identifiable information from the student's education records to the Attorney General of the United States or to his designee in response to an *ex parte* order in connection with the investigation or prosecution of terrorism crimes specified in sections 2332b(g)(5)(B) and 2331 of title 18, U.S. Code.[11] An *ex parte* order is an order issued by a court of competent jurisdiction without notice to an adverse party.

In addition to allowing disclosure without prior written consent or prior notification, this provision amends FERPA's record keeping requirements [20 U.S.C. §1232g(b)(4); 34 C.F.R. §99.32]. As a result, FERPA, as amended, does not require a school official to record a disclosure of information from a student's education record when the school

---

[11] These statutes define federal crimes of terrorism as offenses calculated to influence the conduct of government such as destruction of aircraft, assassination, arson, hostage taking, destruction of communications lines or national defense premises, and use of weapons of mass destruction.

makes that disclosure pursuant to an *ex parte* order. Further, an educational agency or institution that, in good faith, produces information from education records in compliance with an *ex parte* order issued under the amendment "shall not be liable to any person for that production."

A copy of the new statutory language follows this guidance. The Department will be working with the Department of Justice in the implementation of this new provision. In addition to this guidance, we will be amending and updating the FERPA regulations to include this new exception to the written consent requirement. You should address any questions you have on the new amendment to ferpa@ed.gov.

Lawfully Issued Subpoenas and Court Orders

FERPA permits educational agencies and institutions to disclose, without consent, information from a student's education records in order to comply with a "lawfully issued subpoena or court order" in three contexts [20 U.S.C. §1232g(b)(1)(J)(i) and (ii), (b)(2)(B); 34 C.F.R. §99.31(a)(9)]. These three contexts are:

① **GRAND JURY SUBPOENAS**—Educational agencies and institutions may disclose education records to the entity or persons designated in a federal grand jury subpoena. In addition, the court may order the institution not to disclose to anyone the existence or contents of the subpoena or the institution's response. If the court so orders, then neither the prior notification requirements of §99.31(a)(9) nor the recordation requirements at 34 C.F.R. §99.32 would apply.

② **LAW ENFORCEMENT SUBPOENAS**—Educational agencies and institutions may disclose education records to the entity or persons designated in any other subpoena issued for a law enforcement purpose. As with federal grand jury subpoenas, the issuing court or agency may, for good cause shown, order the institution not to disclose to anyone the existence or contents of the subpoena or the institution's response. In the case of an agency subpoena, the educational institution has the option of requesting a copy of the good cause determination. Also, if a court or an agency issues such an order, then the notification requirements of §99.31(a)(9) do not apply, nor would the recordation requirements at 34 C.F.R. §99.32 apply to the disclosure of education records issued pursuant to the law enforcement subpoena.

③ **ALL OTHER SUBPOENAS**—In contrast to the exception to the notification and record keeping requirements described above, educational agencies or institutions may disclose information pursuant to any other court order or lawfully issued subpoena only if the school makes a reasonable effort to notify the parent or eligible student of the order or subpoena in advance of compliance, so that the parent or eligible student may seek protective action. Additionally, schools must comply with FERPA's record keeping requirements under 34 C.F.R. §99.32 when disclosing information pursuant to a standard court order or subpoena.

Health or Safety Emergency

FERPA permits non-consensual disclosure of education records, or personally identifiable, non-directory information from education records, in connection with a health or safety emergency under §99.31(a)(10) and §99.36 of the FERPA regulations. In particular, §99.36(a) and (c) provide that educational agencies and institutions may disclose information from an education record "to appropriate parties in connection with an emergency if knowledge of the information is necessary to protect the health or safety of the student or other individuals" and that the exception will be "strictly construed." Congress' intent that the applicability of this exception be limited is reflected in the *Joint Statement in Explanation of Buckley/Pell Amendment*, 120 Cong. Rec. S21489 (Dec. 13, 1974).

Accordingly, the Department consistently has limited the health and safety exception to a specific situation that presents imminent danger to a student, other students, or other members of the school community—or to a situation that requires the immediate need for information from education records in order to avert or diffuse serious threats to the safety or health of a student or other individuals. For example, the health or safety exception would apply to nonconsensual disclosures to appropriate persons in the case of a smallpox, anthrax or other bioterrorism attack. This exception also would apply to nonconsensual disclosures to appropriate persons in the case of another terrorist attack such as the September 11 attack. However, any release must be narrowly tailored considering the immediacy, magnitude, and specificity of information concerning the emergency. As the legislative history indicates, this exception is temporally limited to the period of the emergency and generally will not allow for a blanket release of personally identifiable information from a student's education records. Under the health and safety exception school officials may share relevant information with "appropriate parties," that is, those parties whose knowledge of the information is necessary to provide immediate protection of the health and safety of the student or other individuals [20 U.S.C. §1232g(b)(1)(I); 34 C.F.R. §99.36(a)]. Typically, law enforcement officials, public health officials, and trained medical personnel are the types of parties to whom information may be disclosed under this FERPA exception. FERPA's record keeping requirements (§99.32) apply to disclosures made pursuant to the health or safety exception.

The educational agency or institution has the responsibility to make the initial determination of whether a disclosure is necessary to protect the health or safety of the student or other individuals. However, the Department is available to work with institutions to assist them in making such decisions in order to ensure that the disclosure comes within the exception to FERPA's requirement of prior written consent.

In short, the health or safety exception will permit the disclosure of personally identifiable information from a student's education record without the written consent of the student in the case of an immediate threat to the health or safety of students or other individuals. Of course, a school official, based on his or her own observations, may notify law enforcement officials of suspicious activity or behavior. Nothing in FERPA prohibits a school official from disclosing to federal, state, or local law enforcement authorities information that is based on that official's personal knowledge or observation and not from an education record.

Law Enforcement Unit Records

Under FERPA, schools may disclose information from "law enforcement unit records" to anyone—including federal, state, or local law enforcement authorities—without the consent of the parent or eligible student. FERPA specifically exempts from the definition of "education records"—and thereby from the privacy restrictions of FERPA—records that a law enforcement unit of a school district or postsecondary institution creates and maintains for a law enforcement purpose. A "law enforcement unit" is an individual, office, department, division, or other component of a school district or postsecondary institution—such as a unit of commissioned officers or noncommissioned security guards—that is officially authorized or designated by the school district or institution to: (1) enforce any federal, state, or local law; or (2) maintain the physical security and safety of the school. See 34 C.F.R. §99.8.

FERPA narrowly defines a law enforcement record as a record that is: (i) created by the law enforcement unit; (ii) created for a law enforcement purpose; and (iii) maintained by the law enforcement unit [34 C.F.R. §99.8(b)]. While other components of an educational institution generally can disclose, without student consent, student education records to school law enforcement units (under FERPA's exception for school officials with legitimate educational interests), these records are not thereby converted into law enforcement unit records because the records were not created by the law enforcement unit. Thus, a law enforcement unit cannot disclose, without student consent, information obtained from education records maintained by other components of an educational institution.

Directory Information

FERPA's regulations define "directory information" as information contained in an education record of a student "that would not generally be considered harmful or an invasion of privacy" [34 C.F.R. §99.3]. Specifically, "directory information" includes, but is not limited to the student's name, address, telephone listing, electronic mail address, photograph, date and place of birth, major field of study, dates of attendance, grade level, enrollment status (e.g., undergraduate or graduate, full-time or part-time), participation in officially recognized activities or sports, weight and height of members of athletic teams, degrees, honors and awards received, and the most recent educational agency or institution attended. A school may disclose "directory information" from the education records without prior consent only after giving notice to the student of its directory information policy, and providing parents and eligible students with an opportunity to opt out of having their "directory information" disclosed. See 34 C.F.R. §99.37.

Under FERPA, a school may not comply with a request for "directory information" that is linked to other non-directory information. For instance, a school cannot disclose "directory information" on students of a certain race, gender, or national origin. However, the school could disclose "directory information" on all students (who have not opted out) to law enforcement authorities who may be requesting "directory information."

Disclosures to the Immigration and Naturalization Service (INS)

The Immigration and Naturalization Service (INS) requires foreign students attending an educational institution under an F-1 visa to sign the Form I-20. The Form I-20 contains a consent provision allowing for the disclosure of information to INS. The consent provision states that, "I authorize the named school to release any information from my records which is needed by the INS pursuant to 8 C.F.R. 214.3(g) to determine my nonimmigrant status." This consent is sufficiently broad to permit an educational institution to release personally identifiable information of a student who has signed a Form I-20 to the INS for the purpose of allowing the INS to determine the student's nonimmigrant status. Students that have an M-1 or J-1 visa have signed similar consents and education records on these students may also be disclosed to the INS.

Finally, we anticipate there may be a need for additional guidance in the future on other INS disclosure issues.

Technical Assistance on FERPA

For additional guidance on these or other provisions of FERPA contact the Family Policy Compliance Office at the following address and telephone number:

Family Policy Compliance Office
U.S. Department of Education
400 Maryland Avenue, SW
Washington, D.C. 20202-5901
(202) 260-3887, telephone
(202) 260-9001, fax

Additionally, schools officials may contact the Family Policy Compliance Office by email for quick, informal responses to routine questions about FERPA. That address is: ferpa@ed.gov. The Web site address is: www.ed.gov/offices/om/fpco.

Sincerely,

LeRoy S. Rooker

Director, Family Policy Compliance Office

Public Law 107-56, October 26, 2001; 115 Stat. 272

"Uniting and Strengthening America Act by Providing Appropriate Tools Required to Intercept and Obstruct Terrorism (USA PATRIOT Act) Act of 2001"
Sec. 507. Disclosure of Educational Records. [115 Stat. 367-68]

Section 444 of the *General Education Provisions Act* (20 U.S.C. 1232g), is amended by adding after subsection (i) a new subsection (j) to read as follows:

"(j) Investigation and Prosecution of Terrorism.—

"(1) In general.—Notwithstanding subsections (a) through (i) or any provision of state law, the Attorney General (or any federal officer or employee, in a position not lower than an Assistant Attorney General, designated by the Attorney General) may submit a written application to a court of competent jurisdiction for an *ex parte* order requiring an educational agency or institution to permit the Attorney General (or his designee) to—

"(A) collect education records in the possession of the educational agency or institution that are relevant to an authorized investigation or prosecution of an offense listed in section 2332b(g)(5)(B) of title 18 United States Code, or an act of domestic or international terrorism as defined in section 2331 of that title; and

"(B) for official purposes related to the investigation or prosecution of an offense described in paragraph (1)(A), retain, disseminate, and use (including as evidence at trial or in other administrative or judicial proceedings) such records, consistent with such guidelines as the Attorney General, after consultation with the Secretary, shall issue to protect confidentiality.

"(2) Application and approval.—

"(A) In general.—An application under paragraph (1) shall certify that there are specific and articulable facts giving reason to believe that the education records are likely to contain information described in paragraph (1)(A).

"(B) The court shall issue an order described in paragraph (1) if the court finds that the application for the order includes the certification described in subparagraph (A).

"(3) Protection of educational agency or institution.—An educational agency or institution that, in good faith, produces education records in accordance with an order issued under this subsection shall not be liable to any person for that production.

"(4) Record-keeping.—Subsection (b)(4) does not apply to education records subject to a court order under this subsection."

FPCO Letter to AACRAO on SEVIS

August 27, 2004

Mr. Jerome H. Sullivan
Executive Director
American Association of Collegiate Registrars
 and Admissions Officers
One Dupont Circle, NW, Suite 520
Washington, DC 20036

Dear Mr. Sullivan:

This is in response to your letter to the Family Policy Compliance Office (FPCO), as well as follow-up to the telephone conversation between Ms. Shelley Rodgers of your staff with Dr. Stephen Hunt of the International Affairs Office, in the Office of the Secretary. You asked certain questions about the applicability of the Family Educational Rights and Privacy Act (FERPA) to disclosures to the Immigration and Naturalization Service (INS). On March 1, 2003, INS ceased to exist and its responsibilities relating to student visas transferred to the Department of Homeland Security (DHS), Immigration and Customs Enforcement (ICE).

As you are aware, on April 12, 2002, FPCO issued guidance relating to disclosure of personally identifiable information from students' education records relative to anti-terrorism investigations of law enforcement officials. We noted in that Dear Colleague Letter that we anticipated that there may be a need for additional guidance in the future on ICE disclosure issues. Since that time, the Department has worked closely with ICE on several matters of mutual concern, including the applicability of FERPA to disclosures of information to ICE employees. We provided comments on ICE regulations published in the Federal Register on December 11, 2002, regarding the Student and Exchange Visitor Information System (SEVIS), and will continue to work with them as we develop additional guidance on issues relating to foreign students and exchange visitor program participants. In the interim, we believe, as is explained more fully below, that FERPA does not prohibit the disclosure of information to ICE contractors in order to certify an institution as eligible to participate in SEVIS.

Preliminarily, with regard to your apparent concern about disclosure of student information to ICE contractors rather than directly to the ICE, this Office has previously advised that FERPA does not prevent schools from outsourcing various functions. In particular, schools may disclose FERPA protected information, without consent, to contractors and other agents who have been retained to perform administrative and other professional services so long as the disclosure would be proper if made to a school official performing the same service. Similarly, FERPA does not prevent lawful recipients of protected education records, such as ICE, from using the services of outside contractors to perform services in place of regular employees, such as these site visits to certify institutions for participation in SEVIS. Accordingly, disclosures to ICE contractors retained to perform SEVIS certification visits should be treated as disclosure to ICE itself.

With regard to the broader question concerning access by ICE to education records of foreign students and exchange visitor program participants, § 641(c)(2) of the Illegal Immigration Reform and Immigrant Responsibility Act of 1996 (IIRIRA), as amended, (8 U.S.C. § 1372) provides that FERPA shall not apply to aliens described in subsection (a) of § 641 to the extent that the Attorney General determines necessary to carry out the SEVIS program. In the December 11th regulations, the Attorney General made such a determination. 67 Fed. Reg. 76256, 76270 (December 11, 2002).[12] In effect, ICE regulations, 8 C.F.R. § 214.1(h), state that with respect to F and M nonimmigrant students and J nonimmigrant exchange visitors, the FERPA provisions that might impede the proper implementation of 8 U.S.C. § 1372 and 8 C.F.R. § 214.3(g) are waived to the extent that 8 U.S.C. § 1372 or 8 C.F.R. § 214.3(g) requires the educational agency or institution to report the information.

---

[12] The Homeland Security Act of 2002, Public Law No: 107-296, Title IV, Section 442, transferred to the Assistant Secretary of the Bureau of Border Security the responsibility for administering the program to collect information relating to non-immigrant foreign students and other exchange program participants described in section 641 of the Illegal Immigration Reform and Immigrant Responsibility Act of 1996 (8 U.S.C. 1372), including the Student and Exchange Visitor Information System established under that section.

We also note that § 502 of the Enhanced Border Security and Visa Entry Reform Act of 2002, Pub. L. 107-173, requires ICE, in consultation with the Department of Education, to conduct a review of institutions certified to receive nonimmigrants under § 101(a)(15)(F), (M), or (J) of the Immigration and Nationality Act (8 U.S.C. § 1101(a)(15) (F)(M), or (J)) to determine whether the institutions are in compliance with the recordkeeping and reporting requirements of the Immigration and Nationality Act and IIRIRA.

We believe that Congress did not intend for the privacy protections under FERPA to impede ICE in carrying out the SEVIS program. Therefore, our advice to AACRAO is that institutions generally may not use FERPA in order to refuse to comply with requests from ICE relative to participation in SEVIS.

However, you specifically asked about the collection by ICE of the following information:

Common data elements being requested by the INS (now ICE) site-visit contractors are (a) all directory information for international students (b) citizenship (c) list of courses taken by each student (d) reason for separation from an institution if the student is no longer enrolled, etc. Information is being requested on enrolling students without status yet and enrolled students with active current status. Some of the requested information is required by SEVIS, some—like schedule of classes for each student—is not.

First, we note that SEVIS is not limited to enrolled students with active current status. Rather, the IRRIRA, as amended, applies to aliens who either have status or are applying for the status of nonimmigrants under § 101(a)(15) (F), (M), or (J) of the Immigration and Nationality Act. 8 U.S.C. § 1372(a)(1).

The IRRIRA, as amended, also requires institutions to report to ICE any failure of an alien to enroll in an institution of higher education or other approved educational institution or the scheduled commencement of participation by an alien in a designated exchange visitor program. 8 U.S.C. § 1372(a)(4).

Second, the issue of "directory information" is not relevant in this situation. In the instant case, ICE has broad, independent authority under the IRRIRA, as amended, (and does not need to request directory information) to receive the following information on foreign students and exchange program participants: A) the identity and current address in the United States of the alien; B) the nonimmigrant classification of the alien and the date on which

a visa under the classification was issued or extended or the date on which a change to such classification was approved by the Attorney General; C) in the case of a student at an approved institution of higher education, or other educational institution, the current academic status of the alien, including whether the alien is maintaining status as a full-time student, or in the case of a participant in a designated exchange visitor program, whether the alien is satisfying the terms and conditions of the program; D) in the case of a student at an approved institution of higher education, or other educational institution, any disciplinary action taken by the institution against the alien as a result of the alien's being convicted of a crime, or, in the case of a participant in a designated exchange visitor program, any change in the alien's participation as a result of the alien's being convicted of a crime; E) the date of entry and port of entry; F) the date of the alien's enrollment in an approved institution of higher education, other approved educational institution, or designated exchange visitor program in the United States; G) the degree program, if applicable, and field of study; and, H) the date of the alien's termination of enrollment and the reason for such termination (including graduation, disciplinary action, and failure to re-enroll). 8 U.S.C. § 1372(c)(1).

The ICE regulations further specify that: "an approved school must keep records containing certain specific information and documents relating to each F-1 or M-1 student to whom it has issued a Form I-20A or I-20M while the student is attending the school and until the school notifies the Service, ...that the student is not pursuing a full course of study.... The designated school official must make the information and documents required by this paragraph available to and furnish them to any ICE officer upon request. The information and documents that the school must keep on each student are as follows:

(i) Name.

(ii) Date and place of birth.

(iii) Country of citizenship.

(iv) Current address where the student and his or her dependents physically reside. In the event the student of his or her dependents reside on or off campus and cannot receive mail at that location, the school may provide a mailing address.

(v) The student's current academic status.

(vi) Date of commencement of studies.

(vii) Degree program and field of study.

(viii) Whether the student has been certified for practical training, and the beginning and end dates of certification.

(ix) Termination date and reason, if known.

(x) The documents referred to in paragraph (k) of this section.

(xi) The number of credits completed each semester.

(xii) A photocopy of the student's I-20 ID copy."

8 c.f.r. 214.3(g), as amended by 67 Fed. Reg. 76256 (December 11, 2002).

Thus, FERPA does not prohibit the nonconsensual release to ICE of the alien's field of study, degree program, number of credits, and other items of information enumerated in § 214.3(g). In addition, we are informed that the Department of Homeland Security is presently drafting regulations governing the SEVIS certification process and identifying additional reporting requirements incident to that process. During the pendancy of that rulemaking process, the Department will refrain from any enforcement action under FERPA under circumstances where an educational agency or institution has provided any education records to officers of the Department of Homeland Security at its request to carry out the SEVIS program.

I trust that this is responsive to your inquiry.

Sincerely,
LeRoy S. Rooker, Director
Family Policy Compliance Office

ICE Sample Information Request
Form for Foreign Students

U.S. IMMIGRATION & CUSTOMS ENFORCEMENT
OFFICE OF INVESTIGATION

FAX

Student Exchange Visitor Information System

126 Northpoint Dr.
Houston, TX 77060

TO:	{Institution's Name}
PHONE:	{Institution's Phone}
FAX:	{Institution's Fax}
FROM:	Investigative Assistant, Sharon Benge Sevis ID Sharon.benge@dhs.gov XXXXXX
PHONE:	(281) 774-4979
FAX:	(281) 774-5986
DATE:	March 17, 2010
COVER+:	
SUBJECT:	The below listed student is under investigation by U.S. Immigration & Customs Enforcement. We are requesting a copy of Form I-20, dates of enrollment at your Institution, copy of transcripts and a letter indicating the current status for the following individual: (student name); DOB: (XX/XX/XXXX); COC: (name of country). Kindly provide these documents via fax, and mail original to U.S. Immigration & Customs Enforcement, at the above address within three business days.

If you require additional information, please contact Investigative Assistant Sharon Benge, at (281) 774-4979. Your assistance is greatly appreciated. Thank you.

WARNING! This facsimile transmission cover sheet and any documents that accompany it are intended only for the individual or entity it is addressed to and may contain information that is privileged, confidential and exempt under applicable law. If the reader of this message is not the intended recipient, YOU ARE HEREBY NOTIFIED that any dissemination, distribution or copying of this communication is strictly prohibited. If you received this communication in error, please notify us immediately by telephone and return the original message to us at the address above via the U.S. Postal Service.

Appendix L
··················

State Laws Relating to FERPA

State Security Breach Notification Laws
As of December 9, 2009

Forty-five states, the District of Columbia, Puerto Rico and the Virgin Islands have enacted legislation (listed below) requiring notification of security breaches involving personal information.

State	Statute
Alaska	Alaska Stat. § 45.48.010 et seq.
Arizona	Ariz. Rev. Stat. § 44-7501
Arkansas	Ark. Code § 4-110-101 et seq.
California	Cal. Civ. Code §§ 56.06, 1785.11.2, 1798.29, 1798.82
Colorado	Colo. Rev. Stat. § 6-1-716
Connecticut	Conn. Gen Stat. 36a-701(b)
Delaware	Del. Code tit. 6, § 12B-101 et seq.
Florida	Fla. Stat. § 817.5681
Georgia	Ga. Code §§ 10-1-910, -911
Hawaii	Haw. Rev. Stat. § 487N-2
Idaho	Idaho Code §§ 28-51-104 to 28-51-107
Illinois	815 ILCS 530/1 et seq.
Indiana	Ind. Code §§ 24-4.9 et seq., 4-1-11 et seq., 2009 H.B. 1121
Iowa	Iowa Code § 715C.1 (2008 S.F. 2308)
Kansas	Kan. Stat. 50-7a01, 50-7a02
Louisiana	La. Rev. Stat. § 51:3071 et seq.
Maine	Me. Rev. Stat. tit. 10 §§ 1347 et seq., 2009 Public Law 161
Maryland	Md. Code, Com. Law § 14 3501 et seq.
Massachusetts	Mass. Gen. Laws § 93H-1 et seq.
Michigan	Mich. Comp. Laws § 445.72
Minnesota	Minn. Stat. §§ 325E.61, 325E.64
Missouri	Mo. Rev. Stat. § 407.1500
Montana	Mont. Code § 30-14-1701 et seq., 2009 H.B. 155, Chapter 163
Nebraska	Neb. Rev. Stat. §§ 87-801, -802, -803, -804, -805, -806, -807
Nevada	Nev. Rev. Stat. 603A.010 et seq.
New Hampshire	N.H. Rev. Stat. §§ 359-C:19, -C:20, -C:21

State	Statute
New Jersey	N.J. Stat. 56:8-163
New York	N.Y. Gen. Bus. Law § 899-aa
North Carolina	N.C. Gen. Stat § 75-65
North Dakota	N.D. Cent. Code § 51-30-01 et seq.
Ohio	Ohio Rev. Code §§ 1347.12, 1349.19, 1349.191, 1349.192
Oklahoma	Okla. Stat. § 74-3113.1 and 2008 H.B. 2245
Oregon	Oregon Rev. Stat. § 646A.600 et seq.
Pennsylvania	73 Pa. Stat. § 2303
Rhode Island	R.I. Gen. Laws § 11-49.2-1 et seq.
South Carolina	S.C. Code § 39-1-90
Tennessee	Tenn. Code § 47-18-2107
Texas	Tex. Bus. & Com. Code § 521.03
Utah	Utah Code §§ 13-44-101, -102, -201, -202, -310
Vermont	Vt. Stat. tit. 9 § 2430 et seq.
Virginia	Va. Code § 18.2-186.6
Washington	Wash. Rev. Code § 19.255.010
West Virginia	W.V. Code §§ 46A-2A-101 et seq.
Wisconsin	Wis. Stat. § 134.98 et seq.
Wyoming	Wyo. Stat. § 40-12-501 to -502
District of Columbia	D.C. Code § 28- 3851 et seq.
Puerto Rico	10 Laws of Puerto Rico § 4051 et. seq.
Virgin Islands	V.I. Code § 2208

TABLE NOTES: States with no security breach law: Alabama, Kentucky, Mississippi, New Mexico, and South Dakota.

Chart above taken from the National Conference of State Legislatures, accessed March 11, 2010 at www.ncsl.org/Default.aspx?TabId=13489

NCSL Contact: Pam Greenberg, NCSL Denver Office, pam.greenberg@ncsl.org, 303-364-7700, ext. 1413

The 2009 Florida Statute

Accessed from the Official Internet Site of the Florida Legislature on March 11, 2009
at www.leg.state.fl.us/Statutes/index.cfm?App_mode= Display_Statute&Search_String=&URL=Ch1006/Sec52.HTM.

In 2009, Florida amended their education code to align with FERPA. The amended code (included below) also protects the privacy of applicant records. Florida also amended its open records law to exempt from disclosure any records subject to FERPA. The result of this is that release of directory information in Florida is no longer subject to the Florida open records law.

Title XLVIII
K-20 EDUCATION CODE
Chapter 1006
SUPPORT FOR LEARNING

1006.52 Education Records and Applicant Records

(1) Each public postsecondary educational institution may prescribe the content and custody of records that the institution may maintain on its students and applicants for admission. A student's education records, as defined in the Family Educational Rights and Privacy Act (FERPA), 20 U.S.C. s. 1232g, and the federal regulations issued pursuant thereto, and applicant records are confidential and exempt from s. 119.07(1) and s. 24(a), Art. I of the State Constitution. For the purpose of this subsection, applicant records shall be considered to be records that are:

(a) Directly related to an applicant for admission to a public postsecondary educational institution who has not been in attendance at the institution; and

(b) Maintained by a public postsecondary educational institution or by a party acting on behalf of the public postsecondary educational institution.

(2) A public postsecondary educational institution may not release a student's education records without the written consent of the student to any individual, agency, or organization, except in accordance with and as permitted by the FERPA. Education records released by public postsecondary educational institutions to the Auditor General or the Office of Program Policy Analysis and Government Accountability, which are necessary for such agencies to perform their official duties and responsibilities, shall be used and maintained by the Auditor General and the Office of Program Policy Analysis and Government Accountability in accordance with the FERPA.

(3) This section is subject to the Open Government Sunset Review Act in accordance with s. 119.15 and shall stand repealed on October 2, 2014, unless reviewed and saved from repeal through reenactment by the Legislature.

The 2008 Virginia Law

Accessed from the Virginia General Assembly Legislative Information System on March 11, 2010 at http://leg1.state.va.us/cgi-bin/legp504.exe?081+ful+HB1058ER2.

The Virginia law below, enacted in 2008, requires Virginia public institutions of higher education to provide parents of dependent students access to their student's education records.

Virginia Acts of Assembly—Chapter

An Act to amend and reenact § 23-9.2:3 of the Code of Virginia, relating to release of educational records.

[H 1058]

Approved

Be it enacted by the General Assembly of Virginia:

1. That § 23-9.2:3 of the Code of Virginia is amended and reenacted as follows:

§ 23-9.2:3. *Power of governing body of educational institution to establish rules and regulations; offenses occurring on property of institution; state direct student financial assistance; release of educational records.*

A. In addition to the powers now enjoyed by it, the board of visitors or other governing body of every educational institution shall have the power:

1. To establish rules and regulations for the acceptance and assistance of students except that (i) individuals who have failed to meet the federal requirement to register for the selective service shall not be eligible to receive any state direct student assistance; (ii) the accreditation status of a Virginia public high school shall not be considered in making admissions determinations for students who have earned a diploma pursuant to the requirements established by the Board of Education; and (iii) the governing boards of the four-year institutions shall establish policies providing for the admission of certain graduates of Virginia community colleges as set forth in § 23-9.2:3.02.

2. To establish rules and regulations for the conduct of students while attending such institution.

3. To establish programs, in cooperation with the State Council of Higher Education and the Office of the Attorney General, to promote compliance among students with the Commonwealth's laws relating to the use of alcoholic beverages.

4. To establish rules and regulations for the rescission or restriction of financial aid, within the discretionary authority provided to the institution by federal or state law and regulations, and the suspension and dismissal of students who fail or refuse to abide by such rules and regulations for the conduct of students.

5. To establish rules and regulations for the employment of professors, teachers, instructors and all other employees and provide for their dismissal for failure to abide by such rules and regulations.

6. To provide parking and traffic rules and regulations on property owned by such institution.

7. To establish guidelines for the initiation or induction into any social fraternity or sorority in accordance with § 18.2-56.

8. To establish programs, in cooperation with the State Council of Higher Education for Virginia and the Office of the Attorney General, to promote the awareness and prevention of sexual crimes committed upon students.

B. Upon receipt of an appropriate resolution of the board of visitors or other governing body of an educational institution, the governing body of a political subdivision which is contiguous to the institution shall enforce state statutes and local ordinances with respect to offenses occurring on the property of the institution.

The governing bodies of the public institutions of higher education shall assist the State Council of Higher Education in enforcing the provisions related to eligibility for financial aid.

C. The board of visitors or other governing body of every public institution of higher education in Virginia shall establish policies and procedures requiring the release of the educational record of a dependent student, as defined by 20 U.S.C. § 1232g, to a parent at his request.

D. In order to improve the quality of the Commonwealth's work force and educational programs, the governing bodies of the public institutions of higher education shall establish programs to seek to ensure that all graduates have the technology skills necessary to compete in the 21st Century and, particularly, that all students matriculating in teacher-training programs receive instruction in the effective use of educational technology.

Bibliography

American Association of Collegiate Registrars and Admissions Officers. 2001. *The Solomon Amendment—A Guide for Recruiters and Student Records Managers*. Washington, D.C.: AACRAO.

———. 2005. 2005 Survey of AACRAO Member Institutions on FERPA Policies and Practices. Washington, D.C.: AACRAO.

———. 2010. *Retention of Records: Guide for Retention and Disposal of Student Records*. Washington, D.C.: AACRAO.

American Association of Collegiate Registrars and Admissions Officers and National Association of College and University Attorneys. 1984. *Legal Guide for Admissions Officers and Registrars*. Washington, D.C.: AACRAO and NACUA.

American Jurisprudence. 1991 (2d ed.). Volume 81. Rochester, NY: Lawyers Cooperative.

Ault, R.L. 1993. To waive or not to waive? Students' misconceptions about the confidentiality choice for letters of recommendation. *Teaching of Psychology*: 20: 44–45.

Baker, M.G. 1987. The teacher's need to know versus the student's right to privacy. *Journal of Law and Education* (Winter) 16: 71–91.

Baker, Thomas R. 1997. Inaccurate and misleading student hearing rights under FERPA. *West's Education Law Reporter* (February 6) 114: 72.

Burd, Stephen. 2000. College allowed to tell parents about alcohol use. *The Chronicle of Higher Education*. 46(45): A31.

CAUSE. 1997. Privacy and the Handling of Student Information in the Electronic Networked Environments of Colleges and Universities, A White Paper.

Curran, R. 1988. The law, computers, and student privacy. *CUPA Journal*. (Fall) 39: 37–45.

Davis, T.E., et al. 1987. Writing letters of recommendation: The struggle continues. *The Teacher Educator*. (Spring) 22: 27–30.

Dobbins, K.W. 1987. Student and Administrator Knowledge and Perception of the Buckley Amendment at Kent State University. Doctoral dissertation, Kent State University.

Ericson, J. L. 1993. Real world, pretend universities. *Educational Record*. (Winter) 74: 43–48.

Essex, Nathan L. 2000. Confidentiality and student records: Ten ways to invite legal challenges. *The Clearing House* (May/June) 73: 259–261.

Fry, Bobbye G. 1999. An Academic Dilemma: Student Records, Faculty Access, and the Family Educational Rights and Privacy Act. Doctoral dissertation, Texas Tech University.

Fulkert, Ronald F., and K. G. Kerstron. 2000. Limiting your liability in the classroom. *Business Education Forum*. 55(1): 42–45.

Garfinkel, S. L. 1987a. An introduction to computer security, Part I. *Practical Law*. (September) 39–48.

———. 1987b. An introduction to computer security, Part II. *Practical Law*. (October) 57–67.

Holder, H. 1990. Buckley Amendment—Help or Hindrance for Postsecondary Institution Admissions Officers. Doctoral dissertation, George Washington University.

Hollander, P.A. 1992. Student records. *New Directions in Student Services*. (Fall) 59: 49–59.

Internal Revenue Code of 1954. Section 152 (including amendments and applicable sections of the Tax Reform Act of 1976). 1976 edition of the Internal Revenue Code of 1954, with permission from Prentice Hall, Inc., Englewood Cliffs, N.J. 07632.

Johnson, T. P. 1993. Managing student records: The courts and the Family Educational Rights and Privacy Act of 1974. *West's Education Law Reporter* (February 11) 79: 1–18.

Lauren, Barbara. 2006. *The Registrar's Guide: Evolving Best Practices in Records and Registration*. Washington, D.C.: American Association of Collegiate Registrars and Admissions Officers.

Leatherman, Courtney. 2000. Universities wield privacy law in clashes with T.A. unions. *The Chronicle of Higher Education*. 47(9): A12–A13.

McDonald, Steven J., (ed.). 1999. *The Family Educational Rights and Privacy Act: A Legal Compendium*. Washington, D.C.: National Association of College and University Attorneys.

McIntyre, Gregory N. 1989. Post-1974 Trends in Students' and Teachers' Rights to Control Information about Themselves. Doctoral dissertation, University of Georgia.

Mawdsley, Ralph D. 1996. Litigation involving FERPA. *Education Law Reporter*. (September 6) 675–692.

Morley, Robert. 1996. Killing the electronic messenger. *CAUSE/EFFECT*. (Spring): 43, 53.

Nolan, J. and J. Nolan-Haley. 1990. *Black's Law Dictionary* (6th ed.). St. Paul, MN: West Publishing.

Pechman, Ellen, and E. O'Brien. 1994. Issues in Educational Data Confidentiality and Access. Paper prepared for the National Center for Education Statistics and the National Forum on Education Statistics Steering Committee on Technology (January 6).

Pennsylvania Rules of Court. 1991. St. Paul, MN: West Publishing.

Quann, C. James and T. D. Ratcliff 1997. An argument for and a case study of recording significant disciplinary actions on student transcripts. *College and University*. 73(1): 2–6.

Rapp, James A. 1995. *Education Law, Volume 3: Student Records*. New York: Matthew Bender and Co.

Rooker, LeRoy S. 1989. Family Educational Rights and Privacy Act (FERPA). Paper presented at the annual meeting of the American Association of Collegiate Registrars and Admissions Officers, Chicago, Illinois, April 18.

———. 1991. Paper presented at the annual meeting of the American Association of Collegiate Registrars and Admissions Officers, Honolulu, Hawaii, April 15.

———. 1993a. October 4 letter to Richard Rainsberger, Registrar, Carnegie Mellon University.

———. 1993b. December 3 letter to Joseph Roof, Dean of Admissions and Records Systems, Seminole Community College.

———. 1999. August 2 letter of technical assistance to National Student Loan Clearinghouse. Available at: <www.ed.gov/policy/gen/guid/fpco/ferpa/library/herndonva.html>.

———. 2000. Family Educational Rights and Privacy Act (FERPA). Paper presented at the annual meeting of the American Association of Collegiate Registrars and Admissions Officers, New Orleans, Louisiana, April 10.

———. 2001. May 29 letter to Hunter College re: Posting grades by last four digits of social security number. Available at: <www.ed.gov/policy/gen/guid/fpco/ferpa/library/hunter.html>.

———. 2002. April 12 *Dear Colleague* letter (re: Recent Amendments to Family Educational Rights and Privacy Act Relating to Anti-Terrorism Activities).

———. 2004a. October 6 letter to Auburn University.

———. 2004b. October 19 Letter to Miami University re: Disclosure of Information Making Student's Identity Easily Traceable. Available at: <www.ed.gov/policy/gen/guid/fpco/ferpa/library/unofmiami.html>.

———. 2004c. November 5 letter to University of Wisconsin-River Falls re: Student Account Identifiers. Available at: <www.ed.gov/policy/gen/guid/fpco/ferpa/library/uwisc.html>.

Rothenberger, J. 1994. Transmission Security and Acknowledgment. Paper presented at the AACRAO SPEEDE Workshop, October, Madison, Wisconsin.

Schuerman, William C. 1980. *A Model Institutional Policy on the Privacy of Student Records in Compliance with the Family Educational Rights and Privacy Act of 1974 as Amended.* Doctoral dissertation, American University.

Selingo, Jeffrey. 2000. Colleges say privacy laws hinder class-rank admissions plans. *The Chronicle of Higher Education.* 47(7): A47.

Siegler, Gregory E. 1996. What should be the scope of privacy protections for student health records? A look at Massachusetts and federal law. *Journal of Law and Education.* 25(2): 237-66.

Solomon Amendment. January 13, 2000. (Military Recruiting and Reserve Officer Training Corps Program Access to Institutions of Higher Education, Department of Defense Billing Code 5000–04, Office of the Secretary, 32 C.F.R. Part 216, RIN 0790-AG42).

Tanaka, Paul. 1995. *The Permissibility of Withholding Transcripts Under the Bankruptcy Law.* Washington, D.C.: National Association of College and University Attorneys.

Tener, M. 1992. The Buckley Amendment: Student-athlete 'privacy.' *Scholastic Coach.* (Fall) 61: 13.

The West Group. 2000 (rev. ed.). *Federal Civil Judicial Procedures and Rules, Title 28—Judiciary and Judicial Procedure.*

Tidwell, J. A. 1986. Educator's liability for negative letters of recommendation. *Journal of Law and Education.* 15: 479-83.

Trubow, G. B. *Law Enforcement Information and the Family Educational Rights and Privacy Act.* American Bar Association.

Turner-Dickerson, Madalyn. 1997. The Family Educational Rights and Privacy Act of 1974 as Amended: Knowledge, Practices and Perceptions. Doctoral dissertation, University of Pittsburgh

United States Department of Education. 1993. *SPEEDE/ExPRESS: An Electronic System for Exchanging Student Records.* National Center for Education Statistics. Washington, D.C.: NCES.

USA PATRIOT Act of 2001. Public Law 107–56; 115 Statute 272, Section 507.

Van Tol, J. (ed.) 1989. *College and University Student Records: A Legal Compendium.* Washington, D.C.: National Association of College and University Attorneys.

Index
· · · · · · · · · ·

A

academic standing 21, 55, 83

access

  admissions files 21–2, 73, 80

  agent (representing the student) 24, 33, 45, 54, 76, 177, 207, 223

  alumni 22, 29

  computer 23, 33–4, 37, 42, 121, 205, 229

  e-mail requests 27, 95, 118, 121, 124, 202, 229

  parents(s) 17–8, 27, 36–7, 61, 71, 97, 182

  research 31, 40, 54, 66, 68, 78, 83, 157–8, 170, 173–4, 177, 220, 241–2, 294, 325

  security 34, 37, 58, 75, 79, 93–5, 169, 329–330

  student rights to 2, 13–5, 21–2, 26, 32, 34, 52, 55, 61, 63, 66–7, 71, 75, 85, 97, 100, 137, 296, 298

  student worker 33, 120

  victim of crime, by viii, 4, 10, 16, 26, 60, 69, 157, 174, 238, 301

accrediting agencies (disclosure to) 16, 58, 60, 68, 156, 174

Act. See FERPA

admissions files 21–2, 80, 183–80

agency. See also agent(s) 7, 9, 11, 22, 24, 31, 33, 41, 65, 139–40, 152, 163, 167, 185, 189–90, 212, 214, 217, 219–23, 227–8, 238–9, 253, 260, 263, 286, 310, 313, 316, 321, 325, 335

agent(s)

  definition of 7, 11, 24, 33, 42, 65, 76, 223

  designating 66, 201

alumni record(s) 7, 22, 29, 57, 59, 62, 75, 166

amendment (of records) vii–viii, 1–2, 4, 11, 13–5, 18–9, 25, 30, 54, 57, 59, 63, 87–8, 95, 98, 116–8, 151, 153, 177, 183, 255, 287, 289, 343

amendments (2009) 2–3, 26, 40, 143, 165

anecdotal notes 42, 68

annual notification

  distance learners 5

  policy (on campus) 1, 5, 13–4, 16, 22, 45, 63–4, 94, 178, 223, 233, 248, 302

appeal, student 19, 25

attendance

  dates of 2, 8, 24–5, 64, 138, 148, 188, 218, 221, 266, 335

  "In attendance." See also enrolled student. 2–3, 5, 7–9, 11, 13–4, 21–2, 24–5, 31, 35, 64, 97, 144, 152, 165–6, 175, 181, 187–90, 193–4, 211, 217–8, 220–1, 248, 266, 277, 335, 342

B

biometric record 3, 7, 11, 37, 150, 172–3

Buckley Amendment. See FERPA, historical background

C

Campus Sex Crimes Prevention Act 3, 171, 255–6

CFR. See Code of Federal Regulations

challenge to records. See also amendment (of records) 13, 18–9, 23, 137, 153

Clery Act 4, 7, 159, 174, 301

Code of Federal Regulations 1, 7, 52, 172–3, 322–3, 342–3

complaints

  filing viii, 2, 13, 22, 54, 60, 63, 94, 151, 162, 177, 204–5, 209, 274

  procedure 141, 162

compliance, requirements for viii, 5, 9, 13, 33, 63–7, 79, 139–41, 155, 160, 169, 200, 210, 213, 234, 236, 243, 249, 251, 308, 317, 324, 338

computer access 23, 33–4, 37, 42, 121, 175, 202, 205, 207, 209, 229

confidentiality ix, 4, 15, 28, 33–4, 43, 53, 65, 83, 119, 174, 236, 242, 269, 272, 286, 336

credentials

  electronic transmission of 9, 28, 39, 229

  fax transmission of 28–9, 55, 74, 340

crime of violence

  alleged perpetrator of a 2, 7, 16, 69, 174, 237–9, 260, 280

  definitions of 2, 4, 7–8, 16, 60, 69, 75, 97, 174, 237–9, 260–1, 280

crisis situations and emergencies viii, 4, 10–1, 16, 28, 30, 36–7, 40, 52, 56, 58, 60, 69, 72, 77–8, 100, 139, 157–8, 160, 167, 170, 174, 205–9, 249, 301–2, 304, 309, 312–14, 316, 318–9, 334

D

data

  breach(es) 41, 79–80, 175, 234, 236

  system requirements 34, 38, 79, 161, 194

databases, state 73, 243

dates of attendance 2, 8, 24–5, 55, 57, 59, 64, 84, 88, 138, 148, 188, 218, 220–1, 266, 289, 304, 335

deceased students 24, 55, 76, 96, 300

degrees, verification of 32, 42, 45, 87, 98, 168

de-identifying information (on records) 4, 8, 157, 170–1, 173, 239, 258, 264–5

Department of Education ii, 2–4, 10, 27, 165, 211, 218, 243, 260, 296, 298, 310, 336–7, 339

dependency status 2, 55, 80, 182, 305

destruction of information. See also records retention 15, 18, 24, 39, 58, 60, 93, 152, 235

directory information

  categories of 14, 17, 70, 138

  definition of 2–4, 8, 14, 16–7, 21, 23–5, 27, 35–6, 38, 41–5, 52, 58, 60, 64–5, 72–3, 75–6, 79, 81, 94, 97, 99, 138, 149, 165–6, 169, 174–5, 178, 187–90, 196–8, 200–1, 205–6, 211, 217–7, 253, 266, 285, 335, 342

  disclosure of viii, 2–4, 8, 14, 16–7, 19, 23–7, 35–6, 40, 42–5, 52–3, 55, 58, 60, 63–4, 70, 72–3, 85–7, 90, 95, 97–8, 138, 157, 159, 161, 165–6, 174–5, 188–90, 195–205, 205–6, 218–21, 253–4, 266, 285, 289, 303–4, 325, 335–6

  notification of (by institution) 14, 63–5, 89, 189, 341

  opt out 8, 10, 17, 25, 35, 108, 111–2, 161, 165, 174–5, 188–90, 200–1, 206, 289, 304, 335

  religion as 25, 40

  standards for defining 8, 14, 24

  telephone inquiries for 25, 40

  withholding viii, 14, 42, 53, 83, 89, 95

disciplinary action 2–3, 8, 10, 25, 34,
    74–5, 141, 148, 151–2, 160, 162, 239,
    258, 262, 264, 277, 279–80, 338
disciplinary hearing records 2, 4,
    56, 69, 75, 97–8, 274, 302
disclosure
    authorized government officials, to
        viii, 2, 16, 34, 39, 67, 155, 160, 249
    educational agencies or institutions, to
        other vii, 1, 3–4, 10–1, 13, 16–7, 30,
        38–9, 43, 45–7, 62, 67–70, 83, 139,
        151, 154–61, 165, 167–9, 174, 188–9,
        192–95, 197, 200–2, 205, 207–9,
        211–3, 218, 220, 223, 225, 227–30,
        232, 238, 246, 249–53, 255–8, 260,
        263, 270–3, 277, 279–81, 283–5, 289,
        300–2, 310, 314, 317, 322, 325, 333–5
    emergencies (health and safety)
        4, 10, 16, 30, 40, 58, 60, 147,
        157–8, 160, 167, 174, 206–7, 209,
        249, 301–2, 304, 314, 334
    exceptions vii, 3, 13, 16–7, 26, 31–2,
        35, 39–40, 48, 52, 54, 57, 59, 61,
        64, 71, 74, 78, 94, 165, 167–5,
        170–1, 173–74, 177, 181, 188, 192,
        194, 200–1, 208–9, 211, 223, 225–6,
        229, 239, 242, 246, 249–51, 254,
        260, 266, 270, 278–80, 285, 289, 297,
        303, 310, 312, 314, 316, 319, 334–5
    Juvenile Justice System
        147, 155, 161, 249
    legal actions, in response
        to 68, 156, 249, 281
    parents of dependent students, to 5,
        16, 36, 58, 60, 130, 167, 181, 284
    personally identifiable information,
        of vii–viii, 2–4, 7, 10–2, 13, 16–7,
        19, 23–4, 27–8, 30–3, 35–6, 38–40,
        42–5, 54, 61, 67–8, 70, 73, 86, 147,
        151, 154, 156–61, 165–7, 170, 173–4,
        177, 181, 187–8, 192, 194–5, 197–8,
        200, 205–9, 212–3, 216, 219, 223,
        227–9, 231–2, 234, 236, 238–43, 249,
        252–3, 256–61, 263–4, 266–7, 270–2,
        277, 279, 282, 284–9, 291, 293–6, 298,
        301, 303, 310, 312, 325, 333–5, 337
    postsecondary feedback to
        high schools 38–9
    recordkeeping of 10, 24, 39–40,
        47, 147, 158, 226, 230, 333–5
    third party, to a. See also agent(s) 2,
        17, 19, 27, 40, 159, 218–20, 225,
        229, 246, 251, 272–3, 284–5,
        291, 293, 314, 324–5, 333
    U.S. Attorney General 2,
        156, 171, 225, 245, 336
    without written consent
        courts, to 97, 249, 334
        drug and alcohol violations 142
        final results of a disciplinary
            proceeding 2, 8, 26, 69, 157,
            238, 260–1, 279–80, 301
distance education vii–viii, 4–5,
    15, 26, 35, 38, 45, 79, 100, 165

E

email
    addresses 26, 42, 49, 64,
        76, 83, 89, 99, 298
    transcript requests 28–9, 38, 55,
        67–8, 70, 74, 77, 85, 91, 229
EDI 9
education institution ii, vii–viii, 1–6,
    7–12, 13–8, 21–42, 44–7, 51–5, 57–63,
    65–76, 78–83, 85–8, 93, 96–100,
    137–41, 147–63, 165–78, 181–2, 184–5,
    187–95, 197–8, 200–2, 205–9, 211–4,
    216–20, 222–3, 225, 227–30, 232–6,
    238–9, 241–2, 246, 249–58, 260–1,
    263–4, 266–8, 270–3, 275, 277, 279–86,
    288–9, 293, 296–302, 304, 306, 309–10,
    313–9, 323, 325, 328–9, 331–9, 342–4
education records. See also record
    academic transcripts 55
    amending 2, 25, 147, 153, 281, 334
    computer access to 23, 33–4, 37, 42,
        121, 175, 202, 205, 207, 209, 229
    deceased students, of 24, 300
    definition of ii, 1–5, 7–9, 11, 13–8, 21–5,
        27, 29, 31–8, 41–5, 52, 57–63, 65–6,
        68–76, 79, 81, 93–4, 97, 99, 148–50,
        152, 155, 163, 165–75, 181, 185, 188–9,
        193–4, 196–8, 200–3, 205–12, 214,
        216–23, 225–8, 230–2, 234, 238–9,
        241–2, 249, 251, 253, 255, 260–1,
        263, 266, 268, 270, 275, 277–81,
        285–6, 291, 296, 310–1, 313–6, 318–9,
        322–3, 325, 334–5, 337–9, 342
    destruction of 8, 15, 24, 39, 43,
        161–2, 164, 170, 235, 333
    disclosure of vii–viii, 1–5, 8, 13, 15–9,
        23–8, 30–1, 34, 37, 39, 41, 43–7, 54,
        58, 60–2, 67–72, 80, 83, 108, 132,
        147, 151, 154, 157–8, 160–1, 165–75,
        177, 188, 192–4, 197–202, 205–14,
        216–20, 223, 225–7, 229–33, 235–6,
        238–9, 241, 245–6, 249, 251–9, 260,
        262–4, 268–70, 272–3, 277–86, 288,
        291, 293–6, 298, 300–2, 304, 310,
        312, 314–6, 318, 322–5, 333–6, 342
    electronic transmission of
        27–8, 38–9, 229–30, 322
fax transmission of 29, 44, 55
independent requests for 170, 324
institutional rights viii, 13, 39, 51,
    53, 57, 59, 66, 151, 153, 177, 333
law enforcement, related to viii,
    1–2, 10, 19, 23, 31, 37, 46–7, 62–3,
    65, 67, 138–9, 147, 152, 168, 208,
    225, 235, 238–9, 251–2, 260, 283,
    302, 316, 318, 334–5, 337, 339
letters of recommendation,
    contained in 15, 34, 57–60,
    67, 87, 137, 152–3, 166, 185
parental and spousal access
    to 17, 27, 36, 182
permission to release 28–9, 34,
    36–7, 39–41, 43, 51–2, 58, 60, 65,
    67–70, 72, 74–8, 80–1, 83–4,
    86–7, 90–2, 98–100, 104–5
reviews by student members of
    institutional committees 46
safeguarding 4, 23–4, 41, 79, 169,
    172, 175–6, 179, 234–5, 323
security. See confidentiality
student rights vii–viii, 1, 4,
    13–5, 36, 147, 152, 167, 177
Electronic Data Interchange. See EDI
electronic signatures 27–8,
    96, 166, 198, 321–5
electronic technology ix, 26–7,
    93, 166, 198, 235, 321
electronic transmission. See also EDI
    posting of grades via 26, 28, 38, 74
emergencies 147, 160, 174, 208
employee records 9, 21, 51, 62, 66, 74–5,
    80–1, 87, 92, 138, 149, 168, 205–7,
    209, 216–7, 220, 243, 316, 336
enforcement 1–2, 4–5, 10–1, 23, 29, 31–2,
    37, 41, 47, 65, 73, 75, 168, 170–1, 173,
    175, 206–9, 223, 225, 237–9, 242–3, 251,
    255, 260, 315, 318–9, 334–5, 337, 339
enrolled student 5, 9–12, 17, 21–2, 27,
    35, 39–40, 42–3, 51, 53, 55, 60, 64,
    70, 73–4, 78, 84, 94, 97, 155, 160–1,
    166, 169, 171, 183, 190, 192–4, 200–1,
    214, 217, 234, 256, 279, 329, 338
ex parte order viii, 3, 9, 12, 16, 46–7,
    142, 156, 171, 333–4, 336

F

facsimile. See fax transmission
faculty 10–1, 23, 26, 28–9, 32, 34,
    51, 53, 57–9, 61, 63, 65–7, 69–74,
    76–7, 79–80, 82–5, 87–91, 94–5,
    97, 100, 210, 222–3, 234
Family Educational Rights and
    Privacy Act of 1974. See FERPA

Family Policy Compliance Office 14
FAQs 53
fax transmission 340
Federal Rules of Civil Procedure
    (subpoenas) 47, 245–6
fees 23, 216, 330
FERPA
    applicability 3, 170, 187–8, 207, 222,
        241, 257, 324, 327–8, 334, 337
    at a glance vii
    audit (self-assessment) 93
    brochure (sample) 54, 301, 303
    changes and additions (2000) ii, 2
    definitions 2, 7, 14, 52, 66,
        165, 190, 305, 310, 327
    enforcement 4, 23, 29, 31, 37,
        62, 175, 206, 237, 242–3, 254,
        260, 302, 316, 335, 339
    exam 83, 98, 227
    historical background 1, 183,
        207, 212, 286–7, 289, 334
    key terms and concepts 51–2, 61, 70–1
    "musts" and "mays" 6, 52, 61, 70–1
    policy (on campus) 94–5, 205
    technology, impact on ix
    workshop/presentation
        (sample) 61, 63, 66, 83, 90
Final Regulations (1988). See
    Regulations, the: Final
financial aid viii, 5, 10, 16, 29–30, 33,
    55, 60, 68, 76–7, 81, 88, 90, 100, 137,
    155, 207, 225–6, 323–4, 343–4
financial hold 45
frequently asked questions. See FAQs

G
Gonzaga University v. John Doe 3, 74, 97
grades
    email, sending via 26, 28, 38, 74
    permission to access 36
    permission to release 37
    phone request for 40
    posting of 27–8, 38–9, 51, 58, 62, 74,
        80, 82–3, 97, 166, 175, 179, 227–8
    sharing (with another
        institution) 26–7, 36, 52
graduate rights 22, 27, 30, 216–7
graduation rates. See Student
    Right-to-Know Act of 1990
grievances. See challenge to records

H
health care. See also emergencies
    ii, 10, 30, 33, 309–16, 319
Health Insurance Portability &
    Accountability Act. See HIPAA

hearing, legal request for 18–9, 22,
    54, 63, 117–8, 153–4, 160, 177
Higher Education Amendments of 1992 1
HIPAA i–ii, 10, 30–1, 35,
    222–3, 302, 309–19, 325

I
ICE viii, 11, 41, 302, 337–6
Immigration and Naturalization
    Service requests 335, 337
inspection of records limitations
    14–5, 23, 54, 147, 152–3, 185, 303
institution of postsecondary education
    vii–viii, 2–5, 9–12, 16–7, 25, 27, 35–9,
    52, 57, 59–60, 80, 137–8, 152–3, 155,
    157, 159, 161, 165–71, 173–4, 176,
    181, 185, 188–9, 192, 197, 205–6, 217,
    222–3, 227, 229–30, 232, 234–5, 238,
    246, 251, 257, 260–1, 266, 279–81,
    283–4, 293, 296, 298–302, 304, 309–10,
    313–6, 323, 329, 333, 335, 341–2
institutional obligations
    access to records 37, 169, 232
    notification 51, 191, 223, 254, 331
    recordkeeping 11, 40, 147, 158–9,
        169, 173–4, 203, 230, 322, 338
institutional policy, FERPA 1, 16, 18,
    21–2, 24, 29, 34, 36–7, 42, 64, 76,
    85–6, 88, 93–4, 96, 100, 167, 175,
    187–9, 193, 197, 205, 216, 223, 230, 236,
    238, 241, 257, 263, 279, 310, 333, 342
Internal Revenue Code of
    1954 181, 284, 304–5
IRS summons 31, 68, 251–2

K
key terms and concepts,
    FERPA 51–2, 61, 70–1

L
law enforcement
    agencies/units viii, 2, 9–10, 23, 31–2,
        46, 54–5, 57, 59, 62–3, 65, 86–7,
        138–9, 149, 151–2, 156–7, 162, 168,
        171, 177, 207–8, 223, 237–9, 254–5,
        260, 302, 316, 318, 334–5, 339
    records viii, 1–2, 9–10, 19, 23, 31, 37,
        46–7, 55, 57, 59, 62–3, 65, 67, 75,
        87, 138–9, 149, 151–2, 168, 172, 175,
        208, 225, 235, 238–9, 251, 260, 283,
        301–2, 316, 318, 334–5, 337, 339
    subpoenas 2, 31, 46–7, 68,
        225, 251, 254, 334
legal actions 2–3, 46, 48, 68,
    156, 164, 249, 270, 281

legitimate educational interest 14, 18,
    21–5, 29, 32–4, 41, 45, 52, 58, 60, 66,
    72, 75, 79, 93–4, 97, 167, 169, 194,
    197–8, 205, 207, 209, 223, 285
letters of recommendation 15, 34, 57–60,
    67, 86–7, 137, 152–3, 166, 183, 185

M
media access ix
medical records viii, 30–1, 35, 57, 59, 62,
    72, 87, 97, 208, 213–4, 222–3, 268,
    301–2, 309–13, 316, 319, 325, 334
missing/lost student information 234–6

N
non-directory information. See also
    personally identifiable information
    disclosure of 17, 28, 36, 39, 44, 52–3,
        67–8, 70, 86, 161, 188, 334, 336
non-disclosure
    requests 30, 35–6, 42–3, 53,
        64, 94–5, 99–100, 113–4
    students' rights of 52–3
    telephone inquiries 40
notes. See also recordkeeping
    anecdotal 42, 68
    sole possession 42, 55, 62–3, 72
notification to students vii, 1–2, 5, 12,
    13–4, 18–9, 22, 26, 33, 38–9, 45–6, 51,
    54, 57, 59, 61, 63–8, 70–1, 74–6, 79–80,
    88–90, 94–6, 99, 127, 147, 151, 167, 175,
    177, 188–9, 206–7, 233, 235, 247–8, 302

O
open records laws 5–6, 21, 25, 44, 71, 341
opt out 8, 10, 17, 25, 35, 108,
    111–2, 161, 165, 174–5, 188–90,
    200–1, 206, 289, 304, 335
Owasso Independent School
    District v. Falvo (2002) 3, 296

P
parent
    definition of 3, 11, 36, 62, 66, 68, 72,
        97, 150, 152, 167, 172, 217, 219, 227,
        238–9, 253, 261, 263, 310, 313, 315, 335
    FAQs of 69, 303–4
    notifications/disclosures to 2, 4,
        16–7, 27, 36, 40, 51–2, 58, 60–1, 68,
        71–2, 106, 130, 156–7, 159–60, 167,
        181, 200, 217, 241, 246, 249, 253,
        270, 278, 281, 284, 302, 312–4, 323
    requests 18, 69, 154, 181
    rights of ii, 9, 27, 36–7, 51–2, 57,
        59, 61, 70, 85, 100, 137, 150, 167,
        181, 195, 217, 227, 238, 242, 246,

257, 260, 270, 279, 281, 283–4,
    286, 293, 296, 298, 302–4, 333
party 2, 4–5, 8, 11, 16–8, 21, 24, 27, 29, 32–4,
    37, 43, 45, 52, 79, 97, 166, 168, 171, 173–5,
    188, 197–9, 201–2, 206, 208, 211–2,
    218–9, 222, 225–6, 232, 234, 251, 261, 263,
    266, 268, 270, 278, 285, 310, 325, 342
penalties for violations. *See also*
    enforcement 5, 40, 174
personal identification
    numbers(s). *See* PINs
personal identifier. *See also* personally
    identifiable information 8, 11, 24,
    41–2, 62, 87, 124, 150, 166, 188, 196–9,
    227, 239, 241, 258, 261, 264, 288, 297
personally identifiable information
    definition of 3–4, 7, 11, 14, 24, 31, 33,
        35–6, 42, 52, 62, 68, 76, 79, 97, 99,
        149–50, 152, 167, 170, 172, 189, 198,
        212, 219, 223, 227–8, 238–9, 253,
        260–1, 263, 286, 291, 310, 325, 335
    disclosure of vii–viii, 2–4, 10–2, 13,
        16–7, 19, 24, 27–8, 30–3, 35–6,
        38–40, 42–5, 54, 61, 67–8, 70, 73,
        86, 147, 151, 154, 156–61, 165–7, 170,
        173–4, 177, 188, 192, 194–5, 197–9,
        200, 205–9, 212–3, 216, 219, 223,
        227–9, 231–2, 234, 236, 238–43,
        249, 252–3, 256–61, 263–4, 266–7,
        270–2, 277, 279, 282–9, 291, 293–6,
        298, 301, 303, 310, 312, 325, 333–7
PINs 8, 37–8, 44, 51, 65, 149,
    166, 173, 198, 233, 235, 324
posting of grades (by faculty) 28,
    51, 58, 74, 80, 82–3, 97
Postsecondary Feedback Act 39
postsecondary feedback to high
    schools. *See also* Postsecondary
    Feedback Act 38–9
postsecondary institution. *See also*
    Institution of Postsecondary Education
    vii–viii, 2–5, 9–12, 16–7, 25, 27, 35–7, 39,
    52, 57, 59–60, 69–70, 80, 137–8, 147–50,
    152–3, 155, 157, 159, 161, 165–71, 173–6,
    181, 185, 188–90, 192–3, 197, 205–6,
    217, 222–3, 227, 229–30, 232, 234–5,
    238, 246, 251, 257, 260–1, 266, 279–81,
    283–4, 289, 293, 295–6, 298, 300–2, 304,
    309–10, 313–6, 323, 329, 333, 335, 342
prior notification (subpoenas)
    31, 46–8, 225, 252, 334
Privacy Act of 1974. *See* FERPA
public information. *See*
    directory information
purging of requests for access, records of
    disclosure, and education records. *See*
    also destruction of information 24

R

recommendations. *See* letters
    of recommendation
record 1, 3–4, 7–8, 11, 13–6, 18, 21–4, 27,
    29, 32–5, 38, 43–5, 52, 58, 60, 66, 69,
    72–4, 76, 79, 81, 97, 166, 170–1, 173–4,
    188, 193–4, 196–7, 201–3, 207, 209,
    218–9, 223, 225–6, 241–2, 251, 261, 275,
    279, 285, 296, 315, 318–9, 323, 334–5
recordkeeping. *See also* records retention
    disclosures, of 10, 24, 39–40, 47,
        147, 158, 169, 226, 230, 333–5
    technology 10–1, 203
records
    redisclosure of vii, 40, 155, 168, 173,
        213, 225, 251, 271, 281, 284–5, 287–9
    retention 15–6, 22, 24, 39, 58, 60, 73, 93
Regulations, the
    2009 (amended) 2–3, 26, 40, 147, 165
    Final (1988) 1
religious organization requests 41
requests, records of. *See* recordkeeping
research 31–2, 40, 43, 54, 65–6, 68, 76,
    78, 83, 157–8, 170, 173–4, 177, 207,
    220, 223, 241–2, 294–5, 316, 325, 331
rights
    parents, of ii, 9, 27, 36–7, 51–2, 57,
        59, 61, 70, 85, 100, 137, 150, 167,
        181, 195, 217, 227, 238, 242, 246,
        257, 260, 270, 279, 281, 283–4,
        286, 293, 296, 298, 302–8, 333
    postsecondary level, at the i–ii, viii,
        27, 36–7, 39, 52, 57, 59–60, 70, 151,
        177, 181, 246, 284, 301–2, 304, 333
    students, of
        admitted vs. enrolled 5, 9, 12, 21–2
        after graduating 12, 22, 30, 35, 39, 44,
            57, 59, 65, 75, 82, 84, 89, 216–8, 279
        amend records, to vii–viii, 4,
            13, 19, 63, 151, 153, 177
        at a glance vii
        deceased 24, 96, 300
        limitations 15, 185
        non-disclosure 14, 42, 53, 64, 99
        review records, to vii–viii, 14–5,
            21, 36, 45, 54, 58, 60–1, 63, 82–3,
            85, 87, 89, 165, 185, 275, 310, 314
        waivers 15, 137, 271

S

safeguarding (of education
    records) 4, 23–4, 41, 79, 169,
    172, 175–6, 179, 234–5, 323
scholarships (financial aid) 29, 77, 225
school official(s) i, 2–4, 8, 11, 14, 16–7,
    21–3, 25, 32–5, 38, 41, 44–5, 52, 58, 60,
    65–6, 72, 75, 94, 165–9, 173, 175, 194,

196–8, 201, 203, 205–10, 212, 218, 223,
    232, 249, 260, 266, 318, 321, 334–5, 337
security v, viii, 1, 7, 10–1, 23, 27, 29, 33–4,
    37, 41, 44, 55, 58, 74–5, 79, 87, 93–5,
    100, 119, 151, 159, 168–9, 172–5, 196,
    231, 234–6, 256, 301–2, 309–11, 319, 321,
    323–5, 328–30, 332, 335, 337–9, 341
SEVIS ii, viii, 11, 41, 302, 333, 337–40
social security number
    attendance verification using 25
    posting grades by 38, 51, 58,
        62, 82–3, 97, 227
sole possession records viii, 2, 9, 11, 42,
    55, 57, 59, 62–3, 72, 97, 138, 149
Solomon Amendment, the ii, viii, 11–2,
    42–3, 78, 82–3, 97, 298, 327, 329–30
staff, education of 61, 95, 286
state
    databases 73, 243
    education agency requests 41, 158
    law, conflict with i, 5–6, 44, 142,
        162, 187, 190, 208, 216, 277–9
    open records laws 5–6, 13–4, 21–2,
        26, 44–5, 71, 73–5, 97, 180, 260
student identification number(s) vii–
    viii, 2–5, 7–12, 13–4, 16–7, 19, 21–46,
    49, 52–5, 57–9, 61–71, 73, 75–80,
    82–9, 93–100, 123, 149, 154–61,
    165–7, 169–77, 181–2, 187–92, 194–202,
    205–9, 211–2, 216, 218–23, 227–43,
    249–50, 252–4, 257–61, 263–7, 270–4,
    277, 279, 282–9, 291, 293–8, 300–3,
    309–12, 314, 317, 323–5, 330, 333–40
student recruiting information. *See also*
    Solomon Amendment, the viii, 11–2,
    42–3, 78, 82–3, 97, 298, 327, 329–30
Student Right-to-Know Act of 1990 12, 44
student(s)
    committees, serving on 32, 46,
        54, 65, 83, 89, 177, 207, 223
    definition of ii, v, 2–5, 7–8, 11, 13–8,
        21–5, 27, 29, 32–5, 37–8, 41, 43–5, 52,
        58, 60, 64–6, 69, 72–6, 79, 81, 93–4,
        97, 165–71, 173–5, 181, 187–90, 193–4,
        196–9, 200–3, 205–12, 217–9, 222–3,
        225–7, 230–2, 234, 237–8, 241–2,
        248–9, 251, 260–1, 263, 266, 268, 270,
        275, 277–81, 285, 296, 310, 315, 318–9,
        322–3, 325, 327, 334–5, 337, 339, 342
    dependent, as viii, 5, 16–8, 26, 36,
        55–6, 58, 60, 68, 72–3, 82–3, 85–6,
        95, 97–8, 130–1, 139, 156, 167, 181–2,
        279–80, 284, 302, 304, 314, 343–4
    directories viii, 3, 8, 14, 17, 21, 23–5,
        27, 30, 35, 40–4, 53, 57–60, 63–5,
        70, 76, 78–9, 83–4, 86, 89, 91, 94–5,
        98–9, 138, 149, 159, 161, 165–6,

174–5, 188–91, 196–201, 205–6, 218, 266, 285, 289, 324, 329, 335, 338

dual-enrolled ii, 27, 80, 127, 192, 194

eligible 2–5, 11, 17, 21, 23–4, 27, 41, 45, 52, 81, 167, 174, 181, 188, 190, 194, 197–8, 200–2, 206, 211, 217–9, 223, 227, 234, 238, 249, 251, 260, 263, 266, 275, 279, 281, 285, 296, 310, 315, 323, 325, 334–5, 337

files. *See* education records

former (rights of) 5, 14, 30, 83–4

IDs vii–viii, 2–5, 7–12, 13–4, 16–7, 19, 21–46, 49, 52–5, 57–9, 61–71, 73, 75–80, 82–9, 93–100, 123, 149, 154–61, 165–7, 169–77, 181–2, 187–92, 194–202, 205–9, 211–2, 216, 218–23, 227–43, 249–50, 252–4, 257–61, 263–7, 270–4, 277, 279, 282–9, 291, 293–8, 300–3, 309–12, 314, 317, 323–5, 330, 333–40

limitations of rights vii–viii, 14–5, 53–4, 67, 153, 185, 270

notification. *See* Notification to students

records. *See* Education records

statement (addition to record) 18–9, 23, 36, 39, 66, 74, 76, 82, 92, 120, 133–4, 154, 182, 239, 271–2, 285, 288, 291, 294

waiver of rights 15, 34, 58, 60, 67, 90, 137, 153, 185, 195, 268, 270–7, 281–8, 286

subpoenas 2, 8, 12, 15, 31, 46–9, 68, 73, 88, 96–8, 139–40, 171, 180, 225, 251, 253–4, 285, 334

T

telephone inquiries 25, 40

terms, definitions of crimes of violence 2, 7, 161, 163

time limits

appeal of hearing results 19

complaint, to file a 63, 162–9

conflicting laws, notification of i, 5, 44, 144, 162, 180, 187, 190, 216, 219, 277–9

providing access to records, for 14, 21, 44 5, 54, 66, 177

response to DoD regarding institutional policies 330

subpoena

objection to 48

response to 40, 46–9, 55, 73, 82, 87, 96–8, 156, 159, 245, 252, 254, 334

training materials ii, 28–9, 51, 94, 96, 162

transaction sets 310

transcript directory 48

transcript(s) 26–9, 37–8, 45, 48, 53, 55, 66–8, 70, 74, 77, 79–80, 84–5, 91–2, 100, 127, 129, 166, 168, 170, 189, 197, 229–30, 245, 287, 294 5, 303, 325, 340

U

U.S.C. 12

U.S. Immigration and Customs Enforcement Office. *See* ICE

United States Code. *See* U.S.C.

United States v. Miami University and Ohio State University 3, 25, 29, 262, 264, 279

USA Patriot Act viii, 3, 12, 16, 47, 141, 171, 333, 336

V

verification requests 40, 42, 45

Veterans Administration (disclosure to) 67

W

waiver of rights 15, 34, 48, 58, 60, 67, 71, 90, 137, 153, 183, 185, 195, 268–73, 281–2, 286

Web

posting grades on the 38, 74, 175

related sites 53

teaching 26

work–study 32, 85–6, 100

written complaints. *See* complaints

written consent viii, 5, 13, 16, 19, 21–2, 25, 28–9, 32–3, 44, 46–7, 55, 63, 65–70, 94, 139–41, 160, 165, 173–5, 194, 200–2, 210–1, 219, 225–6, 228, 230–1, 234, 238–41, 246, 250–7, 259, 263, 266–8, 277–80, 283, 291, 295, 297, 303, 323–4, 334